Studies in Celtic History XX

CHRIST IN CELTIC CHRISTIANITY:
BRITAIN AND IRELAND
FROM THE FIFTH TO THE TENTH CENTURY

STUDIES IN CELTIC HISTORY

ISSN 0261–9865

General editors
Dauvit Broun
Máire Ní Mhaonaigh
Huw Pryce

'Studies in Celtic History' aims to provide a forum for new research into all aspects of the history of Celtic-speaking peoples throughout the whole of the medieval period. The term 'history' is understood broadly: any study, regardless of discipline, which advances our knowledge and understanding of the history of Celtic-speaking peoples will be considered. Studies of primary sources, and of new methods of exploiting such sources, are encouraged.

Founded by Professor David Dumville in 1979, the series is now relaunched under new editorship. Proposals or queries may be sent directly to the editors at the addresses given below; all submissions will receive prompt and informed consideration before being sent to expert readers.

Dr Dauvit Broun, Department of History (Scottish), University of Glasgow, 9 University Gardens, Glasgow G12 8QH

Dr Máire Ní Mhaonaigh, St John's College, Cambridge CB2 1TP

Dr Huw Pryce, School of History and Welsh History, University of Wales, Bangor, Bangor, Gwynedd LL57 2DG

For titles already published in this series
see the end of this volume

CHRIST IN
CELTIC CHRISTIANITY

BRITAIN AND IRELAND
FROM THE FIFTH TO THE
TENTH CENTURY

MICHAEL W. HERREN AND SHIRLEY ANN BROWN

THE BOYDELL PRESS

First published 2002
The Boydell Press, Woodbridge

ISBN 0 85115 889 7

The Boydell Press is an imprint of Boydell & Brewer Ltd
PO Box 9, Woodbridge, Suffolk IP12 3DF, UK
and of Boydell & Brewer Inc.
PO Box 41026, Rochester, NY 14604–4126, USA
website: www.boydell.co.uk

A catalogue record for this book is available
from the British Library

Library of Congress Cataloging-in-Publication Data
Herren, Michael W.
    Christ in Celtic Christianity: Britain and Ireland from the fifth to the tenth
century/Michael W. Herren and Shirley Ann Brown.
        p.cm. – (Studies in Celtic history; 20)
    Includes bibliographical references and index.
    ISBN 0-85115-889-7 (alk. paper)
        1. Ireland – Church history – To 1172.   2. Great Britain – Church
history – To 449.   3. Celtic Church.   I. Brown, Shirley Ann.   II. Title.
III. Series.
BR749.H47 2002
274.1'02–dc21   2002018579

This publication is printed on acid-free paper

Typeset by Joshua Associates Ltd, Oxford
Printed in Great Britain by
St Edmundsbury Press Ltd, Bury St Edmunds, Suffolk

CONTENTS

List of Illustration   vii

Prologue   ix

Introduction   1

I   The Growth and Development of Monasticism in the British Isles   21

     Britain: 400–700   22
     Ireland: 450–850   30
     Monasticism in Anglo-Saxon England: 599–*ca* 750   38
     Additional Texts   44

II   The Theology of Christ in Insular Christianity   47

     Expressions of Orthodoxy   47
     Heresy: 51
         Arianism   51
         Pelagianism   52
         The 'Three Chapters' controversy and Columbanus   53
         Monothelitism   54
         Quattuordecimans and Judaisers   56
     Additional Texts   65

III   Pelagianism in Britain and Ireland   69

     The Pelagian Movement   69
     Pelagian Writings   70
     Doctrines   71
     Survivals of Pelagianism in Britain and Ireland: 80
         Britain in the fifth and sixth centuries   80
         Ireland in the seventh, eighth and ninth centuries   87
         Northumbria in the eighth century   97
     Additional Texts   101

IV   The Common Celtic Church   104

     Some Evidence for a Common Church   104
     Scripturalism   106
     'Judaising Tendencies'   109
     Literary Culture   115
     The Sacraments   122

	Ostracism	130
	Additional Texts	134
V	Christ Revealed in the Texts	137
	Christ the Perfect Monk	140
	The Heroic Christ (Harrower of Hell)	151
	Christ the Wonder-Worker	160
	Christ the Judge	174
	Additional Texts	178
VI	Non-Representational Images of Christ	186
	The Cross	191
	The Cult of the True Cross	195
	The Ringed 'Celtic' Cross:	199
	The Ahenny crosses	201
	The Anglian Crosses:	206
	Acca's cross at Hexham	207
	Bewcastle and Ruthwell crosses	209
	Symbols for Christ in Manuscripts	213
	Cross Carpet Pages:	215
	The Books of Durrow and Kells	215
	The Lindisfarne Gospels	217
	The Lichfield Gospels	220
	Four Evangelist Symbols/Cross Pages	220
	The Monogram of Christ	224
	Additional Texts	232
VII	The Representational Images of Christ	234
	Christ as the Ideal Monk:	236
	The Ruthwell cross	236
	The Book of Kells	243
	The Crucified Christ	250
	Christ as Judge and Conqueror of Hell:	260
	The second coming	261
	The last judgement	264
	The Militant Christ and the Harrowing of Hell	268
	Christ the Wonder Worker	270
	Additional Texts	276
	Epilogue	278
	Appendix: *Precamur patrem*	284
	Bibliography and Abbreviations	289
	Index	305

ILLUSTRATIONS

Plates 1–8 appear between pp. 212 and 213, 9–16 between pp. 244 and 245.

1. Ahenny, Co. Tipperary. North cross, west Face. (Photo: S.A. Brown)
2. Double-cross carpet page, Book of Durrow; Dublin: Trinity College Library MS 57, fo. 1v. (By permission of the Board of Trinity College Dublin)
3. Double-cross carpet page, Book of Kells; Dublin: Trinity College Library MS 58, fo. 33r. (By permission of the Board of Trinity College Dublin)
4. Cross carpet page, Lindisfarne Gospels; London: British Library MS Cotton Nero D.IV, fo. 2v. (By permission of the British Library)
5. Four-evangelist-symbols cross page, Book of Durrow; Dublin: Trinity College Library MS 57, fo. 2r. (By permission of the Board of Trinity College Dublin)
6. *Chi Rho* page, Barberini Gospels; Vatican: Biblioteca Apostolica, Barberini MS lat. 570, fo. 18. (Photo Archivio Fotografico, BAV)
7. *Chi Rho* page, Book of Armagh; Dublin: Trinity College Library MS 52, fo. 33v. (By permission of the Board of Trinity College Dublin)
8. *Chi Rho* page, Book of Kells; Dublin: Trinity College Library MS 58, fo. 34r. (By permission of the Board of Trinity College Dublin)
9. Ruthwell cross, Dumfriesshire. (a) Mary (Magdalene) at Christ's feet, (b) Christ standing on the beasts. (Photo: S.A. Brown)
10. Christ on Mount Olivet, Book of Kells; Dublin: Trinity College Library MS 58, fo. 114r. (By permission of the Board of Trinity College Dublin)
11. The temptation of Christ, Book of Kells; Dublin: Trinity College Library MS 58, fo. 202v. (By permission of the Board of Trinity College Dublin)
12. Athlone crucifixion plaque, Dublin: National Museum of Ireland. (By permission of the National Museum of Ireland)
13. Crucifixion of Christ, St Gall Gospels; St Gallen: Stiftsbibliothek, Cod. 51, p. 266. (By permission of the Stiftsbibliothek, St Gallen)
14. The second coming of Christ, St Gall Gospels; St Gallen: Stiftsbibliothek, Cod. 51, p. 267. (By permission of the Stiftsbibliothek, St Gallen)
15. The enthroned Christ, Book of Kells; Dublin: Trinity College Library MS 58, fo. 32v. (By permission of the Board of Trinity College Dublin)
16. Monasterboice, Co. Louth. Cross of Muiredach, *psychostasis*/harrowing of hell. (Photo: S.A. Brown)

Figures

Prepared by Bojana Videkanic

i.	Incised cross forms, Clonmacnois	194
ii.	Vine motif with cross:	
	(a) Acca's cross at Hexham	208
	(b) Bewcastle cross, upper north side	208
	(c) Bewcastle cross, middle south side	208
	(d) Bewcastle cross, bottom south side	208
iii.	Inhabited vine motif:	
	(a) Ruthwell cross	210
	(b) South (Muiredach's) Cross, Monasterboice	210
	(c) Barberini Gospels, XPI page, detail	210
iv.	Inhabited vine/text: Book of Kells, fo. 19v, detail	214
v.	Crucifixion slab from the Calf of Man	256

PROLOGUE

If a book can be inspired by a song, this one was inspired by 'Is that all there is?', famously sung by Miss Peggy Lee. While this book is not about existential *angst*, the question of the song's title is aptly posed with regard to Celtic Christianity, and more generally to Insular Christianity in the early middle ages. From Bede to historians of the twenty-first century it has been widely accepted that Christians in the early British and Irish Churches were wholly orthodox in matters of faith. The questions debated were confined to 'practical issues' such as Easter tables, equinoxes, epacts, consecrations, triple immersions and tonsures. To be sure, these issues caused plenty of trouble in their day, but to persons living in the twenty-first century, including those still seriously interested in the history of Christianity, they look like a tempest in a teapot. Is that all there *was*?

This book began with the project of defining the images of Christ that were prevalent in the British Isles, and more specifically in Celtic Britain and Ireland from the fifth century to the tenth. It became apparent that one could not achieve this goal simply by looking at poems and pictures without an ideological context for their interpretation. The most fundamental task was to investigate the character of Christian theology prevalent in Britain and Ireland from the fifth to the tenth century, and to look for continuity and change. But how could this be achieved if there was no theology to study, but only epacts and haircuts? Is that all there *was*?

Previous speculation regarding the spiritual roots of Celtic Christianity has tended to look to the distant East, the monastic theology of Egypt being a particularly favoured focus. We followed a different path of investigation, deciding to look for those clues that were directly under our noses, by which we understood the evidence found in the indigenous religious culture of Britain and Ireland. Of course, Christianity was transplanted to Britain by someone (probably *not* Joseph of Arimathea), but it developed a life of its own and produced a religious literature. Focussing on theology, we examined a substantial sample of religious writings produced in Britain and Ireland down to about 900, with some further post-holing beyond. These include historical writings, canon collections, penitentials, monastic rules, scriptural commentaries and works on scriptural questions, saints lives, letters and a variety of works less easily classified. We also took stock of books on religious topics that were imported into Britain and Ireland – at least as far as this was possible, given the rudimentary state of our knowledge of 'books known to the Britons and Irish'.

In our survey of religious literature (or works with relevance to religion) we decided to go beyond those writings produced in Britain and Ireland, and to include works written by Britons and Irishmen who spent a portion of their lives on the continent, notably Pelagius, Faustus of Riez and

Columbanus. The writings of all three came back to the British Isles and enjoyed varying levels of circulation. In the case of Pelagius, we were struck by the fact that not only did his works circulate in Britain, Ireland and also Anglo-Saxon England, there was also scattered evidence for the presence of the Pelagian heresy first in Britain, then in Ireland from the fifth to the seventh centuries. If there was no smoke coming from the gun, the barrel and the chamber were certainly hot. Our search for 'more' thus began with Pelagius, and in fact ends there. The thesis of this book is that Celtic Christianity and its Christological images were formed in the matrix of the controversy surrounding Pelagius and his divergent views on grace and redemption. This in turn created a theological spectrum that differentiated Britain and Ireland from the European continent.

As authors of this hypothesis we are aware of its controversial character. We were less cognisant – until more recently – of the conflicting perceptions surrounding the notion of 'Celtic Christianity' which are current in various parts of the British Isles today. In some regions it is possible to obtain an advanced degree in 'Celtic Christianity', a fact pointing to the respectability of the term and its content. But there is also New Age 'Celtic Christianity', a phenomenon not only flourishing in the British Isles, but known to have reached North America and other parts of the world. This is certainly not respectable in academic circles. Indeed, there is now an academic sub-industry dedicated to abolishing the notion of 'Celtic Christianity' alto-gether, whether it be found in its popular or academic manifestation. We shall have more to say about this matter in our Introduction; here we shall simply assert that communication sometimes requires the use of terms that may be currently unfashionable, but still maintain the power to convey ideas effectively and are preferable to circumlocutions. 'Celtic Christianity' is one such term, as is 'British Isles' and even 'mankind'. To abandon such inclusive terms entirely leads to communicative dysfunctionalism – an endless series of qualifications that makes the completion of sentences all but impossible. This has been brilliantly demonstrated by Professor John Cleese in his *Life of Brian,* which, incidentally, also touches on Christianity.

As already stated, the aim of our book is to show that debate over practical issues was *not* all there was to Celtic Christianity. We recognise that some of the ideas proposed in this book – the Pelagian hypothesis and probably also the notion of a 'common Celtic Church' in the fifth and sixth centuries – may be unpopular in some quarters. We did not write to satisfy current academic opinion, much less to give aid or comfort to groups or individuals hoping to appropriate congenial conclusions to their own interests. New Age fans of Celtic Christianity may well be horrified by our depiction of a hell-oriented Irish Church, and Catholic theologians may be dismayed by our characterisation of Celtic Christianity prior to the *Romani* movement in Ireland. If others are pleased with our conclusions because they can be seen to serve a sectarian or other agenda, their pleasure will bring no pleasure to us. Our purpose has been strictly to re-evaluate an historical situation, and to attempt to effect a shift in the discussion of religious issues in the British Isles during a period which we believe not to have been fully understood. We have attempted to portray Pelagius sympathetically without agreeing with his views; the same applies to our construction of the common Celtic Church. We neither cheer nor lament the Romanisation of Ireland, nor shed tears over the passing of a Golden Age. We prefer light on the Celts to Celtic twilight.

When we were nearing the end of our work on this book, we had the privilege of seeing a selection of Gustav Klimt's masterpieces beautifully exhibited in the National Gallery of Canada in Ottawa. In a gold square above the oil-on-canvas rendition of *Nuda Veritas* are painted the words of Schiller:

> KANST DU
> NICHT ALLEN
> GEFALLEN DURCH
> DEINE THAT UND DEIN
> KUNSTWERK =
>   MACHT ES
> WENIGEN RECHT.
> VIELEN GEFALLEN
> IST SCHLIMM.

These words doubtless overstate our own attitudes and intentions, and we do not pretend to have created a *Kunstwerk*. Yet Schiller's text does indeed support the representation of *Veritas*. The pursuit of truth, certainly of historical truth, requires that one abandon the aim of pleasing. It also requires that one cease to care about appropriations of one's scholarly findings, as these lie beyond all human control.

If we bring any special advantages to our book – apart from those occasioned by our respective disciplines – it is our status as outsiders. It is easier to 'think outside the box' – to use the current jargon – if one is not inside the box. Perhaps more than any other subject falling generally in the category 'medieval studies', the investigation of the religious culture of the British Isles in the transition from antiquity to the middle ages has become the preserve of scholars working in English, Irish, Scottish and Welsh universities. This, of course, has not always been the case. Up to about 1980 there were highly significant contributions by German, French and Belgian scholars. One thinks of Zimmer, Bischoff, Gougaud, Grosjean and Wilmart, to name but some. North Americans, most notably J.F. Kenney and J.T. McNeill, also made signal contributions. However, full-scale studies of early Insular religion by scholars based outside the British Isles appear to be in decline, particularly during the last two decades or so. It may well be that globalisation has divided as much as united us. Europe and North America, united in trade, seem more inward-looking than before when it comes to engaging with history beyond the very recent past. We hope that the present book will be viewed as a tentative effort at correcting this state of affairs.

It remains to say something about our collaboration, and to thank those who have helped us. Michael W. Herren wrote Chapters I–V and the Appendix; Shirley Ann Brown wrote Chapters VI and VII. The Prologue, Introduction and Epilogue are a joint effort. We as authors collaborated on every aspect of the present book, and there is nothing in these pages that does not represent our jointly considered opinion.

We offer our warm thanks to Charlie Wright, who read this book in an earlier draft, and to Paul Meyvaert and Anthony Harvey who helped us with specific points. Jennifer Reid, a doctoral candidate at the Centre for Medieval Studies, University of Toronto, assisted us with the typing and proof-reading of citations in the original languages. Our greatest debt is to the editors of Studies in Celtic History: Dauvit Broun, Máire Ní Mhaonaigh and Huw Pryce. They did far more than is expected of series editors, not only challenging us at many points and calling for both clarification and qualification, but also buttressing our arguments with references to primary evidence that we had neglected and to secondary literature of which we were unaware, tracking down incomplete references, even faxing or mailing pages of publications that had not yet arrived in Toronto. We should also like to express our sincere appreciation to the author of the very thoughtful 'specialist report'. We took *nearly* all of the good advice offered in the report as well as that in the reports of the series editors. That we did not take it all is hardly the fault of their authors, and they must surely be absolved of the responsibility for the flaws remaining in this book.

Finally, a word about our intended audience. Within the constraints of a scholarly series reputed for its severe standards, we have striven to write a book that is accessible to all readers interested in early Celtic Christianity. English translations of passages in Latin, Greek and Irish are always given in the body of the text; long quotations in the original languages have been placed at the end of each chapter, so as not to burden pages with excessively long footnotes. We have concentrated on primary sources and have tried to restrict the secondary literature cited to publications that offer important breakthroughs or significant dissenting opinions, or valuable bibliographies. We have also tried to write clearly and in a reader-friendly style. *Lector, vale*!

Michael W. Herren   Toronto, September 2001
Shirley Ann Brown

INTRODUCTION

This book is about the *nexus* of two subjects: the images of Christ, and Christianity as it was conceived and practised in the Insular Celtic regions in late antiquity and the early middle ages. Our work presents a model of early Celtic Christianity and its development from the early fifth to the end of the ninth century or beginning of the tenth century. The topics include institutional Christianity, theology and religious practice. We argue that the character of Christianity that emerges from our analysis determined the range of Christological images found in literature and art produced in the Celtic areas. We hope to demonstrate that the form of Christianity and of Christological images experienced both continuity and change over the period studied, reflecting continuity and change in the theological and spiritual outlook. The first four chapters are devoted to the problem of characterising 'Celtic Christianity' in the period examined; the last three deal specifically with the images of Christ. Of these, the first deals with images drawn from literary evidence; the last two, with images drawn from the visual arts. This introduction provides an outline of our thesis and defines terms used later in the book. We have reserved detailed argumentation and the presentation of evidence for the ensuing chapters.

Our geographical focus is the Celtic areas of the British Isles: Britain (modern Wales and Cornwall and areas now in northern England) and Ireland with its extensions into Iona. Because of the late nature of the evidence, Brittany receives only intermittent attention, and that chiefly where it provides evidence bearing upon Britain and Ireland. However, for historiographical reasons it is essential to include Anglo-Saxon England in this study. The English writers Aldhelm and Bede, who wrote in the late seventh and early eighth centuries, provide invaluable information for our assessment of British and Irish beliefs and practices in their day. Indeed, as all modern scholars of early Insular history are aware, it would be impossible to write anything very meaningful about the Celtic regions without recourse to these sources, particularly Bede. However, English writers were not simply detached observers of the Celtic scene; they were also deeply influenced by it. Irish missionaries and teachers converted Northumbria, in which Bede lived, and were also influential in Wessex and Kent, where Aldhelm circulated. The Celtic and Anglo-Saxon worlds reveal commonalities in such areas as school curriculum and handwriting as well as shared religious values, including the privileging of the monastic life and an ideal of sanctity based upon asceticism. In this book we use the convenient term 'Insular' to denote the common features of the Celtic and Anglo-Saxon religious cultures. However, while recognising common characteristics in the two groups, we remain cognisant of the obligation to point out significant contrasts.

1

Any attempt at a serious study of the religious thought of this period must confront the gaps in both the written and material record. In the period *ca* 450 to *ca* 630, which is – for reasons soon to be explained – the privileged period of this book, written evidence is at a premium, and material evidence very thin. Early British and Irish writers tell us a good deal about their thoughts, opinions and feelings, but less about their history, and this usually in the terse format of annals. For any connected account of this period we must turn to Bede's *Ecclesiastical History of the English People*, finished in 731. However Bede seems to have known only a few sources written before his own lifetime to which we in the twenty-first century do not have access. Even with regard to the history of his own day, he was limited by his geography and his contacts. He appears to have had very little first-hand knowledge of Britain, and though he says quite a lot about Ireland and the Irish, he only rarely mentions place-names in Ireland, or the names of Irish persons who did not travel to England. He knew a number of Irish sources written in Latin, but does not mention Irish works written in the vernacular. He knew about Columba, because Columba was connected to his own island, but nothing about Patrick or Brigit. Fortunately, we possess British and Irish works written in the fifth, sixth and seventh centuries which can be used to supplement Bede's account, which, to be fair, was concerned primarily with the religious life of his own people. However, the (mainly Latin) British and Irish sources themselves are scant for the period *ca* 400 – *ca* 630, becoming richer only after about the middle of the seventh century, and then almost entirely in Ireland. The record for Britain is especially dark after about 600, picking up again only in the later eighth and ninth centuries and augmented by sources emanating from Brittany. The Irish record is also deficient, but in different places. The fifth century is illuminated almost solely by the writings of St Patrick, the sixth is plagued by problems pertaining to the date of the evidence, while the writings of Columbanus – arguably the first Hiberno-Latin writer known by name – are difficult to evaluate because nearly all of these that survive were written on the continent between *ca* 600 and 615. To make matters worse, the Irish annals are unreliable for the fifth and sixth centuries.[1] A continuous record of datable texts written in Ireland begins only with Cummian in the 630s.

The material record is similarly lacunose. For the period *ca* 400 – *ca* 650 there is no evidence for the production of religious art in either Britain or Ireland. We get written descriptions of religious art in Ireland only from a little past the mid-seventh century. Moreover, scholars cannot agree about the dates of many of the religious art objects that have survived from the Insular region in the period we are considering (the early fifth century to the late ninth century), and there is continuing controversy over where some of them were produced. In this book we have endeavoured to use datings for art works based on majority opinion. However, given the problems of localisation as well as dating, it would be dangerous to use works of art as evidence for influence of one region upon another, or for a sudden change

---

[1] Smyth, 'The earliest Irish annals'.

in ideology. Rather, the works of art studied here have value largely for showing the continuity of motifs supported in texts of often considerably earlier date. While, ideally, motifs from dated or roughly datable art objects should be juxtaposed with texts of known date, this *desideratum* is unattainable given the gaps in both the material and textual record and the difficulty of dating much of the evidence that has survived. Although we have done our best to privilege evidence (whether textual or art historical) that is at least roughly datable and chronologically not far removed from a period or event under discussion, it has sometimes been necessary to appeal to evidence emanating from later periods. In several cases this evidence challenges the received opinion founded on the interpretation of earlier sources. However, as textual critics have learned, *codex vetustior non (semper) melior*. A radically different historical account from a later period, like a surprising textual variant in a late copy, may be explained either by a writer's access to a source unknown to us or by his or her wilful intervention. It is impossible to decide *prima facie* which is the case. A good textual critic suppresses only that late evidence which *repeats* what is already well established by earlier sources; historians would do well to do the same, if they do not wish to eradicate the chance of new discoveries and new evaluations.

Our book is based on the following model of periodisation for Celtic Christianity: (1) A period of *relative* harmony in theology and practice in Britain and Ireland; this is the period of the 'common Celtic Church' (soon to be defined) that extends from *ca* 450 to *ca* 630. The unity is preserved by a prolonged period of relative isolation from continental Christianity. (2) The dissolution of the common Celtic Church due to contacts between Rome and the south of Ireland. This is the origin of the division of the Irish Church into *Romani* in the south of Ireland, and *Hibernenses* in the north and on Iona; the British Church adheres to the roots put down in the first period and maintains isolation. Missionaries from Iona bring the theology and practices of the *Hibernenses* to Northumbria. This period extends from *ca* 630 to *ca* 750. (3) A synthesis of *Romani* and *Hibernenses* ideals in Ireland under the hegemony of the *Céli Dé* movement and a lessening of contacts with other churches in the British Isles. This period extends from *ca* 750 to *ca* 850. While most textual evidence that we use stops at this point, the mid-ninth century appears to mark the beginning of the Irish monuments known as the 'scripture crosses', which constitute the richest source of religious iconography from any part of the British Isles. We use the evidence of these ninth- and tenth-century crosses on the assumption that, to a considerable extent, they represent continuity of the earlier religious ideology of Ireland, and sometimes, even of the common Celtic Church. To be sure any schema of periodisation entails dangers. Things change at different times in different regions, and there may be pockets of resistance to change in a given region. Moreover – and this must be kept in mind – old ideologies can be found side-by-side with the new.

When we speak of 'Celtic Christianity' we do not mean to imply that Christianity in Celtic regions was influenced, to any noticeable degree, by pre-Christian religious ideology or practice in its official theology or liturgy.

3

One can, of course, easily find such influences in popular manifestations of religion, but these are outside our scope. The term 'Celtic', then, is used in a neutral sense to refer to geographical regions and language groups without the *impedimenta* of racial characteristics. Dom Gougaud's translated title 'Christianity in Celtic lands' would more aptly describe the phenomenon that we wish to discuss – it is just a little ungainly for repeated use. The changes we describe in Celtic Christianity have nothing to do with a greater or lesser degree of 'Celticity', excepting, perhaps, where we see an increased use of the Irish language for religious purposes in the third period described above. Rather, they concern the changing relations between the Christianity of the Celtic lands and that of the other regions of the Western Church. Moreover, by using the term 'Celtic' as a modifier of 'Christianity' we by no means wish to imply that Christianity was identical in all Celtic regions – even during the period of the common Celtic Church (*ca* 450 – *ca* 630). We recognise that the British and Irish apparently never expressed a collective sense of identity as Celts. However, we point out that outsiders tended to lump the Britons and the Irish together with reference to ecclesiastical matters, particularly in the late sixth and early seventh centuries. We have endeavoured to be cautious with the term 'Celtic' used inclusively, and not apply it to beliefs or practices that were uniquely British or Irish.

We expect that some readers will find the notion of a 'common Church' problematic, especially as there was no central authority exercising control over the entire region, whether in the fifth to early seventh centuries, or at any other time. Indeed, even to speak of a 'British Church' or an 'Irish Church' poses grave difficulties.[2] Clearly it is wrong to impose the model of the English Church in Theodore's time or the Frankish Church under the Carolingian kings on the Celtic areas of the British Isles. If anything, the ecclesiastical situation of the Celtic areas was characterised by decentralisation. We considered alternatives to the term 'Church'. For example, we might have simply referred to 'Celtic Christianity' (as in our title). But Christianity is a movement, and movements imply some organising mechanism, so one is no further ahead. We might also have used the plural 'Churches', or resorted to a small-c 'church', or 'churches'. However, we required a term that expressed the commonalities of theology and some significant features of common practice which obtained over a restricted period. In the end, we decided on a small-c for 'common', in order to signal that we did not regard the British and Irish Churches of the fifth and sixth centuries as a formal institution under the leadership of a metropolitan Church.

It is incumbent on us to explain how there may have been any kind of unity in a given region without a central authority. In the case of our common Celtic Church this seems to have been achieved in various ways. First, there appears to have been a shared respect for the authority of influential monastic figures. Early seventh-century evidence shows that the Britons Gildas and Uinniau were regarded as regional authorities, and later evidence points to the influence of Illtud and David. A second mechanism

---

[2] See (J.B.) Stevenson, *The Liturgy*, xi–xiii.

for preserving unity was the advocacy of a common literary culture. We argue that in the common Celtic Church the scriptures were regarded as the highest authority, superseding every other form of authority such as the teachings of the church fathers. We hypothesise that the common Celtic Church was highly restrictive in the kinds of non-scriptural materials it admitted. There seems to have been a bias against theological writings and against hagiographical literature that allowed for the miraculous. With few exceptions, both the use and the composition of scriptural commentaries appears to have been discouraged in the earliest period. Finally, there seems to have been suspicion, even avoidance, of outsiders – particularly those who might be identified as representatives of Roman beliefs and institutions.

In the final analysis, it may be that some historians' ideas of religious unity are governed by anachronistic and anatopic models. One can point to religious cultures elsewhere that have survived intact without centralising institutions such as a supreme pontiff, metropolitan bishops, inquisitorial boards or a 'secular sword'. One thinks of the federation of north Italian churches opposed to the 'Three Chapters' in the sixth and seventh centuries, or of the churches in southern Gaul allied against predestination theology in the fifth and early sixth centuries. The Celtic regions, largely isolated from continental religious trends for 150 years, developed a regional religious culture that was, in some respects, archaic, but in others, innovative. The innovative character of Celtic Christianity was defined by its internal struggle with Pelagianism; the resolution of this struggle produced the common Celtic Church.

The notion of a 'common Celtic Church' presupposes that Christianity in Britain was very similar to that of Ireland from the early fifth to the early seventh century,[3] and simultaneously markedly different from the forms of Christianity in other western areas in the same period, notably Gaul, Italy and North Africa. While 'Celtic Christianity' shared the general Dyophysite Christology of the Western churches, and partook of other features that distinguished Western Christianity from Eastern, it exhibited some theological characteristics which marked it as unique, others which, arguably, received greater emphasis there than elsewhere. We would list as defining theological features the assertion of the natural goodness of human nature, the possibility of a sinless life, the denial of transmitted original sin, categorical denial of predestination, a marked tendency to discount the miraculous, and the reliance on the scriptures as the sole source of religious authority. Salvation could be achieved by all through strict obedience to God's law as revealed by the scriptures. The ability to obey God's law in all respects was fostered by *askesis*.

There were also certain practices which were arguably peculiar to the common Celtic Church: an ambivalence about the eucharist, continuation of sabbath alongside Sunday observance and the existence of a ceremony used as a substitute for infant baptism. We have identified these in addition to the well-known divergent practices in calculating Easter, the form of the tonsure and the consecration of bishops. Not every one of these features can be

---

[3] See, however, Dumville, 'Some British aspects'.

exemplified in written evidence in the period *ca* 450 – *ca* 630. Some of the evidence is found uniquely in texts of Irish origin from the seventh and eighth centuries; we have assumed that this evidence is not indicative of innovation, but rather of continuity from the period of the common Celtic Church. Furthermore, it must be stated frankly that not all of the evidence used is assertive: much of it is found in the form of attacks on what we have called 'defining positions'. Finally, the term 'defining' does not mean the same thing as 'prevalent' or 'predominant'. Certain beliefs and practices may belong to a minority of a given group at a given time, yet they powerfully influence the character of the society in which they are found, and they are notable by their absence or reduced presence in other societies. To invoke a contemporary example: evangelical religion, which is practised by a minority of Americans, plays a disproportionate role in religious and social debate in the United States. However, it is far less influential in neighbouring Canada, and, although not non-existent in the United Kingdom, its influence there would be described as 'marginal'.

The features listed above as 'defining' are, for the most part, central doctrines of Pelagius and his followers. The theological points are clearly identifiable as Pelagian, the features of practice, less so. Admittedly, a reading of the Pelagian corpus reveals mostly absences with reference to the sacraments apart from baptism. Pelagians did not recommend sabbath observance, yet their numerous injunctions to obey all of God's commands provide a foundation for it. Finally, Pelagian opposition to infant baptism is well known, and there is evidence from early Irish canon collections pointing to an alternative ritual to formal baptism of infants. It may be objected, however, that one central feature of Celtic practice was distinctly un-Pelagian: the institution of penitential books and a general reform of the practice of penance permitting the repetition of the rite. By contrast, the Pelagians insisted that no Christian should sin after baptism, and that restitution after a post-baptismal lapse was extremely difficult. What is frequently claimed to be a Celtic innovation in penitential practice thus appears to run counter to the notion of a Church dominated or even heavily influenced by Pelagian ideology. However, it might be more fruitful to see the penitentials as representing a grudging compromise with Pelagian teaching rather than as a denial of its influence. The penances imposed are long and often harsh, and because of their length clash with the Roman-imposed duty of annual communion; moreover, as we shall see, there are texts in the penitentials that set limits to repeatability. At all events, the common Celtic Church was no more monolithic than any other regional church. Some of the best evidence for opposition to, or disapprobation of Pelagians and their ideas is found in the earliest British authors: Patrick and Gildas.

Our very earliest evidence teaches us that in the year 429 the Pelagians in Britain had their own bishops,[4] and these were opposed by 'Catholics' coming from Gaul. It would seem, then, that there was an organised Pelagian Church in Britain for at least some time in the fifth century.

---

[4] Prosper, *Chronicle* s.a. 429 (tr. de Paor, 79).

Evidence for the continuity of the sect in Britain will be discussed in Chapter III. However, it would appear that Pelagians had to share their island with another group: the so-called semi-Pelagians. This group, while partaking of some central theological tenets with Pelagians, allowed a place for the role of grace, including certain types of miracles, and held a different outlook on the sacraments. The semi-Pelagians were closely linked with the monastic movement, particularly the type centred in southern Gaul, which emphasised effort based on an ascetic regimen as the means to salvation. This kind of monasticism appears to have been transplanted into Britain towards the end of the fifth century, and had a major impact on the organisation of Christian life. Texts from the sixth century show that a number of Christian communities included a monastic component. Gildas indicates that there was opposition to the monastic movement in his day, and one wonders if this did not come from the Pelagians, who, although in favour of asceticism, were cool to its organised form, and did not impose celibacy on regular clergy, doubtless for sound scriptural reasons (I Tim. 3:2). Whatever the case, there appear to have been two principal groups which composed the common Celtic Church: Pelagians and semi-Pelagians. The two 'founding groups'– for want of a better term – shared a number of central theological tenets: both believed in the efficacy of free will and the necessity of works for salvation; both opposed the notion of predestination. The semi-Pelagians, however, made a place for grace and advocated the eucharist as needful spiritual food and a regime of repeatable penance. In doing this, they represented a form of Christianity that was, in most respects, similar to that which preceded the acrimonious debate between the Pelagians and Augustine. Thus, what characterises Celtic Christianity, and justifies our use of the term 'defining', is the persistence of *distinctly* Pelagian – as opposed to semi-Pelagian – tenets not only in the period of the common Celtic Church, but in later periods, at least in some regions. There may have been individuals in the period of the common Celtic Church who did not wish to identify with either Pelagian or semi-Pelagian theologies, but one is very hard pressed to find representatives of Augustinian theology, or even of the quasi-Augustinian type that we find in Caesarius of Arles, much before the middle of the seventh century, and then, primarily in the south of Ireland.

It is this 'theological spectrum' – if you will – that separated the British Church from the neighbouring Gaulish Church, and commands the label of a separate 'Church' as distinct from a 'local theology'. While Gaul was famous for raising up or harbouring semi-Pelagian writers – Cassian, Vincent of Lérins, Gennadius and the Briton Faustus of Riez – it boasted no famous Pelagians, though we learn that some Pelagian communities had been suppressed.[5] But more to the point is that some of the fiercest opponents of the Pelagian and semi-Pelagian movements came from Gaul: Prosper of Aquitaine, Germanus of Auxerre and Caesarius of Arles. Prosper wrote an attack on Cassian and defended Augustine against the attacks of Vincent of Lérins. He also applauded the anti-Pelagian

[5] Markus, 'The legacy of Pelagius', 215.

7

crusade in Britain, which was led by Germanus of Auxerre. In the next century, Caesarius established Augustinian theology, shorn of its predestinarianism, in southern Gaul. These agents of Augustinianism had no equivalents in Britain or Ireland. As we shall argue, Patrick was an exception in being theologically at odds with Pelagianism (though this is subtle), but we cannot be sure that his hostility was not the result of a formation in Gaul.

A final point regarding the theology of the common Celtic Church: as already noted, Pelagians recognised only one authority, and this is the divine law, which can be known from the holy scriptures alone. Pelagians implicitly believed that God's law was clear and did not require interpretation; indeed, Pelagian writers thundered against anyone who dared to interpret the law figuratively. The concept of an institution that possessed teaching authority that is additional to the teaching authority of the scriptures was anathema in Pelagian thinking. The semi-Pelagian writings, which focussed heavily on a monastic audience, accorded some authority to the words of venerable abbots, but this authority related almost exclusively to monastic *conversatio*, and was treated more as respected opinion than as a set of commands which could in any way be construed as running counter to scripture. The notion that a local council, or even the universal Church, might command anything that contradicted or undermined what was explicit in scripture would have been unacceptable to both groups. Morever, what was *not* commanded in scripture could not be commanded by men, regardless of their good motives. It would seem that both Pelagians and semi-Pelagians had a considerably reduced notion of the role of the Church in society. Its main task, apparently, was to teach the law and help individuals to understand it and to obey it. After all, it is only through the fulfilment of the whole law that one can be saved.

We know only a little about the organisation of the individual church communities in Britain and Ireland. The earliest canon collections and penitentials imply that some communities on both islands comprised laity, regular clergy and monks. Bishops appear to have exercised the same functions in the Celtic churches as they did elsewhere; there can be no question that their authority in spiritual matters was usurped by heads of monasteries, though there are cases of individuals who simultaneously held abbatial and episcopal positions. Issues of disagreement were resolved at councils, which seem to have been mostly of a regional nature. There was considerable diversity in monastic rules in both Britain and Ireland.[6] Our concern, however, is not primarily church organisation, as this subject has been helpfully addressed in several recent publications.[7]

It is probable, but not certain, that the common Celtic Church was more harmonious in the sixth century than in the fifth. While there is evidence that Pelagians still constituted some kind of identifiable group in the sixth century – its status is extremely difficult to define – the more

---

[6] See now Dumville, 'Saint David'.

[7] Sharpe, 'Some problems'; Etchingham, *Church Organisation*; Charles-Edwards, *Early Christian Ireland*.

moderate semi-Pelagians appear to have gained the upper hand. This is shown by the emergence of organised monasticism and a penitential regime that allowed for repeatability. However, a separate Pelagian strain did not completely disappear. In 640, or just before, a papal letter charged that the Pelagian heresy had been resuscitated in Ireland, and outlined the aspects of the heresy at issue. We do not know what events or writings may have instigated the charge, although it is not improbable that it was connected to the controversy surrounding the introduction of martyrs' relics into Ireland and the practice of miraculous healings. Hiberno-Latin works of the seventh and early eighth centuries, and Irish-language works from a somewhat later period offer abundant evidence for a continuing debate over the central hypotheses of Pelagian-ism and for the continuity of practices that can be explained by reference to Pelagian theology. The upshot of this is that the 'core theology' of the common Celtic Church in the sixth century and in some Celtic regions long afterwards was a mixture of semi-Pelagian and Pelagian elements, and, whereas one might hazard that the milder semi-Pelagian element had become dominant, theological features that are distinctly Pelagian per-sisted, and continued to be 'defining'. This does not imply that there was an organised Pelagian faction (much less a Pelagian Church) in seventh- and eighth-century Ireland. But it does mean that there continued to be individuals who asked hard questions of the 'main-streamers', and that these questions, or counter-positions, reflected the teachings of Pelagius and his followers.

Although Roman or 'Catholic' practices and some beliefs (for example, the use of relics, belief in miracles) gained a foothold in southern Ireland in the seventh century, the core theology dealing with the process of salvation was never seriously challenged. Effort consistently prevailed over grace, and salvation remained a possibility for everyone up to the end of life. Miracles themselves, rejected by strict Pelagians, eventually found a place in the hagiographical literature, where they were often depicted as a reward for a meritorious life rather than as arbitrary acts of divine intervention in human affairs.

So much for our synopsis and definition of the common Celtic Church. Yet before proceeding, some remarks on the history of scholarship are in order. The historiography of the twentieth century has been characterised by a consistently negative reaction to the 'Pelagian thesis' of Celtic Christianity. Despite the promising title, Heinrich Zimmer devoted only a few pages of his *Pelagius in Irland* to the central question of possible Pelagian influence on Irish theology,[8] concentrating instead on a textual study of Pelagius's *Commentary on Paul*. In fact, Zimmer never argued that the Irish – or British Church – subscribed to the tenets of Pelagianism at any time after Germanus's mission to Britain; on the contrary, he thought the Celtic Church (his term) orthodox in all the essentials.[9] Subsequent scholarship

[8] Zimmer, *Pelagius in Irland*, 21–5.
[9] Zimmer, *The Celtic Church*, 19–24, 129–30.

followed Zimmer in focussing on the *fortuna* of this commentary, and concluded that it could not be invoked to prove the continued presence of a Pelagian party or movement.[10] However, it is simply not true, as recently stated, that 'In most discussions of Insular theology there has been a detailed discussion of Pelagius.'[11] With the sole exception of Leslie Hardinge's *The Celtic Church in Britain*, and now Charles-Edwards' *Early Christian Ireland*,[12] no scholarly book on the early Celtic Church written after Zimmer's day has gone beyond a brief mention of Pelagius, and that usually with the intent of dismissing his influence.[13] Several articles have raised the question of Pelagian influence on doctrine, with negative results.[14] It would appear that modern scholars have been content to examine only the very few explicit references to Pelagianism as a heresy or movement in Britain or Ireland, or to trace explicit quotations from Pelagius's writings in British and Irish works.[15] These limited procedures are clearly inadequate. It is only by comparing what is known of Pelagian doctrine with the doctrines enunciated in the surviving monuments of Celtic Christian literature – a time-tested procedure in the study of other periods of the history of theology – that one can attain to any valid conclusions. The procedure requires scholars to familiarise themselves thoroughly with the corpus of a specific theological literature, learning not only its doctrines, but also favoured expressions and privileged biblical passages, then to examine a large sample of *comparanda* with these facts in mind. This is the procedure followed here, and it has yielded a much more positive conclusion than has been obtained heretofore.

The length to which scholars have gone to deny the influence of Pelagianism in Celtic theology is sometimes surprising. In articles written nearly twenty years apart, Charles Donahue advanced the thesis that the *Beowulf* poet – on the assumption that he was a Christian – was influenced by a theological outlook emanating ultimately from Ireland, entailing the principle of *bonum naturale,* that is, the natural goodness of human nature and the possibility of a life lived *naturaliter* without sin.[16] Donahue adduced a number of passages from Hiberno-Latin and Irish vernacular literature to demonstrate the existence of this doctrine in Ireland. However, although *bonum naturale* and the possibility of a sinless life are central dogmas of Pelagianism, Donahue rejected the hypothesis that Pelagianism explained their presence in Irish literature, and sought refuge in the theory of Eastern

---

[10] (J.F.) Kelly, 'Pelagius', 115–17.

[11] O'Loughlin, *Celtic Theology*, 16.

[12] Hardinge, *The Celtic Church*, 61–7; Charles-Edwards, *Early Christian Ireland*, 202–14.

[13] See, however, Bradley, *Celtic Christianity,* 199, for references to popular literature on Pelagius.

[14] (J.F.) Kelly, 'Pelagius'; Ó Cróinín, 'New heresy for old'. Dumville ('Late seventh- or eighth-century evidence', 52) allows for a greater role for the Brittonic Churches in disseminating Pelagius's work than previously supposed, but says little about Pelagian theological influence.

[15] Exceptions are: Ó Néill, '*Romani* influences'; Nerney, 'A study'.

[16] Donahue, 'Beowulf'; *idem*, 'A reconsideration'.

influence, even appealing to Greek theology.[17] J.F. Kelly also reviewed Irish references to *bonum naturale*, but did not regard these as 'classical Pelagianism'.[18] As we shall see, however, when this concept is found, it is usually in the context of anecdotes about gentiles or the pre-Mosaic patriarchs who lived sinless lives under the *lex naturae*. The idea of the possibility of a life lived entirely without sin was so controversial that Pelagius himself hedged his answer when challenged about it. 'The possibility of not sinning' is part and parcel of Pelagian rejection of original sin and the need for any form of grace beyond baptism and instruction, and thus belongs to the central teachings of Pelagius and his followers. Pelagius's positions on these subjects cannot be seen as a simple extension of pre-Augustinian views, as is sometimes maintained.[19] On the contrary, precisely because the Pelagians were pushed by Augustine to define their views in contradistinction to his own, Pelagian positions on nature, the effects of Adam's sin, grace and free will are more radical than the Eastern (Greek) views to which they are often compared.[20] Whereas it is easy to find attestations of the view that a *lex naturae* had been granted to mankind, statements that anyone, gentile or patriarch, had kept it perfectly are extremely hard to find, particularly after the Pelagius–Augustine debate, in which Augustine triumphed unequivocally. Yet, as will be seen, the examples of this assertion in Irish texts are considerable.[21]

One can only speculate as to the reasons for the general scholarly aversion to the Pelagian thesis, especially as it is the right doctrine, in the right place and at the right time. One explanation may be that specialists in early Insular studies have enough to do – and too many languages to learn – to trouble themselves with the complicated history of earlier Christine doctrine, whose study often requires a knowledge of Greek. On this account, the fifth century (in Britain and Ireland) has remained a kind of 'no man's land' for Insular specialists, falling as it does between the end of the Romano-British period and the beginning of what is termed the early middle ages. There is thus a gap between 'Insular' scholarship, which begins in the fifth century at the earliest and works forwards, and patristics, which is regarded largely as the province of ancient history. An exemplary attempt to bridge these fields was made in the recent publication of Archbishop Theodore's biblical glosses carried out by Bernhard Bischoff and Michael Lapidge.[22] But this work was exceptional (in two senses of the word), and there is little evidence of current attempts to overcome the artificial hindrances posed by periodisation and the maintenance of *Fächer*. Given such circumstances, many may deem it best to follow previous authority. If

---

[17] Donahue, 'A reconsideration', 66: 'There is no evidence that Pelagianism as a doctrine was ever a force in Ireland or that it had any direct influence on the formation of the favorable view of the pre-Christian past that was current there.' For his view of Greek influence, see 'A reconsideration', 71.

[18] (J.F.) Kelly, 'Augustine', 142 n. 81.

[19] For example by Markus, 'Pelagianism', 198.

[20] Wickham, 'Pelagianism in the East', 208–9.

[21] These are given in Chapter III, below, 94–7.

[22] Bischoff and Lapidge, *Biblical Commentaries*.

sound scholars have found no evidence for 'real Pelagianism', then surely there is no point in looking for it. That is the charitable explanation. A less charitable one – *ne verum sit!* – is that there may still be scholars in the twenty-first century who cry out with Columbanus, *Nullus hereticus, nullus scismaticus* – certainly not in Britain or Ireland!

An unwillingness to examine the possibility of the continuity of Pelagianism in the British Isles after Germanus is, of itself, unfortunate for the history of doctrine, but there are wider disadvantages for our understanding of early British and Irish Christianity. After claiming that Pelagian doctrine is 'only incidentally a topic touching upon theology in Celtic lands', belonging rather 'to the debates of Italy and North Africa in the early fifth century',[23] Thomas O'Loughlin proceeded to the claim that 'the theological and pastoral work of the early Irish Church constitutes a "local theology"'.[24] In denying the notion of a separate Celtic Church, O'Loughlin states:

Moreover, the 'Celtic Church' notion fails to recognize the most obvious facts: the early [Celtic] theological writers whom we shall examine all sought that theological ideal that the truth was 'what was held always, everywhere, by everyone', and if they had suspected that they were in any way idiosyncratic, they would have been the first to adapt their ideas to that larger group.[25]

This statement appears to miss the point that there is a difference between how heretics think of themselves and what, in fact, heretics are. There is no truly objective criterion of what constitutes a heresy, or for that matter, orthodoxy. It is not meant cynically to assert that orthodox thinkers are people who win a particular debate at a particular time, and heretics are those who lose the decision. In other circumstances, had a few votes at a Church council swung the other way, the result would have been radically different. Following the fine Greek principle 'no one willingly makes a mistake', all those engaged in serious theology believe that they have orthodoxy on their side. Pelagius, Patrick and Columbanus all believed this, as we shall see from their 'professions of faith' given in Chapter II, but, obviously, their opponents did not. Hence, the intention to be orthodox, or the belief that one already is, has little to do with the case. The only thing that matters is the consensus established by the victorious party. In the Insular context, nothing establishes this principle more clearly than the results of the Synod of Whitby. Did the 'Celtic Party' acknowledge that it was in the wrong, or immediately attempt to rectify its error? Inevitably, each side appeals to its own authorities, its own logic, and claims victory, or at least righteousness. Pelagius, who, by all accounts came from Britain, and may have been of Irish descent, was never, or only rarely, seen as a heretic by churchmen in Britain or Ireland. (Anglo-Saxon England viewed him differently, as we shall see.) As already noted, his teachings were vigorously

[23] O'Loughlin, *Celtic Theology*, 16.
[24] O'Loughlin, *Celtic Theology*, 21.
[25] O'Loughlin, *Celtic Theology*, 17.

debated in Britain and Ireland, but the label of 'heresy' was nearly always avoided in internal discussion.[26]

It follows that the contention that the theology of the Celtic regions was merely 'local' must be vigorously challenged.[27] The 'theological spectrum' defined above is markedly different from that of Gaul, and radically distinct from that of North Africa, where devotion to Augustinianism reigned into the sixth century, while the papacy itself, at the end of the fifth century, was reinfected with the Augustinian spirit.[28] Whereas it is certainly true that continental Christianity in the fifth and sixth centuries cannot be described as monolithic, it is just as true that Celtic Christianity was distinctively different from all the Christianities of the Western regions in ways already indicated. It is therefore seriously misleading to compare the difference between early Celtic Christianity and the continental varieties to the different approaches to Thomism found at the Sorbonne, Tübingen or Louvain.[29] This is to trivialise the continuing history of what had been to date the most serious theological conflict in the Western Church.

Whereas the focus of this book is theological rather than institutional, a discussion of early monasticism in the Celtic regions, and generally in the Insular world, is essential to any understanding of the general spiritual outlook and the more focussed issue of Christology which constitutes the second part of the *nexus* mentioned above. Again, it should be stressed that our concern with the organisation of monasteries and their administrative relation to the wider church is peripheral. Our primary interest is in the prevalence of monasticism and its existence as the religious ideal *par excellence*. While Richard Sharpe has shown that there is no reason to think that the jurisdiction over the Irish Church passed to the monasteries,[30] or that abbots usurped the function of bishops, it is indisputable that among Celtic churchmen the monastic life was universally regarded as privileged. It was the life that every Christian should aspire to, and might even be regarded as embodying the 'fulness' of Christianity, with other forms of Christian life being regarded as 'lesser'. As we shall argue, this is an attitude that extends from Patrick and Gildas onwards. So strong was Celtic adherence to the ideal that a form of lay monasticism was offered to those, who on account of marital vows, were unable to achieve a hundred-fold return on their talents!

Although Pelagius himself expressed coolness towards organised monasticism, his principal teaching, emphasising the freedom of the will and the potential of every human being to accomplish his or her salvation, provided the perfect theological foundation for the monastic movement. His contemporary, Cassian of Marseilles, recognised the strength of Pelagius's

---

[26] Markus, 'Pelagianism', 203–4.
[27] O'Loughlin, *Celtic Theology*, 21, describes a 'local theology' as 'distinctiveness . . . relative to a community of belief rather than as the symptoms of sectarianism'.
[28] Markus, 'The legacy', 222–5.
[29] O'Loughlin, *Celtic Theology*, 21.
[30] Sharpe, 'Some problems', 242.

doctrine and incorporated much of it into his own ideal of effort-based monastic life. Cassianic monasticism is rooted in *askesis* ('discipline', 'exercise'). Accordingly, an individual, through understanding and effort, by following prescribed exercises, could attain to spiritual perfection. Those who joined the movement and accepted the challenge of the monastic exercises had a far better chance of achieving salvation than those who remained outside. The language of monastic theology was rich in metaphors for effort and struggle: a recruit could be a *miles Christi*, or an *athleta Dei*. He or she was engaged in a daily contest, *agon*, against the devil, the *antiquus hostis*. At the end of life's contest lay the reward of the *corona*, the *laurus*, or the *palma*.

Early Celtic Christianity – and Western Christianity in general – seems to have laid greater stress on the pains of hell than the joys of heaven. Attaining heaven seems to have brought little more than a sigh of relief. The literature of the age is replete with descriptions of the torments of hell, and the dangers to the soul after it leaves the body. Comparatively little is said about heaven. (One might speculate that one reason for this is that human beings have a common understanding of what constitutes pain, but differ markedly in their definition of pleasure.) Ironically, there was agreement between Augustine and Pelagius, who were poles apart on other issues, that salvation was extremely difficult, and most human beings would end up in hell. It followed – logically from the hypothesis of Pelagius, less so from that of Augustine – that a life of mortification (variously defined) provided the only reliable chance of escape from damnation.

For reasons that are beyond the scope of this book, the late fourth-century ideal of private asceticism gave way to organised monasticism in most regions of the West. Monasteries advanced with the growth of Christianity. The monastery stood as the paragon of Christianity in its fulness, a paradigm of sanctity and token of salvation visible to all the faithful. One must not forget that the Christian movement was about changing people's way of life. While there was hope for those striving to be *perfecti*, care had to be provided for others, namely the laity. The war against paganism in barbarian societies arguably had as much to do with the suppression of violence and free love as it did with the defeat of idol-worship and magic. The layman who forwent his idols but kept his weapons and concubines would have been no further along in the quest for salvation.

True conversion requires of all a total commitment to a Christian way of life; it entails the abandonment of pillage and violence and the direction of human sexuality solely to the procreation of children. For the common Celtic Church, and more generally, throughout early Celtic Christianity, membership in the Church required far more than baptism and attendance at the liturgy. It demanded that the 'faithful laity' attain to a monastic condition to the extent that this was possible, namely by practising sexual abstinence for three forty-day periods each year and by submitting to the guidance of a confessor. As is well known, in Ireland such 'lay monks' acquired the name of *manaig*, derived from the Latin *monachi*. The history of early Celtic Christianity, especially in Ireland, is replete with examples of attempts to restrict the concept of the laity to the 'faithful laity', and regard all others as outside the Church, or as candidates for admission. In the view of numerous ecclesiastical legislators, the Church was all but synonymous with the monastery. If, perhaps, instead of asking the question, 'what was a monastery?', we ask 'who was a monk?', a misunderstanding can be averted.[31]

It is precisely in the context of early Celtic monasticism that the debate between grace and effort takes on importance. A type of grace-based theology that advocates 'love God and do what you will' simply would not do for barbarian societies, where backsliding must have been a constant danger. Thus, even when there is a renewed emphasis on the sacraments and place is found for miracles and relics, the Irish (for whom we have the best evidence) continued to privilege the 'Pelagian' values of good works and obedience to the law. At the spiritual bottom line, God gives his grace to those who deserve it, and miracles are the rewards for a life well lived.

The Christ of early Celtic Christianity was perforce initially the Christ of the Pelagians and semi-Pelagians. In the strictly Pelagian view, he is to be seen primarily as the giver of the New Law and as the ultimate model for human imitation. Thus it is the penitential aspect of Christ – the Christ of the desert and Christ of the cross – that receives greatest attention. Christ's death on the cross was undertaken so that all should die to their sins. Initially, little regard is given to the crucifixion as a redemptive act in the mystical sense. In the Pelagian view, just as all men did not die in Adam, so all men do not rise in Christ. As it is clear that Christ's supreme sacrifice did not and could not accomplish the redemption of all mankind, even though God wills the redemption of all, his mission to the world must have contained a different purpose. This must have been the giving of the New Law and the example of a perfect life. Thus salvation is accomplished by adherence to the law of Christ, by profiting from the instruction he gave, and by imitating his perfect life. We cannot, by virtue of our own wills, imitate Christ's resurrection from the dead, but we can follow in his footsteps into the desert, and onto the cross. Such a characterisation perhaps validates the waggish view of a 'Nestorian Christ saving Pelagian man'.[32]

A semi-Pelagian Christology is not so very different in the essentials, but it is a bit softer around the edges. Christ can be seen as a 'refuge' and is referred to as 'Saviour'. He is sometimes accorded the prerogative of drawing some men to their salvation – a notion that strict Pelagians would deem anathema. And, whereas writers such as Cassian were averse to thaumaturgy, there is a recognition that God can operate in miraculous ways to aid the righteous. Grace, then, is awarded in relation to merit. We may have here the theological foundation of what can be termed a 'monastic miracle': this is not a miracle performed *by* monks, but is rather a supernatural reward conferred *upon* those who have earned it through their sanctity. Insular hagiography has relatively numerous examples of such

---

[31] This is a refocussing of the discussion in Sharpe, 'Some problems', 260–1.
[32] Wickham, 'Pelagianism in the East', 210.

interventions. They often involve the motif of birds or other animals ministering to the needs of the *perfecti*.

As noted above, *Romani* ideas and religious motifs reached southern Ireland by the second quarter of the seventh century, producing a much expanded range of Christological images, drawn from both canonical and apocryphal scriptures. The reading of the gospels was no longer restricted to a selection of Christ's penitential acts and his teachings, but enlarged to include his miracles. The evangelical miracles were supplemented by the apostolic wonders detailed in Acts, and also by thaumaturgical elements from non-canonical literature. It is this extra-evangelical component that creates an image of sanctity strikingly at odds with a Christ based strictly on the canonical gospels. Interestingly, hagiographical literature, which rose fully armed with every kind of thaumaturgical act, was introduced into the Celtic world, and specifically Ireland, shortly after the dissolution of the common Celtic Church. One may have reason to suppose, even if it is not provable in the strict sense, that Pelagian resistance to all forms of grace and the semi-Pelagian preference for 'merited grace' and 'merited miracles' combined to inhibit the development of a genre of writing long popular in Gaul and Italy.[33]

The use of non-canonical gospels introduced by the Irish *Romani* produced an image of Christ that was to be embraced by the entire Insular world. This is the 'heroic Christ', the Christ who overcame Satan in physical combat and harrowed hell. Such a Christ would have been unwelcome in the pre-*Romani* world, and probably in other quarters as well long after the dissolution of the common Celtic Church. Pelagian sympathisers, in particular, would have opposed the introduction of the motif on two grounds: (1) non-canonical scriptures should be avoided on the principle that they undermined the clarity of the divine law; (2) there would have been no need for Christ to release those who had already saved themselves! But the power of this heroic image of Christ upon the imagination and the need to demonstrate divine justice largely overcame any theological resistance. The Christ of the harrowing was to become a popular theme in *Insular* poetry. Versions of the tale are to be found in Irish, Latin and Old English.

In one very important aspect, a *Romani* – and specifically Augustinian – image of Christ clearly triumphed over the ideal of the common Celtic Church. This is in the characterisation of Christ as the judge of the world. Pelagius, and certainly the semi-Pelagians too, believed in Christ as the *iudex aequitatis*. For them, Christ at the end of the world would judge everyone fairly according to each one's deserts. Nothing had been pre-decided. For Augustinians, the purpose of the Last Judgement was simply to reveal the good and the evil to the entire cosmos. Christ's Second Coming was not for the sake of judgement, but of pronouncing sentence. The wicked were not only foreknown, but forejudged. But there is more. Christ does not simply dispense a punishment already expected, he comes to avenge himself on those who caused his scourging and crucifixion! Christ arrives 'red-backed'

---

[33] This point is developed fully in Chapter IV, 118–22.

and carrying his cross.[34] This concept of an 'angry Christ', harmonising with the idea of predestination, is clearly alien to both Pelagianism and semi-Pelagianism, and a sharp departure from the theology of the common Celtic Church.

The 'post-dissolution' world of Celtic Christianity offers a mixture of survivals and radical departures. The teaching, preaching, scripturalist and non-mystical Church we have called 'common Celtic' survived in places for some time, but elsewhere gave way to the advocates of grace, sacraments, miracles and relics. While the differences were originally largely regional, it is likely that these disappeared in favour of a synthesis, or perhaps a series of syntheses. As we shall argue, the *Céli Dé* movement effected one such synthesis. However, the theology of the common Celtic Church was never fully eradicated by the *Romani* in their time, or by later continental influences. Christ remained the Perfect Monk, his sacrifice on the cross prevailed over his resurrection (because the latter could not be imitated), a penitential life was recommended for everyone, and effort and merit continued to be preferred to passivity and grace.

The last two chapters bring visual images of Christ into the discussion of early Celtic Christianity. Early medieval art in the Celtic-dominated areas of Britain and Ireland has received a considerable amount of scholarly attention in the past century, spurred on by the study of manuscript collections and archaeological finds exposed by the farmer's plow. Intricately-worked metal objects of obvious Christian intent, illuminated manuscripts of astonishing complexity, and impressive standing high crosses ascribed to the seventh to tenth centuries attest to a lively and sophisticated artistic component within the religious communities. Currently, there are two main approaches to the study of these works of art. One deals with the material and formal aspects of objects, describing and analysing the techniques of fabrication and design, producing catalogues of formal patterns and elements. This leads to the discussion of dating and origins, issues which are fraught with difficulties because of the lack of specific evidence. The other approach focusses attention on the iconographical interpretation of the images, motifs and symbols. Current iconographical studies have become increasingly linked to the study of liturgical usage and development, and to seeking sources in biblical and exegetical texts. Our discussion seeks to place early Christian Celtic and Insular art into the context of Celtic monastic theology, with emphasis on how Christ in his various aspects was represented. Our approach is primarily iconographic, attempting to establish how the viewers of the time would have reacted to the images before them. Style is brought into the equation as an aspect of the total impact of imagery rather than as a separate study devoid of meaning.

There is ample evidence for a thriving Christian art during the Romano-British period as attested by surviving frescos and mosaics, as well as smaller objects, with obvious Christian content. Christ was represented both

---

[34] See the discussion in Chapters V and VII.

symbolically and realistically. We suspect that the apparent hiatus in the creation of sumptuous religious art for Christian use in the fifth to late-seventh centuries and the absence of images of Christ in the common Celtic Church is due to Pelagian-based strictures against luxury combined with their literal interpretation of the scriptural injunctions against imagery. Although religious imagery was introduced into southern England at the very end of the sixth century with the arrival of Augustine and his entourage, it was some time before religious art became established in northern England or in Ireland. The creation and use of religious art and imagery in Celtic Christianity coincided with the growing influence of the *Romani* and the dissolution of the common Celtic Church after the mid-seventh century. The cult of the Cross was introduced into Britain and Ireland and was manifested in both literary and artistic forms. The hundreds of cross-inscribed pillars and slabs, the latter mostly grave-markers, and the remains of equally numerous stone crosses found in both Ireland and Britain attest to the ubiquitous adoption of the primary symbol of Christ and Christianity. Manuscripts containing the sacred texts required for liturgical and monastic use were produced, many of them lavishly decorated with painted decoration and images. Sumptuous liturgical vessels and shrines to hold relics appeared in abundance.

While the original impetus for the creation and use of religious art may have come from Italy, the motifs chosen and the interpretation of both symbol and image were determined by local conditions and tradition. This led to different manifestations in Anglo-Saxon England and in Celtic areas of Britain and Ireland. Irish churchmen returning to their homeland from Rome, probably in the early 630s, brought with them books, relics and perhaps visual memories, but there is no record that they transported images in their currachs. There is no evidence for the importation of continental artisans into Ireland or of the desire to collect artistic prototypes from the Mediterranean. This is in contrast to the undisputed evidence for both phenomena occurring in the Northumbrian monasteries under the influence of Benedict Biscop and Wilfrid. Perhaps for this reason, change occurred more slowly in the Celtic-dominated areas for some time after the incursion of the *Romani*. The severely iconoclastic aspect of the common Celtic Church seems to have created a religious atmosphere which preferred to symbolise Christ rather than to represent him in a realistic fashion. The Western Church had accepted the practice of representing Christ in his bodily form from the end of the third century, but it was not until the Quinisext Council of 692 that this became canonically entrenched. The Christ figures on the Ruthwell cross, generally accepted as dating from the first half of the eighth century, are perhaps the earliest of the 'realistic' images of Christ in the Insular world where the Celtic and Anglo-Saxon traditions met and melded. While the antique artistic tradition had a strong influence on the Anglo-Saxon establishments from the seventh century on,[35] it had less impact in the Celtic centres. Only gradually was the representation of Christ and his deeds introduced into the Celtic churches, coming to full

---

[35] Henderson, *Vision and Image*, 56–122.

fruition in the series of so-called 'scripture crosses' of the ninth and tenth centuries.

We discuss symbolic and representational images of Christ separately in order to distinguish the inherent differences in thinking underlying these two conceptions of the relationship between image and idea. We argue that the images of Christ, whether symbolic or representational, can only be fully understood if one acknowledges the complexity of meaning transmitted by visual art. On the primary level it attracts attention as an aesthetic object pleasing to the eye, often employing patterns, motifs and images associated with and easily identified by the society which creates it. Hence the retention of the indigenous Celtic decorative motifs such as the spiral and pelta, along with the Germanic and Pictish animal forms and the Roman interlace, combined to form what we call 'Insular' art. These motifs were used in association with religious art, and undoubtedly secular art which had disappeared, creating objects and monuments which are part of a continuing local tradition rather than incursions from a foreign culture. On a 'deeper' level, images and symbols incorporated into the work of art carry a perceptible meaning which must be deciphered by the viewer. Since each viewer responds to a visual stimulus from the standpoint of personal as well as collective experience, it is important to try to recreate the viewpoint of the particular person or group for whom the images were made, locating both the art and the group in a particular place and time. This is particularly important when studying images, such as that of Christ, which appear throughout the Christian world, but which would convey different meanings to different groups. We have adopted the principle that the only reliable path to uncovering the meaning that the images of Christ would have conveyed to the participant in early Celtic Christianity in Britain and Ireland is to study the texts which would have been known to them. This is the only way to arrive at an insight into the spiritual preoccupations and theological leanings of the local population. The use of texts and liturgies known in the Mediterranean and further afield, but for which there is no evidence for their transmission to the Celtic areas we discuss, may be interesting, but in the end yields little of value – hence our reliance upon Irish and local Latin textual traditions, along with scripture and apocryphal writings as the basis from which to interpret the art. We believe that local tradition would be a greater component in forming the visual expression of Celtic Christianity than would a distant and culturally alien source,[36] and that this would be true from the period of the artistic hiatus of the fifth century to the full artistic flowering of the tenth.

We discuss many different ways of representing Christ in symbolic form: the cross, the fish, the sacred monogram, the vine, the tree of life. Since the cross is the most frequently appearing proxy image for Christ, we discuss the nature and development of the cult of the cross which leads to the creation of the stone high crosses of Ireland and Britain. In manuscripts, the cross carpet pages are another manifestation of the same iconography. The singling out of the *Chi Rho* in Matthew is a feature of the luxury gospel

---

[36] See the argument of Stalley, 'European art and the Irish high cross'.

books created in the Celtic monastic centres and is another manifestation of the iconography of Christ. We interpret the representational images of Christ, where he is shown in his human form, in the context of a monastic community, as providing lessons and ideals for the devout Christian in his or her search for salvation. Hence, we discuss the portrayal of Christ as the Ideal Monk, the crucified Christ as both priest and sacrifice, Christ as Judge and conqueror of hell, Christ as the militant hero at the end of time, and Christ the wonder-worker. All of these correspond to what can be found in available textual sources.

By stressing the monastic and devotional component of the chosen images, even if at the expense of downplaying the liturgical connection, we attempt to place the visual images and symbols of Christ in the context of the life and devotion of the Celtic Christian man and woman, whether clerical, monastic or lay, and the aspiration each would have had for his or her own spiritual future. We do not necessarily see text and image in a direct causal relationship – an image need not have been a deliberate illustration of a specific text. In fact, this is seldom the case. Nor must every level of meaning have been intended by the creating artist or the 'patron'. Our arguments are built upon the principle that, in our period, texts are 'absorbed' into a society and become part of the 'collective' way of thinking. An image can recall a number of different associations relayed by texts and culture and can carry multivalent meanings, the comprehension and interpretation of which will be reliant upon the repository of ideas in the viewer's mind. Two of the examples which we invoke are the Christ/Priest of the Athlone Plaque and the Christ/Moses on fo.114r of the Book of Kells. As mentioned earlier, we posit that even though representations of Christ appear late in our historical period, they embody many ideas which had been established much earlier. But it is essential to establish which texts and doctrines could have been known in Celtic areas in the fifth to tenth centuries in order to create a solid basis for interpretative study of the visual imagery. Hence our study of the visual culture of early Celtic Christianity closely follows the preceding study of the theological and religious culture of which it was both product and component.

I

THE GROWTH AND DEVELOPMENT OF
MONASTICISM IN THE BRITISH ISLES

In our Introduction we stated that the Insular world was 'monasticised'. At the same time, we wish to acknowledge that, at least for the Irish Church, there was no such thing as an over-arching monastic structure under which all religious activity was subsumed. We note that even the meaning of the term 'monastery' has been left open to question.[1] In what follows, we examine evidence of a different character, namely that which reveals the promotion of the monastic ideal (expressed in various life-styles) as shown by writers of the three Insular regions. Where possible, we relate this type of evidence to the evidence for the existence of monks and monasteries at various times and in various places. Monastically-oriented texts are, by definition, the writings of an elite about an elite. Those practising the 'perfect life' are very few, yet their influence is great, or, more accurately, made to be great by the opinion-makers. These were the proponents of monastic spirituality, whose writings exercised an influence on the clergy concerned with a verbal translation of Christianity to a wider public, as well as on the artists who created objects that could convey specific meanings to the monk, cleric and lay person.

Monasticism began in Egypt and Syria in the fourth century and rapidly spread westward. By the end of the fourth century it was known in Italy and Gaul. What began with individuals seeking salvation in the desert changed into a variety of social forms. Groups could be very small: a chaste widow living in her own home with her virginal daughter, a married couple living in continence by a shrine, a small group of men living in celibacy on an island. As early as Augustine's day, monastic clergy were attached to episcopal churches, and thus began the long tradition of canons regular.[2] Separate churches for monks and nuns, otherwise known as monasteries, also found early adherents. This was the case at Lérins, an island off the coast of France near present-day Cannes. In some cases monasteries for monks were contiguous to those for nuns – these were the so-called 'double monasteries'. A separated community life – coenobitism – found its perfect model in the monastery and rule of Benedict of Nursia, who flourished in Italy around the middle of the sixth century. This model was destined to win over all of western Europe, yet its influence was limited in the Insular world in the period which we are considering.

[1] Sharpe, 'Some problems', 260–3.
[2] Ladner, *The Idea*, 350–65.

Understanding the precise relationship of a monastic group to the wider religious community composed of non-monastic clergy and laity is difficult. If monks are dedicated to a life of self-perfection, and if they have no sacerdotal powers, how can they serve the overall needs of the Church? A related question is: why were missionaries from the late fourth to the eighth centuries so eager to establish a monastic element in the midst of barbarian converts, to whom the concept of virginity would have been utterly unnatural, if not repulsive? Yet such an intention was obviously in the minds of the most prominent missionaries of the period. It began with Martin of Tours, followed by Victricius of Rouen who converted the pagans of northern Gaul in the late fourth century. It is repeated in Patrick's mission to Ireland in the fifth century, Columba's mission to the Picts in the late sixth century, Augustine of Canterbury's papally-sponsored mission to Anglo-Saxon England beginning in 597, and Columbanus's mission to Gaul and Rhaetia (Switzerland) in the early seventh century. The explanation must lie in the need to have a core of fervent Christians who could serve as role-models for everybody else. A community of *conversi* made up of (married) secular clergy and lay people living in families must have been thought of as simply not viable. Monks and virgins were seen as role-models for the new Christian communities in late antiquity and the early middle ages.[3] Moreover, the presence of institutionalised monasticism offered opportunities beyond baptism to the newly converted and their descendants. Those who sought the holier life had the possibility of spiritual 'upward mobility'.

Britain: 400–700

The origins of monasticism in Britain are extremely difficult to trace. The monastic movement is thought to have reached Britain by *ca* 500.[4] This fact, of course, does not exclude the possibility that small groups of individuals attached to episcopal churches led a monastic life in the manner of canons regular, or that there might have been men or women practising some form of monasticism in remote regions in buildings that have left no trace. Evidence for the first of these possibilities is provided by Gildas who describes the persecution and abuse of religious women by secular bishops.[5] But the situation Gildas describes is apparently contemporary, and thus belongs to the sixth century.

Several possible references to fifth-century Britons in the monastic movement need to be considered. First Nynia, as recounted by Bede, founded a church dedicated to St Martin at Whithorn. Bede tells us that this church was known as *Candida Casa*, as it was made of stone rather than the customary timber.[6] Nynia, whom Bede describes as a bishop who went to

---

[3] Herren, 'Mission and monasticism', 83–4.
[4] Olson, *Early Monasteries*, 4.
[5] Gildas, *The Ruin*, LXVI (tr. Winterbottom, 52).
[6] Bede, *Historia Ecclesiastica*, III.4 (edd. Colgrave & Mynors, 223).

Rome, is credited with the conversion of the southern Picts. Nynia has traditionally been dated to the fifth century – indeed, to the early fifth – on the witness of the twelfth-century writer Ailred of Rievaulx who makes Nynia a contemporary of St Martin. However, considerable doubt now surrounds this early dating. A number of scholars now argue for a sixth-century date for Nynia, and the time of the establishment of *Candida Casa* is also in question.[7] In any case, we know nothing of Nynia's role in promoting monasticism in Britain, and cannot even be sure that the dedication of the foundation to St Martin was contemporary with Nynia or not.

The most important development in the fifth-century British Church involved a Briton who spent his career outside his homeland, as far as is known. This was the heretic Pelagius, whom most contemporary sources called a 'Briton', although Jerome called him 'Irish by race'.[8] It is not impossible that he was a member of an Irish colony established in south-western Wales. He was born early in the second half of the fourth century, most probably educated in Britain, spent his career in Rome and Palestine, was tried for heresy in various places, and finally expelled from Rome in 418.[9] We do not have certain news of him afterwards; his heresy was condemned at Ephesus in 431. Two salient facts about Pelagius concern us: his heresy and its effects in Britain, which will be dealt with in some detail in the following chapters, and the possibility that he was a monk, which concerns us immediately.[10] His closest associate, Coelestius, is described as a monk in one source.[11] In fact, Pelagius was probably not a monk in the sense of one who lived in a community.[12] Moreover, one Pelagian writer even raised doubts about the validity of the monastic movement he saw developing around him:

I want you to be called a Christian, not a monk, and to possess the virtue of your own personal claim to praise rather than a foreign name which is bestowed to no purpose by Latins on men who stay in the common crowd, whereas it is given legitimately by Greeks to those who lead a solitary life.[13]

---

[7] For advocacy of a sixth-century date for Nynia see MacQuarrie, *The Saints of Scotland*, 50–73. For a recent defence of the traditional date see MacQueen, *St Nynia*, 1–31, together with the review article by Broun, 'The literary record'. It has recently been proposed, however, that Nynia should be identified with Uinniau: see Clancy, 'The real St Ninian'. It has not been possible to explore fully the implications of this theory in the current work.

[8] See the references collected in Zimmer, *Pelagius in Irland*, 18–21; also Kenney, *Sources*, 161–3.

[9] For a brief sketch of Pelagius's career, see Rees, *Pelagius*, ix–xv.

[10] See the references in Morris, 'Pelagian literature', 41–2.

[11] Genadius, *De scriptoribus ecclesiasticis*, XLIV (cit. Morris, 'Pelagian literature', 41).

[12] See the references in Rees, *Pelagius*, xiv, nn. 23, 25, 26.

[13] On the Divine Law, IX.3 (tr. Rees, *The Letters*, 102); *De divina lege*, VII. 9 (*PL* XXX.115): 'Ego te Christianum volo esse, non monachum dici, et virtutem propriæ laudis possidere magis quam nomen alienum. Quod frustra a Latinis in turba commorantibus imponitur, cum a Græcis solitarie viventibus legitime deputetur.'

However, Pelagius assuredly led an ascetic life. His theology was a basis of the modified doctrine (semi-Pelagianism) which was espoused by John Cassian and incorporated into his monastic teachings. These doctrines, expressed in the *Institutes* and the *Conferences*, were influential in both Britain and Ireland. Without denying grace, they emphasised effort and proper spiritual discipline as the means to salvation. They had a direct impact on the work of Faustus, a Briton resident in southern Gaul in the fifth century, and of Columbanus, an Irish monk and missionary who wrote monastic literature in the early seventh century.[14]

Pelagius is important to the monastic question for a second reason. Nearly all early monastic writers regarded virginity as the foundation of perfection. Pelagius and his associates did not deny the importance of this virtue, but they placed greater emphasis on poverty, which was to become 'the first perfection' of Cassian and Columbanus. The author of the treatise *On Riches* scoured both Testaments for evidence to prove that a rich man could not be saved. Avarice was the root of all evil. In this work we read:

But lust and gluttony are more easily overcome than avarice, because in their case satiety arouses a certain feeling of repugnance, whereas avarice, since it is insatiable, is never repugnant in those who love it . . . Finally, in many men you will find gluttony and lust overthrown; but even those who censure avarice have great difficulty in entirely subduing it.[15]

Opposition to Pelagianism in Britain may have been fiercer because of Pelagius's teachings on worldly goods than his teachings on grace. Fifth-century evidence provided by Patrick shows that wealth and status were entrenched in ecclesiastical families. Patrick's father was a deacon, who was the son of the priest Potitus, 'who had a small estate'.[16] His father was also a decurion, showing that a civil office could be combined with clerical status.[17] Patrick himself inherited money which he used to finance a private mission to Ireland. Gildas, in the sixth century, wrote a savage attack on the secular clergy living in luxury: 'You desire a bishopric greatly, because of your avarice and not on the pretext of the spiritual advancement it

---

[14] For Columbanus's use of Cassian see Walker, *Sancti Columbani Opera*, ix; also, Stancliffe, 'The thirteen sermons', 105–6.

[15] On Riches, I.3 (tr. Rees, *The Letters*, 175); *De divitiis*, I.4 (*PL* LI.1380–1): 'Facilius tamen uel libido, uel gula, quam auaritia uincitur, quia illa duo cum saturata fuerint, aliquid habere uidentur horroris, haec uero, sicut satiari nescit, ita nunquam suis amatoribus perhorrescit . . . Denique apud multos inuenies gulam libidinemque prostratam, auaritiam uero ipse uix, qui uituperant, deuicere.' The tract *De divitiis* belongs to the group of works known as the 'Caspari Letters'. Some scholars do not think that these came from the pen of Pelagius. However, they closely reflect the thought of Pelagius and employ many of his favourite scriptural quotations. See Rees, *The Letters*, 171–4, and his Introduction. If the work is not by Pelagius, it is probably by his very close associate Coelestius: see Morris, *Pelagian Literature*, 40–1.

[16] Patrick, *Confession*, I (tr. Hood, 41): 'uillulam enim prope habuit' (Bieler, *Libri epistolarum*, I.56).

[17] Patrick, *Letter to Coroticus*, X (tr. Hood, 57).

offers.'[18] Gildas apparently saw the monastic movement as a corrective to the corruption that had set into the secular clergy.[19] Towards the middle of the sixth century, when Gildas was an old man, monasticism had established itself in Britain and had developed factions of its own. Around this time we hear of a controversy involving the rights of monks to bring their private property with them to the monastery. There must have been rigorists who demanded complete renunciation of worldly goods upon entrance. Gildas entered the fray again, this time to plead for moderation:

> But if any monk has a superabundance of wordly things, they should be put down as luxury and riches; but he will not be blamed for owning anything he is compelled to possess by need rather than choice, so as to avoid destitution.[20]

It is possible, then, that for most of the fifth century the monastic movement in Britain experienced stiff resistance from vested interests, compelling British men and women desirous of the life to find it abroad. Faustus is a good example. He seems to have departed his homeland at an early age, as he was already abbot of Lérins in 433; we find him still living in 485.[21] Faustus, who became bishop of Riez, wrote an important treatise on grace as well as letters and sermons, some of which are addressed to monks; these will be examined later.[22]

We glean some important comments about the general character of British Christianity, and some evidence regarding Britons leading a monastic life abroad from Patrick, a Briton who conducted a mission to Ireland in the fifth century. We do not know whether his mission fell into the second third of the fifth century or the last third, as there is much confusion of the record.[23] Patrick's career may have been conflated in the sources with that of Palladius, who was sent as bishop to the Irish by Pope Celestine in 431.[24] Patrick left us two important documents: a *Confession*, which provides a rather patchy first-person account of his life and mission, and the *Letter to Coroticus*, which condemned the killing and capturing of recently converted Christians by a certain British chieftain.[25] The authenticity of these

---

[18] Gildas, *The Ruin*, CVIII.3 (tr. Winterbottom, 77); *De excidio*, CVIII.3 (ed. Winterbottom, 140): 'Vos episcopatum magnopere avaritiae gratia, non spiritalis profectus obtentu cupitis . . .'

[19] Herren, 'Gildas', 75.

[20] Gildas, *Fragments*, IV (tr. Winterbottom, *Gildas*, 81); *Fragmenta*, IV (ed. Winterbottom, 144): 'Quicquid autem monacho de rebus saecularibus superabundat, ad luxurias et divitias debet referri, et quod necessitate, non voluntate habere compellitur, ut non penuria cadat, non illi ad malum reputabitur.'

[21] Bolton, *A History of Anglo-Latin Literature*, I.21.

[22] See below, 79–80.

[23] For recent discussion of the problem of Patrick's dates, see Dumville, *Saint Patrick*, 1–12, 13–18, 29–33, 39–43, 45–50, 51–64.

[24] See especially O'Rahilly, *The Two Patricks*. On Palladius see now Ó Cróinín, 'Who was Palladius?'

[25] Texts and translations in Hood, *St Patrick*, except where otherwise noted; on Coroticus, see Thompson, *Who was Saint Patrick?*, 125–43.

documents has never been impugned, and they remain our best written sources for Patrick's mission.[26]

Patrick has only a little to say about the British Church of his day; his comments, like those of Gildas, are mostly critical.[27] Commenting on his success in convincing young Irish noblewomen to become virgins of Christ, he makes a parenthetical remark about British virgins:

... and nonetheless, their number [of virgins] continues to grow (and as for those of our own race who were born there we do not know the number), and this figure does not include widows and those who practise continence.[28]

In translating the passage, we have kept to its original, rather awkward, word-order. The passage appears to suggest that British Christians were living in Ireland and practising virginity. The placement of the crucial words *et de genere nostro qui ibi nati sunt nescimus numerum eorum* ('and as for those of our own race who were born there we do not know the number') argues in favour of the possibility. These British Christians may have been victims of slave-raids, as was Patrick himself.[29] However, it is also a possibility that Patrick encountered persons who chose to live a religious life in Ireland because of more favourable conditions.

The extent of Patrick's commitment to promulgating the virginal condition is shown clearly in a central section of the *Confessio* (chs. XLI–XLIII), in which the writer notes that in addition to bringing a pagan people to the knowledge of God he also encouraged a considerable number of others, both men and women, to embrace the monastic life. In a remarkable statement, Patrick admits that he was willing to leave his mission and return to his homeland, and would have done so, had it not been for his fear of losing the chief fruit of his work: the spiritual gains of the women whom he had persuaded to become virgins of Christ:

And so it is that even if I wished to leave these women and go to Britain – and I was wholly disposed to do so, partly for the sake of my homeland and family, but not only that, but also to go as far as Gaul to visit the brethren and to see the visage of the holy men of my Lord; God knows how much I desired to do this – but I was bound by the Spirit who declared to me that if I do this, he will mark me as liable at some future time, and I fear to lose the work that I have begun – and not I but Christ the Lord who bade me to come to be with them for the rest of my life ....[30]

We have no sure knowledge of where Patrick acquired his commitment to the idea of a monasticised Church, or put more cautiously, a Church with a

---

[26] Binchy, 'Patrick and his biographers'.

[27] Herren, 'Mission and monasticism', 82.

[28] Patrick, *Confession,* XLII (tr. Herren, 'Mission and monasticism', 79); *Confessio,* XLII (ed. Bieler, *Libri epistolarum,* I.82): '... et nihilominus plus augetur numerus (et de genere nostro qui ibi nati sunt nescimus numerum eorum) praeter uiduas et continentes'. On the difficulties of the passage, see Dumville, 'Some British aspects', 17–18.

[29] Dumville, 'Some British aspects', 17–18.

[30] Patrick, *Confession*, XLIII (tr. Herren, 'Mission and monasticism', 80); Latin text below, 44.

monastic component. Did Patrick go to Gaul and study at the feet of monastic masters? Given the assured dating of Patrick to the fifth century, one wonders how and where at home he could have acquired his orientation. If, for example, Nynia's *Candida Casa* already existed and offered a monastic training in Patrick's day, why did Patrick not mention a desire to visit the brethren there, or somewhere else in Britain, rather than those in Gaul? Surely, the natural construction of Patrick's words is that, next to seeing his homeland and family, his greatest desire was to visit the holy men in Gaul *with whom he had shared a spiritual experience.*

We may gain some insight into the state of monasticism in fifth-century Britain by examining the *acta* of a late fifth-century synod in Brittany. This is the Council of Vannes, which occurred some time between 461 and 491.[31] There are specific provisions for monks: they are not permitted to wander (canon VI); they may not arbitrarily remove themselves to a solitary cell (canon VII); abbots are forbidden to have separate cells and may not rule more than one monastery (canon VIII). Virgins who violate their vows are to be regarded as adulterous and excommunicated (canon IV). Priests, deacons, and subdeacons are forbidden to take wives (canon XI). Penitents who fall back into their old ways are to be excommunicated (canon III). The overall tenor of the text bears a general resemblance to the canon collections and penitentials of sixth-century Britain and seventh-century Ireland. It is addressed to monks, regular clergy (bishops down to subdeacons), and to the general population. It insists that clergy from subdeacon upwards be unmarried. Penitents are treated as a special class. In some ways it resembles the so-called 'First Synod of St Patrick'[32] – both texts, in addition to concerns about wandering clerics and monks and fallen virgins, deal with Christians who go to law in secular courts and those who practise pagan superstitions. They differ, however, on the issue of clerical celibacy; in contrast to the harsh pronouncements of Vannes, the 'First Synod' regards married clergy as normal (canon VI).

Gildas presents us with another enigma. The evidence for his dates is as insecure as those for Patrick. The obits from the Irish annals fall between 565 and 570, but Irish annalistic dates before *ca* 600 are notoriously unreliable.[33] Scholars have reckoned his *floruit* at various times between the second half of the fifth century and the middle of the sixth.[34] However, recent work has argued convincingly that Gildas's writing reveals an intellectual formation more congruous with late Roman secular education than with a monastic formation, and hints at a dating earlier than that given by the annals.[35] At all events, Gildas is an important figure for recording the

---

[31] de Paor, *Saint Patrick's World*, 66–9; evidence for the date is on p. 66.

[32] Ed. Bieler, *The Irish Penitentials*, 54–9. See the discussion below, 31–2.

[33] Smyth, 'The earliest Irish Annals'.

[34] See Dumville, 'The chronology', 61–84, for a defence of the traditional dating of Gildas's *floruit* to the middle of the sixth century.

[35] Lapidge, 'Gildas's education'; see also the detailed study by Kerlouégan, 'Le *De excidio*', 546–79, for Gildas's attachment to the ideal of *Romanitas*. An earlier dating is also advanced by Wood, 'The end of Roman Britain', 23.

transition of British Christianity from an exclusively sacerdotal structure to one that makes a place for monasticism.[36]

Gildas has been credited with several writings, but there are only two of which we can be certain: the *De excidio Britanniae* (*The Ruin of Britain*) and a group of epistolary fragments. The *Preface on Penance* attributed to him is almost certainly spurious, as is the *Lorica*.[37] *The Ruin* is an attack on the laxity of the British secular clergy of the late fifth or early sixth century. The work also contains severe criticism of British kings of the period. The words 'abbot', 'monk', and 'decrees concerning monks' are used in the text, and a sharp contrast is drawn between the *sancti* and the secular clergy, the former represented as the only hope of Britain. Gildas states his desire to be a participant in a distinctive form of spiritual life:

... I beg to be forgiven by those whose life I praise and indeed prefer to all the riches of this world. If it may be so, I desire and thirst to be a participant in that life before I die.[38]

Gildas is, without any doubt, alluding to his desire to become a monk. A life to be preferred 'to all the riches of this world' is the life of poverty, and poverty was the 'first perfection' of Cassian-influenced Celtic monasticism, as a later chapter will show.

The epistolary fragments, written considerably later when Gildas was enjoying the life he sought, treat problems of discipline in the Church; several of these explicitly deal with monastic questions.[39] Gildas reveals himself as a moderate reformer, concerned with preserving evangelical values against the encroachments of asceticism:

Abstinence from bodily food is useless without charity. Those who do not fast unduly or abstain over much from God's creation, while being careful in the sight of God to preserve within them a clean heart (on which, as they know, their life ultimately depends), are better than those who do not eat flesh or take pleasure in the food of this world . . .[40]

The combined evidence of Gildas's writings indicate that within the author's lifetime monasticism had moved from the status of a small protest movement to that of an important institution within Christianity, which was already undergoing differences of spiritual emphasis, if not the presence of factions.

[36] Herren, 'Gildas'.
[37] *Ibid.*, 65–6.
[38] Gildas, *The Ruin*, LXV (tr. Winterbottom, 51–2); *De excidio*, LXV (ed. Winterbottom, 118): 'Mihi quaeso . . . ab his veniam impertiri quorum vitam non solum laudo verum etiam cunctis mundi opibus praefero, cuiusque me, si fieri possit, ante mortis diem esse aliquamdiu participem opto et sitio.'
[39] Sharpe, 'Gildas as a father', 193–205.
[40] Gildas, *Fragments*, II (tr. Winterbottom, 80); *Fragmenta*, II (ed. Winterbottom, 143): 'Abstinentia corporalium ciborum absque caritate inutilis est. Meliores sunt ergo qui non magno opere ieiunant nec supra modum a creatura dei se abstinent, cor autem intrinsecus nitidum coram deo sollicite servantes, a quo sciunt exitum vitae, quam illi qui carnem non edunt nec cibis saecularibus delectantur . . .'

A work of uncertain date, attributed to Gildas in the manuscripts, is the *Preface of Gildas on Penance*.[41] Its references to Roman and British systems of measurement give clear proofs of its place of composition. A harsh and casuistic tone sets it apart from the genuine responses of Gildas on monastic matters (indeed, the two texts appear to contradict each other on the question of excommunication).[42] Many of the canons are aimed specifically at monks, and a monastic community is suggested by a reference to psalm-singing. Canons XVI, XVII, and XXVII enjoin the reporting of offences to abbots.

If we except the quasi-legendary monastic figures of the British Church such as Illtud and David, who left no certain writings,[43] the only other well-known British ecclesiastic of the sixth century is Uinniau (Finnian),[44] who wrote a penitential (perhaps the earliest that survives),[45] and who sent questions to Gildas on various problems relating to monastic practice, to which we have Gildas's replies in the form of epistolary fragments.[46] This Uinniau may well be identical to the bishop Uinniau who taught Columba when the latter was still a deacon.[47] Although his penitential specifically mentions monasteries and monks, it appears to be aimed at churches that include non-monastic clergy. Monks are sharply distinguished from clergy: 'Monks, however, are not to baptise, nor to receive alms. Else, if they do receive alms, why shall they not baptise?'[48] Moreover, Uinniau insists that those in clerical orders maintain chastity. If they have been previously married, they are not to return to their wives or families:

If anyone is a cleric of the rank of a deacon, or of any rank, and if he was formerly a layman, and if he lives with his sons and daughters and with his mate and if he returns to carnal desire and begets a son with his own mate, as he might say, let him know that he has fallen to the depths of ruin and ought to rise; his sin is not less than it would be if he had been a cleric from his youth and sinned with a strange girl, since they have sinned after their vow and after they were consecrated to God, and then they have made a vow void.[49]

Uinniau's text (mid-sixth century?) gives our earliest *insular* evidence of an

---

[41] Bieler (ed.), *The Irish Penitentials*, 60–5.

[42] *Preface*, XII (ed. Bieler, *The Irish Penitentials*, 62–3), and Gildas, *Fragments*, I (tr. Winterbottom, 80; text, 143).

[43] Excerpts from a 'Book of David' are edited by Bieler, *The Irish Penitentials*, 70–3. See now Dumville, 'Saint David of Wales', 12–15, for a discussion of this work and its relation to Gildas's epistolary fragments.

[44] Dumville, 'Gildas and Uinniau'.

[45] Bieler (ed.), *Irish Penitentials*, 74–95.

[46] See above, 28.

[47] Sharpe, *Adomnán of Iona*, 11 (identification based on the *Life*, II.1, tr. Sharpe, 154).

[48] Uinniau, *Penitential*, L (ed. and tr. Bieler, *The Irish Penitentials*, 92–3); *Penitentialis Vinniani* L: 'Monachi autem non debent baptizare neque accipere elimosinam. Si autem accipiant elimosinam, cur non baptizabunt?'

[49] Uinniau, *Penitential*, XXVII (ed. and tr. Bieler, *The Irish Penitentials*, 83); Latin text below, 44.

attempt to require celibacy of those in orders, thereby extending the monastic ideal to all in religious life. (But note the injunctions in the Breton Council of Vannes, canon XI.) A set of Irish canons, discussed below, still makes a place for married clergy. Uinniau also provides our earliest Insular evidence for the imposition of forty-day periods of sexual abstinence on the laity – the so-called 'three Lents' – in addition to other specified times:

> Married people, then, should mutually abstain during the three forty-day periods in each single year, by consent for the time being, that they may be able to have time for prayer for the salvation of their souls . . . and there they shall receive the thirtyfold fruit which the Saviour in the Gospel, in his account (of rewards) has set aside for married people.[50]

Uinniau's penitential thus sets out the fundamentals of a 'monasticised' society. It establishes separate statutes in canon law for monks; it requires that all regular clergy observe the same law of celibacy as monks; it enjoins a partial celibacy on married layfolk – if they cannot live as perfect *continentes*, then let them abstain from intercourse for long periods in order to 'have time for prayer and the salvation of their souls'.[51] The last phrase encapsulates the exact reason why people enter the monastic life in the first place. The sharing of monastic law and monastic *conversatio* with the laity becomes, as it were, an act of grace; it brings them a real possibility of attaining salvation. Uinniau and Gildas together laid the foundations of Celtic monastic culture.

Ireland: 450–850

We know nothing about the state of early monasticism in Ireland apart from what Patrick tells us. We have already noted Patrick's desire to bring women to the state of virginity. He also states explicitly that he converted men to the monastic state:

> And how has it lately come about in Ireland that those who never had any knowledge of God but up until now always worshiped idols and abominations are now called the people of the Lord and the sons of God, and sons and daughters of Irish underkings are seen to be monks and virgins of Christ?[52]

---

[50] Uinniau, *Penitential*, XLVI (ed. and tr. Bieler, *The Irish Penitentials*, 92–3); *Penitentialis Vinniani*, XLVI: 'Oportet enim tres quadragisimas in anno singulo abstinere se inuicem ex consensu ad tempus ut possint orationi uacare pro salute animarum suarum . . . et tunc accipiant xxx fructum quem Saluator in evangelio enumerans et coniugiis deputauit.'

[51] *Ibid.*

[52] Patrick, *Confession*, XLI (tr. Hood, 50); *Confessio*, XLI (ed. Bieler, *Libri epistolarum*, I.81): 'Unde autem Hiberione qui numquam notitiam Dei habuerunt nisi idola et inmunda usque nunc semper coluerunt quomodo *nuper facta est plebs Domini* et filii Dei nuncupantur, filii Scottorum et filiae regulorum monachi et uirgines Christi esse uidentur?'

In his letter to Coroticus he claims that he 'cannot count the number' of the (noble) Irish who became monks and virgins of Christ.[53] But we have no idea of how monks and virgins were governed, or how they fitted into the overall structure of the Patrician Church.

Sixth-century Ireland is poorly documented. Our evidence consists of annals begun in the following century, canons of councils which cannot be securely dated, and the works of Columbanus, written at the beginning of the seventh century, though some might date from the end of the sixth. A recent study, however, has argued for early sixth-century continuity with the Patrician mission, and strongly implied that its dates must be brought into the 490s.[54] The existence of a letter written by a certain Mauchteus, called 'disciple of Patrick' who died in 535 or 537 is attested in several annals; Mauchteus is also cited as a source of an annal entry. The use of these literary remains by annalists arguably shows that educated clerics who had known Patrick had survived into the sixth century. Is it possible to establish continuity with Patrick's 'monastic programme'?

A set of canons professing to be the promulgations of Patrick and his suffragans, Auxilius and Iserninus ('The First Synod of Saint Patrick') is dated variously to Patrick's own times, the sixth century, and the seventh.[55] Those favouring an early date point to several canons that deal with problems posed by paganism, and assume that the persistence of pagan practices supposes an early stage in the history of the Irish Church. A different view holds that the emphasis on the authority of bishops, insistence on the Roman tonsure (canon VI), and the attempt to gain some independence for the Irish Church from Britain (canon XXXIII) argue for a date in the seventh century and *Romani* influence.[56] It would seem, however, that the most important evidence for dating is canon VI:

Any cleric, from ostiary to priest, that is seen without a tunic and does not cover the shame and nakedness of his body, and whose hair is not shorn after the Roman custom, and whose wife goes about with her head unveiled, shall both likewise be held in contempt by the laity and be removed from the Church.[57]

---

[53] Patrick, *Letter to Coroticus,* XII (tr. Hood, 57).

[54] Sharpe, 'Saint Mauchteus'.

[55] Ed. in Bieler, *The Irish Penitentials,* 54–9; separately ed. and tr. by Faris, *The Bishops' Synod.* For a thorough discussion of the dating issue see Hughes, *The Church,* 44–56. Hughes herself favoured a sixth-century date. See now Charles-Edwards, *Early Christian Ireland,* 245–7, who also (cautiously) supports an early date. He also gives a detailed history of the debate. For other recent discussion see Dumville, *Saint Patrick,* 175–8. (I am not convinced by Dumville's suggestion that the synod in question may have been merely local. Canon XXX addresses the mobility of bishops between 'dioceses'.)

[56] Binchy, 'Patrick and his biographers', 45–9.

[57] 'First Synod', VI (ed. and tr. Bieler, *The Irish Penitentials,* 54–5); *Synodus I S. Patricii,* VI: 'Quicumque clericus ab hostiario usque ad sacerdotem sine tunica uisus fuerit atque turpitudinem uentris et nuditatem non tegat, et si non more Romano capilli euis tonsi sint, et uxor eius si non uelato capite ambulauerit, pariter a laicis contempnentur et ab ecclesia separentur.' On the veiling of women in early Irish society see Ní Dhonnchadha, '*Caillech*'.

Whereas the words 'after the Roman custom' (*more Romano*) could easily have been interpolated by later canonists, the most shocking part of the canon has been left intact: it is taken for granted that men in regular orders may have a wife. This stands in contradiction to canon XI of the Council of Vannes (461 × 491), the penitential of Uinniau, and the penitential of Columbanus. It must thus reflect a relatively early phase of the Christianisation of Irish society. The first half of the sixth century, pre-dating the diffusion of Uinniau's penitential and the composition of Columbanus's, strikes us as a plausible time-frame for this collection.

The 'First Synod' presents a picture of ecclesiastical society that is not substantially different from that found in the Council of Vannes and in Uinniau: there are monks and virgins, non-monastic secular clergy, abbots, and bishops. It is difficult to derive an overall picture of ecclesiastical organisation. According to the 'First Synod', monks are subject to an abbot's authority (canon XXXIV), but so, too, are deacons. Bishops are to restrict their authority to their own dioceses (canon XXX), a stricture possibly aimed against the growth of the monastic *parruchia*, from which abbots or bishops might attempt to extend their influence over churches and monasteries (compare canon VIII of the Council of Vannes) outside their immediate episcopal territory. There is also a reference to lay control of churches (canon XXIV):

If a new-comer joins a community, he shall not baptise, or offer the holy sacrifice, or consecrate, or build a church, until he receives permission from the bishop. One who looks to laymen for permission shall be a stranger.[58]

This is an attempt on the part of the synod to limit lay interference with Church policy and practice. Possibly, then, as early as the sixth century, we see the beginning of lay abbacy in Ireland. This institution is bound up with ownership of land. Land in Ireland was essentially inalienable: it remained the possession of the kinship group in perpetuity.[59] If it was given over to the use of 'the saint and his heirs', it nonetheless continued to belong to an extended family, or kin-group. A family was able to retain direct control of lands consigned to churches by appointing one of its members as titular abbot (*princeps* or *airchinnech*), giving him power over the church and its lands in all that pertained to the family interests, while in principle relegating authority in spiritual matters to resident clergy.[60]

A 'monastery' (*urbs*, *civitas*) – or ecclesiastical settlement (to use the more neutral term) – was a community with a broad array of cultural and economic as well as religious functions.[61] The larger monasteries would

---

[58] 'First Synod', XXIV (ed. and tr. Bieler, *The Irish Penitentials*, 58–9); *Synodus I S. Patricii*, XXIV: 'Si quis aduena ingressus fuerit plebem non ante baptizat neque offerat nec consecret nec aecclesiam aedificet †nec permissionem accipiat ab episcopo, nam qui a gentibus sperat permissionem alienus sit.'

[59] (F.) Kelly, *Guide*, 100–1.

[60] See most recently Etchingham, *Church Organisation*, 64–8.

[61] Hughes & Hamlin, *The Modern Traveller*, 1–18. See now the discussion of *civitas* in Charles-Edwards, *Early Christian Ireland*, 119–23.

have had resident bishops as well as lower clergy (priests, deacons, sub-deacons). Also included would have been a group known as the *manaig* (loosely translated as 'lay monks'). These were married folk with families, who provided services to the church in return for pastoral care (the sacraments, burial, prayers for the dead).[62] They lived under the rule of the community, which, in most cases, would have required the observance of three periods of sexual abstinence in the year (the 'three Lents') and appointed fasts. Indeed, the *manaig* may have been so called because, in so far as it was possible for married persons, they lived the life of monks, engaging in sexual intercourse solely for the procreation of children. In many communities they would have been obliged to accept the authority of a confessor in obedience to the rule. In the stricter churches the *manaig* may have been regarded as the only portion of the laity eligible for pastoral care. These were the 'faithful laity'.[63]

It appears that there was considerable choice of holy forms of life.[64] In contrast to strict Benedictinism, which prescribed a single life for all, the Irish monasteries allowed for modified eremiticism (hermit life that does not involve a complete break with a monastery), strict coenobitism, and laxer forms. Priests and bishops were not only welcome in many monasteries and received without suspicion, but were generally a constituent part of the monastic community. The pursuit of different forms of religious commitment at different stages of life, or even simultaneously, was actively encouraged.[65]

Did the Irish Church undergo a transformation at some time in the sixth century? The evidence of Patrick's writings shows that Patrick was personally committed to the monastic movement and viewed monasticism (understood as the *vita perfecta*) as an essential component of his missionary strategy. As far as the evidence goes, however, Patrick did not create separate monastic churches; rather, it appears that he instituted churches under sacerdotal governance that included loosely defined groups of men and women pursuing a more perfect life: monks, virgins, chaste widows and possibly even *continentes* (married persons practising sexual abstinence) – all familiar classes in the organisation of contemporary churches on the continent. Indeed, the concept of a single church containing various classes of persons practising Christianity continued into the seventh century. We read in the *Book of the Angel* (*ca* 650):

In this city of Armagh Christians of both sexes are seen to live together in religion from the coming of the faith to the present day almost inseparably, and to this aforesaid (city) also adhere three orders: virgins, and penitents, and those serving the church in legitimate matrimony. And these three orders are allowed to hear the word of preaching in the church of the northern district on Sundays always; in the southern

---

[62] Etchingham, *Church Organisation*, 239–89.
[63] *Ibid.*, 264–7.
[64] *Ibid.*, 319–62.
[65] This 'openness' contrasts strongly with the Benedictine Rule. For suspicion towards the presence of priests in monasteries see the *Rule*, LX, LXII (tr. Hunter Blair, *The Rule*, 153, 157–9).

basilica, however, bishops and priests and anchorites and the other religious offer pleasing praises.[66]

The institution of the office of abbot is probably post-Patrician. We encounter the term for the first time in canon XXXIV of the 'First Synod'. Separate communities of monks, as opposed to separate monastic churches within a larger community (see the text immediately above), are sometimes harder to identify. In Columba's community on Iona there was emphasis on the 'enclosure' aspect of a monastery – monks were supposed to stay within it.[67] The case for the seclusion of monks is first presented by Columbanus, who was writing at the end of the sixth century and beginning of the seventh.[68] In a letter to the bishops of Gaul he wrote: 'Let none disparage the benefits of silence; for unless they grow lax, the secluded live better than the social, except for that still stricter life [the anchorite's life?] which has the greater reward.'[69] Columbanus also sharply distinguishes clergy from monks:

. . . St Jerome bade bishops imitate the apostles, but taught monks to follow the fathers who were perfect. For the patterns of clergy and of monks are different and widely distinct from one another.[70]

Further evidence of the belief that monks should live in seclusion is provided by the (eighth-century?) 'Second Synod of St Patrick': 'Monks are those who dwell in solitude without worldly resources, under the power of a bishop or an abbot . . . the site of their place is narrow.'[71]

In his *Monks' Rule* Columbanus resorts to the language of the Mediterranean fathers. The path to perfection is paved with the monastic virtues: obedience, silence, temperance in food and drink, poverty, humility, chastity, the choir office (!), discretion, mortification, and, finally, the monk's perfection. These are the works that are to be performed in addition to fulfilling Christ's twofold commandment to love God and one's neighbour as oneself.[72] The thirteen *Instructiones*, or Sermons, deal with a variety of monastic themes, in which the notion of *disciplina* plays a central part. In

---

[66] *Book of the Angel*, XV–XVI (tr. Bieler, *The Patrician Texts*, 187); Latin text below, 44–5. Etchingham, *Church Organisation*, 293–4, rightly observes that the class of penitents mentioned in this text must be distinguished from excommunicated persons performing compulsory penances.

[67] MacDonald, 'Aspects of the monastery', 280–1.

[68] Bullough, 'The career of Columbanus'.

[69] Columbanus, *Letters*, II.8 (ed. and tr. Walker, 20–1); *Epistulae*, II.8: 'Nullus detrahat silentii bonis; nisi enim tepescant, secreti melius vivunt quam publici, excepta austeriore adhuc vita quae maiorem habet mercedem . . .'

[70] Columbanus, *Letters*, II.8 (ed. and tr. Walker, 20–1); *Epistulae*, II.8: '. . . sanctus Hieronymus haec sciens iussit episcopos imitari apostolos, monachos vero docuit sequi patres perfectos. Alia enim sunt et alia clericorum et monachorum documenta, ea et longe ab invicem separata.'

[71] 'Second Synod', XVII (tr. Bieler, *The Irish Penitentials*, 191). Hughes dates this collection to the early eighth century: 'Synodus II S. Patricii', 141.

[72] Columbanus, *Monks' Rule*, preface (tr. Walker, 123).

one sermon, Columbanus refers to monastic training as the *disciplina disciplinarum*: 'This is in fact the training of all trainings, and at the price of present sorrow it prepares the pleasure of unending time and the delight of unending joy.'[73] This training is to be acquired at the feet of spiritual fathers, or elders (*seniores*). For Columbanus, the ideal conditions are provided in a secluded community.

The question of contacts with the outside world was a perennial problem for monasticism. The 'world' posed two obstacles to the true monastic life. The first consisted of bodily temptations; the second, of distraction. Even a monk who did not 'lose his crown' could become so involved in secular affairs as to lose his discipline. Cassian approves of the words of Abbot Abraham:

Therefore it is better for us to go after, with unbroken constancy, the very small fruit of this desert, which no worldly concerns or earthly distractions or swelling vainglory can nibble away at, and no cares about daily needs can diminish, than to pursue greater profits which, even if they have been gotten by the very lucrative conversion of many, are nonetheless devoured by the demands of a worldly way of life and by the daily loss arising from distractions. For 'the little that the righteous has is better than the great wealth of sinners' [Ps. 37:16].[74]

Around the middle of the eighth century a new movement arose under the leadership of Mael Ruain, who died in 792. Members of the movement were known as the *Céli Dé* or culdees ('clients of God'), an indication that their allegiance was not given to the powers of this world. Mael Ruain's monastery was at Tallaght near present-day Dublin. One of the aims of the *Céli Dé* was to achieve a renewal of monastic life. They shared the Columbanian view that monks should be secluded and disengaged from worldly affairs:

He ordered them not to seek news of those who came to them, or even to carry on a conversation with them. . . . Such news, he felt, was the cause of much harm and disturbance in the mind of the one to whom it was told.[75]

Similarly, there was concern about contact with the 'old churches' which had been corrupted by worldliness. A question of whether it was right to receive

---

[73] Columbanus, *Sermons*, IV.1 (ed. and tr. Walker, 78–9); *Instructiones*, IV.1: 'Quae etiam disciplina disciplinarum est, quaeque aeterni temporis iucunditatem et aeterni gaudii amoenitatem praesenti merore comparat.'

[74] Cassian, *Conferences*, XXIV.xiii.4 (tr. Ramsey, 836); *Conlationes*, XXIV.xiii.4 (ed. Pichery, III.185): 'Et idcirco rectius nobis est hunc solitudinis huius tenuissimum fructum indisrupta iugitate sectari, quem nullae saeculares curae, nullae mundanae distentiones, nulla cenodoxiae ac uanitatis adrodat elatio, nullae sollicitudines diurnae necessitatis imminuant (*melius est enim modicum iusto, super diuitias peccatorum multas*).'

[75] Mael Ruain, *The Rule of Tallaght*, XXXIIIb (tr. Ó Maidín, 109); (ed. Gwynn, *The Rule*, 20): 'Do ordaigh dhoibh gan sgeula d'fhiafraighe don mhuinntir thigeadh ar cuairt chuca no do chaint riu, acht na gnothaighi fa ttangadar amhain do dheunamh, do bhrigh gurb mor an urchoid do nid 7 an toirmeasg chuirid ar mheanmain antí da n-aisneidhtear na sgeula sin.'

gifts from sinful clergy was resolved in the affirmative, since 'we have a far greater right to their possessions, should we receive them, than they have, corrupt as they are'.[76]

In addition to chastity and obedience coupled with absolute poverty, the *Céli Dé* monks were encouraged to practise ascetic feats that might have earned the *Romani* charge of Novatianism.[77] According to the Rule of Tallaght, 'No flesh meat was eaten in Tallaght during Mael Ruain's lifetime.'[78] The same prohibition applied to beer. The Rule records a lively debate between Mael Ruain and Dublitir, a rival abbot, over the virtues of beer:

Dublitir answered: 'My monks drink beer, and they will enter heaven along with yours.' 'I am not certain of that', said Mael Ruain, 'but of this I am sure: no monk of mine who pays heed to me and observes my rule will have need of judgement, nor of the cleansing fire of purgatory, because they will already be purified. Not so with your monks; they will have need of the cleansing fire.'[79]

The text shows not only the *Céli Dé* obsession with abstinence from alcoholic drink, it also attests to their confidence in their spiritual training: follow the Rule exactly and your through-ticket to heaven is guaranteed – no waiting, and no unpleasant surprises. Such absolute reliance on human effort will receive attention in the following chapters.

A special feature of *Céli Dé* spirituality was its penitential system. According to Kathleen Hughes, 'The Old Irish Table of Penitential Commutations composed in the second half of the eighth century is almost certainly to be associated with the culdees.'[80] A commutation (Old Irish *arrae*) constitutes a replacement of long periods of fasting (often while in a state of excommunication) with special penances of shorter duration. These would include cross-vigils, standing in water, and flagellations administered by another person. The frequently stated reasons for the commutations was to reduce the amount of time a person spent in excommunication, and thereby cut off from spiritual food and exposed to mortal danger. This system goes hand in hand with the *Céli Dé* emphasis on the sacraments and the liturgy as well as on the roles to be played by priests and bishops. The Rule of the *Céli Dé* is explicit about the importance of bishops:

If the sons of Ireland are to be found within the bequest of Patrick, it is because there is a senior bishop in every important territory in the land. The duty of such a bishop is to ordain men to holy orders, to consecrate churches, and to give spiritual directions to rulers, to those in authority, and to those in holy orders.[81]

---

[76] Mael Ruain, *The Rule of Tallaght*, XXXV (tr. Ó Maidín, 109); (ed. Gwynn, *The Rule*, 20): 'As fearr an ceart atá againne ar a ghabhail, má gheibmid é, ina ata acasan ar a bheith aca, 7 iad go holc.'

[77] 'Second Synod', XIV (tr. Bieler, *The Irish Penitentials*, 189–91).

[78] Mael Ruain, *The Rule of Tallaght*, XL (tr. Ó Maidín, 111); (ed. Gwynn, *The Rule*, 24): 'Nir hitheadh fos mír feola a tTamhlachta riamh re beo Maoile Ruain . . .'

[79] Mael Ruain, *The Rule of Tallaght*, XL (tr. Ó Maidín, 111); Irish text below, 45.

[80] Hughes, *The Church*, 178; also, Binchy *apud* Bieler, *The Irish Penitentials*, 47, 49.

[81] Rule of the Céli Dé, LX (tr. Ó Maidín, 93); *The Rule of Tallaght*, LX (ed. Gwynn,

Moreover, the Rule of the *Céli Dé* clearly defines the obligations of churches to the whole community, religious and lay:

A church is not entitled to the tenth cow or the third part of the revenue payable by another church nor has it any right to the other dues payable to its monks, unless it is faithful to its obligation. These duties are the administration of baptism, the distribution of Holy Communion, and prayers which are rightly offered by the monks for both the living and the dead . . .[82]

The *Céli Dé* were thus a curious blend of *Romani* and *Hibernenses*. Like the *Romani* they placed heavy stress on the regular liturgy and the sacraments and expressed a serious interest in the needs of the laity. They recognised episcopal authority and the importance of having a sufficient number of qualified priests. However, they also looked back to the sixth century and the *Hibernenses* for certain models. One such was an attachment to the Law of Moses; their sabbatarian prohibitions were as strict as those of the Jews.[83] The *Hibernenses* were noted for their incorporation of Mosaic Law into Church canons.[84] The *Céli Dé* also derived from the *Hibernenses* their ideal of rigorous asceticism and spiritual perfection. This induced them to renew their demand for celibacy for all persons leading the religious life. Celibate clergy – deacons, priests and bishops – lived a common life with the monks not in orders. While showing more explicit concern for the needs of the laity than is sometimes found in the earlier periods, the *Céli Dé* were opposed to missionary work. The pilgrimage for Christ, *peregrinari pro Christo*, which for centuries was an ideal of Irish monasticism, was forbidden. The ordained clergy were to take good care of the souls in their territories entrusted to them, but attempt no more.

In the final analysis, there was little that was new in the teachings of the *Céli Dé*. One sees in them the vigorous attempt to fulfil Uinniau's objective to monasticise as much of society as possible, beginning with the seclusion of monks and proceeding to the imposition of monastic vows on the ordained clergy. Beyond the clergy was the laity, who, far from being excluded, were encouraged to live a life that came as close to the monastic ideal as possible. If married couples could not live as *continentes*, they could still practise self control in their conjugal relations. The *Céli Dé* urged the observation of the 'three Lents' and additional sexual abstinence within each week.[85] All of this was known from earlier canon collections. What is new is the sense of

---

The Rule, 80): 'Is de ata anmunna fher nErenn i timna Patraic, co raibe prim-espoc cecha prim-tuathi i nErinn fria hoirdnead oessa graid 7 fri coisecrad eclais, fri hanmchairdine do flaithib 7 oirchinnib 7 d'oes graid.'

[82] Rule of the Céli Dé, LVII (tr. Ó Maidín, 92); *Rule of Tallaght*, LVII (ed. Gwynn, *The Rule*, 78, 80): 'Ni dlige*t* dechmadu na bo chendaith na trian annoti na dire seoit do mháinib mina bet a frithfholaid techta na heclaisi innte do bathis 7 comnai 7 gabal n-ecnairce a manach etir biu 7 marbu . . .'

[83] Hughes, *The Church*, 178–9; see below, 109–15.

[84] See the 'Irish Canons' (*Hibernenses*) (ed. Bieler, *The Irish Penitentials*, 16–75).

[85] Hughes, *The Church*, 177 n. 4.

structure and overall purpose that one finds in *Céli Dé* texts. The story of the *Céli Dé* is a story of monks in the act of creating, if only in their imaginations, a society in which everyone is, to a greater or lesser degree, a monk.

Irish evidence from the sixth to the ninth century shows that the monastic life was the measuring rod by which every other kind of life was judged. It is hard to think of any important ecclesiastic in this period who was not a monk. All of the large churches in these times had a monastic component, however defined. The status of an abbot of a large monastery was equivalent in law to that of a bishop.[86] Monks had enormous influence on the drafting of legislation that affected the clergy and the laity. Monks also wrote the books that set the goals and ideals of every literate person, and reached well beyond via the spoken word to the population as a whole. By their own account they were the cream of the crop. Interpreting the parable in Matthew 13:8, the compiler of the 'Second Synod' records these words: 'Monks and virgins we may count with the hundredfold.'[87]

Monasticism in Anglo-Saxon England: 599–ca 750

Our general picture of monastic Christianity in early Anglo-Saxon England is well informed primarily thanks to Bede's *Ecclesiastical History*, finished in 731. This is supplemented by Bede's other writings and some eighth-century saints' lives. For the latter part of the seventh century we have Aldhelm's writings and the penitential ascribed to Theodore. There is no contemporary witness prior to Aldhelm, who began writing in the 670s, and very little between the later eighth century, when Alcuin's early writings can be used to shed light on England,[88] and the Benedictine Reform of the tenth century, with which we shall not be concerned.

Christianity came to England almost simultaneously from two divergent sources, both of them monasticised. Almost like two wings of an army engaged in a 'pincer movement', soldiers of Christ dispatched from Rome invaded Kent from the sea, while about a generation later another legion of missionaries headquartered at Iona marched southwards into Northumbria. A smaller contingent of monks coming perhaps directly from Ireland made forays into Wessex and parts of southern England.

Augustine and his colleagues, who had been sent by Pope Gregory I, who was himself a monk, established a monastery at Thanet on lands granted by King Æthelbehrt. As Bede notes:

As soon as they had entered the dwelling-place allotted to them, they began to imitate the way of life of the apostles and of the primitive Church. They were constantly

---

[86] (F.) Kelly, *Guide*, 41.

[87] 'Second Synod', XVIII (ed. and tr. Bieler, *The Irish Penitentials*, 192–3); *Synodus II S. Patricii*, XVIII: 'Monachus uero et uirginis cum centissimis iungamus.'

[88] An exception is Aethelwulf's *De abbatibus* (*On the Abbots*). See Lapidge, 'Aediluuf', 162.

engaged in prayers, in vigils and fasts; they preached the word of life to as many as they could . . .[89]

England had monks and missionaries from the beginning, but it did not yet have a bishop. Therefore,

. . . Augustine, the man of God, went to Arles and, in accordance with the command of the holy father Gregory, was consecrated archbishop of the English race by Etherius, the archbishop of that city.[90]

On returning to England Augustine wrote to Gregory a series of requests for advice regarding various problems that arose in the infant Church. The first question was: how should bishops live with the clergy? Gregory's answer, preserved by Bede, was as follows:

But because you, brother, are conversant with monastic rules, and ought not to live apart from your clergy in the English Church, which, by the guidance of God, has lately been converted to the faith, you ought to institute that manner of life which our fathers followed in the earliest beginnings of the Church: none of them said that anything he possessed was his own, but they had all things in common.[91]

Thus the document that might be described as 'the constitution of the English Church' sets forth the ideal of a bishop living a monastic life in community with his clergy. There can be no doubt that Augustine himself was trained as a monk for Pope Gregory states in a letter to King Æthelbehrt:

Our most reverend brother Bishop Augustine, who was brought up under a monastic Rule (*in monasterii regula edoctus*), is filled with the knowledge of the holy scripture and endowed with good works through the grace of God.[92]

Augustine established his episcopal church, dedicated to the Holy Saviour, in the royal city of Canterbury. This church, according to Bede, was extant from Roman times.[93] King Æthelbehrt, at Augustine's behest, built a monastery 'not far from the city', dedicated to SS Peter and Paul.[94]

---

[89] Bede, *Historia Ecclesiastica*, I.26 (edd. and tr. Colgrave & Mynors, 76–7): 'At ubi datam sibi mansionem intrauerunt, coeperunt apostolicam primitiuae ecclesiae uitam imitari, orationibus uidelicet assiduis uigiliis ac ieiuniis ser/uiendo, uerbum uitae quibus poterant praedicando . . .'

[90] Bede, *Historia Ecclesiastica*, I.27 (edd. and tr. Colgrave & Mynors, 78–9): '. . . uir Domini Augustinus uenit Arelas, et ab archiepiscopo eiusdem ciuitatis Aetherio, iuxta quod iussa sancti patris Gregorii acceperant, archiepiscopus genti Anglorum ordinatus est . . .'

[91] Bede, *Historia Ecclesiastica* (tr. Colgrave & Mynors, 81); Latin text below, 45.

[92] Bede, *Historia Ecclesiastica*, I.32 (edd. and tr. Colgrave & Mynors, 112–13): 'Reuerentissimus frater noster Augustinus episcopus in monasterii regula edoctus, sacrae scripturae scientia repletus, bonis auctore Deo operibus praeditus . . .' The date of the letter is 22 June 601.

[93] Bede, *Historia Ecclesiastica*, I.33 (edd. and tr. Colgrave & Mynors, 114–15): 'non longa ab ipsa civitate'.

[94] *Ibid.*

This monastery had its own abbot, a priest named Peter, who was sent on a mission to Gaul, where he drowned. We thereby learn at a stroke that monasteries could exist separately from a bishop's church, that they were ruled by abbots who were in orders, and that abbots could be engaged in missionary work away from their monasteries.

The great bishops known to us from early English history – Augustine, Mellitus, Aldhelm, Wilfrid, Theodore – were monks. Aldhelm and Wilfrid were abbots before they became bishops. Augustine doubtless served *vice abbatis* in his own household. In his *Life of Cuthbert*, Bede accords approval to the form of organisation in which a monastery can hold both a bishop and an abbot with his monks:

And let no one be surprised that, though we have said above that in this island of Lindisfarne, small as it is, there is found the seat of a bishop, now we say also that it is the home of an abbot and monks; for it is actually so. For one and the same dwelling-place of the servants of God holds both; and indeed all are monks. Aidan, who was the first bishop of this place, was a monk and always lived according to the monastic rule together with his followers. Hence all the bishops of that place up to the present time exercise their episcopal functions in such a way that the abbot, whom they themselves have chosen by the advice of the brethren, rules the monastery; and all the priests, deacons, singers and readers, and the other ecclesiastical grades, together with the bishop himself, keep the monastic rule in all things. The blessed Pope Gregory showed that he greatly approved of this mode of life, when Augustine, the first bishop he had sent to the English, asked him in his letters how bishops ought to live with their clergy . . .[95]

Bede seems actually pleased to report that the model established by the holy Irish monk and bishop Aidan agrees in the essentials with the recommendations of Pope Gregory to Augustine, founder of the English Church. We learn from the same passage that Cuthbert, while serving as prior of the community at Lindisfarne, was engaged in teaching both monks and laymen:

So the man of the Lord came to the church or monastery of Lindisfarne, and soon equally by his life and his doctrine taught the monastic rule to the brethren. Moreover in accordance with his custom he also by frequent visits aroused the common people (*uulgi multitudinem*) round about to seek and earn heavenly rewards.[96]

It is likely that for England, just as for Ireland, there was no single model of monastic organisation. Bede's Lindisfarne was one type, but there were others. As noted, Augustine established a separate monastery under an abbot, whom he appointed. This early situation persisted at least down to Theodore's time, when first Benedict Biscop, then Hadrian, were appointed

---

[95] Bede, *Life of Cuthbert*, XVI (tr. Colgrave, 207–9); Latin text below, 45.

[96] Bede, *Life of Cuthbert* (ed. and tr. Colgrave, 208–9); *Vita Sancti Cuthberti*, XVI: 'Igitur ad Lindisfarnensem aecclesiam siue monasterium uir Domini adueniens, mox instituta monachica fratribus uiuendo pariter et docendo tradebat, sed et circunquaque morantem uulgi multitudinem more suo crebra uisitatione ad coelestia querenda ac promerenda succendebat.'

as abbots of SS Peter and Paul. The same Benedict Biscop (whose name was a cognomen and not a mark of ecclesiastical rank), following the example of his famous Italian namesake, managed to become a kind of arch-abbot to twelve abbots serving beneath him.[97] Double monasteries, under the rule of an abbess, were also known. Hilda's monastery at Whitby and Hildelith's at Barking are the most famous examples, but there were others.[98]

Just as there was a variety of organisational types, there was a diversity of monastic rules. The rule introduced by Aidan in Lindisfarne was doubtless based on the rule of the 'mother house' at Iona. The same may be assumed of Melrose. The Benedictine Rule, which was apparently unknown in Ireland, had its advocates in England, particularly the influential Benedict Biscop. Benedict trained at Lérins and professed there, but this may have occurred during or after the period of reform when the mixed Columbanian-Benedictine Rule was introduced.[99] It is probably this mixed rule that was commonly used in Benedict Biscop's monasteries in Northumbria.[100] Given Pope Gregory's expressed preference for bishops living in community with their monks, it is unlikely that a pure Benedictine Rule, with its distrust of priests living in monasteries, would have been widely observed. Furthermore, a strict Benedictinism would not have been consistent with episcopal appointments of abbots, such as we see not only in Bede's Lindisfarne but also in Wessex, where Aldhelm owed his appointment as abbot of Malmesbury to Bishop Leuthere.[101]

Legislation governing monastic organisation was introduced in two prominent places: in the canons of the Council of Hertford, held in September of 673, and in the penitential attributed to Theodore, compiled by a disciple, but reflecting his teaching on many points.[102] The two documents agree with each other in preserving monasteries from episcopal interference, and thus are in sympathy with the Benedictine spirit. Chapter III of the Council is sweeping in its prohibition: 'That no bishop shall in any way interfere with any monasteries dedicated to God nor take away forcibly any part of their property'.[103] Canons of the penitential grant to the monastic community the right of selecting its own abbot (canons I and III). Moreover, the sins or errors of abbots do not give grounds to a bishop to seize monastic property (canon V). Also consistent with Benedictinism is the disapproval expressed against double monasteries in canon VIII:

---

[97] Bede, *History of the Abbots*, VII (ed. Plummer, *Baedae Opera Historica*, 371).
[98] Sims-Williams, *Religion*, 119–20.
[99] Wormald, 'Bede and Benedict Biscop', 144.
[100] *Ibid.*, 144–50.
[101] Lapidge & Herren, *Aldhelm, the Prose Works*, 137.
[102] On the authenticity of Theodore's penitential, see Charles-Edwards, 'The Penitential of Theodore'. Text in Haddan & Stubbs, *Councils*, III.173–204. The penitential cites a number of Greek authorities (Basil, Gregory Nazianzus, Dionysius the 'Areopagite') and frequently compares the customs of the Greek Church to Roman customs.
[103] Bede, *Historia Ecclesiastica*, IV.5 (edd. and tr. Colgrave & Mynors, 350–1): 'Ut, quaeque monasteria Deo consecrata sunt, nulli episcoporum liceat ea in aliquo inquietare nec quicquam de eorum rebus uiolenter abstrahere.'

It is not lawful for males to have female monks, nor for females to have males. Nevertheless, let us not wish to tear down that which is the custom in this country.[104]

The maintenance of monastic vows for newly elected clergy is also strongly recommended in canon XII: 'Any monk whom the community elects for ordination to the priesthood ought not to give up his earlier vow (*priorem conversationem suam*).'[105] Canons XIV–XVI treat the rights of monasteries. Canon XIV affirms the rights of monasteries to serve as hospitals, while canon XVI assigns to clergy rather than monks the right of doling out penances to the laity.[106]

The *Penitential of Theodore*, which cites an Irish source (probably the *Penitential of Cummian*),[107] resembles an Irish penitential in many respects. It uses the terminology of healing vice through contrary virtues that was used in some Irish penitentials and was derived ultimately from Cassian. Penalties are distinguished according to the gravity of the offence and the status of the offender. If a simple monk gets drunk and vomits, he must do penance for thirty days; if a priest or deacon does the same thing, he must do penance for forty; a layman, however, can get away with fifteen days.[108] The *Penitential of Theodore* was exceptionally severe in punishing sexual offences of those in clerical orders. A bishop, priest, or deacon committing fornication must be deposed from office, though not excommunicated (I.ix.1); priests and deacons found in adultery must be expelled from the Church and do penance with the laity for the rest of their days (I.ix.5); anyone with a concubine must not be ordained (I.ix.6). These canons, in effect, require absolute celibacy of all in clerical orders, though doubtless they allow those who have renounced their wives or concubines to be ordained.

Like a number of Irish canonists, 'Theodore' placed rigorous demands on the married laity. Three days' abstinence from conjugal relations was required before taking communion (II.xii.1); sexual abstinence, 'for the sake of prayer', was asked for the forty days of Lent and extended to the octave of Easter (II.xii.2) – a requirement mercifully less strict than that of

---

[104] 'Theodore', *Penitential*, IV.vi.8 (our translation); (edd. Haddan & Stubbs, III.195): 'Non licet viris feminas habere monachas neque feminis viros; tamen nos non destruamus illud quod consuetudo est in hac terra.'

[105] 'Theodore', *Penitential*, II.vi.12 (our translation); (edd. Haddan & Stubbs, III.195): 'Si quis monachus quem elegerit congregatio ut ordinetur eis in gradum presbiterii, non debet dimittere priorem conversationem suam.'

[106] 'Theodore', *Penitential*, II.vi.14,16 (edd. Haddan & Stubbs, III.196): '14. In potestate et libertate est monasterii susceptio infirmorum in monasterium. 16. Nec non libertas monasterii est penitentiam secularibus judicandam, quia proprie clericorum est.' The Latin is imprecise, but the intent is clear. Another canon, II.ii.15, prohibits deacons from assigning penances to the laity; this is reserved to those above that grade.

[107] Charles-Edwards, 'The Penitential of Theodore', 151–2.

[108] 'Theodore', *Penitential*, I.i.2,3,5 (edd. Haddan & Stubbs, III.177): '2. Si monachus pro ebrietate vomitum facit, XXX. dies penitent. 3. Si presbiter aut diaconus pro ebrietate, XL. dies penitent. 5. Si laicus fidelis pro ebrietate vomitum facit, XV. dies penitent.'

Uinniau or the *Céli Dé*. Sexual abstention was also required for three months before the birth of a child and forty days afterwards.

An interesting set of provisions of the Theodoran penitential concerns divorce for the purpose of entering monastic life. Marriages could be dissolved if one partner wished to enter a monastery:

It is not lawful for a man to put aside his wife even if she be a fornicator, unless perhaps he do this for the sake of monastic life. This is Basil's judgement.[109]

Another canon in the same section makes a provision for the remarriage of the partner remaining outside the monastery:

Nevertheless, one partner may give permission to the other to enter into the service of God in a monastery and may remarry (*sibi nubere*), provided it be a first marriage, or so say the Greeks (and nevertheless it is not canonical); but if it take place in a second marriage, remarriage is not lawful as long as the husband or wife is living.[110]

That these canons reflect social reality is proved by actual cases of separation followed by entry into a monastery. A number of cases involve women in royal marriages. Examples include Eanflaed who was married to King Oswiu (642–70), Æthelthryth who was married to King Ecgfrith (670–85), Cuthburg who was married for a time to King Aldfrith. This same Cuthburg may well have been one of the holy women at Barking to whom Aldhelm dedicated his treatise *On Virginity*.[111] Male examples include Benedict Biscop, King Offa of East Anglia, and the monk Dryhthelm (whose vision is discussed in a subsequent chapter). There are also examples of couples who did not agree to separate entering a monastery together.[112]

The Theodoran canons run parallel to most of the Irish collections in their orientation to a life of penance.[113] The clergy must live a monastic life in addition to their pastoral one. The married laity must participate in the life of mortification as far as possible. The marriage bond, whose indissolubility is guaranteed by sacred scripture (Gen. 2:24 and I Cor.7:10–11), and confirmed by the teachings of the fathers, can be broken (by mutual consent) for the sake of a 'greater good'. A single text – a little 'debate poem' of undetermined Insular origin – expresses perfectly the conflict between the married state and the ideal of perfection that must have obtained on both islands between the seventh and at least the ninth century:

[109] 'Theodore', *Penitential*, II.xxi.6 (our translation); (edd. Haddan & Stubbs, III.199): 'Mulieri non licet virum dimittere licet sit fornicator, nisi forte pro monasterio. Basilius hoc judicavit.'

[110] 'Theodore', *Penitential*, II.xxi.8, (our translation); Latin text below, 45.

[111] For a fuller discussion with sources see Lapidge & Herren, *Aldhelm, the Prose Works*, 51–6.

[112] For references and fuller discussion, see Lapidge, 'A seventh-century Insular Latin debate poem', 14–18.

[113] Indeed, they approximate Irish teachings so closely that canons attributed to Theodore are cited in the *Collectio canonum Hibernensium*. See the references gathered in Charles-Edwards, 'The Penitential of Theodore'.

Husband: I wish to turn to God.
         I do not want my wife.
         Lord, I ask this of you:
         I wish to serve you thus.
         Get away from me, woman!

Wife: God has joined us well together;
         My heart rejoices at it.
         This were pleasing in God's eyes.
         My husband at my side.
           O my darling husband!

Husband: O disaster, be gone;
         I do not wish to hear these words!
         If it pleases you to marry
         Go and find another man!
           Get away from me, woman!

Wife: Day and night I'm sad,
         I weep for my sweet husband.
         If God deprives me of you
         You'll no longer lie beside me.
           O my darling husband![114]

Additional Texts

30. Patrick, *Confessio*, XLIII (ed. Bieler, *Libri epistolarum*, I.82): 'Vnde autem etsi uoluero amittere illas et ut pergens in Brittaniis – et libentissime *paratus eram* quasi ad patriam et parentes; non id solum sed etiam usque ad Gallias uisitare fratres et ut uiderem faciem sanctorum Domini mei: scit Deus quod ego ualde optabam, sed *alligatus Spiritu*, qui mihi *protestatur* si hoc fecero, ut futurum reum me esse designat et timeo perdere laborem quem inchoaui, et non ego sed Christus Dominus, qui me imperauit ut uenirem esse cum illis residuum aetatis meae . . .'

49. Uinniau, *Penitentialis Vinniani*, XXVII (ed. Bieler, *The Irish Penitentials*, 82): 'Si quis fuerit clericus diaconis [*sic*] uel alicui⟨us⟩ gradus et laicus ante fuerit ⟨et⟩ cum filiis et filiabus suis et cum clentella habitet et redeat ad carnis desiderium et genuerit filium ex clentella propria sua, ut dicat, sciat se ruina maxima cecidisse et exsurgere debere; non minus peccatum eius est ut esset clericus ex iuuentute sua et ita est ut cum puella aliena peccasset, quia post uotum suum peccauerunt et postquam consecrati sunt a Deo et tunc uotum suum inritum fecerunt.'

66. *Liber Angeli*, XV–XVI (ed. Bieler, *The Patrician Texts*, 186): '(15) In ista uero urbe Alti Machæ homines Christiani utriusque sexus relegiossi ab

---

[114] Lapidge, 'A seventh-century Insular Latin debate poem', 23; Latin text below, 46. Lapidge's article provides some interesting Old Irish poetic parallels to the debate poem.

initio fidei hucusque pene inseparabiliter commorari uidentur, cui uero praedictae tres ordines adherent uirgines et poenitentes ⟨et⟩ in matrimonio ligitimo aeclesiae seruientes. (16) Et his tribus ordinibus audire uerbum praedicationis in aeclesia aquilonalis plagae conceditur semper diebus dominicis, in australi uero bassilica aepiscopi et praesbiteri | et anchoritae aeclessiae et caeteri relegiossi laudes sapidas offerunt'.

79. *Mael Ruain, The Rule of Tallaght*, XL (ed. Gwynn, *The Rule*, 24): "Ibhid mo mhuinnter-sa', ar . . . Dublitir, 'lionn, ⁊ biaidh siad a bhflaithios De fa re do mhuinntire-si'. 'Ni fhuil a fhois agam', ar Maol Ruain, 'acht ata a fhois-so agam', ar se, 'gach duine dom mhuinntir eisdfios riom-sa ⁊ coimheudfas mo riaghail ni bhia riachdanas aca breitheamhnas do bhreith orra na teine bhratha da nglanadh, ar an adbhar go mb*eid* siad glan chena. Ní mar sin dod mhuinntir-si biaidh ni aca ghlanfus teine bhratha.'

91. Bede, *Historia Ecclesiastica*, I.27 (edd. Colgrave & Mynors, 80): 'Sed quia tua fraternitas monasterii regulis erudita seorsum fieri non debet a clericis suis in ecclesia Anglorum, quae auctore Deo nuper adhuc ad fidem perducta est, hanc debet conuersationem instituere, quae initio nascentis ecclesiae fuit patribus nostris; in quibus nullus eorum ex his / quae possidebant aliquid suum esse dicebat, sed erant eis omnia communia.'

95. Bede, *Vita Sancti Cuthberti*, XVI (ed. Colgrave, *Two Lives*, 206, 208): 'Neque aliquis miretur quod in eadem insula Lindisfarnea, cum permodica sit et supra episcopi et nunc abbatis et monachorum esse, locum dixerimus, re uera enim ita est. Nanque una eademque seruorum Dei habitatio, utrosque simul tenet, immo omnes monachos tenet. Aidanus quippe qui primus eiusdem loci episcopus fuit monachus erat, et monachicam cum suis omnibus uitam semper agere solebat. Unde ab illo omnes loci ipsius antistites usque hodie sic episcopale exercent officium, ut regente monasterium abbate, quem ipsi cum consilio fratrum elegerint, omnes presbiteri, diacones, cantores, lectores, caeterique gradus aecclesiastici, monachicam per omnia cum ipso episcopo regulam seruent. Quam uiuendi normam multum se diligere probauit beatus papa Gregorius, cum sciscitanti per litteras Augustino quem primum genti Anglorum episcopum miserat, qualiter episcopi cum suis clericis conuersari debeant . . .'

110. Theodore, *Penitential*, II.xii.8 (edd. Haddan & Stubbs, III.199): 'Potest tamen alter alteri licentiam dare accedere ad servitutem Dei in monasterium et sibi nubere, si in primo conubio erit, secundum Grecos; et tamen non est canonicum; sin autem in secundo, non licet vivente viro vel uxore. Maritus si se ipsum in furtu aut fornicatione servum facit vel quocunque peccato, mulier si prius non habuit conjugium, habet potestatem post annum alterum accipere virum; digamo non licet.'

114. *Debate Poem on Divorce* (ed. Lapidge, 'A seventh-century Insular Latin debate poem', 23):

Ad Deum uertere uolo,
Uxorem meam ego nolo.
Domine, hoc tibi rogo:
Tibi sic seruire uolo.
   Recede a me, uxor!

Bene nos iunxerat Deus;
Congaudet animus meus.
Placuisset hoc in Deum:
Maritus in latus meum.
   Dulcis iugalis meus!

Calamitas, regredere:
Ista uerba nolo audire!
Si te delectat nubere,
Alium uirum perquire.
   Recede a me, uxor!

Die atque nocte doleo,
Propter uirum carum fleo.
Si tibi me fraudat Deus
Non dehinc iaces in latus.
   Dulcis iugalis meus!

II

THE THEOLOGY OF CHRIST IN INSULAR CHRISTIANITY

In a world where the tenets of inherited Christianity were probably not understood by the vast majority of the laity and only imperfectly by many clerics and monks, the complicated dogmas dealing with the nature of Christ that arose in the fourth and fifth centuries must have been incomprehensible to all but a very few – learned writers such as Gildas in Britain, Cummian in Ireland, and Aldhelm and Bede in England who show close acquaintance with the history of dogma. However, there are various indications that the Insular world did not entirely escape the effects of the heresies that cropped up on the continent between the fourth and seventh centuries. Writers on both islands took special pains to insist upon their orthodoxy, particularly in matters relating to the Trinity and to the nature of Christ. Involvement in these disputes – however marginal they may seem at first glance – played a role in shaping official theology, but perhaps more importantly, in defining the activities and concerns that constituted Insular Christology and the literary and artistic images of Christ to be examined here.

Expressions of orthodoxy

From the beginnings of Insular Christianity, prominent ecclesiastics were eager to demonstrate their freedom from all taint of heresy and show their solidarity with the central teachings of the Roman Church. This is embodied in the form of a 'profession of faith' – a more or less detailed statement of 'correct' beliefs which is sometimes coupled with anathematisations of heresies. The defensive character of these professions always relates to the individual claimant, but in some cases, as we shall see, there is a clear awareness on the part of the professing person that he is defending the beliefs and practices of his region. Moreover, such professions do not occur in a vacuum. Two of the three earliest professions – those of Pelagius and Columbanus – were addressed to popes; a third – that of Patrick – was sent to unnamed authorities in Britain. In all three cases we have to do with some charge of heresy, divergent practice, or misconduct. As we noted in our Introduction, praise of orthodoxy and the assertion of one's own orthodoxy are not synonymous with *being* orthodox. Professions of faith may contain many assertions that are consistent with the teachings of the universal Church, but often there is simultaneously an attempt to screen from view, or to overbalance the more dubious doctrines ascribed to their authors, or even to use the claim to personal purity of faith as a plea for forgiveness in the event of a misdemeanour.

Pelagius, knowing that pressures had been applied on Pope Innocent I to excommunicate him, sent him a lengthy list of doctrines in which he professed to believe. It begins as follows:

I. We believe in God the Father almighty, creator of all things visible and invisible.

II. We believe in our Lord Jesus Christ through whom all things were created, true God, the only-begotten, not created or adopted, but begotten, of one substance with the Father, which the Greeks call *homoousion*, and thus in all things equal to God the Father, so that he is not inferior temporally (that is, coming into existence after the Father), nor in rank, nor in power. We confess him who was begotten to be as great as him who begot.

Pelagius goes on to express his approval of numerous points of doctrine respecting both the Trinity and the person and nature of Christ:

IX. Moreover we confess that there is a single person of the Son in Christ, so that we should say that he is two perfect and whole substances, that is, of God and of humanity, which is constituted out of soul and body; and, just as we condemn Photinus, who professes that there was only a bare man in Christ, so too we anathematise Apollinaris and his ilk, who say that the Son of God did not take anything at all from human nature . . .

Pelagius went out of his way to show that even his teaching on free will, to which we shall devote considerable attention in the next chapter, was in conformity with Catholic teaching:

XXV. We profess free will in this way, so as to say that we always require the aid of God, and that they are in error who say with the Manichaean that a man cannot avoid sin, as much as they who assert with Jovinian that a man cannot sin; for each of them takes away the freedom of the will. We, however, assert that a man always has the possibility of sinning as well as of not sinning, so that we always profess that (this possibility) belongs to free will.[1]

There is a remarkable profession of faith near the beginning of Patrick's *Confession*:

For there is no other God, nor ever was before nor will be hereafter except for God the Father, unbegotten, without beginning, from whom is all beginning, possessing all things, as we have learned; and his son Jesus Christ, whom we declare to have existed always with the Father, before the beginning of the world spiritually with the Father, begotten ineffably before all beginning; and by Him were made things visible and invisible; he was made man; He conquered death and was received up into

---

[1] Pelagius, *Profession of Faith* (our translation); Latin text below, 65. Pelagius's *Profession of Faith* may owe its general structure to Rufinus's *Liber de fide*, which adopted the strategy of beginning with orthodox pronouncements on the Trinity and the nature of Christ. For the hypothesis that Rufinus may have been the 'first Pelagian', see Bonner, 'Rufinus'.

heaven to the Father and he gave Him all power over every name of things in heaven and on earth, that every tongue should confess to Him that Jesus Christ is Lord and God; in whom we believe, and we look to His imminent coming, as judge of the living and the dead, who will render to each one according to his deeds; and He poured out on us abundantly His Holy Spirit, the gift and pledge of immortality, who makes those who believe and obey to be sons of God and heirs alone with Christ; Him we confess and worship as one God in the Trinity of sacred name.[2]

Patrick's *Confession* was addressed to unnamed authorities in Britain. Its purpose was to defend his mission against charges of misconduct (specifically, profiteering) as well as against questions about his authority to conduct it. In such cases it may have not been unusual to add the suspicion of heresy to more substantial charges.

A century or so after Patrick, Columbanus in a letter to Pope Boniface IV declared:

For all we Irish, inhabitants of the world's edge, are disciples of Saints Peter and Paul and of all the disciples who wrote the sacred canon by the Holy Ghost, and we accept nothing outside the evangelical and apostolic teaching; none has been a heretic, none a Judaiser, none a schismatic; but the Catholic Faith, as it was delivered by you first, who are the successor of the holy apostles, is maintained unbroken.[3]

The tone of the text strongly indicates that Columbanus is replying to allegations or suspicions. In a much different context, the same writer, in a series of instructions or sermons to his monks, opens with a discourse on the Trinity. Columbanus asserts in the preface to his first sermon that right belief is the foundation of salvation: 'I desire that what is the basis of all men's salvation should be the foundation of our talk . . .' And then he continues:

Let each man then who wishes to be saved believe first in God the first and last, one and three, one in substance, three in character; one in power, three in person: one in nature, three in name; one in Godhead, Who is Father and Son and Holy Spirit, one God, wholly invisible, inconceivable, unspeakable . . .[4]

---

[2] Patrick, *Confession*, IV (tr. Hood, 41–2); Latin text below, 65–6. For the literature on 'Patrick's creed' see Bieler, *Libri epistolarum*, II.97 n. 22.

[3] Columbanus, *Letters*, V.3 (ed. and tr. Walker, 38–9); *Epistulae*, V.3: 'Nos enim sanctorum Petri et Pauli et omnium discipulorum divinum canonem spiritu sancto scribentium discipuli sumus, toti Iberi, ultimi habitatores mundi, nihil extra evangelicam et apostolicam doctrinam recipientes; nullus hereticus, nullus Iudaeus, nullus schismaticus fuit; sed fides catholica, sicut a vobis primum, sanctorum videlicet apostolorum successoribus, tradita est, inconcussa tenetur.'

[4] Columbanus, *Sermons*, I.2 (ed. and tr. Walker, 60); *Instructiones* I.2: 'Credat itaque primum omnis qui vult salvus esse, in primum et in novissimum Deum unum ac trinum, unum substantia, trinum subsistentia; unum potentia, trinum persona; unum natura, trinum nomine; unum numine, qui est Pater et Filius et Spiritus Sanctus, Deus unus, totus invisibilis, incomprehensibilis, ineffabilis . . .' The authenticity of the sermons attributed to Columbanus has been demonstrated by Stancliffe, 'The thirteen sermons'.

The profession of faith is also expressed as literary topos. We find an abbreviated profession in the hymn *Altus prosator*, attributed to Columba:

> The exalted Creator, Ancient of Days, and Unbegotten One
> was without a first beginning, or a foundation;
> he is, and he will be for unending ages.
> [His] only-begotten Christ, and the Holy Spirit,
> are co-eternal with him in the everlasting glory of Godhead.
> We do not assert that there are three gods, but speak of one God
> retaining our faith in the three most glorious Persons.[5]

And in the *Lorica* of Laidcenn we find the invocation:

> Help me, O unity in Trinity,
> Take pity on me, O Trinity in unity.[6]

Even more remarkable, perhaps, is Tírechán's *Life of Patrick*, which portrays the saint propounding teachings about the Trinity to Irish pagans who were encountering Christian teaching for the first time:

... He has a son, coeternal with him, similar to him; The Son is not younger than the Father nor is the Father older than the son, and the Holy Spirit breathes in them; the Father and the Son and the Holy Spirit are not separate.[7]

Whatever one makes of this explanation, its formulation shows the belief of seventh-century writers in the importance of orthodoxy and in the importance of imparting *right belief* to pagans encountering Christianity for the first time. To paraphrase Columbanus, orthodoxy is the basis of all men's salvation.

The English Church, too, was concerned with preserving orthodox teaching and gave this objective an institutional framework. At the Council of Hertford in 673, the decision was taken to conduct a bi-annual, or – in adverse circumstances – an annual synod at Clovesho (a place not identified) to deal with all matters of doctrine and practice. A provision of one of these regularly held synods required that priests know the *symbolum fidei* (the Nicene Creed) and be able to explain it in their own language.[8] More significantly, the English Church held a Council at Hatfield in 679 with Archbishop Theodore presiding; the Council affirmed its allegiance to all the doctrines proclaimed at the five major ecumenical councils: Nicaea in 325,

---

[5] *Altus prosator*, I (tr. Carey, 33); Latin text below, 66. For an attribution of the *Altus prosator* to seventh-century Iona see (J.B.) Stevenson, 'Altus Prosator', 368.

[6] Laidcenn, *Lorica*, lines 1–2 (ed. and tr. Herren, *The Hisperica Famina II*, 76–7):
> Suffragare   Trinitatis unitas
> Unitatis miserere   Trinitas.

See Hill, 'Invocation of the Trinity'.

[7] Tírechán, *Life*, XXVI.11 (ed. and tr. Bieler, *The Patrician Texts*, 142–3): 'Filium habet coaeternum sibi, consimilem sibi; non iunior Filius Patri nec Pater Filio senior, et Spiritus Sanctus inflat in eis; non separantur Pater et Filius et Spiritus Sanctus.'

[8] Council of A.D. 747, X (edd. Haddan & Stubbs, III.366).

50

Constantinople I in 381, Ephesus in 431, Chalcedon in 451 and Constantinople II in 553. To these was added a profession of acceptance of the decrees of the first Lateran Council in 649, conducted by Pope Martin I,[9] which will be discussed below. The promulgation of the Lateran Conference along with the '*filioque*-clause' shows that the English Church was concerned to be at one with contemporary Roman pronouncements in matters of faith.

Heresy

Despite their geographical position, the Insular Churches did not escape the main dogmatic disputes that raged on the continent. Five controversies in particular deserve our attention; in rough chronological order they are: (1) Arianism in Britain; (2) Pelagianism in Britain and Ireland; (3) the 'Three Chapters' affair which involved the Irish on the continent in the early-seventh century; (4) the Monothelite heresy that spanned most of the seventh century and involved the See of Canterbury; (5) the Quattuordeciman charge brought against the British and Irish churches. Arianism, the 'Three Chapters', and Monothelitism are all centrally Christological. Pelagianism, in its dogmatic aspect, is not; however, as one works outwards from the central notions of nature and free will to the edges of its teachings, there are major implications for the Pelagian conception of Christ. On the other hand, to be charged with being a 'Fourteener' (Quattuordeciman) was tantamount to being accused of apostasy. It brought with it the taint of Judaism and the utter rejection of Christ.

Arianism

Arius (?256–336) taught the subordination of the Son to the Father, meaning that he was not consubstantial with the Father, and did not share in the creation. For Arius, the Godhead was indivisible, and thus the notion of consubstantiality of persons in the Trinity undermined monotheism itself. The Son must therefore be of a different order of existence from the Father. Moreover, only the Father was uncreated; this means that the Son is the creation of the Father. He therefore has no direct knowledge of, or communion with, the Father. Such terms as 'Word of the Father' and even 'Son of the Father' were only courtesy titles. The Arians defended their position with such scriptural passages as 'the first-born of all creation' (Col. 1:15) and 'the Father is greater than I' (John 14:28).[10] Along with other heresies such as Adoptianism and Nestorianism, Arianism elevated the humanity of Christ over his divinity. Arius's doctrine was condemned at the Council of Nicaea in 325. None the less, it was widely influential, especially amongst the Germanic peoples who invaded western Europe. It was still extant in Lombardy in the early seventh century.

British bishops took part in several councils dealing with the heresy, and

---

[9] Bede, *Historia Ecclesiastica*, IV.17 (tr. Colgrave & Mynors, 387); see (H.) Chadwick, 'Theodore', 88.

[10] (J.N.D.) Kelly, *Early Christian Doctines*, 230.

there is even some evidence of reluctance on their part to approve the term *homoousion*.[11] Our best authority for the presence of the heresy in Britain is Gildas (later paraphrased by Bede):

This pleasant agreement between the head and limbs of Christ endured until the Arian treason, like a savage snake, vomited its foreign poison upon us, and caused the fatal separation of brothers who had lived as one. And as though there were a set route across the ocean there came every kind of wild beast, brandishing in their horrid mouths the death-dealing venom of every heresy, and planting lethal bits in a country that always longed to hear some novelty – and never took firm hold of anything.[12]

Gildas's phrase 'agreement between the head and limbs of Christ' refers, of course, to the correct relation between Christ's divinity and humanity. Although Gildas does not mention Pelagius or his heresy by name, it is interesting that he believed that Arianism paved the way for other virulent heresies in Britain. Clearly the most 'lethal' of these was Pelagianism. That there is an Arian strain in Pelagianism will be argued at a later point.

Pelagianism

Pelagius has already been introduced in the context of monasticism and in this chapter as the author of a profession of faith. Even though he claimed to be orthodox and to accept the doctrines of the consubstantiality of Christ with the Father and the Holy Spirit and the undiminished quality of his divinity and humanity, there are numerous aspects of his theology that contradict – or, at least, undermine – these claims. Pelagius's special formulation of the doctrine of free will had a serious impact on his Christology, heavily emphasising Christ's humanity at the expense of his divinity, and even placing restrictions on the human aspect of Christ. The evidence for the persistence of Pelagianism in the British Isles will be discussed fully in the next chapter.

The 'Three Chapters' controversy and Columbanus

The so-called 'Three Chapters' controversy, which arose in the middle of the sixth century immediately after the Fifth Ecumenical Council (Constantinople II, 553), at first glance, would seem to be entirely a continental matter. Indeed, the eye of the storm was in Italy and affected, principally, Aquileia and Lombardy in their relations with Rome, and Rome in its relation to Byzantium. To understand something of the controversy, one must look back to the Fourth Ecumenical Council (Chalcedon, 451) at which the heresy of Eutyches (Monophysitism), was condemned. The Monophysites maintained that Christ possessed only a single nature, which was divine. The Council, however, defined Christ as one person (hypostasis) in two natures (human and divine). After Chalcedon, many in the eastern Church believed

---

[11] Haddan & Stubbs, *Councils*, I.7–11; see especially the testimony of Hilary of Poitiers, 9.
[12] Gildas, *The Ruin*, XII.3 (tr. Winterbottom, 20); Latin text below, 66. Cf. Bede, *Historia Ecclesiastica*, I.8 (tr. Colgrave & Mynors, 59–61).

that the Council had gone too far in the direction of the opposite heresy, Nestorianism, which at times appeared to say that 'Christ's soul was independent of the incarnate Word.'[13] The controversy caused a great deal of civil disturbance, ultimately leading the emperor Justinian to convoke Constantinople II (the Fifth Ecumenical Council) with a view to redressing the balance.

Three writers (with their texts) were of particular concern to those with leanings to a single-nature theory (or who, at least, were opposed to the emphasis on a double nature). These constitute the 'Three Chapters'; they were the person and work of Theodore of Mopsuestia, the writings of Theodoret of Cyrrhus against Cyril of Alexandria, and the letter of Ibas of Edessa to Maris the Persian. These 'Nestorian' texts, along with the person of Theodore of Mopsuestia, were condemned by the Fifth Council, and the *acta* subscribed to by Pope Vigilius (under pressure from Justinian). Vigilius had originally resisted the condemnation of the Three Chapters (an act consistent with western support for the Council of Chalcedon), but the long version of the acts of the council's decisions did not survive. To many in the West Vigilius had simply betrayed the cause. The result was the Aquileian Schism,[14] a movement committed to maintaining the formulae of Chalcedon (as interpreted in the West, particularly by the *Tome* of Pope Leo) and to undoing Constantinople II.

Papal policy between the Fifth Council and the papacy of Gregory I vacillated between appeasing Byzantium and defending western theological commitments. Gregory himself pursued a similar course, but in a more subtle fashion. While publicly maintaining his defence of Constantinople II, he agreed to let the memory of the Council lapse in the written record and to refer to the first four synods only.[15] Gregory's policy seemed to be directed not only to the concerns of the Aquileians, but also – and perhaps even more crucially – to the task of mollifying the Lombard court, whose king, Agilulf, was Arian. It has been plausibly suggested that the emphasis placed on Christ's humanity in the condemned Nestorian texts (the Three Chapters) would have been more appealing to Arians in Lombardy (and hence more useful to their conversion) than the single-nature hypothesis favoured by Byzantium.[16]

The Irish monastic founder Columbanus, who arrived on the continent probably around 600, entered the fray on behalf of his patron, the Lombard king Agilulf, from whom he had obtained land at Bobbio to build a monastery. Writing to Gregory's successor, Pope Boniface IV, at some time between 612 and 615, Columbanus issued an appeal for a new council

---

[13] As phrased by (H.) Chadwick, 'Theodore', 89. For a history of the period after the Council of Chalcedon up to Constantinople II, see Gray, *The Defence of Chalcedon*.

[14] See Cuscito, 'Aquileia e Bisanzio', for a survey of the schism up to the time of Columbanus.

[15] For a detailed discussion see Gray & Herren, 'Columbanus and the Three Chapters', 163–4.

[16] Walker, *Sancti Columbani Opera*, xxx.

to resolve the issue of the Three Chapters once and for all.[17] His objective in writing was clear: King Agilulf was apparently wavering in his commitment to the Arian faith, but was in doubt about the stance of the papacy (and the Western Church) regarding the nature of Christ. He called upon Columbanus to intercede in the issue. Columbanus presented the case to the pope as a window of opportunity for the conversion of the king; pressing decisions were needed, and an end to the conciliatory policies ascribed to Vigilius and openly espoused by his successors.

Columbanus's understanding of the theological issues entailed in the Three Chapters controversy (and its forerunners) was, by his own admission, incomplete, and doubtless governed by the coded language adopted by his contemporaries in Italy.[18] In his Letter to Pope Boniface he signals his own theological stance to potential readers in Rome, Milan, and Aquileia:

For if, as I have heard, some do not accept two natures in Christ, they are to be accepted as heretics rather than as Christians; for Christ Our Saviour is true God eternal without time, and true man without sin in time. Who in His divinity is co-eternal with the Father and in His humanity is younger than His mother. Who born in the flesh never left heaven, remaining in the Trinity lived in the world; and thus, if it was written at the Fifth Council, as someone has told me, that a man who adores two natures has his prayer divided, the writer is divided from the saints and separate from God. For we, in respect of the unity of the Person, in Whom it pleased the fullness of deity to reside bodily, believe one Christ, His divinity and humanity, since He Who descended is He Himself who ascended above every heaven that He might fill all things. If any think otherwise about the Lord's Incarnation, he is a foe to the faith, and fit for scorn and anathema from all Christians . . .[19]

One might be entitled to wonder about Columbanus's phrase 'remaining in the Trinity',[20] the very type of formula that could give rise to the criticism that 'a man who adores two natures has his prayer divided'. Whatever may be said of Columbanus's theological skills, this bold formulation of western Dyophysitism resonates in the spirituality of the Insular world. It gives full scope to Christ's human nature: the sufferings of the man are in no way assuaged by the Person in the Trinity. Such a Christology is wholly consistent with a monasticism founded on the imitation of Christ. The *imitatio Christi* is truly possible because humanity, not divinity, is the model.

Monothelitism

The Monothelite controversy, which occupied a large part of the seventh century, may be viewed as a direct continuation of the controversy over the divine and human nature of Christ. The Monothelites held that Christ's will could not be divided, and therefore he must possess a single divine will.

---

[17] Columbanus, *Letters*, V (ed. Walker, 36–57). This is the same letter in which Columbanus defends the orthodoxy of the Irish; see above, 49.

[18] See, generally, Gray & Herren, 'Columbanus and the Three Chapters'.

[19] Columbanus, *Letters*, V.13 (tr. Walker, 53); Latin text below, 66. Columbanus's word for 'nature' is *substantia*, which translates the Greek *hypostasis*.

[20] This formula is also employed in *Precamur patrem*, XVIII; see below, 287, and Lapidge, '*Precamur patrem*'.

Official Monophysitism – otherwise known as the heresy of Eutyches – remained condemned, along with the opposite heresy, Nestorianism. However, Monophysite leanings remained strong, especially in the East, and new arguments were found for their validation. The challenge to the Dyophysite theology that Christ possessed both a human and a divine will was potentially damaging, as it pointed to a conflict in the psyche of the Incarnate Word. If Monophysites, reborn as Monothelites, could stump their opponents on this question, the door would be opened to a full-scale reinstatement of a single-nature Christology.

In 633, a temporary consensus on the question was reached in the East, when Cyril, the patriarch of Alexandria, found a magic formula in the term *energeia*. Christ indeed had two natures, but these were united in the *energeia* ('actualisation') of a single person, and were incapable of conflict or tension.[21] This formula received the endorsement of Pope Honorius and the patriarch of Constantinople, but was soon undermined by hardline Chalcedonians and Monophysites. In the West, leading Dyophysites such as Sophronius and Maximus the Confessor put pressure on Pope Martin I, who convoked a Lateran Council in 649 to deal with the problem. Cyril's formula was condemned on the predictable ground that it denied Christ's full humanity. The emperor Constans II would have none of this. In 653, an imperial force was dispatched, Martin was arrested and tortured, and a conclave summoned to elect a new pope.[22]

The conflict continued to rage until 680, when Pope Agatho participated in the synod known as Constantinople III. In the meantime, his predecessor Vitalian had appointed Theodore of Tarsus, a monk resident in Rome, as archbishop of Canterbury. Michael Lapidge has argued plausibly that this Theodore was none other than the *Theodorus monachus* who subscribed to the *acta* of the Lateran Council of 649.[23] He has suggested further that Pope Vitalian's hesitation in consecrating Theodore and insistence that he be superintended by Abbot Hadrian was founded not on the suspicion that he was a Monothelite (as some have assumed), but on his concern, based on close knowledge of preceding events, that his pronounced Dyothelite views would provoke imperial wrath.[24] The death of Emperor Constans II brought a sea change in the East, and made it possible for Pope Agatho to convoke a Lateran Council in Rome in 680 as a prelude to Constantinople III, which started in the same year. Just prior to this activity Archbishop Theodore summoned the English bishops to Hatfield, at which the Lateran Council of 649 was added to the list of the five ecumenical synods whose articles required assent.

---

[21] (H.) Chadwick, 'Theodore', 90–1.

[22] Herrin, *The Formation*, 252–9.

[23] Lapidge, 'The career', 23–4.

[24] *Ibid.*, 25–6. Vitalian's hesitation is known from Bede, *Historia Ecclesiastica*, IV.1 (edd. and tr. Colgrave & Mynors, 330–1): '. . . ne quid ille contrarium veritati fidei Graecorum more in ecclesiam cui praeesset introduceret'. Hadrian was to 'take great care to prevent Theodore from introducing into the church over which he presided any Greek customs which might be contrary to the true faith'.

In his summary account of the Synod of Hatfield, Bede repeats what is almost certainly Theodore's own gloss on the section requiring assent to the formulae of Martin I's Lateran Council: 'And we glorify our Lord Jesus just as they (those present at Martin's Council) glorified him, adding and subtracting nothing.'[25] This can only be interpreted to mean that nothing can be added or taken away from Christ's divinity or his humanity. It thus seems clear that Theodore was imbued with the same enthusiasm for a Dyophysite Christology that infected Martin, Maximus the Confessor and Sophronius – men he doubtless had known personally in Rome. Because Dyophysitism must restore an imbalance created by Monophysitism, it naturally stresses the human nature of Christ. The concern with the human aspect is reflected in Theodore's own biblical exegesis, which is strongly Antiochene, or 'historical', in character.[26]

Quattuordecimans and Judaisers

In the earliest Christian period, Easter, understood as Christ's resurrection, did not enjoy status as a separate feast. Among Christian Jews the observance of the Lord's sacrifice would have coincided with the Jewish feast of the Passover, and this situation may well have obtained for other Christians. We hear of the first attempt to separate Passover from Easter towards the end of the second century. The Church historian Eusebius reported that in the time of Pope Victor:

> . . . the dioceses of all Asia, as from an older tradition, held that the fourteenth day of the moon, on which day the Jews were commanded to sacrifice the lamb, should always be observed as the feast of the life-giving Pasch, contending that the fast ought to end on that day, whatever day of the week it might happen to be. However, it was not the custom of the Churches in the rest of the world to end it at this point, as they observed the practice, which from Apostolic tradition has prevailed to the present time, of terminating the fast on no other day than on that of the Resurrection of Our Saviour. Synods and assemblies of bishops were held on this account, and all with one consent through mutual correspondence drew up an ecclesiastical decree that the mystery of the Resurrection of the Lord should be celebrated on no other day but Sunday and that we should observe the close of the paschal fast on that day only.[27]

From the outset it is clear that two sets of issues had to be disentangled: first, whether Easter was meant as the celebration of Christ's sacrifice or rather his resurrection, and, if the first, if this was to be seen as the fulfilment of the Jewish Passover;[28] second, however Easter is interpreted, whether it

---

[25] Bede, *Historia Ecclesiastica*, IV.17 (*ibid.*, 386–7): '(Et) glorificamus Dominum nostrum Iesum, sicut isti glorificauerunt, nihil addentes uel subtrahentes . . .'

[26] Bischoff & Lapidge, *Biblical Commentaries*, 243–4.

[27] Eusebius, *Ecclesiastical History*, V.23 (cit. *Catholic Encyclopedia*, V.28); Greek text below, 66–7.

[28] See Charles-Edwards, *Early Christian Ireland*, 401–2: 'For the early Christian there was no great problem; for them the Passion and Resurrection of Christ were part of a single process of salvation . . .' This assessment appears to underestimate the problem of conflating the two events.

should coincide with the day of Passover, or be separate from it, and always be celebrated on a Sunday (the day Christ chose for his resurrection). As we shall have occasion to see, the failure to identify at the start what religious event was observed in Easter led to further strife and confusion. Note that Eusebius himself, like nearly every Christian writer (and preacher) before and after him, uses the term 'paschal' (derived from the Greek word *pascha* translating the Hebrew *pesach*, 'Passover') to denote Easter.

Pope Victor came down on the side of the regular observance of Easter on a Sunday. From that time forwards, those who kept Easter at the same time as Passover, that is, on the fourteenth day of the Jewish month of Nisan, were referred to as 'Quattuordecimans' (Fourteeners) and frequently labelled 'Judaisers'. The Council of Nicaea (325) condemned the Quattuor-decimans and insisted that all Christians observe Easter on the same day, namely on a Sunday. However, differences in calculating *which* Sunday persisted for a long time, with different systems prevailing in different places. It appears that the principle was accepted in the early-fourth century that Easter Sunday should follow the fourteenth moon of Nisan. A further principle was enunciated to the effect that each year the pope would send out a letter to all the Churches enjoining the day for the common celebration.[29]

The Quattuordecimans persisted for some time, however, particularly in the Asian regions of Lydia and Phrygia. In the West there was a Quattuordeciman element among the Novatians. The Council of Ephesus (431) was concerned with Fourteeners who wanted to be reconciled with the universal Church. As we shall see, there is some evidence that the Pelagians espoused the Quattuordeciman cause; their belief in the inviolable authority of the scriptures (as witness to the will of God) might well have led many of their followers to sacrifice and consume the paschal lamb on the fourteenth day of Nisan, on whatever day of the week it should occur.

At some point early in the seventh century, Bishop Laurence (the successor to Augustine of Canterbury), Mellitus and Justus wrote a letter to the bishops and abbots of Ireland; part of it is cited by Bede:

The apostolic see, according to customs in all parts of the world, directed us to preach to the heathen in these western regions, and it was our lot to come to this island of Britain; before we knew them we held the holiness of both of the Britons and of the Irish in great esteem, thinking that they walked according to the customs of the universal church: but on becoming better acquainted with the Britons, we still thought that the Irish would be better. But now we have learned from Bishop Dagan when he came to this island and from Abbot Columban when he came to Gaul that the Irish did not differ from the Britons in their way of life. For when Bishop Dagan came to us he refused to take food, not only with us but even in the very house where we took our meals.[30]

---

[29] 'Easter Controversy', *Catholic Encyclopedia*, V.229; see also Kenney, *Sources*, 210–16; and Charles-Edwards, *Early Christian Ireland*, 391–415.

[30] Bede, *Historia Ecclesiastica*, II.4 (tr. Colgrave & Mynors, 147); Latin text below, 67.

We learn two important facts from this letter: (1) the Irish and the Britons did not differ from each other in their way of life (*conversatio*);[31] (2) they excommunicated from their table those who differed from them. Bede explains that Laurence sent the letter because he had noticed that:

they did not celebrate the festival of Easter at the proper time but . . . held that the day of the Lord's resurrection should be observed from the fourteenth to the twentieth day of the paschal moon.[32]

Laurence's letter is a forerunner of Aldhelm's letter to Geraint, king of Devon and Cornwall, and his bishops, arguably written in the early 670s.[33] Aldhelm wrote at the behest of a synod of bishops 'out of almost the entirety of Britain' to urge the bishops of Devon and Cornwall (and their king) to enter into unity with the 'Catholic Church' in the matters of a common Easter and common tonsure.[34] Aldhelm takes Laurence's concerns a step farther. He implies that the British clergy are Quattuordecimans, that is, 'they celebrate the feast of Easter on the fourteenth moon along with Jews who blaspheme Christ and trample on the Gospel in the manner of swine'.[35] The Roman Church regarded Quattuordecimans as heretics, and not merely as a group with a divergent ritual, and thus his charge is a serious one.[36] If Aldhelm's letter was written at the behest of the Council of Hertford (672), then its main reference is to chapter I.4: 'That we all keep Easter Day at the same time, namely on the Sunday *after* the fourteenth day of the moon of the first month.'[37]

Some time after 706, Ceolfrid, abbot of Wearmouth-Jarrow, wrote to Nechtan, king of the Picts, regarding the correct way of calculating Easter and the correct manner of the tonsure. Bede provides a long and detailed paraphrase.[38] Ceolfrid does not use the term 'Quattuordeciman' or charge the Picts with heresy. On the contrary, the whole tenor of his letter is aimed

---

[31] Bede was not alone in speaking of the Britons and the Irish as a unity; see Walsh & Ó Cróinín, *Cummian's Letter*, 72–5.

[32] *Ibid.*; Bede, *Historia Ecclesiastica*, II.4 (edd. and tr. Colgrave & Mynors, 146): '. . . ut non suo tempore celebrarent sed . . . a quarta decima luna usque ad uicesimam dominicae resurrectionis diem obseruandum esse putarent . . .'

[33] Lapidge & Herren, *Aldhelm, the Prose Works*, 140–3.

[34] *Ibid.*, 155–60.

[35] *Ibid.*, 158; Aldhelm, *Epistolae*, IV (ed. Ehwald, 484): '. . . quarta decima luna cum Judeis Christum blasphemantibus et margaritas evangelii ritu porcorum calcantibus paschae solemnitatem peragunt . . .' Unfortunately, Aldhelm does not make it clear whether he is accusing the Britons of celebrating Easter on the fourteenth moon, regardless of the day of the week on which it falls, or simply of observing Easter Sunday when it happens to occur on the same day as the Passover, that is, on the fourteenth moon.

[36] *Ibid.*, citing Augustine, *Concerning Heresies*, XXIX.

[37] Bede, *Historia Ecclesiastica*, IV.5 (edd. and tr. Colgrave & Mynors, 350–1): 'Ut sanctum diem paschae in / commune omnes seruemus dominica post quartamde-cimam lunam mensis primi.' The 'first month' referred to is the Jewish lunar month known as Nisan. The fourteenth moon is the full moon.

[38] Bede, *Historia Ecclesiastica*, V.21 (edd. and tr. Colgrave & Mynors, 534–51).

at rebutting certain arguments advanced by the Picts (and, presumably, their Irish teachers). The main thrust of his brief is that Christians must celebrate Easter on the Sunday that falls in the third week of Nisan, that is between the fifteenth and twenty-first moons. He advances a variety of arguments, primary of which is that the practice fulfils both the old and the new laws. It follows the old law by adopting the first month and by keeping the seven-day feast of unleavened bread (*azyma*). It obeys the new because Christ himself chose Sunday as his day of resurrection.

Because Christ is regarded as 'our Passover sacrificed for us' (I Cor. 5:7, cited by Ceolfrid), the challenge for Ceolfrid was to prove that it is not necessary to obey the letter of Exod. 12:5: 'And you shall keep it [the lamb] until the fourteenth day of this month: and the whole multitude of the children of Israel shall sacrifice it in the evening.' (Exodus goes on to say that everything should be eaten the same night, and nothing left over in the morning.) Ceolfrid counters:

. . . it is not commanded that the Passover should be kept on that day, but it is commanded that the lamb should be sacrificed on the evening of the fourteenth day, that is on the fifteenth day of the moon, which is the beginning of the third week, when the moon appears in the sky . . .[39]

The entire tone of Ceolfrid's letter is defensive: it is clear that he is arguing against opponents who argue that Ceolfrid and his adherents celebrate the paschal feast in a manner contrary to the stated law of God.

The Quattuordeciman charge *is* introduced, this time in the context of Ireland, by a papal letter. This is the missive of Pope-elect John, to a group of mostly northern Irish bishops and abbots, dated to 638.[40] Bede cites the beginning of it:

The writings which were brought by envoys to Pope Severinus of holy memory were left with the questions contained in them unanswered when he departed this life. These we re-opened so that no obscurity should remain uncleared in questions of such import, and we discovered that certain men of your kingdom were attempting to revive a new heresy out of an old one and, befogged with mental blindness, to reject our Easter in which Christ was sacrificed for us, contending with the Hebrews that it should be celebrated on the fourteenth day of the moon.[41]

Like Aldhelm's letter to Geraint, the pope-elect's letter says nothing of lunar limits, but deals only with the matter of celebrating Easter on the fourteenth moon along with the Jews. Similar language is used by the Irishman

---

[39] Bede, *Historia Ecclesiastica*, V.21 (edd. and tr. Colgrave & Mynors, 536–7): '. . . non tamen in ipsa die quarta decima pascha fieri praecipiatur, sed adueniente tandem uespera diei quartae decimae, id est quinta decima luna, quae initium tertiae septimanae faciat, in caeli faciem prodeunte, agnus immolari iubeatur . . .'

[40] For this date rather than the usual 640 see Walsh & Ó Cróinín, *Cummian's Letter*, 5. For the identities of the various churchmen addressed in the pope-elect's letter see Plummer, *Baedae Opera Historica*, II.112–13.

[41] Bede, *Historia Ecclesiastica*, II.19 (tr. Colgrave & Mynors, 201); Latin text below, 67. See Walsh & Ó Cróinín, *Cummian's Letter*, 18–47.

Cummian, who, in his treatise on the paschal controversy, cites Pseudo-Cyril:

... so that we may not be deceived in the moon of the First Month and so that we should celebrate Easter on the following Sunday, and not keep it on the fourteenth moon with the Jews and heretics who are called Thesserescedecate.[42]

The question is thus: Was the Easter controversy of the seventh century waged only over the correct lunar limits, or did the British and the Irish always celebrate Easter on the same day as the Passover (on the fourteenth moon), hence earning them the reproach of 'Judaiser'? Bede's report of Laurence's concern that the British and the Irish celebrate Easter between the fourteenth and twentieth moons (of Nisan) argues for the former alternative. These limits could be seen as heretical, since the fourteenth moon would sometimes occur on a Sunday which coincided with the Passover. This explains why the Western Church insisted on the lunar limits 15–21: a coincidence with the Jewish Passover would thus never occur. The term 'Quattuordeciman' in this instance would be hyperbolic – a term of abuse used to slander contemporary opponents with the opprobrium of an old heresy. Most scholars have understood the controversy in this light, and they would find additional authority in a letter of the same Abbot Columbanus mentioned by Laurence. Columbanus argued for the limits 14–20 against both the Western and Eastern Churches.[43]

Against this evidence, however, are the reports of the pope-elect and Aldhelm, who make no mention of lunar limits and speak only of celebrating Easter on the fourteenth moon along with the Jews. The normal construction of their words is that the Britons and the Irish celebrated on that moon only. However, some very important evidence remains to be considered, namely the account of the Synod of Whitby (664), at which the Irish and the Roman parties presented their cases respecting the correct date of Easter. Bishop Colmán was the main spokesman for the Irish, while the priest Wilfrid represented the Roman case. After a discussion of the tradition of the apostles in observing Easter – John following strict Mosaic law, Peter waiting for the Sunday after Passover – the argument turns to lunar limits. Wilfrid puts the case against Colmán:

For John who kept Easter according to the decrees of the Mosaic law, took no heed of the Sunday; you do not do this, for you celebrate Easter only on the Sunday. Peter celebrated Easter Sunday between the fifteenth and the twenty-first day of the moon; you, on the other hand, celebrate Easter Sunday between the fourteenth and the twentieth day of the moon.[44]

---

[42] Cummian, *Letter*, lines 226–9 (edd. and tr. Walsh & Ó Cróinín, 88–9); *De controversia Paschali*, lines 226–9: 'ut non fallam⟨ur in⟩ luna primi mensis et celebre⟨mus⟩ pascha in sequenti Dominico, et non faciemus in luna .xiiii. cu⟨m⟩ Iudaeis et hereticis, qui dicuntur thesserescedecadite'.

[43] Columbanus, *Letters*, I.3–4 (ed. Walker, 2–7).

[44] Bede, *Historia Ecclesiastica*, III.25 (tr. Colgrave & Mynors, 303); Latin text below, 67; see discussion in Charles-Edwards, *Early Christian Ireland*, 398.

It is clear enough, then, that the Irish celebrated Easter on a Sunday, and thus, as Wilfrid charged, were not strict observers of the law of Moses, and thus also not Quattuordecimans in the original sense of the term. By observing Easter on a Sunday, the Irish tried to fulfil the example of the gospel: 'And in the end of the sabbath, when it began to dawn towards the first day of the week, came Mary Magdalen and the other Mary, to see the sepulchre' (Matt. 28:1). By allowing Easter to coincide with Passover in some years they attempted to fulfil the command of the law: 'This month shall be to you the beginning of months: it shall be first in the months of the year' (Exod. 12:2); 'And you shall keep it (the pasch) until the fourteenth day of this month: and the whole multitude of the children of Israel shall sacrifice it in the evening' (Exod. 12:6). Bede clinches the case, and refutes those who believed that the Irish were real Quattuordecimans:

> They (the Irish) did not always observe it on the fourteenth day of the moon, with the Jews, as some believe, but they celebrated it always on the Sunday, though not in the proper week. Being Christians they knew that the resurrection of our Lord, which happened on the first day after the sabbath, must always be celebrated on that day; but, rude barbarians as they were, they had never learned when that particular first day after the sabbath, which we now call the Lord's Day, should come.[45]

Bede, however, may have been speaking of the Irish (and Britons?) of his own time or within recent memory. There is some late evidence relating to the sixth century that shows that some Irish were Quattuordecimans in the strict sense. For the year 704 the Fragmentary Annals of Ireland has:

> In this year the men of Ireland accepted a single regulation and rule from Adamnán, regarding the celebration of Easter on Sunday, the fourteenth of the moon of April, and regarding the wearing of Peter's tonsure by all the clergy of Ireland; for there had been great disturbance in Ireland until then, that is, many of the Irish clergy were celebrating Easter on Sunday, the fourteenth of the moon of April, and were wearing the tonsure of Peter the Apostle, following Patrick. Many others, however, were following Colum Cille, celebrating Easter on the fourteenth of the moon of April no matter on which day of the week the fourteenth happened to fall, and wearing the tonsure of Simon Magus.[46]

It has been argued that the so-called 'Fragmentary Annals' were compiled in the eleventh century.[47] However, the origin of much of the material has yet to be fully analysed or properly dated. Nonetheless, an examination of the 'foreign notes' in this entry for 704 ascertained that it is based almost entirely on Bede's *Historia Ecclesiastica*.[48] However, as we have just shown, Bede defended the Irish against the serious charge of being

---

[45] Bede, *Historia Ecclesiastica*, III.4 (tr. Colgrave & Mynors, 225); Latin text below, 67.

[46] *Fragmentary Annals*, CLXVI, s.a. 704 (tr. Radner, 55–7); Irish text below, 67–8. Adomnán's *Life of Columba* is silent on the Easter controversy except at *Life* I.3 where the saint prophesies strife among the churches in Ireland over the question.

[47] Radner, *Fragmentary Annals*, xiii.

[48] von Hamel, 'Foreign notes'.

true Quattuordecimans. One might therefore speculate that the charge that Columba (Colum Cille) 'celebrated Easter on the fourteenth of the moon of April *no matter on which day of the week the fourteenth happened to fall*' was derived from an Irish *Romani* tradition. The veracity of the charge cannot be denied out of hand. At the very least, the claim is compatible with the evidence we have of Columba's continuing to celebrate the sabbath additionally to the Lord's Day.[49]

Perhaps, however, not enough attention has been paid to the question of the meaning of Easter. It is important to note that Pope-elect John's and Ceolfrid's letters referred to Easter as Christ's sacrifice, reflecting Paul's text of I Corinthians and a long tradition in the Christian Church of identifying Easter with the pasch/Passover (note Graeco-Latin *pascha,* which stands for both 'Passover' and 'Easter'). Cummian, writing in 632 or 633,[50] perceived the problem and very intelligently attempted to separate the pasch from the resurrection: 'I found that the Apostle spoke thus concerning the sacrifice of Christ, not concerning the resurrection, saying: "For Christ, our Paschal lamb, has been sacrificed" (I Cor. 5:7).'[51] Cummian proceeds to draw the logical conclusion of his distinction:

Hence the entire church of the East has reverently allotted three weeks for the most holy feasts of Our Lord Jesus Christ, that is (a week) to the Passion, (a week) to the Sepulture, and (a week) to the Resurrection: from the 14th to the 20th moon for the Passion, from the 15th to the 21st for the Sepulture, and the 16th to the 22nd for the Resurrection, consecrating a week for reverence of the Lord's Day. For, if the fourteenth moon were assigned to the Resurrection, as you do, then the thirteenth would fall on the Sepulture and the twelfth on the Passion, in an inverted order.[52]

For this reason, the Jewish Passover might be allowed to coincide with Good Friday, but not with Easter. Wilfrid, in his speech reported by Bede, makes a similar point:

But when Peter preached at Rome, remembering that the Lord rose from the dead and brought to the world the hope of the resurrection on the first day of the week . . .[53]

Bede skilfully creates a dichotomy between the followers of Peter, who by celebrating Easter on Sunday validate the gospel and the resurrection, and the followers of John, who remain mired in the Old Law and identify Easter with the Passover. By linking Wilfrid and the Roman party to Peter, he

---

[49] See below, 109–10.
[50] For this date and a general chronology of the paschal controversy in Ireland in the early seventh century, see Walsh & Ó Cróinín, *Cummian's Letter,* 6–7.
[51] Cummian, *Letter,* lines 23–5 (edd. and tr. Walsh & Ó Cróinín, 58–9); *De controversia Paschali,* lines 23–5: 'Et inueni hoc apostolum de immolatione Christi non de resurrectione commemorasse ⟨di⟩centem: *Etenim pascha nostrum immolatus est Christus.*'
[52] Cummian, *Letter,* lines 80–5 (edd. and tr. Walsh & Ó Cróinín, 67–9); Latin text below, 68. See Walsh & Ó Cróinín's discussion, 25–9.
[53] Bede, *Historia Ecclesiastica,* III.25 (edd. and tr. Colgrave & Mynors, 302–3): 'At uero Petrus cum Romae praedicaret, memor quia Dominus prima sabbati resurrexit a mortuis ac mundo spem resurrectionis contulit . . .'

points to the identification of that party with the gospel and the true Church. By linking Colmán and the Irish to John, he points to the identification of the Irish with the law of Moses. Bede causes Wilfrid to answer Colmán with these words: 'Far be it from me to charge John with foolishness: he literally observed the decrees of the Mosaic law when the Church was still Jewish in many respects.'[54]

Two very large issues are entailed in the paschal controversy. The first is the definition of the law for a Christian. Precisely what is the relevance of the Old Law expressed in the Old Testament to Christians who believe in the gospel? The second is the question of who has authority to interpret the law? The first question troubled the Church from the beginning. Christ's claim to fulfil the law rather than abolish it (Matt. 5:17) provided a principle to which all might appeal, yet the saying may have raised more problems than it solved. Did it mean that the commandments of Christ were to be added to the Old Law, and if so, to *all* of the Old Law? Which of the versions of the ten commandments was one to follow? Was a Christian bound by the same dietary restrictions as a Jew? Should Christians be circumcised? And so on. Columbanus, in his letter to Pope Gregory on the paschal reckoning, defends the Irish position with the words of Deuteronomy 4:2: 'You shall not add to the word that I speak to you, neither shall you take away from it'; and the same text runs further: 'Keep the commandments of the Lord your God which I command you.' If one adds to this the words of Christ, 'He who hears my words and does them, he it is who loves me' (John 14:21), then all of the injunctions of the Bible found in both testaments must be followed. Such a viewpoint was probably the minority position in the first six centuries of Christian history. Even though both testaments were accepted as the word of God, the Old Testament was read and interpreted much more selectively than the New. The Romanising Cummian was aware of these divergent approaches. With help from Paul and Jerome, he struck at his opponents:

Again Jerome: 'Moses dying', he says, 'is mourned'; Jesus is buried on the Mount without tears. I would mourn for those who die in the Law, crucifying the Lord under the fourteenth moon, but I would receive those rising again with Christ in the Gospel.[55]

The second problem is closely related to the first. For those who believed that the totality of the law had to be followed, there was no room for interpretation. The law is the law, and no one may take away from it or add to it. Moreover, God's law, expressed in commandments ('thou shalt, thou

---

[54] Bede, *Historia Ecclesiastica*, III.25 (edd. and tr. Colgrave & Mynors, 300–1): '"Absit" inquit "ut Iohannem stultitiae reprehendamus, cum scita legis mosaicae iuxta litteram seruaret, iudaizante adhuc in multis ecclesia".' See Charles-Edwards, *Early Christian Ireland*, 411–12.

[55] Cummian, *Letter*, lines 180–3 (edd. and tr. Walsh & Ó Cróinín, 80–1, citing Jerome, *Adversus Iovinianum*, I:22 [*PL* XXIII:251]); *De controversia Paschali*, lines 180–3: 'Item Ieronimus: "Moyses," inquit, "moriens plangitur; Iesus" absque lacrimis "in monte" sepelitur. In lege morientes sub .xiiii. luna Dominum crucifigentes plangam, sed cum Christo resurgentes in euangelio suscipiam.'

shalt not') is clear enough. It is all in the Bible for everyone to read. This kind of 'scripturalism' places opponents on the defensive. It helps to explain why Ceolfrid worked so hard to 'explain away' the injunctions of Exodus 12. It also helps to explain why Cummian invoked the aid of Jerome against the unnamed 'Quattuordecimans'. In his *De exodo in vigilia Paschae* (*On Exodus on the Vigil of Easter*) Jerome warns against eating the figural lamb outside of the precept of the law, that is, *outside of the universal Church*.[56] This is another way of saying that God's law is by no means self-evident; it is to be understood as the universal (Roman) Church understands it. The magisterium of the Church founded by Christ is supreme and final.

Cummian's treatise shows that the debate between the Romanisers and the Celtic churches had as much to do with the source of authority as it did with the celebration of Easter. Cummian addresses his opponents directly:

Meanwhile I cry out: 'Whoever is joined to the chair of St Peter is mine.' Therefore either two deceive or all deceive. 'Troubles on all sides of me!' (Dan. 13:22). If I shout this with Jerome, interpreter of divine Scripture and opponent of all heretics, I am opposed by you. If I do not cry out, I am excommunicated by the universal Catholic Church, to which the authority of binding and loosing was given by God.[57]

However, it should be emphasised that the dispute over final authority did not pertain to the claims of rival churches or sects, but rather to the conflict between the authority of the scriptures and the authority of a church – any church. This places the Insular Easter controversy in a new light, changing its focus from a debate about lunar limits and Easter tables to the much more fundamental issue of *magisterium*. The curious Quattuordeciman controversy that occupied the Insular world in the seventh and eighth centuries played a central role in the development of the concept of Christ. By their attempt to adhere more closely to the Law of Moses, the Fourteeners were seen to push Christ's resurrection into the background, and to keep it subject to the Old Law.[58] Ultimately, this delimitation of Christ was more important than the date of Easter. 'Moses is mourned, Jesus is buried without tears.'

The heterodox movements which grew up in the British Isles at various times from the fourth to the seventh century had one important feature in common: they privileged Christ's human nature over his divine. This is clear enough in the case of Arianism, but perhaps is not so obvious in the

---

[56] Jerome, *De Exodo in vigilia Paschae* (*CCSL* LXXVIII.536–7), cit. by Cummian, *Letter*, lines 101–7 (edd. and tr. Walsh & Ó Cróinín, 73).

[57] Cummian, *Letter*, lines 144–9 (tr. Walsh & Ó Cróinín, 79); Latin text below 68.

[58] An expected allusion to the canonical account of the resurrection is omitted in the (seventh-century?) hymn *Precamur patrem*, which describes the life of Christ from his birth to his second coming; see the translation in the Appendix, esp. stanzas xviii–xxxix, 287–8. The resurrection is also omitted in the acount of New Testament miracles given in Pseudo-Augustine, *On the Miracles of Holy Scripture*; see the discussion below, 164. Moreover, the resurrection is ambiguously represented in Irish iconography to the tenth century; see discussion in Chapter VII.

case of the Pelagians who professed an orthodox Christology. Yet, as we will try to show, Pelagian emphasis on Christ's role as law-giver, teacher and model of conduct left little room for a divine Redeemer, the second person of the Trinity. One charge brought against the Quattuordecimans is that they celebrated the pasch without Christ, that is before his resurrection from the dead, effectively undercutting the miraculous nature of the resurrection, and hence, Christ's divinity. From the standpoint of an eastern Monophysite, these heresies (along with Nestorianism) are the end of a slippery slope that starts with Dyophysitism – the affirmation that Christ is equally God and equally man. It is easy for such a delicate balance to be destroyed in favour of the all-too human. A non-transcendent, heavily humanised Christ, however, suited the objectives of Insular monasticism. God's saints are commanded to imitate Christ in all things – or, at least in all things allowed to men. But men can only imitate men, they cannot imitate God.

Additional Texts

1. Pelagius, *Libellus Fidei*, I, II, IX, XXV (*PL* XLVIII. 488–91): 'I. Credimus in Deum Patrem omnipotentem, cunctorum visibilium et invisibilium conditorem. II. Credimus et in Dominum nostrum Jesum Christum, per quem creata sunt omnia, verum Deum, unigenitum, et verum Dei Filium, non factum aut adoptivum, sed genitum, unius cum Patre substantiæ, quod Græci dicunt [ὁμοούσιον], atque ita per omnia aequalem Deo Patri, ut nec tempore, nec gradu, nec potestate possit esse inferior. Tantumque esse confitemur illum qui est genitus, quantus est ille qui genuit. IX. Sic autem confitemur in Christo unam Filii esse personam, ut dicamus duas esse perfectas atque integras substantias, id est, Deitatis et humanitatis, quæ ex anima continetur et corpore; atque ut condemnamus Photinum, qui solum et nudum in Christo hominem confitetur, ita anathematizamus Apollinarem et ejus similes, qui dicunt Dei Filium minus aliquid de humana suscepisse natura; et vel in carne, vel in anima, vel in sensu assumptum hominem, his propter quos assumptus est fuisse dissimilem, quem, absque sola peccati macula, quæ naturalis non est, nobis confitemur fuisse conformem. XXV. Liberum sic confitemur arbitrium, ut dicamus nos semper Dei indigere auxilio: et iam illos errare qui cum Manichæo dicunt hominem peccatum vitare non posse, quam illos qui Joviniano asserunt hominem non posse peccare; uterque enim tollit arbitrii libertatem; nos vero dicimus hominem semper et peccare, et non peccare posse, ut semper nos liberi confiteamur esse arbitrii.'

2. Patrick, *Confessio*, IV (ed. Bieler, *Libri epistolarum*, I.58–60): 'Quia non est alius Deus nec unquam fuit nec ante nec erit post haec praeter Deum Patrem ingenitum, sine principio, a quo est omne principium, omnia tenentem, ut didicimus; et huius filium Iesum Christum, quem cum Patre scilicet semper fuisse testamur, ante originem saeculi spiritaliter apud Patrem ⟨et⟩ inenarrabiliter genitum ante omne principium, et per ipsum facta sunt uisibilia et inuisibilia, hominem factum, morte deuicta in caelis ad

Patrem receptum, *et dedit illi omnem potestatem super omne nomen caeles-tium et terrestrium et infernorum et omnis lingua confiteatur ei quia Dominus et Deus est Iesus Christus*, quem credimus et expectamus aduentum ipsius mox futurum, *iudex uiuorum atque mortuorum, qui reddet unicuique secun-dum facta sua*; et *effudit in nobis habunde Spiritum Sanctum, donum* et *pignus* immortalitatis, qui facit credentes et oboedientes ut sint *filii Dei* et *coheredes Christi*: quem confitemur et adoramus unum Deum in trinitate sacri nominis.'

5. *Altus prosator*, I (ed. and tr. Carey, 33):
    Altus Prosator, Uetustus/ Dierum, et Ingenitus,
    erat absque origine/ primordii et crepidine;
    est et erit in saecula/ saeculorum infinita,
    cui est unigenitus/ Christus et Sanctus Spiritus
    coaeternus in gloria/ dietatis perpetua.
    Non tres deos depromimus,/ sed unum Deum dicimus
    salua fide in personis/ tribus gloriosissimis.

12. Gildas, *De excidio*, XII.3 (ed. Winterbottom, 93): 'Mansit namque Christi capitis membrorumque consonantia suavis, donec Arriana perfidia, atrox ceu anguis, transmarina nobis evomens venena fratres in unum habitantes exitiabiliter faceret seiungi, ac sic quasi via facta trans oceanum omnes omnino bestiae ferae mortiferum cuiuslibet haereseos virus horrido ore vibrantes letalia dentium vulnera patriae novi semper aliquid audire volenti et nihil certe stabiliter optinenti infigebant.'

19. Columbanus, *Epistulae*, V.13 (ed. Walker, 52): 'Nam si, ut audivi, aliqui in Christo duas substantias non credunt, heretici potius quam Christiani credendi sunt; Christus enim salvator noster verus Deus aeternus sine tempore et verus homo absque peccato ex tempore est, qui iuxta divinitatem coaeternus est patri et iutxta humanitatem iunior est matre, qui natus in carne, nequaquam deerat caelo, manens in trinitate vixit in mundo; et ideo, si scriptum est in quinta synodo, ut quidam mihi dixit, quod, qui duas substantias adorat, orationem suam divisam habeat, ille divisus est a sanctis et separatus est a Deo, qui scripsit. Nam nos pro unitate personae, in qua complacuit *plenitudinem divinitatis inhabitare corporaliter*, unum Christum credimus, divinitatem eius et humanitatem, quia *qui descendit ipse est, qui ascendit super omnes caelos, ut adimpleret omnia*. Si quis aliter de incar-natione Domini senserit, hostis est fidei et abominandus est omnibus Christianis ac anathematizandus.'

27. Eusebius, *Historia Ecclesiastica*, XXIII.1–2 (ed. Lake, I.502–4):
Ζητήσεως δῆτα κατὰ τούσδε οὐ σμικρᾶς ἀνακινηθείσης, ὅτι δὴ τῆς ᾽Ασίας ἁπάσης αἱ παροικίαι ὡς ἐκ παραδόσεως ἀρχαιοτέρας σελήνης τὴν τεσσαρεσκαι-δεκάτην ᾤοντο δεῖν ἐπὶ τῆς σωτηρίου πάσχα ἑορτῆς παραφυλάττειν, ἐν ᾗ θύειν τὸ πρόβατον ᾽Ιουδαίοις προηγόρευτο, ὡς δέον ἐκ παντὸς κατὰ ταύτην, ὁποία δᾶν ἡμέρᾳ τῆς ἑβδομάδος περιτυγχάνοι, τὰς τῶν ἀσιτιῶν ἐπιλύσεις ποιεῖσθαι, οὐκ ἔθους ὄντος τοῦτον ἐπιτελεῖν τὸν τρόπον ταῖς ἀνὰ τὴν λοιπὴν ἅπασαν οἰκουμένην

ἐκκλησίαις, ἐξ ἀποστολικῆς παραδόσεως τὸ καὶ εἰς δεῦρο κρατῆσαν ἔθος φυλαττούσαις, ὡς μηδ᾽ ἑτέρᾳ προσήκειν παρὰ τὴν τῆς ἀναστάσεως τοῦ σωτῆρος ἡμῶν ἡμέρᾳ τὰς νηστείας ἐπιλύεσθαι, σύνοδοι δὴ καὶ συγκροτήσεις ἐπισκόπων ἐπὶ ταὐτὸν ἐγίνοντο, πάντες τε μιᾷ γνώμῃ δι᾽ ἐπιστολῶν ἐκκλησιαστικὸν δόγμα τοῖς πανταχόσε διετυποῦντο ὡς ἂν μηδ᾽ ἐν ἄλλῃ ποτὲ τῆς κυριακῆς ἡμέρᾳ τὸ τῆς ἐκ νεκρῶν ἀναστάσεως ἐπιτελοῦντο τοῦ κυρίου μυστήριον, καὶ ὅπως ἐν ταύτῃ μόνῃ τῶν κατὰ τὸ πάσχα νηστειῶν φυλαττοίμεθα τὰς ἐπιλύσεις.

30. Bede, *Historia Ecclesiastica*, II.4 (edd. Colgrave & Mynors, 146): 'Dum nos sedes apostolica more suo, sicut in uniuerso orbe terrarum, in his occiduis partibus ad praedicandum gentibus paganis dirigeret, atque in hanc insulam, quae Brittania nuncupatur, contigit introisse, antequam cognosceremus, credentes quod iuxta morem uniuersalis ecclesiae ingrederentur, in magna reuerentia sanctitatis tam Brettones quam Scottos uenerati sumus; sed cognoscentes / Brettones, Scottos meliores putauimus. Scottos uero per Daganum episcopum in hanc, quam superius memorauimus, insulam, et Columbanum abbatem in Gallis uenientem nihil discrepare a Brettonibus in eorum conuersatione didicimus. Nam Daganus episcopus ad nos ueniens non solum cibum nobiscum sed nec in eodem hospitio, quo uescebamur, sumere uoluit.'

41. Bede, *Historia Ecclesiastica*, II.19 (edd. Colgrave & Mynors, 200): 'Scripta quae perlatores ad sanctae memoriae Seuerinum papam adduxerunt eo de hac luce migrante, reciproca responsa ad ea, quae postulata fuerant, siluerunt. Quibus reseratis, ne diu tantae quaestionis caligo indiscussa remaneret, repperimus quosdam prouinciae uestrae contra orthodoxam fidem nouam ex ueteri heresim renouare conantes pascha nostrum, in quo immolatus est Christus, nebulosa caligine refutantes et XIIII luna cum Hebreis celebrare nitentes.'

44. Bede, *Historia Ecclesiastica*, III.25 (edd. Colgrave & Mynors, 302): 'Iohannes enim, ad legis Mosaicae decreta tempus paschale custodiens, nil de prima sabbati curabat; quod uos non facitis, qui nonnisi prima sabbati pascha celebratis. Petrus a quinta decima luna usque ad uicesimam primam diem paschae dominicum celebrabat; quod uos non facitis, qui a quarta decima usque ad uicesimam lunam diem dominicum paschae obseruatis . . .'

45. Bede, *Historia Ecclesiastica*, III.4 (edd. Colgrave & Mynors, 224): '. . . quem tamen et antea non semper in luna quarta decima cum Iudaeis, ut quidam rebantur, sed in die quidem dominica, alia tamen quam decebat ebdomada, celebrabant. Sciebant enim, ut Christiani, resurrectionem dominicam, quae prima sabbati facta est, prima sabbati semper esse celebrandam; sed ut barbari et rustici, quando eadem prima sabbati, quae nunc dominica dies cognominatur, ueniret, minime didicerant.'

46. *Fragmentary Annals*, CLXVI (ed. Radner, 54, 56): 'Isin bliadhain si ro fhaomhsad fir Eireann aonsmacht 7 aoinriagail do gabhail ó Adhamhnan um celeabhrad na Casg ar Dhomhnach, an ceathramhadh dec esga April 7 im

corunugh[adh] Peadair do bheith for cleirchibh Eireann uile. Uair bá mór an buidhreadh ra bhaoí in nEir*inn* gonige sin, .i. buidhean do chleircibh Eir*eann* ag celeabra*d*h na Cascc ar Dhomhnach an ceathram*h*a*d* deag esga April, 7 coronughadh Peadair Apstoil ar slio*cht* Phatricc. Buidhean eile dno ag secheamh Colom Cille, .i. Caiscc do celeabhr*ad* ar cethram*ad* déc esga april gibe laithe sea*cht*muine ar a mbeit[h] an ceat[h]ramhadh décc 7 coronughudh Simoin Druadh forra.'

52. Cummian, *De controversia Paschali*, lines 80–5 (edd. Walsh & Ó Cróinín, 66–8): 'Unde orie⟨ntalis tota aecclesia⟩ tres ebdomadas tribus sacratissimis solennitatibus Domini ⟨nostri Iesu⟩ Christi uenerabiliter, id est passioni, sepulturae, resurrectioni, deputau⟨it⟩: passioni a .xiiii. in .xx.; sepulturae a .xv. in .xxi.; resurrectioni a ⟨.x⟩vi. in .xxii. lunam, septimanam pro reuerentia Dominici diei consecrans. Quia si .xiiii. luna resurrectioni deputetur, ut uos facitis, .xiii. in sepultura et .xii. in passione, prepostero ordine, fiet.'

57. Cummian, *De controversia Paschali*, lines 144–9 (edd. Walsh & Ó Cróinín, 78): '"Ego interim clamito si quis cathedrae sancti Petri iungatur meus est ille. Aut ergo duo mentiuntur aut omnes. *Angustiae michi undique*". Si ego hoc clamauero cum Ieronimo, diuinarum scripturarum interprete et omnium hereticorum impugnatore, a uobis impugnor. Si non clamauero, ab uniuersali aecclesia catholica excommunicor, cui alligand⟨i sol⟩uendique aucto⟨ritas a Deo data est.'

III

PELAGIANISM IN BRITAIN AND IRELAND

Pelagius was introduced in Chapter I in the context of the monastic movement, and mentioned in Chapter II as the author of a profession of faith. Here we shall examine his doctrines in the wider context of Christian dogma and establish him as a part of a broader activity. We shall then consider the evidence for the continuity of Pelagianism in Britain and Ireland and attempt to show its influence on the character of the common Celtic Church.

The Pelagian movement

Pelagianism is sometimes thought of as a one-man heresy, but it is now clear that Pelagius himself belonged to a wider movement. Despite the fact that his name is given to the doctrine, it is not completely certain that he was the instigator.[1] Other participants included Rufinus the Syrian, Julian of Aeclanum (an Italian bishop) and Coelestius, who was possibly a compatriot of Pelagius.[2] It should also be recalled that John Cassian, the leader of the 'semi-Pelagians', did not follow at some later date, but was contemporary with the main Pelagian movement.

For our purposes, it might be useful to regard the Pelagians as a broad group, embracing the semi-Pelagians on the left (if you will), Pelagius himself in the centre, and the hard-liner Coelestius on the right. While modern theologians may object to this re-classification of semi-Pelagians and Pelagians, it may claim some historical validity. Throughout the history of Christianity, theological polemicists frequently resorted to tarring their opponents with the brush of a heresy that was similar, but not identical, to the doctrine under attack. Throughout the fifth century it was convenient to lump together Pelagians and semi-Pelagians alike as 'enemies of grace'. This held especially true of Prosper of Aquitaine, the most vigorous champion of Augustinianism after Augustine himself, and a figure closely concerned with suppressing Pelagianism in any form in Britain and Ireland. In *Contra Collatorem* ('Against Cassian') Prosper repeatedly accused Cassian of stirring up the ashes of a dead doctrine, or attempting to snatch victory from the jaws of defeat.[3] Although Prosper occasionally acknowledged

[1] See Rees, *The Letters*, 1–7, 20–5; Bonner, 'Rufinus', 31.
[2] Morris, 'Pelagian literature', 41–2.
[3] See generally *Contra Collatorem*, I.2 (tr. De Letter, 71–2).

differences between Cassian and the Pelagians,[4] he took greater pleasure in pointing out their similarities. While differences between 'pure Pelagians' and semi-Pelagians doubtless persisted throughout the period of the common Celtic Church and even afterwards, the two groups formed a loosely compatible spectrum of belief and practice that differentiated early Celtic Christianity from Christianity in other regions.

Unlike so many heterodox teachings of the period, Pelagianism did not hinge on technicalities. Working outwards from the central doctrines of the goodness of created nature and the freedom of the will, it embraced the questions of moral laws, the scriptures, the way to salvation and the nature of Christ. Far from being a one-issue doctrine, Pelagianism involved the total human personality in its relations to God and the world. The doctrines deeply influenced the mindset of many who would have been horrified to think of themselves as heretics. Indeed, it can be argued that Pelagianism began as a traditionalist movement, in tune with the spirituality of the pre-Augustinian Christian Church.[5]

Pelagian writings

The attribution of writings to Pelagius and his followers has been the subject of a long scholarly debate.[6] It is axiomatic that when doctrines are condemned, the writings that contain them are also doomed. Copies of heretical works can be preserved principally by circulating them pseudonymously – usually under the name of orthodox authorities. Pelagian writings survive mainly in two collections known as the 'Evans Letters' and the 'Caspari Corpus'.[7] Fortunately, detailed paraphrases of Pelagian teachings are also given in the works of the orthodox fathers who attack them. Thus we know a great deal about the teachings of Pelagius and his followers from Augustine, Orosius, Marius Mercator and Jerome. Moreover, the orthodox fathers often give the names of heretical writings in their own works. Hence modern scholars have a basis for identifying texts with suspicious teachings that travel under the name of Augustine, Jerome or some other Father.

Only three extant texts can be assigned to Pelagius with certainty. These are the *Profession of Faith* (cited in Chapter II), a *Commentary on the Epistles of*

---

[4] See, for example, *Contra Collatorem*, III.1 (tr. De Letter, 76): 'You have invented some hybrid third system . . . and so you neither find approval with our enemies nor keep in one mind with us'; (*Sancti Prosperi Aquitani*, I.171): 'tu informe nescio quid tertium . . . quo nec inimicorum consensum adquireres, nec in nostrorum intelligentia permaneres'.

[5] See Markus, 'Pelagianism', 198: 'As so often happens, the conflict of heresy and orthodoxy is not one between an established and generally accepted doctrinal tradition and attempts to subvert, change or modify it by innovation. It is rather a conflict between elements crystallised out of a pre-existing, undifferentiated range of acceptable doctrinal options.'

[6] For a review of the problem see Rees, *The Letters*, 12–20; Morris, 'Pelagian literature'.

[7] Rees, *The Letters*, 12–20.

Paul and the *Letter to Demetrias*.[8] Sayings ascribed to Pelagius can be gleaned not only from patristic sources, but also from the record of the Synod of Diospolis, which preserved a series of heterodox statements imputed to both Pelagius and Coelestius.[9] (This useful record helps us identify differences of emphasis between the two.) Fragments of other works thought to be Pelagian also survive.[10] When we are not referring to the three texts named above, we shall use the term 'Pelagian writing' to cover any of the identified works emanating from the formative period of the movement.

Doctrines

Pelagian doctrine developed in the first two decades of the fifth century in reaction to Augustine's doctrine of grace as enunciated in Book X of Augustine's *Confessions* and his *De trinitate*. Pelagian teachings are contextualised in the spiritual instruction given to virgins, chaste widows and others practising some form of asceticism. There it is asserted that man can achieve salvation by his own free will.[11] In sharp opposition to Augustine and his followers, Pelagians defined grace as created nature itself (which includes the freedom of the will), the laws of Moses and Christ, and instruction. To these they added baptism with penance as the sole aspect of grace that lies outside human free will – although it may be accepted by a man, it was God who offered it in the first place.[12] These aspects of 'grace' are available to all, not just to a select few. God is no respecter of persons (Rom. 2:11); he wills the salvation of all; he foresees but does not predestine. Nor is man doomed by his own nature, since he is not predisposed to sin on account of the fall of Adam. Adam's sin is not transmitted, even though his disobedience found many imitators.[13] In theory, it is possible for an individual to live a complete life without sin.[14]

[8] Morris, 'Pelagian literature', 27–8. For more generous views of Pelagius's output see Evans, *Four Letters*, and de Plinval, *Pélage*, 44–5. For a recent opinion regarding the authorship of the treatise *Honorificentiae tuae* (tr. Rees, *The Letters*, 148–56), see Ó Cróinín, 'Who was Palladius?', 223–31.

[9] Translated in Rees, *Pelagius*, 135–9. Pelagius's and Coelestius's *dicta*, along with the Synod's *responsa*, are preserved in Augustine's *De gestis Pelagii*.

[10] For example, *On the Hardening of the Heart of Pharaoh* (*PL supp.* I.1506–39).

[11] Pelagius, *To Demetrias*, II–III (tr. Rees, *The Letters*, 37–9).

[12] See especially Pelagius's remarks on Romans 3:23 (tr. de Bruyn, *Pelagius's Commentary*, 81): 'Without the works of the law, through baptism, whereby he has freely forgiven the sins of all, though they are undeserving'; *Expositio in Romanos* 3:23 (ed. Souter, I.32–3): 'Sine legis operibus per baptismum, quo omnibus non merentibus gratis peccata donauit.'

[13] See especially *On the Christian Life*, XIII.2 (tr. Rees, *The Letters*, 121): 'I find that there was no disbelief in him (Adam) but only disobedience, which was the reason why he was condemned and why all are condemned for following his example'; *De vita Christiana*, XIII.2 (*PL* XL.1043): 'In quo nihil fuisse incredulitatis invenio praeter solam inobedientiam, cuius causa ille damnatus est, et omnes suo damnantur exemplo.'

[14] See Pelagius's (cagey) remarks addressed to the Synod of Diospolis (415),

The concept of nature is central to Pelagian thought; it embraces the whole of God's creation including the human will. Scripture attests to the goodness of created nature (note the repeated citation of Gen. 1 'and God saw that it was good').[15] There is a detectable resistance to the notion that God interferes with creation (by means of miracles) after it is created. The Synod of Diospolis records the following statement attributed to Coelestius: 'Adam was created mortal and would have died whether he sinned or not.'[16] This is a direct denial of the idea that man's condition in the garden before the fall was supernatural (or preternatural). One text calls grace 'miracles which are concealed in the divine law',[17] seemingly depriving both grace and miracles of existence.

Nature also plays a major role in the idea of law. In addition to the two laws given by God, that is the law of Moses and the law of Christ, there is a natural law. Pelagius himself developed this doctrine fully in his commentary on Romans, at Rom. 2:14–16, and also in his *Letter to Demetrias*. This is the law written on the hearts of men; its existence is proved by the acts of both virtuous gentiles and Jews who lived before the law of Moses. Pelagius cast the 'three laws' in a chronological mould. First comes the natural law; when this was 'forgotten' by men, it was replaced by the law of Moses (the second law) and finally the law of Christ (the third). Although Pelagius sometimes uses the standard formula 'under grace' or 'age of grace' to refer to the period after Christ, he always makes us to understand that by grace nothing more than the New Law is meant. The phrase 'instructed by grace' is a shibboleth of Pelagianism.[18]

The whole of God's law is promulgated in the scriptures. It consists of the 'law' (pentateuch), the prophets and the gospels; one text, *On Bad Teachers*, adds the apostles.[19] Despite the greater textual emphasis given the first three parts, there can be no question that 'the Apostles' was given equal status by Pelagius as a part of the divine law. This is shown by the particularly heavy weight accorded the authority of the Pauline epistles. God's law, with the aid of instruction, is thus available to everyone, as is the knowledge of the

---

chapter VI (tr. Rees, *Pelagius*, 136), and Jerome's *Letter to Ctesiphon*, CCCXXXIII.3 (tr. Fremantle *et al.*, 273). See also the tract *On the Possibility of Not Sinning* in Rees, *The Letters*, 164–70.

[15] See Pelagius, *To Demetrias*, III (tr. Rees, *The Letters*, 39): 'Whence can these good qualities come to them [*sc.* the pagan philosophers], unless it come from the good of nature?'; *Ad Demetriadem*, III (*PL* XXX.18): 'Unde autem illis [var. haec] nisi de naturae bono?'

[16] *Synod of Diospolis*, VIIa (tr. Rees, *Pelagius*, 136); Augustine, *De gestis Pelagii*, XXXIII (edd. Urba & Zycha, 111): 'Adam mortalem esse factum, qui siue peccaret, siue non peccaret, esset moriturus.'

[17] *On the Hardening of the Heart of Pharaoh* (our translation); *De induratione cordis pharaonis* (*PL supp.* I.1508): '. . . mirabilia quae obtecta sunt a lege divina . . .'

[18] Pelagius, *To Demetrias*, III (tr. Rees, *The Letters*, 39), VIII.4 (tr. Rees, *The Letters*, 45); *On Romans*, 7:4 (tr. de Bruyn, 101).

[19] Pelagius, *To Demetrias*, IX.2 (tr. Rees, *The Letters*, 45); *On Virginity*, VII.2 (tr. Rees, *The Letters*, 77); for the addition of the apostles see *On Bad Teachers* XI.1 (tr. Rees, *The Letters*, 229).

penalties for their infraction. No Christian can plead ignorance. The operative principle of Pelagian exegesis is the literal acceptance of all of God's laws enunciated in scripture. Any attempt to 're-construe' the law texts of the Bible is designated 'false exegesis'.[20] The Bible also contains many paradigms of behaviour to be emulated or avoided. Individuals are encouraged to read and meditate upon the scriptures for the lessons they contain. Pelagian writers assumed, with most other Christian thinkers, that persons and events in the Old Testament prefigure those in the New. Pelagian writings, however, sometimes employ allegory to explain narratives, but never to explain the law. This is because God's law must be seen as unambiguous, especially as he means us to fulfil it in every particular, and the consequences of disobedience are so dire – any sin that is not absolved in this life is punishable by death (eternal hell fire)!

Because no Christian was permitted to sin after baptism, the Pelagians opposed infant baptism and defended the ancient practice of the Church insisting on a long period of preparation.[21] Unlike Augustine, they did not believe that baptism was needed to undo the effects of original sin, since there were none. Baptism absolved all the previous sins of the individual, and at the same time entailed the commitment to sin no more. This commitment must be taken extremely seriously. If one happened to fall after baptism, sin could be atoned for only through long and arduous penance. The rigour of the Pelagian position on this matter led others to believe that Pelagians did not believe at all in the forgiveness of sin;[22] this must have prompted Pelagius's statement to the contrary in his *Profession of Faith*: 'A man, should he fall after baptism, can be saved through penance, if he believes.'[23] A couple of Pelagian texts speak of an allotment of sins for each individual, implying that there is a limit to God's mercy.[24] Pelagian writings refer rarely to sacraments other than baptism as these would be superfluous in the divine dispensation.[25]

Despite their optimistic view of human nature and the belief that God's commands can be fulfilled,[26] the Pelagians reached a pessimistic conclusion

[20] *On Bad Teachers*, XI.1 (tr. Rees, *The Letters*, 229): '. . . it is easier to adulterate them [the laws] by clever but perverse exegesis than to fulfill them faithfully'; *De doctoribus malis*, XI.1 (*PL supp.* I.1434): '. . . facilius sit illa peruersae expositionis ingenio conrumpere, quam fideliter adinplere'. This remark seems to have been directed against the opinion that the law might be interpreted spiritually, of which we have a clear example in Augustine's *City of God*, XX.28 (tr. Bettenson, 955–6).

[21] Under duress, Pelagius acknowledged that infants might be baptised; see Pelagius's *Profession of Faith*, article XVII (*PL* XLVIII.490).

[22] See especially the exceptionally stern remarks regarding sin after baptism in *On the Christian Life*, XIII.4 (tr. Rees, *The Letters*, 122).

[23] Pelagius, *Profession of Faith*, XVIII (our translation); *Libellus fidei*, XVIII (*PL* XLVIII.490): 'Hominem, si post baptismum lapsus fuerit, per poenitentiam credentem posse salvari.'

[24] *On the Christian Life*, IV (tr. Rees, *The Letters*, 111); Pelagius, *On Romans*, 9:22 (tr. de Bruyn, 119).

[25] See below, 126.

[26] Pelagian writings insist that God, who is just, could never have commanded what he knew to be impossible; see Pelagius, *To Demetrias*, XVI.2 (tr. Rees, *The Letters*,

regarding the possibility of salvation. Even though it was possible in theory not to sin (as numerous passages assert), the reality was very different. This is reflected in Pelagius's defence of his words about not sinning attributed to him by the Synod of Diospolis:

I did indeed say that a man can be without sin and keep the commandments of God, if he wishes, for this ability has been given to him by God. However, I did not say that any man can be found who has never sinned from his infancy to his old age . . .[27]

Ironically, the law, seen as stages of grace for man, while it does indeed save, imposes higher thresholds of performance with the advent of each stage. The command to be perfect and the demand of obedience to the entire law (as enunciated in both testaments) impose conditions that are almost impossible to fulfil. Even trivial sins can be punished with eternal damnation – we are reminded of Christ's warning that even to call our brother 'fool' makes us liable to the fires of Gehenna (Matt. 5:22).[28] Similarly, the refusal to perform Christ's commands respecting charity will earn the words at the last judgement: 'Depart from me ye cursed . . .' (Matt. 24:41). In effect, the law was a two-edged sword for the Pelagians as it was for Paul, but it is unclear to what extent they recognised this. Ironically, the Pelagians would have agreed with Augustine that most men will be damned;[29] their disagreement was confined to the cause.

In recommending the kind of life that true Christians should live, Pelagian writings lay stress on the various available forms of sexual abstinence (virginity, chaste widowhood, chaste marriage), which was a common theme of nearly all Christian writers of the period. However, Pelagians insisted with Paul that these were a matter of choice, not a command. Several texts place special stress on poverty. In the treatise *On Riches* the author viewed avarice, rather than gluttony or lust, as the root of all evil.[30] The proof of this is that most men are able to subdue the latter, but overcome the former only with the greatest difficulty. The drive to acquire wealth frequently leads to every kind of crime, and the possession of wealth often creates arrogance in the heart of the possessor. The writer assembled a plethora of scriptural injunctions against the acquisition of wealth, and set

---

53), XVI.3 (tr. Rees, *The Letters*, 53–4); *To an Older Friend*, IV (tr. Rees, *The Letters*, 150); *On the Possibility of Not Sinning*, II.2 (tr. Rees, *The Letters*, 166–7).

[27] Cited in Rees, *Pelagius*, 136; Augustine, *De gestis Pelagii*, X (22) (edd. Urba & Zycha, 75–6): 'Dixi quidem, proprio labore et Dei gratia posse hominem esse sine peccato; sed quam dicam gratiam optime nostis, et legendo recolere potestis, quod ea sit, in qua creati sumus a Deo cum libero arbitrio. . . . Non autem diximus quod inueniatur aliquis ab infantia usque ad senectam, qui nunquam peccauerit.'

[28] *On Bad Teachers*, XII.1 (tr. Rees, *The Letters*, 232–3).

[29] For Pelagian recognition of the difficulty of attaining salvation see *On Virginity*, VII.2 (tr. Rees, *The Letters*, 76); *On the Divine Law*, V.1 (tr. Rees, *The Letters*, 95); *To Celantia*, X (tr. Rees, *The Letters*, 132); *On Bad Teachers*, XII.1 (tr. Rees, *The Letters*, 122–3).

[30] *On Riches*, I.3 (tr. Rees, *The Letters*, 175).

great store by Christ's words, 'It is easier for a camel to go through the eye of a needle than for a rich man to enter the kingdom of heaven' (Matt. 19:24). Without any doubt, there is strong social comment in the tract which, arguably, exceeds the usual bounds of theological discourse.

Finally, Pelagian teaching entails a peculiar kind of Christology. Because of its focus on law and instruction as the truest forms of grace, Christ's chief importance lies primarily in the fact that he is the giver of the New Law, and secondarily in that he is the model whom we are to imitate as far as possible. A direct connection is made between the obedience to the law (which is the will of God) demanded of us and Christ's obedience to the will of the Father. Commenting on Rom. 5:19 ('For as by the disobedience of one man, many were made sinners . . .'), Pelagius wrote: 'Just as by the example of Adam's disobedience many sinned, so also many are justified by Christ's obedience.'[31] At a single stroke, Pelagius undermines the basis for the doctrine of transmitted original sin and exploits Paul to support his own notion that the most important act of Christ was his act of obedience, by which 'many shall be made just' (Rom. 5:19). Arguably, attaching too much importance to Christ's obedience to the will of the Father leads to theological dangers. In the first place, it is implied that it is Christ's example of obedience that justifies us (when we follow it)[32] rather than the grace flowing from his death. This is made wholly transparent in the treatise *On the Divine Law*:

Those who have been redeemed by Christ's passion through his dutifulness to his Father have been redeemed to this end that, by keeping the laws of their Redeemer, they may prepare themselves for the life laid up for them in heaven, and there they may in no way be said to arrive redeemed, unless they follow the commands laid upon those who seek to obey, as it is written: 'If you would enter life, keep the commandments' (Matt. 19:17).[33]

Secondly, stressing the obedience, hence the 'sonship', of Christ is a way of implying that Christ may not be consubstantial with the Father. For example, what is one to make of Pelagius's comparison of God's (sexual) resuscitation of Abraham, accomplished through faith, with his raising up of Christ?[34] Did Christ also require faith in his Father to raise him? Despite

---

[31] de Bruyn, *Pelagius's Commentary*, 95; Pelagius, *Expositio in Romanos*, 5:19 (ed. Souter, I.48): 'Sicut exemplo inoboedientae Adae peccauerunt multi, ita et Christi oboedentia iustificantur multi.'

[32] See also the Pelagian treatise *On the Hardening of the Heart of Pharaoh*: 'Christ our Redeemer suffered in order to leave us the example of his suffering' (our translation); *De induratione cordis pharaonis* (*PL supp.* I.1516): '. . . redemptor noster passus est Christus, ut nobis suae passionis exemplum relinqueret.'

[33] *On the Divine Law*, IV.2 (tr. Rees, *The Letters*, 94); *De divina lege*, IV.2 (*PL* XXX.108–9): 'Qui paterna pietate Christi passione redempti sunt et qui ad hoc redempti sunt, ut redemptoris jura servantes ad vitam se in cælo repositam præparent: ad quam redempti licet nullo modo pervenire dicantur, nisi ea quae jubentur obsequii competentibus exsequantur, sicut scriptum est: *si vis ad vitam ingredi, serva præcepta.*'

[34] Pelagius, *On Romans*, 4:17–24 (tr. de Bruyn, 87–8). For New Testament references to Jesus's 'having been raised', see O'Collins, *Christology*, 86–7, 94–5.

Pelagius's protestations in his *Profession of Faith*,[35] we may have here a strain of the Arian mindset which Gildas claimed to have left its impact on British Christianity.[36]

The views and writings of Pelagius and his followers were vigorously opposed by Augustine, who not only wrote against them, but manoeuvred to bring about their condemnation. The Pelagian doctrine, so commendable in many particulars, by denying grace as God's beneficent intervention in human history, and substituting the law for grace, posed an extreme institutional as well as theological threat. If grace does not exist, what need is there for the sacraments (other than baptism) which dispense grace, and if sacraments are not needed, what need is there for a Church? Moreover, Pelagian teachings empowered the individual to read and understand the law for him or herself, thereby reducing the role of the religious teacher.

Charges were brought against Pelagius and his close associate Coelestius at the Synod of Diospolis, where they avoided condemnation. However, the two were condemned in the following year at Councils held in Milevis and Carthage. In 418 they were finally excommunicated by Pope Zosimus. The views of Coelestius were officially condemned at the ecumenical Council of Ephesus held in 431.[37]

Augustine triumphed, and Pelagius ('the heresiarch') died in disgrace some time after 418. However, there were many in the Church who viewed with alarm Augustine's teachings on grace, transmitted original sin, perverted human will and predestination. What role is left for human effort? None, apparently. Augustine and the Pelagians were in agreement that the vast majority of mankind would end up in hell, but their explanations for this unhappy phenomenon were very different. The Pelagians attributed it to human obstinacy, hard-heartedness, foolishness and bad habits[38] (all of which were in the individual's power to control and overcome), while Augustine believed that there was nothing to be done but to rely on God's grace. Yet it had to be admitted that in the face of universal pessimism the Pelagians offered a ray of hope. Moreover, to accept Augustine's views in their strictest formulation was tantamount to counselling moral laxness: you might as well enjoy yourself in this life, because you haven't got a hope in hell in the next!

The strict Augustinian view of grace and free will collided head-on with the ethos of the burgeoning western ascetic movements of the late fourth and early fifth centuries. People were drawn to the ascetic life, whether in communities or privately, not because they wished to punish themselves in this life before they went to hell, but precisely because they believed that, by limiting their enjoyment of the present life, they ran a much better chance of

---

[35] Cited above, 48.

[36] See above, 51–2.

[37] For a summary of the Pelagian controversy with the dates of councils and tracts, see Rees, *Pelagius*, 140–2.

[38] Pelagius offers a developed notion of habit and its relation to sinfulness in his *On Romans* at 7:17–20 (tr. de Bruyn, 104).

avoiding hell and attaining salvation. The term 'ascetic', of course, does not mean 'self-punishing' *per se*, but rather 'relying on exercise or discipline'. The true ascetic believes that, by practising particular corporal and spiritual exercises, he or she may attain to spiritual advancement, which, in turn, leads to salvation. Such a belief implies the ability of the intellect to recognise the necessary exercises and the freedom of the will to carry them out. The principles of Pelagianism were attractive in early monastic circles because of their emphasis on the role of the will and of the correct *conversatio* ('way of life') in the process of salvation. Pelagius develops this point clearly and cogently in his *Letter to Demetrias*:

Whenever I have to speak on the subject of moral instruction and the conduct of a holy life, it is my practice first to demonstrate the power and quality of human nature and show what it is capable of achieving . . . The best incentive for the mind consists in teaching it that it is possible to do anything which one really wants to do.[39]

The role of the will and its relation to grace was a central issue for the semi-Pelagian writer John Cassian, who trained with monks in Egypt and elsewhere in the East before settling in Marseilles where he founded two monasteries.[40] Clearly, if the monastic ideal of perfection was to have any meaning, the means of achieving it had to be thoroughly understood. Cassian examined the problem of grace and free will in Book XII of his *Institutes*, and more deeply in his Thirteenth Conference – the *Conferences* was a work of twenty-four dialogues on monastic themes, written between 426 and 429.[41] It is very probable that the Thirteenth Conference was written with Augustine's doctrine of grace, by then fully enunciated, in mind.[42]

The Thirteenth Conference picks up the theme of the Twelfth, namely, the possibility of attaining true chastity. Near the beginning of the Conference, Germanus (not to be confused with Germanus of Auxerre) rejects the idea that everything must be ascribed to grace:

This tends toward the destruction of free will and seems to stand in opposition to a good understanding of it that we cannot hastily reject. For we see that many Gentiles, who certainly do not deserve the grace of divine assistance, shine with the virtues not only of temperance and patience, but even – which is more wonderful – with that of chastity. How can it be believed that their free will was fettered and that these things were bestowed on them by the gift of God when they were in fact followers of worldly wisdom and not only completely ignorant of the grace of God but even of the true

---

[39] Pelagius, *To Demetrias*, II.1 (tr. Rees, *The Letters*, 36–7); *Ad Demetriadem*, II.1 (*PL* XXX.16): 'Quoties mihi de institutione morum, et sanctæ vitæ conversatione dicendum est, soleo prius humanæ naturæ vim qualitatemque monstrare, et quid efficere possit . . . Optima enim animi incitamenta sunt, cum docetur aliquis posse quod cupiat.'

[40] For the career of Cassian, see Stewart, *Cassian*, 3–26.

[41] Ramsey, *The Conferences*, 8.

[42] This Conference, also known as *De protectione Dei*, was the impetus for Prosper's attack on Cassian in the work *Contra Collatorem* ('Against Cassian'), written in 432 or just afterwards; see De Letter, *Prosper of Aquitaine*, 8–9.

God himself, as we know from the course of our reading and from the teaching of certain persons? They are said to have possessed the purest chastity thanks to their own laborious efforts.[43]

Germanus's position is wholly consistent with 'pure Pelagianism'. Note that Pelagius argued in several places that there were righteous men even before the law of Moses – Abel, Noah, Enoch, Melchisedech, Job – and goes even farther to assert that there is a law written on the hearts of men that was available even to the gentiles:

This is the law which the apostle recalls when he writes to the Romans, testifying that it is implanted in all men and written as it were on the tablets of the heart. For when gentiles who have not the law do by nature what the law requires, they are a law to themselves, even though they do not have the law.[44]

The remainder of the Thirteenth Conference is given to the reply to Germanus by Chaeremon, who proves to be Cassian's spokesman. Chaeremon first refutes Germanus's contention that the gentiles could achieve true chastity – their sexual continence belonged to the act alone, and not to the intention, and therefore was only partial. And, while men can accomplish certain things on their own, 'human frailty can accomplish nothing which pertains to salvation'.[45] The first part of Chaeremon's reply gives the impression that he wishes to defend the Augustinian position that grace is all, but the speaker subtly shifts his ground towards an equal balance between grace and free will:

These things [grace and free will] are mixed together and fused so indistinguishably that which is dependent on which is a great question as far as many people are concerned – that is, whether God has mercy on us because we manifest the beginnings of a good will, or we acquire the beginnings of a good will because God is merciful. For many who hold to one of these alternatives and assert it more freely than is right have fallen into different self-contradictory errors. For if we said that the beginning of free will was up to us, what was there in Paul the persecutor and in Matthew the tax-collector, one of whom was drawn to salvation while intent upon the blood and torment of the innocent, the other upon violence and the plunder of public property? But if we said that the beginnings of a good will were always inspired by the grace of God, what should we say about the grace of Zacchaeus and by the devotion of the thief upon the cross? By their own desire they brought a certain force to bear on the heavenly kingdom . . .[46]

Chaeremon does not explain the precise relation between grace and free will, or how one operates on the other. He simply insists on the necessity of both

---

[43] Cassian, *Conferences*, XIII.4 (tr. Ramsey, 469); Latin text below, 101.

[44] Pelagius, *To Demetrias*, IV.2 (tr. Rees, *The Letters*, 40); *Ad Demetriadem*, IV.2 (*PL* XXX.19): 'Hujus legis, scribens ad Romanos, meminit Apostolus: quam omnibus hominibus insitam velut in quibusdam tabulis cordis scriptam esse, testatur: *Cum enim*, inquit, *gentes, quæ legem non habent, naturaliter quæ legis sunt, faciunt: hujuscemodi legem non habentes, ipsi sibi sunt lex.*'

[45] Cassian, *Conferences*, XIII.6.1 (tr. Ramsey, 470); *Conlationes*, XIII.6 (ed. Pichery, II.153–4): '. . . nec aliquid humanam fragilitatem quod ad salutem pertinet'.

[46] Cassian, *Conferences*, XIII.xi.1 (tr. Ramsey, 476–7); Latin text below, 101.

for salvation. Moreover, siding with the Pelagians against Augustine, he claims that the will is truly free (and not inclined to evil on account of Adam's sin):

For it must not be believed that God made the human being in such a way that he could never will or be capable of the good. He has not allowed him a free will if he has only conceded that he wills what is evil and be capable of it but not of himself either will the good or be capable of it . . . Finally, in the words of the Apostle it is very clearly stated that after Adam's sin the human race did not lose the knowledge of the good: 'When the Gentiles, who do not have the law, naturally do the things of the law, they who do not have the law are a law unto themselves', etc.[47]

Another important representative of the semi-Pelagian doctrine was Faustus, born in Britain around 410, trained as a monk at Lérins, later bishop of Riez, dying around 490.[48] Faustus wrote an important treatise entitled *On Grace*.[49] In it he follows the same general strategy as Cassian in the Thirteenth Conference: he attacks Pelagius for arguing that man can be saved solely by his will and for opposing infant baptism, then proceeds to level his big guns against Augustine's doctrine of predestination. Faustus argued that if every mortal was predestined to one eternal condition or another, then prayer is pointless.[50] And, if prayer is useless, why did Christ institute it?[51] Like Cassian in the Thirteenth Conference, Faustus gives special weight to Paul's words (I Cor. 15:10):

But by the grace of God I am what I am; and his grace in me hath not been void, but I have laboured more abundantly than all they; yet not I, but the grace of God in me.

Faustus construes the text in this way: 'Note that he did not say "I without grace" or "grace without me", but "the grace of God in me"',[52] thus giving equal value to grace and freely-initiated works. In a particularly vehement (and clearly anti-Augustinian) passage, he wrote:

[47] Cassian, *Conferences*, XIII.xii.1 (tr. Ramsey, 478) citing Rom. 2:14–16; Latin text below, 101. Note that Pelagius cites the same text in his *Letter to Demetrias*; see above, 78.

[48] For Faustus's career, see Weigel, *Faustus*. Recent work has attempted to modify the view that Faustus was a semi-Pelagian, arguing that he, while sharing a Pelagian anthropology and rejecting predestinarianism, goes farther than his early fifth-century predecessors in accommodating Augustinian views of grace. See Tibiletti, 'Libero arbitrio', and Smith, *De gratia*, esp. 219–32. We find it difficult to assent to the contention of (O.) Chadwick, *John Cassian*, 127, that: 'The leaders of the [semi-Pelagian] school were not half-way to being disciples of Pelagius . . . Augustine stood far nearer to them than Pelagius.'

[49] Faustus, *De gratia* (*PL* LVIII.783–836). Zimmer, *Pelagius in Irland*, 21 showed that this work as well as Faustus's treatise on free will reached Britain through the agency of a fellow countryman named Riocatus, a bishop and monk.

[50] Faustus, *De gratia*, I.4 (*PL* LVIII.790).

[51] *Ibid.*

[52] Faustus, *De gratia*, I.6 (*PL* LVIII.792): 'Non dixit ego sine gratia vel gratia sine me, *sed gratia Dei mecum.*'

Therefore when the destroyer of free will in both directions [sc. for good or ill] declares that all things are decreed and fixed through predestination, he also nullifies the final remedy of penance with his uncompromising attitude of impiety. And how does he who denies mercy preach grace? How does he who removes the help of God proclaim his gift? How does he who seeks to exclude the bounty of the scriptures dare to rely on their witness?[53]

The influence of the semi-Pelagians lasted well beyond the lifetime of Faustus,[54] for Caesarius of Arles found it necessary to convoke a council at Orange in 529 in order to secure their condemnation. The first eight canons of the council drew on the writings of Augustine for support; Caesarius himself wrote a treatise reaffirming the Augustinian doctrine of grace.[55] Augustine's triumph was total, at least officially. Unofficially, there must have been countless believers who continued to have faith in the efficacy of their own efforts. Nothing is more telling of this fact than the earlier condemnation of Augustine's 'predestination heresy' by the anonymous 'Chronicle of 452'.[56]

Survivals of Pelagianism in Britain and Ireland

Britain in the fifth and sixth centuries

Pelagianism was closely associated with Britain from the beginning. Pelagius himself was certainly a resident of Britain before he went to the continent.[57] As we have seen, another Briton, Faustus, was a force – even if attenuated – in the semi-Pelagian movement. Yet another Briton, Fastidius, is credited by Gennadius with the Pelagian writing called *On the Christian Life*, although this is dubious.[58] But even should this attribution prove incorrect, there

---

[53] Faustus, *De gratia*, I.11; (our translation); (*PL* LVIII.799–800): 'Igitur dum liberi interemptor arbitrii in alterutram partem omnia ex praedestinatione statuta et definita esse pronuntiat, etiam suprema remedia poenitentiae sensu abruptae impietatis evacuat. Et quomodo praedicat gratiam qui misericordiam negat? Quomodo videtur asserere Dei donum, cujus tollit auxilium? Quomodo audet de Scripturis praesumere testimonia, qui Scripturarum conatur excludere beneficia?' The concept of *misericordia*, God's mercy, seems to have been especially favoured by the semi-Pelagians. Logically, it did not accord well with 'pure' Pelagian theology, or with late Augustinianism.

[54] For a helpful survey of the Pelagian and semi-Pelagian controversies from the death of Augustine to 529 see Markus, 'The legacy of Pelagius'.

[55] *On the Opinions of the Lord Caesarius against Those Who Explain Why God Gives Grace to Some but not to Others* (ed. Morin, 'On the opinions', 481–5). See Pelikan, *The Christian Tradition*, I.327–9. For an account of the theological issues (and the politics) of the Council of Orange see Klingshirn, *Caesarius*, 140–3. For a convenient resumé with bibliography see Pontal, *Histoire des conciles mérovingiens*, 94–9.

[56] *Chronica minora*, I.650 (ed. Mommsen); see Wood, 'The end of Roman Britain', 18.

[57] See above, 23.

[58] See Evans, 'Pelagius, Fastidius'; also Rees, *The Letters*, 105–6.

remains the contemporary suspicion that Fastidius, 'bishop of the Britons', was an adherent of Pelagius.[59] Finally, Gildas, writing at some time in the sixth century, approvingly quotes a passage from the Pelagian work *On Virginity*, and refers to its author as *quidam nostrum*, ('one of us'),[60] surely meaning a Briton.

Although it cannot be proved that Pelagius himself returned to Britain after leaving it for the continent, nonetheless, his teaching reached his native land at an early stage, certainly within his lifetime.[61] By the second quarter of the fifth century Pelagianism had made powerful inroads into Britain. In 429 certain authorities in the British Church invited Germanus of Auxerre and Lupus of Troyes to confute the teachings of the Pelagians.[62] This they did successfully, and, at the same time performed miracles using the relics of the saints.[63] Some time later there was a resurgence of Pelagianism in Britain, and Germanus was called upon once again to do battle against the heresy. On this occasion the leaders of the heretics were allegedly banished.[64]

Two years after Germanus's first visit to Britain, Pope Celestine decided to send Palladius as bishop to 'the Irish believers in Christ'.[65] Prosper, in his work *Contra Collatorem* ('Against Cassian'), records that Pope Celestine, who had successfully suppressed Pelagianism in Britain, 'while thus endeavouring to keep that island in the Catholic faith, he ordained Palladius to be bishop of the Irish and so draw this pagan nation to the Christian fold'.[66] It should be noted that Palladius, the bishop sent to the Irish, was almost certainly the same Palladius who persuaded Pope Celestine to send Germanus to Britain in his first mission against the Pelagians.[67] It has been argued on the basis of Patrick's reference to a group of British Christians resident in Ireland, that Celestine may have feared that the Pelagian heresy had already

---

[59] Rees, *The Letters*, 105.

[60] Gildas, *The Ruin*, XXXVIII.2 (tr. Winterbottom, 37); cf. *On Virginity*, VII.2 (tr. Rees, *The Letters*, 77); *On Bad Teachers*, XIII.1 (tr. Rees, *The Letters*, 233).

[61] Note that Prosper, *Contra Collatorem*, XXI.2 (tr. De Letter, 134) praised Pope Celestine for freeing Britain from 'some enemies of the grace of God, who took refuge there *as* in the land of their birth'. De Letter's translation is misleading. There is no word corresponding to 'as' in Prosper's Latin as reported (without variants) by Venice/2: 'quando quosdam inimicos gratiae solum suae originis occupantes'. See de Plinval, *Pélage*, 57–63; Charles-Edwards, *Early Christian Ireland*, 204.

[62] Prosper, *Chronicle*, s.a. 429 (tr. de Paor, *Saint Patrick's World*, 79); Bede, *Historia Ecclesiastica*, I.17 (edd. and tr. Colgrave & Mynors, 54–5); Constantius, *Vita Germani*, III.12–18 (ed. and tr. Borius, *Constance de Lyon*, 170–1).

[63] Bede, *Historia Ecclesiastica*, I.17–20 (edd. and tr. Colgrave & Mynors, 54–65).

[64] Bede, *Historia Ecclesiastica*, I.21 (edd. and tr. Colgrave & Mynors, 64–7); Constantius, *Vita Germani*, V.25 (ed. and tr. Borius, 170–1).

[65] Prosper, *Chronicle*, s.a. 431 (tr. de Paor, *Saint Patrick's World*, 79); (*PL* LI.595): 'Scotos in Christum credentes'

[66] Prosper, *Contra Collatorem*, XXI.2 (tr. De Letter, 134); (*PL* LI.271): '. . . dum Romam insulam studet servare Catholicam, fecit etiam barbaram Christianam'.

[67] Prosper, *Chronicle*, s.a. 429 (tr. de Paor, *Saint Patrick's World*, 79).

spread to Ireland through the agency of British missionaries.[68] Palladius, well-known for his tough anti-Pelagian stance, was the ideal choice of a bishop.

Patrick himself does not mention Pelagians by name, and there is no hint of direct engagement with any heretical teaching. Yet in his two surviving writings he continually portrays himself as the instrument of God's grace and assigns nothing to his own design. By his frequent citations of Paul's Letters, particularly Corinthians, he aligns himself with 'the vessel of election'.[69] It would appear that he is addressing Pelagian elements among his detractors, when he says '. . . (God) is no respecter of persons and he chose me for this task'.[70] The theme of God's impartiality, so dear to Pelagians, must be subordinate to the higher teaching of the divine will acting through human agents.

Indeed, there are numerous passages in Patrick's writings that show his deep-rooted belief that his actions are motivated by grace, not by will. Here is one of the most striking:

On the other hand I did not go to Ireland of my own accord, until I was nearly at the end of my strength; but this was really rather to my own good, since as a result I was reformed by the Lord, and he fitted me to be today what was once far from me, that I should be concerned and busily active for the salvation of others, whereas at that time I took no thought of my self.[71]

The phrase 'until I was nearly at the end of my strength' (*donec prope deficiebam*) almost certainly refers to Patrick's attempt to resist God's grace. And, similarly, in the *Letter to Coroticus*:

Did I come to Ireland without God's favour or according to the flesh? I am obliged by the Spirit not to see any of my kinsfolk. Did it come from me that I show devout mercy towards the very people which once took me captive and harried the slaves of my father's house, male and female?[72]

Patrick's notion of being obliged (*alligatus*) to the Spirit expresses itself, as it were, in terms of possession. Just as a demoniac is possessed by a devil so that he no longer has any self control, so, by his own description, Patrick is possessed by the Spirit who eerily resides 'above Patrick's inner self':

---

[68] Dumville, 'Some British aspects', 16; Charles-Edwards, 'Paladius, Prosper and Leo the Great', 7–8; Charles-Edwards, *Early Christian Ireland*, 202–5.

[69] See Bieler, *Index locorum, loci biblici*, in *Libri epistolorum*, 116. For an important discussion of Patrick's use of Paul's writings see Nerney, 'A study, II', 14–21.

[70] Patrick, *Confession*, LVI (tr. Hood, 53); *Confessio*, LVI (ed. Bieler, *Libri epistolarum*, I.88): '. . . *personam non accipit* et elegit me ad hoc officium . . .' Further examples of Patrick's use of anti-Pelagian polemic are given in Nerney, 'A study, II', 23–5.

[71] Patrick, *Confession*, XXVIII (tr. Hood, 47); Latin text below, 101–2.

[72] Patrick, *Letter to Coroticus*, X (tr. Hood, 56–7); *Epistola ad Milites Corotici*, X (ed. Bieler, *Libri epistolarum*, I.96): 'Numquid sine Deo uel *secundum carnem* Hiberione ueni? Quis me compulit? *Alligatus* sum *Spiritu* ut non uideam aliquem *de cognatione mea*. Numquid a me piam misericordiam quod ago erga gentem illam qui me aliquando ceperunt et deuastauerunt seruos et ancillas domus patris mei?'

And again I saw him praying within me and I was, as it were, inside my own body and I heard Him above me, that is to say above my inner self, and He was praying there powerfully and groaning, and meanwhile I was dumbfounded and astonished and wondered who it could be that was praying within me, but at the end of the prayer He spoke and said that He was the Spirit . . .[73]

It is abundantly clear from these and other passages that Patrick's defence before his elders is that his mission to the Irish was not a voluntary act of disobedience (*non sponte*), but simply an act of submission to God's irresistible grace. If we assume, as most authorities have, that Patrick's *Confessio* was addressed to superiors in Britain at some point in the fifth century, we must allow for the possibility that Patrick was arguing the case for grace and God's irresistible will against the proponents of voluntarism,[74] in other words, against Pelagian sympathisers, or even – if we allow an early date for Patrick's mission – against Pelagian clergy. Surely Patrick's repeated appeal to his utter lack of control in the decision to go to Ireland points in this direction.

If we assume an anti-Pelagian context for Patrick's *apologia*, then one of the great riddles of Patrician scholarship can be solved. This is the vexing question of Patrick's sin, alluded to in the *Confessio*:

After thirty years they found a pretext for their allegations against me in a confession which I had made before I was a deacon. In a depressed and worried state of mind I mentioned to a close friend what I had done as a boy one day, indeed in the space of one hour, because I was not yet proof against temptation. I do not know, God knows, whether I was fifteen years old at the time, and I was not then a believer in the living God, nor had I been from infancy. But I remained in death and unbelief till I was severely chastened and in truth humiliated by hunger and nakedness, and every day too.[75]

Speculation has centred on what type of sin Patrick committed in his youth that could have blocked his elevation to the episcopate. Patrick does not tell us *what* sin it was, but he does tell us *when* the sin was committed: it was while he was in a state of 'death and unbelief', that is, before he was baptised. We can learn much by shifting our question from what to when.[76] First, Patrick's line of defence was clearly constructed to meet any accusation that he had sinned after baptism (note the Pelagian shibboleth 'No

---

[73] Patrick, *Confession*, XXV (tr. Hood, 46); Latin text below, 102.

[74] Note the statement imputed to Pelagius at the *Synod of Diospolis*, II (tr. Rees, *Pelagius*, 135): 'All men are governed by their own will.' Augustine, *De gestis Pelagii*, III (5) (edd. Urba & Zycha, 56): 'omnes uoluntate propria regi'.

[75] Patrick, *Confession*, XXVII (tr. Hood, 46); Latin text below, 102. I have had to alter Hood's translation here since he erroneously translated Patrick's words *neque ex infantia mea* which follow on *et Deum vivum non credebam* as 'nor had I done *since* earliest childhood', which gives the impression that Patrick had been a pious young child who lost his faith in adolescence. But Patrick's Latin is very clear: he did not believe in God when he was fifteen, nor did he *from* infancy (*neque ex infantia*)! (MWH).

[76] I am particularly grateful to Dr Anthony Harvey (Royal Irish Academy) for this perceptive observation (MWH).

Christian is permitted to sin'). As baptism removes all sins, Patrick would have been pure at the time he was preparing for the diaconate, and hence the revelation of his youthful sin should have had no relevance to his ecclesiastical career. Secondly, we learn from the same passage that Patrick did not receive baptism as an infant (*sed in morte . . . mansi*), even though his father was a deacon and his grandfather a priest. This would imply that the views of Patrick's own clerical progenitors were in harmony with Pelagian teaching, at least insofar as baptism was concerned. There is much else in the *Confessio* and the *Epistola ad Coroticum* to show that Patrick was in rebellion against the kind of Christian formation he received from his immediate family and which he knew in his homeland. Patrick must thus be viewed as a convert to a theology based on grace. Whether this conversion came solely from personal experience, or was developed in some location other than Britain is outside the scope of this study.

Positing Patrick's writings as anti-Pelagian also permits us to understand his concern to dismiss his detractors' charge of rusticity and inadequate education:

Therefore I have long had it in my mind to write but have in fact hesitated up till now, for I was afraid to expose myself to the criticism of men's tongues, because I have not studied like others, who have successfully imbibed both law and Holy Scripture alike and have never changed their language from infancy but have always been bringing it nearer to perfection.[77]

It would seem that there are two issues here: Patrick's inability to express himself adequately in the Latin language and his questionable knowledge of the scriptures. Patrick speaks later (*Confession*, XI) of his 'ignorance and slow tongue'. If he had prepared for the diaconate under Pelagian teachers, these deficiencies would have been regarded as a severe detriment to any further promotion, for Pelagians believed that without a sure knowledge of the laws contained in the scriptures, salvation was impossible.[78] The priest or bishop responsible for the instruction (and, potentially, the salvation) of others must necessarily possess a secure knowledge of Holy Writ himself and the power to communicate it accurately. Patrick was painfully aware of the reason used for blocking his mission (and presumably his episcopate): 'Not that they were being malicious . . . it was because of my lack of education'.[79] Patrick's best defence was to refute his enemies with the scriptures, citing II Cor. 3:2–3: 'It [the law] has been written in your hearts not with ink but with

---

[77] Patrick, *Confession*, IX (tr. Hood, 42); *Confessio*, IX (ed. Bieler, *Libri epistolarum*, I.61): 'Quapropter olim cogitaui scribere, sed et usque nunc haesitaui; timui enim ne *incederem in linguam* hominum, quia non didici sicut et ceteri, qui optime itaque iura et sacras litteras utraque pari modo combiberunt et sermones illorum ex infantia numquam mutarunt, sed magis ad perfectum semper addiderunt.'

[78] See the *Synod of Diospolis*, I (tr. Rees, *Pelagius*, 135): 'A man cannot be without sin, unless he has acquired a knowledge of the Law'; Augustine, *De gestis Pelagii*, I (2) (edd. Urba & Zycha, 52): 'non posse esse sine peccato nisi qui scientiam legis habuerit'.

[79] Patrick, *Confession*, XLVI (tr. Hood, 51); *Confessio*, XLVI (ed. Bieler, *Libri epistolarum*, I.84): '. . . non ut causa malitiae . . . propter rusticitatem meam . . .'

the Spirit of the living God.'[80] Patrick simultaneously exhibits his impugned command of the scriptures and hoists the Pelagians on their own petard by alluding to the law of nature, that is, the law given to men before the tablets of Moses or the commandments of Christ written in the gospels.

When we turn to sixth-century Britain, an examination of some epistolary fragments, now accepted as genuine,[81] shows that Gildas was indeed aware of a group showing close affinities to Pelagian teachings.[82] In the tirade of fragment III he blasts the arrogance of certain ones who: 'Meditating on their lofty principles, they prefer slaves to masters, the common people to kings, lead to gold, iron to silver, the elm-prop to the vine.'[83] This passage surely is meant to recall several themes in the treatise *On Riches*. A major leitmotif in this latter work is the equality of all mankind:

Get rid of the rich man, and you will not be able to find a poor one. Let no man have more than he really needs, and all will have as much as they need, since the few who are rich are the reason for the many who are poor.[84]

And again:

Observe whether the rich man enjoys the benefit of this air of ours more than the poor, whether he feels the sun's heat more or less, whether larger drops descend upon the rich man's field than on the poor man . . .[85]

Inequality applies not only to wealth, but also to status:

You may see the servant sitting where the master stood, and judging where he was judged. What is this, Christian? What is this disciple of Christ? This is not the pattern given by your teacher. He stood humbly before the tribunal; *you* sit on the tribunal, above those who stand before you, propped up by your pride, ready to judge.[86]

---

[80] Cited at *Confession*, XI (tr. Hood, 43).

[81] Sharpe, 'Gildas as a father', 196–8.

[82] Gildas's witness might well be valid for the late fifth century or early sixth rather than the mid-sixth, where his work is often dated. For early dating, see Wood, 'The end of Roman Britain', 3; Lapidge, 'Gildas's education', *passim*; Herren, 'Gildas', 77.

[83] Gildas, *Fragments*, III (tr. Winterbottom, 80); *Fragmenta*, III (ed. Winterbottom, 143–4): 'Dum principalibus decretis meditantur, servos dominis, vulgus regibus, auro plumbum, argento ferrum, (vineae) ulmum praeferunt.'

[84] *On Riches*, XII.1 (tr. Rees, *The Letters*, 194). I have modified the translation slightly (MWH); *De divitiis*, XII.2 (*PL supp.* I.1401): 'Tolle diuitem et pauperem non inuenies. Nemo plus, quam necessarium est, possideat, et, quantum necessarium est, omnes habebunt. Pauci enim diuites pauperum sunt causa multorum.'

[85] *On Riches*, VIII.3 (tr. Rees, *The Letters*, 183). I have modified the translation here (MWH); *De divitiis*, VIII.3 (*PL supp.* I.1389): 'Vide, si aeris huius beneficio plus diues quam pauper abutitur, si solis calorem amplius minusue persentit . . . si maiores guttae super agrum diuitis quam super agrum pauperis defluunt.'

[86] *On Riches*, VI.2 (tr. Rees, *The Letters*, 179). I have modified the translation here (MWH); *De divitiis*, VI.2 (*PL supp.* I.1385): 'Videas, seruum sedere, ubi dominus stetit; et ubi ille iudicatur, hic iudicat. Quid est, Christiane? quid est Christi discipule? Non haec tui est forma doctoris. Ille ante tribunal humilis stetit; tu in tribunali, superba elatione subnixus, super stantes sedes iudicaturus.'

In answer to the objection that gold and silver are the creations of God:

... God created the things which we have just now mentioned (gold and silver) along with the rest of his creation, yet not in order that one man should become wealthy by the possession of unlimited affluence while another is tormented by excessive poverty, but that all should possess impartially and with equal rights what the source of all justice has granted them.[87]

Gildas may have employed hyperbole in saying that his adversaries *prefer* slaves to masters, lead to gold, and so forth, but he certainly hit upon themes that were distinctly Pelagian, namely the inequality of men and the injustices created by the attainment of wealth and rank. In a final salvo Gildas remarks: 'For they do not observe that the position of the stars in the sky, and the duties of the angels, are unequal.'[88] To this he adds, '. . . not observing what the gospel, but rather *what the will, commands*'.[89] Followers of Pelagian teachings appear to have been alive and well in Gildas's day. Corroboration for the persistence of Pelagianism in late fifth-century Britain is also provided in the *Passio Albani*, linking the cult of St Alban to Germanus's visit to Britain and the propogation of the miraculous.[90]

The probability that Gildas's censures relate to Pelagians is reinforced by some later British (Welsh) evidence. Rhygyfarch (d. 1099), in his *Life of St David*, wished to leave us in no doubt that Pelagianism as a sect persisted well after Germanus's second visit to Britain:

Since even after Germanus's second visit of help the Pelagian heresy was recovering its vigour and obstinacy, implanting the poison of a deadly serpent in the innermost reaches of our country, a general synod is assembled of all the bishops of Britain. In addition to a gathering of 118 bishops, there was present an innumerable multitude of priests, abbots, clergy of other ranks, kings, princes, laymen and women . . . Thereafter, after the passage of subsequent years, another synod is assembled, called the Synod of Victory, in which a number of bishops, priests and abbots were called together, and reaffirmed the decisions of its predecessor . . .[91]

This text alleges that not one, but two synods (Brefi and Victory) were needed to suppress Pelagianism after Germanus's second visit. The *acta* of

---

[87] *On Riches*, X.10 (tr. Rees, *The Letters*, 191); *De divitiis*, X.9 (*PL supp.* I.1397): 'Constat . . . Deum praedicta creasse cum omnibus, non tamen, ut unus infinita possidendi adfluentia locuples fieret, alius nimia conflictaretur inopia, sed ut omnes aequali lance et pari iure possiderent, quod aequitatis auctor indulserat.'

[88] Gildas, *Fragments*, III (tr. Winterbottom, 81); *Fragmenta*, III (ed. Winterbottom, 144): 'Non intendentes statum siderum in caelo inaequalem esse et angelorum officia inaequalia.'

[89] *Ibid.* I have modified Winterbottom's translation here ('what they want') in order to bring out the full impact of the Latin: 'q*uod* voluntas *iubet*' (MWH); *Fragmenta*, III (ed. Winterbottom, 144): '. . . non intendentes quod evangelium sed quod voluntas iubet'. For the Pelagian principle that everyone is ruled by the will, see above, 83 n. 74.

[90] Wood, 'The end of Roman Britain', 12–13.

[91] Rhygyfarch, *Life of St David*, XLIX, LV (tr. (J.W.) James, 43–4, 46); Latin text below, 102.

neither synod survive. However, nine canons of a synod entitled *Altera Sinodus Luci Victoriae* (*The Second Synod of the Grove of Victory*) have come down to us.[92] The word *Altera* surely implies that a *First Synod* (*Prima Synodus*) had taken place (compare the *First* and *Second Synod of St Patrick*). The fact that the extant canons of the *Altera Synodus* deal exclusively with penitential questions and say nothing about Pelagianism is thus irrelevant to the matter of Rhygyfarch's source. Rhygyfarch refers only to a *Synodus Victoriae* (surely the *First Synod*), of which no independent record survives. Further, one should not invoke Rhygyfarch's transparent attempt to connect the account of the synods with David's election as archbishop 'of the whole Britannic race' as an argument for denying the historicity of Brefi and Victory.[93] It has been shown that Rhygyfarch knew a *Rule of David*, which, thanks to a parallel in Gildas, can be demonstrated to derive from David's day, that is, some time in the sixth century.[94] This, of course, proves only that Rhygyfarch had access to one ancient source; it does not prove that he had the *acta* of the synods of Brefi and Victory. On the other hand, there are no compelling arguments against the historicity of these synods. Whatever his motives for promoting the claims of St David, it is difficult to believe that Rhygyfarch completely invented the details of two councils, especially as they point to the embarassing presence of heresy in his homeland.

Ireland in the seventh, eighth and ninth centuries

In the seventh century, a claim is made for the resurgence of Pelagian doctrine, this time in Ireland. Bede cites a letter written *ca* 638 by the Pope-elect John IV to several Irish bishops and abbots in northern Ireland on the subject of the date of Easter *and* the revival of Pelagianism. The passage cited here is a continuation of the same pope-elect's letter regarding the Quattuordeciman heresy, cited above:[95]

And this also we have learnt that the poison of the Pelagian heresy has of late revived amongst you; we therefore exhort you utterly to put away this kind of poisonous and criminal superstition from your minds. You cannot be unaware that this execrable heresy has been condemned; and not only has it been abolished for some two hundred years but it is daily condemned by us and buried beneath our perpetual ban. We exhort you then not to rake up the ashes amongst you of those whose weapons have been burnt. For who can fail to execrate the proud and impious attempt of those who say that a man can live without sin and that, not by the grace of God, but by his

---

[92] Ed. and tr. Bieler, *The Irish Penitentials*, 68–9.

[93] (N.K.) Chadwick, 'Intellectual life', 134, 138–46.

[94] For Rhygyfarch's knowledge of the *Rule of David* see Dumville, 'Saint David', 12–17; for David's (obscure) chronology see *ibid.*, 26.

[95] See above, 59. Zimmer, *Pelagius in Irland*, 22–4, demonstrated that the linking of Pelagianism to divergence in Easter practice had already been projected backwards to the year 455 by Irish annalists, citing Conell Mageoghagan's 1627 translation of the lost Annals of Clonmacnoise for s.a. 451 (*recte* 455): 'The Resurrection of our Lord was celebrated the 8 of the Calends of May by the Pelagion [*sic*] heresy.' See (D.) Murphy, *The Annals of Clonmacnoise*, 70.

own will? . . . For all other men [except Christ] were born with original sin and are known to bear the mark of Adam's trangression. . . .[96]

Dáibhí Ó Cróinín, in a penetrating article,[97] sought to explain the passage by demonstrating a link to the first part of the letter, which deals with the Quattuordeciman issue. Here is his conclusion:

To the Roman curia, therefore, anyone who advocated (or seemed to advocate) celebration of Easter on the fourteenth of the moon was preempting the pasch and, by the same token, denying the efficacy of the Resurrection as the true instrument of man's redemption. Thus were the Irish seen to be resuscitating the 'uirus Pelagianae hereseos,' though in fact they were doing no such thing.[98]

There is surely a link between the Quattuordeciman and Pelagian heresies. The link is strengthened by reference to Cummian's insistence that Easter is the celebration of the Lord's resurrection, not his passion.[99] To allow Passover and Easter to fall together at any time is to interpret Easter as the observance of Christ's sacrifice (Christ as the prefigured lamb) rather than his triumph. Pelagian literature repeatedly refers to Christ's sacrifice as the supreme example to be imitated by men. However, the Pelagians excluded rising from the dead from those acts of Christ which can be imitated: 'Why are we born of married women, not of virgins? Or why do our dead not rise again on the third day?'[100] There are very few references to Christ's resurrection in the Pelagian corpus.[101] As we have seen, in his commentary on Romans Pelagius himself referred to Christ having *been raised* by the Father (exploiting Paul's language), and draws a parallel to the resuscitation of Abraham's body as an example of faith. Quattuordecimans also shared with Pelagians the belief in the primacy of the law as it is presented in the scriptures.

Important as the above is, it should not be forgotten that the pope-elect speaks directly to the central dogmas of Pelagius and his followers as shown in the quotation above. It is admittedly difficult to find texts which prove that anyone in Ireland asserted Pelagian teachings as boldly as they are stated in the pope-elect's letter. However, numerous texts from the seventh to ninth century show either the influence of Pelagian thought, or polemical engagement with it. One of the earliest examples of influence can be found in Columbanus's *Sermon XI*:

A grand distinction for man is the likeness of God, if it is preserved; but again, it is a great damnation to defile the image of God. For if he prostitutes for the opposite

---

[96] Bede, *Historia Ecclesiastica*, II.19 (tr. Colgrave & Mynors, 201–3); Latin text below, 102.

[97] Ó Cróinín, 'New heresy'.

[98] *Ibid.*, 516.

[99] See above, 62.

[100] *On the Divine Law*, X.1 (tr. Rees, *The Letters*, 103).

[101] A rare example occurs in *On Riches*, XIII.2 (tr. Rees, *The Letters*, 196). The author uses the uncharacteristic phrase *resurrectionis gratiam* ('grace of the resurrection').

employment what he has received from the breath of God, and corrupts the blessing of his nature, then he perverts the likeness of God and destroys it as far as in him lies; yet if he employs the virtues planted in his soul to a proper end, then he will be like to God. So whatever virtues God sowed in us in our original state, He taught us in the commandments to restore the same to Him . . . But he loves God who observes His commands; for He said, 'If you love Me, keep My commands' (John 14:15).[102]

The words 'blessing of nature' (*beneficium naturae*) can be construed as innately Pelagian, since Pelagians regarded our good human nature as a facet of 'grace'. Although Pelagians only occasionally refer to the 'image of God', the phrase is put to use in the *Commentary on Romans* in the same way as it is here; commenting on the word 'corruption' in Rom. 8:21, Pelagius wrote: 'It shall no longer serve those who have corrupted the image of God (in themselves).'[103] It is clear that Columbanus was in tune with the Pelagians by thinking of human nature as good, even virtuous. It is implied here that men corrupt their own originally good natures. We conserve the image of God by following his precepts. Grace does not play a role. The core doctrine is Pelagian.[104]

That the Pelagian issue was in the air towards the middle of the seventh century is evidenced by two Hiberno-Latin texts. A commentary on Mark, attributed to a certain Cummian[105] and possibly contemporary with the pope-elect's letter,[106] mentions 'free will' in three places, and 'grace' in several more. It is worthwhile looking at these. At Mark 9:22, 'And Jesus says to him, "If you can believe"', the author remarks, 'This points to the

---

[102] Columbanus, *Sermons*, XI.1 (ed. and tr. Walker, 107); Latin text below, 102–3.

[103] Pelagius, *On Romans*, 8:21 (tr. de Bruyn, 110). The words in brackets belong to the interpolated text; *Expositio in Romanos*, 8:21 (ed. Souter, I.66): 'Iam non seruiet eis qui dei [in se] imaginem corruperunt.'

[104] Note, however, Columbanus's allusion to original sin elsewhere: *Sermons*, V.1 (ed. and tr. Walker, 84–5). For a discussion of the term *imago* and its possible sources in Columbanus's Sermons see Stancliffe, 'The thirteen sermons', 106–8. Stancliffe omits consideration of a Pelagian source. Walker, 107 n. 1 observes that the distinction between *imago Dei* and *similitudo Dei* is owed to Irenaeus, *Adversus Haereses*, V.6.1. Irenaeus's possible influence on Irish spirituality is developed by Stancliffe, 'The miracle stories', 103–4. Note, however, the very limited circulation of the Latin version of Irenaeus's work prior to the late middle ages: Siegmund, *Die Überlieferung*, 90.

[105] Bischoff, 'Wendepunkte', 257–9. But note the strictures of Cahill, 'Is the first commentary on Mark an Irish work?'; also Gorman, 'A critique', 180–1. See also (J.F.) Kelly, 'Pelagius, Pelagianism, and the early medieval Irish'. Bischoff (*ibid.*) proved that a commentary by a certain Cummian on Mark existed and was known in the Carolingian period; the question is whether the version translated and discussed by Cahill is identical with the one mentioned in Bischoff's manuscript (Angers 55). I tend to the view that the text is Irish and from the first half of the seventh century (MWH). See now the review of Cahill's recent edition (*CCSL* LXXXII) by Löfstedt, who also favours an Irish attribution: 'Review', 434–6.

[106] Cahill dates the work to the first half of the seventh century. See Cahill, *Expositio Evangelii*, 120–1.

fact of free will.' At 11:4, commenting on the sense of 'meeting of two ways', the author adds: 'hesitating in free will between life and death'. At 12:1, 'he went to a far country', the author comments: 'the leaving on a journey on the part of God represents the freedom of our will'.[107]

The author also pays attention to passages that connote the grace of God. At Mark 1:4, commenting on 'baptising', he writes:

Grace is given through baptism, by means of which sins are graciously forgiven. It is said, 'What you have freely received, freely give' (cf. Matt. 10:8). And the Apostle says, 'By grace you are saved, through faith, and not of yourselves. The gift is God's . . . lest anyone boast' (cf. Eph. 2:8–9).[108]

Commenting on Mark 1:7 'there comes one more powerful than I', the author writes:

Who is more powerful than the grace by which sins are washed away? Surely the one who forgives seven and seventy times (cf. Matt. 18:22). Grace indeed comes first but forgives only once through baptism. Now, mercy has arrived for wretches from Adam to Christ for 77 generations, even up to 144,000 (cf. Apoc. 14:1).[109]

The writer distinguishes here between grace (represented in baptism) and mercy. Grace, which is prior in time, forgives only once, because one is not allowed to sin after baptism, while the chronologically later mercy of Christ forgives seven and seventy times. 'Grace' is an interpretation of John's Hebrew name – grace thus preceded mercy, as John the Baptist preceded Christ. But the passage may well imply more. Baptism – at least for adults – requires human cooperation and thus the exercise of free will. But the divine mercy extended to the just who perished before the coming of Christ, operates efficiently without any activity on the part of the recipient. The author has added a new level of complexity to the schema

---

[107] *On Mark*, 9:22, 11:4, 12:1 (tr. Cahill, *The First Commentary*, 75, 84, 89); (ed. Cahill, *Expositio Evangelii Marci*, 52): '. . . peregrinatio Dei, libertas nostri arbitrii'.

[108] *On Mark*, 1:4 (tr. Cahill, *The First Commentary*, 28–9); (ed. Cahill, *Expositio Evangelii Marci*, 8): 'Per baptismum enim gratia datur quia peccata gratis dimittuntur. Unde dicitur quod "gratis accepistis gratis" date. Et Apostolus ait, "gratia salui estis per fidem, et hoc non ex uobis, Dei enim donum est", "ne quid glorietur".' Compare Pelagius, *On Romans*, 3:24: '. . . through baptism, whereby he has freely forgiven the sins of all, though they are undeserving' (tr. de Bruyn, *Pelagius's Commentary*, 81); *Expositio in Romanos*, 3:24 (ed. Souter, I.32–3): '. . . per baptismum, quo omnibus non merentibus gratis peccata donauit'.

[109] *On Mark*, 1:7 (tr. Cahill, *The First Commentary*, 31); lines 102–7 (ed. Cahill, *Expositio Evangelii Marci*, 10): 'Quis fortior est gratia qua peccata abluuntur? Ille nimirum qui "septies" et "septuagies" remittit peccata. Gratia prior quidem est sed semel remittit per baptismum. Misericordia uero in miseros ab Adam usque ad Christum per lxxvii generationes et usque ad "cxliiii milia" prouenit.' The Marcan commentator's emphasis on divine mercy, coupled with his attempts to balance grace and free will, place him fairly firmly at the semi-Pelagian end of our theological spectrum.

'law of nature', 'law of Moses', 'law of grace'. By linking baptism to John ('Grace'), and mercy to Christ, he implies that the Pelagian philosophy of history is not fully Christian because it fails to acknowledge the final stage (mercy) and hence to fully acknowledge Christ! Ultimately, the Marcan commentator attempts to confront and confute the Pelagian teaching that the dispensation of grace ends with baptism.[110] That this teaching was still debated in seventh- and eighth-century Ireland is shown by other texts. The Würzburg commentator on Paul at II Cor. 1:15, explaining Paul's use of the phrase 'second grace', writes: 'What is the first grace? Easy to answer. It is the grace of forgiveness of sins through baptism. This is the second grace: forgiveness of sin through repentance.'[111] The Pelagian doctrine that no Christian is permitted to sin (after baptism) and the teaching of quotas of sin assigned to each person made the possibility of repentance problematic. Tírechán, who composed a Life of Patrick *ca* 700, portrays the bishop posing questions of faith to his catechumens; one of them is 'Do you believe in penance after sin?'[112] The anti-Pelagian character of this profession of faith is shown even more clearly by the question, 'Do you believe that through baptism you can cast off the sin of your mother and father?'[113]

A revealing text for the study of seventh-century Irish attitudes towards the nature of grace is the *De mirabilibus sacrae scripturae* (*On the Miracles of Holy Scripture*), written in 655 in southern Ireland by a monk writing under the name of Augustine.[114] Using examples from both the Old and the New Testaments, the writer sets out to examine the nature of miracles. The main problem for him was to reconcile God's creative power with his continuing governance of the universe and hence to prove the existence of miracles. Someone had raised the problem: if God completed his creation on the sixth day, then rested 'from all his work' on the seventh day, according to scripture, how can it be that he continues to work in the universe on a

---

[110] See Pelagius, *On Romans*, 3:24 (tr. de Bruyn, 81). Baptism is the sole exception to the teaching that grace consists of nature and the law.

[111] *Codex Paulinus Wirziburgensis* (ed. and tr. Stokes & Strachan, I.593): '. . . *rad dilgutha (pe)chthe tre baithis* (is)hed *arrath ta(n)ise dilgud pectho (t)re aithirgi*'.

[112] Tírechán, *Life of Patrick*, XXVI (ed. and tr. Bieler, *The Patrician Texts*, 144–5); *Vita Sancti Patricii*, XXVI: 'Si poenitentiam creditis post peccatum?'

[113] Tírechán, *Life of Patrick*, XXVI (ed. and tr. Bieler, *The Patrician Texts*, 144–5); *Vita Sancti Patricii*, XXVI: 'Si creditis per babtismum patris et matris iecere peccatum?' Although we have argued above, 82–5, that Patrick's genuine writings are anti-Pelagian in tone, it strikes us as likely that Tírechán's conception of Patrick's questions to his catechumens reflects the pre-occupations of the late seventh or early eighth century.

[114] Pseudo-Augustine, *On the Miracles of Holy Scripture* (*PL* XXXV.2149–200); see Kenney, *Sources*, 275–7. This work is also edited and translated in an as-yet-unpublished dissertation: MacGinty, 'The treatise'. The date and milieu of this text were definitively established by Esposito, 'On the Pseudo-Augustinian treatise', 196–8. Gorman's objections to Esposito ('A critique', 192–3 n. 29) cannot be substantiated; see the reply by Herren, 'Irish biblical commentaries', 401–4; and, in more detail, by Ó Cróinín, 'Bischoff's *Wendepunkte*', 212–16.

daily basis? Pseudo-Augustine answers the question by distinguishing between *opus* and *labor*. God indeed had completed and perfected his *opus*, but he did not cease from *labor*. Thus he continues to govern the natures he perfected.

All of this seems to be aimed at confuting adherents of the view that if God completed (in the sense of 'perfected') his creation, there would be no need for his continued administration of the world, and hence there could be no miracles or grace. Chapter II of the first book deals expressly with sin and penance. The author summarises his views in a crucial passage: 'By the clemency of the Creator and through the passion of Christ, man is recalled to that blessedness to which as a sinner he (had) not yet come.'[115] Pseudo-Augustine then goes on to show that miracles are not irrational and do not contravene the order of created nature. In an interesting example from the Old Testament, the turning of Lot's wife into a pillar of salt, he argues that salt is already present in the body (in tears, for example), and thus the event recorded in scripture is not out of harmony with nature.[116]

Pelagians taught that miracles – an aspect of heavenly grace – interfere with human free will; certainly this idea was ascribed to Coelestius at Diospolis: 'Will is not free if it stands in need of God's help, since everyone has it in his own will to do or not to do something.'[117] As already noted, the same synod attributed to Coelestius the statement: 'Adam was created mortal and would have died whether he sinned or not.'[118] The intent of the statement was twofold: (1) to deny that sin was transmitted; (2) to contradict prevailing notions that man went from a preternatural condition in the garden to a natural one (and thus experienced a change in his essence). Pseudo-Augustine surely had Coelestius's statement (or one very like it) in mind when he wrote:

Enoch was indeed without death and kept apart from the life of men throughout almost the entire age of the world, so that it might be shown how men, even though they generated offspring, might be transfigured into a spiritual life without death, if they had not sinned. But even though he still lives and is kept apart for a long time, nevertheless he shall not be able to avoid the debt of death which we all received in Adam . . . Yet in this case a new nature is not begotten in a single man, but the pristine and general (nature) of all men is governed. For it is obvious to those who consider the history of the book of Genesis that it was given to every man to live not

---

[115] Pseudo-Augustine, *On the Miracles of Holy Scripture*, I.2 (ed. and tr. MacGinty, II.15); *De mirabilibus sacrae scripturae*, I.2 (*PL* XXXV.2154): 'Clementia . . . Conditoris homo ad illam beatitudinem, ad quam peccans adhuc non pervenit, per passionem Domini revocatur.'

[116] Pseudo-Augustine, *On the Miracles of Holy Scripture*, I.11 (ed. and tr. MacGinty, II.42–3); *De mirabilibus sacrae scripturae*, I.11 (*PL* XXXV.2160).

[117] *Synod of Diospolis*, IXh (tr. Rees, *Pelagius*, 138); Augustine, *De gestis Pelagii*, XVIII (42) (edd. Urba & Zycha, 98): 'non esse liberum arbitrium, si dei indigeat auxilio, quoniam in propria uoluntate habet unusquisque aut facere aliquid aut non facere'.

[118] Cited above, 72.

only for a long time but even forever, if death did not obliterate the boundaries of nature on account of the sting of sin.[119]

Here we have a major point of contention between Pelagians and their opponents. Pelagians did not believe that God would change Enoch's nature because he was virtuous any more than he would change Adam's nature because he had sinned. The Pelagian writer Rufinus the Syrian discussed Enoch's and Adam's fate and arrived at this conclusion with reference to Adam:

If, therefore, Adam and Eve had observed God's command, they would certainly never have tasted death. However, when they ignored his command, not from being immortal were they made mortal; but, since they were mortal, they alienated themselves from the immortality promised to them by God.[120]

Rufinus also argued that if Adam and Eve had been immortal from the beginning, they would never have been tempted by the fruit forbidden by God, since 'he who has been made immortal does not need food at all'.[121] Rufinus invokes nature to support his argument: 'Therefore, if indeed Adam and Eve were *by nature* immortal, they would never have tasted the tree which had been forbidden by God.'[122]

In combatting the Pelagians of his day, Pseudo-Augustine espoused the doctrine of original sin and the necessity of the passion of Christ in God's plan for salvation.[123] His stated preference for a literal reading of the narrative portions of the Bible as against an allegorical interpretation strengthened his anti-Pelagian stance, since thus miracles must be accepted as real events that cannot be rationalised. Whereas Pelagians were literalists with regard to the law, they favoured allegory or figurative interpretations to explain narratives they disliked, such as the notion that God made Abraham rich,[124] or that he hardened the heart of Pharaoh.[125] One Pelagian text even uses allegory to equate miracles with the law:

[119] Pseudo-Augustine, *On the Miracles of Holy Scripture*, I.3 (our translation); Latin text below, 103. Pseudo-Augustine doubtless borrowed the distinction between creating and governing from Augustine, *De genesi ad litteram*, XII.4.12; see MacGinty, 'The treatise', I.100–1.

[120] Rufinus, *Liber de fide*, XXX (ed. and tr. Miller, 96–7): 'Adam igitur et Eva, siquidem mandatum Dei servassent, numquam profecto gustassent mortem. Mandato autem minime servato, non ex immortalibus mortales facti sunt; sed, cum mortales essent, promissa sibi a Deo immortalitate semetipsos alienarunt.'

[121] Rufinus, *Liber de fide*, XXX (ed. and tr. Miller, 96–7): 'quod qui immortalis facta est cibo penitus non eget'.

[122] Rufinus, *Liber de fide*, XXX (ed. and tr. Miller, 96–7): 'Adam igitur et Eva, siquidem immortales naturaliter essent, numquam de ligno gustassent quod a Deo prohibitum fuerat.' Bonner, 'Rufinus', 40–1, rightly notes differences between Rufinus's and Coelestius's views on Adam's condition. However, on the issue of the possibility of transformed nature they would have been at one.

[123] Ó Néill, 'Romani influences', 284.

[124] *On Riches*, IX.4–5 (tr. Rees, *The Letters*, 185–6).

[125] *On the Hardening of the Heart of Pharaoh*, XIV (*PL supp.* I.1513). The elect should be understood typologically as figuring Christ; they achieve victory through the conquest of vice.

And how else can grace be understood except as miracles which are concealed in the divine law and revealed to us? On behalf of which the prophet David cries out: 'Open thou my eyes: and I will consider the wondrous things of thy law' (Ps.118:18).[126]

The evidence of *On the Miracles of Holy Scripture* shows clearly that the core teachings of Pelagianism continued to be debated more than fifteen years after Pope-elect John's letter to the Irish hierarchy.

The question of whether a man could live without sinning was of major concern to the Pelagians. While the movement consistently defended the possibility with vigour, it also conceded the difficulty of the proposition. There is evidence of the continuity of this question, which, unfortunately, is hard to date. In a Celtic-Latin poem known as the *Adelphus adelpha meter*, written some time between the seventh and early tenth centuries, we find a series of three-line stanzas containing seemingly conventional moral propositions: the deceptiveness of this life, the traps of the flesh, the requirement to do good and avoid evil, the terrors of hell, and the like. The language is very difficult, and the meaning is not clear at every point. Two stanzas in particular relate to the 'possibility of not sinning':

> Accomplished (?) is the pure man,
> the wise combatant
> who is justified without a slip.

and:

> I marvel in my mind
> that I did not see on earth
> a man without blemish.[127]

If the gloss (*peritus*) is sure in the first line of the first stanza, then the stanza seems to be saying that not sinning is a possibility, however rarely it is fulfilled. The second stanza excludes the possibility, but yet the author 'marvels' as to the reason. The two stanzas read together seem to encapsulate Pelagius's own position on this most basic problem. God, if he is truly just, cannot give us laws if he knows that we cannot fulfil them.[128] On the other hand, the succession of laws poses an ever heavier burden, and even small offences are liable to hell fire. Pelagius himself admitted at Diospolis: 'I did not say that any man can be found who has never sinned from his infancy up to his old age.'[129] The rest of the poem, with its emphasis on

---

[126] *On the Hardening of the Heart of Pharaoh*, VI; *De induratione cordis Pharaonis*, VI (*PL supp*. I.1508): 'Et quae potest alia intellegi gratia, nisi mirabilia quae obtecta sunt in lege divina, quae revelantur nobis? Pro quibus clamat propheta David: *Revela oculus meos, Domine, et considerabo mirabilia de lege tua.*'

[127] *Adelphus adelpha*, lines 49–51, 55–7 (tr. Herren, *The Hisperica Famina II*, 109); Latin text below, 103.

[128] See above, 73 n. 26.

[129] *Synod of Diospolis*, VI (tr. Rees, *Pelagius*, 136); Augustine, *De gestis Pelagii*, X (22) (edd. Urba & Zycha, 75–6): 'Non autem diximus quod inueniatur aliquis, ab infantia usque ad senectam, qui nunquam peccauerit . . .'

obedience to the law of God and the difficulty of obtaining forgiveness after baptism is consistent with a Pelagian theological outlook.[130]

There are several examples in late seventh-century Irish texts of gentiles who kept the law of nature, apparently without any assistance of divine grace. Muirchú, in his Life of Patrick, mentions 'the swineherd of a man who was good by nature, although a pagan, whose name was Díchu'.[131] Even more striking are two passages occurring in Adomnán's Life of Columba that concern the conversion and baptism of pagans who had conserved natural goodness throughout their lives. The first is a prophecy by Columba regarding a certain Artbranan:

My children, strange to tell, today in this place, on this plot of ground, a certain pagan old man, who has preserved natural goodness throughout his whole life, will be baptised, and will die, and will be buried.[132]

The second example is analagous to the first; it concerns the baptism of another pagan named Emchath:

Let us hasten towards the holy angels that have been sent from the highest regions of heaven to conduct the soul of a pagan, and who await our coming thither so that we may give timely baptism, before he dies, to that man, who has preserved natural goodness through his whole life, into extreme old age.[133]

It is remarkable that both Muirchú and Adomnán provide the names of their examples of *naturale bonum* in each case, as though it were necessary to support the claim of natural goodness and the possibility of a sinless life against the sceptics – in effect, venturing to provide the very kind of proof which Pelagius hesitated to give! The Adomnán examples, moreover, are especially instructive in that they support the central claim of Pelagianism that a perfect life is possible without baptism, or any form of grace other than the grace of nature.

Finally, there is an unambiguous mention of a Christian man who did not

---

[130] *Adelphus adelpha*, lines 46–8 (ed. and tr. Herren, *The Hisperica Famina II*, 108–9): 'The Lord does not absolve [from us] the sins of his saints; save me, O my God!':
  Quirius [apemon] anomias u
  apollit agion autu:
  soson me, o theos mu

[131] Muirchú, *Life of Patrick*, I.11(10).4 (ed. and tr. Bieler, *The Patrician Texts*, 78–9): 'porcinarius cuiusdam uiri natura boni licet gentilis, cui nomen erat Dichu'. See Donahue, 'Beowulf', 267.

[132] Adomnán, *Life of Columba*, XXXIVb (edd. and tr. Anderson & Anderson, 274–5): 'Mirum dictu Ó filioli hodie in hac huius loci terrula quidam gentilis senex, naturale per totam bonum custodiens vitam, et baptizabitur et morietur et sepelietur.' See Donahue, 'Beowulf', 267.

[133] Adomnán, *Life of Columba*, CXIVb (edd. and tr. Anderson & Anderson, 492–3): 'Properemus, ait, sanctis obviam angelis qui, de summis caeli regionibus ad praeferendam alicujus gentilici animam emisi, nos illuc usque pervenientes exspectant, ut ipsum naturale bonum per totam vitam usque ad extremam senectutem conservantem priusquam moriatur opportune baptizemus.' See Donahue, 'Beowulf', 267.

sin; this is found in an entry in the *Martyrology of Tallaght*, a *Céli Dé* work written *ca* 800:

> Building a wall, cross vigil,
> Prostration, pure prayer, . . .
> The virtue of Becan, without aught of sin.[134]

Many of the pieces of Irish evidence for survivals of Pelagian thought are, as we have seen, anti-Pelagian in tone. This seems clear enough from the passages cited from the *First Commentary on Mark, On the Miracles of Holy Scripture*, Tírechán's *Life of Patrick*, and the Würzburg *Commentary on Paul's Letters*. Pelagius is rarely openly attacked, but his ideas are contradicted or undermined. Moreover, some texts reveal a vacillation between a grace-based and a nature-based explanation for sanctity. Muirchú's story of the British virgin Monesan, who maintained virginity against family coercion, has two explanations: the first is the assistance of the Holy Spirit, the second is nature, 'following in this the example of Abraham'.[135] In a similar vein, the composer of the *Altus prosator* cannot decide whether sin is a matter of nature or nurture: 'so that men . . . steeped in bad examples and crimes, . . .'[136] The notion of being imbued with crimes (= sin) is rather clumsily linked to bad example. The one seems to point to Augustinian inherited sin, the other to Pelagian voluntarism. Such texts serve to make it clear that Pelagian dogmas were at the very centre of exegetical and theological discussion – whether a man can live without sin, whether sin is transmitted through the blood line, whether penance is possible after baptism, and, perhaps most importantly, whether God interferes with the nature he created and deemed good. Indeed, nature is at the centre of the Irish Pelagian debate. The Pelagian doctrine of natural law is highlighted in the 'Irish Canons' (*Canones Hibernenses*):

The people of Israel had to be ruled by the Ten Commandments of the law, since for the sake of these God smote the Egyptians with ten plagues; therefore are there ten commandments. Where are the precepts in the law which God did not command? (For example) Jethro the kinsman of Moses told Moses to choose seventy leading men who would judge the people with Moses; and this is the judgement (to the effect) that if we find judgements of the heathen good, which their *good nature* teaches them, and it is not displeasing to God, we shall keep them.[137]

And finally, one of the Irish glossators of Jerome's *Preface to the Psalms*

---

[134] *Martyrology of Tallaght* (tr. O'Dwyer, *Céli Dé*, 142); (edd. Best & Lawlor, 104):
  Sním casil crossigell
  slechtain irnaigthi idan.

  .   .   .   .

  Buaid Becgain cen (cu)it (c)inad.
[135] Muirchú, *Life of Patrick*, I.27(26) (ed. and tr. Bieler, *Patrician Texts*, 98–101).
[136] *Altus prosator*, VIII (ed. and tr. Carey, 38): 'ne malis exemplaribus imbutis, ac sceleribus'. (I should be inclined to read *imbuti*, agreeing with *homines*, which occurs further down [MWH].)
[137] *Irish Canons*, III.8 (tr. Bieler, *The Irish Penitentials*, 169); Latin text below, 103.

could write: 'It is in the nature of every man to do good and to avoid doing evil.'[138]

Northumbria in the eighth century

Turning to Northumbria, we find important evidence that Pelagian writings were in circulation around the turn of the eighth century, and that Pelagianism was still a living issue. In a substantial preface to his *Commentary on Canticles*, Bede notes that several works attributed to Julian of Eclanum, one of the major architects of the Pelagian movement, were making the rounds, and that it was incumbent on him to warn readers of their dangers:

> Before I begin my commentary on Canticles aided by heavenly grace, I thought that readers should first be warned to take great care when they read some short works by Julian of Eclanum, a bishop from Campania, which he composed on the same book [of holy scripture], lest on account of his abundance of seductive eloquence they fall into the pit of baneful doctrine.[139]

Bede goes on to discuss Julian's *On Love* (*De amore*), a work written against Augustine, which summarises the principal tenets of Pelagianism. Bede's detailed exposition leads us to believe that he had access to this work by Julian in addition to the commentary on Canticles. An important aspect of Bede's exposé of *On Love* is the criticism that the insistence on understanding the divine law (contained in the scriptures), at the expense of everything else, for all practical purposes, excludes the illiterate from the salvation process.[140]

Bede then discusses a third work written by Julian entitled *On the Good of Constancy* (*De bono constantiae*), directed against the Manichaeans. Bede provides several extensive quotations from this work, showing that he had a copy of the work – or a set of excerpts from it – on his desk. The second excerpt is of some incidental interest, as it shows how deeply rooted in Stoicism Pelagian theology was: 'No one ever can be truly harmed except by himself, nor is there anything through which a man might be made wretched, except he wills it.'[141]

Bede goes on to discuss the *Letter to Demetrias*, which has been mentioned several times already. The letter had been used earlier by Aldhelm

---

[138] *The Milan Glosses on the Psalms*, fo.14c (edd. and tr. Stokes & Strachan, I.12) n. 12: 'atá inaicniud chaich denum maith 7 imgabail uilc dodenum'.

[139] Bede, *On Canticles*, *preface* (our translation); *In cantica canticorum*, *praefatio* (edd. Hurst & Hudson, *Bedae Opera Exegetica*, IIB, 167): 'Scripturus iuuante gratia superna in cantica canticorum primo ammonendum putaui lectorem ut opuscula Iuliani Eclanensis episcopi de Campania quae in eundem librum confecit cautissime legat ne per copiam eloquentiae blandientis foueam incidat doctrinae nocentis . . .'

[140] *Ibid.*

[141] Bede, *On Canticles*, *preface* (our translation); *In cantica canticorum*, *praefatio* (edd. Hurst & Hudson, *Bedae Opera Exegetica*, IIB, 174): '. . . nemini uere umquam noceri nisi a se ipso potest nec est prorsus aliquid quo quisquam inuitus fiat miser'.

who was apparently oblivious of its authorship.[142] Bede, however, was fully aware of the heretical content of the work; he expresses considerable annoyance that it has been circulating under the name of Jerome, rather than its rightful author, whom he believed to be Julian:[143]

> But in the book which he wrote to the virgin Demetrias regarding the institution of virginity he reveals the same thoughts regarding the power of free will. Some of us who read this book rashly believe that it was written by the holy and catholic teacher Jerome, not recognising that the sweetness of its caressing eloquence and perversity of seductive heresy clearly prove that this is not his [Jerome's] work, but rather that of Julian . . .[144]

Bede finishes his preface to Canticles with a repeated warning on the dangers of Julian's *opuscula*. There therefore can be little doubt that Julian's certain writings and at least one other Pelagian work (the *Letter to Demetrias*) were in circulation in early eighth-century Northumbria, and that they were sufficiently well known to give cause for alarm.

The author or authors of the Pseudo-Bedan *Collectanea*, the contents of which have been dated to the eighth century and to a Celtic or Celtic-influenced milieu,[145] included a section of a letter circulating under Jerome's name in which Pelagius is listed as one of the 'twelve luminaries of the Church'; there it is stated: 'Pelagius is a talking point among the faithful, and to me likewise it is a grievous matter.'[146] While, of course, this sentence repeats an earlier work, its inclusion in the *Collectanea* and the categorisation of Pelagius as one of the 'twelve luminaries' attest to contemporary interest in this figure.

The evidence for Pelagian survivals must be considered in the light that Pelagius's own commentary on the Pauline Epistles was widely known in Ireland in the eighth and ninth centuries, and almost certainly in the seventh as well.[147] That this commentary did not circulate anonymously as elsewhere, but under Pelagius's own name, is proved by numerous *nominatim* citations. As noted above, he is cited very frequently in the Irish collection of glosses to Paul's Epistles found in a Würzburg manuscript dated *saec.*VIII/IX. On the basis of linguistic evidence, the date of the Irish material of the first hand in Würzburg can be pushed back to *ca* 700, while the Latin glosses may be older.[148] Further references to Pelagius are found in the Book of Armagh's prologues to the Pauline Epistles and the *Collectio Canonum Hibernensium*.[149] In the ninth century, Sedulius Scottus used Pelagius's commentary for his own commentary on the

---

142 Lapidge & Herren, *Aldhelm, the Prose Works*, 196 n. 26.
143 The work is actually by Pelagius; see above, 70–1.
144 Bede, *On Canticles, preface* (our translation); Latin text below, 103.
145 Bayless & Lapidge, *Collectanea Pseudo-Bedae*. For the date and milieu see 1–12.
146 Tr. Bayless & Lapidge, 170–1; *Collectanea Pseudo-Bedae*, CCCXXVI: 'Pelagius apud fideles sermo est, de quo etiam et mihi grauis causa . . .'
147 Zimmer, *Pelagius in Irland*, 25.
148 Stokes & Strachan, *Thes. Pal.*, I.xxiii.
149 Kenney, *Sources*, 249, 643, 662. Further references in de Bruyn, *The Commentary*, 28 n. 185. See also Zimmer, *Pelagius in Irland*, 24–5.

Pauline Epistles.[150] One of the principal manuscripts on which the text of the commentary is based was written, in part, by an Irish scribe.[151] There is also some new-found evidence that Pelagius's commentary was known in Britain (Wales) in the eighth century.[152] None of this proves that the commentary was continuously available in Ireland from Pelagius's own lifetime, but it was in all probability available there by the time of the pope-elect's letter.[153] Even if no other genuine Pelagian text was to hand, one could extract a large part of Pelagian theology from it.

It was not necessary to lapse into formal heresy to become a Pelagian (or semi-Pelagian) by temperament. Columbanus could write:

What is the best thing in the world? To please its Creator. What is his will? To fulfil what He commanded, that is, to live rightly and dutifully and to seek the Eternal; for duty and justice are the will of Him Who is dutiful and right. How do we reach this goal? By application . . . What helps to maintain this practice? Understanding . . .[154]

Here 'application' translates the Latin *studium*, which has a wide range of meanings: 'effort', 'exertion', 'assiduity', 'zeal'. This is supplemented by 'understanding', which guides 'application'. Columbanus does not mention the grace of God, where one would most expect it. This un-Pauline and un-Augustinian notion of the path to salvation has biblical roots: it lies at the heart of Old Testament moral theology and it finds New Testament support in the so-called Catholic Epistles, especially the Epistle of James. Obedience to the law and faith in God demonstrated through good works are the central themes of James's Epistle.

A central text for the understanding of Irish spirituality is the so-called *Alphabet of Piety*, written in Old Irish.[155] It has been argued that this work was written in the opening years of the seventh century, but this is not certain.[156] At the beginning of the work the constituents of holiness are mentioned. The first of these is 'faith with deeds' (no. 1). 'Temperate zeal' is the 'practice of the clergy'. Whoever learns it 'shall have the kingdom of heaven' (no. 3). The road to eternal life commences with the possession of the proper spiritual attributes: fear of God and love. Love brings one to the

---

[150] Frede, *Pelagius*, 87–155.
[151] Karlsruhe, Landesbibliothek, MS Augiensis CXIX; see Kenney, *Sources*, 663.
[152] Dumville, 'Late seventh- or eighth-century evidence'.
[153] Zimmer, *Pelagius in Irland*, 25.
[154] Columbanus, *Sermons*, III.1 (ed. and tr. Walker, 72–3); *Instructiones*, III.1, *Qualiter monachus Deo placere debet*, I: 'Quid in mundo optimum est? Auctori eius placere. Quid est eius voluntas? Complere quod iussit, hoc est, recte vivere et pie aeternum quaerere; pietas enim et aequitas pii et recti voluntas est. Ad id quomodo pervenitur? Studio. . . . Ad hoc conservandum quid iuvat? Intellectus . . .'
[155] *Apgitir Chrábaid* (ed. and tr. Hull).
[156] For an early seventh-century date see Ó Néill, 'The date and authorship', esp. 214–15. For doubts about a date this early see McCone, *Progress*, 34–5. McCone's argument, based on stylistic considerations, can be supported by a theological point: the reference to 'unity of the Catholic Church' (no. 12). This suggests that the poem, in the version which has come down to us, had passed through the hands of the *Romani*.

holy deed, and the holy deed 'entails eternal life in heaven' (no. 5). There is no notion of an elect; salvation is available to everyone. It is only necessary to obey the commandments and observe the law of love:

Anyone, therefore, who shall fear God and who shall love Him and who shall fulfil His will and His commandment, shall have honour in the presence of men in this world and shall be blessed along with God in the next world (no. 8).[157]

This generalisation is later subjected to the restriction that a person 'be in the unity of the Catholic Church' (no. 12). The sequence of grace (expressed as the help of Christ) and works might be classified as semi-Pelagian: 'Who is nearest to God? He who meditates on him. Whom does Christ help? Him who does good' (no. 37).[158]

This is a long way from the notion of 'irresistible grace' which we find in pro-Augustinian authors such as Prosper of Aquitaine. For the author of the *Alphabet of Piety*, the help of God exists for those who earn it. Coelestius would not have approved of such a formula – he wanted to be rid of grace in any form; however, the wily Pelagius might have liked it. For him, one may require the help of God, so long as the will remains free.[159] (Grace must remain resistible!) Thus the spectrum of Insular Celtic theology ranged from soft forms of semi-Pelagianism (largely identified with effort-based monasticism) to the 'hawkish' views of a Coelestius, with Pelagius somewhere in the middle, albeit closer to Coelestius. Augustinians were very thin on the ground before at least 655, when Pseudo-Augustine wrote *On the Miracles of Holy Scripture* alluding to the genuine works of Augustine.

To conclude: the influence of Pelagianism in the British Isles throughout the period we are considering was substantial – indeed, 'defining', as we claimed in the Introduction. We know too little about Church affairs in fifth-century Britain to argue that Pelagians were numerically in the majority or excerised control over the whole region – we may simply have a case of the 'tail wagging the dog'. However, even after the alleged suppression of Pelagianism by Germanus, it would appear that the movement persisted in some form. Even if doubts persist regarding Rhygyfarch's evidence that they were suppressed only in the time of St David, and then with difficulty, we have Gildas's more reliable witness that a closed group subscribing to identifiable Pelagian tenets persisted into the sixth century. In the seventh century a pope-elect charged that the heresy had been revived among the northern Irish. Moreover, we know that important Pelagian texts were copied and circulated throughout both islands, sometimes pseudonymously, sometimes not, into the ninth century. But most significantly, throughout our entire

---

[157] *Alphabet of Piety*, VIII (ed. and tr. Hull, 60–1); *Apgitir Chrábraid*, VIII: 'Nach duine didu ad-āigfedar Dia 7 nod-cechra 7 comalnabthar a thoil 7 a thimnae, bid airmitiu dó fīad doīnib ī-síu 7 bid findbadach la Dīa hī-thall.'

[158] *Alphabet of Piety*, XXXVII (ed. and tr. Hull, 76–7); *Apgitir Chrábraid*, XXXVII: 'Cīa nessam do Dīa? Int-ī immod-radai. Cīa frisa congai Crīst? Frisinn-í do-gní maith.'

[159] Pelagius, *Profession of Faith*, XXV (*PL* XLVIII.491).

period we find numerous citations from writers on both islands that either support or attack the chief tenets of Pelagianism. Pelagius continued to be 'a talking point among the faithful'! It is fair to say that Pelagian thought influenced – and disturbed – the Churches of the British Isles for more than four centuries. This 'pure' Pelagian strain, while persisting in its own form, harmonised with the milder type usually known as semi-Pelagianism, creating a theological consensus that provided the foundation of the common Celtic Church, and, to some degree, survived its dissolution. An understanding of British, Irish and even Northumbrian Christology requires the acceptance of this basic fact.

Additional Texts

43. Cassian, *Conlationes*, XIII.4 (ed. Pichery, II.151–2): '. . . abrupte a nobis potest inprobari, illud uidetur obsistere quod ad destructionem liberi tendit arbitrii. Nam cum multos gentilium, qui utique diuini adiutorii gratiam non merentur, non solum frugalitatis atque patientiae, sed, quod magis mirum est, etiam castitatis uideamus fulgere uirtutibus, quomodo captiuato liberae uoluntatis arbitrio dei munere conlatae illis fuisse crendendae sunt, cum utique mundanae sapientiae sectatores non solum dei gratiam, sed ipsum etiam uerum deum penitus ignorantes, quamtum uel serie lectionis uel quorundam traditione cognouimus, summam castimoniae puritatem proprii laboris industriae possedisse dicantur?'

46. Cassian, *Conlationes*, XIII.11 (ed. Pichery, II.162): 'Et ita sunt haec quodammodo indiscrete permixta atque confusa, ut quid ex quo pendeat inter multos, magna quaestione uoluatur, id est utrum quia initium bonae uoluntatis praebuerimus misereatur nostri deus, an quia deus misereatur consequamur bonae uoluntatis initium. Multi enim singula haec credentes ac iusto amplius adserentes uariis sibique contrariis sunt erroribus inuoluti. Si enim dixerimus nostrum esse bonae principium uoluntatis, quod fuit in persecutore Paulo, quod in publicano Matthaeo, quarum unus cruori ac suppliciis innocentum, alius uiolentiis as rapinis publicis incubans adtrahitur ad salutem? Sin uero a gratia dei semper inspirari bonae uoluntatis principia dixerimus, quid de Zacchaei fide, quid de illius in cruce latronis pietate dicemus, qui desiderio suo uim quandam regnis caelestibus inferentes . . .'

47. Cassian, *Conlationes*, XIII.12 (ed. Pichery, II.64–6): 'Nec enim talem deus hominem fecisse credendus est, qui nec uelit umquam nec possit bonum. Alioquin nec liberum ei permisit arbitrium, si ei tantummodo malum ut uelit et possit, bonum uero a semet ipso nec uelle nec posse concessit. . . . Denique non amisisse humanum genus post praeuaricationem Adae scientiam boni etiam apostoli sententia euidentissime declaratur, qua dicit: *cum enim gentes, quae legem non habent, naturaliter ea quae legis sunt faciunt, hi legem non habentes ipsi sibi sunt lex . . .*'

71. Patrick, *Confessio*, XXVIII (ed. Bieler, *Libri epistolarum*, I.73): 'Contra,

Hiberione non sponte pergebam, *donec*, prope *deficiebam*; sed hoc potius bene mihi fuit, qui ex hoc emendatus sum a Domino, et aptauit me ut hodie essem quod aliquando longe a me erat, ut ergo curam haberem aut satagerem pro salute aliorum, quando autem tunc etiam de me ipso non cogitabam.'

73. Patrick, *Confessio*, XXV (ed. Bieler, *Libri epistolarum*, I.72): 'Et iterum uidi in me ipsum orantem et eram quasi intra corpus meum et audiui super me, hoc est super *interiorem hominem*, et ibi fortiter orabat gemitibus, et inter haec *stupebam et ammirabam et cogitabam* quis esset qui in me orabat, sed ad postremum orationis sic effitiatus est ut sit Spiritus . . .'

75. Patrick, *Confessio*, XXVII (ed. Bieler, *Libri epistolarum*, I.73): '*Occasionem* post annos triginta *inuenerunt me aduersus* uerbum quod confessus fueram antequam essem diaconus. Propter anxietatem maesto animo insinuaui amicissimo meo quae in pueritia mea una die gesseram, immo in una hora, quia necdum praeualebam. *Nescio, Deus scit*, si habebam tunc annos quindecim, et Deum uiuum non credebam, neque ex infantia mea, sed in morte et in incredulitate mansi donec ualde castigatus sum *et in ueritate humiliatus sum a fame et nuditate*, et cotidie.'

91. Rhygyfarch, *Life of St David*, XLIV, LV (ed. (J.W.) James, 21, 24): 'Quia uero post Sancti Germani secundo auxilia Pelagiana heresis suae obstinationis neruos ueluti uenenosi serpentis uirus intimis patriae compaginibus inserens reuiuiscebat, uniuersalis cunctorum Brytanniae episcoporum synodus colligitur. Collectis itaque centum decem et octo episcopis, innumerosa affuit multitudo presbiterorum abbatum ceterorum ordinum, regum, principum, laicorum (uirorum, feminarum) . . . . Deinde succedente temporum serie alia colligitur synodus cui nomen Victoriae, in qua collecta episcoporum, sacerdotum, abbatum turba, ea quae in priori firmauerant.'

96. Bede, *Historia Ecclesiastica*, II.19 (edd. Colgrave & Mynors, 200, 202): 'Et hoc quoque cognouimus, quod uirus Pelagianae hereseos apud uos reuiuescit; quod omnino hortamur, ut a uestris mentibus huiusmodi uenenatum superstitionis facinus auferatur. Nam qualiter ipsa quoque execranda heresis damnata est, latere uos non debet, quia non solum per istos ducentos annos abolita est, sed et cotidie a nobis perpetuo anathemate sepulta damnatur; et hortamur ne, quorum arma conbusta sunt, apud uos eorum cineres suscitentur. Nam quis non execretur / superbum eorum conamen et impium, dicentium posse sine peccato hominem existere ex propria uoluntate et non ex gratia Dei? . . . Nam ceteri homines cum peccato originali nascentes testimonium praeuaricationis Adae . . .'

102. Columbanus, *Instructiones*, XI.1, *De disciplina* (ed. Walker, 106): 'Magna dignitas homini Dei similitudo, si conservetur; sed grandis iterum damnatio Dei imaginis violatio. Quod enim accepit de flatu Dei, si in contrarium depravaverit usum, et beneficium naturae contaminaverit, tunc Dei similitudinem corrumpit, et quantum in se est delet; si autem animae

insitis virtutibus usus fuerit in rectum, tunc Dei erit similis. Quascumque ergo Deus in nobis in prima nostra conditione virtutes seminavit, ipsas ei reddere nos praeceptis docuit. . . . Deum autem diligit qui eius mandata custodit; dixit enim, *Si diligitis me, mandata mea servate.*'

119. *De mirabilibus sacrae scripturae*, I.3 (*PL* XXXV.2155): 'Enoch vero sine morte, per totius pene saeculi tempus remotus ab hominum conversatione custoditur, ut in eo qualiter hominum homines si non peccarent, generata prole commutarentur in vitam spiritualem sine morte, ostenderetur. Sed licet longo reservatus tempore adhuc vivat; mortis tamen debitum, quod omnes in Adam sumpsimus, vitare non poterit. . . . Attamen in hoc non nova natura uni homini gignitur: sed pristina et generalis omnium hominum gubernatur. Insitum enim omni homini in prima conditione Geneseos libri historiam considerantibus esse apparet, ut non solum longo tempore, sed etiam perpetuo viveret, nisi peccati aculeo mors naturae metas exterminaret.'

127. *Adelphus adelpha*, lines 49–51, 55–7 (ed. Herren, *The Hisperica Famina II*, 108):

Raxas est ci⟨b⟩ro merus,
agonitheta frunemus,
qui sine labe fit iustus.

. . . .

Tamaxo in mente mea
minus idon in terra
antrophum sine macula.

137. *Canones Hibernenses*, III.8 (ed. Bieler, *The Irish Penitentials*, 168): 'Populus Israel debuerat constringui .x. mandatis legis dum causa ipsorum percusit Deus Egyptum .x. plagis; ideo decim mandata sunt. Ubi sunt in lege praecepta quae Deus non praecipit? Iethro socer Moysi elegere .lxx. principes qui iudicarent populum cum Moysi, et hoc indicium est, quia si inuenerimus iudicia gentium bona, que natura bona illis docet et Deo non displicet, seruabimus.'

144. Bede, *In cantica canticorum, praefatio* (edd. Hurst & Hudson, *Bedae Opera Exegetica*, IIB, 175): 'Sed et in libro quem ad Demetriadem uirginem Christi de institutione uirginitatis scripsit haec eadem de potentia liberi arbitrii quomodo sentiat pandit. Quem uidelicet librum non nulli nostrum studiose legentes sancti et catholici doctoris Hieronimi esse temere arbitrantur minime peruidentes quod et suauitas eloquentiae demulcentis et hereseos peruersitas seducentis manifeste probat hoc illius opusculum non esse, quin potius . . . edidit . . . Iulianus . . .'

IV

THE COMMON CELTIC CHURCH

Some evidence for a common Church

It is our hypothesis that there was a common Church in Britain and Ireland in the period *ca* 450 – *ca* 630.[1] This period embraces the time from the alleged expulsion of the leaders of the Pelagian heresy (discussed in the previous chapter) down to the intrusion of Romanising elements in Ireland and the establishment of a Roman Church in Anglo-Saxon England. After the expulsion of the 'heresiarchs' from Britain it may be assumed that a separate Pelagian Church, with its own bishops and clergy,[2] ceased to exist; yet, if we can trust Rhygyfarch's *Life of St David*, the heresy was not finally suppressed in Britain before some point around or after the mid-sixth century. Even after this, Pelagian ways of thought, which many Britons doubtless never viewed as heretical, persisted. Combining with the effort-based semi-Pelagianism that lay at the heart of the nascent monastic movement, they formed the matrix of theology and ecclesiastical practice in Britain. The early Christian community in Ireland, which may be as old as the fourth century, may have already included Pelagian sympathisers in its numbers, and the papally-sponsored mission of Palladius may have been ineffective in its effort to eradicate them. We can only assume that the continuing presence of British clergy in Ireland in the fifth and sixth centuries reinforced patterns of belief which may have looked like pollution to outsiders, but remained as invisible as the surrounding air to natives. Whereas there was never a central ecclesiastical government for the British and Irish Churches of this period, and local differences may have developed, there was surely a common set of beliefs and practices that demarcated the 'transmarine' Church from the continental.

The common Celtic Church developed its peculiarities through isolation. After the departure of Roman forces from Britain in 410, the Church of Rome would have been much reduced in her ability to enforce decrees in that region. It is noteworthy that the two campaigns against the Pelagian heresy

---

[1] For a theoretical discussion and an attempt to delimit this term, see the Introduction, 3–9.

[2] Prosper, *Chronicle*, s.a. 429 (tr. de Paor, 79): 'The Pelagian Agricola, son of the Pelagian Bishop Severianus, insidiously corrupted the churches of Britain with his teachings'; *Properi Tironis Epitoma Chronicon* (ed. Mommsen, 472): 'Agricola Pelagianus, Severiani episcopi Pelagiani filius, ecclesias Brittaniae dogmatis sui insinuatione corrumpit.'

in Britain were carried out from Gaul rather than Rome. Prosper of Aquitaine alluded to the remoteness of Britain and its reputation as a retreat for the 'enemies of grace'.[3] The contacts between the British Church and the continent, so well attested in the fourth century,[4] dwindle in the fifth and sixth centuries. Evidence for their renewal resumes with the Irishman Columbanus, whose mission to the continent began in 590 and whose writings date mostly to the period 600–15.[5]

Evidence for close contact between the British and Irish Churches in the sixth century is relatively plentiful. We have already seen that a British bishop Uinniau taught Columba while the latter was a deacon.[6] Further, we noted the influence of Uinniau's penitential on the penitentials of Columbanus and Cummian. Indeed, Uinniau's little book charted the course of the Irish Church from the sixth to the ninth century, most particularly with regard to the creation of a monasticised clergy and 'paramonastic' laity.[7] The *Annales Cambriae* records a visit of Gildas to Ireland in 565, and he is quoted by Columbanus (*ca* 600) as well as by the compilers of canon collections.[8] Already in the sixth century Irish ecclesiastics felt it necessary to place controls on the influx of British clergy: 'A cleric who comes from the Britons without a letter, even though he lives in a community, is not allowed to minister.'[9]

In the opening years of the seventh century, Archbishop Laurence (in Bede's account) could still speak of a common *conversatio* for the British and the Irish, just as Cummian might make mention of *Britonum Scottorumque particula* (a small part [sect?] of the British and the Irish).[10] By his use of the

---

[3] Prosper, *Contra Collatorem* ('Against Cassian'), XXI.2 (tr. De Letter, *Prosper of Aquitaine*, 134): '. . . he banned from that remote corner of the Ocean some enemies of the grace of God who took refuge there as in the land of their birth'; (*PL* LI.271): '. . . quando quosdam inimicos gratiae solum suae originis occupantes, etiam ab illo secreto exclusit oceani'. See above, 81 n. 61.

[4] Haddan & Stubbs, *Council*, I.44: 'A.D. 450–547 (No records)'. The editors go on to explain that there are no available contemporary records for the period, but they note material in much later historiographical and hagiographical sources. Gildas, the next source cited, is silent on continental contacts. Note, however, Patrick's references to Christians in Gaul at *Confession*, XLIII, and *Letter to Coroticus*, XIV. For a recent survey of contacts between the British Isles and the continent in the fifth and sixth centuries see (J.B.) Stevenson, *The Liturgy*, xxvii–xxxv.

[5] See most recently Bullough, 'The career of Columbanus'.

[6] See above, 29.

[7] We adopt Colmán Etchingham's useful term; see his *Church Organisation*, 290–318.

[8] Kenney, *Sources*, 177; also Sharpe, 'Gildas as a father'.

[9] *First Synod*, XXXIII (tr. Bieler, *The Irish Penitentials*, 59); *Synodus I S. Patricii*, XXXIII (ed. Bieler, *The Irish Penitentials*, 58): 'Clericus qui de Britanis ad nos uenit sine epistola, etsi habitet in plebe, non licitum ministrare.' For our early dating of this collection, see above, 31–2.

[10] Bede, *Historia Ecclesiastica*, II.4 (tr. Colgrave & Mynors, 144–7); Cummian, *On the Easter Controversy*, lines 109–10 (tr. Walsh & Ó Cróinín, *Cummian's Letter*, 72–5).

word *particula*, Cummian, writing around 632 or 633, apparently refers to a group comprising the British Church and the *Hibernenses*, now confined mostly to northern Ireland and Iona, and thereby identifies himself with the 'majority' of the southern Irish, who were Romanisers. His letter provides us with a terminus for the dissolution of the common Celtic Church. It belongs, apparently, at the head of a series of seventh- and eighth-century Insular texts that insist on unity with the universal Church of Rome, or contrast the practices of the British and the Irish with those of the 'Catholic faith'. Besides Cummian's letter these include the anonymous *On Festivities* (*De sollemnitatibus*), the version of the *Alphabet of Piety* (*Apgitir Chrábaid*) that has survived, Aldhelm's letter to Geraint and, above all, Bede's *Ecclesiatical History*. Is it possible to reconstruct the *conversatio* of this Church before it broke into 'particles'?

Scripturalism

It has already been argued that the British Church (and by extension the pre-Romanising Irish Church) was oriented towards a theology that ranged between semi-Pelagian and Pelagian. It has further been shown that the monastic movement had a foothold in Britain at least by the turn of the sixth century, and was well established by mid-century. British monasticism was rooted in the semi-Pelagian teachings of Cassian and Faustus. However, British Christianity (whether monastic or lay) was governed by a total reliance on the authority of the scriptures, the corollary of which was a marked distrust of any theology that was not scripturally based. This reliance, of course, is wholly consistent with both Pelagianism and semi-Pelagianism. Both of these theologies warned that it must never be forgotten that God revealed his law through the written word. The complete law is contained in the scriptures, and examples are given in both testaments to help us in our quest for perfect obedience to the law. Support for the nexus between knowledge of the scriptures and perfection can be found in the scriptures themselves. Paul wrote (II Tim. 3:15–17): 'And because from thy infancy thou hast known the holy scriptures, which can instruct thee to salvation . . . That the man of God may be perfect, furnished to every good work.'

Pelagian texts refer to four sources of the divine law: the law (Pentateuch), the prophets, the gospels and the apostles.[11] The question for Pelagians was the same as the one posed for many early Christians: how do the parts of the law relate to each other, and to what extent are we bound by each? One could take one of two basic approaches to this problem: appeal to Christ's words as given by Matthew 5:17, 'I am not come to destroy the law or the prophets. I am not come to destroy, but to fulfil.' Alternatively, one could turn to Paul's Letter to the Romans, which puts the (Old Testament) law in a subordinate position, and sometimes forcefully suggests that Christians should ignore it. The authority of Paul's text presented so great an obstacle

---

[11] See the discussion in Chapter III, above, 72.

to Pelagius that he felt compelled to explain it away in his commentary to the work. Ultimately, the tension between 'Jewish Christianity', which remained beholden to the law, and a more New Testament style of Christianity was never really resolved. The radical attempt by Marcion around the middle of the second century to impose a 'sunset law' on the Old Testament and remove it entirely from the canon of the Christian Bible ended in failure. Subsequently, Christians were faced with the dilemma of what portions of the law to accept, and what to reject. Nearly all Christians agreed that they were required to obey the commandments given to Moses, by which they understood the Ten Commandments. Beyond that, the question was tricky in the extreme.

For the Pelagians, however, the matter was clear-cut, at least in principle. Pelagius himself seems to have left no doubt about what laws were to be obeyed:

What he says above is: 'Do everything'; so we are not to select some of God's commandments as if to suit our fancy but to fulfil them without exception, nor to spurn some of his instructions as being mean and insignificant tasks but to have regard in all matters for the majesty of the one who gives them.[12]

Commenting on Matthew 5:20 'Unless your righteousness exceeds that of the scribes and Pharisees, you should not enter the kingdom of heaven', the author of *On Bad Teachers* wrote:

For the righteousness of Christ's disciples will be able to stand out above that of the scribes and Pharisees, as long as they have fulfilled not only the precepts given to the scribes and Pharisees by Moses and the prophets but also the commandments given by Christ.[13]

In an extended exegesis of the passage, the writer concludes that Jesus's words were not to be taken as irony. It is difficult to reach any conclusion other than that the writer believed that every commandment entered into the scriptures (from the law to the apostles) must be fulfilled, whether it be a prohibition or a command to do something. He proceeds to give a catalogue of God's punishments for seemingly small infractions of commandments: Adam and Eve were punished with death for eating fruit; Miriam was covered with leprosy for slandering Moses; the sons of Aaron were consumed by fear for offering fire that was unsuitable; a man gathering sticks on the Sabbath was stoned to death; Uzzah was slain by

---

[12] Pelagius, *To Demetrias*, XVI.1 (tr. Rees, *The Letters*, 52); *Ad Demetriadem*, XVI.1 (*PL* XXX.30): '*Omnia*, inquit, *facite*. Non enim quasi ad arbitrium nostrum, quædam ex mandatis Dei debemus eligere, sed generaliter universa complere. Nec aliqua præcepta ejus quasi vilia munuscula ac parva contemnere; sed imperantis in omnibus majestatem aspicere.'

[13] *On Bad Teachers*, X.1 (tr. Rees, *The Letters*, 227); *De doctoribus malis*, X.1 (*PL supp.* I.1431): 'In hoc enim discipulorum Christi plus quam scribarum et Pharisaeorum poterit eminere iustitia, si non ea tantum, quae per Moysen et prophetas scribis Pharisaeisque praecepta sunt, uerum etiam, quae per Christum sunt mandata subpleuerint.'

a lethal blow for touching the ark, even though he did so to prevent it from falling.[14]

When discussing commandments, Pelagius and his followers invariably confined themselves to the Ten Commandments, or to Christ's special orders, or to prohibitions of the past, such as the examples cited above. What would they have said to issues such as circumcision – a major question in Paul's Letter to the Romans? Here precisely is where theory foundered on the shoals of particulars. In his commentary on Romans 2, Pelagius treads closely in the footsteps of Paul in arguing for 'the circumcision of the heart' over against the physical removal of the foreskin. He consigns physical circumcision to its own day – it is an act deserving to be set in a time-capsule, interesting, but without further relevance:

[Circumcision] is of value in its own day. It is of value as a sign, if righteousness, of which it is a 'seal', accompanies it (Rom. 4:11); without righteousness the rest will be superfluous. Or . . . if it enabled the Jew to live and escape destruction in infancy, before he came to an age of understanding. Or: Because he set it in the law, one discovers, upon close examination, that when the circumcision of the flesh ends the true circumcision of the heart will come.[15]

Alert readers of Pelagian works would have realised the contradiction. It is illogical to advocate the (literal) obedience to the whole law of God, and at the same time, to regard certain commands and prohibitions of the Old Law as no longer valid. To follow Pelagian teachings to the letter, it would be necessary to observe all the prohibitions and commands in the law, prophets, gospels and apostles, including the law of circumcision and dietary restrictions. Pelagius, apparently, wanted to have it both ways: to teach simultaneously the unity of God's law and the superiority of the New Law to the Old. Another way of looking at the problem is to realise that Pelagius and his friends never bothered to scan the whole of the scriptures to see where God's injunctions contradicted each other, at least potentially. The theory of the 'three laws – those of nature, Moses and Christ' was presented as seamless, whereas, in fact, as Paul and Marcion recognised, the contradictions were even more egregious than the agreements.

However, just as one can make whole cloth of Augustine's contradictory statements, one can do the same with Pelagianism. In the end, it is the broad principles – the teachable theology – that really counts. The preacher expounding Pelagian teachings in church will inevitably concentrate on the dogma of obeying the entire law. For the congregation, the law must be viewed as divinely ordained from all eternity, and without contradiction. As has been noted, for Pelagians, it is the authority of him who commands

---

[14] *On Bad Teachers*, XIII.1–2 (tr. Rees, *The Letters*, 233–4).

[15] Pelagius, *On Romans*, 2:25 (tr. de Bruyn, 75); *Expositio in Romanos*, 2:25 (ed. Souter, I.26): '. . . prodest tempore suo, signum prodest, si iustitia, cuius est "signaculum," adsit; ceterum sine illa superfluum erit. Siue: . . . quia uiuere faciebat Iudaeum et in infantia non exterminari ante quam saperet. Siue: Quia in lege facit esse, [qua] perspecta inuenitur, carnis circumcisione cessante, uera[m] illa[m] cordis esse uentura[m].'

which counts the most, not the particular commandment.[16] It is thus the duty of the believing Christian to see the divine law as unitary, lying at the very core of his or her Christianity, and to find its direct application to daily life.

'Judaising tendencies'

It is precisely in the applications that we see the hand of Pelagius in the unfolding of Celtic Christianity. In the virulently anti-Jewish world of the sixth to eighth centuries, the British and Irish Churches preserved a deep regard for the most Jewish aspects of Christianity. This is not because Pelagian theology was consciously Judaising, but because it was scriptural-ist. We have already seen how close adherence to the law led to the 'Quattuordeciman heresy', whether practised strictly, or, as more usually, in a compromising fashion.[17] This Celtic practice may seem an oddity to some, but, in fact, it is wholly consistent with sabbatarianism, which was the norm in the common Celtic Church until the Romanising period. Both go back to the same root: literal observance of Old Testament law. As for sabbatarianism, it is important to recall Exodus 20:8: 'Remember that thou keep holy the sabbath day.' The Church in the first five centuries maintained the distinction between the sabbath (*sabbatum*) and the Lord's Day (*dies dominica*), and many Christians observed both days for a long time, strictly observing the prohibitions against work or travel on the sabbath (Saturday), while worshipping on the Lord's Day (Sunday). However, a series of councils held in Gaul (at Arles, Orleans and Mâcon) throughout the sixth century imposed a variety of rules affecting Sunday observance that had the effect of sabbatising the Lord's Day.[18] The prohibition of labour on a Sunday became secular law in England in the late seventh century, and in the Carolingian kingdom in 789.[19]

The isolation of the British Church throughout the sixth century may have shielded it from the effects of the new Sunday canons, though we have no direct evidence. We do know, however, that the church on Iona at least in Columba's time continued the separate observance of the sabbath and Sunday, as Adomnán causes Columba to remind us:

This day is called in the sacred books 'Sabbath', which is interpreted 'rest'. And truly this day is for me a Sabbath, because it is my last day of this present laborious life. In it after my toilsome labours I kept Sabbath; and at midnight of this following venerated Lord's day, in the language of the Scriptures I shall go the way of the fathers. For now my Lord Jesus Christ deigns to invite me.[20]

---

[16] Cited above, 107.

[17] See the discussion above, 60–2.

[18] *Dictionnaire d'archéologie chrétienne et de liturgie*, IV.938–43, 950–6; see also van Dam, *Leadership and Community*, 287–8.

[19] See the evidence collected in Anderson & Anderson, *Adomnan's Life of Columba*, 26–7.

[20] Adomnán, *Life of Columba*, CXXVIb–CXXVIIa (tr. Anderson & Anderson, 523); Latin text below, 134.

Adomnán wrote approximately a century after Columba's death, but his testimony appears to be confirmed by a passage in *Amra Choluimb Chille*, arguably composed in 597 on the occasion of Columba's death: 'He used to perform no fasting that was not according to the (heavenly) King's law.'[21] Other evidence in Adomnán's work shows that the Iona monks did not sabbatise Sunday; further, the tenth-century Irish Life of Adomnán indicates that his successors resisted the trend even longer.[22]

Predictably, the attempt to preserve the letter of Exodus 20:8–11 while acceding to commonly accepted Christian observance emanated from the *Hibernensis* party, which most closely reflected the practice of the common Celtic Church, whereas the impetus to obliterate a separate sabbath observance and incorporate it into Sunday came from the Roman party. Curiously, when the battle was finally resolved in favour of a single observance (that is, a sabbatised Sunday), the penalties imposed on infractions of 'the Law of Sunday' appear as rigorous as any imposed by the Old Law. Writing of the Sunday observance of the *Céli Dé* of the eighth to ninth century, Kathleen Hughes remarked:

The culdees also kept Sunday much as though it had been the Jewish Sabbath. No work was done on Sunday, not even the gathering or preparation of food. Bread must be baked and fruit and vegetables must be picked before Sunday began; not even a single apple might be lifted from the ground. Food brought from a distance on Sunday might not be eaten by the religious. Journeys might not normally be undertaken, though short distances (a thousand paces) were legitimate to watch over the sick, administer communion, attend mass, and other 'urgent matters', and many culdees occasionally went farther. Sunday, the Lord's Day, was to be as free as possible from any worldly activity. One man, who 'happened to stay in the bath a while after vespers on Saturday', had to undergo a special fast.[23]

The laws for Sunday observance were promulgated not only in the monastic rules such as the 'Monastery of Tallaght', but also in a special tract on Sunday observance, *Cáin Domnaig* ('The Law of Sunday'). This work contains the so-called 'Letter of Jesus concerning Sunday Observance'; examples of punishment for the transgression of Sunday; and *Cáin Domnaig* itself, a law tract dealing with the observance of Sunday and the punishments for violations.[24]

The (earlier) separate observation of the sabbath and the 'Quattuordeci-

---

[21] *Amra Choluimb Chille*, XCVII (ed. and tr. Stokes, 272–3): 'Ní oened ní na bu recht rig.' One of the glosses to the passage states (*ibid.*): 'he fasted not on Sundays' ('i. ní aened i ndomnaigib'). For the early date of the *Amra* see Herbert, *Iona, Kells and Derry*, 9–10 and n. 5.

[22] Anderson & Anderson, *Adomnan's Life*, 29. See *Betha Adamnáin*, XIII (9) (edd. and tr. Herbert & Ó Riain, 57). The passage describes Adomnán's restoring to life a sheep-dog which had accidentally been cooked with one hundred sheep given to the monastery! The miracle took place on a Sunday.

[23] Hughes, *The Church*, 178–9.

[24] A discussion of these texts and their relations is provided in McNally, '*Dies dominica*'. For what may be the earliest Irish tract on Sunday observance see *Precamur patrem*, discussed and translated in the Appendix.

man' celebration of Easter may not have been the only examples of Jewish practice regarding festivities in the common Celtic Church. An acephalous letter called *De sollemnitatibus et sabbatis et neomeniis* (*On Festivities, Sabbaths and New Moons*),[25] assigned variously to Jerome and Columbanus, is now argued to be an anonymous Irish work of the seventh century.[26] The letter is addressed to an unnamed *venerabilis papa*, and the author calls himself a *peregrinus*. That Columbanus himself was not the writer of this letter is clear enough from the use of the 'orthodox' Easter reckoning rather than that of the Irish (84-year) cycle.[27] But there are other grounds for dissociating the work from Columbanus. The gist of this writer's brief is an assault on 'those persons who, though they appear superficially as Christians, yet in the ungodliness in their leanings towards Judaism, do not fear to rend the body of Christ'.[28] Columbanus, in sharp contrast, defended the following of Jewish practice in some matters as of no account to Christians. In his famous Letter to Pope Gregory he wrote:

We ought not to hold Easter with the Jews? What relevance has it to reality? Are we really to believe that the reprobate Jews hold Easter now, considering that they are without a temple, outside Jerusalem, and that Christ then prefigured has been crucified by them? Or are we really to believe that the Easter (*Pascha*) of the fourteenth moon is rightly theirs, and not to confess that it is the Passover (*Phase*) of God himself who instituted it, and who alone clearly knows the mystery by which the Fourteenth Moon was chosen for the Exodus.[29]

On Festivities is a general attack on Christians who follow Jewish observances because they believe that they are commanded by the law. Citing the prophets Esdras and Isaias along with Romans (10:4), the writer declares:

My soul hates your festal days and new moons and Sabbaths and the Lord declares that he did not command these things, while it is clear that He enjoined them in the law. What else is shown in these words, than that when Christ [who was] the end of the law came, He did not command them to be kept according to the letter?[30]

The author proceeds to deal with Christ's ending of the sabbath when he healed a cripple, and with Christ's abolition of Passover through his resurrection on the fifteenth (rather than the fourteenth) day. But other Jewish feasts are also discussed: the Sabbaths of the Trumpets, the Day of

---

[25] Ed. and tr. Walker, *Sancti Columbani Opera*, 199–207.
[26] Ó Cróinín, 'The computistical works', 266–9.
[27] *Ibid.*, 268.
[28] *On Festivities*, VIII (ed. and tr. Walker, 206–7); *De sollemnitatibus*, VIII: '. . . qui cum in superficie Christiani videantur, per Iudaici sensus impietatem corpus Christi . . . scindere non metuunt'.
[29] Columbanus, *Letters*, I.4 (ed. and tr. Walker, 6–7); Latin text below, 134.
[30] *On Festivities*, I (ed. and tr. Walker, 198–9); *De sollemnitatibus*, I: '*Dies festos vestros et neomenias et sabbata odit anima mea*, et haec se Dominus non mandasse pronuntiat, cum ipsum in lege haec praecepisse manifestum est. In quibus verbis quid aliud ostenditur, quam quod, cum *Christus finis legis* advenerit, ea secundum litteram custodiri non mandaverit?'

Atonement and the Feast of Tabernacles.[31] The writer bids Christians to understand these feasts as figuring Christ:

Now this perhaps may mean, that since we at the end of the age are consecrated by the sacrament of a threefold liturgy (by the trumpet of preaching, by the faith of the Gospel, and by the sprinkling of the blood of Jesus Christ, in which is true propitiation), now that the time of the law is finished we should not cease to learn, and gathering the fruits of good works, resting from every evil work, bearing persecution by the grace of the sevenfold Spirit, we should deserve to reach the reckoning of the eighth beatitude.[32]

There is evidence, however, that certain Irish Christians did not interpret as allegory the injunctions to celebrate at least one of these feasts. The Sabbaths of Trumpets is connected to the offering of the first fruits at the beginning of the harvest. In the so-called 'Irish Canons' (*Canones Hibernenses*) we find excellent evidence for the continuation of this practice, with only a slight accommodation to the requirements of Christian institutions:

To know what is the amount of the first fruits, that is, an omer; as others (say), it is nine loaves or twelve loaves . . . Of vegetables, as much as the hand can hold. These things ought to be presented at the beginning of the harvest, and they were offered once in the year to the priests at Jerusalem. In the new (dispensation), however, each person to the monastery of which he is a monk.[33]

Tithes and dietary restrictions also played important roles in the *conversatio* of the common Celtic Church. The section of the 'Irish Canons' that treats first fruits also deals with tithes. Tithes apply to animals as well as crops. The first-born of animals is to be offered, 'however, of those animals only which may be sacrificed'.[34] A list of animals that may be sacrificed is given in *On Festivities*; there the author insists on the spiritual (allegorical) nature of sacrifices:

I had determined to say a little about the sacrifices, which containing in themselves a type of the Victim Who as the true Priest, ought to be offered by us also in a spiritual manner to the Lord. For by the calf is meant our toil, by the sheep innocence, by the he-goat the mortification of fornicating lust, by the she-goat which feeds in the lofty pasture the life of contemplation . . . And all these things, whether festal or sacrificial, are commanded by the law to be celebrated and offered in one place, since all things are of value only when they are performed in the unity of the Church without any error of schism.[35]

[31] *On Festivities*, V (ed. and tr. Walker, 205).
[32] *On Festivities*, V (tr. Walker, 205). Latin text below, 134–5.
[33] 'Irish Canons', III.5 (tr. Bieler, *The Irish Penitentials*, 168–9); *Canones Hibernenses*, III.5: 'Sciendum quantum est pondus primitiarum, hoc est gomor; ut alii, .i. viiii. panes uel .xii. panes . . . De oleribus uero quantum pugnus capere potest. Hae res initio estatis reddi debent, et semel in anno ad sacerdotes Hierusalem offerebantur. In nouo autem unus quisque ad monasterium cui monachus fuerit.'
[34] 'Irish Canons', III.3 (tr. Bieler, *The Irish Penitentials*, 166–7); *Canones Hibernenses*, III.3: '. . . autem animalium tantum quae licita sunt immolari'.
[35] *On Festivities*, VII (tr. Walker, 205–7); Latin text below, 135. For works insisting on unity with the universal Church see above, 106.

Whether this text was aimed against the actual sacrifice of animals given as tithes in Ireland or elsewhere cannot be proven. The 'Irish Canons' insist, however, that the only animals that may be given as tithes are those that were regarded as sacrificial animals under the Old Law. What is certain is the requirement for all, except absolute paupers, to tithe:

Further, as others say: if he has too little property for a tithe . . . he shall not pay tithes. Further, as others (say): How is it proper for anyone to offer tithes to the Lord if he has nought but one cow or ox? He shall divide the value of the cow in ten and given the tenth part to the Lord . . .[36]

Dietary restrictions based on the Old Law are also recorded in the *Canones Hibernenses*, and may derive from the common Celtic Church. Here, however, adherence to the letter is less strict. Carrion is to be altogether avoided, as are animals that taste human blood. Cisterns contaminated by corpses, whether human or animal, are to be drained and purified. Beyond these general principles, however, application of the Old Law is either lax or non-existent. Swine may be eaten (provided they are not carrion), and there is no prohibition against eating crustaceans, provided they are not decomposed.[37] In this domain, culture and economy prevail over religious absolutism.

One of the most remarkable aspects of the entire Irish tradition is its claim to have lived under all three laws, to wit, the law of nature, the law of Moses (or circumcision) and the law of Christ. The notion of three successive laws, though not exclusive to the Pelagians, is prominent in their writings. Pelagians, being products of the ancient world, believed that the original goodness of the human race was corrupted over time. In his *Letter to Demetrias* Pelagius writes:

In a word, as long as nature which was still comparatively fresh was in vigorous use and long habituation to sinning did not draw a dark veil, as it were, over human reason, nature was set free and left without law; but when it had become buried beneath an excess of vices and, as if tainted with the rust of ignorance, the Lord applied the file of the law to it, and so, thoroughly polished by its frequent admonitions, it was enabled to recover its former brilliance.[38]

---

[36] 'Irish Canons', III.6–7 (tr. Bieler, *The Irish Penitentials*, 168–9), based on Lev. 27:8; *Canones Hibernenses*, III: '6. Item ut alii: Si minus decimo substantiam habuerit, non reddet decimas. 7. Item ut alii: Quo modo conuenit offere decimas aliquis Domino si non habuerit nisi unam uacam uel bouem? Diuidat praetium uacce in .x. et det decimam partem Domino; sic et reliqua.' On the tithing requirements in Ireland and England in the seventh and eighth centuries see Kottje, *Zum Einfluss*, 64–8.

[37] See the 'Canons of Adamnan' (tr. Bieler, *The Irish Penitentials*, 176–81).

[38] Pelagius, *To Demetrias*, VIII.2 (tr. Rees, *The Letters*, 44); *Ad Demetriadem*, VIII (*PL* XXX.23): 'Denique quamdiu recentioris adhuc naturae usus uiguit: nec humanae rationi velut quamdam caliginem, longus usus peccandi obduxit, sine lege dimissa est natura. Ad quam Dominus nimiis jam vitiis obrutam, et quadam ignorantiae rubigine infectam, limam legis admovit, ut hujus frequenti admonitione expoliretur, et ad suum posset redire fulgorem.'

It turned out, however, that the doctrine of the successive laws was a point of vulnerability for the Pelagians. True enough that the natural law was given to all, and that Christ came to save all men, but surely the law of Moses was reserved for God's chosen people alone. This objection is made forcefully by Jerome:

> Or lastly make your own the favorite cavil of your associate Porphyry, and ask how God can be described as pitiful and of great mercy when from Adam to Moses and from Moses to the coming of Christ He has suffered all nations to die in ignorance of the law and of His commandments. For Britain, that province so fertile in despots, the Scottish tribes, and all the barbarians round about as far as the ocean were alike without knowledge of Moses and the prophets. Why should Christ's coming have been delayed to the last times?[39]

It was very possibly in the context of patristic criticism of the Pelagian doctrine of successive laws and the reference to barbarian peoples, particularly the British and Irish, that the legend of the translation of the law of Moses to Ireland was created and diffused. Its aim was doubtless to show that the Irish benefitted from the 'grace' of the law of Moses at a time when all other peoples excepting the Hebrews themselves lived under the law of nature (in the time of its diminished effectiveness). The (ninth-century?) *Sanas Cormaic* ('Cormac's Glossary') reports the tale of Caí Cáinbrethach:

> . . . the pupil of Fenius, he is the disciple who went to the Sons of Israel to learn Hebrew, and he was the judge with the fleet of the Sons of Mil [the ancestors of the Irish]. And the reason why he is called Caí Cáinbrethach [C. of the good judgements] is that he gave judgements of the [Mosaic] law and that is why they are abundant in Irish law.[40]

Later traditions place Caí in the company of Moses crossing the desert.[41]

While some Christians (like the author of *On Festivities*) believed that the gospel of Christ supplanted the Old Law, and others believed that the New Law was superior to the Old (even if it did not supplant it), some portion of the Irish, doubtless influenced by the notion of successive laws promulgated to counteract the decline of human nature, seem to have regarded the Old Law as primary. We see this attitude, for example, in the writings of Virgilius Maro Grammaticus:

---

[39] Jerome, Letter CXXXIII (tr. Fremantle, 278); Latin text below, 135.

[40] Tr. Ó Corráin, 'Irish vernacular law', 290; *Sanas Cormac*, 'Bráthchæi' (ed. Stokes, *Three Irish Glossaries*, 7): '. . . dalta Feniusa F[arsad]. ise indescipulsin rosiacht mec Israheil frifóglaimm nÆbhra. 7 ise babretheam laloinges mac Milid. isaire asberair Cæi Cænbrethach de fobith itbretha rechta nosberead. 7 isaire atimdha isinbelra.' This legend of the *translatio legis* is doubtless older than the glossary in which it first occurs. Compilers of glossaries may invent explanations and even etymologies; they do not, as a rule, make up stories. For recent work on 'Cormac's Glossary', see Russell, 'The sounds of a silence'.

[41] Ó Corráin, 'Irish vernacular law', 288–9. Hennig, 'The literary tradition', 256, attaches the Caí Cáinbrethach legend (as expanded in a commentary on the *Senchas Mór*) to the Irish Synchronism (s.a. 721), which attempted to harmonise Irish and Jewish history.

For whoever defends this art of the philosophers (which we regard very much as a rival) in such a way that they subject the authority of the first law of the Hebrews to it, a more recent sect, however much adorned, expends all its audacity to no purpose.[42]

Virgilius makes the surprising point that secular learning and philosophy (whatever he means by the term) are subject, not to the teachings of the gospels, the fathers, or the universal Church, but to the Pentateuch. In a somewhat similar vein, the author of the grammatical tract known as *Anonymus ad Cuimnanum* defines the 'science of religion' as 'knowing the law, understanding the prophets, believing in the gospel, and not over-looking the apostles'.[43] The formula accords equal importance to the four divisions of scripture, but the law and the prophets receive first mention, implying (perhaps unwittingly) that Christianity is founded upon Judaism rather than that Judaism prefigures Christianity. This notion is embedded even more deeply in the statement of the anonymous commentator on Mark 1:21: 'We, the children of the synagogue, are healed of this by the hand of discipline, and the elevation of our desire.'[44]

Literary culture

To acquire the 'science of religion' – to use the phrase of the Anonymous – it was essential to be able to read the texts that imparted the required knowledge. A church that encouraged its holiest members to 'meditate on the law of the Lord night and day' was obliged to establish the conditions that would make the fulfilment of the injunction possible. The ideal of the literate monk had not been universal. Even the Benedictine Rule did not enjoin private study, nor require literacy of all its members, since the recommended oral readings at mealtime could have been carried out by a select number of lectors.[45] In the Pelagian view, however, only by being literate could one read and meditate upon the scriptures, from which alone God's will is made known.[46]

---

[42] Virgilius Maro Grammaticus, *Epitomae*, I.2 (our translation); (ed. Polara, 4): 'Etenim quicumque hancce, quam nos valde aemulum putamus, ita defendunt peritiam filosophorum, ut auctoritatem primae Hebreorum minulae huicce quam-vis ornatae recentiori sectae postferant, incassum omne suum expendunt auda-tum.'

[43] *Anonymus ad Cuimnanum. Expositio latinitatis*, I (edd. Bischoff & Löfstedt, 11): 'Scientia . . . pietatis est nosse legem, intellegere prohetas, euangelio credere, apostulos non ignorare.'

[44] *On Mark*, 1:21 (tr. Cahill, *The First Commentary*, 39); *Expositio Evangelii Marci*, 1:21 (ed. Cahill, 17): '. . . nos filii synagogae per manum disciplinae et levationem desiderii sanamur.' It seems likely that the author of the Markan commentary was in some way remarking on the prevalent Judaising tendencies. Cahill, in the Introduction to his edition of the Commentary, 63–4, has (in our opinion erroneously) set the commentary in a milieu where Jews were prevalent.

[45] Benedict, *Rule*, XXXVII (tr. Hunter Blair, 105–7).

[46] Pelagius, *To Demetrias*, IX.2 (tr. Rees, *The Letters*, 45).

The ideal of universal literacy for clerics and those practising the ascetic life was diffused together with British Christianity. Columbanus enjoined his monks to 'pray daily, toil daily, and daily read'.[47] The power of the letter for Celtic Christians is expressed in a seventh-century depiction of Patrick teaching the heathen by holding up written tablets in his hands like Moses.[48] To this image one might contrast Bede's depiction of Augustine of Canterbury showing a picture of Christ on a panel – after the Roman fashion – to the English he hoped to convert.[49]

Although British (and common Celtic) Christianity was a religion of the book, requirements were kept simple in the earliest stages. The scriptures were, far and away, the most important source of spiritual food. Pelagius, writing to Demetrias, advises the following course:

. . . at one time, therefore, let the sequence of heavenly history instruct, at another a holy song of David delight, at another the wisdom of Solomon inform, at another the rebukes of the prophets arouse; at another the perfection of the evangelists and apostles unite you with Christ in a life of complete sanctity.[50]

Aldhelm, whose earlier education was in an Irish school,[51] similarly exhorted the nuns of Barking:

. . . roaming widely through the flowering fields of scriptures, traverse (them) with thirsty curiosity, now energetically plumbing the divine oracles of the ancient prophets foretelling long in advance the advent of the Saviour with certain affirmations; now scrutinising with careful application the hidden mysteries of the ancient laws miraculously drawn up by the man [Moses] . . . now exploring wisely the evangelical story [the four Gosples], expounded through the mystical commentaries of the catholic fathers . . .[52]

Significantly, Aldhelm's additional recommendation to employ 'catholic' commentaries while reading the scriptures places him in a world that has moved out of the Pelagian, or semi-Pelagian, framework into a Romanising

---

[47] Columbanus, *Monks' Rule*, III (ed. and tr. Walker, 126–7); *Regula Monachorum*, III: '. . . Cottidie orandum est, cottidie laborandum, cottidieque est legendum'.

[48] Tírechán, *Life of Patrick*, II.2 (tr. Bieler, *The Patrician Texts*, 123).

[49] Bede, *Historia Ecclesiastica*, I.25 (tr. Colgrave & Mynors, 74–5).

[50] Pelagius, *To Demetrias*, XXIII.2 (tr. Rees, *The Letters*, 61); *Ad Demetriadem*, XXIII.2 (*PL* XXX.37): 'Nunc te igitur ordo instruat coelestis historiæ: nunc sanctum David oblectet canticum: nunc Salomonis erudiat Sapientia: nunc ad timorem Domini increpationes incitent prophetarum: nunc Evangelica et Apostolica perfectio te Christo in omni morum sanctitate conjugat.'

[51] On this point see Orchard, *The Poetic Art of Aldhelm*, 4.

[52] Aldhelm, *On Virginity*, IV (tr. Lapidge & Herren, 61–2); *De virginitate*, IV (ed. Ehwald, 232): '. . . per florulenta scripturarum arva late vagans bibula curiositate decurrit, nunc divina priscorum prophetarum oracula certis adstipulationibus iamdum salvatoris adventum vaticinantia enixius investigando, nunc antiquarum arcana legum ab illo mirabiliter digesta . . . nunc quadrifaria evangelicae relationis dicta misticis catholicorum patrum commentariis exposita . . .' As noted by Lapidge & Herren, 196 n. 26, Aldhelm knew Pelagius's *Letter to Demetrias*, although he was unaware of the authorship of the work.

one. Note that Cassian had advised his monks to lay aside scriptural commentaries and to achieve a true knowledge of the scriptures through fasting and prayer.[53]

While Pelagius recommended to Demetrias a comprehensive reading of the scriptures, it is clear that he and his close associates favoured a more limited range. Most striking is their reliance on the sapiential texts, particularly Ecclesiasticus (Sirach). There is also relatively heavy dependence on the Letters of the Apostles: James, I-II Peter, I-III John; Jude is missing. These moralising texts from both testaments make fitting accompaniment to the Gospel of Matthew, which is far and away the most frequently cited of the four.[54] The preference for Matthew's gospel accords with Pelagian emphasis on the law and the commandments of Christ, Christ as fulfilment of the law, the enjoining of perfection, the disapproval of riches and the like. The Pelagians also favoured the Psalms, which is fitting in an ascetic context. Paul is more heavily used than one might anticipate, but once Pelagius had explicated Paul in a way so as to sound more Pelagian than the Pelagians themselves, he was rendered harmless. Acts was rarely appealed to, and there was virtually no interest in the Apocalypse.

There is some evidence for the continuity of this programme of scriptural reading by the Irish in the late sixth to early seventh centuries. The readings favoured by Columbanus are not so very different from those of the Pelagians: sapiential texts, the Psalms, heavy use of Matthew, vis-à-vis the other gospels, lots of Paul, the apostolic letters and only one doubtful example of use of the Apocalypse.[55] Columbanus's older contemporary Columba (Colum Cille) bequeathed no certain writings, but we learn from *Amra Choluim Chille* that:

> He made books of the law known, books *ut* Cassian loved,
> The battle of *gula* he won.
> The books of Solomon he followed them.[56]

We see here the continuing popularity of the sapiential books – Proverbs, Ecclesiastes, Wisdom (Solomon), Ecclesiasticus (Sirach) – from Pelagius to Cassian to Columba. It has also been shown that Proverbs and Ecclesiasticus were important sources for the author of the *Alphabet of Piety*.[57]

Whatever the precise reading programme prescribed in early British and

---

[53] Cassian, *Institutes*, V.34 (ed. and tr. Guy, 244–5); *Institutiones*, V.34: 'quibus rursum naturali redditis sanitati ipsa scripturarum sanctarum lectio ad contemplationem uerae scientiae abunde etiam sola sufficiat, nec eos conmentationum institutionibus indigere . . .' See Hardinge, *The Celtic Church*, 33. Note, however, that Jonas (*Vita Columbae*, I.3, ed. Krusch, 158) attributes to Columbanus a commentary on Psalms, written while he was still in Ireland. This work has never been satisfactorily identified, although references to it survive in library catalogues: see Kenney, *Sources*, 200–3.

[54] See the index of biblical references in Rees, *The Letters*, 349–57.

[55] See the biblical index in Walker, *Sancti Columbani Opera*, 216–22.

[56] *Amra Choluimb Chille*, LV–LVII (ed. and tr. Stokes, 254–5): 'Sluinnsi*us* leig libru ut car Caisseoin/ Catha gulae gailais/ Libru Solman sexus.'

[57] Ó Néill, 'The date and authorship', 208–10. See above, 99–100.

117

Irish Churches, we may well imagine that reading consisted primarily of the scriptures. Certainly, Patrick's reading, if at all typical for fifth-century Britain, appears to be thus limited.[58] He mentions only two subjects which he and his contemporaries studied in (a British) school: law (*iura*) and holy scripture.[59] Even Gildas, the brightest star in the firmament of the sixth-century British Church, displays a very limited knowledge of works other than the Bible – Rufinus's translation of Eusebius's *Ecclesiastical History*, a few works by Jerome, the Life of Martin by Sulpicius, Cassian, tags of Vergil.[60] He cites one Pelagian work.[61] Evidence for the use of scriptural commentaries in sixth-century Britain is very limited, apart from the possibility that Pelagius's Commentary on Paul was circulating there. The writings of Faustus of Riez were also known.[62]

The literature produced in sixth-century Britain is sparse and limited in character. Gildas's *The Ruin of Britain* is atypical, not only for its style and learning, but also for its genre. Essentially, the sixth-century British Church produced only three types of writing: penitentials, monastic rules and monastic instructions in epistolary form.[63] These were the dominant genres also in the opening years of the seventh century in Ireland. To these the Irish added poems of religious instruction written in both Latin and the vernacular, for example, a poem in praise of St Patrick (*Audite omnes amantes*), Columbanus's poem *On the World's Impermanence* (in Latin),[64] possibly the *Alphabet of Piety*,[65] and the poem on Columba's virtues (*Amra Choluim Chille*),[66] the last two in Old Irish. Sermons or *Instructiones* were also introduced by Columbanus.[67] When one considers the available range of Christian literary genres, the common Celtic menu is surprisingly limited. With the exception of Columbanus's lost Psalm commentary noted above,[68] apparently very few scriptural commentaries were produced

---

[58] There are hints of the use of others writings, including Augustine's *Confessions* and the *Pastor Hermas*: see Dronke, 'St Patrick's reading', 37–8. See also Bieler, 'The place of St Patrick'. For doubts that Patrick knew Augustine's *Confessions*, see Shanzer, 'Iuvenes', 170–9.

[59] Patrick, *Confession*, IX (tr. Hood, 42).

[60] Identified by Winterbottom, *Gildas*, 156–9. For a more generous view, see Kerlouégan, *Le De excidio*, 71–100.

[61] On Virginity, VI, or alternatively, *On Bad Teachers*, XIII.1.

[62] See above, 79 n. 49.

[63] With the exception of Gildas's genuine writings, all of this material is reproduced in Bieler's *The Irish Penitentials*. One should, of course, take into account the problem of survival: see especially Sims-Williams, 'The uses'. Still, the paucity of sixth-century British material is remarkable, especially when compared to the quantity of works surviving from sixth-century Gaul and seventh-century Ireland, especially after *ca* 630.

[64] Ed. and tr. Walker, 182–5.

[65] Ed. Hull, '*Apgitir Chrábaid*'. For strictures on the date of this work see above, 99.

[66] Ed. Stokes, 'The Bodleian *Amra Choluimb Chille*'.

[67] Ed. and tr. Walker, 60–121; see Stancliffe, 'The thirteen sermons'.

[68] See 117 n. 53. In the absence of an identified work it is impossible to determine whether Columbanus's 'commentary' is a commentary in the proper sense, or simply a set of explanatory glosses typical of many Irish productions down to the

in Celtic lands before the middle of the seventh century.[69] Hagiography is also absent before that time, at least in the usual form of saints' lives replete with miracles and prodigies of all types. However, *Amra Choluim Chille* and *Audite omnes amantes*[70] enumerate the virtues and good works of Columba and Patrick respectively.[71] As already noted, the miracle-rich Life of Samson of Dol, earlier assigned to the seventh century, is now convincingly dated to the middle of the eighth. There are also no theological tracts *per se* until 655, when *On the Miracles of Holy Scripture* appeared.

What can explain the narrowness of literary interests in the pre-*Romani* Celtic world? Literacy obviously had not disappeared, despite the relative scarcity of literary remains. The explanation may lie in a deliberate decision to exclude certain types of writing. The lives of the saints were not recommended reading because they contained accounts of miracles, and miracles are, in Pelagian terms, manifestations of grace, making God a respecter of persons and overriding the natural capabilities within men. The semi-Pelagians were also averse to miracles. If one relied on a miraculous cure, one would do nothing for oneself. If one attempted to perform such a cure, one ran the risk of becoming arrogant.[72] Scriptural commentaries should be eschewed because they often contain false exegesis, and this is particularly dangerous with regard to the law – it has the potential to imperil salvation.[73] Interestingly, the Pelagians trusted a virtuous ascetic to read and interpret the scriptures for him- or herself, as the frequent citation of Psalms 1:2 shows. It would be better to read on one's own, or under the guidance of a right-minded teacher, than to employ the 'commentaries of the Catholic fathers'. There one might encounter not only the false allegorisation of the law, but also the pernicious doctrine of grace, a concept that contained the potential to undermine self-reliance and to encourage either presumption or despair. Most especially, the Pelagian elements within the Church would

---

Carolingian Age. On the general character of such readers' aids see Contreni and Ó Néill, *Glossae Divinae Historiae*, 58–72.

[69] Even this is controversial. For a positive assessment of Irish exegetical activity see Bischoff, 'Wendepunkte'; however, see Gorman, 'A critique of Bischoff's theory'. Various replies to Gorman were made: Herren, 'Irish biblical commentaries', (C.) Wright, 'Bischoff's theory', and Ó Cróinín, 'Bischoff's *Wendepunkte*'.

[70] This poem was edited by Bieler, 'The hymn of St Secundinus'; there is now an English translation by Carey, *King of Mysteries*, 147–61. For the date and authorship see Herren, 'An early Irish precursor', and Orchard, '*Audite omnes amantes*'. Orchard re-edits and translates the poem, providing additional parallels to those advanced by Bieler.

[71] A possible exception to the didactic and strictly moralising character of late sixth-to early seventh-century Irish poetry is the hymn *Precamur patrem*, anthologised in the late seventh-century Antiphonary of Bangor (ed. Warren, *Antiphonary of Bangor*, II.5–7); see Curran, *The Antiphonary of Bangor*, 50–8. This poem is translated and discussed in the Appendix. See now Herren, 'The role'.

[72] See especially Cassian, *Conferences*, XV.vi (tr. Ramsey, 541–2).

[73] For false exegesis of the law see especially *On Riches*, X.1, XI.11 (tr. Rees, *The Letters*, 187, 204).

have been anxious to prohibit the writings of Augustine, the notorious pedlar of grace. Inevitably, these were introduced into Ireland by the *Romani*.[74] Jerome found a place much earlier. Gildas knew him, and Columbanus made much fuller use of him than of Augustine.[75] Despite their strong anti-Pelagian stance, Jerome's letters and scriptural comment-aries contain much that is congenial to an effort-based asceticism.

Thus, the warring Christian, striving against the enemy to attain salva-tion, did not require a large library. The scriptures, as noted, contain the whole law of God, as well as the necessary examples of righteous behaviour. Works of instruction, such as Cassian's *Conferences* and Gildas's epistles, teach correct *conversatio*. Together with the scriptures, they instruct the reader how to avoid evil and do good. Should one happen to fall, however, medicine was available in the form of penance. The penitentials prescribe the needful physics.

Finally, we note that the writing of saints' lives did not get underway in Celtic regions until after the mid-point of the seventh century.[76] Saints' lives are, above all, affirmations of God's power to work his will through human agents. The proof of this power is in the miracles wrought by the saints, which are, in turn, imitations of the miracles wrought by Christ. It is interesting to note that the beginning of this literary genre would coincide with the consolidation of the *Romani* movement in Ireland around the middle of the seventh century, or a little before. It also may be argued that that the relatively late rise of the thaumaturgical saint's life was closely connected to a view of Christ as heroic ascetic, an image held to in opposition to that of Christ as a healer and miracle worker. The innovative character of the prose Hiberno-Latin saints' lives – Cogitosus's Life of Brigit, Muirchú's and Tírechán's Lives of Patrick and Adomnán's Life of Columba – is pointed up by comparison with the earlier poems *Amra Choluim Chille* and *Audite omnes amantes*, dating probably *ca* 600, which practically exclude miracles and concentrate on the accomplishments and virtues of Columba and Patrick, their respective subjects.[77]

The absence of miracle-oriented hagiography in the period of the common Celtic Church is consistent with the little we know about the Pelagian attitude to miracle cures. Bede tells us that Pelagian clerics of the fifth century did not engage in acts of healing, but referred requests to their

---

[74] (J.F.) Kelly, 'Augustine', 141, notes only two citations of Augustine in the writings of Columbanus. These occur in Letter IV, addressed to Pope Boniface when Columbanus was based at Bobbio and had access to a continental library. The next datable citations occur in *On the Miracles of Holy Scripture*, an 655. MacGinty, 'The treatise', I.99–109, views Pseudo-Augustine's debt to Augustine as one of general inspiration rather than direct verbal borrowing.

[75] See the index of classical and patristic sources in Walker, *Sancti Columbani Opera*, 221–2.

[76] Sharpe, *Medieval Irish Saints' Lives*, 8–18; Stancliffe, 'The miracle stories', 87.

[77] See Herren, 'The role'. It has recently been observed by Clancy, 'Columba', 3, that even for the seventh-century lives before Adomnán, 'there is a notable lack of posthumous miracles, little discussion of relics . . .'

orthodox opponents.[78] In Bede's view, this unwillingness to heal (and, particularly, to heal with the help of saints' relics) contributed to the undoing of the Pelagians and the triumph of orthodoxy.[79] The semi-Pelagians were apparently just as reticent. Their attitude, as usual, is based on the concept of spiritual training. In Cassian's Fifteenth Conference we read:

And indeed it is a greater miracle to tear out the remains of lasciviousness from one's own flesh than to cast out unclean spirits from the bodies of others. It is a more significant sign to control fierce movements of anger by the virtue of patience than to command the princes of the air. It is better to have kept devouring sadness from one's own heart than to have expelled bodily illness and fever from another's.[80]

Opposition to miracle and healings was also based on the principle that faith is purely individual and cannot be transmitted from one person to another: '. . . for when the grace of God is dispensed it is certainly not bestowed because of someone else's faith . . . but because of the person's own zeal'.[81]

Credence in miracles and belief in the power of the relics of the saints to accomplish them began with Irish visits to Rome, probably *ca* 630, and the importation into Ireland of the relics of the martyrs in the same time-frame. The evidence comes from Cummian, a decidedly *Romani* source:

And they [the Irish visitors] were in one lodging in the church of St Peter with a Greek, a Hebrew, a Scythian and an Egyptian at the same time at Easter, in which we differed by a month. And so they testified to us before the holy relics, saying, 'As far as we know, this Easter is celebrated throughout the whole world'. And we have tested that the power of God is in the relics of the holy martyrs and in the writings which they brought back. We saw with our own eyes a totally blind girl opening her eyes at these relics, and a paralytic walking and many demons cast out.[82]

This is followed by the *Book of the Angel* (*ca* 650), which makes reference to:

the blood of Jesus Christ, the redeemer of the human race, on a linen cloth, together with the relics of the saints in the southern Church, where there rest the bodies of holy men from abroad who had come with Patrick from across the sea.[83]

---

[78] Bede, *Historia Ecclesiastica*, I.18 (edd. Colgrave & Mynors, 58–9).
[79] *Ibid.*
[80] Cassian, *Conferences*, XV.viii (tr. Ramsey, 543); *Conlationes*, XV.8 (ed. Pichery, II.218): 'Et re uera maius miraculum est de propria carne fomitem eradicare luxuriae quam expellere inmundos spiritus de corporibus alienis, et magnificentius signum est uirtute patientiae truculentos motus iracundiae cohercere quam aeriis principibus imperare, plusque est excluisse edacissimos de corde proprio tristitiae morsus quam ualetudines alterius febresque corporeas expulisse . . .'
[81] Cassian, *Conferences*, XV.ii.1 (tr. Ramsey, 538); *Conlationes*, XV.2 (ed. Pichery, II.211): '. . . non pro alterius fide . . . sed pro unius cuiusque studio dei gratia dispensante conceditur'.
[82] Cummian, *Letter*, lines 280–8 (ed. and tr. Walsh & Ó Cróinín, 94–5); Latin text below, 135.
[83] *Book of the Angel*, XIX (ed. and tr. Bieler, *The Patrician Texts*, 186–9): '. . . extat sacratissimus sanguis Iesu Christi redemptoris humani generis in sacro lintiamine

While the use of primary relics of the Roman martyrs had clearly taken hold before the middle of the seventh century, there seems to have been some resistance among the Irish to venerating the primary relics of their own saints.[84] In any event, it is clear that by the middle of the seventh century the south of Ireland and Armagh were at one with the continent with respect to the veneration of martyrs' relics and even their use for healing. One might suspect that resistance to these trends in the northern churches (apart from Armagh) explains – at least in part – Pope-elect John's letter dealing with the resurgence of Pelagianism. That belief in miracles was a serious issue in seventh-century Ireland is clearly shown by *On the Miracles of Holy Scripture*, written in 655.

The sacraments

An important manifestation of Pelagian theology in the common Celtic Church is the treatment of the sacraments. Pelagius himself conceded that baptism was a manifestation of God's grace, in that it was within God's power alone to grant it to men.[85] It was absolutely essential for the forgiveness of sin, that is, the sins an individual commits during his lifetime. Indeed, there is no other kind of sin. The sin of Adam's disobedience to God's command may have been imitated by countless men, but it was not inherited.[86] The acceptance of baptism brought with it the forgiveness of sins and the commitment to sin no more. Through baptism one becomes a Christian, and, 'no Christian is allowed to sin'.[87] On this account, Pelagians were at one with those Christians before Augustine's time who believed that baptism should be deferred to a mature age (when one was less likely to sin) and only received after a suitably long preparation. They were therefore opposed to infant baptism. There is an indication, however, that Pelagians may have performed on infants a ritual that was similar to baptism, because we find what looks like a retraction in Pelagius's own *Profession of Faith*: 'We hold one baptism which we assert should be administered with the same words for infants as those used also for adults.'[88]

---

simul cum sanctorum reliquiis in aeclessia australi, ubi requiescunt corpora sanctorum peregrinorum de longue cum Patricio trans marinorum caeterorumque iustorum!'

[84] See Clancy, 'Columba', 3–6; Charles-Edwards, *Early Christian Ireland*, 348.

[85] See especially Pelagius's comment on Romans 3:24 (tr. de Bruyn, 81): 'Without the works of the law, through baptism, whereby he has freely forgiven the sins of all, though they are undeserving'; *Expositio in Romanos*, 3:24 (ed. Souter, I.32): 'Sine legis operibus per baptismum, quo omnibus non merentibus gratis peccata donauit.'

[86] See above, 71.

[87] *On Virginity*, XI.3 (tr. Rees, *The Letters*, 820).

[88] Pelagius, *Profession of Faith*, XVII (our translation); *Libellus fidei*, XVII (*PL* XLVIII.490): 'Baptisma unum tenemus quod iisdem sacramenti verbis in infantibus quibus etiam in majoribus asserimus esse celebrandum.' On Pelagius and

The ritual in question may well have been the benediction of infants or young children in lieu of baptism. If this is the case, then we have evidence for survival of this ritual in seventh-century Ireland, for the practice is condemned in a canon from the *Penitential of Cummian*:

One who instead of baptism blesses a little infant shall do penance for a year . . . or atone with bread and water. If, however, the infant dies having had such a blessing only, the homicide shall do penance according to the judgement of a council.[89]

Further, we see evidence for an insistence on the continuation of the catechumenate. This is opposed, or rather, undermined by a canon of a seventh- or eighth-century (*Romani*) synod: 'On the eighth day they are catechumens. Thereafter they are baptised on the solemn feast days of the Lord, that is at Easter, Pentecost, and Epiphany.'[90] In all probability, it was the *Hibernenses* who insisted on maintaining the age-old distinction between catechumens and fully-fledged Christians; hence the need of their *Romani* opponents to pay lip-service to the term 'catechumen', even if emptied of all content. Thus it is likely that pre-Augustinian attitudes towards baptism survived in Ireland, whether or not Pelagian teachings were the direct cause.

Penance had no sacramental standing in Pelagian theology apart from baptism, which was the ultimate token of the forgiveness of sin. It is only with reluctance that Pelagians admitted the possibility of salvation for one who had lapsed after baptism. In the *Profession of Faith* Pelagius wrote: 'A man who falls after baptism can be saved through penance, if he believes.'[91] However, such a statement is scarcely representative of Pelagian thinking on the question and must be viewed in the context of Pelagius's desire to evade condemnation. One may justifiably assume that a post-baptismal penitential rite was not a feature of any Pelagian-controlled Church, whether in Britain or elsewhere. It is therefore surprising to learn that sixth-century Britain was in all likelihood the place where a ritual of repeatable penance was created,

---

infant baptism see Ferguson, *Pelagius*, 50. For the notion that Pelagians regarded infant baptism as 'benedictory' see (J.N.D.) Kelly, *Early Christian Doctrines*, 359, with references; see also Pelikan, *The Christian Tradition*, I.316–18.

[89] Cummian, *Penitential*, XI.19 (ed. and tr. Bieler, *The Irish Penitentials*, 128–9); *Penitentialis Cummiani*, XI.19–20: '19. Benedicens infantulum uice baptismi annum . . . peniteat siue cum pana et aqua expleat. 20. Si uero mortuus fuerit infans sub tali tantum benedictione, iudicio senatus peniteat homicida ille.' See below, nn. 93, 94.

[90] *Second Synod*, XIX (ed. and tr. Bieler, *The Irish Penitentials*, 192–3); *Synodus II S.Patricii*, XIX: 'Octauo die caticumini sunt. Postea solemnitatibus Domini baptizantur, id est Pascha et pentecostem et Aepiphania.' That the text clearly refers to the age of those to be baptised is shown by the rubric: 'Qua etate baptizandi sunt.' A requirement to baptise infants on the eighth day goes back at least to Cyprian, who apparently thought that this was dangerously late. See his *Epistola* LXIV.4–5 (ed. Bayard, II.215–16) and the discussion in Pelikan, *The Christian Tradition*, I.291–2.

[91] Pelagius, *Profession of Faith*, XVIII (our translation); *Libellus fidei*, XVIII (*PL* XLVIII.490): 'Hominem, si post baptismum lapsus fuerit, per poenitentiam credhans [*sic*] posse salvari.'

and manuals were written to assist its implementation. The oldest surviving penitential book, the *Penitentialis Vinniani*, is attributed to Uinniau, who has been identified with the author of queries on monastic practice sent to Gildas and also with the teacher of Columba.[92] If these identifications withstand scrutiny, then our oldest penitential probably belongs to the mid-sixth century. Its very existence denotes the end of any possible monopoly exercised by the Pelagian party on the spirituality of the common Celtic Church. This is also shown by Canon XLVII which prescribes a penance for parents who, through their neglect allow a child to die unbaptised, thus 'occasioning the loss of a soul',[93] while Canon XLVIII censures clerics who refuse to receive a child (*paruulum*) in baptism.[94] The work concludes with a brief epilogue which employs the language of 'remedies' and 'cures' espoused by Cassian. The metaphor of sickness and remedy implies the possibility of repeated sin and the need for repeated penance.[95]

While Pelagian writers were loath to spell out specific penances for specific offences, no such reticence was to be found among the authors of the earliest British penitentials. Indeed, it is very possible that the development of the penitential handbook, with its fixed prescriptions, was a means of countering hard-line Pelagian thinking. Perhaps it was the need to satisfy the most rigorous in this sect that explains the harsh character of many of the penances imposed. We note, for example, that the 'Synod of North Britain' prescribed draconian penances for sexual sin:

Anyone who sins with a woman or with a man shall be sent away to live in a monastery of another country and shall do penance, after he has confessed, for three years in confinement; and afterwards, as a brother subject to the altar of that monastery he shall do penance at the discretion of his teacher; if he is a deacon, for one year; if a presbyter, for three years; if a bishop or abbot, for seven years, each being deprived of his order.[96]

Penances could entail exile, confinement, harsh sleeping or lodging conditions, and, almost always, an unpleasant dietary restriction such as living on bread and water. Long penances for serious sins almost invariably implied

---

[92] See 29.

[93] *Penitentialis Vinniani*, XLVII (ed. and tr. Bieler, *The Irish Penitentials*, 92–3): 'Si quis fuerit cuius paruulus absque baptismum abscesserit et per neglegentiam perierat, magnum est crimen animam perdere . . .'

[94] *Penitentialis Vinniani*, XLVIII (ed. and tr. Bieler, *The Irish Penitentials*, 92–3): 'Si autem clericus non susciperit paruulum, si ex una plebe fuerit, annum integrum peniteat cum pane et aqua.'

[95] Note that *Penitentialis Vinniani*, XLVII (ed. and tr. Bieler, *The Irish Penitentials*, 92–3) states: '. . . quia nullum crimen quod non potest redimi *quamdiu sumus in hoc corpore*'. See the useful discussion by O'Loughlin, *Celtic Theology*, 56–60.

[96] *Synod of North Britain*, I (ed. and tr. Bieler, *The Irish Penitentials*, 66–7); *Synodus Aquilonalis Britaniae*, I: 'Cum muliere uel cum uiro peccans quis expellatur ut alterius patriae cenubio uiuat, et peniteat confessus .iii. annis clausus, et postea frater illius altari subiectus anno uno diaconus, .iii. presbiter, .vii. episcopus et abbas suo quisque ordine priuatus doctoris iudicio peniteat.'

excommunication, that is, debarment from the regular church service and communion until the penance was completed.[97] Some communities provided special churches, or sections of a church, for penitents. Penance was therefore generally not regarded as a sacrament, but rather as the actions that must be performed to restore the sinner 'to the altar and table' after excommunication. By the late seventh or eighth century a *Romani* canon mentions absolution by a bishop, bringing us closer to the realm of the sacramental.[98]

In general, it would seem that penance in the common Celtic Church was designed as a kind of compromise between the unbending Pelagian principle that 'no Christian is permitted to sin' – or at least, that there are narrow limits to forgiveness – and the need to accommodate the realities of human nature. We occasionally detect in the penitentials a sensitivity to potential Pelagian criticism, as in Uinniau's surprising exegesis of Proverbs 24:16: 'Seven times a just man falleth and ariseth.' The *Penitentialis Vinniani* explains the text thus:

. . . that is, after seven years of penance he who fell can be called just and in the eighth year evil shall not lay hold of him, but for the remainder (of his life) let him preserve himself carefully lest he fall, since, as Soloman saith, 'as a dog returning to his vomit becomes odious, so is he who through his own negligence reverts to sin'.[99]

It is probably due to defensiveness such as this that penances were long and harsh. Very often they exceeded the limits of a year and thus made the demand of the (Roman-imposed) Easter duty impossible to fulfil. Yet the early canons consistently call for completion of penances prior to restoration to 'altar and table'. This shows in turn that the sacramental character of the eucharist was either less heavily valued in the period of the common Celtic Church, or that it was regarded as a mark of perfection rather than as essential spiritual food.[100] This attitude changed significantly under the *Céli Dé*, who introduced the system of commutations: short but very unpleasant penances in place of long ones. In *The Old Irish Table of Commutations* one of the principle reasons for this change was: '. . . in order to (be free to)

---

[97] The paradigm for the completion of long penances is the tale of Librán in Adomnán, *Life of Columba*, II.39 (tr. Anderson & Anderson, 421–3). See the discussion by Etchingham, *Church Organisation*, 290–1.

[98] *Second Synod*, VIII (ed. and tr. Bieler, *The Irish Penitentials*, 186–7): 'We ought to believe that those who have lapsed from the faith are not to be absolved unless they are received with imposition of hands by a bishop'; *Synodus II S.Patricii*, VIII: 'Non absoluendus autem lapsos a fide credamus nisi per inpositionem manus episcopi.' Interestingly, Augustine and other Latin Church fathers also did not refer to penance as a 'sacrament'; see Grundy, *Books*, 195 with nn. 65, 66.

[99] *Penitentialis Vinniani*, XXI (ed. and tr. Bieler, *The Irish Penitentials*, 80–1); see Latin text below, 135.

[100] A notable exception is the praise for Patrick as a priest who gave the eucharist to the faithful: *Audite omnes amantes*, 'I'-stanza (ed. and tr. Carey, 154).

approach the Body and Blood of Christ by restricting (the period of) penance'.[101]

Pelagian texts rarely mention the eucharist,[102] and there are no citations of John 6:54, 'Except you eat the flesh of the Son of Man, etc.', or John 15:1, 'I am the true vine', in either the Evans Letters or the Caspari Corpus. The omission of the first text is curiously inconsistent with Pelagian theology, because it omits a command of Christ ('go to communion or you will not be saved'). The ignoring of the eucharist by Pelagians is probably best explained by their repugnance towards the miraculous, as it constitutes a mutation of created nature, which God had proclaimed good.[103] Likewise lacking in the Pelagian corpus are the synoptic gospel accounts of Christ's institution of the eucharist: Matt. 26:26-7, Mark 14:22-5, Luke 22:19-20.

The allaying of Pelagian aversion to the miraculous may underlie the so-called 'inverted formula' of the eucharist found in a number of texts of Irish origin.[104] In this formula bread and wine are not changed into God, but God changes himself into bread and wine. A good example occurs in the First Commentary on Mark at Mark 14:22: 'He transfigures his body into the bread . . . He turns his blood into a chalice mixed with wine and water.'[105] This formula may owe its existence to a curious piece of casuistry. While God, having found created nature good, would not deign to change the true nature of bread and wine, nonetheless he, being omnipotent and not subject to the laws of nature, is free to transfigure himself in any way he chooses. The inverted formula may thus have been an attempted compromise between rigorous Pelagian naturalism and the earliest formulations of transubstantiation.

In general, one sees in the canons and spiritual writings from the period of the common Celtic Church (and sometimes even later on) a minimalist attitude towards the eucharist. It is indeed mentioned in the early penitentials, but usually in the context of rules governing infractions (spitting out

---

[101] *The Old Irish Table*, VI (tr. Binchy *apud* Bieler, *The Irish Penitentials*, 278); *De arreis*, VI (ed. Meyer, 488): '. . . ar cuinnriuch chuirp *Chríst* 7 a fhola tria cuinnriuch peinni'.

[102] Pelagius, in *To Demetrias*, V.1 (tr. Rees, *The Letters*, 40), refers to 'the Lord's sacrament' in his discussion of Melchisadek as a type of the priesthood of Christ: '[Melchisadek] expressed the mystery of the body and blood by the sacrifice of bread and wine'.

[103] See above, 72, 91-4.

[104] McNamara, 'The inverted eucharistic formula'. The 'inverted formula', of course, appears to be a variant of the idea of transubstantiation, which was not a doctrinal issue before the ninth century. However, the notion of substantial change is adumbrated in various patristic texts. See the index under 'Eucharist' in Pelikan, *The Christian Tradition*, I.

[105] *On Mark*, 14:22 (tr. Cahill, *The First Commentary*, 105); *Expositio Evangelii Marci*, 14:22 (ed. Cahill, 62): 'Transfigurat corpus suum in panem . . . format sanguinem suum in calicem uino et aqua commixtum'. For a precursor of the 'orthodox' description of the transubstantiation, see Blathmac, *Poems*, stanza 203 (ed. and tr. Carney, 68-9).

the host, vomiting the host because of drunkenness, etc.).[106] Concern for the respect of the host, it is true, implies that Mass and communion were a regular component of Christian life in Britain and Ireland in the sixth and early seventh centuries, yet one searches the early texts in vain for recommendations of frequent communion. Even the *Romani* 'Second Synod of St Patrick' provides only a vague endorsement of taking communion, though it insists on the fulfilment of the Easter obligation:

After a proving of the flesh it is to be taken, but especially on the even of Easter; for he who does not communicate at that time is not a believer. Therefore short and strict are the seasons (of penance), lest the faithful soul perish, by abstaining from the medicine for so long a time, for the Lord saith: 'Except you eat the flesh', etc.[107]

Such minimalism contrasts sharply with contemporary practice in the eastern and western rites, for which we have the seventh-century testimony of the *Penitential of Theodore*:

1. The Greeks, both clergy and laity, communicate every Sunday. Those who do not communicate for three Sundays are excommunicated according to the canons.
2. The Romans also communicate (every Sunday), if they wish; however, those who do not want to are not excommunicated.[108]

Confirmation of Theodore's testimony is provided in Walafrid Strabo's *Libellus de exordiis et incrementis quarundam in observationibus ecclesiasticis rerum* (*The Origins and Development of Some Matters relating to the Clergy*) which provides a capsule history of attitudes towards the frequency of communication.[109] Walafrid makes it plain that weekly communication had been a common practice in the Church for centuries, and daily communion had also been known for some time. He confirms Theodore's statement regarding the Greek practice of excommunication of those who fail to communicate within three Sundays. However, the only Irish penitential that repeats this injunction is the so-called *Bigotian Penitential*,[110] which is heavily dependent on Theodore, and therefore of doubtful value as an independent witness to Irish practice. A description of what was closer to the

---

[106] For example, 'Gildas', *Penitential*, VII–VIII (ed. and tr. Bieler, *The Irish Penitentials*, 60–3); Cummian, *Penitential*, XI (*ibid.*, 130–3). See Bieler's index s. *sacrificium*.

[107] *Second Synod*, XXII: 'Of taking the Eucharist after a fall' (ed. and tr. Bieler, *The Irish Penitentials*, 192–3); *Synodus II S.Patricii*, XXII: 'Post examinationem carceris [*recte*; carnis ?] sumenda est, maxime autem in nocte Paschae, in qua qui non communicat fidelis non est. Ideo breuia sunt et stricta apud eos spatia, ne anima fidelis interiat tanto tempore ieiuna medicinae, Domino dicente: *Nisi manducaueritis carnem . . .*'

[108] 'Theodore', *Penitential*, XII.1,2: 'On the communion of the Eucharist or the Sacrifice' (edd. Haddan & Stubbs, III.186): '1. Greci omni Dominico commonicant cleri et laici, et qui III. Dominicis non commonicauerint excommonicentur, sicut canones habent. 2. Romani similiter communicant qui volunt, qui autem noluerint non excommunicantur.'

[109] Walafrid Strabo, *The origins and development*, XXI (tr. Harting-Correa, 114–23).

[110] *Bigotian Penitential*, ⟨II⟩.9 (ed. Bieler, *The Irish Penitentials*, 218).

norm for the faithful laity (those living in lawful wedlock and adhering to a confessor) is given in the *Old Irish Penitential*: 'continence during the three lents of the year . . . *if* he goes to the Sacrament on Christmas Day and Easter Day and Whitsun Day'.[111]

Once again the *Céli Dé* shed light on attitudes and practices that may have been much older; some texts, as shown below, appeal to ancient tradition. A visible thread running through this literature is the notion that the eucharist is something to be given to meritorious folk and refused to the sinful and undeserving. In one work, weekly reception of the eucharist was an ideal for monks to attain to by stages:

During their first year they received it once, on the feast of Christmas. The following year they received only at Easter. The third year they received at Christmas and Easter. In the fourth year they received five times – Christmas, Epiphany, Easter, Low Sunday, and Pentecost. The fifth year they received every forty days in addition to the feasts mentioned above. In the sixth year they became monthly communicants. The following year they received once a fortnight and finally became weekly communicants.[112]

The Rule of Tallaght records a debate over the administration of *viaticum*:

The fathers of old used to say that Holy Communion should not be given to persons of imperfect life in danger of death, even when they renounced their sins. The reason was that they regarded this conversion as something inspired by fear of death, and not really an act of free will, or a desire to abandon sin.[113]

The notion that the eucharist must be merited, and that sinners should not be allowed to receive it even *in extremis*, had critics even among the semi-Pelagians. In his Twenty-third Conference Cassian quotes with approval the words of a certain Theonas:

Yet we should not keep away from the Lord's communion because we know that we are sinners, but we should hasten to it all the more avidly for the sake of our soul's healing and our spirit's purification . . .[114]

---

[111] *The Old Irish Penitential*, II.36 (tr. Binchy *apud* Bieler, *The Irish Penitentials*, 265); *The Old Irish Penitential*, II.36 (ed. Gwynn, 'An Irish penitential', 150–1) '. . . denma in trib corgusaib na bliadna . . . ma[ni] theis di sacarbaic ar notlaicc 7 caiscc 7 cengciges'. Binchy's translation depends upon the emendation of Gwynn's *mani* to *ma*. Binchy made this correction in his personal copy of Gwynn's text to which I had access. Clearly the emendation is necessary for sense (MWH).

[112] *The Rule of the Céli Dé*, XIII (tr. O'Dwyer, *Céli Dé*, 88); Irish text below, 135.

[113] Mael Ruain, *Rule of Tallaght*, XIII (tr. Ó Maidín, 103–4); (ed. Gwynn, *The Rule*, 10): 'Adeirdís na sean-aithri nar ghnath sacramuint do tabhairt don lucht neamhfhoirbthi a n-airteagal bhais ge go ttiobradaois freitech ris na peac*adh*aibh, air do mheasdaois nach dá ndeóin acht re heagla an bháis do bheirdis an freitech sin, 7 nach d'fhonn cul do chur ris na peac*adh*aibh . . .'

[114] Cassian, *Conferences*, XXIII.xxi.2 (tr. Ramsey, 812–13); *Conlationes*, XXIII.xxi.2 (ed. Pichery, III.167): 'Nec tamen ex eo debemus nos dominica communione suspendere, quia nos agnoscimus peccatores, sed ad eam magis ac magis est propter animae medicinam ac purificationem spiritus auide festinandum . . .'

Then a sharp attack on contrary minds:

These people are guilty of a more arrogant presumption than they themselves seem to avoid, because they judge themselves worthy of receiving them when they do receive them. But it is more righteous for us to receive the sacred mysteries every Sunday as a remedy for our sickness . . . than to be puffed up with a foolish attitude of heart and to believe that we are worthy to participate in them even once a year.[115]

All this suggests that some elements in the Irish Church for an extended period held attitudes towards the eucharist that differed markedly from those on the continent, both East and West. The absence of a recommendation for frequent communion, and the connection of the eucharist to the worthiness of the recipient point to a reticence to accept Christ's sacrament as freely given grace.[116] Is it too daring to suggest that the root of this attitude is Pelagian? When the Markan commentator turns to allegory to explicate the eucharist, he draws from the storehouse of Pelagian formulas: 'The bread is the present church. It is accepted in faith, blessed in number, broken in sufferings, given in examples, taken in teachings.'[117]

A *possible* shift in Irish eucharistic theology may be perceived in the 'Tract on the Mass' in the Stowe Missal, usually assigned to *ca* 800.[118] The text is, however, difficult to interpret, as it is written mostly in figurative language (using the Old Irish word *fiugor*, 'figure'), though sometimes its discourse dispenses with figurative terminology, as in section IX: 'The Host on the paten (is) Christ's Flesh on the tree of the Cross.'[119] Section XVIII is of particular interest, as it associates the confractions of the Host, placed in the shape of a cross, with the different elements of the Church community: bishops, priests, subgrades, anchorites and penitents (*aes na aithirge*), young clerics, innocent children, lawfully married folk, 'and those that go not before to communion'.[120] The importance of the text seems to lie in the emphasis it places on the reception of the eucharist and its inclusive message to the entire Church community. It is not entirely clear that it represents a

---

[115] Cassian, *Conferences*, XXIII.xxi.2 (tr. Ramsey, 812–13); Latin text below, 136.

[116] An exception is found in the inclusion of the *Hymnus quando communicant sacerdotes* in the (late) seventh-century Antiphonary of Bangor (ed. Warren, II.10–11). The hymn treats the eucharist as Christ's gift and views it as a universal means to salvation. See (J.B.) Stevenson, *The Liturgy*, lxii–lxiii.

[117] *On Mark*, 14:22 (tr. Cahill, *The First Commentary*, 104); *Expositio Evangelii Marci*, 14:22 (ed. Cahill, 62): '. . . quod est ecclesia praesens, quae accipitur in fide, benedicitur in numero, frangitur in passionibus, datur in exemplis, sumitur in doctrinis'.

[118] *The Tract on the Mass in the Stowe Missal* (edd. and tr. Stokes & Strachan, II.252–5). For a recent discussion of the text, with helpful bibliography, see O'Loughlin, *Celtic Theology*, 128–46.

[119] *The Tract on the Mass in the Stowe Missal* (edd. and tr. Stokes & Strachan, II.253): 'Indoblae forsinméis colind cr*ist* hi crann cruche.'

[120] *The Tract on the Mass in the Stowe Missal* (edd. and tr. Stokes & Strachan, II.255): '7 doaes na tet dolaim ria*m*'.

retreat from the primarily penitential language of earlier texts, or a full espousal of a theology of spiritual refreshment, though this might be argued. These two ideas seem to be held in tension in section XIX, the conclusion of the work:

This is what God deems worthy, the mind to be in the symbols of the mass, and that this be thy mind: the portion of the Host which thou receivest (to be) as it were a member of Christ from His Cross, and that there may be a cross of labour on each (in) his own course, because it unites to the crucified Body. It is not meet to swallow the particle without tasting it, as it is improper not to seek to bring savours into God's mysteries.[121]

The first part of this passage shows that the eucharist is thus absorbed into the context of the penitent's life of effort. Christ gave all men and women the example of his suffering and embodied it in his teaching. Is this the essence of one's faith? Pelagius would have nodded and smiled. However, the language of union 'with the crucified Body' and savouring 'God's mysteries' appears to point in a new direction. It represents a balance between individual effort and penance and the grace of God that flows from the sacrament.

Ostracism

The common Celtic Church was xenophobic and ostracising. It avoided, if at all possible, contact with outsiders, and it was prone to excommunicate its own members, even for minor infractions. If no Christian is permitted to sin (that is, after baptism), then true Christians must not associate with known sinners. If they do so, they sin themselves.[122] While ostracism and excommunication are enjoined in the scriptures and implemented throughout Christian history, the practice was strongly marked in the Celtic Churches of the early period. It was certainly a major issue in the sixth-century British Church. Of the ten fragments of Gildas's letters which have been preserved, three censure the excessive application of excommunication.[123]

On excommunication Gildas says:

Noah did not wish to keep his son Ham, teacher of the magic art, away from the ark or sharing his table. Abraham did not shrink from Aner and Eschcol when he was warring with the five kings. Lot did not curse the banquets of the Sodomites . . . Our

---

[121] *The Tract on the Mass in the Stowe Missal*, XVIII (edd. and tr. Stokes & Strachan, II.255): 'Iss*ed tr*a asbrig ladia menmae dobuith hifigraib i*n*offr*ind* 7 corophe tomen*m*me indrann arafoemi din obli amail bith ball dicr*ist* assachroich 7 ara*m*bé croch sa(it)hir for cach arith fein ore noenigether frisi*n*chorp crochthe. Nitechte aslocod i*n*parsa cena*m*laissiuth amal nan coer cen saigith mlas hirruna dé.' See O'Loughlin, *Celtic Theology*, 136–45.

[122] Some examples of Pelagian support for ostracism: *On Virginity*, VII.3 (Rees, *The Letters*, 77): *On the Christian Life*, IX.2 (*ibid.*, 116); *To an Older Friend*, II.1 (*ibid.*, 152); *On Riches*, XIX.3 (*ibid.*, 205–6),

[123] Gildas, *Fragments*, I, III, VII (tr. Winterbottom, 80–2).

Lord Jesus Christ did not avoid eating with publicans, so as to save all sinners and whores.[124]

In fragment VII, Gildas enunciates the principles according to which one should practice excommunication ('from the communion of our altar and table'): the offences must be proven, and they must be major.[125]

In mentioning Christ, Gildas certainly meant to appeal to the principle of the *imitatio Christi*, dear to all Christians, and also important to Pelagians.[126] However, for Pelagians, the principle of *imitatio* was always subordinate to the principle of obedience to the law. Examples were given in the scriptures to clarify the law, not to supersede it.[127] The supremacy of God's law over example is made transparent in the following passage:

I am aware that not everything which is becoming to our Lord is becoming to us, his servants; but lest we may appear to be offering an insult to the Lord by using a comparison which places him on a level with his servants, let me perhaps begin my reply to you in another fashion, Why are we born of married women, not of virgins? Or why do our dead not rise again on the third day? The lord, who forbade us to take an oath, often did so himself . . . but we servants may not swear, being forbidden to swear by the law of the Lord.[128]

Thus, even the imitation of Christ is potentially sinful, if it contravenes the law! The treatise *On Riches* explicitly mentions the error of reading the scriptures as (merely) a series of examples:

Lay nothing to the fact that at that time all things were done by way of an example, as the apostle says: 'For these things happened to them as an example for us' (I Cor.

---

[124] Gildas, *Fragments*, I (tr. Winterbottom, 80); *Fragmenta*, I (ed. Winterbottom, 143): 'De excommonicatione dicit Gildas: Non Noe Cham filium suum magicae artis scribam aut arca aut mensae communione voluit arcere. Non Abraham Aner et Hescol in debellatione quinque regum exhorruit. Non Loth Sodomitarum convivia execratus est. . . . Non dominus noster Iesus Christus publicanorum convivia devitabat, ut omnes peccatores et meretrices salvaret.'

[125] Gildas, *Fragments*, VII (tr. Winterbottom, 82); *Fragmenta*, VII (ed. Winterbottom, 145): '. . . a communicatione altaris et mensae . . .'

[126] Examples of the injunction to imitate Christ in Pelagian literature: Pelagius, *To Demetrias*, XXVII.4 (tr. Rees, *The Letters*, 67); *On the Divine Law*, IV.2 (*ibid.*, 94); *On the Christian Life*, I.1 (*ibid.*, 108), VI.1 (*ibid.*, 112–13); *To Celantia*, XII (*ibid.*, 133); *To an Older Friend*, IV (*ibid.*, 150); *On Riches*, V.3 (*ibid.*, 178–9); *On Bad Teachers*, XVIII.3 (*ibid.*, 243–4); Pelagius, *On Romans*, 4:24 (tr. de Bruyn, *Pelagius's Commentary*, 88); Pelagius, *On Romans*, 5:10 (*ibid.*, 92); Pelagius, *On Romans*, 6:11 (*ibid.*, 98); Pelagius, *On Romans*, 8:10 (*ibid.*, 108).

[127] See especially Pelagius, *On Romans*, 3:21 (tr. de Bruyn, 81): 'The righteouness which has been given to us freely by God, not acquired by our effort, has been made plain without the written law, and, having lain hidden in the law, has been revealed with greater clarity through the examples of Christ'; *Expositio in Romanos*, 3:21 (ed. Souter, I.32): 'Sine lege litterae iustitia manifesta[ta], quae nobis gratis a deo donata est, non nostro labore quaesita, et apertius per exempla Christi euidentiora patefacta, quae lateba[n]t in lege.'

[128] *On the Divine Law*, X.1 (tr. Rees, *The Letters*, 103); Latin text below, 136.

10:11). For now no man has to have his wife fashioned for him out of his rib in his sleep . . . nor must he be supplied with a concubine as well as a wife simply because Abraham had a concubine as well as a wife . . . [129]

Pelagians even went so far as to speak of the imitation of Christ and the act of shunning in a single breath:

. . . and to live, humble and gentle by the example of Christ, shunning the company of evil men to the extent that you do not even take any food with fornicators or the envious or detractors or drunkards or the grasping.[130]

Ultimately, excommunication must be performed, because the law itself enjoins it:

This the blessed apostle also makes abundantly clear by commanding that we must not even break bread with sinners, saying: 'If any one who bears the name of brother among you is guilty of immorality or greed, or is an idolater, reviler, drunkard, or robber – not even to eat with such a one' (I Cor. 5:11).[131]

As for excommunicating or ostracising for small sins, Pelagians would appeal to the principle:

But it is never a light matter to despise God even in small things, since he pays regard not only to the nature of a sin, but to the extent to which it brings contempt upon his person; and for this reason a man must attend not only to the nature of a command but to the greatness of the one who gives it.[132]

The injunction to ostracise excommunicated persons is to be found in what is probably the earliest Irish canon collection: 'If any cleric has been excommunicated by someone and some other person receives him, both

---

[129] *On Riches*, IX.3 (tr. Rees, *The Letters*, 185); *De divitiis* IX.3 (*PL supp.* I.1391): '. . .Taceo, quod illo in tempore omnia figuraliter gerebantur, dicente apostolo: *Haec enim in figura nostri contingebat illis.* Neque enim idcirco nunc cuiquam nostrum aut per soporem coniux de lateris costa . . . formanda est, aut praeter uxorem etiam concubina adhibenda . . . quia Abraham praeter uxorem concubinam habuit.'

[130] *On Virginity*, VII.3 (tr. Rees, *The Letters*, 77); *Exhortatio ad sponsam Christi*, VI (*PL* XVIII.81): '. . . et humilis ac mitis Christi vivas exemplo: malorum consortia in tantum vitans, ut eum fornicatoribus, aut avaris, aut maledicentibus, aut invidis, aut detractoribus, aut ebriosis, aut rapacibus nec cibum capias'.

[131] *On the Christian Life*, IX.2 (tr. Rees, *The Letters*, 116); *De vita christiana*, IX.2 (*PL* XL.1039): 'Hoc et beatus Apostolus evidentur ostendit, qui nec panes cum peccatoribus frangi præcepit, dicens: *Si quis frater cognominatur inter vos fornicator, aut avarus, aut idolis serviens, aut maledicus, aut ebriosus, aut rapax, cum ejusmodi nec cibum sumere.*'

[132] *On the Divine Law*, V.1 (tr. Rees, *The Letters*, 95); *De divina lege*, V.1 (*PL* XXX.110): 'Quamquam leve numquam ait, Deum etiam in exigua contemnere, qui non tantum ad qualitatem peccati respicit, sed ad personæ contemptum. Propter quod homini non solum intendendum est, quale sit quod jubetur, sed quantus sit ille qui jubet.' Ironically, Gildas cited approvingly a similar passage; see above, p. 81.

are to perform the same penance.' And: 'If a Christian has been excommunicated, not even his alms are to be accepted.'[133]

Despite the efforts of such writers as Gildas and Uinniau to create a more inclusive and forgiving atmosphere in the common Celtic Church, a culture of purity and exclusivity persisted. Evidence for its survival after the dissolution of the common Celtic Church comes from late seventh-century Britain. Aldhelm, writing to King Geraint and the clergy of Dyfed, complained:

> How very different from the Catholic Faith and what a departure from the evangelical tradition it is that bishops of Dyfed, on the other side of the strait of the River Severn, glorying in the private purity of their own way of life, detest our communion to such a great extent that they disdain equally to celebrate the divine offices in church with us and to take courses of food at table for the sake of charity . . . But indeed, should any of us, I mean Catholics, go to them for the purpose of habitation, they do not deign to admit us to the company of their brotherhood until we have been compelled to spend the space of forty days in penance.[134]

We have painted here a picture of a Church that was profoundly scripturalist, in the sense that no authority superseded the text of the Bible, not even the Church of Rome. The scriptures contain the entire law (and will) of God, and are given to men for their salvation. The laws of both testaments are (in principle) to be observed without exception, small commands as well as great. On account of the authority of the scriptures one observes the Pasch on the fourteenth moon, not the fifteenth. On the same account one avoids nearly all activity on the sabbath day, which is a Saturday. The scriptures also demanded tithes. Moreover, we may well imagine (although the evidence is only negative) that on account of the scriptures, no one was allowed to make a graven image of anything on heaven or earth or in the waters or under the earth (Exod. 20:21).[135] In time adjustments were made. Easter was to be celebrated always on a Sunday, although this would occasionally rather than regularly occur on the fourteenth moon, and the sabbath (Saturday) prohibitions were moved to Sunday. Dietary restrictions were generalised and adapted to the requirements of local economies; graven images were introduced. Still one sees an attempt to bend the letter of the scriptures as little as possible.

We have noted other characteristics as well. These can generally be subsumed under the category 'devaluation of grace'. The common Celtic Church which we have posited eschewed the miraculous and discouraged involvement with it, whether this entailed performing miraculous cures or simply reading about them. It also took a restrictive view of the role of the

---

[133] *First Synod*, XI–XII (ed. and tr. Bieler, *The Irish Penitentials*, 56–7); *Synodus I S.Patricii*, XI–XII: '11. Quicumque clericus ab aliquo excommunicatus fuerit et alius eum susciperit, ambo coaequali penitentia utantur. 12. Quicumque Christianus excominicatus fuerit, nec eius elimosina recipiatur.'

[134] Aldhelm, *Letter* IV (tr. Lapidge & Herren, 158). Latin text below, 136.

[135] See the discussion in Chapter VI, 190–1.

sacraments, which it viewed not as panaceas for human frailty, but rather as symbols of the merits of human nature. One 'merits' baptism only after a long period of preparation as a catechumen; likewise, one approaches the eucharist in stages related to experience and achievement. There may have been a spiritual elite, located in the clergy and in the monastic element (the 'hundredfold'), but there was no elect. All who were baptised could be saved through faith and the merits of good works; those who fell could be saved through faith and penance.

Gradually, infant baptism took its place alongside the older practice of a long catechumenate preceding adult baptism, and a repeatable ritual of penance for post-baptismal sins appears to have been well established by the sixth century. But infant baptism was not accepted in all quarters, as a number of canons prove, and the belief that there were limits to the repeatability of penance seems to have persisted. Even when the common Celtic Church seems to have overcome the hegemony of the Pelagian party, it never completely managed to eradicate Pelagian ways of thinking. Lacking a common government, there was no single set of rules in force throughout the areas concerned. Local synods produced local sets of canons, and every *abbas* was master in his own house – 'tot abbates, quot regulae'. But beneath this real diversity was an equally real theological unity that affirmed the ability of every human being to achieve his or her own salvation through good works and strict obedience to the law. What place was there for Christ in all this?

Additional Texts

20. Adomnán, *Vita Columbae*, CXXVIb–CXXVIIa (edd. Anderson & Anderson, 522): 'Haec in sacris voluminibus dies sabbatum nuncupatur, quod interpraetatur requies. Et vere mihi est sabbatum haec hodierna, quia hujus praesentis laboriosae vitae / mihi ultima est, in qua post meas laborationum molestias sabatizo. Et hac sequenti media venerabili dominica nocte, secundum eloquia scripturarum, patrum gradiar viam. Jam enim dominus meus Jesus Christus me invitare dignatur'.

29. Columbanus, *Epistulae*, I.4 (ed. Walker, 6): 'Cum Iudaeis Pascha facere non debemus? Quid ad rem pertinet? numquid Iudaei reprobi Pascha facere credendi sunt nunc, utpote sine templo, extra Ierusalem, Christo tunc figurato ab eis crucifixo? aut numquid ipsorum esse recte credendum est decimae quartae lunae Pascha, et non potius Dei ipsius instituendis Phase esse fatendum est, scientisque solius ad purum quo mysterio decima quarta luna ad transcensum electa est?'

32. *De sollemnitatibus*, V (ed. Walker, 204): 'Hoc autem fortasse significare potest, ut quia nos in fine saeculi trinae invocationis sacramento sumus consecrati – tuba praedicationis, evangelii fide, et aspersione sanguinis Iesu Christi, in qua vera propitiatio est – finito legis tempore, discere non cessemus, et, congregatis novis bonorum operum fructibus, ab omni opere

malo quieti, per septiformis spiritus gratiam persecutione sustentata, in octavae beatitudinis numerum pervenire mereamur.'

35. *De sollemnitatibus*, VII (ed. Walker, 204, 206): 'De sacrificiis pauca dicere decreveram, quae cum hostiae veri pontificis in se figuram continent, a nobis etiam Domino spiritaliter offeri debent. Per vitulum enim labor noster, per ovem innocentia, per hircum mortificatio fornicariae voluptatis, per capram, quae in sublimi pastu pascitur, vita theorica, per arietem opus praedicationis quae agnos bono pastori generat, per turturem castitas solitariae mentis nemini praeter Christum iunctae, per columbam perspicacior intuitus sacramentorum, per panem soliditas praeceptorum, per similam sinceritas vitae, per vinum et sal veritas praedicationis, per oleum fomenta caritatis intelliguntur. Quae omnia sive festa sive sacrificia in uno loco celebrari et offerri lex iubet, quia tunc omnia prosunt, cum in unitate ecclesiae sine ullo schismatis errore peraguntur.'

39. Hieronymus, *Epistolae*, CXXXIII (*PL* XXII.1157–8): 'Et ad extremum quod solet nobis objicere contubernalis vester qua ratione clemens, et misericors. Deus ab Adam usque ad Moysen, et a Moyse usque ad adventum Christi passus sit universas gentes perire ignorantia Legis et mandatorum Dei. Neque enim Britannia fertilis provincia tyrannorum, et Scoticae gentes, omnesque usque as Oceanum per circuitum barbarae nationes Moysen Prophetasque cognoverant. Quid necesse fuit eum in ultimo venire tempore . . .?'

82. Cummian, *Letter*, lines 280–8 (ed. and tr. Walsh & Ó Cróinín, 94–5): 'Et in uno hospicio cum Greco et Hebreo, Scitha et Aegiptiaco in aecclesia sancti Petri simul in pascha, in quo mense integro disiuncti sumus, fuerunt. Et ante sancta sic testati sunt nostris, dicentes: "Per totum orbem terrarum hoc pascha, ut scimus, celebratur". Et nos i⟨n r⟩eliquiis sanctorum martyrum et scripturis quas attulerunt probauimus inesse uirtutem Dei. Uidimus oculis nostris puellam caecam omnino ad has reliquias oculos aperientem, et paraliticum ambulantem, et multa demonia eiecta.'

99. *Penitentialis Vinniani*, XXI (ed. Bieler, *The Irish Penitentials*, 80–1): '*Septies cadit iustus et resurgit*, id est post ⟨septem⟩ annos penitentie potest iustus uocari qui cecidit et in octauo non obtinebit eum malum, sed de cetero seruet se fortiter ne cadat, quia, sicut Solamon dicit, *sicut canes* [sic] *reuertens ad uomitum suum hodibilis fit ita qui* per neglegentiam suam *reuertitur ad peccatum suum*.'

112. *Rule of the Céli Dé*, XIII (ed. Gwynn, *The Rule*, 66, 68): 'Inti teti *prius* do midnocht, do shacarbaicc namá theit 7 ni théit do chailech, 7 ni theit *interum usque ad finem anni*. Teit iarum di midnocht di[a] bliadna, 7 do churp na cásc arabarach. *Tertia uice*, di midnocht 7 di churp na casc 7 notlac *Tertia uice*, ar notlaic 7 dí cháisc 7 cingcedis. *Quinto anno*, ar sollamnu 7 cind .xl. oidche beos. *Sexto anno*, cind cech mís. *Septimo anno*, cind cech coecthiges. *Post .uii. anno*[s] is and teit cech domnaig.'

115. Cassian, *Conlationes*, XXIII.xxi.2 (ed. Pichery, III.167–8): 'Qui profecto maiorem arrogantiae praesumptionem, quam declinare sibi uidentur, incurrunt, quia uel tunc cum ea percipiunt dignos se esse perceptione diiudicant. Multo autem iustius est ut cum hac cordis humilitate, qua credimus et fatemur illa sacrosancta mysteria numquam pro merito nos posse contingere . . . quam ut uana persuasione cordis elati uel post annum dignos eorum participio nos esse credamus.'

128. *De divina lege*, X (*PL* XXX.116): 'Scio primum non omnia nobis convenire servis, quæ Domino conveniunt, ne in comparatione famulorum, Domini videatur injuria. Alioquin forsitan reclamare incipiamus: cur non de virginibus, sed de mulieribus generamur? Juravit, scio, saepe Dominus, qui nos jurare prohibuit . . . nobis potest, juravit Dominus quasi Dominus, quem jurare nemo prohibeat: nobis quasi servis jurare non licet, qui Domini nostri lege jurare vetamur.'

134. Aldhelm, *Letter* IV (ed. Ehwald, 484): 'Illud vero quam valde a fide catholica discrepat et ab evangelica traditione discordat, quod ultra Sabrinae fluminis fretum Demetarum sacerdotes de privata propriae conversationis munditia gloriantes nostram communionem magnopere abominantur in tantum, ut nec in ecclesia nobiscum orationum officia celebrare nec ad mensam ciborum fercula pro caritatis gratia pariter percipere dignentur! . . . Ast vero, si quilibet de nostris id est catholicis ad eos habitandi gratia perrexerint, non prius ad consortium sodalitatis suae adsciscere dignantur, quam quadraginta dierum spatia in penitendo peragere compellantur.'

V

CHRIST REVEALED IN THE TEXTS

A broad range of Christological images was available in the British Isles in the fifth to tenth centuries. Some of these belonged to Christianity of every period, namely, Christ the Judge and Christ the Wonder-Worker. Others were peculiar to certain times and places; for example, the image of Christ the true Sun, a favourite image of the late Roman world, was utilised by some of the earliest Insular writers.[1] The kingship of Christ, ambiguous in the gospels, took on broader form in the time of Constantine as Christ 'king of kings',[2] then narrowed again to simple kingship – or high kingship – in the barbarian realms. The notion of the ascetic Christ, Christ crucified or Christ the Perfect Monk,[3] was emphasised in the fourth century and became a central image of the middle ages. All of these have some foundation in the canonical gospels. Out of the apocryphal writings came the tale of the harrowing of hell, which gave rise to the Heroic Christ. The apocrypha must also be credited for broadening the image of Christ the Wonder-Worker.

Clearly, none of these images had its origins in the Insular world (including the period of the common Celtic Church). However, inevitably, the Insular world favoured some images above others, and in some cases even imparted to them a peculiarly Insular form. Here we have selected four images for special consideration: Christ the Perfect Monk, the Heroic Christ, Christ the Wonder-Worker, and Christ the Judge. These images function together in a kind of symbiosis. The Christ who will judge us at the end of the world has also given us a model for our salvation: Christ the Perfect Monk. Up until the end of our lives it is possible to follow Christ as our guide and to invoke his aid. Only when we are no longer in our present bodies must we fear him as our Judge. In between these two are images representing different aspects of the supernatural: God's redemptive aid and his power to heal. Thus Christ moves from the realm of the human and accessible through the heroic and beneficent to the divine and transcendent being who is beyond all supplication.

The most substantial and enduring images of the common Celtic Church, and indeed of the Insular world, were the first and last of these. Only by becoming Christ the Perfect Monk in time will it be possible to fulfil all the commands of the law and thus successfully evade the terrible censure of

---

[1] For example, Patrick, *Confession*, LIX (tr. Hood, 34); Gildas, *The Ruin*, VIII (tr. Winterbottom, 18).

[2] Pelikan, *Christ*, 46–56.

[3] *Ibid.*, 95–121.

Christ the Judge at the end of time. The Heroic Christ and Christ the Wonder-Worker are images created in reaction to the narrowness of Christ the Perfect Monk – the protest of grace against unlimited self-reliance. The harrower of hell is, in principle, a particularly un-Pelagian image of Christ, since the redemptive act of harrowing denies that the just who lived before Christ were capable of saving themselves. A wonder-working Christ is just as bad, since he is at odds with the Christ who assisted in creating the good nature of the world. Yet these 'newer' images of grace do not replace the 'old' image of asceticism and effort. Rather, they exist with it in complementarity, if not in total harmony.

All imaging of Christ is necessarily based on a selective reading of the canonical or apocryphal scriptures. Each image requires that some texts be highlighted, others ignored. The common Celtic Church, whose theology fell into the Pelagian to semi-Pelagian spectrum that we have described, emphasised Christ's acts of asceticism and his role as judge of all mankind at the end of the world. It also stressed his position as teacher and lawgiver, and downplayed or ignored entirely his thaumaturgical acts, including the resurrection. As we have seen, there appears to have been confusion as to which event of religious history was commemorated at Easter: was the *paschal* celebration a re-enactment of Christ's sacrifice prefigured by the *paschal* lamb (and the Jewish passover), or was it specifically the anniversary of his resurrection from the dead? If the latter, did Christ raise himself, or was he raised by the Father? A poem on the life of Christ, widely attributed to Hilary of Poitiers, is preserved in the late seventh-century Antiphonary of Bangor. In stanza XXVIII of this *Hymnus Sancti Hilarii de Christo* we read: 'He announces to the apostles that on the third day he returned from the dead, raised by his Father's right hand.'[4] This formulation of the resurrection is compatible with Pelagius's own exegesis of the event given in his Commentary on Romans.[5] While this formula does not deny Christ's resurrection in an absolute sense, it undermines his image as a wonderworker, as rising from the dead is the greatest wonder of all.

Given the small body of texts that survives from the period of the common Celtic Church, it is difficult to establish with certainty the point at which Christ's resurrection, as well as his other miracles, came to the foreground in either or Britain and Ireland. There is no question of their ever having been categorically denied; rather, it is a matter of their not being openly promulgated in works of a didactic character. Gildas, for example, whose ample work *The Ruin of Britain* is a veritable *catena* of biblical texts from chapter XXXVII to the end at chapter CX, refers to the resurrection only

---

[4] *Hymnus Sancti Hilarii*, XXVIII (ed. Warren, *Antiphonary of Bangor*, II.4):
> Seque a mortuis paterna
> Suscitatum dextera
> Tertia die redisse
> Nuntiat apostolis.

See the discussion of this hymn by Curran, *The Antiphonary*, 22–34. I am not persuaded by his arguments that the work is Irish (MWH).

[5] Above, 75–6. See also Danielou, *Théologie*, 109–10.

once, citing I Peter 1:3–5.[6] Nearly all of the other texts he uses are concerned with obedience to God's law, warnings of punishment for disobedience, the imitation of Christ, giving good example and the like. Texts dealing with miraculous occurrences are conspicuous by their absence. The poem in praise of St Patrick, *Audite omnes amantes*, says nothing of Christ's resurrection and mentions only the miracles that serve as figures of the eucharist.[7] A mixed case is the hymn *Precamur patrem*, which lists some of Christ's major miracles and treats them factually, but neglects any mention of the canonical resurrection.[8] Although this work has been ascribed to Columbanus, it should be noted that Columbanus, one of the last voices of the common Celtic Church, never discusses miracles in his genuine works, and mentions the resurrection of Christ only in the context of the Easter reckoning.

If the Commentary on Mark attributed to a certain Cummian is indeed Irish and written in the fourth or fifth decade of the seventh century, as we think likely,[9] then we may have in it a discernible turning point in respect of Christ's miracles and his resurrection. The author devotes an entire chapter to an exposition of Mark's account of the resurrection.[10] No attempt is made to subordinate the resurrection to Christ's sacrifice, or to portray it in a reductive way, that is, as the action of the Father upon the Son. Moreover, throughout the commentary, miracles are treated as real events, and not merely as figures of the sacraments or the law. The validation of Christ's canonically attested miracles paves the way for the introduction of miracle-filled saints' lives into Ireland in the ensuing decades.

Ironically, however, at the very point when Christ's resurrection is accorded full recognition,[11] it was forced into the background once again by the widespread enthusiasm accorded to the aprocryphal motif of the harrowing of hell. While the canonical resurrection and the harrowing can be made compatible in creeds, the two events sit uneasily together when combined in a narrative. By interpolating the harrowing into the canonical account, Christ is made to get out of his tomb, descend into hell, rescue the just souls, take them to heaven, then climb back into his tomb just in the nick of time to rise at dawn on Sunday. Given this exhausting scenario, it must have been tempting for some Irish Christians to simplify the sacred narrative by conflating Christ's resurrection – and even his ascension – with the harrowing (!), using this logic: in order to harrow hell, Christ, when he brought the just souls to heaven, had already ascended. Why would he have to *rise* from his tomb? Why would he have gone back into it? And why

[6] Gildas, *The Ruin*, CVI.2 (ed. and tr. Winterbottom, 76, 139).
[7] For the early date of this poem see Herren, 'An early Irish precursor', 97; for miracles see Herren, 'The role'.
[8] See Appendix, 284–8.
[9] See above, 89 n. 105.
[10] *The First Commentary*, XVI (tr. Cahill, 127–31); *Expositio Evangelii Marci*, XVI (ed. Cahill, 78–83).
[11] Several collects venerating the resurrection and linking Christ's resurrection to ours are included in the Antiphonary of Bangor. For a discussion of these and their possible association to Spanish collects see Curran, *The Antiphonary*, 140–1.

would he have returned to earth just to ascend all over again? Why not excise the redundant elements in the conflated account? A simplification of sacred history of this kind seems to underly the narrative of Christ's life found in *Precamur patrem.*

The reading of the gospels – and the consequent imaging of Christ – remained a selective affair. In the period of the common Celtic Church discussion of Christ's miracles and resurrection was generally avoided. In the post-dissolution period, miracles and the resurrection were quickly accorded a place, in Romanised areas; yet for some, the canonical account of the resurrection seemed to have slipped out of focus. In its stead, in clear view, stood the motif of the harrowing of hell, which compactly embraced Christ's resurrection and ascension, and may even have comprised the redemption.

Christ the Perfect Monk

The canonical gospels provide plentiful support for the Christ who privileged the ascetic life and bade others to follow him. At Matt. 16:24 (Mark 8:34) Christ gave the ultimate definition of discipleship: 'If any man come after me, let him deny himself, take up his cross and follow me.' The cross has nearly always been the central symbol of Christianity, but it can be interpreted in two very different ways: as the means by which the grace of the Redemption flowed to the world, or, as the ultimate symbol of self-mortification. The first interpretation looks to grace, the second, to effort. The entirety of the life of Christ might be read as an example of self-mortification, and a summons to the life of effort according to Christ, 'by whom the world is crucified to me and I to the world' (Gal. 6:14). As Columbanus declared:

. . . for this is the truth of the gospel, that the true disciples of Christ crucified should follow him with the cross. A great example has been shown, a great mystery has been declared; the Son of God willingly . . . mounted the cross as a criminal, leaving to us, as it is written, an example that we should follow his footsteps.[12]

The gospels may also be scanned for evidence that Christ privileged the ascetic life above the ministry. Christ's public life was preceded by a forty-day fast in the desert and ended in crucifixion. His ministry was punctuated by brief disappearances for the sake of prayer (for example, Matt. 14:23), and before his death on the cross he deserted his disciples to pray alone (Matt. 26:36). In one gospel account, Jesus appears to resist the start of his ministry: 'My hour is not yet come' (John 2:4). In other places he is portrayed as fleeing the crowds to pray (Luke 5:16). Notably, the man

---

[12] Columbanus, *Letters*, IV.6 (ed. and tr. Walker, 30–1): '. . . haec est enim veritas evangelii, ut veri Christi crucifixi discipuli eum sequantur cum cruce. Grande exemplum ostensum est, grande sacramentum declaratum est: Dei filius voluntarius . . . crucem ascendit ut reus, *relinquens nobis*, ut scriptum est, *exemplum, ut sequamur vestigia eius.*'

chosen to prepare the way of Christ is portrayed as a solitary preaching in the desert. Matthew (3:4) describes John the Baptist as follows: 'And the same John had his garment of camels' hair, and a leathern girdle about his loins; and his meat was locusts and wild honey.'

We have argued that the monastic life, understood as the *vita perfecta*, represented the apex of Christian aspirations in the Insular world. For nearly all, it must have seemed the surest road to salvation, and some would have said the *only* road. The elevation of monastic *conversatio* above other forms of life can be found in the exegesis of the New Testament. Commenting on Mark 1:45 ('but he was in the desert places') the first Markan commentator writes:

Certainly Jesus was not made known to all those who in wide-open places serve their own praises and wishes. However, he does show himself to those who, like Peter, go out into the desert places which the Lord chose for prayer and for feeding the people, who forsake the love of the world and who give up everything they possess, so that they may say, 'The Lord is my inheritance' (Ps. 119:57).[13]

And, in an Irish commentary on Luke:

The New Testament takes its origin from the desert, namely from John and from Jesus. It was a new event to fast and preach in the desert. And the holy monks followed this rule of the desert. Thus it behooves us to flee the crowds of vices and to enter the secrets of perfection.[14]

Christ's – and hence, our – crucifixion to the world can be derived from the gospels in two opposing ways. The first is restrictive. Christ's purely penitential acts must be seen as overriding everything else. His fasting in the desert, his flight from crowds, his engagement in prayer, and his suffering are what really matter. The rest is distraction. The second view is inclusive. Penitence embraces not only acts of mortification and prayer performed in solitude, it also encompasses acts performed on behalf of the spiritual welfare of others. The first view is propounded most eloquently by Cassian. For him, acts of mortification were not an end in themselves, but rather the means by which the striving monk attained to the contemplation of God. If the contemplation of God is the most perfect activity available to humans in this life, why should one who practises it interrupt the joy for the sake of other things, even if the actions are beneficial? In his exposition of the gospel account of Martha and Mary Cassian writes:

Martha and Mary are very beautifully portrayed in the Gospel as examples of this attitude and manner of behavior. For although Martha was indeed devoting herself to a holy service, ministering as she was to the Lord himself and to his disciples, while

---

[13] *On Mark*, 1:45 (tr. Cahill, *The First Commentary*, 40); Latin text below, 178.

[14] *On Luke* (tr. Meyvaert, 'A new perspective', 133); *Commentatio in Lucam*, IV.1 (ed. (J.F.) Kelly, *Scriptores Hiberniae Minores*, 29): 'A deserto nouum testamentum oritur, id est, ab Iohanne et Christo. Quod res noua erat ieiunia et praedicatio in deserto. Et hanc deserti regulam sancti monachi sequebantur. Bene ad nos conuenit turbas uitiorum fugire et secreta perfectionis adire.' For the Irish origin of this text see Bischoff, 'Wendepunkte', 261–2.

Mary was intent only on spiritual teaching and was clinging to Jesus's feet, which she was kissing and anointing with the ointment of a good confession, yet it was she whom the Lord preferred, because she chose the better part, and one which could not be taken from her.[15]

The inclusive view, that the penitential life might combine mortification with compassion for one's neighbour, is expressed in a seventh-century text known as the *Cambrai Homily*, written in a mixture of archaic Old Irish and Latin. Commenting on the words of Matt. 16:24, 'If any man come after me', etc., the author writes:

... we carry the cross of Christ in two ways, both when we mortify the body through fasting, and when, out of compassion for him we regard the needs of our neighbour as our own. A person who has compassion for the needs of his neighbour truly carries the cross in his heart, as Paul says: 'Bear one another's burdens, and so fulfil the law of Christ' (Gal. 6:2).[16]

The notion that the penitential life must embrace a concern for the spiritual welfare of others also finds support in the writings of Gregory the Great. Here Gregory joins contemplation with spiritual good works:

For unless holy preachers were to descend from that boundlessness of inward contemplation that they embrace, by bending, as it were, to our infirmity with humble preaching, they would surely never beget sons in the faith.[17]

Bede, doubtless drawing on Gregory, forges a similar link between contemplation and public ministry:

And when [teachers] reveal publicly to the faithful what they have seen in private, they fill all the inner recesses of the temple as windows do with the sunlight they let in.[18]

Here it should be pointed out that Gregory and Bede drew a line between contemplation and spiritual good works, whereas the (Irish) Cambrai

---

[15] Cassian, *Conferences*, I.viii.2–3 (tr. Ramsey, 147); Latin text below, 178.
[16] *The Cambrai Homily*, fos. 37c–d (tr. Ó Maidín, 140); (edd. Stokes & Strachan, II.245): '. . . duobus modis crucem Domini baiulamus, cum aut per abstinentiam carnem efficiamus, aut per conpassionem proximi necessitatem illius nostram esse putamus; qui enim dolorem exhibet in aliena necessitate crucem portat in mente, ut Paulus ait: portate onera uestra inuicem, sic adimplebitis legem Christi . . .' For this work see Stancliffe, 'Red, white and blue martyrdom', 21–3.
[17] Gregory, *Moral Interpretation of Job*, XXX.13.48 (tr. DeGregorio, 27–8); *Moralia in Iob*, XXX.xiii.48 (ed. Adriaen, 1523): 'Nisi enim praedicatores sancti ab illa immensitate contemplationis internae quam capiunt, ad infirmitatem nostram humillima praedicatione quasi quadam incuruatione descenderent, numquam utique in fide filios procrearent.' An abbreviation of this work was made in Ireland around the middle of the seventh century by Laidcenn of Clonfert-Mulloe (ed. Adriaen, *Egloga*).
[18] Bede, *On the Temple*, I (tr. DeGregorio, 29); *De templo*, I (ed. Hurst, *Bedae Opera Exegetica*, IIA, 162): 'Qui dum ea quae in occulto uident publice fidelibus pandunt quasi suscepto lumine solis fenestrae cuncta templi penetralia replent.'

homilist distinguished between bodily mortification and compassion for one's neighbour, each being a type of penance. These separate classifications need to be related to the concept of the *imitatio Christi*. The evangelical accounts portray Christ fasting and praying in solitude, and they show him teaching and ministering to the people. But did the evangelists depict Christ in contemplation? Bede apparently thought so:

The Lord in the midst of preaching and administering spiritual goods to mankind removed his mind's eye from external things and directed it to the contemplation of both heavenly and internal light.[19]

Of course, one is free to believe that Christ, when he prayed in solitude, also engaged in contemplation. Yet the concept of contemplation, a spiritual activity which unites man to God, was in all probability foreign to the framers of the gospels. Its projection upon Christ is the work of the Greek fathers and their western spokesman John Cassian, who wrote in his First Conference (quoting Abbot Germanus):

You see, then, that the Lord considered the chief good to reside in *theoria* alone – that is, in divine contemplation. Hence we take the view that the other virtues, although we consider them necessary and useful and good, are to be accounted secondary, because they are all practised for the purpose of obtaining this one.[20]

It would seem that Columbanus in his *Monk's Rule* followed Cassian's general outline in positing 'three perfections', leading to 'affection for things divine':

Thus then nakedness and disdain of riches are the first perfection of monks, but the second is the purging of vices, the third the most perfect and perpetual love of God and unceasing affection for things divine.[21]

In his little poem *On the World's Impermanence* Columbanus lists the three impediments to the three perfections in the same order as in the *Rule*:

> What to bestow for Christ
> they will not, all misers
> lose out of season . . .

[19] Bede, *Commentary on Samuel*, I (our translation); *Commentatio in Samuhel*, I (ed. Hurst, *Bedae Opera Exegetica*, II.35): 'Dominus inter praedicandum ministrandumque spiritalia mortalibus suspensum ab exterioribus oculum mentis in supernae atque intimae lucis contemplatione defigebat.'

[20] Cassian, *Conferences*, I.viii.2–3 (tr. Ramsey, 47); *Conlationes*, I.viii.2–3 (ed. Pichery, I.86): 'Uidetis ergo principale bonum in theoria sola, id est in contemplatione diuina dominum posuisse. Unde ceteras uirtutes, licet necessarias et utiles bonasque pronuntiemus, secundo tamen gradu censendas esse decernimus, quia universae huius unius patrantur obtentu.' For Columbanus's use of Cassian, see Stancliffe, 'The thirteen sermons', 105.

[21] Columbanus, *Monks' Rule*, IV (ed. and tr. Walker, 126–7); *Regulae*, IV: 'Ideo ergo nuditas et facultatum contemptus prima perfectio est monachorum, secunda vero purgatio vitiorum, tertia perfectissima dei continuata dilectio ac divinorum iugis amor . . .'

Beware, my little son,
the forms of women,
through whom death enters,
no light destruction . . .

From earthly things lift up
your heart's eyes;
love the most loving hosts of angels . . .[22]

It is not too speculative to assume that Columbanus's 'first and second perfections' were practised for the sake of the third, which approximates Cassian's (and Germanus's) 'prime good: contemplation'.

It is tempting to equate Columbanus's 'affection for things divine' with contemplation; but this is apparently not contemplation in any intellectual or mystical sense:

Therefore seek the supreme wisdom, not by verbal debate, but by the perfection of a good life, not with the tongue but with the faith which issues from singleness of heart . . .[23]

Elsewhere Columbanus states that the contemplation of God is possible only through the contemplation of his creation:

Seek no farther concerning God; for those who wish to know the great deep must first review the natural world. For knowledge of the Trinity is properly likened to the depths of the sea . . . If then a man wishes to know the deepest ocean of divine understanding, let him first if he is able scan that visible sea, and the less he finds himself to understand of those creatures which lurk between the waves, the more let him realise that he can know less of the depths of the Creator . . .[24]

In the end, it must be admitted that little more turns upon the words 'affection for things divine' than the desire for heaven, the reverse side of the coin bearing the inscription 'avoid hell'. God's creation cannot be fathomed, much less God himself. The direct contemplation of God is therefore futile. In *Sermon III*, Columbanus proceeds: 'What then are we to do? Let us love and seek them (namely, good and eternal things) even when unknown, lest perhaps we neglect them and lose them forever.'[25] In other words, put your trust in heaven, and devote your whole life to actions that will lead you there. These actions are nothing else than self-mortification, 'dying to oneself'. The purpose of this life is to do penance, while there is still time!

---

[22] Columbanus, *On the World's Impermanence* (tr. Walker, 182–5). Latin text below, 178. On Columbanus's authorship of this poem see Schaller, 'De mundi transitu', 254, who noted parallels in content and style between the poem and the *Sermons* (*Instructiones*).

[23] Columbanus, *Sermons*, I.5 (ed. and tr. Walker, 64–5); *Instructiones*, I.5: 'Quaere ergo scientiam summam non verborum disputatione sed morum bonorum perfectione, non lingua sed fide, quae de cordis simplicitate procedit . . .'

[24] Columbanus, *Sermons*, I.4 (tr. Walker, 65); Latin text below, 178–9.

[25] Columbanus, *Sermons*, III.3 (ed. and tr. Walker, 76–7); *Instructiones*, III.3: 'Quid ergo faciemus? Vel ignota amemus et quaeramus, ne forte in perpetuum ea ignoremus et perdamus . . .'

The life of angels is not on this earth but in heaven, and there is little place for the kingdom of heaven on earth.[26] In place of Cassian's *theoria* stands only *askesis* – monastic discipline. One can imitate Christ's *askesis*, but not his imputed contemplative prayer. However, in his last two sermons Columbanus shows that he has received at least a glimpse of the mystical ideal of unity with God in this life. A passage in *Sermon XII* is particularly instructive:

> . . . and let us unweariedly beseech, request, and pray for the unspeakable mercy of the righteous and good God from the bottom of our heart through Jesus Christ his Son, that he may deign so to inspire us with His love, that he join us to Him for eternity, weld us together inseparably, raise us from the ground, unite our senses to heaven all the time that we are stationed in this body of death . . .[27]

Note, however, that even this passage occurs in the context of a warning about the final judgement. Similarly, one should remark that while the earliest account of the life of Columba records his conversations with angels[28] and his access to a vision of the Godhead,[29] the same work informs us that his mission to Alba was conducted not out of love of the divinity, but 'for dread of the infernal regions'.[30]

Bede, who was indebted to Gregory, and doubtless influenced by Cassian also made the attempt to incorporate contemplation into the *vita perfecta*. Yet, invariably, he found the effort daunting. Sometimes he equated it with an extension of prayer. At all events, it should not be attempted by any except the most advanced. In his Commentary on Canticles Bede depicts Christ scolding the human soul for attempting to comprehend heavenly mysteries: 'Turn the eyes of your mind away from the contemplation of My divine majesty and essence, since those very things cause me to vanish.'[31] Despite the somewhat considerable influence placed upon the anchoritic life

---

[26] See the excellent discussion of the 'kingdom of God' in Ladner, *The Idea*, 107–32; also the preceding pages dealing with the 'return to paradise': 63–107; see also Stewart, *Cassian the Monk*, 55–60: 'Cassian allows that a monk can anticipate something of heavenly beautitude in contemplation' (*ibid.*, 58). For a more optimistic view of contemplation in the Irish tradition see Stancliffe, 'The miracle stories', 103.

[27] Columbanus, *Sermons*, XII.2 (ed. and tr. Walker, 112–13); *Instructiones*, XII.2: 'et Dei pii et boni ineffabilem misericordiam de profundo cordis nostri per Iesum Christum Filium suum infatigabiliter deprecemur, rogemus, oremus, ut ita nobis suam dilectionem inspirare dignetur, ut nos ei in aeternum coniungat, inseparabiliter conglutinet, humo elevet, caelo societ interim sensus nostros quamdiu simus in hoc *mortis corpore* constituti.' See Stancliffe, 'The thirteen sermons', 131–5, for development within the series of sermons.

[28] *Amra Choluimb Chille*, XLVII (ed. Stokes, 180–1).

[29] *Amra Choluimb Chille*, XLV (ed. Stokes, 178–9).

[30] *Amra Choluimb Chille*, CXIV (ed. Stokes, 280): 'Ar íffurn i n-Albu omun'.

[31] Bede, *On Canticles*, IV (tr. DeGregorio, 31); *In cantica canticorum*, IV (ed. Hurst & Hudson, *Bedae Opera Exegetica*, IIB, 303): 'Auerte oculos tuos a me quia ipsi me auolare fecerunt.' See DeGregorio's discussion of Bede and the theme of contemplation, 26–34.

in both Irish and English hagiography, the solitary life, appearances to the contrary, did not entail contemplation in the Greek or Cassianic sense.[32] *Theoria* was a concept that was never really understood by Insular writers. When they spoke of the *vita theorica* as against the *vita practica*, what they nearly always meant was *askesis*.

It cannot be stressed too often that all Christian *askesis* is grounded in the imitation of Christ. The three great monastic precepts, poverty, chastity and obedience, are founded on Christ's poverty, his chastity, and his obedience to the will of his Father. The common Celtic Church gave poverty pride of place: it was the 'first perfection' for both Cassian and Columbanus. It also held status among Pelagians because it was a command of Christ, or at least a command for those seeking perfection: 'If thou wilt be perfect, go sell what thou hast, and give it to the poor, and thou shalt have treasure in heaven: and come follow me' (Matt. 19:21). There is no command to be virginal. However, to the commandments of the Old Law dealing with fornication, adultery and other sexual sins, Christ added the injunction not to sin in one's heart: 'Whosoever shall look on a woman to lust after her hath already committed adultery with her in his heart' (Matt. 5:28). Columbanus repeated this text in his *Monk's Rule*, and added: 'A monk's chastity is indeed judged in his thoughts.'[33] Christ's strict censure of sexual sin was reinforced by his own example of virginity and that of his mother and his closest disciple. This example is beautifully expressed in an Anglo-Latin rhythmical poem of the seventh century:

Christ, having suffered the cross and the hiding-places of death, himself a virgin commended a virgin to a virgin for safe-keeping.[34]

Finally, Christ gave the example of perfect obedience to the will of his Father. In the place of Gethsemani he prayed: 'Father, if it be possible, let this chalice pass from me. Nevertheless not as I will, but as thou wilt' (Matt.

---

[32] See especially Cassian, *Conferences*, IX.xxv.1 (tr. Ramsey, 345–6), discussing 'fiery prayer': 'This transcends all human understanding and is distinguished not, I would say, by a sound of the voice or a movement of the tongue or a pronunciation of words. Rather, the mind is aware of it when it is illuminated by an infusion of heavenly light from it, and not by narrow human words, and once the understanding has been suspended it gushes forth as from a most abundant fountain and speaks ineffably to God, producing more in that very brief moment than the self-conscious mind is able to articulate easily or to reflect upon'; Latin text below, 179. See Stewart, *Cassian the Monk*, 47–55, 117–18.

[33] Columbanus, *Monks' Rule*, VI (ed. and tr. Walker, 128–9); *Regulae: de castitate*, VI: 'Castitas vero monachi in cogitationibus iudicatur . . .'

[34] Cited in Aldhelm, *On Virginity*, VII (tr. Lapidge & Herren, 64); *De virginitate*, VII (ed. Ehwald, 235):

      Christus passus patibula
      Atque leti latibula
      Virginem virgo virgini
      Commendabat tutamini.

26:39). Christ's perfect obedience led to his ultimate mortification. Obedience and mortification are likewise intimately connected in the thought of Columbanus:

Thus there is a threefold scheme of mortification: not to disagree in mind, not to speak as one pleases with the tongue, not to go anywhere with complete freedom. Its part is ever to say to a senior, however adverse his instructions, not as I will but as thou wilt, following the example of the Lord and Saviour, Who says, I came down from heaven, not to do My will but the will of Him Who sent Me, the Father.[35]

We have now looked at several models of the imaging of Christ coupled with his *imitatio*. It is important to recall that before the work of imitation can begin, one must have a sure idea of what or whom one is imitating. Cassian's Christ appears to be unidimensional – the Christ of the desert who preferred Mary to Martha, the *vita theorica* over the *vita practica*. For Cassian, *askesis* was not an end in itself, but a means to the goal of perfect *theoria*:

Ascending from the contemplation of these persons, someone who is still advancing will arrive with his help at that which is also called 'one' – namely the vision of God alone, so that, when he has gone beyond even the acts of holy persons and their wonderful works, he may be fed on the beauty and knowledge of God alone.[36]

A very different view of Christ was advanced by the Cambrai homilist. Christ was all about penance, but penance included both self-mortification and compassion for one's neighbour. Indeed, the second is needed to fulfil the law of Christ, as the homilist reminds us. This twofold character assigned to penance would appear to explain the same homilist's distinction between 'white and green (or blue) martyrdom':

This is the white martyrdom to man, when he separates for the sake of God from everything he loves, although he suffer fasting or labour thereat. This is the green martyrdom to him, when by means of them (fasting and labour) he separates from his desires, or suffers toil in penance and repentance.[37]

Separation from all that one loves (white martyrdom) could be seen to entail a pilgrimage for Christ (*peregrinatio pro Christo*), a (possibly permanent)

---

[35] Columbanus, *Monks' Rule*, IX (tr. Walker, 141); Latin text below, 179.

[36] Cassian, *Conferences*, I.viii.3 (tr. Ramsey, 47–8); *Conlationes*, I.viii.3 (ed. Pichery, I.87): 'A quorum contemplatione conscendens is qui adhuc in profectu positus est ad illud quoque quod unum dicitur, id est dei solius intuitum ipso adiuuante perueniet, ut scilicet etiam sanctorum actus ac ministeria mirifica supergressus solius dei iam pulchritudine scientiaque pascatur.'

[37] *The Cambrai Homily*, fo. 38a (edd. and tr. Stokes & Strachan, II.247): 'issí in bánmartre du duiniu intain scaras ar Dea fri cach réet caris, cé rucésa áini nú laubir n-oco. issí ind glasmartre dó intain scaras fria thola leó *uel* césas sáithor i ppennit ocus aithrigi.' The Irish word *glas* is best rendered as 'blue' since it is a translation of the Latin *hyacinthinus* (MWH).

separation from family and homeland in order to ensure the salvation of others. Separation from desires (green or blue martyrdom) could be taken to mean the quest for spiritual perfection through mortification, without any change of location.[38]

However one understood the *vita theorica* – whether in the pure Cassianic sense, or simply as another term for *askesis*, the tension between the individual's quest for perfection and his or her sense of duty to the spiritual welfare of others was always there. If it was present in Christ the model ('My hour is not yet come'), it must surely be present in his followers. Cassian's ideal of the person who 'will live solely on the beauty and knowledge of God' created the anchoritic ideal which had a great effect on the Insular world. Unlike the life of the Benedictine monk which remained ever the same, the Insular monk had his or her spiritual retirement to look forward to. In his *Ecclesiastical History* Bede gave us two vignettes to express this ideal: the lives of the Irishman Fursa and the Englishman Dryhthelm. Of Fursa he wrote:

. . . he preached the word of God in Ireland for many years until, when he could no longer endure the noise of the crowds who thronged to him, he gave up all that he seemed to have and left his native island. He came with a few companions through the land of the Britons and into the kingdom of the East Angles, where he preached the Word and there, as we have said, built a monastery. Having duly accomplished this, he longed to free himself from all worldly affairs, even those of the monastery itself; . . . and, being free from all worldly cares, he resolved to end his life as a hermit.[39]

Dryhthelm, like Fursa, was given a vision of the afterlife, and as a consequence devoted the rest of his life entirely to mortification. Bede gives us some precise details of his 'retirement':

The man was given a more secret retreat in the monastery where he could freely devote himself to the service of his Maker in constant prayer, and as his retreat was on the banks of a river, he often used to enter it in his great longing to chastise his body, frequently immersing himself beneath the water; he would remain thus motionless, reciting prayers and psalms for as long as he could endure it, while the water of the river came up to his loins and sometimes up to his neck . . . And so until the day he was called away, in his unwearied longing for heavenly bliss, he subdued his aged body with daily fasts and led many to salvation by his life and words.[40]

It happened that one of Bede's sources for the life and vision of Dryhthelm was a certain priest Haemgisl.[41] Bede drew a parallel between the visionary monk-priest and the reporter by making a point of Haemgisl's mode of

---

[38] For a different view see Stancliffe, 'Red, white and blue martyrdom'.

[39] Bede, *Historia Ecclesiastia*, III.19 (tr. Colgrave & Mynors, 275, 277); Latin text below, 179.

[40] Bede, *Historia Ecclesiastia*, V.12 (tr. Colgrave & Mynors, 496, 498); Latin text below, 179.

[41] Bede, *Historia Ecclesiastia*, V.12 (tr. Colgrave & Mynors, 496, 498).

retirement: 'He is still alive, living in solitude in Ireland and supporting his declining years on a scanty supply of bread and cold water.'[42]

In his *Life of St Cuthbert*, Bede gives one of the fullest accounts of an anchorite's life available from this period. The saint was granted a long period in the kind of retirement he had hoped for before being recalled to serve as bishop:

Now after he had completed many years in that same monastery, he joyfully entered into the remote solitudes which he had long desired, sought, and prayed for, with the good will of that same abbot and also of the brethren. For he rejoiced because after a long and blameless active life, he was now held worthy to rise to the repose of divine contemplation.[43]

Cuthbert's 'repose of divine contemplation' was not undisturbed. After removing himself from the outer precincts of the monastery to a remote island called Farne, he was immediately engaged in a form of spiritual combat:

No one had been able to dwell alone undisturbed upon this island before Cuthbert the servant of the Lord, on account of the phantoms of demons who dwelt there; but when the soldier of Christ entered, armed with the 'helmet of salvation, the shield of faith, and the sword of the spirit which is the word of God, all fiery darts of the wicked one' were quenched . . .[44]

Cuthbert then busied himself with constructing his hut, which he built in such a fashion that he 'could see nothing except the sky from his dwelling, thus restraining both the lust of the eyes and of the thoughts and lifting the whole bent of his mind to higher things'.[45] At first he permitted visits from the brethren, and even imposed upon them to help him dig his well. But he gradually cut himself off from the society of men:

Then, when his zeal for perfection grew, he shut himself up in his hermitage, and, remote from the gaze of men, he learned to live a solitary life of fasting, prayers and

---

[42] Bede, *Historia Ecclesiastia*, V.12 (ed. and tr. Colgrave & Mynors, 496–7): '. . . superest et in Hibernia insula solitarius ultimam uitae aetatem pane cibario et frigida aqua sustentat'.

[43] Bede, *Life of St Cuthbert*, XVII (ed. and tr. Colgrave, *Two Lives*, 214–15); *Vita Sancti Cuthberti*, XVII: 'At postquam in eodem monasterio multa annorum curricula expleuit, tandem diu concupita, quaesita, ac petita solitudinis secreta, comitante praefati abbatis sui simul et fratrum gratia multum laetabundus adiit. Gaudebat namque quia de longa perfectione conuersationis actiuae, ad otium diuinae speculationis iam mereretur ascendere.'

[44] Bede, *Life of St Cuthbert*, XVII (ed. and tr. Colgrave, *Two Lives*, 214–15); *Vita Sancti Cuthberti*, XVII: 'Nullus hanc facile ante famulum Domini Cuthbertum solus ualebat inhabitare colonus, propter uidelicet demorantium ibi phantasias demonum. Verum intrante eam milite Christi, armato *galea salutis, scuto fidei, et gladio spiritus quod est uerbum Dei, omnia tela nequissimi ignea extincta . . .*'

[45] Bede, *Life of St Cuthbert*, XVII (ed. and tr. Colgrave, *Two Lives*, 216–17); *Vita Sancti Cuthberti*, XVII: '. . . quatinus ad cohibendam oculorum siue cogitationum lasciuiam, ad erigendam in superna desideria totam mentis intentionem, pius incola nil de sua mansione praeter coelum posset intueri'.

vigils, rarely having conversation from within his cell with visitors and that only through the window. At first he opened this and rejoiced to see and be seen by the brethren with whom he spoke; but, as time went on, he shut even that, and opened it only for the sake of giving his blessing, or for some other definite necessity.[46]

The remainder of the episode is taken up with a series of miracles, all of which illustrate the ministrations of nature to the man of God to help him maintain his self-sufficiency. Eventually the report of the miracles is bruited about, with the predictable result that his solitude was ruined.

The topoi of these Bedan examples may be expanded as follows: (1) a holy monk, who has completed an active life, desires to escape his disciples and retire in solitude; (2) he chooses a place remote from his regular community and attempts to cut himself off from human contact; (3) he builds a dwelling and practises a life of self-sufficiency, though he sometimes is aided by 'miraculous nature' (ministrations by birds and other animals); (4) when not engaged in providing for his very simple needs he practises a life of prayer and ascetic discipline, often tending to extreme forms; (5) in some cases (following the lives of the Desert Fathers) there are temptations and struggles with demons; (6) in some cases, the retirement is interrupted due to external troubles, reports of miracles (bringing crowds), or because of a calling to ecclesiastical office. In these cases, retirement must be postponed and resumed when possible. Sometimes there is resistance to the call to service, at other times expressions of regret.

Cuthbert is arguably the most complete 'projection' of Christ. He was a priest as well as a monk and anchorite, and, at different periods held monastic office (*praepositus* and abbot) and high clerical office (bishop). Bede describes his pastoral work while still a priest as follows:

Now he was wont to penetrate those parts especially and to preach in those villages that were far away on steep and rugged mountains, which others dreaded to visit and whose poverty as well as ignorance prevented teachers from approaching them. And giving himself up gladly to this pious labour, he attended to their instruction with such industry, that, leaving the monastery, he would often not return home for a whole week, sometimes even for two or three weeks, and even occasionally for a full month; but he would tarry in the mountains, summoning the rustics to heavenly things by the words of his preaching as well as by the example of his virtue.[47]

In addition to teaching Cuthbert also performed healings and was himself the recipient of miraculous aid.[48] Cuthbert thus embodied Bede's ideal of the holy life of prayer and penance joined to the fullest expression of the pastoral care. Yet his preference was for 'the better part'. Of all the early Insular saints Cuthbert comes closest to the Christ of the gospels.[49]

---

[46] Bede, *Life of St Cuthbert*, XVIII (ed. and tr. Colgrave, *Two Lives*, 221); Latin text below, 179–80.

[47] Bede, *Life of St Cuthbert*, IX (ed. and tr. Colgrave, *Two Lives*, 187); Latin text below, 180.

[48] See below, 172–3.

[49] See especially Stancliffe, 'Cuthbert'; also Thacker, 'Bede's ideal'.

The Heroic Christ (harrower of hell)

We have noted that the Greek tradition was receptive to the possibility of achieving the kingdom of God in some measure in this life. By contrast, Western monasticism – and Western Christianity generally – was much more single-minded: its kingdom of God was certainly not of this world. What might be called the 'salvation ethic' lay at the heart of the western monastic movement. What matters most for the individual Christian is his or her personal salvation in the next life. The present life can be viewed only as a period of trial; as Augustine put it, 'And so long as he [man] is in this mortal body, he is a pilgrim in a foreign land, away from God.'[50] Augustine, the most influential Western theologian of the late Roman Empire, propounded what may be termed a Western theology of hell. It was a place of eternal torment, and most people would end up there:

In contrast with this, however, the wretchedness of those who do not belong to this City of God will be everlasting. This is called also 'the second death', because the soul cannot be said to be alive in that state, when it is separated from the life of God, nor can the body, when it is subjected to eternal torments.[51]

And,

But it does not mean that all who die in Adam will be members of Christ, for the great majority of them will be punished with the second death, which is for ever.[52]

We have noted that Augustine was not alone in his pessimistic outlook. Pelagius's countervailing optimism regarding man's ability to save himself was undermined by his own theology of law. The strictness of the twofold law required an almost superhuman effort to fulfil it. Without the help of grace other than baptism, a person's chances under Pelagius were as poor as they were under Augustine. The pervading pessimism regarding human destiny in the afterlife had a profound effect in shaping Western monasticism. If only a few could be saved, then it was essential that the Church concentrate its efforts on those individuals who displayed a potential for salvation. By definition, these were the people who voluntarily

---

[50] Augustine, *City of God*, XIX.14 (tr. Bettenson, 873); *De civitate Dei*, XIX.14 (ed. Welldon, II.427): 'Et quoniam, quamdiu est in isto mortali corpore, peregrinatur a Domino . . .'

[51] Augustine, *City of God*, XIX.28 (tr. Bettenson, 894); *De civitate Dei*, IX.28 (ed. Welldon, I.448): 'Eorum autem, qui non pertinent ad istam ciuitatem Dei, erit e contrario miseria sempiterna, quae mors etiam secunda dicitur, quia nec anima ibi uiuere dicenda est, quae a uita Dei alienata erit, nec corpus, quod aeternis doloribus subiacebit.' Augustine devotes a large part of Book XXI to detailing the pains of hell and who will suffer them; also, in explaining that God is justified in consigning sinners to eternal torments.

[52] Augustine, *City of God*, XIII.23 (tr. Bettenson, 540); *De civitate Dei*, XIII.23 (ed. Welldon, II.74): '. . . non quia omnes, qui in Adam moriuntur, membra erunt Christi (ex illis enim multo plures secunda in aeternum morte plectentur) . . .'

chose to live a rigorous Christian life in a controlled environment. Thus it was the monastic community (broadened to include a portion of the laity) that could provide the conditions of salvation. *Extra monasterium nulla salus* would have made a good motto for the Western Church of the period studied here.

The Irish Church and the English Church as well were very much hell-oriented.[53] They continually reminded their members that the pains of hell were so fearsome that they must be avoided at all cost. Indeed, the avoidance of hell appears to have played a greater role in eschatological consciousness than the attainment of heaven. The prospect of winning the prize of salvation brought with it a potential sigh of relief rather an anticipated sense of joy. This attitude is revealed in a number of prayers that speak of evading narrow straits and treacherous shoals. One of the earliest instances is found in the eulogy for Columba in an invocation of the recently departed saint: 'May he waft me past tortures.'[54] Then in a mid-seventh-century Irish school text known as the *Hisperica Famina* we read:

> I pray the Ruler of the boundless sphere, –
> Who has created the mass of the world with his benign power,
> envelops the rim of the earth with the sea's girdle, ...
> and establishes for masses of men the rewards of His holy kingdom, –
> grant a stout ship
> to me as I sail through the stormy strait,
> that I may escape the baneful judgement.[55]

Another salient example occurs in an Irish-language litany, the *Litany of Jesus*, in which Christ is adjured in the name of various saints, angels, and other holy persons to perform the following on behalf of the suppliant:

That Thou will take me under Thy protection and defence and care, to preserve and protect me from demons and all their promptings, against all the elements of the world, against lusts, against transgressions, against sins, against the crimes of the world, against the dangers of this life, and the torments of the next, from the hands of enemies and every terror, against the fire of hell and doom, against shame before the face of God, against attacks (lit. seizures) of demons, that they may have no power over us at the entry of the other world . . .[56]

Essentially this prayer is very like a *lorica* ('breastplate'), which might be described as the most basic form of private prayer in the Insular Churches.[57] An important example of this genre is the *lorica* written by Laidcenn of Clonfert-Mulloe, who died in 661. The suppliant asks:

---

[53] (C.) Wright, *The Irish Tradition*, 132–74. For a general discussion of the origins of the Christian view of the afterlife see Le Goff, *The Birth of Purgatory*.

[54] *Amra Choluimb Chille*, CXLI (ed. and tr. Stokes, 414–15): 'Rodom – sinsea sech riaga'.

[55] *Hisperica Famina*, A.561–70 (tr. Herren, *The Hisperica Famina I*, 109); Latin text below, 180.

[56] *Litany of Jesus* – I (ed. and tr. Plummer, *Irish Litanies*, 35–7); Irish text below, 181.

[57] See especially Hughes, 'Some aspects'.

May Christ strike a firm covenant with me:
let fear and fright fasten on the foul fiends.[58]

These and other *loricae*, as well as the closely related litanies, demonstrate the almost exclusively personal nature of private prayer.[59] One prays for oneself. One beseeches – or adjures – Christ to come to one's aid against the powers of demons, who work harm in this life and endanger the soul at the moment of death. Even the act of praising Christ is directed to avoiding the pitfall of hell. In the *Rule of Tallaght* we read:

Just as a condemned man, standing at the gallows awaiting execution, must sing the praises of the king together with pleadings in the hope of pardon, so do we sing the praise and lamentations in the *Beati* to the King of heaven, hoping for deliverance from hell.[60]

This obsession with hell is further revealed in the vision literature of the Irish, written mostly in the vernacular. Vision literature was not an invention of the Irish Church. Rather it is an extension of the apocalyptic literature that began in the intertestamental period (for example, the Book of Daniel, Book of Enoch) and was readily taken over by Christianity. Only one New Testament apocalyptic text (Apocalypse/Revelation) is canonical, but there was a number of other quite influential non-canonical texts such as the *Apocalypse of Paul* that purported to reveal privileged visions of the afterlife. This work and others, such as the *Apocalypse of Peter*, were known and used by Irish scholars.[61]

Irish vision literature began early. Almost certainly the earliest attested instance in Irish literature is an economical reference to Columba's 'journey in flesh to heaven' in *Amra Choluimb Chille*.[62] Bede summarised a vision drawn from a *libellus* containing the Life of the Irishman Fursa. In Bede's précis, Fursa, when ill, was twice taken from his body, the first time to see the heavenly hosts and hear them singing. In his second journey, while still protected by angels, he is attacked by demons who hurl fire at him and accuse him of taking over the property of a sinner. The angels offer a verbal defence of Fursa, but did not save him from the effects of the fire, which he wore after he was restored to his body.[63] The apparent purpose of the vision was to illustrate the dangers that befall the disembodied soul between the point of death and judgement. The narrow straits of this life are replicated in the afterlife.

The concern with the afterlife and especially the horrors of hell was just as powerful among the English. Bede records at length yet another

---

[58] Laidcenn, *Lorica*, lines 27–8 (ed. and tr. Herren, *The Hisperica Famina II*, 78–9):
    Christus mecum   pactum firmum feriat:
    timor tremor   tetras turbas terreat.
[59] See especially (K.) Hughes, 'Some aspects'.
[60] Mael Ruain, *The Rule of Tallaght*, XXXII (tr. Ó Maidín, 108); Irish text below, 180.
[61] McNamara, *The Apocrypha*, 102–9.
[62] *Amra Choluimb Chille*, CXXXV (ed. and tr. Stokes, 410–11): 'intech hi coluain co ether'.
[63] Bede, *Historia Ecclesiastica*, III.19 (edd. and tr. Colgrave & Mynors, 270–5).

eschatological vision, this one granted to the monk Dryhthelm, who, detached from his body, was granted visions of hell, purgatory and paradise.[64] The terrors of hell (comprising cold as well as heat) exercised a salutary effect on the simple monk:

When in winter time the broken pieces of ice were floating round him, which he himself had had to break in order to find a place to stand in the river or immerse himself, those who saw him would say, 'Brother Dryhthelm, – for that was his name – however can you bear such bitter cold?' He answered them simply, for he was a man of simple wit and few words, 'I have known it colder.' And when they said, 'It is marvellous that you are willing to endure such a hard and austere life', he replied, 'I have seen it harder.' And so until the day he was called away, in his unwearied longing for heavenly bliss, he subdued his aged body with daily fasts and led many to salvation by his words and life.[65]

Bede provides his own very vivid description of hell in the poem *On the Day of Judgement*:

> Eternal Gehenna is a place filled with black fire;
> Freezing cold mingles at the same time with glowing flames.
> Now ovens [assault] weeping eyes with excessive heat,
> Now they [attack] gnashing teeth with terrible cold.
> In such alternating miseries wretches pass eternity
> Immersed in dark night and pitch-black gloom.[66]

Perhaps the best known and most influential of Irish vision texts is the Irish-language *Fís Adamnáin* (*Vision of Adomnán*). It has been attributed to the tenth or eleventh century,[67] but it reflects motifs already well known in earlier Irish literature. The work has been aptly described as 'An Irish Precursor of Dante'[68] – not without good reason, as the following excerpt shows:

Near those people is another large group in terrible pain. These are bound to fiery columns, with a sea of fire around them up to their chins, and burning chains in the form of serpents around their waists. Their faces are ablaze with pain. Those who are in such torment are sinners, those who have slain their kin, destroyers of the Church of God, and merciless ecclesiastical leaders who rule over shrines of the saints to gain the donations and tithes of the Church, making this treasure their own particular property rather than that of the invited and needy ones of the Lord. There are large crowds standing continually in dank pools to their belts. Short icy cloaks are around them. Never do the belts stop or cease from scalding them with both cold and heat. Surrounding them is a host of demons with fiery clubs, beating them over the head, and continually threatening them. The countenances of the wretched ones are all turned northward, with a harsh sharp wind directly on their faces, along with every other evil. Red showers of fire rain down on them every night and every day,

---

[64] Bede, *Historia Ecclesiastica*, V.12 (edd. and tr. Colgrave & Mynors, 488–99).
[65] Bede, *Historia Ecclesiastica*, V.12 (edd. and tr. Colgrave & Mynors, 499); Latin text below, 180–1.
[66] Bede, *On the Day of Judgement* (our translation); Latin text below, 181.
[67] McNamara, *The Apocrypha*, 126.
[68] Boswell, *An Irish Precursor*.

and they cannot avoid them, but must eternally suffer them with weeping and lamentation.[69]

One would expect that a vision of the damned would be highly tangential to the theme of the death and bodily assumption of Mary. Yet we find that hell is a central motif in an Irish version of the *Transitus Mariae* (*Ascension of Mary*), a work of a later period based on a text known possibly as early as the seventh century.[70] After the archangel Michael had raised up Mary's body into the clouds, the apostles asked Christ to keep his promise and show them a vision of hell. Christ then bade Michael to reveal hell. After a series of suitably horrifying depictions of punishments:

Jesus and Mary came to them and asked Michael to cease to point out the pains of hell. When the inhabitants of hell saw Mary and Christ they lamented, saying: 'O Mary, mother of the illustrious one, implore your son to grant us relief from our pains.' Christ answered them and said: 'I was crucified for your sakes, my side was pierced, and a crown [of thorns] placed on my head. You, however, rejected the ten commandments of the law of God, in defiance of my teaching. Why, therefore, should I grant you a respite?' Then Mary knelt on the ground, bared her right breast and shed copious tears on the earth, beseeching her son to come to the aid of those in hell. Then Christ said: 'In honour of Mary, of the apostles, and of Michael, I will grant them a respite from their pains for three hours every Sunday.' Then Jesus said: 'Let you close hell.' They closed hell at his command.[71]

Augustinian Christianity taught that all would have been consigned to torment, or at least to the eternal deprivation of the sight of God, had not Christ been sent from heaven to redeem man from the effects of his sins. A central canonical proof-text is St Paul: 'For since it was a man who brought death into the world, a man also brought resurrection of the dead. As in Adam all men die, so in Christ all will be brought to life' (I Cor. 15:21–2).

Paul, who stands at the beginning of Christian teaching, should not be held responsible for the doctrine that the just as well as the wicked who preceded the reign of Christ would be separated from God at the moment of death and imprisoned somewhere removed from God's sight – a place usually thought to exist beneath the earth.[72] This notion developed as a response to the question, what was the fate of souls before the advent of grace? Logically enough, if Christians were taught to believe that salvation was impossible before the redemption through Christ, then it follows that even just men such as Abraham and Moses could not be saved. However, God must be *seen* to be just as well as to *be* just, so it was incumbent upon him at the very moment of the redemption to rescue the good souls from the underworld, where they were not supposed to suffer, but could not share in the benefits of the redemption until it actually occurred. And so it transpired

---

[69] *Vision of Adomnán*, XXXI–XXXII (tr. Herbert & McNamara, 144); Irish text below, 181.

[70] McNamara, *The Apocrypha*, 122–3, 183–5.

[71] *Ascension of Mary*, LIV (tr. Herbert & McNamara, 130); Irish text below, 181.

[72] However, see Paul's allusions to Christ's descent collected by MacCulloch, *The Harrowing*, 45–7.

that already in the early centuries Christ's descent into hell had become a widespread belief – one that was eventually incorporated as an article of faith into the canons of the Council of Toledo (633) and into the Apostle's Creed in the eighth century.[73] Significantly, the phrase *descendit ad inferos* ('he descended to those below') is found in a creed contained in the late seventh-century *Antiphonary of Bangor*.[74]

Here it is important to interject that hard-line Pelagians such as Coelestius specifically rejected Paul's words in I Corinthians; he countered: 'The whole human race neither dies through Adam's death or transgression nor rises through the resurrection of Christ.'[75] He also stated: 'there were men without sin before Christ's coming'.[76] To the likes of Coelestius, if Christ's sacrifice was not necessary for mankind's salvation, surely there would have been no requirement to rescue the just who died before his passion. If, as we have argued, a Pelagianist outlook survived in both the British and Irish Churches at least up to the period of the *Romani* in Ireland (second quarter of the seventh century), one can well imagine that there would have been resistance to treating the *descensus ad inferos* as doctrine on the ground that the just who lived before Christ had already saved themselves. On the other hand, the belief that Christ descended into hell to save the just would have certainly provided an effective bulwark against the late Augustinian doctrine that all who died without baptism, regardless of their circumstances, would be consigned to eternal hellfire. Such a consideration probably outweighed Pelagian-based scruples regarding the use of the non-canonical biblical texts that supported the doctrine of the descent,[77] and the more central theological point that there were sinless men before Christ's coming who required no extra help for salvation. It is, however, one thing to believe that Christ descended to the righteous who died before the age of grace, another to believe that he fought a battle with Satan in order to free them. The military

---

[73] Dumville, 'Biblical apocrypha', 301.

[74] Antiphonary of Bangor, XXXV (ed. Warren, II.21): 'Descendit ad inferos.' See MacCulloch, *The Harrowing*, 72. For other credal references to the descent, see *ibid.*, 67–82.

[75] *Synod of Diospolis*, VII (tr. Rees, *Pelagius*, 136); I have modified Rees's translation slightly. Augustine, *De gestis Pelagii*, XI (24) (edd. Urba & Zycha, 78): 'quod neque per ⟨mortem uel⟩ praeuaricationem Adae omne genus hominum moriatur; neque per resurrectionem Christi omne genus hominum resurgat'.

[76] *Synod of Diospolis*, VII (tr. Rees, *Pelagius*, 136); Augustine, *De gestis Pelagii*, XI (23) (edd. Urba & Zycha, 76): 'quoniam ante aduentum Christi fuerunt homines sine peccato'.

[77] The use of apocryphal books would almost certainly have been opposed in the period of the common Celtic Church. Pelagians certainly maintained a strict view of the canonical books of the Bible. This was entailed by their central belief that the scriptures contained the whole law of God, and thus to tamper with the canon was to tamper with the law itself. See especially Pelagius's *Profession of Faith*, XIX; our translation: 'We accept the New and the Old Testament in the number of books which the authority of the holy Catholic Church hands down'; *Libellus fidei*, XIX (*PL* XLVIII.691): 'Novum et vetus testamentum recipimus in ea [*recte* eo] librorum numero quem sanctae Catholicae Ecclesiae tradit auctoritas.'

aspect of the harrowing motif seems to have been given special prominence in the Irish accounts.

The motif of the harrowing of hell was highly influential in the Insular world. The earliest Irish evidence, dating from the seventh century, if not earlier,[78] is the hymn *Precamur patrem*: 'He extricates the first human creation, gnawed for nearly six thousand years by the deathly knots of hell, with its righteous offspring cast down by cruel death as punishment for [the crime of] the apple, and on his return mercifully restores each of the ancient inhabitants to paradise.'[79] Whereas there can be no doubt that the author employed the harrowing motif, it is also certain that he did not use a standard Latin version of the *Gospel of Nicodemus*, at least as we know it from manuscripts of the ninth century and later. In *Precamur patrem* Christ not only rescues souls from the underworld, he personally escorts them to heaven. In the *Gospel of Nicodemus*, this task is assigned to the archangel Michael.[80] Moreover, *Precamur patrem* neglects to mention Christ's resurrection, whereas this is a major concern of the *Gospel*.[81]

The motif next occurs in the *Poem to Mary and her Son* by Blathmac, whose activity is now dated to the period 750–70.[82] Against the older view that Blathmac knew the *Gospel of Nicodemus* it has been recently pointed out that Blathmac's account of the harrowing deviates in important ways from that of the *Gospel*.[83] Nonetheless, it is clear that Blathmac knew some version of the *descensus* story:

It is he who suffered on the cross, who was buried beneath cold stone, and who went after that on a visit to Hell.

He was victorious from fighting that, his battle with the Devil. Miserable Devil, his strength was crushed; a great prey was taken from him.

It is your son, Jesus, who cast seven chains about his neck and bound him (no falsehood!) in the depths of his dwelling.

He then returned to his body when he cast off the great attack, and he arose (bright tidings!) on Easter after three days.[84]

It is important to note that Blathmac has incorporated an account of the

---

[78] Even if this hymn is not (as argued by Lapidge, '*Precamur patrem*') by Columbanus, its composition can have taken place no later than the end of the seventh century, the *terminus ante quem* of the compilation of the Antiphonary of Bangor: see Appendix, below 284–8.

[79] *Precamur patrem*, XXXIII–XXXV. Latin text below, 181–2.

[80] *Gospel of Nicodemus*, XXV (ed. Kim, 46).

[81] *Gospel of Nicodemus*, XXVII (ed. Kim, 47–8).

[82] Carney, *The Poems*, xix. For a recent argument that Blathmac's poems represent the spirituality of the *Céli Dé* see Lambkin, 'Blathmac and the Céili Dé'.

[83] Dumville, 'Biblical apocrypha', 308, represents the older view. This has recently been challenged by Dooley, 'The *Gospel*', 371–2.

[84] Blathmac, *Poem to Mary and her Son*, stanzas 174–7 (tr. Carney, 59, 61). Irish text below, 182. Unlike the *Precamur patrem* poet, Blathmac felt obliged to ensure that the canonical account of the resurrection was fully represented and not conflated with the harrowing. See the discussion above, 139–40.

canonical resurrection with the harrowing. In contrast to the author of *Precamur patrem*, Blathmac omits alike the narrative of Christ's ascension to heaven with the souls of the just, and the alternative account of his consignment of them to Michael found in the *Gospel of Nicodemus*.

A perhaps surprising appropriation of the harrowing motif is to be found in the poems of John Scottus Eriugena, written in the period 859–70.[85] This Irish scholar, known primarily for his writings on theology and philosophy and his translations from the Greek, left a small corpus of poems in Latin and Greek. In a collection of short 'epyllions', Christ is the hero and it is his deeds that provide the proper matter for the Christian poet. The theme of the harrowing is treated in several poems. A vivid example is no. 6:

> The great light of the world flashes triumphant out of Hell;
>   dying death is dumbfounded by the beginnings of life.
> The furies bound, the fates gather round from all sides,
>   astonished by the doleful moans of the Styx.
> Then the prince of the abyss seeks the accustomed arms
>   by which he subdued the human race to his power.
> But as soon as he sees the broken threshold in crumbling ruins
>   he flees in shock and terror to the depths of his house.
> Yet even through the dark caverns the tyrant could not escape:
>   his foe, more powerful than he, entered and bore off his vessels.
> Soon he is seized, captured, bound taut with chains,
>   overpowered, restrained and cast from the seat
> Where the prince of the world once sat on high,
>   a savage and voracious beast, for aeons unvanquished.
> But the conqueror of the world, solitary and peerless
>   dashed him completely and crushed his head.[86]

The theme of Satan's anger over his failure to recognise Christ finds a reprise in another poem of John's:

> Ah! who accosts me? Who, mighty in arms,
> Dares to join battle with the prince of the world?
> Is it he who was fixed to a tree and immured in a tomb,
>
>   .   .   .   .
>
> The one consigned to death and slain by a Roman prince?
> That was my doing, I own it; I brought it all about.
> His virtue and humble power deceived me, fool that I am![87]

The harrowing was also a dominant theme in Old English poetry. A poem in the Exeter Book is devoted to the subject.[88] In this work John the Baptist acts as a narrator who first addresses the multitude of faithful and tells them that the advent of Christ is at hand (noting that Christ would come to hell

---

[85] Herren, *Iohannis Scotti Eriugenae Carmina*, 24–5.

[86] John Scottus, *Poems*, VI.1–16 (tr. Herren, *Iohannis Scotti Eriugenae Carmina*, 81); Latin text below, 182.

[87] John Scottus, *Poems*, IX.43–8 (tr. Herren, *Iohannis Scotti Eriugenae Carmina*, 93); Latin text below, 183.

[88] *The Exeter Book*, *Poems*, XXIV (ed. and tr. Mackie, II.172–81).

six months after his own demise).[89] In the last part of the poem he addresses
Christ, offering the thanks of all who 'wait in these bonds'.[90] Bridging the
Irish and the English tradition is a poem in the Book of Cerne, compiled
around the first quarter of the ninth century.[91] The poem is the prayer of the
saints held in captivity in the underworld. First the assembled saints beseech
Christ who releases them all save Adam and Eve. There follows the prayer of
Adam, who is then released. Finally, Eve pleads forgiveness for 'the sins of
my youth'.[92] Although there is no description of armed combat with Satan –
the poem concentrates entirely on the pleas of the saints – there is an implicit
connection between the militant Christ who conquers Satan and the
protection of his flock. Indeed, this connection applies to all the embodi-
ments of the harrowing motif. Christ, in defeating Satan, has preserved the
just from his ravages. This notion extends to the present and future. The
armoured Christ who descended unto the dead continues to ward off the
devil from all who seek deliverance. Hence there is a direct connection
between Christ the Hero, who acted at one point in salvation-history, and
Christ the Breastplate (*lorica*), the refuge of all who are still in this life.

Whereas the *Gospel of Nicodemus* itself and the prayer in the Book of
Cerne de-emphasise (or omit entirely) martial combat, the Irish accounts
from Blathmac through John Scottus and onwards highlight this aspect. In
an Irish version of *the Descent*, Christ shatters the gates of hell, pervades the
gloomy underworld with his divine light, seizes Satan, binds him, and casts
him into the depths of hell.[93] There Satan is reproached by his 'officials' for
not having foreseen the result of Christ's crucifixion. Finally, Christ gives
authority to Satan over hell 'in place of Adam and his righteous descen-
dents',[94] then 'took Adam by the hand and brought him out of Hell, and all
his children and all the blessed followed'.[95]

The heroic Christ, who had his origins in the classical world, lived on in
the barbarian kingdoms. Indeed this was not only fitting, it was a social
necessity. The divine man who could break down the gates of hell and bind
Satan was a powerful role model for the Christian engaged in a life and
death struggle with the forces of darkness. Had no one been able to conquer

[89] *The Exeter Book*, *Poems*, XXIV, lines 26–32 (ed. and tr. Mackie, II.172–5).
[90] *The Exeter Book*, *Poems*, XXIV, lines 59–138 (ed. and tr. Mackie, II.176–81); line
    61 (ed. Mackie, II.176): '. . . on þissum bendan bidan . . .'
[91] The collection of poems and prayers was assembled in the time of Æthelwald,
    bishop of Lichfield (818–830): see Kuypers, *The Prayer Book*, xi–xiv; text: 196–8.
    The poem on Christ's descent has been re-edited by Dumville, 'Liturgical drama'.
[92] *The Prayer Book* (ed. Kuypers, 198, lines 17–18).
[93] *Irish Gospel of Nicodemus*, VI(XXII)–VII(XXIII) (tr. Herbert & McNamara,
    82–4).
[94] *Irish Gospel of Nicodemus*, VII(XXIII).3 (tr. Herbert & McNamara, 84); *Stair
    Nicoméid*, XXII (ed. (I.) Hughes, 42): '. . . i nn-inad Ádaim ⁊ a chlaindi fíreóin[e]'.
[95] *Irish Gospel of Nicodemus*, VIII(XXIV).2 (tr. Herbert & McNamara, 85); *Stair
    Nicoméid*, XXIV.2 (ed. (I.) Hughes, 42): '. . . ⁊ ro gab láim Ádaim tug les a
    hIfreand hé ⁊ ro leanastair a chland ⁊ na huile naem hé'. For a helpful survey of
    later Irish accounts of the harrowing, and of the use of the (Latin) *Gospel of
    Nicodemus*, see Dooley, 'The *Gospel*', 373–401.

Satan, the world would have been filled with despair. It is an interesting question why the angel Michael, who appears so often as a combatant against the devil in apocryphal literature, is relegated to the sidelines. Christ takes on the work himself, possibly because the harrowing had become, in contemporary terms, the focal point of the redemption. Since Christ alone could accomplish the redemption, he alone could bring the souls of the just out of hell. Christ proves that Satan is not invincible, and by doing this, bids rigorous Christians to overpower Satan in their own lives.[96] It is because Christ overcame Satan in his own person that the Insular Christian prays to him for protection at the moment of death, when perils to the soul are the greatest.

There is a second reason why a heroic Christ enjoyed widespread popularity in the Insular world. Insular Christianity was based in barbarian societies, Celtic and Germanic. Both groups placed heavy emphasis on individual heroism. In the process of explaining the Christian God, it would have been essential to lay stress on his physical power. A Christ who was crucified could be seen as a weakling. A Christ who could rise from the grave is admirable indeed, but such a feat is the trick of druids: it is achieved through magic rather than valour and strength. It is only the Christ who with his own hands can overcome the cosmic dragon who can earn the reverence of heroes and kings.

Christ the Wonder-Worker

The theology of Christ's miracles begins properly with the gospels themselves. The first step is to observe where the miracles occur. In the synoptic gospels the miracle collections are found between the two great penitential phases of Christ's life: his forty days in the desert and his crucifixion. As noted, the Gospel of John, which omits the account of the temptation of Christ, nonetheless supplies a clear boundary between his earlier life and his miracles in his account of the wedding feast at Cana. Monastic advocates could find support in John for their belief that miracles (and Christ's public life in general) played a subordinate role to Christ's periods of penance.

The framers of the gospel stories were doubtless possessed of far different thoughts. The miracles of Christ were an extremely important aspect of his life and mission. They were meaningful because they manifested the power of God. At the same time they revealed God's goodness and love for suffering mankind. The so-called evangelical miracles are almost invariably directed to alleviating human misery and thus proving God's love for his children, while simultaneously demonstrating that Christ possesses the power of God.[97]

The public miracles of Christ were used by the writers of the New Testament to prove that he was the Messiah and the Son of God. They

---

[96] See especially Ailerán, *Interpretatio Mystica et Moralis*, CCLXXX–CCLXXXV (ed. and tr. Breen, 51–2). For text, see 283.

[97] See O'Collins, *Christology*, 54–9, with bibliography.

also were seen as testimonies to his resurrection. The point is made explicit in a speech by Peter in Acts:

Men of Israel, listen to me: I speak of Jesus of Nazareth, a man singled out by God and made known to you through miracles, portents, and signs which God worked among you through him, as you well know. When he had been given up by you, by the deliberate will and plan of God, you used heathen men to crucify and kill him. But God raised him to life again, setting him free from the pangs of death, because it could not be that death should keep him in his grip (Acts 2:22–4).

The power to perform miracles – a power that comes directly from God – was passed on to the apostles to establish them as heirs to the authority of Christ and continuators of his work on earth. Christ enjoined the twelve: 'Heal the sick, raise the dead, cleanse lepers, cast out devils. You received without cost; give without charge' (Matt. l0:8). The apostolic inheritance of this power is confirmed in Acts:

They met constantly to hear the apostles teach, and to share the common life, to break bread, and to pray. A sense of awe was everywhere, and many marvels and signs were brought about through the apostles (Acts 2:42–4).

Thus the apostles not only were meant to follow Christ's teachings, virtuous way of life and suffering, but to replicate his special powers as well.

The Book of Acts is a central text for the study of Christian attitudes to thaumaturgy, because it documents a basic departure from evangelical strictures on the exercise of *exousia*. Christ's 'evangelical miracles' were nearly always beneficial to others (healing, raising the dead). Sometimes, however, they were directed merely to the demonstration of his divine power (for example, walking on water). There are no examples of maleficent acts against humans. (The whipping of the temple money-changers described in John 2:14–16 cannot be described as a miracle.) The few examples of non-beneficent miracles are directed against plants and animals (causing the fig tree to shrivel, sending a possessed herd of swine over a precipice). Christ did not curse any individual nor utter a self-fulfilling prophecy of death.

It is precisely in this regard that the image of the *virtus Christi* shifts abruptly. Peter, the head of the apostles and head of the community of Christians, extends the power of Christ to embrace seemingly maleficent actions against humans. To be sure, many of Peter's miracles are beneficent. Peter cures the sick simply with his shadow and casts out unclean spirits (Acts 5:15–16). In these actions he follows in the steps of his Master. However, the well-known story of Peter and the couple Ananias and Sapphire (Acts 5:1–12), discussed approvingly by Pseudo-Augustine as an example of 'apostolic power in Christ',[98] imputes terrible powers of prophecy and punishment to the chief of the apostles that are without parallel in the gospels. Prophecy is accompanied by cursing in the famous tale of Peter and Simon Magus: 'Keep thy money to thyself, to perish with thee, because thou hast thought that the gift of God may be purchased with money' (Acts 8:20).

The apocryphal Passions of Peter and Paul, which continue the story of

[98] Pseudo-Augustine, *On the Miracles of Holy Scripture*, III.17 [*PL* XXXV.2201–2].

the two founders of the Church where the canonical Acts leaves off, after Paul's arrival in Rome, developed the story of Peter and Simon Magus into the tale that is familiar to us from paintings, films, and novels. It sets up an extended power contest between Peter and Paul on one side and Simon on the other in the presence of the Emperor Nero. Simon conjures large hounds to attack and devour Peter, but Peter had foreseen this, and has some barley bread, which he has blessed, concealed in his sleeve, and producing it, makes the dogs vanish. The episode ends with the well-known flying episode in which Peter imprecates Christ at the moment of Simon's leap from the tower not to bear the magician up. Simon fell, and his body was broken into pieces. Prior to this Peter had predicted Simon's eternal damnation.[99]

The dark side of Christian *exousia* which we see developing in the canonical Acts and to a fuller extent in the apocryphal Acts of the Apostles is eventually extended to Christ himself. Just as apocryphal Acts of the apostles fill in details of the apostles' lives not given in canonical texts, so, too, apocryphal gospels were written to complete the life of Christ. Infancy narratives were especially popular. One very influential account occurs in the so-called Infancy Narrative of Thomas. In this text, the boy Jesus, depicted in the care of Joseph, caused a Pharisee to wither and die because he had emptied out a pool which Jesus had made.[100] In the *Irish Gospel of Thomas*, the withering and death is applied to a boy who destroyed one of Jesus's playthings.[101] Thus the benign Christ of the canonical gospels acquires some of the darker sides of power associated with the apostles exemplified in both the canonical and apocryphal Acts.

Augustine, in Book XXII of his monumental *City of God*, outlines a theology of miracles.[102] He begins with a premise which most orthodox believers would accept: that the miracles of Christ were performed to confirm the truth of the greatest miracle of them all: Christ's resurrection from the dead. Augustine goes on to show that miracles of all kinds continue up to his own time; these consist not only of the miracles performed in the time of the martyrs, but also ones known personally to him. He speculates that God, 'who is active in temporal events', can achieve these in various ways – all beyond mortal comprehension. However, 'they all testify to the faith in which the resurrection to eternal life is proclaimed'.[103] Augustine, of course, takes no account of non-canonical miracles. The examples of contemporary miracles which he reports – healings and resuscitations from the dead – are consonant with the evangelical miracles. His intent in reporting them is to show the continuity of God's mysterious workings in the world. These did not end with Christ, or the apostles, or the martyrs.

As shown in the two previous chapters, the work *The Miracles of Holy Scripture* by the so-called 'Irish Augustine' was written to refute the doctrine

---

[99] (M.R.) James, *The Apocryphal New Testament*, 470. For an Irish version, see *The Acts of Peter and Paul* (tr. Herbert & McNamara, 102–4).

[100] *Gospel of Thomas*, V (tr. (M.R.) James, 60).

[101] *Irish Gospel of Thomas*, VIII–X; XI–XII (tr. Carney, 93).

[102] Augustine, *City of God*, XXII.8–9 (tr. Bettenson, 1033–48).

[103] Augustine, *City of God*, XXII.9 (tr. Bettenson, 1048).

that miracles were not possible. It is by no means improbable that Pseudo-Augustine knew the genuine Augustine's *City of God*.[104] The writer's unnamed opponent(s) had argued that God had completed nature at the end of the creative process and could do nothing to interfere with its workings, because, in doing so, 'he would create new nature'. Pseudo-Augustine counters this with the statement that when God rested from creation he did not cease to govern what he created, but in doing this he does not create anything new:

And on the seventh day he who never ceases from the regimen of governance rested from the work of creation. Therefore, he who was then the creator should now be understood as God our governor; and thus, even if we see something new coming into being among created things, God should be thought not to create a new nature in them, but to govern that which he first created.[105]

The third of Pseudo-Augustine's three books is devoted to the miracles of Christ, with the very last section given over to the miracles of Peter in the Acts of the Apostles. In this book, as in the first two, the author uses a two-pronged stick to beat his opponent(s). First, he shows that God never does anything counter to the nature he has created (for example, Lot's wife is not subjected to anything new when she is turned into a pillar of salt, because salt is already present in the body). Secondly, for many of the miracles discussed, the author draws parallels to other parts of scripture, thus compelling his antagonist(s) to deny the veracity of increasingly larger tracts of the Bible. Pseudo-Augustine works from two closely linked exegetical principles: (1) scripture does not lie,[106] and (2) the historical sense of scripture must be given pride of place:

Moreover, we have taken care also in this work to set out an ordered reckoning of historical events only, putting aside figural interpretations, since, in these passages where we have touched on some matters historically, multiple interpretations are held [to be possible]; and if [we drew] from them to discuss every passage, we would present to our readers a work [entailing] more and longer books. But we have thought it especially [fitting] to omit [such interpretations] in a rather casual fashion,[107] since whatever writers have concerned themselves with explaining these passages have adhered to the mystical and allegorical senses, that is, the figural explanations that are found in them.[108]

---

[104] See the remarks of MacGinty, 'The treatise', I.107–9.

[105] Pseudo-Augustine, *On the Miracles of Holy Scripture*, I.1 (our translation); Latin text below, 183. It is important to note that Pseudo-Augustine here departs radically from Augustine's theology of miracles outlined in *The City of God*, XXI.8 (tr. Bettenson, 980): 'for how can an event be contrary to nature when it happens by the will of God, since the will of the great Creator is the nature of every created thing? A portent, therefore, does not occur contrary to nature. But contrary to what is known of nature'; Latin text below, 183.

[106] Pseudo-Augustine, *On the The Miracles of Holy Scripture*, III.12 [*PL* XXXV.2200] (ed. MacGinty, II.172): 'Scriptura vera est, quia mentiri non potest.'

[107] Reading *neglegentius* with MacGinty for Migne's *neglegentibus*.

[108] Pseudo-Augustine, *On the Miracles of Holy Scripture, preface* (our translation); Latin text below, 183.

This passage shows simultaneously that allegorical exegesis was popular among seventh-century Irish writers,[109] and that some writers who discussed scriptural miracles employed this method of interpretation at the expense of the literal.

Near the beginning of his book on the miracles of Christ,[110] where he discusses how the star of Bethlehem could draw the Magi to Christ's birthplace, Pseudo-Augustine is careful not to violate his principle that God does nothing contrary to created nature. He proposes three possibilities: (1) the star was a real star; (2) the star was in fact an angel disguised as a star; (3) the star was the Holy Ghost posing as a star. The first alternative is discarded because the star of Bethlehem does not behave as stars should (they cannot desert their accustomed courses). However, either of the second alternatives is viable, because, as scripture shows repeatedly, angels appear to men in altered form, and, as scripture shows at least once, the Holy Ghost does likewise (in the form of a dove at Christ's baptism). The notion that the Holy Spirit would prefer to disguise himself as a star (which is possible since he is God) rather than change the nature of a star by forcing it to veer from its course is consistent with the theory behind the inverted formula of the eucharist discussed above.[111]

Pseudo-Augustine discusses numerous miracles imputed to Christ in the gospels, including the raising of Lazarus from the Dead.[112] This latter is discussed in the context of all the resuscitations from the dead found in both testaments. Curiously, there is no separate discussion of Christ's resurrection itself – Pseudo-Augustine proceeds from his general discussion of resuscitations to the topic of the 'saints rising from their tombs' (III.14) and the recondite subject of 'the Lord's food after the resurrection' (III.15). A possible explanation for the omission is that none of Pseudo-Augustine's opponents wished to tackle directly this central doctrine of the faith. The author of *The Miracles of Holy Scripture* concludes his work with a very brief section on the miracles of Peter (III.16–17). In the final chapter he alludes overtly to the transference of Christ's thaumaturgical power to the apostles: 'Behold how much apostolic power is in Christ when Peter accused a hale Ananais (and) bound him with death through such a great force of speech.'[113] By concluding his work with Peter's miracles as attested by Acts, Pseudo-Augustine opened the door to accepting the miracles performed by the disciples after Christ's ascension (*translatio imperii*), and ultimately, to the accounts of thaumaturgy contained not

---

[109] There appears to be a widespread impression based on Bischoff's 'Wendepunkte' that Irish exegesis was characteristically Antiochene. A more careful reading of Bischoff's article shows this to be incorrect.

[110] Pseudo-Augustine, *On the Miracle of Holy Scripture*, III.4 [*PL* XXXV.2195] (ed. MacGinty, II.156–60).

[111] See above, 126.

[112] Pseudo-Augustine, *On the Miracles of Holy Scripture*, III.12 [*PL* XXXV.2199] (ed. MacGinty, II.170–4).

[113] Pseudo-Augustine, *On the Miracles of Holy Scripture*, III.17 [*PL* XXXV.2202] (ed. MacGinty, II.176): 'Ecce quanta est apostolica virtus in Christo, sanum Ananiam dum Petrus arguit per sermonis tantum imperium, morte ligavit.'

only in the Roman martyrologies, but also in the numerous lives of more recent saints that were emanating from the western continent. The date of his work (655) corresponds closely to the composition of the earliest lives of Irish saints composed in Ireland, or, more accurately, to the time of composition of their sources.[114] The earliest extant Irish lives date from after the middle of the seventh century: Cogitosus's *Life of Brigit*, Muirchú's *Life of Patrick*, Tírechán's *Life* of the same saint, and Adomnán's *Life of Columba*.[115]

As noted, a significant number of apocryphal texts was known in Ireland at a relatively early period. The Acts of Peter and Paul and the Infancy Narrative (or Gospel) of Thomas were among the texts received. There is a twelfth-century Irish poetic version of this latter work, which may be based on an original text datable to *ca* 700.[116] The early Irish hagiographers modelled their saints on a composite image of Christ based upon both the canonical and the apocryphal gospels. Although the usual evangelical miracles, including healing, are indeed portrayed, a heavy emphasis is placed upon spectacular wonders such as resuscitating the dead.[117] Injury and the inflicting of death through cursing are also represented, as are self-fulfilling prophecies of doom. These acts qualify as *imitatio Christi* if we broaden the image of Christ to include actions represented in apocryphal works such as the Infancy Gospel of Thomas.[118] The group of wonders is expanded once again to include both the canonical and apocryphal acts of the apostles, particularly of Peter and Paul. This opens the way for power contests before kings, such as that between Peter and Simon Magus, and for the receiving of revelations, particularly those involving the nature of the afterlife, as was granted to Paul.

A few examples of the features just mentioned should prove instructive. A power contest such as that between Peter and Simon Magus before Nero is paralleled in a Patrick life. In Muirchú's *Life of Patrick* the contest involves the apostle of the Irish and a druid, with King Láegaire as judge:

. . . After this contest between the druid and Patrick in the king's presence, the king said them: 'Cast your books into the water, and he whose books remain unharmed, him we shall adore.' Patrick answered, I will do so, and the druid said, 'I do not want to undergo a test of water with him; for water is a god of his.' He had heard no doubt that Patrick baptised with water. And the king replied: 'Agree (to ordeal) by fire.' And Patrick said: 'I am ready to do so. . . . you yourself, and one of the boys in my service together with you shall go into a divided and closed house, and you shall wear my garment and my boy shall wear yours, and so you two together will be set on fire and be judged in the presence of the Highest.' And this plan was accepted, and a house was built for them, half of green wood and half of dry wood, and the

---

[114] Sharpe, *Medieval Irish Saints*, 14–15.

[115] *Ibid.*, 9–14.

[116] McNamara, *The Apocrypha*, 52–3. The Irish version of the infancy Gospel of Thomas is edited and translated by Carney, *The Poems*, 90–105; see also his Introduction, xv–xviii, for a possible date.

[117] Picard, 'The marvellous', 92.

[118] Dumville, 'Biblical apocrypha', 305.

druid was placed in the green part of the house and one of holy Patrick's boys, Benignus by name, wearing the druid's garb in its dry part; then the house was closed from the outside and in the presence of the whole crowd was set on fire. And in that hour it so happened through the prayer of Patrick that the flame consumed the druid together with the green half of the house, and nothing was left intact except the chasuble of holy Patrick, which the fire did not touch. On the other hand, happy Benignus and the dry half of the house experienced what has been said of the three young men: the fire did not even touch him, and brought him neither pain nor discomfort; only the garb of the druid, which he had donned, was burned in accordance with God's will.[119]

Patrick also dealt with druids by cursing them. Tírechán recounts the tale of Patrick and Énna's armed struggles against a group of druids. To make matters easier for Énna:

Patrick stood up and raised his left hand to God in heaven and cursed the (chief) druid, and he dropped dead in the midst of his druids, and he was consumed by fire before the eyes of all as a sign of punishment. And the people scattered all over Mag Domnon, when everyone saw the miracle and (Patrick) baptised many on that day . . .[120]

Patrick did not reserve his curses for humans alone. Like the Christ of the canonical gospels, he also cursed objects in nature. Patrick cursed several rivers, depriving them of fish, while blessing others, with a predictable consequence. He cursed the River Séle because two of his disciples were drowned in it. This was done 'in order to perpetuate the memory of his power (*uirtutis*)'.[121]

While cursing was a special prerogative of Patrick, prophecy was the particular attribute of Columba in Adomnán's account. Here prophecy entails not only the ability to predict the future, but also to see present events occurring at a distance. Adomnán devotes a short section to Columba's remarkable gift:

Along with the miracles that, by the gift of God, this man performed while he lived in mortal flesh, he began from his youthful years to be strong also in the spirit of prophecy; to foretell future events; to declare absent things to those present, because although absent in body he was present in spirit and able to observe what took place far away. For according to the words of Paul, 'he who clings to the Lord is one spirit'. So too, as this holy man of the Lord, Columba, himself admitted to a few brothers who once questioned him closely about this very thing, in some speculations made with divine favour the scope of his mind was miraculously enlarged, and he saw plainly and contemplated, even the whole world as it were caught up in one ray of the sun.[122]

[119] Muirchú, *Life*, I.20.8–13 (tr. Bieler, *The Patrician Texts*, 95–7); Latin text below, 183–4.
[120] Tírechán, *Life*, XLII.5–6 (tr. Bieler, *The Patrician Texts*, 157); Latin text below, 184.
[121] Tírechán, *Life*, XLVI.5 (tr. Bieler, *The Patrician Texts*, 161).
[122] Adomnán, *Life of Columba*, *Preface* (Xb) (tr. Anderson & Anderson, 205); Latin text below, 184. Stancliffe ('The miracle stories', 89) classifies the gift of prophecy among the 'vertical miracles' – 'those which portray the saint in direct contact with the divine sphere'. These are contrasted with 'helping miracles'.

It is interesting to compare the two seventh-century Lives of Patrick with that of Adomnán's *Life of Columba*. Muirchú and Tírechán are inclined to emphasise Patrick's role as missionary, teacher, and thaumaturge at the expense of his personal holiness. Of course, he is a 'man of God' and a *sanctus*, yet he does not engage often in acts of sanctity as judged by monastic standards. Muirchú's account offers more monastic images than does Tírechán's, which seems bent on ignoring them altogether. But the two accounts agree in stressing the founding of churches, ordaining clergy and performing wonders. Patrick also teaches: he provides his new clergy with an alphabet and sometimes even a copy of a book of scriptures written in his own hand. Yet he is more inclined to impose a penance than to perform a penitential act himself. As a bishop he exerts his authority over monks and converts men and women to the monastic life, but there is little in either account that shows him as monastic in his own life.[123]

Adomnán's picture of Columba combines traditional Celtic asceticism with the 'new' Romanising emphasis on thaumaturgy and special powers. While the Columba of the life possessed many of the powers associated with Patrick and performed similar miracles, he was also a model of the penitential life:

Living as an island soldier for thirty-four years, he could not pass even the space of a single hour without applying himself to prayer, or to reading, or to writing or some kind of work. Also by day and by night, without any intermission, he was so occupied with unwearying labours of fasts and vigils that the burden of each several work seemed beyond the strength of one man. And with all this he was loving to everyone, his holy face ever showed gladness, and he was happy in his inmost heart with the joy of the Holy Spirit.[124]

It is highly probable that the *Vita Columba*'s concern with thaumaturgy of different sorts reflects the interests of Adomnán and the late seventh century. As noted, the earliest account of Columba's life, *Amra Choluim Chille* written probably *ca* 600, has remarkably few references to the miraculous in any form. Furthermore, as Máire Herbert has persuasively argued, the *Liber de virtutibus sancti Columbae*, composed by Cumméne Ailbe (Cummeneus Albus) between 623 and 640, represents a tradition of Columba peculiar to the Iona monastic community that contains very few 'heightened' accounts of the saint's feats of holiness.[125]

Perhaps the most unusual of all the Irish saints was Brigit. She was the subject of several lives, including one in Irish. The earliest extant life, that by Cogitosus, was written probably not long after the middle of the seventh century. Like the early Patrick lives, it is a Romanising text. In advancing the claim of Kildare to be the 'head of almost all the

---

[123] Stancliffe, 'The miracle stories', 96, notes: 'One very basic point is to discriminate between Lives of bishops on the one hand, and those of monks on the other.'

[124] Adomnán, *Life of Columba*, preface (Xb) (tr. Anderson & Anderson, 187); Latin text below, 184.

[125] Herbert, *Iona, Kells and Derry*, 16–26.

churches',[126] it welds the institution of the monastic *paruchia* to the fanciful notion of an archiepiscopal seat:

By the merits of both, their episcopal and conventual see spread on all sides like a fruitful vine with its growing branches and struck root in the whole island of Ireland. It has always been ruled over in happy succession according to a perpetual rite by the archbishop of the bishops of Ireland and the abbess whom all the abbesses of the Irish revere.[127]

Cogitosus's work is occupied largely with Brigit's miracles. Brigit here and in the other lives is as mild and kindly as Patrick is terrifying. Her miracles consist of healings, restoration of lost and stolen animals, fertility of crops and animals, mitigation of birth pangs, almsgiving and the like. Despite her connection with fertility (doubtless based on her pagan model), her legend is made to fit into a Christological framework. In two miracles involving the curing of the blind and the dumb, explicit comparisons are made with the life of Christ:

After the Lord's example, she too opened the eyes of the man born blind. For the Lord has bestowed his powers and works on his members . . . And following the example of our Saviour who ordered the little ones to come to him, she took the girl's hand in her own . . .[128]

A striking comparison to Christ occurs in the 'quasi-eucharistic' miracle involving the changing of water into ale: 'For he who changed the water into wine at Cana in Galilee also changed water into ale through the faith of this most blessed woman.'[129] It might be observed that Brigit's miracle involved ale rather than wine so that the implication of priestly power in a woman might be avoided; this would gibe with her summoning a man to her monastery to fulfil the priestly powers that she lacked. It should perhaps be noted that a later life, written in the vernacular, alleges that *she* was raised to episcopal rank by a bishop 'intoxicated with the grace of God'. Finally we note a general comparison with Christ reminiscent of John 20:30–1: 'And so, confirming her teaching by signs

[126] Cogitosus, *Life, preface*, IV (tr. Connolly & Picard, 11).
[127] Cogitosus, *Life, preface*, VI (tr. Connolly & Picard, 12); *Vitae Sanctae Brigidae Virginis, praefatio*, VI (*PL* LXXII.777–8): '. . . amborum meritis sua cathedra episcopalis et puellaris, ac si vitis frugifera diffusa undique ramis crescentibus, in tota Hibernensi insula inolevit. Quam semper Archiepiscopus Hiberniensium episcoporum et abbatissa, quam omnes abbatissae Scotorum venerantur, felici successione et ritu perpetuo dominantur.'
[128] Cogitosus, *Life*, XI.2 (tr. Connolly & Picard, 16); *Vitae Sanctae Brigidae Virginis*, XI.2 (*PL* LXXII.780–1): 'Nam secundum exemplum Domini et haec oculos caeci nati aperuit. Sua enim nomina et opera membris Dominus largitus est suis . . . Salvatoris nostri jubentis exemplo parvulos ad se venire, filiae manum retinens manu sua . . .'
[129] Cogitosus, *Life*, VIII.2 (tr. Connolly & Picard, 15–16); *Vitae Sanctae Brigidae Virginis*, VIII.2 (*PL* LXXII.780): 'Ille enim, qui in Cana Galilaeae aquam convertit in vinum, per huius quoque beatissimae feminae fidem aquam mutavit in cervisiam.'

and miracles, she addressed the people with salutary words seasoned with divine salt.'[130]

Of the three great Irish saints, Brigit comes closest to the 'evangelical Christ' in terms of miracles. Although her status as a virgin is given due emphasis, Cogitosus says very little about her religiosity. There is no attempt to bring her into line with male saints famous for their asceticism. Brigit, like Patrick, reflects the Christ of the public ministry. But unlike Patrick's, her activity is entirely benign.

We may summarise Irish directions as follows. The early Irish Church down to *ca* 650, imbued with Pelagianist notions inherited from the common Celtic Church, doubtless resisted the introduction of hagiographical writing because of its frequent inclusion of miracle tales. Miracles, whether portrayed in saints' lives or in the scriptures themselves, entailed the notion of God's grace, and thus undermined the freedom of the will. Under the influence of the mostly southern *Romani*, who probably began to be active in the second quarter of the seventh century, hagiography was encouraged. Cogitosus's *Life of Saint Brigit*, our earliest extant example of a saint's life written in Ireland, reflects a group of miracles consistent with the canonical gospels. The other three lives, written somewhat later, represent a new departure. Not only is thaumaturgy a consistent feature of all three, there is also a marked emphasis on sensational miracles. These go well beyond the evangelical examples and embrace miracles drawn from both the canonical and the apocryphal Acts of the Apostles as well as apocryphal gospels.

Interest in the lives of the saints arose in England only a little later than in Ireland. This fact does not reflect a resistance to the miraculous, but points simply to the later development of literary activity in Anglo-Saxon England. In the south of England, the impetus for this interest was provided by sources deriving from the continental Church. Aldhelm, writing in Wessex in the late seventh century, drew from martyrologies and saints' lives, in addition to both the Old and New Testaments, to illustrate his *On Virginity*, a treatise addressed to the noble nuns of Barking. The models of virginity included the gospel writers, the early popes, fathers of the Church, the desert fathers, monastic founders such as Benedict, and martyrs, both male and female. All of the cases emphasise steadfastness in chastity, especially the willingness to accept martyrdom to preserve it. The accounts of the lives given by Aldhelm generally include miracles as well as descriptions of personal virtue and courage. Aldhelm recognises neither English saints nor Celtic ones in his collection. The collection is rigorously monastic in tone, even if only a portion of the figures discussed may justly be categorised as such. Chastity, the foundation of all monastic life, is the greatest virtue and the *sine qua non* of salvation. Indeed chastity, asceticism, and martyrdom are perhaps the chief, if not sole, reflections of the life of Christ. The

---

[130] Cogitosus, *Life*, XVII.3 (tr. Connolly & Picard, 18); *Vitae Sanctae Brigidae Virginis*, XVII.3 (*PL* LXXII.782): '. . . et sic signis et virtutibus sua confirmans, doctrina, [*recte* suam confirmans doctrinam] sermonibus salutaribus, et sale divino conditis, plebem exhortata est'.

inclusion of miracles is directed to showing God's favouring of the chosen saint and the power of God.

Aldhelm was a vigorous partisan of Roman orthodoxy. However, the first stage of his education was Irish, and he worked in an environment where Irish clerics, teachers and scholars were still active.[131] He may therefore have had an (unreformed) Irish audience in mind when he constructed his defence of a miracle wrought by Apollonius:

And, no sooner had the word been spoken than Christ, with his usual compassion in abundance for his hungry servants, sent to the cave-entrance porters whom none of them had seen before, bearing such an abundance of delicacies, that they were plentifully nourished with this divinely-sent gift of food up to the day of Pentecost . . . That this, moreover, was a donation of heavenly munificence, rather than a gift of human generosity, is deduced from the following by the most evident proofs . . .[132]

Aldhelm used miracles and defended their authenticity (possibly against Pelagian-influenced Irish doubt). Moreover, he wished to avoid another Irish fault: the use of miracles drawn from or modelled on non-canonical sources. Writing about St Paul he cites the *Apocalypse of Paul*:

. . . even though the so-called *Revelatio Pauli* says foolishly that he came to the delights of flowering Paradise in a golden ship. But divine law forbids the followers of the catholic faith to believe more, in any respect, than what the judgement of canonical truth promulgates, and the decrees of the orthodox fathers in decretal writings have sanctioned the utter rejection and complete banishment of the other absurdities of the apocrypha as being a cacaphanous thunder of words.[133]

Like hagiographers before and after him, Aldhelm makes a connection between a saint's miracles and his or her sanctity. *On Virginity* defines sanctity narrowly as persistence in life-long chastity, and so the connection to thaumaturgy is expressed in terms of that ideal:

John, the author of the fourth part of the (Gospel) story, . . . also restored to their original state of vitality two corpses of dead people whom a lethal venom had

---

[131] Herren, 'Scholarly contacts', 29–30.

[132] Aldhelm, *On Virginity*, XXXVIII (tr. Lapidge & Herren, 105); *De virginitate*, XXXVIII (ed. Ehwald, 289, 290): 'et dicto citius pro foribus vestibuli tantas diliciarum affluentias gerulis, quos numquam noverant, gestantibus solita pietate Christus familicis suis tam ubertim contulit, ut usque ad ⟨diem⟩ pentecosten . . . Quod autem caelestis munificentiae stipendium potius quam humanae liberalitatis exenium fuerit, ex hoc certissimis experimentis colligitur . . .'

[133] Aldhelm, *On Virginity*, XXIV (tr. Lapidge & Herren, 81); *De virginitate*, XXIV (ed. Ehwald, 256): '. . . licet revelatio quam dicunt Pauli in nave aurea florentis paradisi dilicias eundem adisse garriat? Sed fas divinum vetat catholicae fidei sequipedas plus quippiam, quam canonicae veritatis censura promulgat, credere et cetera apocriforum deleramenta velut horrisona verborum tonitrua penitus abdicare et procul eliminare orthodoxorum patrum scita scriptis decretalibus sanxerunt.'

suddenly laid low with the cruel onslaught of death; and so, flourishing in chastity, he persisted in blessedness up to the snowy whiteness of old age.[134]

The Northumbrian Bede and his contemporary Stephanus, both active towards the end of Aldhelm's career, depart sharply from the hagiographical practice of the West Saxon bishop. Both follow contemporary continental trends by writing separate lives of individual saints (as opposed to a collection of hagiographical vignettes) and by looking to the recent past as well as to their own environment for their models. Moreover, neither writer limits his work to illustrating a single ideal (such as chastity). Both attempt to give a rounded account of their subjects' characters and achievements.

Bede's hagiographical activity found a twofold expression: first, in the writing of individual lives; secondly, in his *Ecclesiastical History* and *History of the Abbots*. His separate lives include a work on the life and passion of the martyr Felix and another on Anastasius, which is lost. He also compiled a double work (one in prose, one in metre) on the life of St Cuthbert.[135] In the *Ecclesiastical History of the English People* there are numerous individual biographies of holy men and women, which occur, as it were, as *excursus* in the chronological framework. There one can find a summary of the activities of Fursa, Aidan, Cuthbert, Wilfrid and Hilda as well as other holy men and women active in the missionary and monastic life of the islands. Because Bede was writing a history, he concentrated on the more factual side of the activities of the saints, particularly their contributions to teaching and learning and the life of the Church.

In his hagiographical writings, however, Bede was as interested in miracles and wonders as anyone else. His greatest piece of hagiography is a 'double work' (*opus geminatum*) on St Cuthbert, who also features prominently in the *Ecclesiastical History*. Cuthbert was an Englishman who spent most of his life, apart from itinerant preaching, in Irish foundations: Farne, Melrose, and Lindisfarne, of which he was bishop for a brief period. Although given to asceticism, Cuthbert was an active missionary and preacher. The fact that this saint also occupies four chapters in the *History* (IV.27–30) shows his great importance to Bede as a model of sanctity and contributor to ecclesiastical life. As already noted, Cuthbert was unrivalled in his passion for penitential solitude, for vigils and fasts. When offered the bishopric at Hexham, first refusing, he then sought a transfer to Lindisfarne, where earlier as prior, 'he had trained many a life under the Rule' (*Ecclesiastical History*, IV.27). Despite Cuthbert's attachment to an Irish rule and spirituality, he was a model figure for Bede in that he governed Lindisfarne as a monastic bishop after the fashion of Augustine at Canterbury.[136]

---

[134] Aldhelm, *On Virginity*, XXIII (tr. Lapidge & Herren, 80); *De virginitate*, XXIII (ed. Ehwald, 254–5): 'IOHANNES, quadripertitae scriptor historiae . . . Gemina quoque defunctorum cadavera, quos letale virus crudeli mortis exitio perniciter prostraverat, in pristinum vitae statum restituit et sic in castitate florens usque cicneam vetulae senectutis canitiem feliciter permansit.'

[135] Bede lists his writings (with some omissions) at the end of *Ecclesiastical History*; see Colgrave & Mynors, 566–71, with notes.

[136] See above, 40.

In Bede's hagiographical account of Cuthbert, the saint takes on many of the aspects of his Irish prototypes: he is particularly strong in prophecy and foresight, but invariably uses his extraordinary power to avert evil and accomplish good. In this he differs from Patrick and Columba, who, as noted, often used their powers in apparently maleficent ways. Cuthbert had great power over nature, like Patrick and Columba, but used it to the benefit of mankind by calming the sea and driving away birds from crops. He was ministered to by angels, but also by creatures of nature such as birds and otters. In his benignity and closeness to nature he resembles Brigit. In his vigour in spreading the word of God he comes closest to Patrick. In his asceticism he is most like Columba. Of all the early Insular saints, Cuthbert is the most inclusive in the *imitatio Christi*. He exhibits Christ's power in his prophecy, exorcisms, and control of nature; he shows Christ's love of mankind by preaching, teaching, and healing; he follows in the steps of Christ in the penitential life.

In a very important sense, the Cuthbert of Bedan hagiography is 'new life' for the Insular world. The image of sanctity is made to serve central evangelical values that are often overlooked in the Irish lives. For all his resemblance to Irish prototypes, Cuthbert reflects a benevolent Christ seldom found in the Irish models. In chapter 22 of the prose life we encounter through Cuthbert the wonder-working Christ who taught the commandments of love:

Now many came to the man of God, not only from the neighbourhood of Lindisfarne but also from the remoter parts of Britain, having been attracted by the report of his miracles; such people declared to him either the sins they had committed or the temptations of devils to which they were exposed, or else revealed the common troubles of mankind by which they were afflicted, hoping that they could get consolation from a man of such sanctity. Nor did their hope deceive them . . . he had learned how to lay bare before tempted men the manifold wiles of the ancient foe, by which the soul that is without brotherly or divine love may be easily entrapped.[137]

Bede's ideal is purged of the more negative extensions of heavenly power that originate in the canonical Acts and greatly increase in the apocryphal gospels and acts. In Bede's *Life of Cuthbert*, we have no doubt that the saint works through the power of God; equally, there is no doubt that the saint imitates Christ only in those acts and personal characteristics that are sanctioned in the gospels, or at least, are consistent with the central values conveyed in them. Thus, just as Christ was ministered to by angels after his forty-day fast and temptation (Matthew 4:11), Cuthbert received the ministrations of nature after his own life-threatening spiritual exercise:

Cuthbert left the monastery . . . and went down to the sea; . . . going into the deep water until the swelling waves rose as far as his neck and arms, he spent the dark hours of the night watching and singing praises to the sound of the waves. When daybreak was at hand, he went on to the land and began to pray once more, kneeling

---

[137] Bede, *Life of St Cuthbert*, XXII (ed. and tr. Colgrave, *Two Lives*, 229); Latin text below, 184–5.

on the shore. While he was doing this, there came forth from the depths of the sea two four-footed creatures which are commonly called otters. These, prostrate before him on the sand, began to warm his feet with their breath and sought to dry him with their fur, and when they had finished their ministrations they received his blessing and slipped away into their native waters.[138]

As a final example of early English hagiography we note Stephanus's *Life of Wilfrid*, written after Wilfrid's death in 709, but probably before 720.[139] In many respects, this work impresses one as closer in spirit to Bede's *Ecclesiastical History* than to his hagiographical works. Only minimum space is devoted to miraculous occurrences. Stephanus concerns himself singlemindedly with detailing the events in Wilfrid's career as priest, abbot, bishop, and missionary. The writer has a keen eye for the politics of the day and likes to portray his subject as central to them. A recent study has argued that one of Stephanus's aims was to create an anti-ideal to Cuthbert: the apostolic authority figure and community-minded minister over against the inward-looking ascetic.[140] This is plausible. The few miracles mentioned in the Wilfrid *Life* are pastoral, beneficent, and strictly detached from any 'taint' of asceticism. In portraying a resuscitation miracle, Stephanus explicitly compares Wilfrid to the evangelical prototype, then makes a direct connection to the *cura animarum*:

Then the holy bishop, not doubting the power of Christ, and hearing her faith like that of the Syro-Phoenician woman, uttered a prayer, and when he had placed his hand on the dead body it breathed again forthwith, receiving the spirit of life. So he baptised the child which had been brought to life again . . .[141]

In the course of the seventh century Christ the wonder-worker was introduced to the Insular world through the dual channels of exegesis and hagiography. By the middle of the seventh century Pelagian-inspired resistance to the miraculous, whether represented in the scriptures or the lives of the saints, had been overcome. Once the genie was out of the bottle, it took on many shapes. Manifestations ranged from the strictly evangelical to the para-evangelical (consistent with the gospel miracles) and well beyond to the apocryphal. The once predictably benign Christ of the canonical gospels could be induced to perform actions (either through manifestations in the apocryphal texts or, indirectly, through the saints) that Matthew, Mark, Luke, and John never contemplated. But for Insular hagiographers, as for the gospel writers, wonders were not recounted for their own sake. In the Insular world they were made to fit closely with religious ideals: chastity

[138] Bede, *Life of St Cuthbert*, X (ed. and tr. Colgrave, *Two Lives*, 189, 191); Latin text below, 185.
[139] Colgrave, *The Life of Bishop Wilfrid*, x.
[140] Foley, *Images of Sanctity*, 107–31.
[141] Stephanus, *Life of Bishop Wilfrid*, XVIII (ed. and tr. Colgrave, *The Life of Bishop Wilfrid*, 38–9); *Vita Sancti Wilfridi*, XVIII: 'Tunc ille sanctus pontifex indubitata Christi virtute, et fidem eius secundum Syrophenissam mulierem audiens, oratione facta, manum ponens super cadaver mortui, et statim respiravit et spiritum vitae recepit. Resuscitatum itaque et baptizatum . . . infantem . . .'

and other forms of asceticism as well as the *cura animarum*. In the first instance they validate the merits of the saint; in the second they prove the power of God.

Christ the Judge

Christ who will judge the living and the dead at the end of the world is the absolute focal point of Insular spirituality. The *perfecti* do not contemplate God as God in the abstract, but as their judge. To think of God at all is to contemplate the last judgement and the state of one's soul when that dreaded event occurs. This is why Benedict Biscop decorated his church of St Peter with scenes from the Apocalypse: it was so that every person (whether lettered or not) might examine his conscience, mindful of that final examination![142]

Christ's ascension into heaven, his last act visible to humans, is directly connected to his future act as judge of the world: 'This Jesus who is taken up from you into heaven shall so come, as you have seen him going into heaven' (Acts 1:11). This text combines the gospel accounts of the foretelling of the last judgement (Matt. 24.30: '. . . and they shall see the Son of man coming in the clouds of heaven . . .') with the description of the ascension (Mark 16:19: 'And the Lord Jesus . . . was taken up into heaven, and sitteth on the right hand of God'). Thus we read in the Apostle's Creed: 'He ascended into heaven, is seated at the right hand of the Father, whence he shall come to judge the living and the dead.'

In a certain sense, the ascension marks the boundary between Christ the man and Christ who is God. From a theological point of view, of course, such an interpretation is false, since Christ does not cease to be God while he is in the flesh.[143] Yet the linear narrative of the gospels must have given rise to the apprehension of a chronological boundary between Christ's humanity and divinity. This linear apprehension would obtain particularly in the West, where rigorous adherence to Dyophysitism often led to a privileging of Christ's human nature.[144] As the human Christ turns into the divine at the point of the ascension, he changes from a soul-friend to a remote, unapproachable deity. Where he was once imminent in the world, he is now transcendent beyond the stars. Yet, miraculously, as long as an individual human is still in the flesh, he can still beseech Christ for protection – indeed, he can do so up to the very point of death. At the last judgement, however, with the abolition of the world and time, only the transcendent Christ remains. Christ at this point is implacable.

There were, essentially, two differing views of Christ's disposition at the point of the last judgement. The first is that of the *iustus iudex* ('just judge'),

---

[142] Bede, *History of the Abbots*, VI (ed. Plummer, *Bedae Opera*, 370). For a full discussion of the passage see below, 235.

[143] The theologically correct Western view was apprehended by Columbanus: *Letters*, V.13 (ed. and tr. Walker, 52–3).

[144] See Chapter II, especially 64–5.

or *iudex aequitatis* ('judge of fairness').[145] At the end of the world Christ will judge each person impartially according to his merits. The outcome is not predetermined, and everyone approaching the judgement throne comes in total terror and uncertainty of his fate. Here we have the idea of the weighing of souls, or rather, of merits. If a man's good exceeds his evil, then he is saved; otherwise, he is damned. It should be noted that in popular spirituality the notion of salvation being attained through a preponderance of good had replaced the stricter, and indeed orthodox, idea that anyone who dies in the state of mortal sin was damned, however great his merits in life. We find the popular view already entrenched in seventh-century Ireland. Near the end of his *Lorica* Laidcenn wrote:

> until, God willing, I reach old age
> and erase my sins with my good deeds.[146]

This belief would certainly not have been approved by Augustine, nor indeed Pelagius. In fact, Pelagius or one of his associates had stated the reverse: '. . . the crime of transgression takes away the merit gained by a deed well done'.[147] However, even with their much stricter ideas about the attainment of salvation, the Pelagians believed in what we today would call 'a level playing-field'. God has elected no one in advance; otherwise: '. . . neither good nor bad actions belong to us, and the result will be that neither does guilt bring punishment, nor are good deeds praised'.[148] Thus, God retains his neutrality to the end and so Christ can be seen as the *iustus iudex*. This is the judge depicted in *Precamur patrem*: 'Whom (*sc.* Christ) we expect to come as a just judge to render each his achievement'.[149] Columbanus, in his *Sermons*, paints a terrifying picture of the last judgement and notes that at that point the mercy of Christ is no longer operative; yet he insists on the absolute impartiality of the *iustus iudex* and thus appears to speak as a late voice from the common Celtic Church.[150]

The second view portrays Christ not as engaged in the scrutiny of the merits of the 'living and the dead', but as calling those to him who are predestined to life, and condemning to hell those who are ordained to death. This view is essentially grounded in Augustine, who bases his

---

[145] See Meyvaert, 'A new perspective', 135–8.

[146] Laidcenn, *Lorica*, lines 89–90 (ed. and tr. Herren, *The Hisperica Famina II*, 88–9):
   . . . donec iäm   deo dante seneam
   et peccata   mea bonis deleam.

[147] *On the Divine Law*, IV.4 (tr. Rees, *The Letters*, 94–5); *De divina lege*, IV.4 (*PL* XXX.109): '. . . transgressionis crimen benefacti meritum tollat'.

[148] *On the Divine Law*, VII.1 (tr. Rees, *The Letters*, 98); *De divina lege*, VII.1 (*PL* XXX.112): '. . . nec bona ad nos pertinent hac ratione, nec mala; et sic erit, ut nec culpa poenam habeat, nec benefacta laudentur'.

[149] *Precamur patrem*, XXXIX (ed. Warren, II.7):
   Quem expectamus
   Affuturum judicem
   Justum cuique
   Opus suum reddere.

[150] Columbanus, *Sermons*, IX.1–2 (ed. and tr. Walker, 98–9).

theology of the last judgement on John 5:29: 'And they that have done good things shall come forth unto the resurrection of life; but they that have done evil unto the resurrection of judgement.' Here the term 'judgement' is used in its most negative sense, as Augustine himself points out: 'This is "judgement" in the sense in which he [John] used the word a little before, meaning "condemnation".'[151] For Augustine, there are thus two resurrections: the first, the resurrection of the soul, which is in the here and now; the second, is the resurrection of the body, which is at the end of the world. Those who do not experience the first resurrection, do not rise to life in the second resurrection, but to judgement.[152] These likewise experience two deaths (Apoc. 20:14).

Augustine uses the 'Son-of-Man' imagery in developing his theology of the last judgement. Again, this is based on John: 'And he hath given him power to do judgement because he is the Son of man.' The previous verses (John 5:22–3) read:

For neither doth the Father judge any man, but hath given all judgement to the Son. That all men may honour the Son, as they honour the Father. He who honoureth not the Son honoureth not the Father, who hath sent him.

Augustine interprets these verses as follows: 'Here he [Christ] is showing that he will come to judge in the body in which he came to be judged; that is the point of saying, "because he is the Son of Man".'[153] Since, in this very passage, Augustine uses 'judge' to mean 'condemn', we can understand the passage to mean that Christ will come to condemn in the body in which he was condemned. We may thus imagine Christ returning to the world not in the glorified body of the resurrection, but in the body of the crucifixion. He therefore returns to the world not as an impartial judge, but as a wronged divinity seeking vengeance.

An angry crucified Christ 'judging' mankind is attested in Irish texts, and can almost certainly be regarded as an aspect of *Romani* theology. Blathmac gives a graphic image: 'At the angry coming of your son with his cross on his reddened back, that at that time you save any friend who shall have keened him.'[154] The image is repeated in the *Saltair na Rann* version of the *Signs before Doomsday*: 'The outstanding king will rise, so that he is visible to all, with his red oppressive cross on his back in the sight of

---

[151] Augustine, *City of God*, XX.6 (tr. Bettenson, 905); *De civitate Dei*, XX.6 (ed. Welldon, II.459): 'Hoc est illud iudicium, quod paulo ante, sicut nunc, pro damnatione . . .'

[152] Augustine, *City of God*, XX.6 (tr. Bettenson, 906–7).

[153] Augustine, *City of God*, XX.6 (tr. Bettenson, 905); (ed. Welldon, II.459): 'Hic est ostendit, quod in ea carne ueniet iudicaturus, in qua uenerat iudicandus. Ad hoc enim ait: Quoniam filius hominis est.'

[154] Blathmac, *Poem to Mary and her Son*, stanza 142 (tr. Carney, 49):
Fri tuidecht do maic co feirc
cona chroich fria ais imdeirc,
ara soírthat lat in tan
nach carae nod-coínfedar.

176

all.'[155] Blathmac extends the vengeance of Christ to include satisfaction for the martyrs:

For what those men [the martyrs] have suffered in the torturing of their bodies they shall have keenest vengeance; they are not clients of (a lord of) bad oaths.

For splendid Christ has risen; he is eternally safe in the eternal kingdom; the leader with great hosts, the triumphant one, victorious in battle, will avenge them.[156]

In this passage we seem to have a blend of the image of the angry Christ at the last judgement with the binding of Satan and the reign of the martyrs in the 'first resurrection' described in Apocalypse 20. The Heroic Christ, or *Christus militans*, has been absorbed into the image of Christ the Judge.[157] He returns to the world not to judge (in the neutral sense) but to condemn and punish. This concept of Christ the Judge was also uppermost in the mind of Bede. In his poem *On the Day of Judgement* he spoke of the 'wrath of the judge' (*judicis iram*), and, in a pair of lines:

> Then his ardour for revenge does not care to spare anyone
> Except him who approaches cleansed of all sin.[158]

In the last analysis, the most enduring Celtic image of Christ was Christ the Perfect Monk, combining the desert and the cross. It was only by following this Christ that one might at least have a chance of escaping the wrath of Christ the Judge who will come at the end of the world. In these two images Christ is divided between his human and his divine nature. Christ's humanity is represented in the man who practised mortification and died on the cross. His full divinity is restricted largely to his eschatalogical role. The divine Christ who rose from the dead at Easter and ascended into heaven is largely missing, or ambiguously represented, in the earliest period of our enquiry. Likewise there is a strong initial resistance to his role as a wonder-worker, as is reflected in the halting development of miracle-filled saints' lives in seventh-century Ireland. In the second half of the seventh century this aspect of Christ's *exousia* is fully accepted and augmented from accounts in non-canonical sources. However, the gospel accounts of the divine Christ on earth from his resurrection to ascension is overshadowed, and to some extent replaced, by the heroic Christ, the harrower of hell; indeed, the divine man who conquers Satan

---

[155] *Signs before Doomsday*, LXIV (tr. Herbert & McNamara, 158); (ed. Stokes, *Saltair na Rann*, lines 8269–72):
> Atre in rí robúadach
> conidfoidreich doib huile,
> *con*chroich deirg do dúalaig
> *fri*aaiss fiadgnúis achduine.

[156] Blathmac, *Poem to Mary and her Son*, stanzas 256–7 (tr. Carney, 87); Irish text below, 185.

[157] See the discussion in Chapter VII, below, 262.

[158] Bede, *On the Day of Judgement* (our translation); *De die iudicii* (*PL* XCIV.635):
> Nec vindex ardor cuiquam tunc parcere curat
> Sordibus ablutus veniat nisi ab omnibus illuc.

and hell is not fully transcendent. Because he engages in an *agon*, in which he can potentially suffer, he retains something of his humanity even in the underworld; his combat with the devil can be imitated by all *milites Christi* who are still in this life. Ultimately, western Dyophysitism, which was so strongly represented in the theology of the British Isles, created a Christ who was 'human, all too human', even in his aspect where he should be most divine. Where is the Christ of the resurrection? Hard to find. But the human Christ we have described surely spoke to barbarian kingdoms, where wizards might still be found, and where violence was all but impossible to contain.[159]

Additional Texts

13. *Expositio Evangelii Marci*, I.45 (ed. Cahill, *Expositio Evangelii Marci*, 18): 'Certe non omnibus manifestus est Iesus qui latis atque plateis seruiunt laudibus, et propriis uoluntatibus, sed ostendit se is qui foris cum Petro exeunt; et in desertis locis quae elegit Dominus ad orandum et ad reficiendum populum, qui deserit dilectionem mundi et deserit omnia quae possident ut dicant, "Portio mea Dominus".'

15. Cassian, *Conferences*, I.viii.2–3 (ed. Pichery, I.86): 'Huius mentis uel actus figura etiam in euangelio per Martham et Mariam pulcherrime designatur. Cum enim Martha sancto utique ministerio deseruiret, utpote quae ipsi domino eiusque discipulis ministrabat, et Maria spiritali tantummodo intenta doctrinae Iesu pedibus inhaereret, quos osculans bonae confessionis liniebat unguento, praefertur tamen a domino, quod et meliorem elegerit partem et eam quae ab ea non possit auferri.'

22. *Carmen de transitu mundi*, lines 13–16, 61–4, 89–92 (ed. Walker, 182–4):

> Quod pro Christo largiri
> Nolunt, omnes avari
> Inportune amittunt . . .
>
> Caveto, filiole,
> Feminarum species,
> Per quas mors ingreditur,
> Non parva pernicies.
>
> De terrenis eleva
> Tui cordis oculos;
> Ama amantissimos
> Angelorum populos . . .

24. Columbanus, *Instructiones*, I.4 (ed. Walker, 64): 'Amplius non requiras de Deo; quia volentibus altam scire profunditatem rerum ante natura

---

[159] Etchingham, *Church Organisation*, 299–318; also, see McCone, *Pagan Past and Christian Present*, esp. ch. 9, 'Druids and Outlaws', 203–32.

consideranda est. Trinitatis enim scientia profunditati maris merito comparatur . . . Si quis ergo scire voluerit profundissimum divinae cognitionis pelagus, istud visibile ante si possit pervideat, et quanto minus cognoscere se noverit de his quae intra mare latent, tanto plus intellegat minora se scire posse de auctoris profunditate.'

32. Cassian, *Conlationes*, IX.xxv.1 (ed. Pichery, I.61–2): '. . . quae omnem transcendens humanum sensum nullo non dicam sono uocis nec linguae motu nec ulla uerborum pronuntiatione distinguitur, sed quam mens infusione caelestis illius luminis inlustrata non humanis atque angustis designat eloquiis, sed conglobatis sensibus uelut de fonte quodam copiosissimo effundit ubertim atque ineffabiliter eructat ad deum, tanta promens in illo breuissimo temporis puncto, quanta nec eloqui facile nec percurrere mens in semet ipsam reuersa praeualeat.'

35. Columbanus, *Regulae*, IX (ed. Walker, 140): 'Mortificationis igitur triplex est ratio: non animo discordare, non lingua libita loqui, non ire quoquam absolute. Suum est semper dicere seni quamvis contraria iubenti, *Non sicut ego volo, sed sicut tu vis*, iuxta exemplum domini salvatoris qui ait, *Descendi de caelo, non ut faciam voluntatem meam, sed voluntatem eius qui me misit patris.*'

39. Bede, *Historia Ecclesiastia*, III.19 (edd. Colgrave & Mynors, 274, 276): '. . . multis annis in Scottia uerbum Dei omnibus adnuntians tumultus inruentium turbarum non facile ferret, relictis omnibus quae habere uidebatur, ab ipsa quoque insula patria decessit, et paucis cum fratribus per Brettones in prouinciam Anglorum deuenit, ibique praedicans Verbum, ut diximus, monasterium nobile construxit. Quibus rite gestis, cupiens se ab omnibus saeculi huius et ipsius quoque monasterii negotiis alienare . . . et ipse ab omnibus mundi rebus liber in anchoretica conuersatione uitam finire disposuit.'

40. Bede, *Historia Ecclesiastica*, V.12 (edd. Colgrave & Mynors, 496, 498): 'Accepit autem in eodem monasterio locum mansionis secretiorem, ubi liberius continuis in orationibus famulatui sui Conditoris uacaret. Et quia locus ipse super ripam fluminis erat situs, solebat hoc creber ob magnum castigandi corporis affectum ingredi, ac saepius in eo supermeantibus undis inmergi; sicque ibidem quamdiu sustinere posse uidebatur, psalmis uel precibus insistere, fixusque manere ascendente aqua fluminis usque ad lumbos, aliquando et usque ad collum. . . . Sicque usque ad diem suae uocationis infatigabili caelestium bonorum desiderio corpus senile inter cotidiana ieiunia domabat, multisque et uerbo et conuersatione saluti fuit.'

46. Bede, *Vita Sancti Cuthberti*, XVIII (ed. Colgrave, *Two Lives*, 220): 'Deinde increscente studio perfectionis includitur in suo monasterio, atque ab hominum remotus aspectibus, solitariam in ieiuniis orationibus et uigiliis discit agere uitam, rarum cum aduenientibus de intus habens colloquium, et hoc per fenestram. Qua primitus aperta et uideri a fratribus, et fratres quos

alloquebatur ipse uidere gaudebat, exin praecendente tempore et ipsam obclusit, nec nisi dandae benedictionis uel alterius cuiuslibet certae necessitatis gratia reserabat.'

47. Bede, *Vita Sancti Cuthberti*, IX (ed. Colgrave, *Two Lives*, 186): 'Solebat autem ea maxime loca peragrare, illis predicare in uiculis, qui in arduis asperisque montibus procul positi aliis horrori erant ad uisendum, et paupertate pariter ac rusticitate sua doctorum prohibebant accessum. Quos tamen ille pio libenter mancipatus labori, tanta doctrinae excolebat industria, ut de monasterio egrediens, sepe ebdomada integra, aliquando duabus uel tribus, nonnunquam etiam mense pleno domum non rediret, sed demoratus in montanis plebem rusticam uerbo predicationis simul et exemplo uirtutis ad coelestia uocaret.'

55. *Hisperica Famina*, A.561–70 (ed. Herren, *The Hisperica Famina I*, 108); *De Oratione*:
>   Supernum uasti posco herum poli, –
>   qui mundanam almo numine condidit molem,
>   tithico terrestrem obuallat limbo crepidinem,
>   humanos lecto restaurat uernaculos incremento,
>   gla⟨u⟩cicomas folicia strue tegit amurcas,
>   florigeros alit de tellure culmos,
>   almi gibrarum turmis collocat premia throni, –
>   mihi aestiuum nauiganti fretum
>   robustam concede puppim,
>   ut furibunda euadam discrimina.

56. *Litany of Jesus – I* (ed. Plummer, *Irish Litanies*, 34–5): 'Co *n*imragba *f*or greis 7 dítin, 7 dethidin, do*m* imdegail, 7 do*m* imditen, *ar* demnaib *cona* [n]ulib aslaigib, 7 *ar* uile dulib *in* domui*n*, *ar* tholaib, ar th*ar*gabalaib, *ar* pecdaib, ar *im*arbasaib in betha, *ar* gaibthib in chent*air*, *ar* pianaib *in* altair, do lamaib namut 7 ce*ch*a agesta, *ar* thenid ifirnd 7 bratha, *ar* enechcreca fiad ghnúis Dé, *ar* chomthet*ar*rachta ndemna, ar na docoemsat ní dún fri hit*ach*t ind altair.'

60. Mael Ruain, *The Rule of Tallaght*, XXXII (ed. Gwynn, *The Rule*, 18): 'Ionnamhail, . . . do bhiadh neach fá bhun croiche do chom a chrochda, an moladh do gheunadh se don righ do bhiadh da chrochadh 7 neimheile (.i. tuirsi) do geunadh se ris ag iarr*aidh* a shaorta air, as a letheid sin do mholadh 7 do nemeile do nimid-ne re ri nime annsa bhiaid far sáoradh o phianaibh ifrinn.'

65. Bede, *Historia Ecclesiastica*, V.12 (edd. Colgrave & Mynors, 498): 'Cumque tempore hiemali defluentibus circa eum semifractarum crustis glacierum, quas et ipse aliquando contriuerat, quo haberet locum standi siue inmergendi in fluuio, dicerent qui uidebant: "Mirum, frater Drycthelme" (hoc enim erat uiro nomen), "quod tantam frigoris asperitatem ulla ratione tolerare praeuales", respondebat ille simpliciter (erat namque

homo simplicis ingenii ac moderatae naturae): "Frigidiora ego uidi." Et cum dicerent: "Mirum quod tam austeram tenere continentiam uelis", respondebat: "Austeriora ego uidi." Sicque usque ad diem suae uocationis infatigabili caelestium bonorum desiderio corpus senile inter cotidiana ieiunia domabat, multisque et uerbo et conuersatione saluti fuit.'

66. Bede, *De die iudicii* (*PL* XCIV.636):
>Ignibus aeternae nigris loca plena gehennae,
>Frigora mista simul ferventibus algida flammis.
>Nunc oculos nimio flentes ardore camini,
>Nunc iterum nimio stridentes frigore dentes.
>His miseris vicibus miseri volvuntur in aevum,
>Obscuras inter picea caligine noctes.

69. *Fís Adomnan* (edd. Bergin and Best, 73): 'Atat dano drem mór aile and hi comfocus dond lucht sin 7 is adbul a pian. Is amlaid iarom atát i cumriuch fri colomna tentide. Muir tened impu connice a smecha. Slabrada tentide imma medón fo deilb natrach lassait a ngnússi osin péin. Is iat iarom filet isin phéin sin pecdaig 7 fingalaig 7 áes admillte ecailse Dé 7 airchinnig etrócair bíte ós inchaib martra na nnáeb for danaib 7 dechnadaib na hecailsi. 7 dogníat dona indmasaib selba sainrudcha sech aígedu 7 aidlicnechu in Comded.'

Atát dano and slóig móra ina sesam do gréss i llathachaib círdubaib connice a cressa cochaill gerra aigreta impu. Ní anat 7 ní thairiset tría bithu, acht na cressa oca loscod eter úacht 7 tess. Slúaig demna na mórthimchiull 7 pluic thentide ina llámaib ocá mbúalad ina cend 7 siat ic sírthacra fríu. A n-aigthe uile ma trúag fothúaid 7 gáeth garb goirt ina firetan maróen ri cach n-olc. Frassa derga tentide oc ferthain forro cach n-aidche 7 cach laí. 7 ní chumgat a n-imgabáil acht a fulang tria bithu sír oc coí 7 ic dogra.'

71. *Transitus Mariae, ad fin.* (ed. Donahue, 54): 'Tainig crist agus araen agus adubairt re michel: scuir do thaisbeannadh pian ifirnn, o conncadar lucht ifirnn muire agus crist do-rinnidar toirsi agus crist do-rinnidar toirsi agus adubradar: a muiri maithair na soillsidh guidh ar do mac fa urtacht do tabairt duinn o na pianuibh a-fuilmuid.

Do-fregair crist doibh agus is edh ro-raidh: ro-crocadh misi ar bar son-si agus do tolladh mo thaebh agus do-coronadh mo ceann, sibsi *uero* ro-obabair .x. n-aithneadha reachta de tar m'forceadul-sa agus cad fa-tiubruinn cumsanadh daibh? Is ann sin do-leig muire a glun ar lar agus do-nocht a cich deas agus do-leig deora troma co lar agus do-guibh a mac fa oirithin do tobairt do lucht ifirnn.

Is ann sin adubairt crist: do-ber-sa a n-onoir muiri agus na n-easbul agus micil cumsanadh re tri uairib gach domnaidh doib ar a pianaibh. Atbert Isu: dunaid iferrn. do-duinsid ifernn ar a forail-sean.'

83. *Precamur patrem*, XXXIII-XXXV (ed. Warren, II.7):
>Corrosum nodis
>Annis fere millibus

Extricat sensis
Inferi feralibus.

[Et] protoplastum
[Probr]osa soboli
Abjecta mali morte
Saeva ultrice.

Quemque antiquum
Paradiso incolam
Recursu suo
Clementer restituit.

84. Blathmac, *Poem to Mary and her Son*, stanzas 174–7 (ed. Carney, 58, 60):
Is é ro-chés frisin croich,
buí adnacuil fo huarchloich,
ocus do-dechuid iar sin
du chuaird isnaib hifernaib.

Robu coscrach diä chur,
a gleten fri diäbul;
demun truag ro-decht a blat,
tucad airi a mórbrat.

Is do mac Ísu ro-lá
ima muin secht slabrada
ocus cotn-áraig – ní gó! –
I n-íchtur a thegdaiseo

Táraill iarum a chorp leis
ó ru-llá de in móirgreis,
ocus as-réracht – scél nglé! –
diä Cáscc iar tredensea.

86. Johannes Scottus Eriugenae, *Carmina* VI, lines 1–16 (ed. Herren, *Iohannis Scotti Eriugenae Carmina*, 80):
Emicat ex Erebo lux mundi magna triumphans:
    Primitias uitae ⟨mors⟩ moribunda stupet.
Prosiliunt Furiae, concurrunt undique Parcae:
    Mirantur tristem congemuisse Stygem.
Ille dein princeps baratri petit arma sueta,
    Quis genus humanum subdidit ipse sibi:
Sed mox ut uidit ruitantia limina fracta,
    Territus, attonitus, fugit ad ima domus.
Non tamen euasit tenebrosa per antra tyrannus:
    Fortior intrauit, qui sua uasa tulit.
Attractus, captus, uinctus, strictusque catenis,
    Detentus, domitus, pulsus ab arce, prius
Qua mundi princeps elatus sederat, olim
    Bestia saeua, uorax indomitaque diu.

Sed uictor mundi praestantior omnibus unus
Totam collisit comminuitque caput.

87. Johannes Scottus Eriugenae, *Carmina* IX, lines 43–8 (ed. Herren, *Iohannis Scotti Eriugenae Carmina*, 92):
Eheu quis mihi congreditur, quis fortis in armis
Audax committit mundi cum principe bellum?
Illene confixus ligno septusque sepulchro . . .

. . . .

Addictus morti, Romano principe caesus?
Hoc egomet feci, fateor, totumque peregi:
Me stultum latuit uirtus humilisque potestas.

105. Pseudo-Augustine, *De mirabilibus sacrae scripturae*, I.1 [*PL* XXXV.2151-] (ed. MacGinty, II.8): 'Et in die septimo requievit ab opere creationis, qui nunquam cessat a gubernationis regimine. Tunc ergo creator, nunc gubernator Deus intelligendus est: ac per hoc etiamsi novi aliquid in creaturis exoriri videamus, non creare ibi novam naturam, sed gubernare olim creatam Deus putandus est.'

Augustine, *De civitate Dei*, XXI.8 (ed. Welldon, II.536): 'Quo modo est enim contra naturam, quod Dei fit uolunate, cum uoluntas tanti utique conditoris conditae rei cuiusque natura sit? Portentum ergo fit non contra naturam, sed contra quam est nota natura.'

108. Pseudo-Augustine, *De mirabilibus sacrae scripturae, praefatio* [*PL* XXXV.2151–22] (ed. MacGinty, II.3): 'Praeterea etiam in hoc opere curavimus, ut sepositis adhuc figurarum intellectibus, rerum tantum modo gestarum rationem et ordinem exponeremus. Quoniam in his locis de quibus historica narratione quaedam tetigimus, multiplex sensuum intellectus habetur; et si de ipso per singula disputaremus, plurimos libros et longioris laborem operis legentibus praeberemus. Sed hoc praecipue negligentius omittere idcirco rati sumus, quoniam quicumque auctores haec loca explanare curaverunt, mystico allegoriarum intellectui, hoc est, figurali expositioni, quae in his reperta est, adhaeserunt.'

119. Muirchú, *Vita Sancti Patricii*, I.20.8–13 (ed. Bieler, *Patrician Texts*, 94–6): 'His autem omnibus gestis in conspectu regis inter magum Patriciumque ait rex ad illos: "Libros uestros in aquam mittite et illum cuius libri inlessi euasserunt adorabimus". Respondit Patricius: "Faciam ego", et dixit magus: "Nolo ego ad iudicium aquae uenire cum isto; aquam enim deum habet"; certe audiuit babtisma per aquam a Patricio datum. Et respondens rex ait: "Permitte per ignem." Et ait Patricius: "Prumptus sum." At magus nolens dixit: "Hic homo uersa uice in alternos annos nunc aquam nunc ignem deum ueneratur." Et ait sanctus: "Non sic, sed tu ipse ibis et unus ex meis pueris ibit tecum in separatam et conclaussam domum et meum erga te et tuum erga me⟨um puerum⟩ erit uestimentum et sic simul incendemini ⟨et iudicabimini⟩ in conspectu Altissimi." Et hoc consilium insedit et aedificata est eis domus cuius dimedium ex materia uiridi et alterum dimedium ex arida

facta est, et missus est magus in illam domum in partem eius uiridem et unus ex pueris sancti Patricii B⟨en⟩ineus nomine cum ueste magica in parte domus aridam; conclussa itaque extrinsecus domus coram omni turba incensa est. Et factum est in illa hora orante Patricio ut consumeret flamma ignis magum cum demedia domu uiridi permanente cassula sancti Patricii tantum intacta, quam ignis non tetigit. Felix autem Benineus e contrario arida, secundum quod de tribus pueris dictum est, non tetigit eum ignis omnino neque contristatus est nec quicquam molestiae intulit cassula tantum magi quae erga eum fuerat non sine Dei nutu exusta.'

120. Tirechán, *Vita Sancti Patricii*, XLII.5–6 (ed. Bieler, *Patrician Texts*, 156): 'Et ecce uir sanctus surrexit Patricius et eleuauit manum sinistram Deo caeli et maledixit magum, et cecidit mortuus in medio magorum eius, et exustus est ante faciem omnium in uindictae signum. Et dispersus est uulgus in totum campum Domnon, cum uiderunt omnes homines hoc miraculum, et babtizauit multos in illa die.'

122. Adomnán, *Vita Sancti Columbani, praefatio* (Xb) (edd. Anderson & Anderson, 204): 'inter ea miracula quae idem vir domini in carne mortali conversans deo donante perficerat, ab annis juvenilibus coepit etiam profetiae spiritu pollere, ventura praedicare, praesentibus absentia nuntiare, quia quamvis absens corpore praesens tamen spiritu longe acta pervidere poterat. Nam juxta Pauli vocem, "qui adheret domino unus spiritus est". Unde et idem vir domini sanctus Columba, sicut et ipse quibusdam paucis fratribus de re eadem aliquando percunctantibus non negavit, in aliquantis dialis gratiae speculationibus totum etiam mundum veluti uno solis radio collectum sinu mentis mirabiliter laxato manifestatum perspiciens speculabatur.'

124. Adomnán, *Vita Sancti Columbani, praefatio* (IVb) (edd. Anderson & Anderson, 186): 'Per annos xxxiiii. insulanus miles conversatus nullum etiam unius horae intervallum transire poterat quo non aut orationi aut lectioni vel scriptioni vel etiam alicui operationi incumberet. Jejunationum quoque et vigiliarum indefesis laborationibus sine ulla intermisione die noctuque ita occupatus ut supra humanam possibilitatem unius cujusque pondus specialis videretur operis. Et inter haec omnibus carus hilarem semper faciem ostendens sanctam, spiritus sancti gaudio in intimis laetificabatur praecordiis.'

137. Bede, *Vita Sancti Cuthberti*, XXII (ed. Colgrave, *Two Lives*, 228): 'Ueniebant autem multi ad uirum Dei non solum de proximis Lindisfarnensium finibus, sed etiam de remotioribus Brittaniae partibus fama nimirum uirtutum eius acciti, qui uel sua quae commisissent errata, uel demonum quae paterentur temptamenta profitentes, uel certe communia mortalium quibus affligerentur aduersa patefacientes, a tantae sanctitatis uiro se consolandos sperabant. Nec eos fefellit spes. Nanque nullus ab eo sine gaudio consolationis abibat, nullum dolor animi quem illo attulerat redeuntem comitatus est. Nouerat quippe mestos pia exhortatione refouere, sciebat

angustiatis gaudia uitae coelestis ad memoriam reuocare, fragilia saeculi huius et prospera simul et aduersa monstrare, didicerat temptatis multifarias antiqui hostis pandere uersutias, quibus facile caperetur animus, qui uel fraterno uel diuino amore nudatus existeret . . .'

138. Bede, *Vita Sancti Cuthberti*, X (ed. Colgrave, *Two Lives*, 188): 'At ille egressus . . . descendit ad mare . . . Ingressusque altitudinem maris, donec ad collum usque et brachia unda tumens assurgeret, peruigiles undisonis in laudibus tenebras noctis exegit. Appropinquante autem diluculo, ascendens in terram denuo coepit in litore flexis genibus orare. Quod dum ageret, uenere continuo duo de profundo maris quadrupedia quae uulgo lutraeae uocantur. Haec ante illum strata in arena, anhelitu suo pedes eius fouere coeperunt, ac uillo satagebant extergere. Completoque ministerio, percepta ab eo benedictione patrias sunt relapsa sub undas.'

156. Blathmac, *Poem to Mary and her Son*, stanzas 256–7 (ed. Carney, 86):
Anro-chésasat ind fir
diä riagad i corpaib,
bethus dígal dígrais de;
nídat céili drochluige.

Ar as-réracht Ísu án,
isin bithflaith is bithslán;
dos-fí in soismid sluagach,
in coscrach, in cathbuadach.

VI

NON-REPRESENTATIONAL IMAGES OF CHRIST

During the first centuries of Christianity, there was a continuing and often bitter debate as to the propriety of representational art in the service of the new religion. Although the Christian West created and employed representational religious art in the form of painting and sculpture from at least the third century on, the Christian East remained wary of its acceptance. Opposing viewpoints and policies were forcefully promulgated during the great iconodule/iconoclastic controversies of the eighth century. The reluctance to allow representations of Christ, the central figure and focal point of the religion, was undoubtedly at first due to the influence of Judaism on Christianity – note the injunction in the decalogue against graven images (Exodus 20:4). Two additional reasons came to play: Christ's divine nature could not be truly captured in the form of mere human flesh and portraying him as a man would be a denial of his true nature as the Son of God, Second Person of the Trinity, the almighty Redeemer and Messiah; and, since the older religions of the Mediterranean portrayed their gods as ideal human beings, doing the same for Christ would place him in concert with these gods, thus denying his essential difference. These reasons, combined with the intermittent fear of persecution and the desire to retain the notion of a special, or even secret, society within the larger population, led, very early in the history of Christianity, to the adoption of certain signs and symbols by which the adherents could both identify themselves and profess their allegiance to Christ. As a substitute for the figure of Christ, who could not be truly represented, the fish, the vine, and the cross, along with the *Chi Rho* monogram became the most common and universally employed symbols. The fish was chosen as a proxy image of Christ because its Greek spelling (*IXΘYΣ*) formed an acrostic of a profession of faith (*Ἰησοῦς Χριστὸς θεοῦ Υἱὸς Σωτήρ*) 'Jesus Christ Son of God and Saviour'. The vine could represent Christ because of the words which John used in reference to him: 'I am the true vine' (John 15:1). The cross became the other widely used substitute image of Christ since it had come to signify Christ's triumph over death and the accompanying promise of personal salvation and eternal life as the reward for the true believer. The sacred monogram, of course made use of the first two letters of the Greek *Christus* (*XPIΣTOΣ*).

With the spread of Christian belief into the West, and its manifestation in the funerary art of the catacombs from the third century on, the idea of representing Christ in human form gradually came to be accepted. At first, Christ would be represented, somewhat paradoxically, under the guise of the very deities he was supplanting. Christ as Orpheus, Christ as Hercules, Christ as Apollo, Christ as Sol Invictus, Christ the Teacher-Philosopher, can be seen in conjunction with the most popular of all images, Christ as the Good Shepherd. The central religious meaning of these images was the role Christ played in the resurrection of the dead and as the protector of his flock. Old Testament scenes of divine intervention and rescue, such as the stories of Noah, Jonah, Daniel and the Three Youths in the fiery furnace, represent the promise of salvation through Christ.

In the early fourth century, during the reign of the emperor Constantine, Christianity was adopted as the *de facto* state religion for the Roman empire. It was formally proclaimed as such by Theodosius the Great in the Edicts of 388 and 392.[1] With the backing of the imperial treasury, formal Christian art and architecture was a creation of the age of Constantine and his successors. As a result, the role and nature of religious art in Christianity changed dramatically. Since the emperor could no longer be accepted as divine within the confines of Christian monotheism, Christ became the divine king of heaven and earth, from whom all power and might flow; the emperor became his representative on earth, and the earthly court was a reflection of the divine court. The imposing and regal figure of Christ, clad in imperial purple and gold,[2] appeared in the paintings and mosaics of the huge churches which were erected throughout the now-Christian empire. Christ the Good Shepherd gave way to Christ the King. The originally loosely organised Christian Church became institutionalised and centralised, with the emperor frequently playing a crucial role in Church affairs. A thriving Christian figural art became evident in both East and West. Pilgrim commerce ensured that souvenir items, often embossed with religious insignia and figures, enjoyed a wide dissemination.

But it was otherwise in Britain and Ireland. Given the fact that Christianity existed in Celtic Britain from Roman times and in Ireland from the fifth century or just before, how does one explain the apparent lack, from the fifth century until the middle of the seventh, of contemporary religious artifacts upon which deliberate artistic attention and care had been consciously devoted? When Celtic Christianity began in western Britain around or before 500, there would have existed an established tradition of Romano-British Christian art.[3] The Water Newton hoard of fourth-century silver plate is evidence that care and expense had in some instances been directed towards the production of liturgical vessels.[4] Romano-British silver spoons inscribed with the *Chi Rho* and *Alpha* and *Omega* were found in the Mildenhall Treasure[5] while others have been

---

[1] Theodosian Code, XVI.1.2 (tr. Hillgarth, *Christianity and Paganism*, 46–7) imposed Christianity as the religion of the empire; the same Code, XVI.10.12 (*ibid.*, 47–8) outlawed all forms of pagan worship.

[2] See Henderson, *Vision and Image*, 122–35, for a discussion of the imperial appropriation of purple.

[3] Thomas, *Christianity*, 85–95; Boon, 'The early church'; Frend, *Archaeology*, 375–8.

[4] Frend, *Archaeology and History*, 147–50; also, Frend, *Archaeology*, 377; Painter, *Water Newton*.

[5] Brailsford, *Mildenhall*, 14.

given a provenance from Monmouthshire and Staffordshire.[6] A number of deposited *agapé* vessels have been found,[7] including those discovered in a Roman house in Caerwent – this fourth-century group included a flanged pewter bowl with the *Chi Rho* incised into the bottom.[8] The mosaic floor found at the Roman villa at Hinton St Mary (Dorset) which featured the image of Christ along with the *Chi Rho*, and the handsome floriated cross which was the centrepiece of a mosaic at the Wemberham villa in Yatton (Somerset)[9] attest the fourth-century development of a thriving religious art incorporated into the villas owned by Christian families. Farther afield, the wall fresco with the garlanded *Chi Rho* and orans figures from the villa at Lullingstone (Kent) provides additional surviving evidence of the use of both symbolic and figural art in the service of Romano-British Christianity. The baptism of a woman represented on the lead tank from Walesby (Lincolnshire) reflects both the liturgy and the ornamentation of ritual objects.[10]

In the fifth to seventh centuries, the continental Christian world was creating a wealth of objects decorated with religious images and liturgical objects that were richly ornamented. Yet apparently, the common Celtic Church did not see fit to transpose any of this to the objects needed for ritual purposes, or for Christian instruction. Primitive stone monuments with incised crosses continued the earlier tradition of carved uprights in both Britain and Ireland, but this cannot be construed as a concerted effort to produce a Christian art. Certain penannular brooches, such as the Hunterston Brooch[11] which contains an obvious cross form, may attest Christian ownership; but these cannot be connected with ecclesiastical purposes, and their dating is still contested.[12] Of the surviving obviously religious items the earliest may very well be the two tiny house-shrines, from Bobbio[13] and Clonmore[14] respectively, which have tentatively been dated to the seventh century – these are modest in their applied decoration.

There appears to be a break in surviving material evidence which would attest that a deliberate, luxurious Christian art was being created for use in the early Celtic Church. The lack of religious art would make the common Celtic Church distinct in practice from its Romano-British predecessor. The accidents of survival have been suggested as the reason for the lack of material evidence. The post-Roman economic decline has been invoked as the possible explanation for the cutting back or even cessation of artistic production. While these may have been very important factors, can they fully account for a two-hundred-year hiatus in artistic production not only

---

[6] Boon, 'The early church', 23 n. 41.
[7] *Ibid.*, 24 nn. 55, 57.
[8] *Ibid.*, 17–18.
[9] *Ibid.*, 22 n. 35.
[10] Frend, *Archaeology*, 377–8.
[11] Youngs, *The Work of Angels*, illus. p. 75.
[12] (R.B.K.) Stevenson, 'Brooches and pins'.
[13] Ryan, 'Decorated metalwork'.
[14] Bourke, 'The Blackwater shrine'.

in Britain, but also in Ireland, which was arguably a province of the British Church for much of this period? The technology and ability were there, as evidenced by the continuing production of secular metalwork, but in both regions there is no major religious artifact which exhibits a conscious policy of creating a precious religious art for Church usage in the period from *ca* 450 to *ca* 630.

This striking lacuna is twofold: not only is there the lack of liturgical items made of precious materials, but there seems also to have been a resistance to the use of figural images of Christ. Rather, we see a preference for diagrammatic symbols such as the cross and the monogram. Two additional determining factors which may help explain this lacuna should be taken into consideration: the isolation of the Celtic Church and the effects of Pelagianism.

It is well attested that the Romano-British bishops had taken part in the Church synods and meetings of the fourth century and would thus have been very familiar with the use of lavish and precious materials in the creation of both liturgical objects and religious art, as well as the growing preference for figural art that was widespread on the continent. These missions might have provided the conduit whereby such tendencies were transferred to the Church at home. After the Roman withdrawal from Britain, there is no evidence that British bishops continued to travel to Rome or to attend Church meetings on the continent. Continental churchmen (such as Germanus of Auxerre) occasionally visited Britain, but this was in order to combat heresy. This isolation continued until the early seventh century and may help to explain why the Churches in both Ireland and Britain did not adopt the concerted use of religious art during this period.

But the apparent lacuna can perhaps better be explained by looking at the Pelagian nature of the common Celtic Church. Among the most important tenets of Pelagian thought is an unflinching hostility towards every expression of luxury. In the treatise *On Riches*, possession or use of material things other than the bare necessities of life is designated by the word *avaritia*, the root of all evil.[15] Gold and silver may be God's creation, but the possession of them is not needful to existence:

> But who was it then that made gold and silver? . . . whose command was it that brought all things forth? Was it not God's? . . . I say that riches are not gold or silver or any other created thing but the superfluous wealth that is derived from unnecessary possessions.[16]

The imitation of Christ commences with the imitation of his poverty:

---

[15] *On Riches*, IV.1 (tr. Rees, *The Letters*, 176); *De divitiis*, IV.1 (*PL* LI.1382): 'Radix enim omnium malorum est avaritia.'

[16] *On Riches*, X.9 (tr. Rees, *The Letters*, 190); *De divitiis*, X.9 (*PL* LI.1398): 'Quis igitur aurum, quis fecit argentum? . . . uel cuius imperium uniuersa produxit? nonne Dei? . . . Ego enim diuitias, ut iam superius definitum est, non aurum non argentum, non aliam quamcunque creaturam, sed superuacuam non necessariae possessionis adfluentiam dico.'

In what manner then are we to imitate Christ? In poverty, if I am not mistaken, not in riches; in humility, not in pride; not in worldly glory; by despising money, not by coveting it.[17]

Moreover, God himself is displeased with the use of luxury items in his worship: 'For I have not made you to labour over frankincense or to buy me incense with silver nor have I desired the fat of your sacrifices.'[18] Pelagian teachings on this point almost certainly helped to fashion the outlook of the common Celtic Church. Survivals of this attitude can be detected as late as the later seventh century. Tírechán notes that Patrick had brought the required liturgical items across the Shannon: bells, chalices, patens, altar stones, books of the law and gospel books.[19] None of these is described as luxurious or decorated. This stands in sharp contrast to Aldhelm's contemporary description of the very luxurious vessels used at Bugga's church in Anglo-Saxon England,[20] to Wilfrid's use of gold and purple silk hangings in his church at Ripon,[21] and to Cogitosus's description of the lavishly decorated church of St Brigit in Kildare.[22] Thus Patrick's mission is credited with an austerity coinciding with earlier Pelagian ideals, perhaps reflecting a consciousness of the earlier, more austere attitude lingering as late as the period when Tírechán wrote and the restriction against sumptuous religious art had been eased.

As noted earlier, the Pelagians believed that a strict, literal interpretation of, and adherence to, the law of Moses was one of the requirements for salvation. This included the stricture against the representation of God and even of created nature.[23] In addition, the policy was very clearly stated by Cassian in his Tenth Conference on Prayer when he argued against Egyptian monastic anthropomorphism, the imaging of God/Christ in human form. He warned against changing 'the glory of the incorruptible God into the likeness of an image of a corruptible man'.[24] He argues that only the mind that is bereft of any representation of a God with human shape, either in the form of an actual icon or an immaterial mind-image, can truly ascend to

---

[17] *On Riches*, X.1 (tr. Rees, *The Letters*, 187); *De divitiis*, X.1 (*PL* LI.1394): 'In quo ergo Christus nobis imitandus est? In paupertate, nisi fallor, non in diuitiis, in humilitate, non in gloria saeculi, non concupiscendo, sed contempnendo.'

[18] *On Riches*, IX.2 (tr. Rees, *The Letters*, 184–5); *De divitiis*, IX.2 (*PL* LI.1391): 'Non enim ad hoc te feci, ut laborares in thure, uel mercareris mihi argento incensum, nec adipes sacrificiorum uestrorum concupiui.'

[19] Tírechán, *Life*, II.1 (tr. Bieler, *The Patrician Texts*, 123).

[20] Aldhelm, *Ecclesiastical Poems*, III (tr. Lapidge & Rosier, 49).

[21] Bede, *Historia Ecclesiastica*, V.19 (edd. Colgrave & Mynors, 528–9).

[22] Cogitosus, *Life*, XXXII (tr. Connolly & Picard, 25–6).

[23] 'Thou shalt not make to thyself a graven thing, nor the likeness of any thing that is in heaven above, or in the earth beneath, nor of those things that are in the waters under the earth' (Exodus 20:4).

[24] Cassian, *Conferences*, X.v.1 (tr. Ramsey, 375); *Conlationes*, X.v.1 (ed. Pichery, II.79): '. . . gloriam incorruptibilis dei in similitudinem imaginis hominis corruptibilis'. See generally, *Conferences*, X.ii.2- X.v.1

God in prayer. His doctrine of imageless prayer admits no place for images either as objects for contemplation or for didactic purposes. Although they were contrary to the Western Church's practice, Cassian's writings were known in the Christian Insular world by the sixth century. Although the oft-postulated post-Roman economic slide and the apparent isolation from Rome may have been factors, we argue that the strictures against sumptuous art and the representation of the Divine may have been a leading cause of the cessation of any real development and use of religious art in the common Celtic Church.

Pelagian and Cassianic strictures against representation may very well have given added distinction to a Church set in an indigenous culture which enjoyed a long history of artistic and decorative forms based primarily on abstract and geometric patterns and motifs. With direct Roman influence absent for so long, and with a long period in which Pelagian ideas had been influential, when the Celtic Church finally turned its attention to the creation of religious art in the seventh century, it is not surprising that it seems to have preferred the use of non-representational symbols for Christ: primarily the cross and the sacred name.

The cross

Throughout the Christian world, the image of the cross was the most frequently employed proxy image for Christ. Personal devotion to the cross and its invocation in daily life was encouraged from the third century when Tertullian recommended the use of the 'sign of the cross', the tracing of its shape upon the forehead, at every stage of daily activity. In the fourth century, in imitation of a practice adopted by St Anthony, the sign of the cross also became a visible weapon in the battle against the snares of the devil, a fortification for the beleaguered Christian.[25] The religious significance of the cross changed, in parallel step with the evolving conception of Christ. The cross retained its reference to Christ's triumph over death and the hope of eternal salvation, but under Constantine, it also became the formal manifestation of the universal triumph of the Christian Church, in both the religious and political arenas. The cross was deemed suitable for this purpose as the result of divine intervention and revelation, as recorded by Eusebius, bishop of Caesarea, to whom the event had been recounted by Constantine himself. In 312, during the struggles for supreme control of Rome, Constantine and his army came to a final, decisive encounter with the forces of his arch-rival, Maxentius, at the Milvian Bridge over the Tiber outside Rome. Constantine, a non-Christian, prayed to the gods for help before the crucial battle. Then, 'He claimed that he saw with his own eyes around mid-day, as the sun inclined to the west, the trophy of the cross in heaven infused with light and standing above the sun and bearing an inscription of this sort: "by this

---

[25] McEntire, 'The devotional context', 347–8.

conquer".'[26] The victorious Constantine accepted this as a manifestation of the great power of the Christian God and as a key to the successful revamping of the divided and troubled empire over which he assumed control. The role of Christ as unifier of the world and abolisher of disruption became an element of Christian thought which could be demonstrated through the visible shape of the cross.

The adoption of the cross as the signifier of Christianity and as the bulwark against the devil in the early medieval British Isles shows a Church in accord with this practice of the greater part of Christendom. Muirchú's seventh-century Life of Patrick demonstrates the devotion to and use of the cross. Muirchú relates how Patrick would sign himself with the 'victorious sign of the cross' a hundred times at every hour of the day and night, and would stop and pray at any cross he encountered on his travels. One day, as the story goes, Patrick was informed that he had missed a cross on the road. Returning to the spot to pray, he discovered it marked a grave. The saint inquired of the deceased if he had lived a Christian life. The dead man remarked that he had been a pagan and that the cross had been intended to mark a Christian burial but had been placed over his grave by mistake. Patrick had not initially seen the cross because it stood on the burial site of a pagan. The cross was transferred to the proper spot.[27] This legend doubtless tells us more about the seventh-century Irish devotion to the cross than about the historical St Patrick. Like the early crosses on Iona, the cross was meant to mark a Christian burial and was a centre for devotion and prayer. In eighth-century Ireland, the *Céli Dé* expanded the sign of the cross to the entire body when they adopted the cross-vigil devotional practice, a combined prayer and penitential stance with arms outstretched, in which the body became the duplicate of the cross.

The cross also satisfied the traditional Celtic preference for art which was non-representational. By the sixth century, its use on personal items provided a Christian label in a society which still had a large pagan component, while its apotropaic power undoubtedly increased its attraction. Crosses will later appear as decoration on locally produced liturgical items such as eucharistic chalices and patens, some as luxurious as the Ardagh chalice and the Derrynaflan chalice and paten. Reliquaries and shrines, such as the Moylough belt shrine and the Irish house shrines, produced in the period from the seventh to the tenth century, are liberally covered with crosses intermixed with snarling dragons' heads and Insular ornamentation, producing powerful invocations of the protection from evil.

Crosses of different configurations are employed for decoration, but the equal-armed cross with slightly flaring ends, often included within a circular frame, is encountered most often. The *Chi Rho*-in-circle had become a very common Christian design during the fourth century, with the circle origin-

---

[26] Eusebius, *Life of Constantine*, I.28 (our translation); *De vita Constantini*, I.xxviii (edd. Caillau & Guillon, VIII.25): 'Horis diei meridianis, sole in occasum vergente, crucis tropaeum in coelo ex luce conflatum, soli superpositum, ipsis oculis se vidisse affirmavit, cum hujusmodi inscriptione: HAC VINCE.'

[27] Muirchú, *Life*, II.1–2 (tr. Bieler, *The Patrician Texts*, 115).

ating in the Roman garland of victory.The motif was popular and appeared with regularity in sarcophagus and mosaic decoration in Italy and other parts of the Mediterranean world.[28] In the fifth and sixth centuries, the garlanded cross appeared with regularity in the mosaics of Ravenna. These designs, with the related cross-in-circle, found their way to the British Isles and clearly became the prototype for the form seen on objects such as the Ardagh chalice and on many of the incised slabs. This form of the cross was easily adaptable for application to these types of items, not only because of the Christian symbolism attached to that particular form of cross, but because it could be designed and cast as a medallion, easy to solder or rivet to the item needing decoration. The Celtic desire to use a circumscribing frame around artistic motifs could be satisfied by employing the circle.

There are two series of monuments found in the British Isles on which the full complexity of the iconography of the cross is reflected: the incised-cross slabs and pillars of Ireland and Iona, and the standing high crosses of Ireland, west Scotland and Northumbria.[29]

There are over one hundred stone slabs existing which are presumed to date from the seventh to the ninth century and which are elaborated with an incised cross.[30] Most of these were grave markers and were probably meant to lie flat on top the burial spot; many carry Irish inscriptions which request a prayer for the deceased person. The crosses display various configurations, different permutations of its Latin or Greek form (*Figure i*). Occasionally the saltire (diagonal) cross is combined with the *Chi Rho* to form a type of sacred monogram. The ends of the arms and stem were often expanded into terminals of differing shapes and a circle sometimes appears to connect the arms. When the equal-armed cross with flaring extremities is created as a cross of arcs within a circle, it can be read either as a cross or as a 'marigold' pattern, a positive–negative image puzzle much loved in Celtic art. Reflecting the spread of Christianity, the crosses also clearly indicate the Christian hope of salvation through Christ.

In addition to these markers, there are also upright slabs and pillars which have been decorated with incised cross forms but which do not seem to have fulfilled a funerary function. These are often taken as evidence of the continuation of the pre-Christian Insular tradition of erecting upright stones to mark locations of specific interest. It has been generally accepted that these stones may have served as focal points or sanctuary markers within monastic sites, or as boundary signals along roads and property limits. Sometimes the stone slab was left in its natural state, and other times it begins to approximate the shape of a cross itself. They range from very crude to very sophisticated in conception and execution. One of the most

[28] One of the earliest sculpted examples can be seen in the central panel of the Passion sarcophagus from the catacomb of Domitilla in Rome, dated to the second half of the fourth century.

[29] The Welsh and Manx monuments are not dealt with here but information can be found in Kermode & Wilson, *Manx Crosses*; and Nash-Williams, *The Early Christian Monuments of Wales*.

[30] Macalister, *The Memorial Slabs*; RACHMS, *Argyll.*

Figure i Incised cross forms, Clonmacnois

satisfying is the slab cross at Fahan Mura (Co. Donegal) which carries an incised cross on either face. In this instance, the crosses are filled with skilfully executed band interlace and the Greek Doxology as sanctioned at the Council of Toledo in 633 was inscribed in the empty space on the north face.[31] Arguably dating from the mid- to late seventh century,[32] this cross slab is one of a series found throughout the northern Celtic areas, including the Christianised areas of Scotland.

The monumental form which is synonymous with Insular Christianity is the free-standing carved stone cross. There are still well over one hundred standing high crosses spread throughout Ireland, Wales, Scotland, northern England and the islands in between, with the greatest number remaining in Ireland. The stone crosses, ranging in height from one metre to almost seven metres, are most often standing in, or close to, their original locations. Although every conceivable type of cross was used in Insular art in its various media, it was the Latin cross which was adopted as the basic form of the standing high cross. This choice may very well have been made because of the sculptural stability offered by the shape which combined a long upright stem and relatively short cross-arm. This provided a prototype which elevated the intersection high above the base and which created a monumental form easily readable from a distance. But the choice of this form most likely was not made by the Insular Christians, who probably adapted an idea which had developed elsewhere.

The cult of the true cross

None of the early high crosses can be securely dated, but it seems reasonable to regard their emergence as a regional manifestation of the widespread and lively cult of the cross which seized the Christian world and which was as strong in north-western Europe as it was in the Mediterranean. On the basis of stylistic analysis and study of the decorative motifs used on them, it has generally been accepted that the standing crosses of the Insular areas cover a long period of production, from the mid- to later seventh century to the twelfth century. It is unlikely that the idea of erecting a monumental cross in the countryside sprang up of its own accord in the Northern Isles. Nor is it likely that it was merely a natural evolution from the earlier pagan pillars. More probably, the development of the Insular high cross was a response to an external stimulus, one which came from the Mediterranean.

Constantine's fourth-century adoption of the cross as the *signum* of Christianity was further justified by the belief in the miraculous, and timely, discovery of the true cross on Golgotha by his aged mother, St Helena. The Shrine of the True Cross, combined with the Church of the Holy Sepulchre, was quickly established by Constantine and his sons. There

---

[31] Cit. Harbison, *The High Crosses*, I.360: Δόξα [sic] καὶ τίμε [sic] Πατρὶ καὶ Υἱῷ καὶ Πνεύματι Ἁγίῳ – Glory and honour to Father and to Son and to Holy Spirit.

[32] See *ibid.*, 376, for dissenting views which place this monument in the ninth or tenth century.

is no detailed description of the original appearance of the reliquary which encased the remains of the true cross, but it is known that a monumental silver cross was erected on the accepted spot of Christ's crucifixion. There is testimony of its existence in Eusebius's *Life of Constantine* and in the account of the pilgrimage of Egeria, a noble lady from late fourth-century Spain who visited the Holy Land and who wrote a vivid account of the homage paid to the true cross on Golgotha.[33] It is also reported by Arculf in *De locis sanctis*:

Towards the east, in the place that is called in Hebrew Golgotha, another very large church has been erected. In the upper regions of this a great round bronze chandelier with lamps is suspended by ropes and underneath it is placed a large cross of silver, erected in the selfsame place where once the wooden cross stood embedded, on which suffered the Saviour of the human race.[34]

Theodosius II had the Sepulchre rebuilt and in 417 erected a monumental gemmed cross on Golgotha, the famous *Crux Gemmata*, made of gilded bronze and studded with jewels and pearls. Pilgrims' accounts note that the cross was protected by a roof and that it stood at the top of a flight of stairs. The martyrium church, the sepulchre inside a great domed rotunda, the shrine of the relics, and the cross of Golgotha were all enclosed within a walled sanctuary. The *Crux Gemmata* of Golgotha appeared in the fifth-century mosaic in the apse of Santa Pudenziana, and later in the mid-seventh-century apse mosaic in San Stefano Rotondo, both in Rome.

With the establishment of the shrines on Golgotha, pilgrims from all over the Roman world travelled to Jerusalem to visit the holy sites. The cult of the cross burgeoned, initiating a whole new industry for the manufacture and sale of devotional mementos and holy souvenirs. Many of these small portable items, such as silver ampullae and flasks, had designs which approximated the appearance of the shrine which had been visited stamped or incised on them. With the return home of these travellers, descriptions of the sites and ceremonies became widespread, and visual motifs were transferred from the Holy Land to distant locations. A schematised depiction of the *Crux Gemmata* elevated on its base and standing under its roof became the reminder of the most sacred spot in Christendom.

In addition to its use as the dominant motif in Christian art, the cross also became the focal point for the outpouring of devotional writing. The *Carmen paschale* of Caelius Sedulius, a fifth-century Roman poet, contains a section advocating devotion to the cross.[35] The poems of Venantius Fortunatus include the famous hymns *Pange lingua* and *Vexilla regis*

---

[33] Egeria, *Travels*, XXIV.1–11 (tr. Wilkinson, 123–5).

[34] Adomnán, *On Holy Places*, V.1 (ed. and tr. (D.) Meehan, 48–9): 'Alia uero pergrandis eclesia orientem uersus in illo fabricata loco qui Ebraicae Golgotha uocitatur; cuius in superioribus grandis quaedam aerea cum lampadibus rota in funibus pendit, infra quam magna argentea crux infixa statuta est eodem in loco ubi quondam lignea crux in qua passus est humani generis Saluator infixa stetit.' See, O'Loughlin, 'Adomnán and Arculf'.

[35] See below, 200.

prodeunt which were first solemnly sung in 569.[36] This tradition was furthered in Charlemagne's court by the Anglo-Saxon Alcuin with his *Ad aram sanctae crucis, Ad sanctam crucem* and *Crux decus es mundi*.[37] Acrostic poems in which the form of the cross was embedded in the lines were popularized by Alcuin and treated with ingenuity by Josephus Scottus, an Irish scholar who accompanied him to the Carolingian court. The tradition was carried on by Rabanus Maurus.[38] Johannes Scottus Eriugena did not write figure poems, but he did write one poem that describes a cross with a halo or garland.[39]

In Anglo-Saxon England, Bede spoke of the relics of the true cross[40] as did Aelfric. But the shining examples of devotion to the cross appear in the eighth-century poem of Cynewulf referred to as the *Elene*,[41] and the famous *Dream of the Rood*. These are all indicative of the widespread popularity of the cult of the cross and its impact on the literary blossoming of the seventh and eighth centuries.

The history of the relics of the true cross and the monumental gemmed cross of Golgotha may have furnished the immediate impetus for the creation of the full-fledged standing stone cross in the British Isles. In 614, the reliquary of the cross was captured by the Persians and carried off. Rescued by the emperor Heraclius, the true cross was returned triumphantly to Golgotha in 628, giving a renewed immediacy to the Feast of the Exaltation of the Cross and that of the Discovery of the True Cross. But the victory was short-lived because the Islamic expansion swallowed up the Holy Land in 638, closing the sacred sites to Christian pilgrimage for the next several decades. However, the primary reliquary of the true cross had been transferred to Constantinople in 638. Unlike the Persians who had burned Jerusalem in 614, the Moslems inflicted little damage on the Holy City; but the holy sites were to remain in Moslem hands until the Crusades. Only in the last quarter of the seventh century could Christian passage to the Holy Land once more be undertaken. When the Holy Land was again accessible to outsiders one of the pilgrims was Arculf, a Gaulish bishop who sojourned in the Near East in 679–82. On his way home by sea, he was purportedly blown off course and fetched up in Iona where he related his experience to Adomnán, the abbot. Adomnán consequently composed his *De locis sanctis* in 683–6, which related Arculf's voyage, and described the holy sites of the East.

The first monumental manifestations of the cult of the cross appearing in the British Isles seems to have been in the form of crosses incised upon upright stones or pillars. These marked spots of particular importance to the

---

[36] See Walpole, *Early Latin Hymns*, 166–77.
[37] See *Alcuini Carmina* in *PLAC* (ed. Dümmler, I.310, 337, 225).
[38] Müller, *Hrabanus Maurus*, 121–34.
[39] John Scottus, *Poems*, II (tr. Herren, *Iohannis Scotti Eriugenae Carmina*, 65–7). See below, 201.
[40] Bede, *Historica Ecclesiastica*, V.16 (tr. Colgrave & Mynors, 509–11).
[41] *Elene* in *The Vercelli Book* (ed. Krapp, 66–102); *Anglo-Saxon Poetry* (tr. Bradley, 164–97).

local community. Adomnán, in his *Vita Columbae*, stated that St Columba erected two crosses on Iona to commemorate the death of a holy monk.[42] This would have occurred between the founding of Iona in 563 and Columba's death in 597 – the story goes on to indicate these crosses were still erect when Adomnán wrote a century later. There is no real possibility of these being the standing crosses which are now on Iona. They may very well have been cross-incised pillars, such as have been found throughout the Christianised areas of Ireland and Dál Riata.

It was during the seventh century that the free-standing wooden cross seems to have had its genesis both in Ireland and in Britain.[43] The Lives of St Patrick written by Muirchú[44] and Tírechán[45] both relate stories about the saint and obviously free-standing crosses but do not describe the material from which they were constructed. In England, Bede wrote that in 634 a wooden cross was set up at Heavenfield to mark a victory of the King Oswald over Caedwalla. This story obviously parallels that of Constantine's victory.[46]

Another momentous event occurred in 701 when Pope Sergius miraculously discovered a relic of the true cross in Rome. This was important since the other remains of the sacred wood were in Constantinople, to where they had been removed before the Moslem takeover of the holy sites. Sergius commemorated the event by elevating the importance of the Feast of the Exaltation of the Cross in the Roman liturgy and locating the main stage for the celebrations in the Church of the Saviour, called the Constantiniana. These happenings were undoubtedly known in Northumbria very quickly for there was a mission from Monkwearmouth-Jarrow, which included Abbot Ceolfrith and his successor Hwaetberht, in the Holy City when they occurred.[47] News would have spread rapidly to the Irish monasteries.

There are no written documents which date the genesis of the standing stone high crosses, but events would support a late seventh- or early eighth-century milieu. It is highly possible that the knowledge of the great upheavals in Jerusalem in the seventh century stirred up by the renewed fervour associated with the Roman cult of the true cross in 701 spurred the sudden, unprecedented building of the stone high crosses. The high cross could be seen as a commemoration of Heraclius's triumphant return of the relics of the true cross to Jerusalem, which ensured its survival. It could serve as a substitute for the monumental cross of Golgotha which fell into Moslem hands soon thereafter. The exaltation of the cross could become a local devotion. As mystical duplicates of the Holy Cross, and as testimony of the presence of Christ, these monumental crosses could serve as centres for local pilgrimage and as gathering places for worship and prayer. With the journey

---

[42] Adomnán, *Life*, I.45 (tr. Anderson & Anderson, 307).
[43] Hamlin, 'Crosses in early Ireland'.
[44] Muirchú, *Life*, I.12, II.1 (tr. Bieler, *The Patrician Texts*, 81, 115).
[45] Tirechán, *Life*, XXXIV.1, XLV.1 (tr. Bieler, *The Patrician Texts*, 151, 159).
[46] Bede, *Historia Ecclesiastica*, III.2 (tr. Colgrave & Mynors, 215–19).
[47] Bailey, *England's Earliest Sculptors*, 49; Gregory, *Liber Pontificalis* (tr. Duchesne, I.374).

to the Holy Land available only to the select few, 'pilgrimages' to the more readily accessible standing crosses could become an accepted alternative. Archaeological evidence seems to indicate that crosses and cross-slabs were set up in several locations in Ireland to mark the sequential prayer stations at holy sites.[48] The liturgical purposes and usage of the later scripture crosses may very well be a development from a simpler devotional function.

As substitutes for the true cross, which was mystically present at each site, the high crosses could serve a number of ancillary purposes. Mostly associated with monastic foundations, they became in time places of refuge and sanctuary;[49] because of their sharing the miraculous powers of the true cross, they could assume an apotropaic function to ward off evil, and later, the Viking enemy. Because their presence created a holy site analagous to Jerusalem, holy men were sometimes buried in the vicinity of the standing crosses and cemeteries grew up around them. In their later development, the stone high cross served as a boundary marker and a market cross. It is worth noting that, in spite of a common impetus, there are two basic types of standing high crosses which are geographically clustered, and which reflect a parallel development. The cross commonly found in Ireland and in Celtic areas of Scotland are of the ringed-cross type; the standing crosses remaining in England are mostly ringless.

The ringed 'Celtic' cross

Most of the extant standing high crosses in Ireland and most of those in areas of Britain and the islands of the Irish Sea which were dominated by Irish monasticism are formed of a tall Latin cross raised up on a pyramidal or stepped base, the cross-arm being joined to the upright by a stone ring. There have been several suggestions made as to the origins of this ringed type of cross. One theory saw the ring as a translation into stone of the struts thought necessary to stabilise earlier large wooden crosses, assuming that the stone crosses developed as a natural sequence from wooden prototypes.[50] Other scholars saw the influence of the Coptic cross (*Crux ansata*) which combined the ancient Egyptian ankh hieroglyph with the cross. Another approach saw the origin of this Insular Christian monument in neolithic and Bronze Age art with the ringed head being a derivation of the wheel or sun disc.[51] It is perhaps preferable to see an origin for the ringed cross in early Christian art, where as noted earlier, the cross-in-circle was a common motif.

There was one more image of the cross in Christian Italy which was more directly relevant to the seventh-century genesis of the Insular ringed high cross – the composite image of the *signum* of victorious Christianity, combined with the cosmic sphere, which was seen repeatedly in imperial Ravenna. In the mosaic of the domical vault of the mid-fifth-century

---

[48] Herity, 'The antiquity'.
[49] Ó Corráin *et al.*, 'The laws', 399.
[50] Ó Ríordáin, 'The genesis'.
[51] Roe, 'The Irish high cross', 213–14.

mausoleum of the empress Galla Placidia the magnificent gemmed gold cross of Golgotha floats in the starry sky, the stars circling it as if it were the immovable polar star, the centre of the universe. That the cross is to be taken as the image of Christ is indicated by the insertion of the *Alpha* and *Omega* signs near the extremities of the cross-arm. An even more dramatic combination of the symbols of the cosmos and the universal victory of Christ is seen in the mid-sixth-century mosaic in the apse of Sant'Apollinare in Classe. There the stars rotate about the intersection of the arms of the monumental *Crux Gemmata*, the whole being circumscribed within the great sphere of the Cosmos. The *Alpha* and *Omega* are once more seen, and a small portrait of Christ marks the centre of the cross. Raised high above the altar and the heads of the faithful, this magnificent image of Christ and Christian universality is one of the most striking sights in Ravenna. On a less ambitious scale, the image of the glorious gemmed cross in the cosmos became popular throughout northern Italy.

The motif and iconography of the cosmological cross had developed from the time of the early Church Fathers. By the fourth century, Gregory of Nyssa had elaborated on the meaning of the cross. For him, the cross is the visible symbol of the four principle extensions of the universe and of its unity in Christ – in his all-embracing gesture on the cross, Christ manifested his power to rule the quadripartite cosmos.[52] The cross becomes through its shape the vision of his omnipotent dominion over all things. Irenaeus of Lyon explained that the parts of the cross enumerate all six spatial directions for they symbolise height and depth, length from east to west, and breadth from north to south.[53] Connecting heaven and earth, Christ draws all people to him.

But more directly pertinent to the Celtic Christian was the fifth-century *Carmen paschale* of Caelius Sedulius, which was known in Ireland from the mid-seventh century. This long poem includes a reference to the cosmological cross of Christ as the world unifier:

> Then, suspended at the top of the branching tree,
> changing the wrath of judgement with his pious devotion,
> He himself was the peace of the cross, and illuminating
> its violent power (wood) with his own limbs,
> He decorated his penalty with honour,
> and gave his punishment as a sign of salvation instead,
> blessing and sanctifying the very torments inside him.
> Lest anyone be unaware that one should venerate the beauty of the cross,
> which happily bore the Lord, whence by a potent reckoning
> it unites the four regions of the four-fold world.
> The brilliant East flashes from the head of the creator,
> The holy feet are licked by the western star,
> His right hand holds the North, his left the middle axis (the South),
> And all of nature lives from the limbs of the Creator,
> And Christ rules with his cross the world compressed on all sides.[54]

---

[52] Ladner, 'St Gregory of Nyssa', 197–201.
[53] *Ibid.*, 204.
[54] *Carmen paschale*, V, lines 182–95 (our translation); Latin text below, 232–3. For

This iconography is paraphrased by Bede, Pseudo-Alcuin and Aelfric. A passage attributed to Pseudo-Alcuin states:

> . . . the very cross contains within itself a great mystery, whose position is such that the upper part extends toward Heaven, and the lower part, fixed in the earth, touches the depths of Hell; its breadth stretches out to the regions of the earth.[55]

That this interpretation of the cross was long-lasting is attested in a poem written in the mid-ninth century by John Scottus Eriugena which proclaims:

> Behold the orb that shines with the rays of the sun,
>   which the Cross of Salvation spreads from its height,
> Embracing the earth, the sea, the winds and the sky
>   And everything else believed to exist far away.[56]

By the mid-seventh century, the actual Golgotha *stauroteca* was no longer easily available to Christian pilgrims, but its image could be seen by northern travellers who visited the churches of Italy. The Irish monasteries sent missions to Rome, particularly during the controversies of the seventh century, and there was a renewed exchange of ideas and objects from one end of the Christian world to the other. It is probable that it was the memory of these images, fortified by the iconography of the cosmological cross already known in Ireland, which produced the prototypical ringed Celtic cross, the contracted cosmic sphere becoming the ring when fashioned in stone. The pattern may have been transmitted through the intermediary of the circle of the cross-in-circle design, which, when converted to three dimensions would have to be contracted to become possible on the free-standing stone crosses. There were two possible solutions – the solid disc at the crossing of the stem and transom as seen in both Ireland and Wales, and the true ring. With the emergence of the Celtic ringed high cross, we have an instance of the *Romani*-influenced response to ideas flowing northward from Italy.

The Ahenny crosses (Plate 1)

The most direct response in the British Isles to the growing cult of the cross and to the troubled history of the true cross can be seen in a group of stone high crosses erected in central Ireland, in the ancient kingdom of Ossory, near modern Kilkenny.[57] Of these seven monuments, the two remaining

---

indications that Caelius Sedulius was known in Ireland see (N.) Wright, 'The *Hisperica Famina*'; and Sharpe, 'An Irish textual critic'.

[55] Cited (W.O.) Stevens, *The Cross*, 69–70.

[56] John Scottus Eriugena, *Poems*, II, lines 1–4 (ed. and tr. Herren, *Iohannis Scotti Eriugenae Carmina*, 64–5); *Carmina*, II:
   Aspice praeclarum radiis solaribus orbem,
      Quos crux saluiflua spargit ab arce sua.
   Terram Neptunumque tenet flatusque polosque
      Et siquid supra creditur esse procul.

[57] Roe, *The High Crosses of Western Ossory*. The group includes the two Ahenny crosses, three at Kilkieran, and one each at Killamery and Kilree. See also, Edwards, 'An early group of crosses'; also, Harbison, *The High Crosses*, I.11–15, 117–20, 121–4, 133–4; II.7–29, 383–98, 404–12, 444–7.

ringed crosses at Ahenny provide the closest parallels to the descriptions of the cross on Golgotha, combined with the cosmic sphere seen in Italian mosaics. As with the greatest majority of monumental crosses, these were situated so that their main sides faced east and west, as did the Golgotha cross.

The crosses are obviously contemporary with each other and stand about three and one-half metres in height, the north cross being the slightly taller. They are raised up on fairly high cubic bases in the shape of truncated pyramids, which are covered with figural relief sculpture. This sculpture has been badly worn by time and the elements and it is now all but impossible to discern the subject matter.[58] The bottom of each cross shaft expands into a rectangular form which, when combined with the upper stage of the base, gives the impression of steps. On top of the north cross is a strange conical cap which may very well not have originally belonged to it. The same can be said of the flat stone now atop the south cross. It is probable that there was some sort of terminal placed on the crown of these monuments and that they have been lost over the centuries. The type of cross exemplified by the Ahenny group combines the elements of the tall Latin cross, the ring, the stepped base and the cap. Although this combination will become the norm by the time the great scripture crosses of the ninth and tenth century are erected and carved, it was by no means a universal formula for the early Irish crosses.[59] This would seem to indicate that in the Ahenny crosses, this combination of all elements must have been deliberate, a response to iconographical demands.

The decoration of these two Ahenny crosses is extraordinarily rich and varied. The surfaces are overspun with abstract ornament, still crisp and clear in definition. All the main patterns found on metalwork and in manuscript illumination associated with Irish foundations can be seen here, carved in stone. This is direct testimony to the unity of the Insular artistic repertoire, regardless of medium and location. The four sides of the shafts are covered with rectangular panels exhibiting what amounts to a veritable catalogue of Insular ornament: spiral compositions terminating in interlocked bird heads, interlace of single and double cords, fret patterns, geometric designs, and even one panel of interlaced human figures. The surfaces of the arcs of the rings are covered with interlace or scroll patterns, while exceptionally well executed band interlace of varying rhythms and spacing expands and contracts to fill the faces of the cross head circumscribed by the ring. A large protruding boss is placed in the central intersection and four other bosses mark the junctions of the ring and the arms.

[58] Harbison, *The High Crosses*, I.11–15, suggests that on the north cross, these are scenes from the story of David and Goliath, Christ with the Apostles, and Adam being given dominion over the animals; while on the south cross the scenes depict Daniel in the Lions' Den, the raised Christ, and two panels of indeterminate horsemen and animals.

[59] (D.) Kelly, 'The relationships', 221, calculated that almost 30% of Irish crosses are ringless, only 1% show indisputable evidence of original capstones, and in 10% of cases, no elevated base is present.

The carving of the Ahenny crosses is obviously the work of a master who must have been trained also as a metal-worker, or at least was intimately familiar with the manufacture and decoration of metal objects. The bosses are covered with spiral ornament and are similar to the small cast bosses used on metalwork as covers for nailheads or rivets. The analogy to metalwork is further extended by the prominent rope moulding which outlines the entire shape of the crosses on both sides, in a fashion similar to the rolled moulding used on complex metal objects to secure the various pieces together.[60]

That the Ahenny crosses are deliberate approximations of decorated metal processional crosses is obvious, and one is even to be seen in the relief carving of a procession on the base of the north cross. But the imitation of descriptions of the great Golgotha cross may have served as the impetus for adapting the form. Starting from the basic knowledge that the *stauroteca* was a monumental gemmed gold cross, the artist converted the prototype into a vision suitable to Irish taste: the *Crux Gemmata* which was enlivened by the designs indigenous to Insular culture. The cubic base which raises the crosses above ground level is reminiscent of the Rock of Calvary itself, which had been carved into a cubic form in Constantine's time so that it would fit into the shrine complex he was building. Descriptions of the Jerusalem shrine also indicated that the cross was approached by steps and that it was covered by a roof. This may explain the steps at the junction of the shaft and the base, and the desire to place a terminating cap or house-shaped shrine on top of the Irish crosses. The connection of the Ahenny crosses with the cross of the crucifixion is intensified by the use and placement of the bosses, which correspond to the five wounds of Christ. The ring is, we have argued, an adaptation of the cosmic sphere seen in Italian mosaics and thus indicative of the universal triumph of Christianity and the unifying power of Christ as represented by the cosmological cross.

The Ahenny crosses cannot be securely dated by any written sources, and suggestions for their origination range from the mid-seventh century to the ninth century. The religious foundation in which they were built was known later as Kilclispeen[61] (Cill Criospín, St Crispin's Church), but nothing is known of its history. The decoration used on the crosses is very close to what can be seen on the Tara brooch, the Ardagh chalice, and in the painting in the Book of Durrow and the Lindisfarne Gospels. Of all these, the only object which may have an even remotely definite dating is the Lindisfarne Gospels. On the basis of the tenth-century colophon inserted into the book, it has been generally accepted that it dates from just before the end of the seventh century. Since both in the Lindisfarne manuscript and on the Ahenny crosses the use of remarkably similar motifs is sophisticated and assured, it seems reasonable to accept a tentative date in the last quarter of the seventh century as a possible earliest date also for

---

[60] Henry, *Irish Art in the Early Christian Period*, 140.
[61] Roe, *The High Crosses of Western Ossory*, 11.

the Ahenny crosses, with the first quarter of the eighth century also an acceptable possibility.[62]

The high standard of the carving on the Ahenny crosses, and on others stylistically associated with them, may be better explained by their close proximity to the important monastery founded at Lismore at the beginning of the seventh century and also to the chief seat of the kings of Ossory,[63] than by a late dating. The close relationship between the monastery and the king would have provided the wealth and organisation necessary for such ambitious artistic undertakings.

It is also very tempting to see a further inference in the suggested emergence of the ringed cross type in this area of Ireland. During the paschal controversy of the seventh century, Pope Honorius had sent an admonishing letter to the Irish exhorting them not to celebrate Easter at a time different from that observed by the ancient and modern churches of Christ throughout the world, and contrary to the synodical decrees of the bishops of the whole world.[64] Representatives of the monasteries in the southern part of Ireland deliberated the question at the Synod convened *ca* 630 at Mag Léne by Cummian. Inconclusive results led to the dispatching of envoys to Rome seeking clarification of the issues and first-hand observation of the Easter celebration. In that year there was a disparity of a month between the Roman and Irish computation of the date of Easter. As a result of the Roman experience, the monastic foundations in the south of Ireland supported the 'Roman' arguments for the computation of the date of Easter, while most of the northern monasteries along with the Irish foundations in Iona and Northumbria clung to the archaic methods. In response to a letter from Ségéne, abbot of Iona, which must have called into question the validity of his support for the Roman calculations, Cummian wrote a letter, *ca* 633, in which he stated:

What, then, more evil can be thought about Mother Church than if we say Rome errs, Jerusalem errs, Alexandria errs, Antioch errs, the whole world errs; the Irish and British alone know what is right.[65]

In 664, the Synod of Whitby settled the question in England in favour of the Roman side, but it was well into the eighth century before the last of the northern Irish foundations finally accepted the judgement and fell in step with Rome. Could it be that these distinctive ringed crosses, erected without

---

[62] Harbison, *The High Crosses*, I.379–82, argues that the Ossory crosses, as represented by the Ahenny group, are contemporary with the ninth-century scriptural crosses and represent a local variant. But they are so completely different in their severe iconoclasm, as far as the decoration on the cross itself is concerned, that we suggest it seems more likely that they stem from a different impetus and time.

[63] Henry, *Irish Art in the Early Christian Period*, 138.

[64] Bede, *Historia Ecclesiastica*, II.19 (tr. Colgrave & Mynors, 199).

[65] Cummian, *Letter*, lines 177–80 (edd. and tr. Walsh & Ó Cróinín, 80–1): *De controversia Paschali*: 'Quid autem prauius sentiri potest de aecclesia matre quam si dicamus Roma errat, Ierosolima errat, Alexandria errat, Antiochia errat, totus mundus errat; soli tantum Scotti et Britones rectum sapiunt.'

precedent in Ossory, so deliberately combining the vision of the *Crux Gemmata* and the shrine of the true cross in Jerusalem with the cosmic symbol of the universality of Christ as unifier seen in the Italian churches, were meant to be statements of the allegiance to Roman supremacy and Church unity which the southern Irish foundations had already embraced but which their northern brothers were resisting?[66] The devotion to and celebration of the new relics of the true cross in Rome in the early eighth century could have served as an immediate impetus for the erection of permanent monuments expressing the Irish participation in the community of the Roman Church.

It is interesting that the beginnings of religious art production in Ireland coincide with the heyday of *Romani* influence, namely the second half of the seventh century and first half of the eighth. In this period we see the creation of the first surviving instances of religious art meant to be lavish and long-lasting, monuments such as the Ahenny crosses and the highly decorated liturgical items such as the Ardagh chalice and the Derrynaflan chalice and paten. The decision to adapt the repertoire of native Insular motifs to the decoration of these crosses, avoiding the figural representation of Christ on the cross and even omitting any use of the more Mediterranean-based symbols for Christ, such as the fish, the vine and the *Chi Rho*, would equate these monuments with the old Celtic culture. This seeming dichotomy leads to an interesting observation.

The decision, taken in centres with a strong Celtic tradition, to retain the native repertoire of abstract ornament rather than to imitate the representational art of the continental Church may signal an attitude which retained the Pelagian-based prejudice against representational art. As was noted in an earlier chapter, Pelagianists claimed that the law was as important as the gospels in attaining salvation, and thus a strict adherence to the Ten Commandments would constitute the minimum observance. The First Commandment is explicit about images: it forbids the representation of not only God, but of created nature as well (Exod. 20:4). While Pelagians allowed allegory for narrative portions of the bible, particularly of the Old Testament, they were literalists when it came to the law.[67] Tírechán's writing provides a contrast between Ireland and Anglo-Saxon England. He describes Patrick preaching to the Irish while holding up written tablets in his hands like Moses,[68] whereas Bede portrays Augustine of Canterbury showing an image of Christ on a panel to the English he hoped to convert[69] – a practice in line with Gregory the Great's own policy on the use of

---

[66] The vexing problem of the relationship between the Ossory crosses and St John's cross in Iona is difficult to solve. (R.B.K.) Stevenson, 'The chronology', argued that the series of ringed crosses began at Iona and spread to southern Ireland. But the fragmentary condition of the St John's cross and the fact that the ring seems to have been added after the cross had been damaged, casts some doubt on its original configuration. We cannot be certain when the stone crosses replaced the wooden crosses said to have been erected by Columba.

[67] *On Riches*, X.4–8 (tr. Rees, *The Letters*, 188–90); see above, 190.

[68] Tírechán, *Life*, II.2 (tr. Bieler, *The Patrician Texts*, 123).

[69] Bede, *Historia Ecclesiastica*, I.25 (tr. Colgrave & Mynors, 75).

images for teaching and conversion.[70] Strict adherence to Old Testament law is also evidenced by a number of seventh- and eighth-century canon collections associated with the *Hibernenses* (the Irish adherents of the common Celtic Church).[71] This retention of the customary thinking of the common Celtic Church may help to explain why, once sumptuary strictures had been eased, the ornamentation on many of the earliest religious artifacts of Irish manufacture remained limited to the decorative and symbolic.

This may explain why the Moylough belt shrine[72] and the Ardagh chalice have toothy dragon heads incorporated into the decoration, and the high cross at Killamery (part of the Ossory group) can include snakelike creatures, for these do not represent truly natural beings. In the instances where human figures were used, as on the otherwise non-pictorial Ahenny crosses, they were relegated to the bases or they were treated as an interlocking decorative device. Images of Christ were never included. This may well be evidence that even as the southern Irish Church moved in the direction of Roman observance, there remained a stubborn streak of Pelagian-based iconoclasm deeply rooted in its psyche.

The Anglian crosses

The great stone crosses erected in Northumbria are testimony to the strength of the devotion to the cross in the areas where the Irish and Anglo-Saxon cultures met and blended, but at the same time produced a certain rivalry. As with the Ahenny crosses, none of the Northumbrian monuments can be securely dated, but they too fit well into the general milieu of the late seventh and early eighth century. Very different in appearance from the ringed 'Celtic cross', the majority of crosses in Northumbria are without rings or decorated bases and are of somewhat taller proportions than the Irish examples. Rather than utilising the form of the tall Latin cross, the Anglo-Saxon monuments generally employ the form of the small equal armed cross placed on top of a tall pillar or stele. The differentiation between the forms is most often accomplished by the use of moulding between the units and by the changing profile of the intersection. Only occasionally is the upper cross a separate piece of stone.[73]

The Anglian monuments provide an alternate iconography to that embodied in the Ahenny crosses. The decoration carved upon their faces is a response to prototypes and models furnished by the Mediterranean tradition, either directly or through Romano-British remains. For the early Church, the cross represented the living Christ, in both his death and in his

---

[70] Harting-Correa, *Walafrid Strabo*, 229; see also 92 n. 95.
[71] See above, 112–13.
[72] Youngs, *'The Work of Angels'*, illus. p. 37.
[73] (D.) Kelly, 'The relationships', 220.

triumph, and it is in certain areas of Northumbria that the grapevine and the inhabited plant scroll, as symbols of Christ, dominate the geometric-based relief carving.

A series of standing crosses and fragmentary cross shafts has been uncovered in the remains of the Anglo-Saxon monasteries of Northumbria – monasteries which were associated with the reforms of Wilfrid, bishop of York. In the mid-seventh century, Wilfrid had attempted to set up a network of monasteries in the northern Anglo-Saxon kingdom which, in both spiritual and political matters, allied themselves very closely with the Church of Rome. This ambition found its artistic expression in the production of manuscripts, such as the Codex Amiatinus, at Monkwearmouth-Jarrow, in which Mediterranean models were imitated in the illuminated pages.[74] On the other hand, in stone carving, the three crosses at Hexham and the cross shafts from Lowther and Heversham all exhibit the desire for a non-figural, symbolic reference to Christ.

Acca's cross at Hexham

The so-called cross of Acca, probably dating from the mid-eighth century, stood in the great Anglo-Saxon monastery at Hexham, one of Wilfrid's foundations in which he attempted to reproduce the grandeur of the Roman Church, and in which the spirit of the art of late Antiquity was evoked. Only the shaft remains of the cross which has become associated with Bishop Acca, Wilfrid's successor at Hexham. In fragmentary state, without its cross arm, it stands 3.57 metres high. On it there is a deliberate and complete rejection of any motif that was traditional in Celtic art. Instead, a regularised vine-scroll is spread over all four sides of the remains of the tall shaft. The designs exhibit a variety of figure-eight vine-scrolls, with symmetrical curling vines and clusters of relatively naturalistic hanging grapes. The spiralling stems on the narrow sides have been formalised into geometric patterns resembling medallions. Models for the plant-scrolls have been cited from Italy and from the Dome of the Rock in Jerusalem; but it is likely that the intermediary for the thin, fine scrolls of the Acca cross was metalwork.[75]

The meaning of the cross itself is augmented by the application of symbols which refer specifically to the role of Christ and his Church in man's salvation. The grapevine-bearing cross is itself the burgeoning stem of the salvific tree of life, supporting yet indistinguishable from Christ, the true vine (John 15:1). Several crosses can be made out, worked into the geometry imposed upon the vines on Acca's cross. On the main face, at about eye-level, four loops form a rudimentary cross (*Figure ii.a*), while on a narrow side, the second spiral from the bottom reveals a marigold/cross-of-arcs puzzle buried within the maze of the linear patterns. With its apparent

---

[74] See Henderson, *Vision and Image*, 56–121, for a discussion of the continuing connection between late antique art and art in Anglo-Saxon England.

[75] Haverfield & Greenwell, *A Catalogue*, 57–9 and illus.; Cramp, 'Early Northumbrian sculpture at Hexham', 128–9, 134–5; Bailey, *England's Earliest Sculptors*, 52–4.

Figure ii.a Acca's Cross Hexham

Figure ii.b Bewcastle Cross, upper
north side

Figure ii.c Bewcastle Cross, middle
south side

Figure ii.d Bewcastle Cross, bottom south side

complete rejection of figural depictions, Acca's cross stands as an almost iconoclastic attempt to represent Christ.[76] But its choice of motifs places it in direct contrast to the contemporary Irish solution to the desire to avoid figural usage in religious art seen on the Ahenny crosses. The eucharistic references of the vine can be seen as indicative of the Northumbrian desire to show allegiance to Rome in all things ritual, but still adhere to the old strictures on representational images of Christ.

Bewcastle and Ruthwell crosses

The two greatest Northumbrian monuments stand about forty kilometres apart, close to the current English–Scottish border, at Ruthwell and Bewcastle. They were obviously created by the same sculptural workshop and exhibit similar iconographic programmes. As always, dating is problematic but the general consensus is that they were early to mid-eighth-century productions. It has been suggested that they might have been intended as a manifestation of the liturgical innovations of Pope Sergius.[77]

Only the tall shaft of the Bewcastle cross stands today. Two sides of the pillar are decorated with framed rectangular panels containing an assortment of interlace designs, a chequerboard pattern and uninhabited vines. The east face is covered with a single tall panel of inhabited vine scrolls, while the west side contains three panels of figural sculpture. The upper interlace panel on the north side (*Figure ii.b*) and the middle one on the south side (*Figure ii.c*) contain negative images of small equal-armed crosses, hidden within the complexity of the knotting. On the south side panels there are interlocking crosses to be found (*Figure ii.d*). These visual puzzles are not unlike what appears on Acca's cross. The vine scrolls use both the motif of the single-stemmed vine and that of the intertwining double vine emerging from roots or pots placed at the corners of the bottom of the frame, once again motifs shared with the Hexham example. On the west side of the Ruthwell cross, the shaft is decorated with a well-executed inhabited vine-scroll in which birds and other animals, six in all, peck at stylised grapes, leaves and flowers (*Figure iii.a*). Appropriated from antique art, this motif was common in early Christian art in Italy and the Near East. In Christian usage, it was interpreted as the union of the eucharistic vine and the *arbor vitae*. The vine-tree-Christ imagery was well established in Christian thought, as reflected in the writing of St Ambrose and the later hymn *Crux benedicta nitet* by Venantius Fortunatus. In Ambrose, Christ is described as 'the new drink brought down from heaven to earth . . .who just like the grape on the vine, hung in the flesh from the wood of the Cross'.[78] In the same vein, Venantius wrote:

---

[76] Wilson, *Anglo-Saxon Art*, 75.

[77] Ó Carragáin, 'Liturgical innovations'.

[78] Ambrose, *On Faith*, I.xx.135 (cit. Ó Carragáin, 'A liturgical interpretation', 33 n. 46); *De fide*, I.xx.135 (*PL* XVI.582): '. . . populum novum de caelo delatum in terram . . . qui sicut uva de vite, ita ille in carne crucis pependit e ligno'.

Figure iii.b South Cross, Monasterboice

Figure iii.a Ruthwell Cross, west
side

Figure iii.c Barberini Gospels, XPI page

You are powerful in your fruitfulness, O sweet and noble Tree, seeing that you bear such new fruit in your branches . . . hanging between your arms is a vine, from which sweet wines flow red as blood.[79]

The cross was, itself, seen as analogous to the tree of life, in contradistinction to the tree of the knowledge of good and evil through which sin had entered creation and brought about the expulsion of man from Eden. In *Romani* eyes, the cross was thus also a symbol of the regeneration of the cosmos which was achieved through Christ's victory in death, and incorporated the renewed hope of man's return to paradise. This transformed tree of life became the symbol of Christ in union with his Church and expresses the harmonious co-existence of all nature in the living God, in the heavenly Eden. The feeding beasts, symbolic of the members of the Church, both in heaven and on earth, are thus partaking of the blood of Christ, both from the vine and from the tree of life, as clearly expressed in John 15:1–6:

I am the real vine, and my father is the gardener . . . No branch can bear fruit by itself, but only if it remains united with the vine; no more can you bear fruit, unless you remain united with me. I am the vine, and you are the branches. He who dwells in me, as I dwell in him, bears much fruit; for apart from me you can do nothing. He who does not dwell in me in thrown away like a withered branch. The withered branches are heaped together, thrown on the fire and burnt.

The vine/tree of life motif thus visualises the efficacy of the eucharist in the hope for salvation, and is also the representation of the paradaisical state to which the Christian aspires. Since the roots of the visual motif were in antique art, it may very well have conveyed the idea of union with the Church in Rome.

The Ruthwell cross is justly the most famous piece of early Anglo-Saxon free-standing sculpture. Once the victim of seventeenth-century iconoclasm, it now stands about five metres high and has been reconstructed inside the protective walls of the parish church. It takes the shape of an equal armed cross atop a tall stele. The narrower north and south sides are covered with the single-stemmed inhabited vine/tree of life motif, very similar to that seen on the shaft of the Bewcastle cross. The broad borders of the vine-laden panels contain the text of a Crucifixion poem written in Anglo-Saxon runes arranged in horizontal lines. For this period, this is a unique instance of a lengthy poetical inscription being incised in stone. Although the lettering is obliterated in spots, a reconstruction is possible:

I. 1. Almighty God stripped himself. When he willed to mount the gallows.
    2. Courageous before all men,

[79] Venantius Fortunatus, *Crux benedicta nitet*, lines 9–10, 17–18 (cit. Ó Carragáin, 'A liturgical interpretation', 33 n. 46); Hymn XXXV (ed. Walpole, 179, 181):
> fertilitate potens, o dulce et nobile lignum,
>   quando tuis ramis tam noua poma geris . . .
> appensa est uitis inter tua bracchia, de qua
>   dulcia sanguineo uina rubore fluunt.

3. I dared not bow
4. but I had to stand fast.

II.   5. I lifted up a powerful king –
6. the lord of heaven I dared not tilt:
7. men insulted the pair of us together; I was drenched with blood
8. poured from the man's side, after he sent forth his spirit.

III.   9. Christ was on the Cross.
10. But eager ones came thither from afar,
11. The noble ones came together. I looked upon all that:
12. I was terribly afflicted with sorrows; I bowed to the hands of the men.

IV. 13. Wounded with arrows,
14. They laid him down, limb-spent; they stood by the shoulders of his corpse;
15. There they looked on the Lord of Heaven, and he rested himself there for a while. Amen.[80]

In the poem, the cross, as a living thing, describes the heroic nature of Christ at the moment of his human death and presents the saviour and lord of heaven to the world. On the Ruthwell cross, this extraordinary devotional poem is augmented by one of the symbols for the living Christ, the inhabited grape vine, which, with its reference to the eucharist, presents the viewer with the central concept that salvation and redemption are to be achieved through the agency of Christ's willing self-sacrifice and the sacrament which re-enacts it. The figural sculpture on the west and east faces presents a further eucharistic iconography which harmonises with the vine imagery, making the Ruthwell cross an eloquent testimony to the central role of the eucharist in salvation.

It can be suggested that the free-standing stone high cross developed contemporaneously in Ireland and Northumbria in the late seventh century or early eighth century as a manifestation of the wide-spread devotion to the primary symbol of Christ. In both southern Ireland and in Northumbria, the monumental stone crosses reflected the communion with the Church in Rome which was espoused independently by the Romanising monasteries in the two regions. The difference in symbols employed to decorate these early crosses however, is striking. The grapevine is one of the oldest of the Mediterranean references to the Blood of Christ and the efficacy of the eucharist. It is notable that the grapevine motif is absent from the decorated Celtic crosses, perhaps for iconographic as well as aesthetic reasons. It has already been noted that the early Celtic Church de-emphasised the eucharist. The popularity of the grapevine motif in the more Anglo-Saxon areas of Britain underscores the contrast between the two Churches. Perhaps, too, the contrast can be made between the Ahenny crosses, with the five bosses placed at the spots of Christ's wounds, thus making them penitential, while the Ruthwell, Bewcastle and Acca's crosses are salvific in their imagery. It is

---

[80] Ó Carragáin, 'The Ruthwell Crucifixion poem', 15–16, 23, 25, 26; Old English text below, 233.

1. Ahenny, Co. Tipperary. North Cross, west face

2. Double-cross carpet page, Book of Durrow, fo. 1v

3. Double-cross carpet page, Book of Kells, fo. 33r

4. Cross carpet page, Lindisfarne Gospels, fo. 2v

5. Four-evangelist-symbols cross page, Book of Durrow, fo. 2r

6. *Chi Rho* page, Barberini Gospels, fo. 18

7. *Chi Rho* page, Book of Armagh, fo. 33v

8. *Chi Rho* page, Book of Kells, fo. 34r

only much later that the vine motif appears in Irish art even though the motif, based on scripture, was known to Blathmac in the mid-eighth century.[81] The plant scroll and inhabited vine are rare in Irish sculpture and are found only on high crosses dating from the later 'scripture' series: Kells South, Clonmacnois South and West, Monasterboice South (*Figure iii.b*), Durrow and Duleek North.[82] The Book of Kells contains two examples of the inhabited vine, much disguised. Fo. 19v incorporates this motif with text, in which a very complicated intertwining of vine, bird, quadruped and letters reflects the Irish appropriation of the antique motif (*Figure iv*).

Symbols for Christ in manuscripts

Several different types of liturgical books would have been used in the Insular monastic world. Lectionaries or missals would have been used for the Mass, and psalters for the Office. Very few of these have survived. Gospel books were meant to be read either privately or publicly as specified by each monastic Rule. But markings and notations in the existing luxury Insular gospel books would seem to indicate that they were also meant for liturgical usage, to be placed on the altar for the celebration of the Mass and perhaps also to be used during the offices for the monastic hours. As such, the question arises as to who would actually get to see the decoration so patiently applied to the sacred text, and what functions these would fulfil, other than identifying passages for lection. Certainly the principle that the text was beautified and made precious for the glory of God and to render homage to the divinely inspired words was one underlying motive. We posit that the images and decorative elements also served a didactic function, to bring out different elements of the text itself, and also to present ideas pertinent to the monastic way of life. The deacon and the priest celebrating the Mass would see the illuminations but there would be no time to contemplate different levels of meaning in the course of the liturgy. Given the size of the luxury books and the small dimensions of the churches, it is very possible that they were exhibited at special times, in a fashion which made them visible to the audience. The congregation could have observed the decorated sacred word either from a stationary position, or perhaps by filing by to get a closer look. Since these books were extraordinary items, produced at an extraordinary cost, they would undoubtedly have been kept under lock and key when not in use. They would have been treated with awe and reverence, the book itself becoming sacred because of the words it contained.

The surviving Insular luxury manuscripts include the Book of Durrow, the Durham Gospels, the Echternach Gospels, the Lichfield Gospels, the Lindesfarne Gospels, the MacRegol Gospels, the Saint Gall Gospel Book,

---

[81] Blathmac, *Poem to Mary and her Son*, stanza 210, describes Christ as 'the tip of the true vine'; (ed. Carney, 70): 'is barr inna fírfine'.

[82] See Edwards, 'The South Cross, Clonmacnois', 26–7, 44–5.

Figure iv Book of Kells, fo. 19v., detail

the Barberini Gospels, and the Book of Kells. Although there is no immutable formula, each gospel often was preceded by a page of over-all abstract decoration or by an Evangelist page, sometimes in combination. A series of expanded initial letters introduced the text of each gospel, in some cases growing to become full-page designs. Eusebian sections and divisions for liturgical readings were marked with marginal notations and often with decorated initials and colour infill.[83] Within the gospel of Matthew, the monogram of Christ, with which the sacred genealogy ends, affords an opportunity for particular attention. Within this system, the complete vocabulary of Insular ornament, Celtic and Germanic, is employed with skill and precision. Zoomorphic and band interlace, spirals and peltas, interact with crosses and vine/tree of life forms. In some instances, full-page illustrations have been inserted within the gospel text. In some books, the representational image of Christ is avoided completely, while in others, Christological symbols have been used alongside representational depictions.

[83] For the functional relationship between text division and decorated letters, see McGurk, *Latin Gospel Books*.

Cross carpet pages

The Books of Durrow and Kells

The Book of Durrow[84] contains only symbolic 'images' of Christ, avoiding any depiction of his corporeal body. In this luxury gospel book, generally thought to have been created in the second half of the seventh century, the cross is the primary visual reference to Christ. Of the six carpet pages in the manuscript, four incorporate obvious crosses. The designer opened his great tome with an elaborate cross carpet page, even before any text was introduced. Fo. 1v[85] (*Plate 2*) exhibits a central panel in which a cross with double cross arms floats against a background of knotted interlace which arranges itself in six instances of cruciform patterns. The six terminals created at the ends of each arm of the main cross are in turn expanded into cross-shapes, while the four corners of the panel are filled with additional equal-armed crosses filled with band interlace. The border around this panel of reiterated crosses is filled with a fatter type of interlace which shifts from loose knots to spiral forms. Colour changes throughout the interlaced bands accentuate the spatial ambiguity of the design. With the exception of the presence of small patterned squares in the centre of each of its rectangular blocks, the main cross is unadorned, its yellow colour visually detaching it from the interlaced ground. This is a formal vision of the cross of Christ, floating not in the starry sky seen in the Mediterranean mosaics, but against a restless complexity born of the Insular imagination. The vision of Constantine has been transformed to appeal to the northern desire for an image expressing constant movement.

The double-armed cross is a most unusual shape in Insular art, surviving only in the pages of the Books of Durrow and Kells. In the Book of Kells[86] there is only one great cross carpet page, fo. 33r[87] (*Plate 3*), situated so that it serves as a companion to the monogram of Christ on fo. 34r. As in the Book of Durrow, the unusual form of the double-barred cross was chosen. In this case, discs are placed at the ends of each arm and at the two intersections, tying the cross design firmly to the borders. These eight circles are filled with exceedingly fine trumpet spiral forms while the panels on the rest of the page received band and animal interlace decoration.

The double-armed cross was adapted from the art of the eastern Mediterranean where it was common. Its meaning was specific. It refers to the fragments and title board of the true cross of Christ's crucifixion which were exhibited on the altar of the church of Golgotha on Good Friday before being moved out of harm's way to Constantinople in 638. The reliquary itself was in the shape of a cross with two cross bars, the so-called

---

[84] Dublin: Trinity College Library, MS 57.

[85] (B.) Meehan, *The Book of Durrow*, 10; Henderson, *From Durrow to Kells*, illus. 2, p. 19.

[86] Dublin: Trinity College Library, MS 58.

[87] (B.) Meehan, *The Book of Kells*, 26; Henderson, *From Durrow to Kells*, illus. 211, p. 145.

Patriarchal Cross.[88] The upper bar contained the remnants of the titulus. This shape became standard in Byzantine art. In the Book of Durrow, the ends of each arm and the two intersecting points have been expanded into rectangular blocks, to produce an eight-lobed form. In the Book of Kells, there are eight circular medallions attached to the cross. Sacred numerology, known to the Irish through the writings of Isidore of Seville, would have lent additional significance to this cross with eight expansions. Eight is the number for resurrection and salvation since Christ rose from the tomb on the eighth day of Passion Week. The true cross, which had been so miraculously discovered, lost, and recovered, was testimony of God's promise of redemption through the sacrifice of Christ. Christ, present in the symbol of the cross, is a fitting image to preface the gospels which contain his words or to introduce the *nomen sacrum*.

The floating cross motif is found in two other carpet pages in Durrow, but in neither case is it as dominant as on the first page of the book. St Mark's gospel is preceded by a carpet page (fo. 85v)[89] comprising fifteen medallions, fourteen of which are composed of band interlace in various colours, laid out on a very dark background. The central medallion contains the cross of arcs/marigold visual puzzle. In this case, the equal-armed cross with splayed arms is a knotted band while the flower petals are filled with a step pattern. In the very centre, a smaller cross is filled with colour to produce a cross within a cross. The cross-in-circle pattern is an omnipresent motif in early Christian art, as stated earlier, and carries with it the reference to the cosmological cross as well as to the imperial victory *signum*. The central image of the cross dominates not because of its size, but because of its colour and placement.

The carpet page which introduces St John's gospel (fo. 192v)[90] in the Book of Durrow presents another rendition of the cosmological cross. This time, it is in the centre of a square panel of reserved vellum, a tiny encircled cross of arcs/marigold within a larger yellow-banded circle filled with knotted interlace. Inserted into the pattern of the interlace are three circular medallions, the same size as the central cross medallion. These are filled with a delicate filigree-like pattern. Given that the interlace within the larger circle is organised into twelve clearly distinct knots, it is probable that the design was meant to represent Christ, the Trinity, and the twelve apostles, all encompassed with the cosmic circle. But was it also meant to be a diagram of the arrangement of the elements making up the dome over the Anastasis itself on Golgotha, which was supported on twelve columns surrounding the tomb of Christ? The design once again is placed against a very dark background, so that it appears to be floating, perhaps in emulation of the great Italian mosaics displaying the cross in the heavens. The panels framing the four sides of the design are filled with quadrupeds, all distinct shapes,

---

[88] Werner, 'The cross-carpet page', 178–80.

[89] (B.) Meehan, *The Book of Durrow*, 48; Henderson, *From Durrow to Kells*, illus. 11, p. 23.

[90] (B.) Meehan, *The Book of Durrow*, 64; Henderson, *From Durrow to Kells*, illus. 41, p. 41.

intertwined into self-biting knotted loops or parade-like groups. There have been a number of suggestions as to possible meaning attached to these beasts: they have been seen as representative of the forces of evil overcome by Christ; they have been given an apotropaic function; it has been suggested that they might be a reference to the forty-two generations before Christ described in Matthew or to the work of the sixth day of creation.[91] They are reminiscent of the type of designs seen on secular metalwork, for instance on the shoulder clasps from the Sutton Hoo hoard, and may be simply a transferral of, in this case Germanic, decorative motifs onto Insular religious art, in the same manner that the spirals were incorporated into the designs on the Ossory crosses.

The last cross carpet page in the Book of Durrow (fo. 248r)[92] is a less obvious iconographically-laden presentation of the cross. It consists of a page of very regular, angular interlace into which are inserted twenty-eight diagonal crosses.[93] Its gold and red colouring emulates the chequered garnet or enamel and gold jewellery and metalwork seen in both Ireland and England.

The Lindisfarne Gospels

The impressive gospel book created at the Northumbrian monastery on Lindisfarne at the end of the seventh century or the beginning of the eighth contains cross carpet pages, evangelist portrait pages which were based on Mediterranean models, and a highly decorated text. Like the Book of Durrow, it does not contain any representation of Christ in human form. It exhibits an even more elaborated devotion to the cross that signifies Christ.

The Lindisfarne Gospels[94] begins in the same fashion as the Book of Durrow with a cross carpet page. In addition, each of the gospels is prefaced by its evangelist portrait, a decorative page featuring a cross, and an *Incipit* with greatly elaborated letters. Fo. 2v[95] (*Plate 4*) exhibits a great Latin cross with six rectangular expansions floating against a background of band interlace differentially coloured to create a pattern of repeated squares. Two squares with cross centres and step-patterns float above the arms of the cross while two vertical rectangles of similar design stand below the arms. This placement reflects Insular crucifixion compositions such as that seen on the Athlone plaque where two seraphs hover over the cross while Longinus and 'Stephaton' stand to either side.[96] The coloured borders around the cross and each of the rectangles, along with the differentiation between the

[91] Henderson, *From Durrow to Kells*, 41. For a discussion of numerology and Irish art see Richardson, 'Number and symbol'.

[92] (B.) Meehan, *The Book of Durrow*, 79; Henderson, *From Durrow to Kells*, illus. 14, p. 25.

[93] For a discussion of the diagonal cross, see 221, 225.

[94] London: British Library, Cotton MS Nero D.IV.

[95] Backhouse, *The Lindisfarne Gospels*, illus. 19, p. 34; Henderson, *From Durrow to Kells*, illus. 137, p. 98.

[96] See discussion in Chapter VII, 251–3.

angular ornamentation of these forms and the more curvilinear interlace, create a composite image which seems to float on top of the background. The chequered diagonal pattern which fills the body of the cross gives it the appearance of jewelled Germanic metalwork. It is reminiscent of a great processional cross, the unoccupied cross of Christ's crucifixion, a response to the Golgotha *stauroteca* itself. It is a parallel to the Durrow gospel book's prefatory cross, the reference to the crucifixion being expressed in a different form. The thin outer border of the panel introduces two motifs not seen in the Book of Durrow – a parade of crouched birds with variegated feathers and long, knotted tails, each grasping in its beak one hind foot of the bird ahead of it, except at the lower corners where the tails are grasped, and corner projections which incorporate dogs' heads and interlace. These animal elements will form a large component of the Lindisfarne designer's decorative repertoire.

In addition to this great prefatory cross page, the Lindisfarne Gospels exhibit a cross carpet page before each of the gospels, each one incorporating a different design. On fo. 26v,[97] the carpet page for Matthew, the large Latin cross, arms extended to touch all four borders, features chalice-shaped extensions radiating from a central disc. In the centre of each cup-like expansion, a white ring highlights a small cross while the little ring in the central circular junction encompasses an eight-petalled marigold design. Both the cross and the background are filled with a complex curvilinear mesh of vines, birds, and beasts, intertwined in the patterns of a knotted and spiral band interlace. The cross seems to be inhabited by sinuous creatures with dog-like heads while the background contains a panoply of birds and quadrupeds, the forms yielding to the demands of spiral and interlace patterning. Once again the delimiting border around the cross form creates the impression that it is floating in front of the background. In spite of its apparent visual impenetrability, this mesh can be identified as a highly abstracted Insular version of the inhabited plant scroll, the tree of life, the symbol of Christ the true vine. The image of the ideal harmony of nature wrought through Christ is recalled here, as it was also expressed in more realistic fashion on the Bewcastle and Ruthwell crosses. But here, no concession is given to its Mediterranean origin, and the Insular desire for abstraction and decoration dominates the visual world.

The cross carpet page for Mark (fo. 94v)[98] is an exercise in discerning interlocking cross forms. At first glance, a short equal-armed cross extends from a central open disc, recalling the head of a ringed 'Celtic cross'. Band interlace in knotted circular configurations links the shape of the cross and its ring to the border of the design. The panels of the background are filled with animal interlace, step-patterns, and trumpet spirals, creating a complete spatial ambiguity among the forms. Colour distribution identifies another equal-armed cross within the interlace-filled ring itself where it appears that

---

[97] Backhouse, *The Lindisfarne Gospels*, illus. 24, p. 42; Henderson, *From Durrow to Kells*, illus. 145, p. 103.

[98] Backhouse, *The Lindisfarne Gospels*, illus. 28, p. 48; Henderson, *From Durrow to Kells*, illus. 148, p. 106.

four short, spreading arms are attached to the inner ring of the central medallion. In the very centre of the composition is a small stepped-design cross similar to designs found on cloisonné jewellery.

Fo. 138v[99] precedes Luke's gospel and exhibits an angular equal-armed cross whose arms end in T-shaped extensions, giving it a family resemblance to the form of the swastika cross. The square panel covering the intersection of the cross carries an inner panel decorated with a complex design of four connected trumpet spirals interlocked with small peltas. This panel is not unlike that seen on the chest of Christ on the Athlone crucifixion plaque where it refers to Christ as the Christian's buckler or breastplate.[100] In this context, it may very well be a reminder of the protective and magical properties of both Christ and the cross. The paired strands between the main spirals form a linear equal-armed cross with diminutive peltas at the intersection as if in imitation of the larger cross in which they dwell. The dominant cross is filled with fine band interlace and seems to float on top of the background which is filled with zoomorphic panels and diagonally-organised fret patterns.

The final cross carpet page in the Lindisfarne Gospels (fo. 210v)[101] introduces the gospel according to John. Here, a very simply shaped equal-armed cross filled with very fine strand interlace occupies the centre of the page, while other T-shaped panels filled with the same design appear to extend the cross outwards towards the edges of the illumination – they resemble the extended arms of the cross on fo. 138v. Other panels of various shapes organise the overall design into a controlled unit, but they are differentiated from the cross by their infill patterns of spirals, swastikas, and diagonal frets. Once again, the cross form and its accompanying panels appear to float over the writhing zoomorphic patterns of the background, created exclusively of interlaced 'Lindisfarne birds'.

There is a marked preference for the equal-armed cross in all the carpet pages from the Lindisfarne Gospels. Even in the two instances where the Latin cross appears, it is apparent that they are actually crosses with arms of the same size, the lower one then being extended by the addition of the design unit. The five great cross carpet pages in this book cannot be seen as merely decorative, for in them the comprehensive iconography of the cross is presented for exhibition and contemplation. They recall not just the sign of the Christian, but also the vision of Constantine, the imitation of the shrine of the true cross and the gemmed cross on Golgotha, the cross in the cosmos, the cross of the crucifixion, the cross bearing Christ as the buckler and the protector of the faithful, and the cross as Christ himself, the tree of life and the true vine.

---

[99] Backhouse, *The Lindisfarne Gospels*, illus. 31, p. 52; Henderson, *From Durrow to Kells*, illus. 156, p. 108.

[100] See discussion on 255–6.

[101] Backhouse, *The Lindisfarne Gospels*, illus. 34, p. 56; Henderson, *From Durrow to Kells*, illus. 159, p. 110.

The Lichfield Gospels

The one surviving cross carpet page (p. 220)[102] in the early eighth-century Lichfield Gospels[103] appears to combine the angular Latin cross shape of fo. 2v of the Lindisfarne Gospels, with a paraphrase of the entangled bird- and quadruped-inhabited vine/tree of life interlace of fo. 26v of the same manuscript. But it is no mere copying, and in the Lichfield cross-page, the bodies of the four birds which inhabit the six square compartments of the cross are placed so as to form diagonal crosses. Once again the cross within a cross puzzle is recalled.

Four evangelist symbols/cross pages

One of the other compositions which adapts the cross to a specific iconography and which appears with regularity in Insular gospel manuscripts as well as in metalwork, is the combination of the cross form and the evangelist symbols. In the Book of Durrow, facing the introductory double-armed cross image, fo. 2r[104] (*Plate 5*) presents a central panel divided into quadrants by an interlace-decorated Latin cross with curvilinearly expanded terminals. The quadrants provide fields for the representations of the symbols of the four evangelists, the carriers of the Word of God, and the means by which Christ is to be known. The composition itself is arranged as a reference to the *maiestas domini* image which had emerged in early Christian art of the Mediterranean. In this prototype, a central representation of Christ enthroned is surrounded by the images or symbols of the four living creatures. It represents aspects of the heavenly vision of Apocalypse 4, in which the shining throne upon which the Divine One sat was surrounded by the twenty-four elders and by the four living creatures, and Apocalypse 5, in which the elders and creatures paid homage to the slain, immortal Lamb on the throne. This vision was itself a fulfilment of the vision of heaven and the living creatures described in Ezechiel 1. In the church of Santa Pudenziana in Rome, the early fifth-century mosaic of the apse displays the enthroned Christ seated before the heavenly Jerusalem and the jewelled cross of Golgotha, accompanied by the four living creatures. In Ravenna, in the almost contemporary mosaic of the dome of the mausoleum of Galla Placidia which shows the great jewelled cross in the starry orb of the cosmos, the four living creatures-cum-evangelist symbols inhabit the pendentives, the four corners of the canopy of heaven.

The *maiestas domini* motif appears in the art of Northumbria on St Cuthbert's wooden coffin where the figure of Christ surrounded by the four evangelical symbols is incised into the cover. But it was the integrated image

---

[102] Henderson, *From Durrow to Kells*, illus. 182, p. 125.

[103] Lichfield: Lichfield Cathedral Library MS 1. The manuscript is alternatively known as the Gospels of St Chad.

[104] (B.) Meehan, *The Book of Durrow*, 15; Henderson, *From Durrow to Kells*, illus. 42, p. 42.

of the *maiestas domini/maiestas Christi/maiestas crucis*, in which the cross replaces a representational image of Christ who signifies the Divine One, that was incorporated into the decoration of the northern gospel books. That the cross was to represent Christ himself is supported by the instance of the four evangelist symbols/cross page (fo. 1v)[105] of the early eighth-century Trier Gospels[106] which incorporates an image of Christ in the central medallion of the cross. Differences seen in the actual sequence of the symbols in the various books reflect the different orders followed, and do not affect the basic iconography of the composition. This type of page makes a fitting preface to the gospels, a reference to the common and equal value placed on the evangelists as witnesses to the hope of salvation through Christ.

The cross on the Durrow four evangelist symbols/cross page is a true Latin cross which retains much of its integrity as a self-standing form.[107] In many of the other appearances of the composition, the cross has been reduced visually to a geometric form used to divide the page into segments, which may tend to obscure the *maiestas domini* iconography to a modern audience. The four evangelist page is absent in the Lindisfarne Gospels, but appears in the Lichfield Gospels (p. 219)[108] where the cross is visually a simple page divider. In the ninth-century MacDurnan Gospels[109] (fo. 1v)[110] the four exotic-looking creatures are disposed around a more dominant cross whose arms extend from the central medallion out to, and into, the perimeter borders of the design panel. This type of cross-divider in which the arms of the cross are the same width as the outer borders occurs again in the Book of Kells. There are three remaining *maiestas domini* pages in this great gospel book, introducing the gospels according to Matthew (fo. 27v),[111] Mark (fo. 129v),[112] and John (fo. 290v).[113] The first two employ the upright cross while the page associated with John exhibits the cross formed of diagonal arms. This so-called saltire cross is a form which will appear often in Irish context, as a reflection of the praying stance of the cross vigil in which the arms are raised upwards toward heaven. It also approximates the form of the *Chi* (X), the first letter of the monogram of Christ. The *maiestas domini*/cross composition also appears on metalwork,

---

[105] Henderson, *From Durrow to Kells*, illus. 130, p. 91.

[106] Trier: Domschatz Codex 61. While this book was created in the Echternach scriptorium, and has definite ties with other Insular manuscripts, this page reflects the influence of Mediterranean models in the realistic depiction of Christ.

[107] Once again, see Werner, 'The cross-carpet page', 209–16, for his argument that this page is associated with references to the *Locis sanctis* on Golgotha.

[108] Henderson, *From Durrow to Kells*, illus. 44, p. 44.

[109] London: Lambeth Palace Library MS 1370.

[110] Henderson, *From Durrow to Kells*, illus. 50, p. 47.

[111] (B.) Meehan, *The Book of Kells*, 8; Henderson, *From Durrow to Kells*, illus. 51, p. 47.

[112] (B.) Meehan, *The Book of Kells*, 40; Henderson, *From Durrow to Kells*, illus. 214, p. 148.

[113] (B.) Meehan, *The Book of Kells*, 38; Henderson, *From Durrow to Kells*, illus. 218, p. 152.

as exemplified on the eighth-century *Soiscél Molaise* book shrine from Devenish Island (Co. Fermanagh), now in the National Museum of Ireland, Dublin.[114]

In the context of their location within the gospel book, these *maiestas domini/maiestas Christi/maiestas Crucis* pages carry the potential for several layers of Christological meaning. The four evangelist symbols refer to the gospels which they introduce and which were contained in these great books. By combining all four symbols on the same page and, in some instances, inserting this composite image before each of the gospels, even in addition to individual evangelist symbol/portrait pages (as in the Book of Kells), the principle of the unity of the gospels and Christ is underscored. Surrounding the cross which represents Christ, the four evangelists witness different aspects of the life of Jesus. Irenaeus of Lyon had written that the lion symbolises Christ's effectual working, leadership, and royal power; the calf signifies his sacrificial and sacerdotal order; the man describes his earthly Incarnation; and the eagle points out the gifts of the Holy Spirit hovering over the Church – the gospels are in accord with these things, among which Jesus Christ is seated.[115] For Irenaeus, the four creatures symbolise both the four individual gospels and Christ in his fourfold manifestations. St Jerome in his commentary on the Gospel of Matthew equated the creatures with specific evangelists based on the nature of the beginning of each gospel – the man with Matthew who writes about the history of Christ as man; the lion with Mark who relates the voice of the lion (Christ) roaring in the desert; the calf with Luke who starts his gospel with the story of the priest Zachary and his temple duties; the eagle with John who soars upwards, treating the Word of God.[116] In his homilies on the Book of Ezechiel written at the end of the sixth century, Gregory the Great incorporated the writings of Irenaeus and Jerome in his exegesis of the four creatures. Gregory built upon these exegetical foundations by writing that the four creatures/evangelist symbols signify Christ himself because by birth he was man, in his death he was akin to the sacrificial calf/ bull, in his resurrection he was a lion, and in his ascension he soared to heaven like the eagle.[117]

The four gospels constitute the basis upon which an understanding of Christ can be reached. The Word of God and the Law which must be followed in order to reach the perfect life are manifest in the text found on the pages. In his homilies, Gregory not only equated the four creatures with Christ and the gospels, but indicated that they also symbolize the *perfecti*, those who had achieved sanctity by adhering to a way of live inspired by the gospels. In homily I.ii.18, he wrote:

---

[114] Henderson, *From Durrow to Kells*, illus. 49, p. 46.

[115] Irenaeus, *Against Heresies*, III.xi.8 (cit. Veelenturf, *Dia Brátha*, 35–6).

[116] Jerome, *Commentary on Matthew Book IV*, preface (cit. Veelenturf, *Dia Brátha*, 37–8).

[117] Gregory, *Homily on the Prophet Ezechiel*, I.iv.1, I.v.1 (cit. Veelenturf, *Dia Brátha*, 39).

the number of all the perfect ones is expressed in the four evangelists, since all who once attain perfection in the Church have learnt from their gospel the justice which makes their perfection.[118]

In homily I.iv.2 Gregory continues the allegory:

For every righteous and perfected person in the path of God is simultaneously a man, a calf, a lion and an eagle. For man is a rational animal. However, a calf is wont to be slaughtered in sacrifice. The lion is a powerful beast . . . The eagle soars to the heights and turns its unblinking gaze to the rays of the sun.[119]

While Irenaeus of Lyon does not seem to have been known directly in Ireland, Jerome certainly was. Gregory the Great was one of the most influential writers on spiritual matters in the early medieval Church and was certainly known to the Irish.[120] His thoughts would undoubtedly have influenced the manner in which a composition such as the cross/evangelist page was interpreted by the devout observer.

In addition to the *maiestas* symbolism seen in the four evangelist symbols/ cross pages, a cosmological interpretation had been established. Irenaeus had likened the gospels to the four winds and the four corners of the world; they were the four pillars of the Church of which Christ, the *Logos*, was the centre.[121] This interpretation is echoed by Gregory who saw the four creatures as an image of the gospels being disseminated to the four regions of the world.[122] The cross was the symbol for Christ, the centre of creation and the Church; but it was also the tree of life, which stood in the middle of paradise, according to the visions of Ezechiel (Ezechiel 17:22–4) and Daniel (Daniel 4:7–14). Thus the cross of the crucifixion stood at the centre of the world. Adomnán describes the column in Jerusalem located where the youth was resurrected when the cross of the Lord was placed upon him as marking the centre of the world since at midday during the summer solstice it casts no shadow. Only three days later does the shadow reappear as the days become shorter. He goes on to quote from the Psalms: 'God our king before the ages hath wrought our salvation in the centre of the earth, this is in Jerusalem.'[123] The cross can be equated with the vision of paradise, in the middle of which

---

[118] Gregory, *Homily on the Prophet Ezechiel*, I.ii.18 (cit. Veelenturf, *Dia Brátha*, 40); *Homilies in Ezechielem* I.ii.18 (ed. Morel, 108): '. . . per euangelistas quatuor perfectorum omnium numerus exprimitur, quia omnes qui in Ecclesia modo perfecti sunt perfectionis suae rectitudinem per eorum Euangelium didicerunt'.

[119] Gregory, *Homily on the Prophet Ezechiel*, I.iv.2 (our translation); *Homilies in Ezechielem* I.iv.2 (ed. Morel, 150): 'Omnis etenim electus atque in uia Dei perfectus, et homo, et uitulus, et leo simul et aquila est. Homo enim rationale est animal. Vitulus autem in sacrificio mactari solet. Leo uero fortis est bestia . . . Aquila ad sublimia euolat et irreuerberatis solis radiis intendit.'

[120] Kerlouégan, 'Grégoire le Grand'.

[121] Irenaeus, *Against Heresies,* III.xi.8 (cit. Veelenturf, *Dia Brátha*, 35–6).

[122] Gregory, *Homily on the Prophet Ezechiel*, I.iii.7, I.iii.15. (cit. Veelenturf, *Dia Brátha*, 39).

[123] Adomnán, *On Holy Places*, I.11. (ed. and tr. [D.] Meehan, 56–7); *De sanctis locis*, I.11: 'Deus autem rex noster ante saeculum operatus est salutem in medio terrae, hoc est in Hierusalem.'

stands the tree of life, the cross thus becomes the source of grace. In the Garden are also the four rivers, to which the four evangelical symbols are allegorically connected, the four streams by which knowledge of Christ is transmitted to the four corners of creation.[124] Representing the centre and pivot of the universe, these pages express a cosmological exegesis which, through the agency of Christ and the gospels, links created life on earth to eternal life in paradise.

The eschatalogical implications of the image of the cross/Christ surrounded by the living creatures/evangelists would not have escaped the viewer as he or she turned the pages of a gospel book to reach the readings for the day. The evangelist/cross page did not represent the last judgement, but the composition which shows the cross being glorified by the four creatures would recall the last days, the second coming of Christ, and the image of paradise. The goal for the Christian on earth was to aspire to join the ranks of the *perfecti*. These evangelist/cross pages not only show the living creatures as giving glory to Christ, but through their equation with the gospels, reveal the way to perfection, and through the symbiotic union of the perfect Christian with the creatures/evangelists, indicate their place in paradise, giving eternal glory to God.

The monogram of Christ

Throughout the Christian world and from the earliest time a tradition had developed of venerating the very name of Jesus, Christ. The Greek word Christ ($X\rho\iota\sigma\tau\acute{o}\varsigma$) which means 'the anointed one', translates the Hebrew word for Messiah. Therefore, the combination of personal name and messianic title encompasses the Christian understanding of the fundamental role played by Jesus in the salvation of mankind. The equating of the reality of existence of Jesus, in both his human and divine nature, with the name, makes the *nomen sacrum* into an object for veneration, since a name is equated with being. The so-called monogram of Christ, which is composed of the first two Greek letters for Christ ($XPI\Sigma TO\Sigma$), the *Chi* and *Rho* (XP), became a universal symbol appearing on all media of Christian art – architectural components, sarcophagi, mosaics, frescos. The entire Christological doctrine is contained within the shorthand of the monogram.

In Latin gospels, the Greek monogram appears intermittently within the Latin text. In many Insular gospel books, the name of Christ which comes at the end of the genealogy in Matthew (Matt. 1:18) is treated as a form for special attention. This may have coincided with liturgical requirements, for this may mark the beginning of the reading for the feast of the Nativity as celebrated in Irish monasteries which used these books.[125] Not only are the letters expanded, but they are often highly decorated. There seems to be an escalation of the decorative element, starting with the Book of Durrow and culminating in the Book of Kells. In all cases, the Greek *Chi Rho* is inserted

---

[124] McNally, 'The evangelists', 120.
[125] Lewis, 'Sacred calligraphy', 141 n. 6; Farr, *The Book of Kells*, 150.

into the Latin text, and as such had to be joined to the Latin 'I' to satisfy the requirement of Latin declensions (*Christi autem generatio*). Although grammatically and technically a Latin I, this third letter of the monogram is visually perceived as a Greek *Iota* (which has an identical shape) because of its linkage to the other Greek letters. This three-letter combination forms the skeleton on which the decorative elements are hung.

Mainstream Christian exegesis on the *nomen sacrum* was extensive and well known in the Insular world, for early Irish exegetes seem preoccupied with the Greek name, its form, and its Latin and Hebrew synonyms. The meanings associated with the letters were multi-layered. The *Chi* was associated with the *crux decussata,* shaped like the Roman numeral X (*decussis*), itself the figure of the cross, an interpretation transmitted to Ireland through the *Etymologiae* of Isidore of Seville.[126] Several early patristic writers had given the *Chi* of the monogram a cosmological significance by linking it with the Platonic idea of a *Chi*-shaped world structure and further equating the *Chi* figure with the power of the *Logos* Incarnate.[127] In Insular monograms, the *Chi* is the dominant form because of its initial position, its size which is greater than the other two letters, and because of the consistent extension of one diagonal arm to encompass several text lines. Artistic choice has made the *Chi/crux decussata* no longer visually identical with the Roman numeral X, but the iconography remains intact.

The *Iota* was also equated with Christ by Augustine, for it is the first letter of *IXθYΣ*, the fish, which mystically incorporates the *nomen sacrum*. He wrote:

Now if you connect the initial letters of those five Greek words, *Iêsous Chreistos Theou Uios Sôtêr* (Jesus Christ, the Son of God, the Saviour) you have the Greek word *ichthus*, which means 'fish', and the allegorical meaning of this noun is Christ, because he was able to remain alive – that is, without sin – in the abyss of our mortal condition, in the depths, as it were, of the sea.[128]

Therefore, both the *Chi* and the *Iota* become symbols for the Incarnation and Resurrection. They are the manifestation of the eternal Christ/*Logos*.[129] The allegorical meaning of the *Iota* developed separately from that of the *Chi Rho* monogram but when it had to be joined to those two letters to form the genitive within the Latin text of the gospels, the developed Christological meaning gave a reason for its decorative elaboration. In several instances, the fish image is actually appended to what appears to be a triple-letter monogram. The mainstream allegorical meanings associated with the sacred

---

[126] Isidore of Seville, *Etymologies*, I.iii.11: 'x is the letter which by its form signifies the cross, and shows the number 10' (our translation); *Etymologiae*, I.iii.11 (ed. Lindsay, n.p.): '. . . X littera, quae et figura crucem significat et in numero decem demonstrat'. For evidence of the Irish familiarity with Isidore see Herren, 'On the earliest Irish acquaintance'.

[127] Lewis, 'Sacred calligraphy', 142–4.

[128] Augustine, *The City of God*, XVIII.23 (tr. Bettenson, 790); Latin text below, 233.

[129] For studies of the exegesis on the monogram see Lewis, 'Sacred calligraphy'.

monogram would underlie its depictions in the Insular gospel books. But several of them also incorporate elements which draw further associations unique to each case.

In the Book of Durrow, the monogram of Christ (fo. 23r)[130] is enlarged but relatively sparsely decorated with dots and spirals, receiving an attention equal to the initial letters of important chapter divisions. The extremities of the monogram's letter forms are expanded by delicately drawn line spirals, trumpets, and peltas, while the wide bands forming the *Chi* are left blank and the *Rho* received two tiny decorated panels. Red dots outline the initials and fill in the spaces between the letters of the first line of text (*autem*) to create a block of colour, setting the monogram out against the relative plainness of the rest of the page. A tiny cross is inked in the upper angle created by the intersection of the arms of the *Chi*, a sure visual sign of the relationship between the cross and the *Chi* or X form. This small cross does not appear in other instances of the monogram and may very well have been individual to the Durrow Gospels. A cross also appears above the *In principio* (*erat verbum*) at the beginning of John's gospel (fo. 193r),[131] and must refer to Christ as *Verbum* (*Logos*).

In the Echternach Gospels[132] the *Chi Rho* in Matthew[133] (fo. 19) has expanded to fill the entire width of the text column and about one-third of the column length. Whereas in the Book of Durrow the *Iota* had remained slightly distinct from the *Chi* and *Rho* forms, here it has been incorporated to form a definite three-letter combination. The curvilinear letter forms are filled with very fine interlace, with the ends extended into spirals, trumpets, and peltas, much as in the Book of Durrow. This is one of the few instances where the horizontal abbreviation bar has been retained. The monogram presented in the Maihingen Gospels[134] is closely related to the Echternach Gospels initials and relates to the text in the same fashion. In addition to the abstract ornament, a bird's head graces the bottom end of the *Rho* while a dog's head terminates the bottom of the *Iota*/I form.[135]

In the Lindisfarne Gospels, the initials of the *Christi autem* on fo. 29[136] have been enlarged so that they cover half the area of the bordered panel on the page, the three letters continuing the pattern of filling the entire width of the text block. The great curvilinear forms are jam-packed with eddies of swirling trumpet spirals and peltas, with knots and braids of band interlace, and, in the case of the *Chi*, with a mesh of birds caught within the tangles formed of their necks and legs. Everything is in constant motion as the great

[130] (B.) Meehan, *The Book of Durrow*, 39; Henderson, *From Durrow to Kells*, illus. 80, p. 65.
[131] (B.) Meehan, *The Book of Durrow*, 65; Henderson, *From Durrow to Kells*, illus. 32, p. 34.
[132] Paris: Bibliothèque Nationale MS lat. 9389.
[133] Henderson, *From Durrow to Kells*, illus. 101, p. 73.
[134] Formerly Schloss Harburg: Coll. Oettingen-Wallerstein; now Augsburg: Universitäts-bibliothek Codex I.2.4.2.
[135] Henry, *The Book of Kells*, fig. 26 left, p. 177.
[136] Backhouse, *The Lindisfarne Gospels*, illus. 26, p. 45; Henderson, *From Durrow to Kells*, illus. 146, p. 105.

monogram of Christ dominates the page and is transformed by the Insular imagination into a celebration of all that is non-Mediterranean. The inflated letters are now closely related to the design of the border framing the text block and receive the same level of attention given to the *Incipit* pages of the gospels. The monogram effectively functions as a break within the text of Matthew's gospel, giving it a new prominence. Attention is drawn to the sacred name for purposes of personal rumination, and perhaps for exhibition. In the closely related, incompleted *Chi Rho* page of the Lichfield Gospels,[137] the left side of the *Chi* has been extended to the entire length of the decorated text panel and functions as a part of the frame of the decoration. This same tendency can be seen in the St Gall Gospels[138] where the *Christi autem* initials,[139] although less refined in their decoration, are once again treated in the same fashion as a Gospel *Incipit*. In this instance, there is an avoidance of animal forms except for a biting dog's head which links the *Rho* and the *Iota*/I.

The Insular gospel book in the Vatican, known as the Barberini Gospels,[140] includes a noteworthy *Christi autem* page[141] in which the three letters cover the entire decorated section of the page, with the following text inserted into the spaces between the uprights of the letters (*Plate 6*). It is most unusual in having the three letters all the same height, so that the *Chi* does not dominate in the fashion seen in the other Insular gospel books. The great initials are filled with panels of spiral and bird interlace, while the ends transmute into the heads and bodies of quadrupeds, and near the bottom right corner, into two hybrid creatures with human faces. In an interesting addition to the common repertoire, the artist has inserted an inhabited vine motif along the left hand border, spanning the distance between the top and bottom terminals of the *Chi* (*Figure iii.c*). The motif is drawn in a surprisingly realistic fashion not totally unlike that seen on the northern Anglian crosses at Bewcastle and Ruthwell, perhaps reflecting the intermingling of Celtic and Anglo-Saxon influence in this book. In this instance, three stems emerge from a small vase. The two side-stems immediately curl into a leaf-ended loop upon which perch the first pair of birds. The central stem grows straight up and splits into three lateral pairs of loops which provide perches for the second set of birds. The vine produces leaves and clusters of berry-like grapes upon which the birds feed. The reference to the eucharistic vine and the tree of life is direct and unveiled. Running parallel to the upright of the *Chi*, which is itself filled with panels of zoomorphic interlace in which the beasts bite each other's bodies and leafy tails, the vine

---

[137] Henry, *The Book of Kells*, fig. 26 below, p. 177; Henderson, *From Durrow to Kells*, illus. 181, p. 124.

[138] St Gall: Stiftsbibliothek Codex 51.

[139] Henry, *The Book of Kells*, fig. 27, p. 178.

[140] Vatican: MS Barberini Lat. 570. Henry, *Irish Art during the Viking Invasions*, 60–1, associates this luxury gospel book with Huigbald, abbot of Lindisfarne from 781 to 802, on the evidence of the colophon on fo. 153r. (M.) Brown, *The Book of Cerne*, 167–8, 172, while not denying a possible Northumbrian origin for Barberini, identifies the book with Mercian manuscript production.

[141] Henry, *The Book of Kells*, fig. 28, p. 179.

motif lends an additional level of reference to the initials themselves. The *Chi* is not only the first letter of the sacred title, it is the cross of salvation itself, the tree upon which the anointed one, the Christ, was raised for the eternal benefit of Man. The *Chi* is itself the tree of life, the eucharistic vine upon which humanity feeds of the spiritual food of the body and blood of Christ. The visual emphasis which is missing from the *Chi* has been compensated for by the careful placement of the inhabited vine motif, which clearly draws attention to the eucharistic metaphor. Upon reflection, one wonders if the placement of the bird mazes in the *Chi* of the Lindisfarne and Lichfield Gospels was meant to be a reference to the inhabited vine, with its eucharistic meaning, uniting the cross of salvation with the sacrament. All three manuscripts were created in monasteries where the Roman influence intermingled with the Celtic. They reflect the marriage between the Insular desire for abstraction and decoration with the Romanising use of Mediterranean motifs and Christology. Dating from the early eighth century, the Lindisfarne and Lichfield Gospels' monograms would reflect an early stage of this integration, a stage at which the strong Celtic heritage was still being retained, alongside the ever-growing movement towards Roman observances. The Barberini Gospels adds the Romanising eucharistic element to the equation.

In the Book of Armagh,[142] a manuscript with restrained textual decoration, the *Chi Rho* in Matthew (fo. 33v)[143] (*Plate 7*) is related to the tradition seen in the Book of Durrow and the Echternach Gospels. The *Chi* and the *Rho* are enlarged but left plain, with the oval formed by the arms of the *Chi* filled with spirals and peltas. Biting animal heads terminate the forms. The *Iota* has been reduced to a simple vertical bar enframed by the upper curve of the *Rho*, grasped in the mouth of the animal's head which terminates the letter. Almost as if to compensate for the downplaying of the *Iota*, a fish has been placed over the monogram, ostensibly to function as the abbreviation mark. In addition to being seen as a substitute for the *nomen sacrum* itself, the fish was also interpreted as symbolic of Christ's resurrection. The fish coming up from the depths to visibility at the surface of the water was taken by several writers as a metaphor for Christ arising from the dead. The fish was also one of the symbols for the body of Christ and the eucharist.[144] The Book of Armagh and the Barberini Gospels may very well be contemporary. This was a time when the value of the eucharist as a help for achieving salvation was being accepted in Irish monasteries and when eucharistic iconography is appearing in Irish art. It may also signal that the resurrection could be alluded to symbolically, but was not emphasised.

In the most exuberantly decorated Insular gospel book of them all, the Book of Kells, which was probably created around the beginning of the ninth century, the *Chi Rho* (fo. 34r)[145] (*Plate 8*), receives its most elaborate

[142] Dublin: Trinity College MS 52.
[143] Lewis, 'Sacred calligraphy', fig. 5.
[144] *Ibid.*, 145.
[145] Henry, *The Book of Kells*, illus. 29; Henderson, *From Durrow to Kells*, illus. 228, p. 160.

decorative treatment. The letters of the monogram have been so inflated that the rest of the text, the '*h generatio*', is squeezed in at the bottom corner, almost as an afterthought. The entire repertoire of Insular ornament is brought into the service of glorifying the sacred name: spirals, trumpets, and peltas; band and zoomorphic interlace formed of birds and quadrupeds; panels of geometric shapes. It is all so densely woven together that it is the equal to the great carpet folios. The monogram floats on the vellum page, forming its own boundaries, except for the lower right edge where a right-angled corner band is filled with panels of decoration.

Of all the decorated monogram pages in Insular gospel books, the Kells page contains the most complex and convoluted iconography. Augmenting the welter of Insular ornament held within the confines of the monogram, the artist has included specific creatures of the sea, land, and air, the earthly and the heavenly realms. An otter with a fish, tucked into the curvature between the bases of the *Rho* and *Iota*, represents marine life. The two cats and four mice nestled between the bottom of the *Chi* and that of the *Rho* represent creatures of the land. Man, another inhabitant of the earth, is included in the motif of the four interlaced human figures occupying the upper panel of the lower corner frame and also by the men caught in the interlace of the diamond-shaped lozenge at the intersection of the great sweeping arms of the *Chi*. The birds and quadrupeds inhabiting several of the other panels and infill sections round out the catalogue of land creatures. Dwellers of the air are identified by the two moths tucked under the curving left shoulder of the *Chi*. To complement the earthly beings, the heavenly realm is represented by three angels placed sideways along the upright of the *Chi*. Near the centre of the composition, the curved upper end of the *Rho* terminates in a man's head with blond hair and a young, slightly bearded face, very possibly a reference to Christ, the centre of the created world. The universality of the power of the anointed one, Christ, is thus graphically referred to here. All creation is united in harmony within the all-encompassing symbol of Christ, his sacred name.

But the range of meaning goes far beyond this to embrace the theology of the eucharist as the Incarnate Christ himself. It would not have escaped attention that the fish was an indication of another title for Christ, the ἰχθύϲ, which was associated with the *Iota*, under whose stem the fish and otter motif was placed. The fish would convey its conventional meaning as the symbol for the body of Christ, the eucharist and the resurrection. The otter would recall the instances of monastic saints' lives where otters provided comfort, companionship, and food in the form of fish to holy hermits, an obvious reference to the eucharist as reward for spiritual perfection. The cat-and-mice motif reiterates the eucharistic meaning with the use of the cross-inscribed wafer which is both being exhibited between the two central mice and consumed by them. But this is probably also a metaphor for Christ as *Logos*. Isidore of Seville expanded upon the symbolism of the mouse by equating the creature with the cyclical waxing and waning of the moon:

The mouse is a wee little animal. Its name (μῦϲ) is Greek, and this is taken over into Latin (*mus*). Some people call them mice because they are born out of the moisture (*hu-more:hu-mure*) of the earth, for a mouse is earth, from which comes *hu-mus*. During the half-moon its liver grows, just as some marine animals grow, then diminishes again with the waning of the moon.[146]

This cosmic cycle was seen to reflect the incarnation, death and resurrection of Christ as testified in the *Hexaemeron* of Ambrose, which may have been known in Ireland. The disc being nibbled by the mice thus stands for both the eucharist and the moon, symbols for the mystical body of Christ. The moon is also a reference to Christ's resurrection.[147] The cats which have caught the two mice holding the wafer/moon would be creatures familiar to the monks. But they also may have reminded them of St Augustine's reference to the cross as the devil's mousetrap, Christ's death being the bait by which the devil was caught. Relating the *Chi*/cross to the mousetrap and the cats to the act of ensnarement would express the mystery of the Incarnation and Resurrection which was completed through disguises and the deception of the devil.

The two moths worked into the design are another reference to the divine metamorphosis of Christ's death and resurrection. Because of their seeming death as larvae, their entombment within the cocoon and their emergence from the chrysalis as transfigured moths, moths and butterflies were an ancient symbol of the soul's immortality as well as Christ's resurrection. Like the mice, the Kells moths appear to be nibbling on a wafer or lozenge which they hold between them, possible another eucharistic symbol. They embody the promise of salvation made possible through the *Logos* Incarnate and the eucharist.

The three angels are directly related to the *Chi*, placed along the extended upright. The pair of flying angels is a revival of the oft-used Mediterranean motif of twinned angels holding aloft a victory garland between them. In Italy, the garland usually encloses a bust-length image of Christ, the apocalyptic Lamb, or the *Chi Rho*. In this case they each appear to be holding a book or scroll, but their close association with the monogram, and thus with Christ, may recall the more direct Mediterranean depictions. The third angel, waistlength, is holding two sceptres or rods, with trilobed ends, a motif which is common in the Book of Kells. There is a final human image, one which has been generally overlooked, worked into the Kells monogram. A single, larger-scale face can be seen peering out from the very top of the upright curved expansion above the intersection of the two arms of the *Chi*. It is placed exactly where the little cross was inserted in the Book of Durrow monogram, and one wonders if it could be a visual reference to link the great initial with Christ himself.

The Christological references seem to be hidden within the forms

---

[146] Isidore, *Etymologiae*, XII.iii.1 (our translation); *Etymologiae*, XII.iii.1 (ed. Lindsay, n.p.): 'Mus pusillum animal. Graecum illi nomen est; quidquid vero ex eo trahitur Latinum fit. Alii dicunt mures quod ex humore terrae nascantur; nam mus terra, unde et humus. His in plenilunio iecur crescit, sicut quaedam maritima augentur, quae rursus minuente luna deficiunt.' The word play between Greek and Latin gets lost in the translation into English.

[147] Lewis, 'Sacred calligraphy', 147–50.

decorating the Kells monogram and invite a close contemplation by those privileged to view it at close range. It works its magic through visual deception, which parallels the idea that the truth of Christ's mission was hidden from the devil and was gradually revealed through the gospels. And so the truths associated with the sacred name are removed from immediate recognition. But at the same time, it incorporates images of animals which had close associations with Insular monastic life and legend: men, fish, otter, cats and mice. Created primarily for a monastic audience, it could be appreciated at different levels.

The monogram in the Book of Kells reflects the multivalent iconography of the sacred name as represented by the *Chi Rho*. It relies upon a complex and erudite knowledge of exegetical writings on the *nomen sacrum* and the meaning of Christ's Incarnation for the salvation of humanity. It presents the messianic purpose of Jesus' Incarnation as the terminus of the many generations of the Old Testament as expounded by Matthew. The Greek *Chi* form is equated with the cross itself, and as such shares the iconography of the cosmic cross. It is the tree of life which simultaneously stands in the centre of paradise eternally yielding fruit and leaves for the healing of the nations (Apoc. 22:2) and furnishes the wood for the cross of the crucifixion. It is the eucharistic vine which feeds the faithful and which unites all of God's creatures with its promise of redemption and salvation. It furnishes the path to heaven. It represents Christ himself. It is located at the heart of the gospel book, the written Law which the faithful Christian is to rely upon in his struggle on earth to reach spiritual perfection. The Book of Kells monogram exhibits the panoply of Christian symbols, including references to grace, sacramentalism and resurrection, which would have been alien to hard-line Pelagian sympathisers. But by the time when it was created, probably in the late eighth or early ninth century, the influence of the Roman Church was well established in the Irish centres. This great gospel-book, which also includes a series of full-page representational images, should best be seen as reflecting a synthesis of Celtic and Roman ideals, a signal of the changed Irish Church.

The lavishness with which key pages in the luxury manuscripts were decorated is a glorification of the Word of God. The desire was probably to increase the awe and reverence felt towards the manifestation of the Sacred Text. These great luxury books were treated like the treasures they were, carefully and jealously guarded and kept in shrines when not in use. The placement of the decoration and its relationship to the text accentuated the cycle of liturgical readings used during religious celebrations. It has been suggested that these great liturgical books with their illuminated pages were placed on the altar and exhibited publicly at certain times during the year.[148]

---

[148] Ó Carragáin, '*Traditio evangeliorum*', 398–403, postulates that, according to the Roman liturgy, during the fourth week in Lent, when the gospels were presented to the catechumens in the '*Apertio aurium*' ceremony, the opening verses of each gospel were chanted to the faithful by the deacon, each followed by a brief sermon explaining the symbol of the evangelist. Whether or not this was a practice in the Celtic churches remains an open question, especially before the ninth century.

The cross carpet pages which introduce the gospels, along with the elaborated initials and the monogram of Christ, may very well have been exhibited before the eyes of the gathered faithful in a monastic setting. This could include not only those in orders and monks, but the faithful laity (*manaig*) who were associated with the monasteries. The several layers of meaning embodied in the various Christological symbols employed in the gospel books would be immediately apparent to the scholars, teachers and educated religious who would be familiar with the aspects of Christ referred to by the symbols of the cross, the tree of life, the vine, the evangelist symbols and the sacred monogram. In spite of the possible occasional exhibition of these great books before the monastic community, their primary audience would be restricted to those who actually handled them: the deacons, priests and lectors. There is no evidence upon which to postulate a real reaching out towards the laity in the non-representational decoration of the luxury liturgical books. The situation might have been very different in the case of the carved slabs and the standing high crosses such as those at Ruthwell and Bewcastle. These latter were obviously public monuments in a truer sense, situated in areas which were easily accessible to the members of the monastic communities they were associated with, and in many cases to the laity itself.

Both classes of monuments are a celebration of Christianity. They are also manifestations of an image of Christ which, not relying upon a familiar human form, avoids a direct involvement with the controversy and confusion concerning the nature of Christ which consumed the continental Churches. This is religious imagery achieving its purpose and meaning by wedding Christianity and Insular culture. The non-representational character of Celtic art was ideally suited to expressing Celtic Christian belief in its early phases. The long-surviving preference for symbolic representations of Christ may indicate the survival of ideas associated with Pelagianism which had been part of Celtic belief for so long. The strong attachment to the Old Law may have carried with it the idea that Jesus, as God, should not be represented in his human form. This gradually changed with the emergence of the *Romani* in the seventh century, but there seems to have been a lingering conservatism where religious art was concerned. The earlier acceptance of direct representations of Christ seen in areas of Anglo-Saxon hegemony reflects the influence of the Roman Church with its tradition of representational art.

Additional Texts

54. Caelius Sedulius, *Carmen paschale*, V, lines 182–95 (ed. Huemer, 128):
> Protinus in patuli suspensus culmine ligni,
> Religione pia mutans discriminis iram,
> Pax crucis ipse fuit, uiolentaque robora membris
> Inlustrans propriis poenam uestiuit honore,
> Suppliciumque dedit signum magis esse salutis,
> Ipsaque sanctificans in se tormenta beauit.

Neue quis ignoret speciem crucis esse colendam,
Quae Dominum portauit colligat orbis.
Spendidus auctoris de uertice fulget Eous,
Occiduo sacrae lambuntur sidere plantae,
Arcton dextra tenet, medium laeua erigit axem,
Cunctaque de membris uiuit natura creantis,
Et cruce conplexum Christus regit undique mundum.

80. Ruthwell Crucifixion Poem (cit. Ó Carragáin, 'The Ruthwell Crucifixion Poem', 15, 23, 25):

1 Ondgeredæ hinæ god alme/g/ttig. Þa he walde on galgu gistiga
2 modig fore allæ men
3 buga ic ni dorstæ
4 ac scealde fæstæ standa

5 Ahof ic riicnæ kyningc.
6 heafunæs hlafard hælda ic ni dorstæ
7 bismæradu ungket men ba ætgadre ic wæs miþ blodi bistemid
8 bigoten of þæs guman sida siþþan he his gastæ sendæ

9 krist wæs on rodi.
10 hweþræ þer fusæ fearran kwomu
11 æþþilæ til anum ic þæt al biheald
12 saræ ic wæs miþ sorgum gidrOEfid hnag ic þam secgum til handa

128. Augustine, *De civitate Dei*, XVIII.23 (ed. Welldon, II.338): 'Horum autem Graecorum quinque uerborum, quae sunt Ἰησοῦς Χριστὸς θεοῦ Υἱὸς Σωτήρ, quod est Latine Iesus Christus Dei Filius Saluator, si primas litteras iungas, erit ἰχθύς, id est piscis, in quo nomine mystice intellegitur Christus, eo quod in huius mortalitatis abysso uelut in aquarum profunditate uiuus, hoc est sine peccato, esse potuerit.'

VII

REPRESENTATIONAL IMAGES OF CHRIST

It was during the eighth century that Christ was first directly represented in Insular art, at a time when the Romanising factions within the Insular Church had gained ascendancy. Both the *Romani* in Ireland and the Anglo-Saxons in Northumbria had been working since the mid-seventh century to establish close ties with Rome in practice and theology. We have already noted the activity in southern Ireland of Cummian, *ca* 630, regarding the questions of the timing of Easter and the authority of Rome.[1] About the middle of the seventh century, probably in Kildare, a cleric who called himself Cogitosus ua hÁeda wrote a *Life of St Brigit* which strings together the legendary anecdotes relating miracles associated with that holy woman. In his section on the rebuilding of the monastic church at Kildare, Cogitosus includes a description of the ornate altar and the tombs in which the remains of Brigit and bishop Conláeth had been laid to rest as being 'adorned with a refined profusion of gold, silver, gems and precious stones, with gold and silver chandeliers hanging from above and different images presenting a variety of carvings and colours'.[2] Interestingly, he also indicates that the main wooden partition which separated the chancel from the nave was 'painted with pictures and covered with wall hangings'.[3] Unfortunately, he does not expand his description to include details of what the images were like, or their meaning. It is interesting to note the possibility that in southern Ireland at least, by the middle of the seventh century there was a decided swerving away from the earlier restriction against sumptuous religious objects and simultaneously the beginning of the acceptance of religious imagery. Kildare was also close to the area where the two Ahenny crosses, with their figural bases, were erected, possibly within the same century.[4]

In Northumbria, John, the precentor of St Peter's in Rome and abbot of the nearby monastery of St Martin, came to Wearmouth with Benedict Biscop upon the latter's return from his fifth trip to Rome in 678–9. Sent by Pope Agatho, John's task was very specific. In addition to investigating the

---

[1] See above, 62–4, 204.

[2] Cogitosus, *Life*, XXXII.1 (tr. Connolly & Picard, 25); *Vita Sanctae Brigidae Virginis*, XXXII.1 (*PL* LXXII.789): '. . . vario cultu auri et argenti et gemmarum, et pretiosi lapidis, atque coronis aureis et argenteis desuper pendentibus'.

[3] Cogitosus, *Life*, XXXII.2 (tr. Connolly & Picard, 26); *Vita Sanctae Brigidae Virginis*, XXXII.2 (*PL* LXXII.789): '. . . imaginibus depictus ac linteaminibus tectus . . .'

[4] See above, 201–2.

beliefs of the English Church and reporting on any lingering taint of heresy, he was to teach the monks the Roman manner of singing and reading aloud during festal celebrations.[5] There appears to have been a loosening of the strict iconoclasm which had been so apparent in the early Celtic Church. In his *History of the Abbots*, Bede reports that the treasures which were brought back to Monkwearmouth-Jarrow from Rome by Benedict Biscop in the late seventh century included:

> . . . painted holy images to adorn the church of Blessed Peter the Apostle which he had built, namely, images of the blessed Mother of God, ever virgin, and also of the twelve apostles, with which he meant to cover the (chancel) arch (*testudinem*) placing them in a row from wall to wall. He also planned to decorate the south wall of the church with pictures from the gospel stories, while he would adorn the north wall with images of the vision in Blessed John's Apocalypse, so that any illiterate person coming into the church, in whatever direction he looked, could always contemplate the lovable face of Christ and his saints – even if only in an image, or else recollect more vividly the grace of the Lord's Incarnation, or else remember to examine his conscience carefully, having, as it were, before his very eyes the danger of that final examination.[6]

With the increasing Mediterranean contact and influence, there evolved a willingness to accept the possibility of representing Christ himself in fully human form, and to use art for a didactic purpose. This seems to have appeared simultaneously in Ireland and Northumbria, although the artists connected to Monkwearmouth-Jarrow moved forward much more quickly. The cross remains the primary symbol associated with Christ and most representations of Jesus, when they appear, remain closely connected to the form of the cross. Crucifixions appear on plaques and in Insular manuscripts during the eighth century. Iconic images of Christ as well as scenes from his life are incorporated into the decoration on some of the earliest sculpted Anglian crosses, such as those at Ruthwell and Bewcastle. Although there are representations of Christ possibly dated to the eighth century found in an Irish context, they remain heavily stylised and fairly restricted until their full adoption on the sculpted high crosses of the ninth and tenth centuries. Perhaps a lingering Pelagian-based tendency which was much stronger in the Irish centres than in the more Romanising Northumbrian monasteries, can be seen underlying this certain Irish reluctance to give Christ an earthly form.[7]

It was not until the advent of the great series of so-called 'scripture crosses' that are spread in groups, mostly throughout the eastern half of Ireland, that the art of Irish Christianity truly embraced the full possibility of representing Christ in his human form. Once this occurred, there was an outpouring of narrative sculpture which concentrated on episodes from the life of Christ, incidents from the Old Testament, or scenes from the lives of selected saints which could be understood as symbolic of Christ's mission on

---

[5] Bede, *Historia Ecclesiastica*, IV.18 (edd. and tr. Colgrave & Mynors, 389).
[6] Bede, *History of the Abbots*, VI (our translation); Latin text below, 276.
[7] See above, 205–6.

earth. Although the presence of bases attests to an originally much larger number of sculpted high crosses, there are substantial extant remains of about thirty-five of these remarkable monuments. Consistently facing east and west, they range up to almost seven metres in height, and are generally associated with monastic settlements. Sometimes produced in clusters both within and without the actual monastic walls, they most likely were used as gathering places for some of the monastic offices and for communal prayer. Erected during the period of the Viking invasions, these monumental free-standing crosses could have been thought of as invocations of God's protection for the monastery. In examining their imagery, we will see that the monastic ideal prevails, not only in the physical function of the artistic monuments, but also in their iconography.

Christ as the ideal monk

The Ruthwell cross

As noted earlier, the narrow sides of the eighth-century Ruthwell cross are covered with the inhabited vine scroll which symbolises Christ in a eucharistic context, accompanied by a runic cross poem. The east and west faces of the cross[8] are divided into a series of panels filled with figural relief carving; Latin inscriptions on the frames are related to the images within the panels. Although there is ongoing discussion concerning the identification and meaning of some of the figures, it is readily apparent that the decoration of this great cross followed a carefully planned icono-graphical programme based upon the Insular monastic theology of Christ and perhaps in correspondence with the Roman liturgy as it might have been performed in Northumbria in the eighth century.[9]

On the east side of the Ruthwell cross the five panels of the shaft depict, in descending order: Martha and Mary (Magdalene) embracing, Mary (Mag-dalene) anointing the feet of Christ, Christ healing a blind man, the annunciation, and the crucifixion. The corresponding panels on the west side represent: St John the Baptist bearing the Agnus Dei, Christ as Judge recognised by the beasts in the desert, the Egyptian hermit-saints Paul and Anthony breaking bread in the desert, and Mary and the Christ Child seated on an ass on the journey from Egypt. The bottom scene is completely obliterated. The crosshead is badly damaged and now reversed, but seems to have contained at least the images of the four evangelists and their symbols as well as that of an enigmatic archer drawing his bow to shoot upwards.

---

[8] The Ruthwell cross has been rebuilt from the fragments into which it was broken in 1642. The difficulties with the reconstruction are decribed in Farrell & Karkov, 'The construction'. In the following discussion we will be referring to what is considered to be the original orientation.

[9] Ó Carragáin, 'The necessary distance'. There is no actual evidence for the use of the Roman liturgy in Ireland or in this part of Britain at this time. Its use is argued because of the results of the Synod of Whitby and from later markings for liturgical readings in the gospel books.

In contrast to the Ahenny crosses and Acca's cross at Hexham, which are almost iconoclastic in character, the Ruthwell cross is an early Insular celebration of fully-developed representational religious art. In the figural depictions, the sculptor has made direct use of models with an obvious Mediterranean origin. Even though the surfaces are worn and damaged, it is still apparent that the forms were carved in a deep relief technique with rounded, plastic contours. Drapery folds, although somewhat schematic, obey the law of gravity and fall in a believable fashion, creating the body volumes. Where the narrative requires it, as in the annunciation and Mary and Martha scenes, the figures turn in space and address each other. This is deliberately and dramatically different in style and artistic concept from the heavily abstracting and symbolic aesthetic that governs most early representations of the human form in Irish Christian art, for example, as seen on the Athlone plaque and the bases of the Ahenny crosses. The direct recalling of Mediterranean realism at Ruthwell (and Bewcastle) was probably the result of the employment of foreign artists using imported models. Stylistically, these monuments reflect the desire to emulate Rome and the Mediterranean as the origin and centre of Christian culture, and appear to be a visual attempt to bring the concept of unity with Rome to the remote Northumbrian landscape.

The religious meaning of the Ruthwell cross would have been understood at several different levels by the various social groups undoubtedly comprising its audience. But the references to the monastic ideal are the most apparent and, at all levels, it is the image of Christ, the ideal monk, which dominates the iconography. The icon-like depiction of Christ standing over the two now rather indeterminate beasts is accompanied by the inscription: 'Jesus Christ, Judge of Fairness. The beasts and serpents recognised the Saviour of the world in the desert' (*Plate 9b*).[10] This recalls multiple scriptural references. Mark 1:13 describes how Christ spent forty days in the desert, in the company of the beasts, was tempted by Satan and administered to by angels. Psalm 90:13 prophesied 'Thou shalt walk upon the asp and the basilisk; and thou shalt trample under foot the lion and the dragon.' Taken together with the psalm's preceding verses which were interpreted as foretelling the temptation of Christ in the wilderness, these words held the promise that God and his angels were ever present as a powerful refuge against the snares of the devil. The 'desert' was the common metaphor for the ascetic monastic life and the Christ who spent forty days in the wilderness before embarking upon his public life was the ideal model for the Insular monk to emulate.[11] But on the Ruthwell cross, the beasts specifically are said to 'recognise' Christ and to pay homage to him. The Old Latin version of the Canticle of Habbakuk brings this idea to the fore: 'You will be known in the midst of two animals.'[12] It is the

[10] IHS X[PS] IUD[E]X [A]EQU[IT]A[TI]S BESTIAE ET DRACON[ES] COGNO-VERVNT IN DESERTO SALVA[TO]REM MUNDI.

[11] See discussion of the Ruthwell text and an Irish exegetical connection in Meyvaert, 'A new perspective', 125–9.

[12] This passage does not occur in the Vulgate version of the Prophecy of Habbakuk.

specified act of recognition which is the key to the intended further meaning of the Ruthwell image of Christ. The Ruthwell animals recognise Christ as the Messiah and Judge, as specified in the accompanying text, just as the soldier Longinus recognised and acknowledged Christ on the cross.[13] All who view the cross are asked to do the same thing. The Ruthwell image of Christ as the perfect monk is also the image of the Christ of the second coming, the just judge, who will judge both the just and the unjust. This combination of the apocalyptic and the ascetic aspects of Christ's image emphasises the monastic ideal of the striving for salvation through the imitation of the perfect, penitential life of Christ. There is the implied message that if you follow Christ into the desert, you will be saved by the fair judge.[14]

Above this image of Christ, St John the Baptist is presented as a fully human model of Christian asceticism for he lived in the desert on locusts and wild honey.[15] As the harbinger of the incarnation of Jesus, John holds up to view the image of the sacrificial Lamb, the *Agnus Dei*, the symbol of Christ. This corresponds to John 1:29 where John the Baptist, upon seeing Christ coming towards him while he was baptising in Bethania, declared: 'Behold the Lamb of God, behold Him who taketh away the sins of the world.' John recognised that the man he was baptising was full of the Holy Spirit and that he was the Son of God (John 1:33–4). John repeated the phrase 'Behold the Lamb of God' the next day before some of his followers, causing two of them to follow Jesus (John 1:35–6). The obvious reference is again to the recognition of Christ, but there is also a eucharistic reference, for Christ is the sacrificial Lamb, offered on the altar for the remission of the sins of mankind. The *Agnus Dei* prayer which was introduced into the Roman mass by Pope Sergius in the late seventh century[16] twice asks the Lamb of God for mercy and then for the bestowal of peace.[17] The apocalyptic meaning apparent in the image of Christ as Judge immediately below is once again established in the intimated link with the image of the wounded Lamb on the throne, glorified by the angels and elders (Apocalypse 5). John the Baptist announced and made known the Christ who was both the ideal of the penitential life and also the Judge who would decide the eternal fate of each person at the last judgement. Taken in conjunction with the image of Christ

---

[13] See below, 251–2.

[14] See above, 174–5.

[15] Meyvaert, 'An Apocalypse panel', has identified this figure as the Divine One from the Apocalyptic vision.

[16] Ó Carragáin, 'Liturgical innovations', 134; Duchesne, I.381 n. 42, sees this as the pope's reaction against canon 82 of the Quinisext Council of 692 which expressly forbade the representation of Christ in the form of a lamb.

[17] 'Agnus Dei, qui tollis peccata mundi, miserere nobis; Agnus Dei, qui tollis peccata mundi miserere nobis; Agnus Dei, qui tollis peccata mundi, dona nobis pacem': 'Lamb of God, who takes away the sins of the world, have mercy on us; Lamb of God, who takes away the sins of the world, have mercy on us; Lamb of God, who takes away the sins of the world, grant us peace.' For the *agnus Dei* motif in Irish literature see Blathmac, *Poem to Mary and her Son*, stanza 208 (ed. and tr. Carney, 70–1).

and the animals, this image would once again emphasise the link between the monastic life and salvation.[18]

The combination of Christ and the two beasts with St John the Baptist and the Lamb was also employed on the west face of the cross at Bewcastle, not far from Ruthwell. In this case, the name *gessus kristtus* has been inscribed in runes on the flat border between the two panels, just over the head of the lower figure, but with obvious reference to both panels. The iconography here was undoubtedly meant to be similar to that of the Ruthwell cross and indicates that these two monuments were planned in conjunction with each other. Indeed, it is generally thought that they were produced by the same team of sculptors. We have seen that apocalyptic vision imagery played a noted role in Benedict Biscop's churches in Northumbria farther to the east. Its use on the crosses at Ruthwell and Bewcastle may reflect the quickly lengthening arm of Romanising influence in north-western Britain.

On the Ruthwell cross, below Christ in the desert, we see the hermit-saints Anthony and Paul of Thebes, sharing the bread delivered daily by the raven, Paul's sole source of sustenance. The accompanying text identifies the scene for the viewer.[19] According to the legend, Anthony had journeyed into the wasteland to visit Paul who had withdrawn from the world. Because of his perfection of the penitential life, Paul received a daily loaf of bread brought to him by a raven sent from God. On the day of Anthony's visit, a double loaf appeared. So as not to rival the other's sanctity, the two hermits decided to break the loaf together. In the Insular tradition, these two saints, Paul and Anthony, were believed to have been the first monks and the founders of the first monastery, effectively establishing the ascetic, eremitical ideal. The notion of the hermit-saints in harmony with the animal world, retiring to the wilderness to achieve a high level of spiritual perfection, in anticipation of the judgement of God, is found often in the Insular saints' lives – the *Life of St Cuthbert* is a good example of this phenomenon.[20] The miraculous delivery of the heavenly bread and the joint halving of it by Anthony and Paul is an obvious eucharistic reference.[21] The halved bread is equated with the bread of the last supper, the body of the crucified Christ and with the breaking of the bread during the consecration of the mass.

In the Celtic monastic tradition, the eucharist is seen as the reward for the monastic withdrawal from life and the attainment of a perfect asceticism. Its regular reception must be gradually attained through an ever-increasing life of penitence and mortification. It is the reward for a perfect life.[22] The working of grace in this way was one of the lingering Pelagian-based concepts which were still to be found in the northern Isles. It is the image of Paul and Anthony which places the overtly eucharistic symbolism of the Ruthwell cross, seen in both the inhabited vine motifs and in the figural

[18] Ó Carragáin, 'Christ over the beasts', 377–403.
[19] SCS PAULUS ET A[NTONINUS] FREGERUNT PANEM IN DESERTO.
[20] Colgrave, *Two Lives of Saint Cuthbert*. See discussion in Chapter V, 149–50.
[21] Ó Carragáin, 'Meeting of Saint Paul and Saint Anthony'.
[22] See above, 128–9.

panels, in the context of Celtic monasticism. This joint depiction of Anthony and Paul was to be adopted as the standard metaphor for the ideal Insular monastic life and appears with great regularity on the shafts of the ninth- and tenth-century scripture crosses which dot the Irish landscape.

The two top panels on the east side of the Ruthwell cross refer to Mary and Martha, the two sisters of Lazarus, and were meant to be icono-graphically complementary. The upper scene shows the two women, identi-fied by a runic inscription as Martha and Mary,[23] embracing. Luke 10:38–42 relates the story of Christ and the apostles' visit to the house of Martha. While Martha was ministering to her visitors, Mary chose to sit quietly at Jesus's feet. When Martha complained that Mary was not helping her, Christ replied: 'Martha, Martha, thou art troubled by many things; but one thing is necessary. Mary hath chosen the best part, which shall not be taken away from her.' Early Christian exegesis on this passage in Luke associated Martha with the active life and Mary with the contemplative life, expressing the tension between the two ideals within the monastic world. Cassian had stated that both are acceptable to God, but the contemplative life, synon-ymous with the meditative monastic life, is preferable.[24] The upper panel was obviously meant to represent these two aspects of monastic existence through the persons of the two sisters, who were described as meritorious women. Their embrace would express the compatibility and unity of the forms of monastic life.

Both are worthy, but perhaps not equal, and the predominance of the contemplative life, as allegorised by the figure of Mary, is indicated in the panel now situated directly below (*Plate 9a*). The lower scene which shows a figure huddled at the feet of a standing, cross-nimbed Christ is accompanied by a long text:

She brought an alabaster box of ointment and standing behind his feet she began to wash his feet with her tears, and she wiped [them] with the hairs of her head.[25]

This is based on Luke 7:37–8:

she . . . brought an alabaster box of ointment; and standing behind at his feet, she began to wash his feet, with tears, and wiped them with the hairs of her head, and kissed his feet, and anointed them with the ointment.

A similar incident is related in less detail in Mark 14:3–9 and Matt. 26:6–13. At John 11:2 we find the passage: 'And Mary was she that anointed the Lord with ointment, and wiped his feet with her hair.' This gave rise to the argument that the anonymous woman (women) of Luke, Matthew and Mark was the same Mary mentioned in John. On the Ruthwell cross, the woman (Mary) is shown humbled at Christ's feet, wiping them with her hair, acknowledging Christ's divinity, an analogy to the image of the beasts at the

---

[23] MARÞA maria M[E]R[ENTES] DOMINNAE.
[24] See above, 141–2; also, Meyvaert, 'A new perspective', 138–9.
[25] A[TT]U[LIT ALA]B[A]STRUM U[NGUE]NTI & S[T]AN[S R]E[TR]O SECUS PEDES EIUS LACRIMIS COEPIT RIGARE PEDES EIUS & CAPILLIS CAPITIS SUI TERGEBAT. See Howlett, 'Inscriptions', 73.

feet of Christ. But there is another relevant layer of meaning. The proximity to the panel of Mary and Martha would further seem to indicate an identification of the female-anointer, with Mary, the sister of Martha. There was also the related issue that this hybrid Mary, Martha's sister, had been equated with Mary Magdalene from whom Christ had cast out seven devils (Luke 8:2). Bede, in his Commentary on Luke, firmly concluded that all these women mentioned – the anonymous anointing woman of Luke, Matthew and Mark, who had been equated with John's Mary, who had been equated with Luke's Mary the sister of Martha and Lazarus, who, by this time, had been equated with Mary Magdalene – were one and the same. In this he was following the conflation of the three as 'Mary Magdalene' which had been established by Gregory the Great.[26]

Because of this symbiotic identification, Mary Magdalene could also take on the dubious character of the woman in the Pharisee's house mentioned in Luke 7. This woman (now identified as Mary) was described by Simon as a notorious sinner. When chided about his willingness to allow a close physical association, Christ responded, 'Many sins are forgiven her, because she hath loved much'; and to her: 'Thy faith hath made thee safe, go in peace' (Luke 7:47–50). Mary Magdalene was one of the women who ministered to Christ and the apostles, the implication being that she repented her past life and reformed her ways. In an eighth-century Anglo-Saxon martyrology, Mary Magdalene is described as a repentant sinner who spent the last decades of her life as a hermit in the desert: Mary Magdalene had become synonymous with Mary of Egypt.[27] By the time the Ruthwell cross was designed, this multi-faceted Mary Magdalene could be seen as the model of the penitential life and the prototype for the holy women and female ascetics in Ireland and England. Insular monasticism exhorted married women and widows, as well as virgins, to flee from the world and to embrace the monastic ideals of penance and mortification of the flesh. The point seems to have been deliberately emphasised on the Ruthwell cross by the inscriptional reference to the tears with which the woman bathed the feet of Jesus. Tears were seen as a symptom of grace by Cassian and were regarded as a true reflection of the movement of the heart towards God.[28] The Ruthwell cross, through its representations of John the Baptist and Mary Magdalene in their close association with Jesus, seems deliberately to have provided ascetic, penitential models for both sexes, models which would help the faithful Christian to imitate Christ, the ideal monk.

At least half of the scenes on the shaft of the Ruthwell cross are associated with the ideals of Insular monasticism. But nothing has been established concerning the early history of the site, and no monastery seems to have

---

[26] Bede, *On Luke*, III.28–42 [*CCSL* CXX, 166–7], (cit. Meyvaert, 'A new perspective', 111 n. 53). See also (J.B.) Stevenson, 'The holy sinner', 25 n. 27.

[27] Herzfeld, *An Old English Martyrology*, 127; see also, Schapiro, 'The religious meaning', 163–4; Orchard, 'Hot lust', 182–4.

[28] (J.B.) Stevenson, 'The holy sinner', 37. For an alternative, feminist view see Farr, 'Worthy women'.

been directly associated with it. Since the Ruthwell cross seems to have been erected outside the immediate vicinity of a known monastery, it may have been a preaching cross, one at which people from various stations in life could congregate for their devotions.[29] It has been suggested that the subjects depicted on the Ruthwell cross correspond to the readings of the Roman liturgy, as performed in Northumbria in the eighth century.[30] As a 'pilgrimage' cross celebrating the Roman liturgy, it could have been used in a ceremony paralleling the Roman commemoration of Christ's death: in Rome, on Good Friday, the pope and clergy went in solemn barefoot procession from St John Lateran to Santa Croce in Hierusalem.

Ruthwell was in the old British kingdom of Rheged, where the seventh century was filled with the struggles between the native British and their Northumbrian-Anglian neighbours. The area had been originally Christianised by the Irish Church with its mixture of coenobitic and eremitical monasticism, an ideal accepted by *Romani* and *Hibernenses* alike. It is this monasticism which is celebrated on the Ruthwell cross, showing the persistence of the ascetic, anchoritic ideal which was so at home in the Celtic provinces. At the same time, it is clear that a compromise was being sought. The shape of the cross itself, which is an equal-armed cross set atop a tall shaft, is not Celtic, but Anglian. The links with the Mediterranean mode of artistic representation make it probable that the impetus for the monument must have come from a place such as Monkwearmouth-Jarrow. The erection of such a cross could not have been the work of isolated monks fasting in the wilderness. It must be representative of the efforts of an organised Church which could accept an Anglian monumental cross, inscribed with an English poem, combined with images referring to the ideals of Celtic monasticism, in an outlying area which had only very recently been taken over by the Anglians.[31] We learn from Bede that in the early eighth century, the number of Christian converts in the area to the near west of Ruthwell grew in such leaps that a new bishopric was established in Whithorn in 731.[32] Given its location, the Ruthwell cross was meant to be a public monument for the laity as well as for the religious communities in the area. To whomever it was directed, the Christ depicted on the Ruthwell cross was the ideal model for the monastic life,[33] symbolised the eucharist, and functioned as the Judge at the second coming. The unity of Christ and the cross was complete and the living cross itself presented the saviour to the faithful, as described in the crucifixion poem inscribed on its

---

[29] Godfrey, 'The place', 346–8; Henderson, *Vision and Image*, 203, argues that the Ruthwell cross may always have been indoors, given its unweathered condition. He does not indicate if he thinks it has been transported from elsewhere or if there was a building on or near the current site.

[30] Ó Carragáin, 'The necessary distance'.

[31] MacLean, 'The date', 54–70.

[32] Bede, *Historia Ecclesiastica*, V.23 (edd. Colgrave & Mynors, 559–61).

[33] Henderson, *Vision and Image*, 207, detects eliptical, typological references to St Cuthbert in the images of Christ on the Ruthwell cross; also, he thinks the intention was to appeal for God's mercy in the name of Cuthbert against the return of the plague; see *ibid.*, 214.

side.[34] When considered as a totality, the imagery presents the idea that a synthesis of grace and effort opens the way to salvation for the true Christian, one who is practising the perfect monastic life.

The Book of Kells

In the Book of Kells there are two full-page miniatures which include representations of Christ and which seem at first glance to be at least partly narrative in character, a concept foreign to earlier Insular manuscript illumination. It has been suggested that this change coincides with the encouragement of narrative religious painting on the continent in the Carolingian court.[35]

The first scene occurs in Matthew's gospel on fo. 114r (*Plate 10*).[36] The large central figure of Christ dominates the composition, standing frontally and staring out at the reader with immense blue eyes. He has no identifying halo. Depicted on a somewhat smaller scale, Christ's two companions stand on either side and gently grasp his forearms – one lays what may appear to be a comforting hand on his left upper arm. They gaze intently at him so that they are both shown in strict facial profile. This scene is often referred to as the Arrest of Christ even though the figures grasping Jesus are clearly not represented as soldiers and the incorprated text does not relate that event. In the framed lunette above Christ's head are written the words: 'Et hymo dicto exierunt in montem Oliveti' – 'After a hymn had been said they left for Mount Olivet' (Matt. 26:30). Because of the direct reference in the text, the picture is alternatively identified as Christ on the Mount of Olives. But this is not a narrative representation of that event either, since the disciples did not remain with Christ that night and according to Matthew 26:37 there should be three of them represented: Peter and the two sons of Zebedee (James and John).

On the facing page the text describes the institution of the eucharist at the last supper (Matt. 26:26–9):

And turning to those dining there, Jesus took bread and blessed it and breaking it, said 'Take this and eat of it all of you for this is my body which will be given for eternal life.' And taking the chalice he raised it and giving it to them said, 'Drink of this all of you for this is my blood of the New Testament which will be shed for you and for everyone for the remission of sins. But I say to you all that I shall not drink again of this fruit of the vine from this day until I drink with you of the new fruit in the kingdom of my Father.'[37]

In subsequent pages the story of the agony in the garden and the betrayal and arrest of Christ is related. But this image is not a straightforward illustration of either the text which it accompanies or the text it anticipates. Rather, it is connected with a range of patristic and Insular exegesis and it

[34] For the text, see above, 211–12.
[35] Harbison, 'Earlier Carolingian narrative'.
[36] Henry, *The Book of Kells*, illus. 45; Henderson, *From Durrow to Kells*, illus. 231, p. 162.
[37] Book of Kells, fo. 113v (Matthew 26:26–9) (our translation); Latin text below, 276.

has been argued that it has possible liturgical connections.[38] We contend that it may refer to, but does not directly represent, Christ on the Mount of Olives, in addition to symbolising the institution of the eucharist. It also encompasses a direct lesson for the monk or holy woman who had the opportunity to meditate upon its form and content.

On each side, the framing pseudo-architecture contains a cross-shaped panel in place of the expected capitals from which the arch springs at the level of Christ's head. The Mount of Olives is visually alluded to by the sinuous vines growing out of vases connected to the horizontal bar of the lunette above the figures. These two vines also refer to the newly-created eucharist as described on the facing page and to Christ as the true vine (John 15:1). Christ's extended arms are supported by his companions so that he assumes the praying position which had been commonly used to distinguish the early Christian *orans* figures. This praying stance was also adopted by the priest celebrating the mass and the eucharist, a reference which would not have been missed by the celebrant reading from the gospel book during the eucharistic liturgy. The priest-celebrant becomes the true imitator of Christ, with his usual two acolytes being identified with the supporting figures in the picture. In the illustration, the body of Christ, synonymous with the host, is held up for the worship of the celebrant, just as he, the celebrant, was holding up the host for veneration during the consecration of the mass. Christ is shown as both the blood-sacrifice required for the remission of sins (Matt. 26:28) as indicated in the text on the facing page, and as the eternal priest[39] whose actions will be repeated at the celebration and reception of the eucharist. The Book of Kells is unique in Insular manuscripts in its singling out of the words of the last supper, which are repeated at the consecration of the eucharist, for such special emphasis and artistic treatment. This specific joining of text and image reflects clearly the acceptance of the efficacious role of the eucharist in the monastic search for salvation.

Christ's legs are angled in such a way that his limbs create the shape of the *Chi*, the first letter of the sacred monogram, and a reference to the cross and Christ's crucifixion. The cross-allusion would have been apparent to the educated monk or could have been pointed out in a sermon. Within the experience of the viewer of this illustration would also be the analogous image of the monk in his devotion, standing with his arms outstretched in the cross-vigil, in imitation of the crucified Christ. This vigil was perhaps the most frequent of the devotions practised by the eighth-century *Céli Dé* and was integrated into their daily lives and prayers as well as featured during feastdays and penitential periods.[40] Any Irish monk would have been familiar with it. The Kells image is a reminder to the monastic viewer that the imitation of Christ was the prime requirement of a life of perfection.

---

[38] Farr, *The Book of Kells*, 104–39; Ó Carragáin, '*Traditio evangeliorum*', 418–24.

[39] See below, 254–5.

[40] Mael Ruain, *The Rule of Tallaght*, VI (tr. Ó Maidín, 101–2) describes one such observance; there are many other references to the practice in this eighth-century text.

9. Ruthwell cross, Dumfriesshire

(a) Mary (Magdalene) at Christ's feet   (b) Christ standing on the beasts

10. Christ on Mount Olivet, Book of Kells, fo. 114r

11. The temptation of Christ, Book of Kells, fo. 202v

12. Athlone crucifixion plaque

13. Crucifixion of Christ, St Gall Gospels, p. 266

14. The second coming of Christ, St Gall Gospels, p. 267

15. The enthroned Christ, Book of Kells, fo. 32v

16. Monasterboice, Co. Louth, Cross of Muiredach, *psychostasis*/harrowing of hell

Matthew's gospel text clearly states that Christ underwent a solitary vigil that long night at Gesthemani, for the three disciples could not stay awake to support him (Matt. 26:36–46). This illustration must then make a different reference. We agree with the principle that this image must have a meaning associated with the text accompanying it and therefore must have a connection with the suffering of Christ at Gesthemani, often seen as synonymous with Mount Olivet. The disposition of the figures may have been typologically inspired by the Old Testament story of the battle between the Hebrews and the Amalekites. Moses and his brothers were watching the fighting from the vantage of an overlooking hilltop. As long as Moses held his arms up, the Hebrews had the advantage; when his arms faltered, the enemy prevailed. Seeing this, Aaron and Hur supported Moses's arms, one on each side, until the sunset when Joshua's victory was assured (Exodus 17:8–17). In the middle ages Moses was viewed as an Old Testament type for Christ, while Amalek was equated with the devil.

The anagogical meaning of this unusual image of Christ in the Book of Kells would have been directed towards its main audience, the Christian dedicated to the monastic life. Christ/Moses here becomes the model and the encouragement for the monk who must withstand the onslaught of Satan and the temptation to succumb to the sin of despair. According to Matthew, Christ was able to overcome the despair which descended upon him in the garden not with the help of his disciples, but because of the ministrations of the angels and the perfection of his willingness to accept God's will (Matt. 26:39–44). Moses, facing the satanic enemy Amalek at Rephidim, had to rely upon the help of his brothers to remain constant and steady and to achieve victory at last. Since the disciples had failed Christ at Gesthemani even after three rebukes, the brethren in the coenibitic monastic life were called upon to imitate Aaron and Hur instead, and to help each other achieve their personal victories over the wiles of the devil.

Painted at a time when the danger of Viking attack was very real, this image in the Book of Kells was also a call for courage and faith and a plea to overcome despair, just as Christ had overcome his despair on the night before his Passion. Some viewers might have been familiar with the episode in Stephanus's *Life of Bishop Wilfrid*, written in Northumbria *ca* 720, in which the saint and his followers were able to withstand the fierce and repeated attacks of a pagan horde by raising their arms in prayer in specific imitation of Moses, Aaron and Hur:

So St Wilfrid the bishop and his clergy on bended knees lifted their hands again to heaven and gained the help of the Lord. For as Moses continually called upon the Lord for help, Hur and Aaron raising his hands, while Joshua the son of Nun was fighting against Amalek with the people of God, so this little band of Christians overthrew the fierce and untamed heathen host, three times putting them to flight with no little slaughter, though, marvellous to relate, only five of the Christians were slain.[41]

The Irish understanding of the militant character of the Mosaic cross stance,

[41] Stephanus, *Life of Bishop Wilfrid*, XIII (tr. Colgrave, 29); Latin text below, 276.

replicated in the cross-vigil, is reflected in its description in the *Rule of Tallaght*: 'The elders formerly called the cross-vigil "The Breastplate of Devotion".'[42]

And so with this one image, the monastic viewers could see themselves in their devotion, and were presented with a complex Christological statement, a reflection upon the establishment of the eucharist, Christ as sacrificial offering, an image of the unity of Christ with the officiating priest at the moment of the consecration during the mass, and the reminder of Christ/Moses as the example for monastic constancy and courage. Exegetical writings of the fifth and sixth centuries equated Moses's praying stance not only with the cross and the Passion of Christ but with the promise of salvation. Gregory the Great saw the pose as a defence against the temptations of the flesh, symbolising the raising of the mind above temptation by means of contemplation and good acts.[43] The Insular monk would clearly understand this directive.

A second set of lessons for the monastic life is embodied in the representation of the temptation of Christ by the devil on fo. 202v (*Plate 11*).[44] The illustration follows immediately after the genealogy of Christ according to Luke – the facing page starts the narration of the Temptation with the text: *IHS autem plenus Spiritus Sancti*: 'Now Jesus, full of the Holy Spirit' (Luke 4:1). Christ is shown in large-scale and half-length perched atop the temple of Jerusalem where he had been led by Satan after spending forty days fasting in the desert beyond the Jordan. Taunted to throw himself from the height and allow himself to be rescued by the angels, Christ's reply was 'Thou shalt not tempt the Lord thy God' (Luke 4:12 from Deuteronomy 6:16). This third temptation is the one most obviously depicted here. The black, scrawny devil is shown in conversation with Christ, while four angels hover over them, two directly over the figures and two in the upper corners of the frame surrounding the picture. The latter pair hold a book each and are depicted in conjunction with a flowering vine growing out of an urn. Groups of four angels are common in the Book of Kells and they must refer to the four archangels most commonly known: Michael, Gabriel, Raphael and Uriel. The temple is depicted as a small Irish-type church or house-shrine. Rather than attempt an imitation of the classical building type, the artist drew on his own experience and produced a fairly accurate description of the type of structure with which he and the readers were familiar.

The two other temptations which Christ overcame are also alluded to. In the first temptation, Satan had commanded Christ to turn a stone into bread so that he could satisfy his hunger after forty days fasting. Christ's reply had been 'It is written that Man liveth not by bread alone, but by every word of God' (Luke 4:4 from Deuteronomy 6:16). Next, Satan had shown Christ all

---

[42] Mael Ruain, *The Rule of Tallaght*, VI (tr. Ó Maidín, 101); (ed. Gwynn, *The Rule*, 6): 'Luireach leiri fá sean-ainm o chein don chrosadh ag na sruithibh.'

[43] Gregory, *In Primum Regum Expositiones*, VI.3–4 [*PL* LXXIX.409B–410A] (as referred to in Farr, *The Book of Kells*, 107).

[44] Henry, *The Book of Kells*, illus. 68; Henderson, *From Durrow to Kells*, illus. 242, p. 169.

the kingdoms of the world and promised to give him dominion over them if he would worship him. Christ had replied, 'Thou shalt adore the Lord thy God, and him only shalt thou serve' (Luke 4:8 from Deuteronomy 6:13, 10:20). The crowd of men to the right of the temple and at the bottom may represent the different nations of the world, over which Christ refused temporal sovereignty.

With this, the monk was warned against the three great temptations of human life which were just as much a danger within the monastery as without. Through the example of the first temptation of Christ, the monk was reminded that the human inclination to satisfy not only hunger, but all carnal desires, must be resisted, that the spiritual life must dominate and this was built upon knowledge of the word of God. As mentioned above, the penances for any carnal sins were severe. In the *Rule of Tallaght*, concerning the intake of food, Mael Ruain had written that it was the practice for one monk to 'read the gospel, the rules, and the lives (miracles) of the saints aloud while the brethren were at table, or eating supper, so that their attention would not be on their food . . . Next day each monk was questioned on the subject of the reading to ensure that they were attentive to what was being read.'[45] The second temptation was a warning against worldly ambition which was seen as being linked directly with the devil; power and authority within monastic life must be separated from personal aggrandisement. The last temptation, that of challenging God to a rescue, was a warning against both bodily and spiritual recklessness. The instructions for monastic observance, penance and asceticism warn against overzealousness and the inclination to attempt more than is reasonable or humanly possible.

The warning against overzealousness was an old issue for the monastic life, as seen in the repeated references made to it by Cassian in *Conference* II. This contains the story of the desert hermit, Heron, who after spending fifty years in ever-more-excessive fasting and self-imposed isolation, was deceived by what he thought was an angel of light (it was actually Satan) into throwing himself into a deep well, thinking that, thanks to his virtues and labours, he could not possibly endanger himself and that he would be miraculously protected from bodily harm. Gravely injured, he died three days later, refusing to believe that he had been deluded by his pride and the devil. It was only after much persuasion that his abbot granted that his death was not a suicide and allowed him a Christian burial.[46] Heron's pride in his overzealous asceticism almost cost him his soul at the very end of his life. The close analogy to the demand of the devil that Christ throw himself from the height of the mountaintop and thus challenge God to perform a miracle upon provocation would have allowed the monk to draw the lesson into his own life and devotional practice. Closer to home, the same warning is illustrated in the *Rule of Tallaght* which relates the story of an anchorite

---

[45] Mael Ruain, *The Rule of Tallaght*, LXXX (tr. Ó Maidín, 122); Irish text below, 276–7. The Irish *fearta* should be translated as 'miracles' rather than 'lives' of the saints (MWH).

[46] Cassian, *Conferences*, II.v.1 (tr. Ramsey, 87–8).

from Clonard, who in his attempt at great asceticism, made seven hundred genuflections each day; Mael Ruain predicted that a time would come before his death when the hermit would not be able to make even a single genuflection; this came to be when the man's legs became so stiff as a result of the repeated and excessive movement that he was unable to bend his knees to perform his devotion.[47]

The temptations of Christ occurred at the end of his forty days of fasting in the desert (Luke 4:1–13) in which he went without food. The monastic life insisted upon the efficacy of the forty days of abstinence, penitence and mortification during the pre-Easter Lent and the pre-Christmas period, in imitation of Christ. The triumph of Christ over the temptations of Satan was seen not only as the promise of help to the monk in overcoming his struggle with the devil but as synonymous with the spiritual struggle of the Church. The connection between Psalm 90 and the temptations of Christ would have been obvious to the monks who recited psalms daily and were aware that the devil had quoted from that psalm when he said: 'For he hath given his angels charge over thee; to keep thee in all thy ways. In their hands they shall bear thee up: lest thou dash thy foot against a stone' (Psalm 90:11–12).[48] Although twisted by the devil, Psalm 90 could also be interpreted as promising God's reasonable protection against all dangers, both physical and spiritual:

. . . . Thou shalt not be afraid of the terror of the night.
(6) of the arrow that flieth in the day, of the business that walketh about in the dark: of invasion, or of the noonday devil . . .
(10) There shall no evil come to thee: nor shall the scourge come near thy dwelling.

These must have been comforting words at a time and place where the Viking invaders were an ever-present and growing danger, and perhaps bolstered the same hope contained in the image of Christ/Moses on fo. 114r.

The monastic lessons embodied in the temptation of Christ are augmented in this depiction. The object which Christ is holding in his hand has been interpreted as a scroll which represents the Torah or the Pentateuch, the source of the scripture which Christ quotes to fend off the devil's attack.[49] The placing of Christ literally as the pinnacle of the temple harmonises with the statement in the anonymous seventh-century Irish commentary on Luke: 'and he placed him on the pinnacle of the temple, that is on the highest seat of the teacher'.[50] Christ, holding the scroll of the word of God, resisting the

---

[47] Mael Ruain, *The Rule of Tallaght*, CIII (tr. Ó Maidín, 129).

[48] Farr, *The Book of Kells*, 68, traces awareness of the connection between Psalm 90 and the temptation of Christ to Augustine's *Commentary on Psalm 90*. This should be treated cautiously since Augustine was not widely used in the Irish Church. See above, 119–20.

[49] Farr, *The Book of Kells*, 51.

[50] *Commentarium in Lukam*, IV.9 (ed. [J.F.] Kelly, *Scriptores Hiberniae Minores*, 33): '*Et statuit eum super* pinnaculum *templi*: Id est, in summa sede doctoris'. Our thanks to Paul Meyvaert for this reference.

devil, is the teacher who addresses the crowd gathered on his right side. Scripture is the weapon which Christ proffers to ward off the demon. Familiarity with 'every word of God', as contained in the Old and New Testaments, may be alluded to by the two books held by the angels. This would have reflected the importance of the close observation of the Law which had been a requirement of the common Celtic Church and a principle of Celtic monastic existence, and which may have had a continuing influence.

The message is reinforced at the bottom of the illumination where a smaller figure of Christ stands in the doorway of the Church/Temple, with a group of men crowded on either side. The temple was also seen as the symbol for the new Jerusalem. This combination of Christ and temple illustrated that the means by which the Christian can overcome his temptations is through his belief in, and imitation of, Christ, and his acceptance of the guidance of the Church. That Christ is the doorway through which the faithful must pass to discover the help they need to combat the devil successfully is reflected in a mid-eighth-century Irish poem ascribed to Blathmac:

> He is overlord of every generation;
> he is the tip of the true vine;
> he is the bright well-lit pathway;
> he is the true door to the eternal kingdom.[51]

Just as Christ was able to resist the temptations of the devil, so the monk must be prepared to do so. The group of twenty-five figures on either side of Christ may very well have been seen as representative of the monastic community, of those very people who were the true Christians, attempting to live the life of perfection demanded by God as the key to salvation.

The last judgement is undoubtedly alluded to by the inclusion of this Christ figure in the doorway of the temple. Synonymous with the Temple, the figure is depicted in the same fashion as is Christ in last judgement scenes on the later scriptural crosses, holding the crossed rod and sceptre. The heavenly Jerusalem, the final and eternal dwelling place of the saved is described in the Apocalypse as having no temple 'since the Lord God Almighty and the Lamb were themselves the Temple' (Apocalypse 21:22–3). Christ is both the Temple and the Church, the Old Law and the New, both required as the means of attaining eternal bliss. Again Psalm 90 provides the key:

(15) He shall cry to me, and I will hear him: I am with him in tribulation, I will deliver him, and I will glorify him.
(16) I will fill him with length of days; and I will show him my salvation.

---

[51] Blathmac, *Poem to Mary and her Son*, stanza 210 (ed. and tr. Carney, 70–1):
> Is forblaith for cach ndíne,
> is barr inna fírfíne;
> é in sét sorchae solus,
> don bithflaith is fírdorus.

In the painted images in the Book of Kells the human figures have been represented through the agency of the indigenous Celtic aesthetic, very different from what was seen on the Ruthwell and Bewcastle crosses. They are not based upon the concept of naturalistic representation which was foreign to the traditional Celtic artist, who primarily saw the decorative and calligraphic element in designs. The figures are flat, two-dimensional designs, conceived of and rendered as coloured line drawings. Human anatomy has been transformed into pattern and colours are arbitrary and in some cases, unnatural.

In these pages, the compositions cannot truly be called narrative, for story-telling is not the main purpose for their inclusion within the text. On the visual level, these pages were meant to decorate the written Word, to elevate it beyond the ordinary, to transform the object into something worthy of reflecting God's glory and of being used in his service. In this way, they would function like the jewels and filigree set into shrines, book-covers and liturgical objects. The liturgical meaning and usage of these illustrations from the life of Christ have been discussed in depth.[52] Because of the multivalent nature of medieval images, the different levels of meaning would be accessible in differing degrees, varying with the preparation with which the viewer approached them. The images were meant to augment the meaning of the text and to serve as catalysts for contemplation and meditation, each viewer bringing his own spiritual and intellectual gifts to the reading. This message of the imitation of Christ as the main means by which salvation is achieved would have been accessible to all who saw the images. But it is highly unlikely that the great luxury gospel books were meant for general public display. They were sacred objects and it is probable that their display would have been kept within the monastic confines. The messages that they held for the Insular monk, man or woman, would have been the important aspect of their effective meaning.

The crucified Christ

Even though Christian art in the Mediterranean accepted the use of the image of Christ from the late fourth century on, his crucifixion was shown only by implication in scenes of his Passion and by the inclusion of the cross.[53] There was a natural reluctance to depict Christ as suffering the humiliating and agonising death of a common criminal. There were also the theological arguments which would have made it unacceptable to represent Christ in fully human form, in a way which might be interpreted as denying his divine nature. These reservations were set aside by the Quinisext Council held in Constantinople in 692, which in canon 82 decreed that Christ was to

---

[52] Farr, *The Book of Kells*, and Ó Carragáin, '*Traditio evangeliorum*'.

[53] The exceptions to this can be seen in the small ivory panel from Rome or southern Gaul depicting the crucifixion of Christ and the suicide of Judas in a suprisingly realistic fashion, which is in the British Museum and dated *ca* 420, and in the Rabbula Gospels of *ca* 590.

be represented only in his human form.[54] This made the realistic representation of Christ and his crucifixion possible. Britain and Ireland were among the first of the Christianised areas of Europe to accept the challenge. One of the earliest sculpted depictions of the crucifixion in the Insular world appears near the bottom of the east face of the shaft of the Ruthwell cross. There are representations of Christ on his cross in eighth-century Insular manuscripts, such as in the Durham Gospel Fragments and the St Gall codex; and in sculpture, on the slab cross at Cardonagh (Co. Donegal) and on the base of the cross of Moone (Co. Kildare), both of which may date from the second quarter of the ninth century.[55] The great scripture crosses of Ireland almost invariably carry a crucifixion on the west face at the crossing.

A formula particular to Ireland and the other Celtic areas for representing Christ's crucifixion seems to have developed by the early eighth century. In addition to observing what was apparently a common iconographical tradition, there are individual attempts to draw attention to particular exegetical strands.[56] One of the most striking examples is the small copper crucifixion plaque, about 21 centimetres in height, which was found near Athlone and is thought to have been a decoration for a book cover or a shrine (*Plate 12*).[57] In the centre, a large figure of Christ with straight, outstretched arms has become synonymous with the cross which supports him: his body and the upright member of the cross are identical, while the horizontal members frame his arms. The upper terminal emerges from his head and the lower terminal contains the feet. The cross and Christ are one, showing the complete merger of symbol and representation. The beardless, living Christ is upright and frontally presented, wearing a long-sleeved tunic, the *colobium*, which extends to his ankles. This robe is decorated at the cuffs and hem and on the skirt with interlace, fret and running spiral designs. The typological model for the robed Christ originated in the east Mediterranean and had appeared in the illumination of Syriac manuscripts, notably the Rabbula Gospels of *ca* 590. There, the long robe denoted a person of consequence and was used in preference to the loin-cloth of the criminal. But there was also an iconographical choice in clothing the crucified Christ in the long robe. It referred to Christ's seamless overgarment (John 19:23) for which the soldiers cast lots, which was itself seen as analogous to Aaron's seamless priest's tunic (Exodus 28:32).

As in the Syriac visual tradition, the figures who had become known as Longinus and 'Stephaton' are placed on either side of the foot of the cross. This became the almost invariable rule in Celtic representations of Christ's crucifixion. The naming of Longinus is non-canonical, first appearing in early apocrypha, in which he was equated with the soldier, who, upon piercing the side of Christ with his lance, caused blood and water to gush forth (John 19:34). This rather matter of fact account is found in the

---

[54] Fritz, 'Quinisexte Concile'.
[55] Harbison, *The High Crosses*, I.375–7.
[56] O'Reilly, 'Early medieval text and image', 84–100, affords an excellent overview of Insular crucifixion iconography and exegesis.
[57] Harbison, 'The bronze crucifixion plaque'.

seventh-century (?) *Evangelium Nicodemi* which translates the Greek *Commentaries of Nicodemus* of *ca* 600: 'But the soldier Longinus, taking his lance, opened his side and blood and water came out from his side.'[58] In eighth-century Ireland, this was combined with the references in the other canonical gospels which refer to the soldier who was converted at the foot of the cross and who proclaimed Christ as God (Matt. 27:54; Mark 15:39; Luke 23:47). In his *Poem to Mary and her Son* Blathmac said:

When they thought thus that Jesus could be approached, Longinus then came to slay him with the spear . . . .

. . .

By the same blood (it was a fair occasion!). Quickly did he cure the fully blind man who, openly with his two hands, was plying the lance.[59]

That physical blindness was referred to in the Irish context, in spite of the patent absurdity of a blind Roman soldier wielding a lance, is visually attested in the depiction of Christ's crucifixion in the eighth-century St Gall Gospels (*Plate 13*) in which a zigzag line extends from the wound in Christ's side down to the eye of Longinus. This reflects full acceptance of the miraculous and the working of grace! The apocryphal curing of Longinus's blindness at the foot of the cross became a reference to both physical and spiritual blindness and to conversion and salvation. Thus, Longinus could be seen as a representative of the true convert, the Christian who was saved by Christ's sacrifice, and who was a witness to his divinity. The two strands of the Longinus story, Latin and Irish, had come together by the time the Irish version of the Gospel of Nicodemus was formulated in the eleventh or twelfth century:

Then one of the soldiers whose name was Longinus came forward. His appearance was such that his face was a flat surface, and he was without eyes. With a great spear he struck Jesus's side, as he had been instructed, for no-one who could see Jesus wished to wound him. Immediately there flowed two streams from Jesus's side, a stream of blood and a stream of water. And Longinus rubbed on his forehead the blood which ran down his spear. Then two clear grey eyes appeared in his head, and when he thus saw the face of Jesus he believed in him, and asked his mercy.[60]

The piercing of Christ's side was regarded as the moment of the creation of the Church and also as a eucharistic symbol, the sacred body fluids being analagous to the water and wine mixture in the consecration chalice.

'Stephaton' was identified with the soldier who, when Christ indicated that he was thirsty, ran and soaked a sponge with vinegar, secured it to the end of his lance and held it up to Christ's mouth (Matt. 27:48; Mark 15:36;

---

[58] *The Latin Gospel of Nicodemus*, X.15–16 (our translation); (ed. Kim, 25): 'Accipiens autem Longinus miles lanceam aperuit latus eius, et exiit de latere eius sanguis et aqua.' This sentence may help to show the origin of the name Longinus: λόγχη, the Greek equivalent of *lancea*, 'lance'.

[59] Blathmac, *Poem to Mary and her Son*, stanzas 55, 58 (tr. Carney, 21); Irish text below, 277.

[60] *Irish Gospel of Nicodemus*, X.1 (tr. Herbert & McNamara, 69); Irish text below, 277.

Luke 23:36; John 19:29).[61] On the Athlone crucifixion plaque, the sponge can be seen as a tiny, lightly incised cup-form immediately below Christ's chin. There is no tradition that 'Stephaton' was converted at the foot of the cross, and thus he came to be seen as a representative of the unbeliever stubbornly clinging to his unbelief even in the presence of God. The piercing of Christ's side was seen by St John as the fulfilment of Messianic prophecy: 'They shall look on him whom they pierced' (John 19:37 and Zacharias 12:10) and thus a revelation of his divinity. The two soldiers, witnesses to, and operatives in, the historical event of Christ's crucifixion exemplify two levels of comprehension: those who see only the apparent physical event and are blind to spiritual insight, and those who perceive its significance as a revelation of divine glory. They also form a parallel to the two thieves who were crucified, one on either side of Christ: one who blasphemed Christ and the other who, recognising Jesus's innocence and asking to be remembered in the heavenly kingdom, is promised a place in Paradise (Luke 23:39–43). In the seventh-century (?) Latin *Gospel of Nicodemus* these men were named Dismas and Gestas.[62] In the Irish *Acts of Pilate*, these men were given the names Dismus and Iasmus. Iasmus, who was crucified on Christ's left side, remained blind to the path to salvation and, like 'Stephaton', refused to recognise Christ. Executed on the right side of Christ, Dismus, like Longinus, was granted spiritual insight and achieved the goal of the true Christian.[63]

It is a truism that, even in narrative scenes, early medieval artists did not aim merely to represent the world of physical action in a given space and time. Religious art was meant to invoke the symbolic and timeless aspects of the symbiotic union of past, present and future. That the depiction of Christ's crucifixion is not meant to refer merely to an historical event occurring in linear time can be inferred from the decision to depict the actions of Longinus and 'Stephaton' as occurring simultaneously. In John 19:28–34, we read that the wine and vinegar had been offered to Christ while he was alive, and that Christ's side was pierced after he was already dead. On the Athlone plaque, the iris of the left eye is visible which would indicate that Christ was meant to be perceived as still alive. But the slight tilt of the head to his left would indicate that he is dead. This indication of Christ being both alive and dead simultaneously has been taken to show the double nature of Christ, the hypostatic union of human and divine. His human nature was dead on the cross, but his divine nature was eternally alive.[64] It clearly indicates the symbolic nature and intent of this scene which is central to Christological thinking.

Two triple-winged angels hover above the arms of the cross, one on either

---

[61] Although iconographers constantly refer to this soldier as 'Stephaton', the source of the appellation is unclear. Dumville, 'Biblical apocrypha', 306 n. 43, indicates that the name does not appear in the Irish context from this period and that in later Irish tradition he is known as Egitianus. We use 'Stephaton' as a convention.

[62] *Latin Gospel of Nicodemus*, IX.5 (ed. Kim, 24).

[63] *Irish Gospel of Nicodemus*, X.1 (tr. Herbert & McNamara, 69).

[64] Veelenturf, *Dia Brátha*, 139–40. The wide-eyed Christ appears clearly in manuscript renditions, less definitely today on the high crosses because of the effects of weathering.

side of Christ's head. They recall their heavenly brethren who ministered to Christ during his time in the desert and during his distress in the garden at Gethsemani, just prior to his Passion (Luke 22:43). As such they are a real, but textually invisible element in the crucifixion narrative. At a deeper level, they evoke an exegetically related series of scriptural texts: the instruction of God to Moses to create two golden cherubim to be placed above the ark of the covenant (Exodus 25:18–20); the description of the ark in Solomon's temple as also having two cherubim accompanying it (III Kings 6:23–8; II Paralipomenon [Chron] 3:10–13); and the prophecy of Habbakuk (in the Old Latin text) that the Lord would be recognised between two animals. These texts were all taken to prophesy Christ's being revealed and glorified on the cross.[65] The artistic source for the composition which places the angels above the crucifixion can be found in the early Christian motif of two flying angels holding aloft a *clipeus* in which a cross or the face of Christ is portrayed. This composition appeared on chancel arches in churches, on the covers of liturgical books and on altar vessels. It denoted the exaltation of the glorified body of Christ with all of its eucharistic and apocryphal connotations.

On the Athlone plaque, the sacerdotal significance of the crucified Christ is indicated by the seemingly strange design which is prominently displayed on his chest. Composed of spirals, it has the appearance of being a shield or an ornamental breastplate. When considered together, this breast ornament and the lavish garment in which Christ is draped are a reference to Christ, the 'anointed one' and eternal priest. He is clad in the 'holy garments' of the Old Testament priest-kings, Aaron and his sons, which includes a long, heavily ornamented robe (Exodus 28:1–5). Over all is attached the breastplate of judgement, as ordained for 'the priest of the Most High God'. It is described as heavily decorated with gemstones and inscribed with the names of the sons of Israel. Through the agency of the pectoral, which was permanently attached to the priestly robes, Aaron was to bear the judgement of the children of Israel on his breast in the sight of the Lord (Exodus 28:15–30). On the Athlone plaque, the sacerdotal pectoral has been rendered as an attached breastplate covered with Celtic decoration. The references to the priesthood of Aaron and Melchisadek, both high priests of the Old Testament seen as prefigurations of the eternal priesthood of Christ, were part of the offertory prayers of the mass. Melchisadek, ancient priest-king of Salem, had offered bread and wine to Abraham, and thus could be seen as foreshadowing the celebration of the eucharist. Within the Irish context, those who spent their lives in, or attached to, a monastic establishment saw themselves as analogous to the Old Testament Levites, the tribe of Moses and Aaron to whom God's laws and observances had been entrusted.[66] The temporal priesthood of the Mosaic Law would be fulfilled in the eternal priesthood of Christ as high priest of a greater and more perfect tabernacle.[67] The exaltation of the eternal priesthood of the crucified Christ, being himself

[65] O'Reilly, 'Early medieval text and image', 90.
[66] Ó Corráin *et al.*, 'The laws of the Irish', 405.
[67] Roe, 'A stone cross at Clogher', 204–5.

both the celebrant and the sacrifice, acknowledged by Longinus and held up to view by the angels, is a fundamental meaning of the crucifixion.

But there may very well have been another layer of meaning attached to the breastplate depicted on the Athlone crucifixion plaque, a meaning rooted within Irish monastic piety. St Paul in his Letter to the Ephesians urged faithful Christians to gird themselves with the 'armour of God' and the 'breastplate of justice' to deter the deceits of the devil and to be able to resist in the evil day (Ephes. 6:11–17). In like spirit, the mid-seventh-century *Lorica* of Laidcenn is a detailed appeal to the heavenly host and to Christ especially, to defend and protect the supplicant against the 'foul demons' and the onslaught of plague, fever, weakness or pain. It is a prayer for a healthy, ripe old age so that Laidcenn, a monk from Clonfert-Molua, will have the opportunity to erase the punishment for his sins with good deeds in preparation for the day of judgement. All parts of the body and its organs are separately mentioned so that none will be missed by the protective spell. The image of Christ as the shield or breastplate is employed a number of times:

Deliver all the limbs of me, a mortal, with your protective shield guarding every member (lines 31–32)
. . .
Then be a most protective breastplate for my limbs and for my inwards' (lines 51–52)
. . .
Protect, O God, with your powerful breastplate my shoulders with their shoulder blades and arms' (lines 55–56)[68]

That the image of the sacerdotal Christ as the *Lorica* or Breastplate of the faithful was widespread can be attested by the inclusion of an elaborately decorated shield on the chest of the crucified Christ on the carved stone slab found on the Calf of Man and now in the Manx Museum (*Figure v*).[69] In addition, the east face of the small cross slab at Clogher (Co. Tyrone) contains what seems to be a disembodied head of Christ jutting directly above a circular shield of broad-band interlacing; while the larger, triangular slab at Knappaghmanagh (Co. Mayo) bears an incised head immediately beneath which is a breastplate bearing a variation of the cross-in-circle.[70] It has already been pointed out in a previous chapter that a carpet page (fo. 138v) in the Lindisfarne Gospels exhibits a cross on which the body of Christ is symbolised by the presence of a decorated square area at the intersection of the beams.[71] This can perhaps be taken to be a symbolic reference to the *Lorica* and to Christ as the Christian's breastplate. One can perhaps speculate as to whether or not the high crosses in Ireland, such as that at Killamery,[72] which bear circular shield-like designs at the crossing

---

[68] Laidcenn, *Lorica* (tr. Herren, *The Hisperica Famina II*, 76–89); Latin text below, 277.

[69] Kermode & Wilson, *Manx Crosses*, plate XVI.

[70] Roe, 'A stone cross at Clogher', illus. VIb, p. 196; and fig. 2, p. 195.

[71] See above, 219.

[72] Harbison, *The High Crosses*, II. figs. 411–12.

Figure v Crucifixion Slab, Calf of Man

rather than a body of Christ were meant to convey the same meaning. Not all representations of the crucifixion make use of the extraordinary breast-plate design with its multi-level iconography, but it is common enough to warrant its own place in the understanding of Insular attitudes towards Christ and his powers. In linking the texts of Exodus, St Paul and Laidcenn with the pectoral exhibited on Christ's body on the cross, the breastplate can be seen to refer to the power of Christ to thwart the evils perpetrated by the devil and to serve as a protection to the faithful soul. The reference to the last judgement is clear in all three texts and was transferred to the iconography of the crucifixion.

Although it does not appear to have been common practice to insert illustrations of Christ's crucifixion in the great eighth-century gospel books, there are at least three instances where it was included. As mentioned earlier, there is an abstracted reference to the crucifixion on fo. 2v. of the Lindisfarne Gospels, the carpet page in which four rectangular panels of decoration are arranged around the uninhabited Latin cross in the same disposition as the angels and soldiers would have been seen in a crucifixion composition.[73] There are two very interesting examples of representational crucifixions in manuscripts: in the Durham Gospels and in the St Gall Gospels. In both cases, Christ's crucifixion is linked very openly to the second coming and the last judgement, emphasising the message which was put more subtly in the Athlone plaque. In the eighth-century Durham Gospels,[74] the crucifixion is a full-page illustration which is inserted at the end of Matthew's gospel on fo. 38v.[75] The living Christ, clad in long multi-layered robes, stares out at the viewer with large open eyes from his

---

[73] See above, 217.
[74] Durham: Cathedral Library MS A.II.17.
[75] Henderson, *From Durrow to Kells*, illus. 114, p. 81.

placement on the cross. The crucified Christ is revealed in all his glory, accompanied by the angels who sing his praises. These angels also integrate the meaning of the Old Testament mercy seat and the presence of God in the Jewish sanctuary with the image of the priestly-robed crucified Christ.[76] The standard composition with two angels and soldiers prevails, but the added inscriptions and letters lend an unusual iconographical clarity. The Greek letters *Alpha* and *Omega* and the words *initium* and *et finis* are paired on either side of the titulus board, a direct use of the Lord's self declaration in Apocalypse 1:8: 'I am alpha and omega, the beginning and the end.' The intended taunt *Hic est IHS rex judaeorum* inscribed on the upper arm of the cross becomes the royal title of Christ enthroned upon the cross. The lengthy inscriptions which run outside the borders of the image make the obvious link between Christ's crucifixion and the last judgement: 'Christ, casting down the author of death, renews our life if we suffer along with him'; and 'He rose from the dead and sits at the right hand of the Father, so that when we have been restored to life, we may reign with him.'[77] The first phrase in particular has pertinence for the monastic viewer who expected to live his life of penitence in imitation of Christ, so that he (she) can sit with God in eternity.

The St Gall Gospel Book,[78] also from the eighth century, draws the connection in more visual terms. A pair of illustrations, the crucifixion and the second coming, face each other at the end of St John's Gospel (*Plate 13*). The crucifixion miniature on page 266 shows a living, open-eyed Christ, whose disjointed head and limbs emerge from a swath of knotted robes, rigidly exposed before the cross. A zigzag line running from Christ's left side down to Longinus's face is an obvious reference to the soldier's awakening spiritual recognition of Christ's messianic identity. The two accompanying angels now hold books, an additional eschatological reference, for they may refer to the books of life and death. The facing page is a schematic second coming (p. 267) with the dominant figure of the glorified, blessing Christ as the Lord holding the Book of Judgement and a small long-stemmed cross (*Plate 14*). An angel standing on either side blows the trumpet call of resurrection. Almost as if this were an ascension scene, twelve human figures carrying books gaze upwards at the Lord.

In all these cases, the recognition of the divinity of Christ on the cross, and hence the messianic purpose of his incarnation and death, links the crucifixion to the second coming of Christ in glory and the day of judgement. Christ on the cross is Christ the sacrifice, the anointed high priest, the enthroned and glorified Christ, Christ the Messiah, Redeemer and Judge. The wound in his side also refers to the institution of the Church, and the sacraments of baptism and the eucharist, sacraments which effect a symbiosis between the participant and Christ. In the ascetic Irish monastic

---

[76] Henderson, *Vision and Image*, 144.

[77] Cit. O'Reilly, 'Early medieval text and image', 89–91: 'Auctorem mortis deiecens, vitam nostram restituens, si tamen compatiamur . . . Surrexit a mortuis, [sedet ad] dexteram patris; ut nos cum resuscitatos simul et regnare [faciat].'

[78] St Gall: Stiftsbibliothek Codex 51.

tradition, baptism initiates the spiritual life in Christ while the eucharist is the reward for achieving a high level of sanctity. Christ is to be recognised and imitated by those who wish to achieve the eternal blessedness of heaven and escape the eternal anguish of hell. But Christ was to be imitated not in the physical actuality of crucifixion, but in his willingness to eagerly accept bodily mortification and penance. In their cross-vigil devotion, the Celtic monks imitated Christ's action and recognised Christ on the cross as their way to salvation, just as did Longinus in his moment of revelation. In their imitation of Christ, the monks aspiring to a final reward in Heaven accept Christ as the armour, the strengthening breastplate in the battle against the ever-present snares of the devil.

The crucifixion of Christ appears at the bottom of the original east face of the shaft of the Ruthwell cross, the only existing indication of its use on a piece of Insular monumental sculpture which can be reasonably dated to the early eighth century. The panel is badly damaged and the composition is difficult to discern, but an early description indicates that there were single figures standing on either side of the cross.[79] It is reasonable to assume that they were Longinus and 'Stephaton' in keeping with the iconographic version which had gained ascendancy in the Insular world. Above Christ's head are two protruberences which have been taken by some to represent *Sol* and *Luna* but are so badly damaged that any identification must remain uncertain.

In Ireland, there are two unusual instances where the crucifixion also appears on the bottom half of a monumental free-standing stone cross. On the top of the west face of the high base of the cross at Moone[80] a slightly abridged version of the crucifixion can be seen. Christ, robed in the long, sleeved *colobium*, stands with his arms outstretched with 'Stephaton' and his sponge to his left and Longinus with a very short swordlike lance to his right. The angels at his head are absent. Below the crucifixion scene, the twelve apostles can be seen lined up in three rows. As in the second coming miniature of the St Gall Gospels, this may be an oblique reference to the ascension, for the apostles, with the exception of St John, were absent at the death of Christ. On the other hand, they witnessed Christ's elevation to heaven. Since the ascension does not seem to have been directly depicted on the Irish high crosses,[81] the inclusion of the apostles here would point to an intention to indirectly represent the ascending Christ as well as the crucified Christ. The figures are all heavily abstracted, rendered as flat rectangular forms from which the neckless, pear-shaped heads emerge. The carving is created at right angles to the granite surface to produce very sharp shadow lines which make the images very easy to read and thus readily comprehensible to the viewers. At Cardonagh, on the current east face of the stem of the

---

[79] Meyvaert, 'An Apocalypse panel', 6, quotes the 1726 description of the cross by Alexander Gordon found in *Itinerarium Septentrionale*, 160–1.

[80] Harbison, *The High Crosses*, II. figs. 514–15.

[81] Harbison, *The High Crosses*, I.290–91, identifies the panel at the top of the west face of Muiredach's Cross at Monasterboice as an ascension rather than its usual identification as Moses, Aaron and Hur.

slab cross, we can see an incised crucifixion in which Christ wears a knee-length robe.[82] The two little figures, one on either side of Christ's head, are probably the angels. The figures standing on either side below his outstretched arms may very well be 'Stephaton' and Longinus although neither carries his identifying attribute. The composition copies the figure disposition of the standard crucifixion format so closely, that even without definite identifying paraphernalia, the figures must have been equated with the soldiers.[83] As on the Moone cross, the figures are highly stylised and resemble human being only in the broadest sense.

In all instances of the representational depiction of the crucifixion of Christ which emanate from Irish centres or centres of strong Irish influence, the figures have been rendered in an abstracted fashion. They do not reflect any influence of Mediterranean artistic sources or models as far as depiction is concerned. Christ and the soldiers only remotely resemble living human beings and there is no concern for a real physical interaction between them or for their existence as three-dimensional objects in space. The style is diametrically opposed to the relative realism seen in the carvings on the Ruthwell cross. This obvious retention, into the ninth century, of the Irish desire to abstract the artistic image, be it animal or human, may very simply reflect the tenacity of an indigenous aesthetic. But the reason for carrying this tendency towards the decorative and abstracted into the realm of human representation may very well be tied to the survival of the earlier, Pelagian-based iconoclastic outlook on imagery.

It was on the series of ninth- and tenth-century scripture crosses of Ireland that the crucifixion was almost universally adopted as a motif for public viewing and contemplation. The crucifixion of Christ was almost always placed at the intersection of the cross arms on the west side. Using the large cross itself as a background, Christ has his arms stretched outward, palms exposed. Longinus with his spear and 'Stephaton' with his lance and sponge/cup are clearly indicated on either side of Christ, and two angels often, but not always, seem to be supporting Christ's head. There will be some variation in compositional arrangement, and the occasional addition of other elements, such as *Sol* and *Luna*, but the scene is always essentially the same.

Christ's clothing varies to include the long *colobium*, short tunic or trousers, or a skin-tight envelope which makes him appear naked. The loin-cloth does not seem to appear in Insular depictions until much later. On the cross of Muiredach at Monasterboice the living Christ is shown apparently naked: a ridge around his ankles may indicate a binding rope but it is also possible that it was meant to be an indication of a long robe.[84] On the nearby very tall West cross, the crucified Christ is clearly depicted as clothed in a long garment, his head drooping to the side in death.[85]

---

[82] *Ibid.*, II. fig. 88.

[83] *Ibid.*, I.32, suggests that these two figures might represent the two thieves crucified along side of Christ.

[84] *Ibid.*, II. figs. 480–81.

[85] *Ibid.*, II. figs. 494, 496.

Obviously, a different tradition of depicting Christ is used from that employed for Muiredach's cross. The living and the dead Christ seem to have had about equal representation on the series of scripture crosses.

In most of these depictions of the crucifixion, the actual cross upon which Christ was elevated is not represented separately. The body of Christ himself becomes the cross, or at least the main part of the cross, as seen in the Athlone plaque. On the high crosses of Ireland, the great stone cross itself bears the crucified Christ. The crucifixion was not represented as an historical narrative, but as a symbol of the sacrifice of the Son of Man and the redemption of humanity. Placing it in the centre of the crosshead, encircled by the cosmic ring, the crucified Christ is the centre of the universe, the font of life from whom all things flow. This is the combined meaning of the cross as expressed earlier by Caelius Sedulius in his *Carmen paschale*, a poem with which the Irish had been familiar since the mid-seventh century and were using in the ninth century.[86] As Christ is elevated on the cross for all to see, his example is offered as the model for penitent Christians, who must emulate the suffering of their Saviour through a pattern of selfless mortification and penance. Only then will they have a chance of passing through the last judgement to achieve the eternal bliss of Heaven.

The eschatological implications of the crucifixion of Christ were plainly understood. It was almost invariably paired with a vision of the second coming or the last judgement on the east face of the Irish high crosses, at the crosshead.

Christ as judge and conqueror of hell

Given the spiritual goals of monasticism, the judgement of the Christian soul, both at death and at the last judgement, plays an important role in the texts used and written in the Insular Church. It is therefore not surprising if the iconography of Christ as Judge is intimately connected with many of the visual images we have already discussed. As noted earlier, the text on the Ruthwell cross identified Christ in the desert, the ideal monk, also as 'Jesus Christ, Judge of Fairness'.[87] The figure with the Lamb in the panel directly above the image of Christ contains apocalyptic references,[88] and the placement of the inscription linking these two panels would seem to refer to both images. In the Durham Gospels, the inscription around the crucifixion refers to the ascended Christ with whom the restored penitent will reign after judgement day, implying that Christ on the cross is also the Judge.

But the depiction of Christ as Judge is unambiguously displayed in the visual renderings of the second coming and the last judgement.

---

[86] See above, 200.

[87] See above, 237–8.

[88] Meyvaert, 'An Apocalypse panel'. The apocalyptic meaning of the Lamb holds true whether the figure is identified as the Divine One or St John the Baptist, although the image of God would make it more direct.

The second coming

As mentioned earlier, the crucifixion miniature (p. 266) in the St Gall Codex, which probably dates to the second half of the eighth century, is paired with a second coming (p. 267). In the latter, Christ, accompanied by two trumpet-sounding angels, is depicted blessing with his right hand, while cradling a large book against his left shoulder and a long-stemmed cross against the right. The two trumpet-blowing angels who accompany the theophanic Christ leave no doubt that the *Secundus Adventus* is being heralded. The juxtaposition of the image of the suffering Christ with that of the glorified Christ establishes the identity of the apocalyptic Judge. Christ's eternal divinity and unity with the Divine One are clearly expressed. The twelve figures lined up in two rows in the bottom half of the page must be synonymous with the twelve apostles, for according to Matthew 19:28, the angels summon the dead to rise up while the Lord appears in heaven with the apostles who will serve as evaluators for the judgement:

And Jesus said to them [apostles]: Amen, I say to you, that you, who have followed me, in the regeneration, when the Son of Man shall sit on the seat of his majesty, you also shall sit on the twelve seats judging the twelve tribes of Israel.[89]

Each of the apostles carries a book, which, given their role as judges, must refer to the books in which the deeds of the individual are inscribed, as detailed in Apocalypse 20:12: 'and the dead were judged by those things which were written in the books, according to their works'. The inclusion of the apostles would seem to reflect the view that the New Law superseded the Old, for they judge Israel.

The presence of the apostles looking upwards at Christ and the angels must also be a reference to the ascension of Christ, which was seen to prefigure the second coming:

And while they were beholding him going up into heaven, behold two men stood by them in white garments. Who also said: 'Ye men of Galilee, why stand you looking up to heaven? This Jesus who is taken up from you into heaven, shall so come, as you have seen him going into heaven' (Acts 1:10–11).

The connection between ascension and second coming was delineated very clearly in the Turin Gospels.[90] In this late eighth-century Irish manuscript, the second coming (fo. 2r) faces a schematised ascension page[91] (fo. 1v) which is perhaps the only instance of this theme actually being depicted in an existing Insular manuscript. As mentioned earlier, in the early Irish Church especially, there is little textual emphasis on the risen Christ or his activities after his death.[92] The miniature is accompanied by the text of Acts 1:11. The angel in the medallion placed among the apostles would be specific to the

[89] For Augustine's treatment of this passage, see *City of God*, XX.5 (tr. Bettenson, 901–2).
[90] Turin: Biblioteca Nazionale, Codex O.IV.20; Henderson, *From Durrow to Kells*, illus. 121, p. 85.
[91] Henderson, *From Durrow to Kells*, illus. 120, p. 84.
[92] See above, 138–40, 164.

ascension. But the upper part of the illumination would seem to make a cross-reference to the second coming, just as the inscribed text does, for the ascending Jesus is shown accompanied by six angels, holding the book, and blessing with his right hand, as he would reappear at the end of time.

The eschatological Christ of the second coming on the facing page is shown standing, full-length, in a rectangular panel in the middle of the composition. He is surrounded by ninety-six figures, eighty-eight of which are depicted knee-length while the remaining eight are full-length. This array of the accompanying multitude is very regularly laid out in individual little boxes arranged in neat rows, just as the twelve apostles on the preceding page are – the visual and iconographical link is obvious. Christ does not carry the book nor does he bless; rather, his arms are folded across his chest and support the figure-length cross placed against his left shoulder. An angel blows its trumpet from the upper right-hand corner of the frame. Interestingly, small ringed cross-heads sprout from the centres of each of the four sides and three heads emerge at the corners not occupied by the angel. It has been suggested that this singular page may represent Matthew 24:30–1:

> . . . and they shall see the Son of Man coming in the clouds of heaven with much power and majesty. And he shall send his angels with a trumpet, and a great voice: and they shall gather together his elect from the four winds, from the farthest parts of the heavens to the utmost bounds of them.

This cosmological aspect of the last event might explain the inclusion of the ringed crosses, themselves bearing a cosmic connotation, as the four corners of the universe and the heads plus the angel as the four winds. The massed human figures would refer to the elect, who gather together for judgement.[93] The cross reminds the viewer of Christ's sacrifice to atone for the sins of humanity and to render salvation possible. But it was also a reminder of the just anger of God who comes to seek retribution, as attested in the 'red oppressive cross' borne by Christ which was included in the poems of Blathmac and in the apocryphal *Signs before Doomsday*.[94] The visual pairing of the ascension and second coming, combined with references to the crucifixion and last judgement once again equates the suffering human Christ on the cross with the triumphant divine Judge of Doomsday, a Judge awesome and vengeful.

The Book of Kells contains an iconic image which can be seen as combining the figure of Christ with that of the apocalyptic enthroned Lord (*Plate 15*). Fo. 32v[95] portrays a full-length figure either seated or standing before a cushioned throne, accompanied by four angels; a closed book is steadied by his right hand in the cradle of the veiled left hand. These are the attributes of the Enthroned One of the vision of St John (Apocalypse 5:1): 'And I saw in the right hand of him that sat on the throne, a book written within and without . . .' The panel in which he stands is circumscribed at the top by a semi-circular arch while the bottom half is formed of

---

[93] Veelenturf, *Dia Brátha*, 81–3.
[94] See above, Chapter V, 176–7.
[95] Henry, *The Book of Kells*, illus. 26; Henderson, illus. 224, p. 157.

a rectangular upright section. The four attending angels are crammed into the two upright rectangles beside the throne. Square panels are placed at the junctions of these forms and at the centre top, so as to create the impression of a cross and half-ring around the figure. In the space created by the lunette around the figure's upper body, a pendant cross is drawn on the central axis, directly over his head, identifying the figure as Christ.

In the semi-circular upper space, a large peacock-like bird stands on either side of Christ, gazing backwards at a cross-inscribed disc on its shoulder. The birds are standing on little knotted vines growing out of chalice-like urns. The components of this composition are taken from the early Christian artistic lexicon as evidenced on numerous sarcophagi and in mosaics. The peacock, whose flesh was believed to be incorruptible, symbolises Christ's immortality and divinity. In early Christian thought the peacock was identified with the phoenix, the mythical bird which rose anew from the ashes of its voluntary funeral pyre as allegorised in the fourth-century poem, *Carmen de ave phoenice*, attributed to Lactantius, a Roman convert to Christianity. By the end of the eighth century, the Latin poem had been reworked into Old English and its Christian symbolism had been augmented by knowledge of *Hexaemeron* V of St Ambrose and the *Commentary on Job* attributed to Bede.[96] In the final section of the poem (lines 546–69), the phoenix in its voluntary death and glorious resurrection is treated as the metaphor of the resurrection not only of Christ, but of all faithful followers, both in soul and body. Thus the peacock, in its relationship with the phoenix, also symbolises Christ's resurrection, and thus the resurrection of the dead at the second coming. The vines, as noted earlier, represent Christ as the true vine and bear a eucharistic significance as the blood of Christ, shed for mankind, flowing from the chalice. The cross-like disposition of the framing elements around Jesus remind the viewer of the cross upon which Christ died, and by extension the blood and water which poured from his pierced side, symbolic of the elements of the eucharist.

This iconic image of the enthroned Christ attended by angels is placed immediately after Matthew's genealogy of Christ and emphasises his divine nature, perhaps in response to the listing of his human lineage. This is the enthroned Lord, Christ in glory, the eucharistic sacrifice, who holds the book in which the names of the elect are written. These elect will rise again on the last day to take their place with him in paradise. The composition is organised as if Christ/the Divine One were placed in the apse of a church, framed by the great chancel arch, an image of the Heavenly Jerusalem.[97] This image faces the great eight-disc cross carpet page, which itself covers the magnificent *Chi Rho* page, both laden with Christological meaning.[98] Taken in combination, this ensemble presents three successive images of Christ, all references to the central role he played in the drama of redemption.

---

[96] 'The Phoenix' in *The Exeter Book* (ed. Krapp & Dobbie, 94–113); *Anglo-Saxon Poetry* (tr. Bradley, 284–301).

[97] Farr, *The Book of Kells*, 145–7.

[98] See above, 215–16, 228–31.

The second coming of Christ is also shown in some instances in a more abbreviated form where the central figure of Christ is surrounded by the symbols of the four evangelists, as seen on St Cuthbert's coffin.[99] This *maiestas Christi* is a partial visualisation of the vision of the Enthroned One surrounded by the four beasts described in Apocalypse 4:6–8 – the subject makes an allusion to the last judgement without actually depicting it. Appearing seldom in Insular sculpture, this composition can be seen on the west side of the crossing of the south cross at Kells, also known as the cross of SS Patrick and Columba.[100] It is located in the place of honour directly above the depiction of the crucifixion on the upper part of the shaft, relating the sacrifice of Christ to the redemption of mankind.

The last judgement

The second coming, as the harbinger of the last judgement, is not usually shown with overt adjudication taking place. The final judgement which will encompass all of humanity is the subject most often displayed on the east face of the scriptural crosses in Ireland. As with the *Secundus Adventus*, it faces the rising sun, the direction from which Christ was expected to reappear. The actual depiction of the weighing of souls and the separation of the saved and the damned first appears in monumental sculpture fairly late in Insular development, coming with the ninth- and tenth-century monuments. The fear and expectation of the last judgement had played a large role in the monastic writings and exegesis of the early Celtic Church, but it was one of the last themes to receive visual representation.

The great last judgement which graces Muiredach's cross at Monasterboice can serve to represent the components of the Insular version of this subject.[101] On the east side of the cross, filling the whole cross head, is the most complex depiction of the last judgement to be seen prior to the erection of the great romanesque tympana of the twelfth century. In the centre is a standing, frontally presented Christ, regally clad in a long robe: this is the formal vision of Christ in glory, Christ the eternal priest, Christ the Judge of righteousness of the second coming at the end of days. He holds a slender cross against his left shoulder and a tau-shaped rod or sceptre over the right, crossed in such a fashion that they form a v-shape around his head. The cross, as we have seen, is the symbol of both Christ's sacrifice and the triumph of his resurrection and thus the symbol of mankind's salvation. The sceptre with its voluted upper terminal, perhaps an evolution from the Celtic pelta, is a natural symbol for rulership and kingship. In manuscripts, this sceptre often terminates in a flowering pelta, a detail which would perhaps have been very difficult to duplicate in stone. The flowering rod is emblematic of Christ's eternal priesthood and testimony of the pact reached between God and Aaron. The flowering branch refers to the story of how God commanded that each of the twelve patriarchal families of Israel should

---

[99] See above, 220–4, for a discussion of the four evangelist symbols/cross pages.

[100] Roe, *The High Crosses of Kells*, 22; Harbison, *The High Crosses*, I.110–11, II. fig. 355, III. fig. 943.

[101] Harbison, *The High Crosses*, II. fig. 473.

place an inscribed branch before the ark in the holy tent. Only Aaron's branch sprouted and flowered, proof that God had chosen Aaron and his descendants (the Levites) to be the priests who could bring offerings before him (Numbers 17; 18:6–7). The stress upon the higher and eternal priesthood of Christ underlies this image on Muiredach's cross, just as it dominates much of the New Testament Letter to the Hebrews. In this Letter, Christ himself replaces the old priesthood of Aaron (Hebrews 4:14–16; 5:10). The ineffectual sacrifices of Levitical worship are replaced by the one uniquely efficacious sacrifice of Christ himself (Hebrews 8:1–9; 9:1–28).

It has been noted earlier that the priesthood of Christ was one of the main features of the iconography of the Athlone plaque and related artistic monuments. But the inclusion on Muiredach's cross of both elements, the flowering rod and the cross, would perhaps indicate that, in distinction to the view expressed in the Letter to the Hebrews, Christ not only unites the Old and the New Laws, but he specifically directed his followers to follow the complete Law in order to achieve perfection and salvation.[102] The image of Christ holding the two stems as if they were sceptres also visualises the several references in the Old Testament to the sceptre-bearing, divine judge who punishes those who transgress Sacred Law (Numbers 17–18; Psalm 109; Isaiah 11:1–4). The Letter to the Hebrews describes the Son of God as bearing the royal sceptre of justice (Hebrews 1:8): 'But to the Son: Thy throne, O God, is for ever and ever: a sceptre of justice is the sceptre of thy kingdom.' Taken together, these texts support a Christ who is the sceptre-bearing divine judge who punishes those who do not follow the guidelines for achieving perfection, directives given in both the Old Testament and the New. A message such as this would find fertile ground among the Irish whose (Old Testament) scripturalism maintained the link between the Christian priesthood and the Levites. But the cross also carries the connotation of the wrathful Christ who is seeking retribution for the suffering inflicted upon his mortal self and his faithful followers by unbelievers through the ages, before, during and after his earthly incarnation. The poem of Blathmac clearly indicates that this vengeful Christ of the second coming is synonymous with the judge of the last reckoning.[103] The cross-bearing Christ is found in most last judgement scenes on the Irish crosses, including the cross of the Scriptures at Clonmacnois, at Durrow, on the cross of SS Patrick and Columba at Kells, and Muiredach's cross at Monasterboice.

The visual image of Christ bearing the flowering rod and the cross seems to have been established in the Insular context by the end of the eighth century as witnessed by its appearance in the Lichfield Gospels. In this codex (p. 218),[104] there is an image of St Luke bearing both what is obviously a flowering sceptre-rod and the cross. The rod has been explained as referring

---

[102] See especially Matt. 19:16–23.
[103] See Blathmac, *Poem to Mary and her Son*, stanzas 142, 256–7 above 176–7 nn. 154, 156 and below, 268 n. 113. More generally, stanzas 244–59 enumerate the classes of the faithful who will be avenged for their sufferings.
[104] Henderson, *From Durrow to Kells*, illus. 180, p. 123.

to the beginning of his gospel which is concerned with Zacharias, the priest of the Old Dispensation, while the cross refers to the apostles and Christianity which replaces Judaism.[105] We suggest that, in a book created in an Irish environment, the emphasis is on the unity of the two Laws rather than on the subordination of the Old to the New.

To the left of the Christ on Muiredach's cross is the angel blowing the trumpet to summon the dead from their graves (I Thessalonians 4:16; I Corinthians 15:51–54), and at his right leg is a small angel reading from the open book in which are inscribed the deeds of men (Apocalypse 20:12). On Christ's right, the projecting arm of the cross is filled with an orderly gathering of sixteen figures, led by another figure reading a book, a trumpeter and by David playing his harp. They face towards their judge and redeemer. On the left arm, a group of the damned is being shoved away from Christ by three devils, the largest of which brandishes a pitchfork and walks on bird's legs. He too appears to be carrying a book. The motif in the upper cross arm above Christ appears to contain three angels reading from another book. The inclusion of books in the last judgement, much less five of them, is exceedingly rare among the Irish crosses. At Monasterboice, they must refer to books of deeds or books of life, perhaps even to the 'book of the devil' in which, according to Irish tradition, are inscribed the sins of the individual.[106] The reference to this book is included in an Irish devotional poem:

> And the devil's book,
> when my life's story has been written,
> may its letters recede
> until my tears drown them.[107]

The message of the judgement is completed by the small scene directly below Christ's feet. At first reading, it appears to be a representation of the weighing of the souls, the *psychostasis*.[108] A scales is suspended from the base of heaven, with a soul seated in one of the bowls. A supine demon is beneath, trying to pull down the other bowl with a hooked instrument. A standing figure has come to the rescue of the soul and has pierced the devil's mouth with a scroll-headed lance (*Plate 16*). In the standard iconography of the *psychostasis*, this figure would be the archangel Michael, God's champion, the defender of the faithful. But another reference may be intended here. The

---

[105] *Ibid.*, 122–3.

[106] Veelenturf, *Dia Brátha*, 112–13; also, Henry, *Irish Art during the Viking Invasions*, 172–3.

[107] Ed. and tr. Ó Cuív, 'Some early devotional verse', 4–6:
> Oc*us* leab*a*r diap*ail*
> ar sgr*i*obb*a*dh mo sg*e*la,
> a lit*ri* ro tr*a*igit
> co mbaidit mo d*éra*

[108] We are attuned to this identification by our familiarity with the carved romanesque tympana of the twelfth century which combine a last judgement and a *psychostasis*, as at Autun cathedral, where the weighing of the souls and the antics of the devil are remarkably similar.

figure defeating the devil is definitely wingless, and the instrument of destruction in his hand bears a direct resemblance to the staff in Christ's hand in the scene above. As previously mentioned, the theme of Christ's descent into the underworld and the harrowing of hell was prominent in Insular literature by this time.[109] We suggest that here, on Muiredach's cross, the viewer was presented with a scene combining the actual weighing of a soul (the *psychostasis*) with the vanquishing of Satan by Christ and the rescuing of the pre-Christian just from hell. The *Descensus*, in which David figures prominently, would also help to explain why he is so prominently displayed, with his harp, leading the saved before Christ the Judge in the scene on the cross-head immediately above. The Latin version relates how David sings his own psalm of praise (97:1–2) as the blessed are led out of the infernal regions:

And the Lord, extending his hand, made the sign of the cross over Adam and over all his saints, and taking the right (hand) of Adam, ascended out of hell and all the saints followed the Lord. Then holy David cried out loudly, saying: 'Sing to the Lord a new song because he has done wonderous things. His right hand has wrought salvation for him and his arm is holy. The Lord has made known his salvation; he has revealed his justice in the sight of the gentiles.'[110]

The incident is elaborated in the later Irish version of the *Descensus* section of the *Gospel of Nicodemus* in which David is given even more prominence, reflecting the continuing Irish interest in his role. The harrowing of hell was a most unusual theme for pictorial usage, and seems to have been represented rarely and only indirectly, as will be discussed shortly.

Among the many scripture crosses bearing a last judgement, none is as complete in its depiction and iconography as Muiredach's cross. They all include at least the figure of Christ as judge and a number of saved and damned. Some are similar to a Christ of the second coming, as on the cross at Durrow.[111] The insistence on the subject attests to the strength of the eschatological concerns of the time. There could be many reasons for this, and one must not discount the influence of millennialism, the fear of the end of the world. It is arguable that the Viking raids and the resulting destruction of so many of the great and important monasteries, including Lindisfarne and Iona, would have turned people's minds to the destruction prophesied as a sign of the coming of the end of the world. Scenes of the last judgement would be a constant reminder to the monastic community of the fate which lay ahead of them all and a spur to a greater and more vigilant observance of their devotional and spiritual exercises.

---

[109] See above, 157–9.
[110] *Gospel of Nicodemus*, XXIV.2 (our translation). See Latin text below, 277.
[111] Harbison, *The High Crosses*, II. figs. 247, 248.

The militant Christ and the harrowing of hell

A most unusual representation of Christ, as *Christus militans*, was given a place of honour on the west cross at Monasterboice.[112] Replacing the more usual last judgement or second coming, this depiction of Christ as the soldier and hero occupies the panel in the centre of the east side of the cross-head. A very large figure of Christ is shown, armed with a shield and sword in his left hand and a spear in his right. He wears a figure-conforming, ankle-length robe as can be discerned from the hemline above the feet. Standing on a triple row of brick-like clouds, he is accompanied by ten men armed with swords and shields, represented on a smaller scale. What might be taken to represent a small angel hovers near his head on his left side. This is Christ, mighty in battle, the Lord of Hosts and King of Glory of Psalm 23, considered prophetic of the second coming of the Son of Man in power and great glory. A harbinger of the last judgement, it is iconographically allied to it, for it refers to the victorious army led by the glorious and heroic 'King of kings and Lord of lords' (Christ) who defeats the armies of the devil in the first battle at the end of time (Apocalypse 19:11–21). In Ireland Blathmac had referred to the final 'war that will be the end of all war' in which Christ will destroy the devil and avenge all the suffering of the saints and martyrs:

For what these men have suffered in the torturing of their bodies they shall have keenest vengeance; they are not clients of (a lord of) bad oaths.

For splendid Christ has risen; he is eternally safe in the eternal kingdom; the leader with great hosts, the triumphant one, victorious in battle will avenge them.[113]

A similar representation of the militant, eschatological Christ with his army appears on what was originally the east side of the shaft of the market cross at Kells (Co. Meath).[114] There is a possible third representation of the *Christus militans* on the much weathered west face of the shaft of the village cross at Tynan (Co. Armagh).[115]

The victory of Christ over Satan at the end of days could be seen as the second defeat of the devil by Jesus. If taken in conjunction with the apocryphal *Gospel of Nicodemus* which was popular in Irish monastic circles, the victorious militant Lord would also be an indirect reference to the harrowing of hell and that initial defeat of Satan by Christ immediately after his mortal death. That the harrowing of hell was a topic familiar to the Irish has been shown[116] and that it carried eschatological

---

[112] *Ibid.*, II. figs. 488, 490.

[113] Blathmac, *Poem to Mary and her Son*, stanzas 256–7 (tr. Carney, 87). Irish text below, 277.

[114] Harbison, *The High Crosses*, II. fig. 336.

[115] *Ibid.*, II. fig. 637. Harbison identifies the similar panels at Monasterboice, Kells and Tynan as David acclaimed King of Israel. See Veelenturf, *Dia Brátha*, 85–8, for a discussion of the varying identifications given to these depictions.

[116] See above, 157–8.

overtones is demonstrated by the fact that it had been combined with the last judgement and *psychostasis* on Muiredach's cross at Monasterboice. The actual first victory of Christ over Satan is only very rarely directly depicted in Irish art – rather it seems to have been approached through a series of allusions. On the market cross at Kells, the panel directly below the representation of Christ and his army portrays Christ's tomb. The two guards seem asleep, but Jesus's shrouded body is clearly still inside the sepulchre, signalling, we contend, that the scene in the panel above refers, not only to the apocalyptic battle, but also to the time between the interment of Christ's body and his resurrection, and thus to his harrowing of hell.[117]

The depiction of Christ in his tomb guarded by soldiers is also found at the bottom of the west face of the shaft of the cross of the Scriptures at Clonmacnois.[118] This time there is no image of Christ and his heavenly army, but in an adjacent position, at the bottom of the north side of the shaft, an image of what might be taken as Christ vanquishing the devil can be discerned.[119] This panel shows a figure in a long robe seated on a small throne, holding what may be a shield on his left arm, grasping a lance in his right hand. This lance, upon which a bird is perched, is thrust into the face of a supine figure at his feet. The vanquished one has his legs straight up in the air in an attitude of defeat, but also in order to conform to the side of the panel. When taken together, these two adjacent panels would imply Christ's descent into hell and his concomitant defeat of Satan.

On the west cross at Monasterboice, the entombed Christ appears at the bottom of the west face of the shaft.[120] The east face of the shaft beneath the *Christus militans* is filled with scenes taken from the Old Testament featuring David, Isaac, Moses, Samuel, Samson, Elijah and the three youths in the fiery furnace.[121] This would recall the necessity of Christ's descent into hell to rescue these heroes and adherents to God's law (except for Elijah and Enoch who were already in heaven), and his victory over the forces of darkness. This is consistent with the belief that those who lived under the law of nature or the law of Moses could be saved, for they would be judged by their adherence to the standards of their era, as formulated in Paul's Letter to the Romans. The figure of Christ in his sepulchre could be taken as signifying the time-frame for the harrowing of hell. Likewise, Christ in his tomb on the bottom of the west face of the shaft of the cross at Durrow[122] is accompanied by panels featuring Old Testament figures, for example, Adam and Eve, Abraham and Isaac, distributed on the sides of the shaft. Images of David as

---

[117] The scene of the entombed body of Christ guarded by the two soldiers, which is found on the crosses at Kells, Monasterboice, Durrow and Clonmacnois, is usually interpreted as a Resurrection. See Stalley, 'European art', 149–53.

[118] Harbison, *The High Crosses*, II. fig. 139.

[119] *Ibid.*, II. fig. 143; Harbison, I.52, identifies this figure as St Anthony defeating the devil in human form.

[120] *Ibid.*, II. fig. 495.

[121] *Ibid.*, II. fig. 488.

[122] *Ibid.*, II. fig. 254.

musician and David killing the lion lie on either side of the image of the glorified Christ of the second coming bearing the cross and the flowering sceptre on the east cross head.[123] Had it not been for the descent of Christ into hell, his vanquishing of Satan and his rescue of the Old Testament figures, David would not have found his place beside the Lord of the second coming. The consistent placing of the entombed Christ at the bottom of the cross shaft may highlight its connection with the harrowing of hell since, according to legend, the cross of the crucifixion had been erected over the burial site of Adam.[124]

Exceedingly rare in Insular art, the armed Christ had appeared in the mosaics of the sixth-century archiepiscopal chapel in Ravenna wearing a cuirass and mailed kilt, trampling the serpent and dragon underfoot. In the drawings in the ninth-century Utrecht Psalter, Christ is armed and accompanied by armed retainers. In Psalm 23, the image of the triumphant Christ at the head of his army is combined with that of the King of kings. The Irish sagas, filled with descriptions of fighting and warfare, along with the narratives of the military victories of the Hebrews furnished in the Old Testament, would be present in an immediate way in the minds of people living in Ireland and northern Britain. It is not surprising to find Christ assuming this military aspect at a time when the monasteries were under physical threat from an outside enemy.

The placement of the *Christus militans* in the middle of the ringed cross-head at Monasterboice, as a companion to the crucifixion on the other side, indicates his eschatological nature. The inclusion of two encounters between St Anthony and the devil, one in the company of St Paul, on the outer extensions of the same cross arms would draw the lessons to the attention of the monastic audience. The monk, holy woman and *manaig*, were all to become *milites Christi* in their striving to overcome their weaknesses and worldliness. *Christus militans* was the model for Christians, who, under the double threat of the devil and the human enemy, must arm themselves for battle.

Christ the Wonder-Worker

The primarily eschatological meaning of these central images of Christ on the Irish scripture crosses is complemented by the plethora of secondary scenes which cover the main faces of the monuments and occasionally spill over onto the narrow sides. There is one existing instance of this occurring in the Insular world before the later ninth century: the great cross at Ruthwell. The Ruthwell cross contains what may very likely be the earliest demonstrated use of narrative scenes in Insular art. In addition to the panels already discussed, the remaining panels contain scenes taken from the life of Christ: annunciation, return from Egypt, crucifixion, Christ healing a blind

---

[123] *Ibid.*, II. fig. 247.
[124] Blathmac, *Poem to Mary and her Son*, stanza 57 (ed. and tr. Carney, 20–1).

man. The iconography of baptism and the eucharist dominate.[125] The water and blood which flowed from the side of the crucified Christ were identified with baptism and the eucharist; one may further detect in these the concept that the Church was born from the side of Christ at the moment when Longinus's spear opened the wound. The healing by Jesus of the man blind from birth reflects the efficacy of baptism and the resulting spiritual awareness, but it also shows that Christ possessed miraculous powers which he did not hesitate to exhibit once he had embarked on his public life. The delivery by the raven of the sustaining bread to SS Anthony and Paul also reflects the efficacious intervention of God into the affairs of man. Scenes such as these indicate the acceptance of miracles and God's grace. However, one should distinguish between the miracles based on the receiver's faith (namely most of the gospel miracles) and miracles based on merit (the monastic miracles). Ruthwell can be seen as presenting a balance between the two types.

The inclusion of narrative scenes at Ruthwell may very well have been an isolated phenomenon. There is no evidence that the practice caught on and was immediately continued elsewhere in Britain and Ireland. The unstinted use of narrative scenes enters into Irish art with the ninth- and tenth-century high crosses, where the list of chosen subjects is long, primarily taken from the scriptures, both canonical and apocryphal.[126] The choice of subject matter reflects the early Insular preference for the Old Testament which was studied both for the understanding it could cast on the New Testament and for moral *exempla*. The story of the fall of man, which necessitated the incarnation of Christ was visualised through the inclusion of the figures of Adam and Eve. The first parents were usually shown naked, standing on either side of the tree of knowledge of good and evil. A very popular topic for illustration, it appears on a large number of high crosses, sometimes in conjunction with the murder of Abel by his brother Cain. The reference to, and acceptance of, original sin is clear and reflects the general moving away from the earlier Pelagian denial of the transmission of guilt. By 750, Blathmac had been able to indicate the belief in original sin in one of his poems:

A blessing on Christ, son of the living God, who has suffered cross and martyrdom; who had atoned on the cross, on the rood, for the transgression of Adam and Eve.[127]

That Adam was later forgiven and brought to salvation by the sacrifice of Christ is seen in another of Blathmac's verses:

---

[125] Ó Carragáin, 'The Ruthwell Crucifixion poem'.
[126] For the distribution of the subjects, see Harbison, *The High Crosses*, I.186–309.
[127] Blathmac, *Poem to Mary and her Son*, stanza 136 (ed. and tr. Carney, 46–7):
      Bendacht for Críst, mac Dé bí,
      ro-chés croich ocus martrai,
      ro-hícc fri croich is fri cross
      Ádaim Éua immarmus.

The flowing blood from the body of the dear Lord baptised the head of Adam, for the shaft of the cross of Christ had aimed at his mouth.[128]

But the most commonly depicted scenes belong to the type known as the 'Help of God' series which includes incidents of deliverance from danger through divine intervention. Mainly from the Old Testament, the scenes most often depicted were Noah's ark, events from the life of David and David as musician, Daniel in the lions' den, the sacrifice of Isaac, and the three youths in the fiery furnace. David appears most often, presumably because he was seen as an ancestor of and prefiguration for Christ. The majority of the narratives show the active and often miraculous intervention of God in a believing person's fate. This is counter to the earlier-held Pelagian idea that a person can achieve salvation only through adherence to the Law and through his own works of penitence and mortification. By the later ninth century these ideas which seem to have been so ingrained in the early common Celtic Church appear to have evolved into a different theology, one in which God's grace dominates. But another interpretation can be argued: the belief that in the harrowing of hell, Christ had freed the just who had preceded him from the bonds of hell and Satan. The various *Descensus ad inferos* describe in detail the group of Old Testament figures who await Christ and laud his arrival. The inclusion of these 'heroes' in the imagery of the high crosses indicates the importance of the universality of the redemption and the belief that the Old Law was a legitimate stage in God's unfolding plan for mankind.

The New Testament was also mined for material to represent on the crosses. The narratives of Jesus's birth, particularly the adoration of the magi and his 'eucharistic' miracles, for example, the wedding at Cana and the multiplication of the loaves and fishes, appear with some regularity while his 'healing' miracles seem to receive little attention. The recounting of Christ's passion and death includes a variety of incidents taken from the biblical account, including the entry into Jerusalem, the betrayal and the mocking. The crucifixion appears almost universally on the scripture crosses.

There seems to be some confusion or ambivalence about representing the resurrection and ascension of Christ. With a few exceptions, neither is treated as an autonomous narrative in the life of the risen Christ. Rather, they are alluded to under the guise of exegetically related topics – as we have seen in the St Gall Gospels where the ascension is implied in the second coming and on the cross of Moone where the twelve apostles witness the crucifixion.[129] The text of the beginning of the resurrection narrative at Luke 24:1 in the Book of Kells, fo. 285r[130] receives special treatment in the form of

[128] Blathmac, *Poem to Mary and her Son*, stanza 57 (ed. and tr. Carney, 20–1):
    Toesca toebraith coimdeth dil
    ro-bathais mullach nÁdaim,
    dég ad-rumedair int eú
    cruchae Críst ina béulu.
[129] See above, 258.
[130] Henry, *The Book of Kells*, p. 89.

a full-page decoration in which the words 'but on the first day of the week'[131] are combined with four angels lounging on the letter forms. Two angels hold books, one brandishes a sceptre, the other a flowering rod, direct references to Christ as seen elsewhere in the manuscript. Christ himself is not depicted.

In the scenes of the entombed Christ at Kells and Monasterboice, a cross rises from the grave between the sleeping soldiers, an image which may be related somehow to the *Apocryphal Gospel of Peter*, in which it is written that at the moment of the resurrection, 'They saw three men come out of the sepulchre, and two of them sustaining the other, and a cross following after them.'[132] This text, possibly originating in Syria before A.D. 200, exists in an eighth- or ninth-century manuscript found in Upper Egypt.[133] It is not known whether or not there was familiarity with the *Gospel of Peter* in Ireland in the ninth and tenth centuries,[134] but the resemblance between the visual image and the text would suggest some commonality. There is an unusual reference to the resurrection to be seen on the entombment panels on the cross at Durrow and the cross of the Scriptures at Clonmacnois where a bird, perched on the edge of the tomb slab, leans over to place its beak into Jesus's mouth, as if to breathe life back into the corpse. The bird may also have been present in the panels at Kells and Monasterboice – the area around the head of Christ has been chipped away in both cases. In early Irish stories it is common that the souls of the dead adopt the shape of birds, as found in *Immram Curaig Maíle Dúin*, *Immram Curaig Ua Corra* and the *Navigatio Brendani*, among others.[135] We suggest that the bird on the tomb might represent the soul of Christ (his divine aspect) returning to his mortal body after the harrowing of hell, as described by Blathmac: 'He then returned to his body when he cast off the great attack, and he arose (bright tidings!) on Easter day after three days.'[136] This may also help to explain the significance of the bird perched on the lance held by the Christ vanquishing the devil on the side of the scripture cross at Clonmacnois – it would represent Christ's divine aspect which descended into Hell and/or refer to the souls which Christ rescued.

In all four representations discussed here, the resurrection narrative is sharpened by the fact that the pairs of soldiers are slumped in sleep with their lances held over their shoulders. But they are not alone – there are always additional figures to be seen beside or above them, which are usually taken to refer to the women approaching the tomb. But the discrepancy with the canonical version of the revelation of the resurrection is obvious – this tomb is not empty! The body of the dead Christ remains. Perhaps these figures represent the heavenly messengers sent to fetch Christ from the tomb as related in the *Gospel of Peter*. If this is the case, then what we have here is

---

[131] 'una autem sabbati ualde delu(culo)'.

[132] *Gospel of Peter*, ix–x. (tr. [M.R.] James, 92–3). This was suggested by Roe, *The High Crosses of Kells*, 28.

[133] Maurer, 'The Gospel of Peter'.

[134] McNamara, *The Apocrypha*, 103.

[135] Strijbosch, *The Seafaring Saint*, 214–15.

[136] Blathmac, *Poem to Mary and her Son*, stanza 177. See above, 182, for the Irish text.

a highly idiosyncratic combination of locally known tradition as transmitted by Blathmac and the apocrypha. There is one other depiction which may correspond to the apocryphal account of the resurrection. On the cross of Muiredach at Monasterboice, the panel on the south arm of the west face seems to depict the two sleeping soldiers, the tomb and cross, with three figures above, presumably representing the risen Christ with his two heavenly companions. In this case, the shrouded body is absent.[137] The Irish literary tradition surrounding the resurrection is confused and contradictory. In the *Precamur patrem* there is no reference to the resurrection, only to the entombment, the harrowing of hell and the escorting of the blessed into heaven,[138] while Blathmac waxes eloquent about the resurrection.

In art there seems to be a certain reluctance to portray the incidents of Christ's earthly life after his resurrection. The ascension does not appear and the favoured subjects chosen leap from his crucifixion straight to the second coming. Perhaps this is because Christ was to be imitated by the monk, but could only be imitated in his human nature. Taken together, the narrative scenes stress the necessity of redemption through the incarnation and sacrifice of Christ on the cross as promised through the ages and the achievement of salvation through the agency of God's help. The *Traditio legis* appears in the group of crosses at Monasterboice, Clonmacnois and Durrow.[139] Christ presents St Peter with the keys to the kingdom of heaven and St Paul with the book of the Law, thereby establishing the Church and the scriptures as the agencies through which man must approach God. The idea that the scriptures (Law) are not the sole authority accommodates *Romani* ideals.[140]

Although the monastic life is held up as the path to salvation, and there were several monastic saints' lives in circulation, hagiography is severely limited in visual art. Saintly models continue to be limited to the representation of events from the lives of the two early hermit saints, Paul of Thebes and Anthony of Egypt. The incident of the two saints breaking bread together is the universally depicted scene, but it has been enhanced by the addition of their various struggles with the devil. As the perceived founders of ascetic monasticism, their joint life is a suitable and immediately identifiable subject for depiction on crosses which were erected in a monastic context. There are no verifiable representations of the Irish saints whose hagiography had already been established in Ireland: Brigit, Patrick and Columba.

With the sculpted high crosses of the ninth and tenth centuries, we see the fairly sudden transformation of Irish art from an essentially ornamental and abstract form into a figurative art obviously meant to be easily 'read'. Unlike earlier relief sculpture, the figures on the scripture crosses have been carved

---

[137] For an overview of the scenes connected to the entombment and resurrection, see Harbison, *The High Crosses*, I.286–90.

[138] See above, 284–8.

[139] Harbison, *The High Crosses*, I.294–5.

[140] See above, 63–4, 115–17.

in terms of a fully-plastic prototype – the human figures are rounded and the anatomy more deliberately observed than before and figures turn towards each other when the context requires. The similarity with contemporary relief sculpture on the continent leads to the conclusion that Carolingian art has made inroads into the Irish domain and has furnished the models for this aesthetic about-face.[141] The extensive communications network between the continental monasteries founded by Irish and Anglo-Saxon missionaries and the Insular establishments would have encouraged the dissemination of both new ideas and models. But even if continental models, Carolingian or early Christian, served as stylistic exemplars for the new narrative art, local tradition would have furnished the sources for the meaning and interpretation.

In the ninth century, the image of Christ, so central to the Christian life, moved from symbol to representation and was expanded to fuller form and meaning. Quite clearly the perceived audience had grown larger to include not only the dedicated religious with his or her devotion, but the broader group of faithful laity gathered around the monastic centres. We can only speculate as to the underlying causes for this new reaching out to the laity as well as the clergy and monks. The influence of the *Céli Dé* is one possible factor. With their combination of a desire to reform monasticism to its original penitential ideals and to reach out to the laity at the same time, to combine the contemplative and the active life, this group may have set the cultural stage for the expansion of the role that public art, such as the sculpted crosses, could play. But it would be wrong to see these crosses primarily as 'bibles for the illiterate in stone'.[142] Indeed their images could be read at a very simple narrative level by the unsophisticated layman and their main importance was their ability to stimulate devotion, an idea contrary to the warnings of Cassian voiced centuries before.[143] But they also carried images laden with a deeper complexity. Their symbolic content and the multivalent levels of interpretation would grow with the observer's knowledge of exegesis, theology and Christology.

The other factor which may have prompted the rapid deployment of the scripture crosses, the popularity of the 'help of God' series and the universal attention given to the eschatological Christ may have been the fear of the impending end of the world. This must have been a very real fear at the time of the Viking raids which wreaked such havoc on the monasteries in both England and Ireland. The devastating attacks in the early ninth century on such venerable sites as Lindisfarne, Iona, Bangor and Armagh, along with the traditions of settled life, and then the renewal of the devastation in 922 must have signalled the advent of the external enemy who could not be turned back. The enduring quality of stone, not easily destroyed or carried off, may have been seen as a means of making permanent the images which expressed the beliefs at the very core of contemporary monastic life and devotion. These monuments which dot the Irish countryside, with their

---

[141] Harbison, 'Earlier Carolingian narrative'.
[142] Roe, *Monasterboice*, 25.
[143] See above, 191.

insistent eschatological messages, focussed people's attention on the fate of their eternal souls. Always, it is the monastic life and its observances which are offered as the only way by which a true Christian can achieve salvation. And this can only be accomplished by the imitation of Christ and obedience to the Law.

Additional Texts

6. Bede, *Historia Abbatum*, VI (ed. Plummer, *Bedae Opera Historica*, I.369–70): '*picturas* imaginum sanctarum quas ad ornandam aecclesiam beati Petri apostoli, quam construxerat detulit; imaginem uidelicet beatae Dei genetricis semperque uirginis Mariae, simul et duodecim apostolorum, quibus mediam eiusdem aecclesiae testudinem, ducto a pariete ad parietem tabulato praecingeret; imagines euangelicae historiae quibus australem aecclesiae parietem decoraret; imagines uisionum apocalipsis beati Iohannis, quibus septentrionalem aeque parietem ornaret, quatinus intrantes aecclesiam omnes etiam litterarum ignari, quaquauersum intenderent, uel semper amabilem Christi sanctorumque eius, quamuis in imagine, comtemplarentur aspectum; uel dominicae incarnationis gratiam uigilantiore mente recolerent; uel extremi discrimen examinis, quasi coram oculis habentes, districtius se ipsi examinare meminissent.'

37. Book of Kells, fo. 113v (Matthew 26:26–9): 'Cenantibus autem eis accipit Iesus panem et benedixit ac fregit deditque discipulis suis dicens accipite edite ex hoc omnes hoc est enim corpus meum quod confringitur pro saeculi uita. Et accipens calicem gratias aegit et dedit illis dicens bibite ex hoc omnes hic est enim sanguis meus noui testamenti qui effundetur pro uobis et pro multis in remissionem peccatorum. Dico autem uobis quia non bibam amodo de hoc gemine uitis usque in diem illum quo illud bibam uobiscum nouum in regno patris mei.'

41. Stephanus, *Vita Wilfridi Episcopi*, XIII (ed. Colgrave, *The Life of Bishop Wilfrid*, 28): 'Igitur sanctus Wilfrithus episcopus cum clero suo, flexis poplitibus genuum et iterum elevatis manibus ad coelum, Domini auxilium perpetravit. Sicut enim Moyses, Hur et Aaron sustentantibus manus eius, Iesu Nave cum populo Dei adversum Amalech pugnante, frequenter Domini protectionem implorans triumphavit, ita et hic isti pauci christiani feroces et indomitos paganos tribus vicibus in fugam versos strage non modica obruerunt, quinque tantum viris, quod mirum dictu est, ex sua parte occisis . . .'

45. Mael Ruain, *The Rule of Tallaght*, LXXX (ed. Gwynn, *The Rule*, 46): 'Fa gnath aca fear ag leugad an tshoisgeil 7 riagla 7 fearta na náomh an feadh bhid na braithri ar a ccuid no ag caithiomh a bproinne, ionnus nach ar a bproinn bhias a n-aire, 7 do ní an fear sin bhios ag an leughthoracht a phroinn fein tráth nona roimhe sin; 7 fiafraighthior iarnabharach do gach

aon diobh creud do leughadh ann, da fheuchain an raibhe aire aige ar an leughthoracht a n-aimsir na proinne.'

59. Blathmac, *Poem to Mary and her Son* (ed. Carney, 20):
stanza 55:   Ó du-ruidmiset am-ne
        Ísu combu thorise
        do-luid Longinus iar sin
        diä guin cosind láigin.

stanza 58:   Dond fuil chétnai – ba cain n-am! –
        is trait ron-ícc in-ógdall,
        ossé díb dornaib co glé
        oc imbeirt inna láigne.

60. *Stair Nicoméid*, X.1 (ed. Dooley, 'The *Gospel*', 382): 'Is and sin da éirich ridire dona ridirib diarbo comainm Loinginus .i. dall 7 is amlaid do boi 7 aenchlaredain aigi gan shuil na cinn. 7 tuc da gai mor fa chomuir a slis Isu amail do sheoladh dho uair nir dhughraic neach da facaidh Isu a goin. 7 do reathastair fo chetoir da thuind asa slis .i. tond fola 7 tond usce 7 an fuil so sil ar fut an gadh do cumail Loinginus da edan hi 7 da fasadar da suil glana gormglasa na cinn 7 mar do-connairc dreach Isu do creid do (LCS do gach ni da nderna 7 da-cuala uadha) 7 do iar trocairi fair . . .'

68. Laidcenn, *Lorica* (ed. Herren, *The Hisperica Famina II*, 80, 82):
lines 31–2:   Mei gibrae   pernas omnes libera
        tuta pelta   protegente singula . . .
lines 51–2:   Deinde esto   lurica tutissima
        erga membra   erga mea uiscera . . .
lines 55–6:   Tege ergo   Deus forti lurica
        cum scapulis   humeros et brachia.

110. *Gospel of Nicodemus*, XXIV.2 (ed. Kim, 45): 'Et extendens Dominus manum suam fecit signum crucis super Adam et super omnes sanctos suos, et tenens dextram Adae ascendit ab inferis et omnes sancti secuti sunt Dominum. Tunc sanctus Dauid fortiter clamauit/ dicens: "Cantate Domino canticum nouum quia mirabilia fecit Dominus. Saluauit sibi dextera eius et brachium sanctum eius. Notum fecit Dominus salutare suum, ante conspectum gentium reuelauit iustitiam suam".'

113. Blathmac, *Poem to Mary and her Son*, stanzas 256–7 (ed. Carney, 86):
stanza 256:   Anro-chésasat ind fir
        diä riagad i corpaib,
        bethus dígal dígrais de;
        nídat céili drochluige.

stanza 257:   Ar as-réracht Ísu án,
        isin bithflaith is bithslán;
        dos-fí in soismid sluagach,
        in coscrach, in cathbuadach.

EPILOGUE

In 418, or immediately afterwards, some British-born advocates of Pelagian teaching – and possibly Pelagius himself – returned to their homeland in the wake of an imperial interdict. Within eleven years they contrived to establish a separate 'Pelagian Church' in Britain, which, in the eyes of their opponents, threatened to undermine British Christianity everywhere. This Church succeeded in building on 'pre-Pelagian' sympathies, and radicalising them in opposition to 'the heresy of Augustine'. In 429, Pope Celestine sent Germanus of Auxerre on a mission to Britain to suppress the movement. However, despite claimed successes, Germanus did not manage to eradicate it, as there was another 'outbreak' in the 440s. In 431, the same pope sent the deacon Palladius to Ireland as the first bishop to the island's Christian community, arguably with the intention of checking any possible occurrence of the heresy there. Later in the fifth century, probably beginning in the early 460s, the Briton Patrick conducted an unsanctioned mission to convert the pagan Irish. His writings show that he was engaged against Pelagian ideas, and it is possible that his superiors, whose accusations he was forced to answer, were of Pelagian sympathies. Towards the middle of the sixth century Gildas remarked on the presence of a group in Britain who displayed Pelagian tendencies, and late evidence tells us that the Pelagians were not finally suppressed in Britain until some time in the sixth century, but that this required two synods. Around 640, a pope-elect charged that Pelagianism had been revived in Ireland.

The Pelagian movement defined the common Celtic Church, which we have envisioned as a set of commonalities of theology and of some features of practice in the British and Irish Churches down to the second quarter of the seventh century. Pelagianism may have dominated this Church for only a short time, but its ideology persisted, in some form, beyond the dissolution of the common Celtic Church in the early part of the seventh century. Its adherents taught the natural goodness of man, that a sinless life was possible not only for the Jewish patriarchs but for gentiles as well, that sin was not transmitted through the blood-line, that grace was not necessary for salvation, that God predestined no one, that all men could be saved if they believed, that salvation was achieved through perfect obedience to the law, and that obedience to the law was fostered by asceticism. The Christ of the Pelagians did not save men and women by dying on the cross, but by his teaching and example he made salvation possible for those who willed it for themselves. The Pelagians opposed the notion of grace in all its forms (save only baptism) and held a minimalist idea of what the Church should be. All men and women were subject to God's law, God's law was revealed completely in the scriptures, and it could not be overturned or modified by any authority, including the Church.

We have seen how this severe doctrine underwent change in the earliest period of Celtic Christianity (down to *ca* 630). The most important changes are probably to be connected to the semi-Pelagian movement. These were the introduction of repeatable penance, supplanting the Pelagian notion that sin committed after baptism was all but impossible to forgive. Infant baptism, opposed by Pelagians, was also introduced. Organised monasticism – in contrast to private asceticism – received special encouragement and came to represent the fulness of Christian life. But the scriptures remained the *fons et origo* of all authority, and the idea of grace or help of God was given only a restricted place.

The long isolation of the common Celtic Church was broken by Irish contacts to the continent, especially to Rome, initially over the matter of the Easter-reckoning. In southern Ireland important events occurred in rapid succession between *ca* 628 and *ca* 633: the Irish Easter-reckoning was replaced with the Roman, the relics of the Roman martyrs were introduced, faith-healings reported, and unspecified writings were sent to Ireland from Rome. Within the next twenty to thirty years other major changes occurred. The Irish themselves took to composing miraculous saints' lives, apocryphal writings were granted acceptance, images found their way into churches, a sabbatised Sunday replaced the separate observance of the sabbath and the Lord's Day, and the idea of unity with the Roman Church took on central importance. Such radical developments undoubtedly generated powerful opposition from ecclesiastics of a Pelagian mind-set, and this opposition in turn may well have occasioned the accusation by Pope-elect John *ca* 640 that the Pelagian heresy had been revived in the northern areas of Ireland. We see the continuation of the struggle in the year 655, when an Irishman employing the name 'Augustine' wrote *On the Miracles of Holy Scripture*, offering a defence of miracles based on nature, almost certainly in opposition to Pelagian-based criticism of the miraculous, namely that it was an assault on the nature which God had created and called good.

Roman ecclesiastical influence on Ireland was rapid and wide-ranging, going far beyond issues of practice such as the Easter-reckoning, the clerical tonsure and the consecration of bishops. By the middle of the seventh century it had affected Armagh, and spread to other areas in the north, probably sooner than is generally recognised. An important water-shed is the Antiphonary of Bangor, dated 680 × 692, and presumably deriving from Bangor itself. Where one might expect a consistent collection of 'conservative' *Hibernensis* materials in a work emanating from a northern centre, this interesting anthology of hymns and collects combines poems that reflect the 'old' values of the common Celtic Church with liturgical pieces imported from the continent and poems displaying *Romani* patterns.

The use of the Latin language and the cult of the Roman martyrs was about all that receded with the *Romani* movement in Ireland which began in the second quarter of the seventh century and lasted approximately to the middle of the eighth century. The shift to the Irish vernacular – so pronounced in works written after the middle of the eighth century – did not entail an attempt to reverse the process of Romanisation. The writings of the *Céli Dé,* who appear to have been the dominant religious movement in

Ireland from the middle of the eighth to the middle of the ninth century, are composed largely in Irish and emphasise the cult of native Irish saints, but otherwise reflect continuity with the Romanisers of the seventh century in such crucial areas as pastoral care and the acceptance of miracles, relics and images. The Christology of the *Céli Dé* reveals a clear shift from the Christ who saves by teaching and example to the Christ who saves by shedding his blood. However, at the same time, the *Céli Dé* movement laid renewed emphasis on the ideals of an earlier period, calling upon all Christians to practice asceticism in their daily lives.

The development of Christological images runs in parallel with theological change. A 'purely Pelagian' Christ comprised the Christ of the desert and the cross (Christ the Perfect Monk) and the giver of the New Law. This Christ saves us by his teaching and example, not by the blood that ran from his wounds. When he comes to judge at the end of the world, he will judge fairly, since he has predestined no one. But beyond the teaching and example of Christ (and the special gift of baptism), God offers no other form of help, since God is no respecter of persons. Thus, the miracles of the Old Testament and even the miracles of Christ cannot be accepted literally, but must be understood as figures of God's law. The resurrection is not a miracle performed by Christ, but an example of what can be accomplished by faith.

The controversy over the law and miracles is closely related to the development of biblical exegesis in seventh-century Ireland. Scholars have tended to regard differing exegetical approaches as a reflection of the late antique division between Alexandrian (allegorical) and Antiochene (historical) exegesis. This has only limited applicability. Pelagian writers showed themselves to be literalist about the law, but they quite freely applied a figural approach to history, particularly to episodes that reflect miraculous intervention in human affairs. Some of their seventh-century Irish opponents followed the opposite procedure. The author of *On Festivities* interpreted the Old Law as a prefiguration of Christian spirituality; the author of *On the Miracles of Holy Scripture* argued against the figural interpretation of miracles and insisted on their factuality.

The earliest Irish hagiography generally reflects the resistance to the miraculous prevalent in both Pelagian and semi-Pelagian writings. Poems about native saints written towards the end of the sixth century and beginning of the seventh lay heavy stress on the virtues of their respective subjects and their good examples, but say next to nothing about miracles. We see evidence of this resistance even as late as *ca* 630 when the *Liber de virtutibus sancti Columbae* was composed. Change occurred after the mid-point of the seventh century, when the first fully-fledged prose lives of Irish saints appear – those of Brigit, Patrick and Columba. But the same writers who are willing to attach almost every type of thaumaturgical act to their subjects also give accounts of native pagans who lived their entire lives in a state of natural goodness, thus revealing new and old ideologies in the same work. Two Irish poems – an earlier in Latin, a later in Irish – deal explicitly with the life of Christ. The first, *Precamur patrem*, probably written in the seventh century, recounts some of Christ's miracles, but neglects his resurrection, substituting in its place an account of the harrowing of hell and Christ's ascension to heaven with the rescued saints. The second poem, Blathmac's *Poem to Mary and her Son*, written probably 750 × 770 under *Céli Dé* influence, includes miracles and the resurrection as well as the harrowing, and espouses the Augustinian image of a vengeful Christ at the last judgement, contrasting with the image of the *iudex aequitatis* (espoused by Pelagians and semi-Pelagians).

The introduction of apocryphal scriptures into Ireland was, arguably, a *Romani* innovation. Doubtless Pelagian-influenced thinkers would have opposed the use of apocrypha on the ground that they reduced the divine law to a state of confusion. Whereas Christ's descent to the dead (omitted in the canonical scriptures) had been introduced into the Apostle's Creed in the seventh century (being viewed as needful to Christian theodicy), the account of his battle with Satan in the underworld might well have been viewed as mythical, and surely as inessential to the salvation process. However, the motif of the cosmic struggle against the devil gripped the imaginations of Irish writers from the seventh century onwards; these were soon followed by writers in Anglo-Saxon England. If the harrowing did not actually replace the redemption or the resurrection in the minds of Christians, it seems to have overshadowed them through the vividness of its imagery. It functioned on one level to elevate Christ to the status of heroic warrior – a highly attractive image in a warlike society – and on another level, to provide the ultimate model for the Christian conducting his own personal war against the devil.

In a general way, one may see the development of the literary images of Christ found in Britain and Ireland as a movement from a highly restrictive view of a human, suffering and purely exemplary Christ to a more inclusive one that embraces some, if not all, of the features of his divine or transcendental nature. Christ's thaumaturgical acts are eventually acknowledged, although there remains a certain ambivalence regarding the resurrection. There is no evidence that the resurrection was deliberately suppressed; rather, it was unconsciously assimilated to the harrowing, in which a Hellenistic 'divine man' was substituted for the Incarnate Word. Christ, the example of our mortification, gives way to a Christ who saves with his blood; yet a fully divine Christ only rarely found full expression in the writings of early Celtic Christianity. Blathmac's poem is a rare example of emphasis on Christ's divinity.

Confirmation of the literary trends is provided, to a considerable extent, by the visual arts, although one must allow for some discrepancies in synchronism due to gaps in the record. The lacuna in the visual record of the fifth and sixth centuries and the first half of the seventh is highly consistent with a theology that was antithetical to the use of images. Pelagians would have opposed images on scriptural grounds, while semi-Pelagians believed that meditative prayer should be accomplished without the assistance of external visual helps. When Celtic religious art took its beginnings around the middle of the seventh century, preference for the abstract and the non-representational was consistent with Pelagian emphasis on the strict observance of the law. The cross in its manifold representations was the primary symbol, but other symbols such as the *Chi Rho* were also prominent. Literary evidence for the existence of painted images in southern Irish churches begins after the middle of the seventh century, but no such early examples survive.

When a fully iconographical form of art was in evidence in Ireland in the eighth century and onwards, it is clear that it had been largely assimilated to a Romanised theology. The blood of the crucified Christ flows directly into the eyes of the blind Longinus, reflecting a miracle based on faith. The hand of God also frees the three boys from the fiery furnace. Alongside these 'faith miracles' are representations of 'monastic miracles', for example, a raven bringing sustenance to Anthony and Paul, who have merited God's help. The notion of meriting the help of God is deeply entrenched in semi-Pelagian theology, and might be regarded as intermediate between the 'pure Pelagian' idea that God has no favourites and the Romanising notion that faith is all that really counts, or alternatively (in a more Augustinian mode), that God helps those whom he wills. Yet the development is anything but linear. In the Book of Kells, thought to have been compiled around the end of the eighth century or beginning of the ninth, we find a striking image of Christ teaching in the temple, holding a scroll of the Torah, and thus reflecting the Pelagian ideology of Christ as giver of the law. Moving in the other direction, one visual image in particular reflects a triumph of Augustinian theology, namely the representation of the last judgement where Christ appears with his cross. This must surely be seen as the avenging Christ who comes to punish those who crucified him as well as those who martyred his saints; the source of this conception goes back at least to Blathmac in the eighth century, and is ultimately based on Augustine's *De civitate Dei.*

One other iconographical point requires attention. This is the almost complete absence of any direct representation of Christ's resurrection. This must be regarded in the contrastive light of the representation of the dead Christ in his tomb. This combination of visual evidence appears to confirm our hypothesis based on literary sources that Christ's resurrection was problematic, and that it was somehow subsumed into the harrowing. This seems to be a uniquely Irish interpretation of the central mystery of Christianity – an interpretation that may have had its origin in the theology of the common Celtic Church and undergone a re-formation at the time when the harrowing motif was introduced, probably via the *Romani.*

In one important Christological aspect, the visual evidence appears to be more sharply focussed than the literary. We refer to the matter of representing Christ's divine nature. The robed Christ with open eyes seen on several crosses might be taken to depict the divine nature of Christ that cannot die. And, though expressing a different theology, the depiction of Christ with one eye open, but with his head tilted in death, might be interpreted as a representation of both natures of Christ: he is dead as a man, but lives as God. Similarly, the presence of a bird 'resuscitating' the dead Christ in the tomb may well point to the concern to represent both of Christ's natures. While literary texts of Celtic origin discuss Christ's place in the Trinity and his consubtantiality, none, apparently, addresses the technical question dear to the Church fathers of how Christ who was always

God could die. Here the relation between the visual and the textual can only be said to be unclear.

Perhaps it is fitting to end with the image of Christ as *lorica*, an image represented in both literature and art, and one that is uniquely Irish in its manifold meaning. The *lorica* is an Old Testament figure of Christ's priesthood, connecting the Levites of the Old Law with the Christian priest of the New. The *lorica* also symbolises the protective aspect of Christ and his love for suffering mankind. Christ the Breastplate is the divine man who heroically conquered Satan and simultaneously the Christ who serves as an example to every Christian fighting his own battle against sin. He is *Christus militans*, teaching us to defend ourselves with a spiritual sword and breastplate and, above all, with the Word of God, which is both the divine law and Christ himself as the Incarnate Word. Ailerán, writing in the mid-seventh century, aptly expressed the meaning of this image to the Christian in his or her quest for eternal salvation:

For invisible enemies must be fought with the spiritual and unseen arms of the soul. Let us therefore put on, according to the apostle, the armour of God, that we may be able to resist on the evil day, and in all circumstances bearing the shield of faith, by which we may extinguish the fiery darts of the evil one, and the helmet of hope also and the breastplate of love and the sword of the spirit, which is the word of God.[1]

---

[1] Ailerán, *Mystical Exposition of the Ancestry of the Lord Jesus Christ*, lines 283–8 (tr. Breen, 51–2): 'Spiritualibus namque et inuisibilibus armis inuisibilis animae contra inuisibiles hostes dimicandum est. Assumamus itaque, secundum apostolum, arma Dei ut possimus resistere in die malo, in omnibus sumentes scutum fidei in quo possimus ignita inimici iacula extinguere, et galeam spei et loricam caritatis et gladium Spiritus, quod est Verbum Dei.'

APPENDIX

PRECAMUR PATREM
A HYMN FROM THE SEVENTH-CENTURY
ANTIPHONARY OF BANGOR

A note on the hymn

This hymn, beginning on fo. 4v and ending on fo. 6v of the Antiphonary of Bangor, is prefaced with the words 'Hymnus apostolorum ut alii dicunt.'[1] The phrase 'ut alii dicunt' can bear its standard meaning, but it is possible that *alii* means 'some' rather than 'others', as is attested in Hiberno-Latin usage.[2] The hymn is composed of forty-two quatrains of non-quantitative verse, usually, but not always, employing the pattern 5p 7pp.[3] Rhyme is irregular.

The poem links the themes of the primacy of the first day (Sunday), the life of Christ and the divine plan for human salvation, which extends from the creation to the last judgement. It does not commemorate any one liturgical event, but celebrates a number of events of sacred history, each related to the other by the fact that it occurs on a Sunday. That Sunday observance is central to the poem's message is shown by detailed comparison with two versions of a short tract entitled *Dies dominica*.[4] In one or both versions the following events which correspond to various stanzas of *Precamur patrem* are alleged to have occurred on Sunday: the first day of creation, the passage of Israel through the Red Sea, the birth of Christ, the miracle at Cana, the miracle of the loaves and fishes, the founding of the Church, the opening of the gates of paradise and the last judgement. The correspondences are given in the notes to the translation.

A perplexing feature of the poem is its omission of any direct reference to the canonical resurrection, especially as this event occurred on a Sunday according to scripture, and is mentioned in both versions of *Dies dominica*.

---

[1] Milan: Biblioteca Ambrosiana, MS C. 5 inf., s. VIIex.; edition in Warren, *Antiphonary of Bangor*, I.4v-6v (diplomatic edition) and II.5–7 (modernised version). For a full description of the manuscript and its contents see Kenney, *Sources*, 706–12; for a detailed discussion of individual hymns, poems and liturgical items see Curran, *Antiphonary of Bangor*. Bibliography in Lapidge and Sharpe, *A Bibliography*, 146–7. The discussion of this poem here, as well as the translation, is based on Warren's modernised version.

[2] Bieler, *The Irish Penitentials*, 37.

[3] Lapidge, '*Precamur patrem*', 262–3.

[4] The title given to the work by its editor, McNally: '*Dies dominica*'.

In the portion of the poem that details the life of Christ (stanzas xviii–xxxix), the crucifixion (stanza xxxi) is followed immediately by a description of the rending of the veil of the temple (stanza xxxii) and then three stanzas detailing the harrowing of hell (xxxiii–xxxv), a reference to the Church triumphant (xxxvi), then the opening of heaven to Christ and the righteous persons rescued from hell (xxxvii) – embellished with an allusion to the Good Shepherd (xxxviii) –, and finally, an indication of Christ's role in the coming judgement (xxxix). One might hypothesise that Christ's resurrection is acknowledged in the notion that, in order to harrow hell, Christ had to leave his tomb. But this is hardly the version of the gospels, and this leaves it doubtful indeed that *Precamur patrem* was composed for the occasion of Easter.[5]

In addition to a source advocating Sunday observance the writer employs an apocryphon which commemorates the harrowing of hell. This apocryphon is certainly not the *Gospel of Nicodemus* as known from Latin manuscripts beginning in the ninth century. This is most clearly shown by the discrepancy regarding the escorting the souls of the just to paradise. In *Precamur patrem* this is performed by Christ himself; in the Latin *Gospel of Nicodemus* the act is performed by the archangel Michael.[6]

It remains to comment briefly on the poem's authorship and date of composition. On the basis of the employment of the rare word *micrologi* (stanza xli) in the same unusual sense as found in Columbanus, and also the use of the Columbanian formula *manens in Trinitate* (stanza xviii), Michael Lapidge conjectured that *Precamur patrem* was written by Columbanus himself as a young man still at Bangor.[7] However, as noted above, it is remarkable that Columbanus's authorship of this poem is not acknowledged in the very collection compiled to celebrate the achievements of the saints of Bangor. Whereas Columbanus's authorship of this work cannot be excluded, it cannot be regarded as proven. We must reckon with the possibility that a later admirer of Columbanus's style and phraseology wrote the poem. Let it suffice that *Precamur patrem* had to be written before 680 × 691, the *terminus ante quem* of the Antiphonary of Bangor.[8] Given the reference to Christ's miracles, the use of an (undetermined) apocryphal source and, especially, the advocacy of Sunday observance, *Precamur patrem* should, in all likelihood, be classified as a *Romani* text, and therefore be dated with greater probability to the period *ca* 630 – *ca* 680. If Columbanus did write this poem, he would have done so after he arrived on the continent. The sabbatising of Sunday in the Gaulish Church beginning *ca* 585[9] coincides closely with Columbanus's arrival on the continent. In the end, one has to be convinced that someone who argued so powerfully for the 'Celtic Easter' against Gaulish ecclesiastics would

---

[5] Lapidge, '*Precamur patrem*', 256.
[6] Above, 157 n. 80. Texts dealing with Christ's escorting of the just souls to paradise are conveniently assembled in Daniélou, *Théologie*, 27.
[7] Lapidge, '*Precamur patrem*', 261.
[8] Curran, *Antiphonary of Bangor*, 197 n. 10.
[9] See the evidence collected in van Dam, *Leadership and Community*, 285–9.

easily have accepted such a radical change to the established practice of the Columban Church and would have promulgated it in a poem.

Translation

i. We beseech the Father, the almighty King, and Jesus Christ and the Holy Spirit too. Alleluia.

ii. Adore God who is perfect in a single substance and threefold in three persons,

iii. (God), the radiance of the source of all lights (those in) the heavens, and those shining in the world.

iv. For just as this first-begotten day flashed to the foundation of the world from the citadel of heaven,

v. So (did) the Word made flesh, the eternal light made in the beginning, sent from the Father to the world.

vi. And (just as) that day first removed the powers of chaos, then, without warning, cast off night from the world,

vii. So he, subduing the ancient enemy, released the world from the knotted bond of death.

viii. (And just as) darkness was over the abyss before that first day of days shone,

ix. Here, when the true light went forth, deep ignorance covered mortal hearts.

x. On the same day, as they say, liberated Israel left the Red Sea behind.

xi. By this we are taught to spurn the deeds of this world and stand firm in the desert of virtues.

xii. (And just as) when Cincres, the cruel enemy, was drowned, they (i.e. the Israelites) eagerly sing praises to God the fiery leader,

xiii. So we, rescued from the straits of evil, are bidden to praise God when our enemies have been destroyed.

xiv. And just as that day was the beginning of light, so he is the start of our salvation.

xv. And just as the first is located in the sense of daylight, the second (is seated) in the heat of faith.

xvi. At the end of the world, after so many wonders, the Saviour will come with great clemency.

xvii. And the elements show these things as clearly as the mouths of priests celebrate them lucidly.

xviii. Born as man in mortal covering, he is not absent from heaven, remaining in the Trinity.

xix. He cries in swaddling clothes, is venerated by the Magi; he flashes among the stars, he is adored in the heavens.

xx. Tiny of stature, he is contained by a manger, (but) in his fist the world can be enclosed.

xxi. He gives a first sign to his disciples: water is changed into the flavour of nectar.

xxii. Then it is fulfilled as spoken through the prophet: 'The lame shall leap' swiftly 'like a deer'.

xxiii. At God's command, the tongues of the mute speak plainly, once the bond is broken.

xxiv. The deaf are healed, the blind and the lepers; the dead are revived when death is crushed.

xxv. He divides five loaves of bread to satisfy (without any doubt!) the same number of thousands of men.

xxvi. After so many examples of divine clemency he was much despised on account of envy's goad.

xxvii. Beseeching (God) he prayed for his enemies, who envied him and hated his life.

xxviii. They took counsel against him who is called the messenger of great counsel.

xxix. With swords they approach him as though he were a thief – (he) who will consign a thief to hell.

xxx. At length he is handed over to human judgement; the immortal one is condemned by a mortal king.

xxxi. Fastened to a cross, he strikes the world in wondrous fashion, and the light of the sun is obscured for three hours.

xxxii. Rocks burst open, the veil of the temple is rent; the dead rise living from their tombs.

xxxiii. He removes the first creation (i.e. Adam), gnawed by the deathly knots of hell for nearly six thousand years,

xxxiv. Together with (his) righteous offspring, cast down by cruel death as punishment for the (crime of) the apple (or: 'sin').

xxxv. On his return he mercifully restores each ancient inhabitant to paradise.

xxxvi. Raising his head, he located the church of his whole body in the Trinity.

xxxvii. Then he commands the princes (i.e. the angels) from heaven to open the eternal gates to the King and his companions,

xxxviii. Bearing the hundredth erring sheep on his own exalted shoulders to the sheepfolds,

xxxix. Whom we expect will come again as our judge to render to each his just due.

xl. I ask, how can we worthily repay (him) for so many and such great gifts?

xli. Why do we, such inarticulate mortals, struggle to enunciate the things which no one can express?

xlii. This one and only greatest thing we pray: have mercy on us, eternal Lord. Alleluia.

Correspondences with Dies dominica

iv. I (359.2): 'Diem autem dominicam primam diem esse dubitari non potest . . .'; II (360.2): 'Dies dominicus dies beatus, quia primus dies fuit.'

v. I (359.16): 'Die vero dominica nativitas Domini'. II (361.27): 'Dies dominicus dies beatus, in qua venit Christus in mundo.'

x. II (360.14): 'Dies dominicus dies beatus, in qua exiit Israel per mare rubrum siccis pedibus.'

xvi. II (361.33–4): 'Dies dominicus dies beatus, in qua veniat Dominus deiudicare vivos ac mortuos.'

xviii. Cf. v.

xxi. I (359.19): 'Die dominica fecit Deus mirabilia in Cannan Galileae.' II (361.1): 'Dies dominicus dies beatus, in qua benedixit Deus vinum in Canan Galilee.'

xxv. I (360.20): 'Die dominica de V panibus et duobus piscibus "Dominus V milia hominum satiavit".'

xxxvi. I (359.14): 'Et in die dominica nata est ecclesia.'

xxxvii. I (359.11–12): 'Die dominica dixit Christus ad angelos: "Aperite portas iustitiae. Et ingressus in eas confitebor Domino".'

xxxix. Cf. xvi.

BIBLIOGRAPHY AND ABBREVIATIONS

BAR   British Archaeological Reports
CCSL   *Corpus Christianorum Series Latina* (Turnhout)
CMCS   *Cambrian Medieval Celtic Studies* (formerly *Cambridge Medieval Celtic Studies*) (Aberystwyth)
CSEL   *Corpus Scriptorum Ecclesiasticorum Latinorum* (Vienna)
JMLat   *The Journal of Medieval Latin* (Toronto and Turnhout)
JRSAI   *Journal of the Royal Society of Antiquaries of Ireland* (Dublin)
KCLMS   King's College London Medieval Studies
MGH   *Monumenta Germaniae Historica*
PL   *Patrologia Latina* (Paris)
PLS supp   *Patrologia Latina, Supplementum*. A. Hamman (ed.) 4 vols. (Paris 1958–74)
PLAC   *Poetae Latini Aevi Carolini* (*Monumenta Germaniae Historica*, Munich)
PRIA   *Proceedings of the Royal Irish Academy* (Dublin)
RCAHMS   Royal Commission on the Ancient and Historical Monuments of Scotland
SC   *Sources Chrétiennes* (Paris)
SLH   *Scriptores Latini Hiberniae* (Dublin)

ADRIAEN, M. (ed.) *Egloga quam scripsit Lathcen filius Baith de Moralibus Iob quas Gregorius fecit CCSL* CXLV (Turnhout 1969)
ANDERSON, A.O. & ANDERSON, M.O. (edd. and tr.) *Adomnan's Life of Columba* (London 1961)
AUTENRIETH, J. & BRUNHÖLZL, F. (edd.) *Festschrift Bernhard Bischoff zu seinem 65. Geburtstag* (Stuttgart 1971)
BACKHOUSE, J. *The Lindisfarne Gospels* (Oxford 1981)
BAILEY, R.N. *England's Earliest Sculptors* Publications of the Dictionary of Old English 5 (Toronto 1996)
BAMMESBERGER, A. & WOLLMAN, A. (edd.) *Britain 400–600: Language and History* (Heidelberg 1990)
BAYARD, M. (ed. and tr.) *Saint Cyprien Correspondence* 2 vols. (Paris 1925)
BAYLESS, M. & LAPIDGE, M. (edd.) *Collectanea Pseudo-Bedae SLH* XV (Dublin 1998)
BERNARD, J.H. & ATKINSON, R. (edd.) *The Irish Liber Hymnorum* 2 vols. Henry Bradshaw Society 12–13 (London 1898)
BEST, R.I. & BERGIN, O. (edd.) *Lebor na hUidre: Book of the Dun Cow* (Dublin 1929)
BEST, R. & LAWLOR, H. *The Martyrology of Tallaght* (London 1931)
BETTENSON, H. (tr.) *St Augustine concerning The City of God against the Pagans* (London 1972)
BIELER, L. 'Ireland's contribution to the culture of Northumbria', in *Famulus Christi* ed. Bonner 210–28

BIELER, L. (ed.) *Libri epistolarum Sancti Patricii episcopi* (Dublin 1993)

BIELER, L. *St Patrick and the Coming of Christianity* (Dublin 1967)

BIELER, L. (ed.) *The Irish Penitentials SLH* V (Dublin 1963)

BIELER, L. (ed. and tr.) *The Patrician Texts in the Book of Armagh SHL* X (Dublin 1979)

BIELER, L. 'The place of St Patrick in Latin language and literature', *Vigiliae Christianae* 6 (1952) 65–98

BINCHY, D.A. 'Patrick and his Biographers, Ancient and Modern', *Studia Hibernica* 2 (1962) 7–173

BISCHOFF, B. (ed.) *Mittelalterliche Studien. Ausgewählte Aufsätze zur Schriftkunde und Literaturgeschichte* 3 vols. (Stuttgart 1966–81)

BISCHOFF, B. 'Wendepunkte in der Geschichte der lateinischen Exegese', in *Mittelalterliche Studien* ed. Bischoff I.205–72

BISCHOFF, B. & LAPIDGE, M. (edd. and tr.) *Biblical Commentaries from the Canterbury School of Theodore and Hadrian* Cambridge Studies in Anglo-Saxon England 10 (Cambridge 1994)

BISCHOFF, B. & LÖFSTEDT, B. (edd.) *Anonymus ad Cuimnanum: Expossitio latinitatis CCSL* CXXIII/D (Turnhout 1992)

BLAIR, J. & SHARPE, R. (edd.) *Pastoral Care before the Parish* (Leicester 1992)

BOLTON, W.F. *A History of Anglo-Latin Literature 1* (Princeton 1967)

BONNER, G. (ed.) *Famulus Christi: Essays in Commemoration of the Thirteenth Centenary of the Birth of the Venerable Bede* (London 1976)

BONNER, G. 'Rufinus of Syria and African Pelagianism', *Augustinian Studies* 1 (1970) 31–47

BONNER, G. *et al.* (edd.) *St Cuthbert, his Cult, and his Community to A.D. 1200* (Woodbridge 1989)

BOON, G.C. 'The early Church in Gwent, I: The Romano-British Church', *The Monmouthshire Antiquary* 8 (1992) 11–24

BORIUS, R. (ed. and tr.) *Constance de Lyon. Vie de Saint Germain d'Auxerre SC* 112 (Paris 1965)

BOSWELL, C.S. *An Irish Precursor of Dante* (London 1908)

BOURKE, C. 'The Blackwater shrine', *Dúiche Néill* 6 (1991) 103–6

BRAILSFORD, J.W. *The Mildenhall Treasure* (London 1964)

BRADLEY, I. *Celtic Christianity: Making Myths and Chasing Dreams* (Edinburgh 1999)

BRADLEY, S.A.J. (tr.) *Anglo-Saxon Poetry* (London 1982)

BREATNACH, L. *et al.* (edd.) *Sages, Saints and Storytellers: Celtic Studies in Honour of Professor James Carney* (Maynooth 1989)

BREEN, A. (ed. and tr.) *Ailerani: Interpretatio Mystica et Moralis Progenitorum Domini Iesu Christi* (Dublin 1995)

BROUN, M. *The Book of Cerne. Prayer, Patronage and Power in Ninth-Century England* (London 1996)

BROWN, D. 'The literary record of St Nynia: fact or fiction?', *The Innes Review* 42.2 (1991) 143–50

BULLOUGH, D. 'The career of Columbanus', in *Columbanus* ed. Lapidge 1–28

BULLOUGH, D. *et al.* (edd.) *Ideal and Reality in Frankish and Anglo-Saxon Society: Studies presented to J.M. Wallace-Hadrill* (Oxford 1983)

CAHILL, M. (ed.) *Expositio Evangelii secundum Marcum CCLS* LXXXII (Turnhout 1997)

CAHILL, M. 'Is the first commentary on Mark an Irish work?', *Peritia* 8 (1994) 35–45

CAHILL, M. (tr.) *The First Commentary on Mark: an Annotated Translation* (Oxford 1998)

CAILLAU, A.B. & GUILLON, M.N.S. (edd.) *Collectio Selecta SS Ecclesiae Patrum = Eusebii Opera* 8 vols. (Brussels 1830)

CAMPBELL, A. (ed.) *Aethulwulf, De abbatibus* (Oxford 1967)

CAREY, J. *King of Mysteries: Early Irish Religious Writings* (Dublin 2000)

CARNEY, J. (ed.) *The Poems of Blathmac, Son of Cú Brettan* Irish Texts Society 47 (Dublin 1964)

CASSIDY, B. (ed.) *The Ruthwell Cross* Index of Christian Art Occasional Papers 1 (Princeton 1992)

Catholic Encyclopedia, edd. C.G.Herbermann *et al.* 15 vols. plus index (New York 1907–14)

CHADWICK, H. 'Theodore, the English church and the monothelite controversy', in *Archbishop Theodore* ed. Lapidge 88–95

CHADWICK, N.K. 'Intellectual life in West Wales in the last days of the Celtic Church', in *Studies in the Early British Church* ed. (N.K.) Chadwick 121–82

CHADWICK, N.K. (ed.) *Studies in the Early British Church* (Cambridge 1958)

CHADWICK, N.K. *The Age of the Saints in the Early Celtic Church* (London 1961)

CHADWICK, O. *John Cassian* (Cambridge 1968)

CHARLES, R.H. *The Apocrypha and Pseudepigrapha of the Old Testament* 2 vols. (Oxford 1913)

CHARLES-EDWARDS, T.M. *Early Christian Ireland* (Cambridge 2000)

CHARLES-EDWARDS, T.M. 'Palladius, Prosper, and Leo the Great: mission and primatial authority', in *Saint Patrick* ed. Dumville 1–12

CHARLES-EDWARDS, T.M. 'The Church in the early Irish laws', in *Pastoral Care before the Parish* edd. Blair & Sharpe 63–80

CHARLES-EDWARDS, T.M. 'The Penitential of Theodore and the *Iudicia Theodori*', in *Archbishop Theodore* ed. Lapidge 141–74

CHARLES-EDWARDS, T.M. 'The social background to Irish Perigrinatio', *Celtica* 11 (1976) 43–59

CLANCY, T.O. 'Columba, Adomnán and the cult of the saints in Scotland', *The Innes Review* 48 (1997) 1–26

CLANCY, T.O. 'The real St Ninian', *The Innes Review* 52 (2001) 1–28

CLARKE, H.B. & BRENNAN, M. (edd.) *Columbanus and Merovingian Monasticism* (Oxford 1981)

COLGRAVE, B. (ed. and tr.) *The Life of Bishop Wilfrid by Eddius Stephanus* (Cambridge 1927)

COLGRAVE, B. (ed. and tr.) *Two Lives of Saint Cuthbert: a Life by an Anonymous Monk of Lindisfarne and Bede's Prose Life* (Cambridge 1940)

COLGRAVE, B. & MYNORS, R. (edd.) *Bede's Ecclesiastical History of the English People* (Oxford 1969)

COLLINGWOOD, W.G. *Northumbrian Crosses of the Pre-Norman Age* (London 1927)

CONNOLLY, S. & PICARD, J.-M. (tr.) 'Cogitosus: Life of Saint Brigit', *JRSAI* 117 (1987) 11–27

CONTRENI, J.J. & Ó NÉILL, P.P. (edd.) *Glossae Divinae Historiae. The Biblical Glosses of John Scottus Eriugena* (Florence 1997)

COOK, A.S. *The Anglo-Saxon Cross* (Hamdon CT 1977)

CRAMP, R. *Corpus of Anglo-Saxon Stone Sculpture in England* vol. I (Oxford 1984)

CRAMP, R. *Early Northumbrian Sculpture* (Jarrow 1965)

CRAMP. R. 'Early Northumbrian sculpture at Hexham', in *Saint Wilfrid at Hexham* ed. Kirby 115–40, 172–9

CURRAN, M. *The Antiphonary of Bangor and the Early Irish Monastic Liturgy* (Dublin 1984)

CUSCITO, G. 'Aquileia e Bisanzio nella controversia dei tre capitoli', in *Aquileia e l'Oriente Mediterraneo* Antichità Altoadriatiche 12 (1977) 231–62

DANIÉLOU, J. *Théologie du Judéo-Christianisme* Histoire des Doctines Chrétiennes avant Nicée 1 (Tournai 1958)

DAVIES, W. 'The myth of the Celtic Church', in *The Early Church in Wales and the West* edd. Edwards & Lane 12–21

DAVIES, W. *Wales in the Early Middle Ages* Studies in the Early History of Britain (Leicester 1982)

DE BRUYN, T. (tr.) *Pelagius's Commentary on St Paul's Epistle to the Romans* (Oxford 1993)

DEGREGORIO, S. 'The Venerable Bede on prayer and contemplation', *Traditio* 54 (1999) 1–39

DE LETTER, P. (tr.) *Prosper of Aquitaine: Defense of St Augustine* (New York 1963)

DE PAOR, L. *Saint Patrick's World: the Christian Culture of Ireland's Apostolic Age* (Dublin 1996)

DE PLINVAL, G. *Pélage: ses écrits, sa vie et sa réforme* (Lausanne 1943)

Dictionnaire d'archéologie chrétienne et de liturgie edd. F. Cabrol & H. Leclercq 15 vols. (Paris 1924–53)

Dictionnaire de théologie catholique edd. A.Vacant *et al.* 15 vols. (Paris 1903–50)

DOHERTY, C. 'The use of relics in Ireland', in *Irland und Europa* edd. Ní Chatháin & Richter 89–101

DOMBART, B. & KALB, A. (edd.) *Sancti Aurelii Augustini Episcopi De civitate Dei* (Stuttgart 1993)

DONAHUE, C. 'Beowulf and Christian tradition: a reconsideration from a Celtic stance', *Traditio* 21 (1965) 55–116

DONAHUE, C. 'Beowulf, Ireland and the natural good', *Traditio* 7 (1949–51) 263–77

DONAHUE, C. (ed.) *The Testament of Mary. The Gaelic Version of the Dormitio Mariae together with an Irish Latin Version* (New York 1942)

DOOLEY, A. 'The *Gospel of Nicodemus* in Ireland', in *The Medieval Gospel of Nicodemus* ed. Izydorczyk 361–401

DRONKE, P. 'St Patrick's reading', *CMCS* 1 (1981) 22–38

DUCHESNE, L. (ed. and tr.) *Le Liber Pontificalis/Texte, introduction, et commentaire* 2 vols. (Paris 1886–92)

DUMVILLE, D.N. 'Biblical Apocrypha and the early Irish: a preliminary investigation', *PRIA* 73 C (1973) 299–338.

DUMVILLE, D.N. 'Gildas and Uinniau', in *Gildas* edd. Lapidge & Dumville 207–14

DUMVILLE, D.N. 'Late seventh- or eighth-century evidence for the British transmission of Pelagius', *CMCS* 10 (1985) 39–52

DUMVILLE, D.N. 'Liturgical drama and panegyric response from the eighth century? A re-examination of the origin and contents of the ninth-century section of the Book of Cerne', *Journal of Theological Studies* n.s. 23 (1972) 374–406

DUMVILLE, D.N. 'Saint David of Wales', Kathleen Hughes Memorial Lectures on Mediaeval Welsh History 1 (Cambridge 2001)

DUMVILLE, D.N. 'Some British aspects of the earliest Irish Christianity', in *Irland und Europa* edd. Ní Chatháin & Richter 16–24

DUMVILLE, D.N. 'The chronology of *De Excidio Britanniae*, Book I', in *Gildas* edd. Lapidge & Dumville 61–84

DUMVILLE, D.N. *et al. Saint Patrick A.D. 493–1993* Studies in Celtic History 13 (Woodbridge 1993)

EDWARDS, N. 'An early group of crosses from the Kingdom of Ossory', *JRSAI* 113 (1983) 5–46

EDWARDS, N. 'The South Cross, Clonmacnois (with an appendix on the incidence of vine-scroll on Irish scuplture)', in *Early Medieval Sculpture in Britain and Ireland* ed. Higgitt 23–48

EDWARDS, N. & LANE, A. *The Early Church in Wales and the West* Oxbow Monograph 16 (Oxford 1992)

EHWALD, R. (ed.) *Aldhelmi Opera* (Berlin 1919, 1961)

ESPOSITO, M. 'On the pseudo-Augustinian treatise *De Mirabilibus Sacrae Scripturae* written in Ireland in the year 655', *PRIA* 35 C (1919) 189–207

ETCHINGHAM, C. *Church Organisation in Ireland A.D. 650 to 1000* (Maynooth 1999)

EVANS, R.F. *Four Letters of Pelagius* (London 1968)

EVANS, R.F. 'Pelagius, Fastidius, and the pseudo-Augustinian *De vita Christiana*', *Journal of Theological Studies* 13 (1962) 72–98

FARIS, M.J. (ed.) *The Bishops' Synod ('The First Synod of St Patrick'): a Symposium with Text, Translation and Commentary* ARCA Classical and Medieval Texts, Papers and Monographs 1 (Liverpool 1976)

FARR, C. 'Liturgical influences on the decoration of the Book of Kells', in *Studies in Insular Art and Archaeology* edd. Karkov & Farrell 127–41

FARR, C. *The Book of Kells: its Function and Audience* The British Library Studies in Medieval Culture (London 1997)

FARR, C. 'Worthy women on the Ruthwell Cross: women as sign in early Anglo-Saxon monasticism', in *The Insular Tradition*, edd. Karkov *et al.* 45–62

FARRELL, R.T. (ed.) *Bede and Anglo-Saxon England* BAR Brit. Series 46 (Oxford 1978)

FARRELL, R.T. & KARKOV, C. 'The construction, deconstruction, and reconstruction of the Ruthwell Cross: some caveats', in *The Ruthwell Cross* ed. Cassidy 35–47

FERGUSON, J. *Pelagius: a Historical and Theological Study* (Cambridge 1965)

FOLEY, W.T. *Images of Sanctity in Eddius Stephanus' Life of Bishop Wilfrid: an Early English Saint's Life* (Lewiston NY 1992)

FONTAINE, J. *et al. S. Grégoire le Grand: Chantilly, centre culturel Les Fontaines, 15–19 septembre 1982, Actes* Colloques Internationaux de Centre National de la Recherche Scientifique (Paris 1986)

FONTAINE, J. & HILLGARTH, J.N. (edd.) *La septième siècle: changements et continuités/The Seventh Century: Change and Continuity* (London 1992)

FREDE, H.J. *Pelagius, der irische Paulustext, Sedulius Scottus* (Freiburg 1961)

FREMANTLE, W.H. *et al.* (tr.) *The Principal Works of St Jerome* A Select Library of Nicene and Post-Nicene Fathers of the Christian Church, 2nd series, VI (Grand Rapids MI 1954)

FREND, W.H.C. *Archaeology and History in the Study of Early Christianity* (London 1988)

FREND, W.H.C. *The Archaeology of Early Christianity: a History* (Minneapolis MN 1996)

FRITZ, G. 'Quinisexte Concile', in *Dictionnaire de Théologie Catholique* 13/2.1581–97

GODFREY, J. 'The place of the double monastery in the Anglo-Saxon minster system', in *Famulus Christi* ed. Bonner 344–50

GORMAN, M. 'A critique of Bischoff's theory of Irish exegesis: the commentary on Genesis in Munich Clm 6302 ("Wendepunkte" 2)', *JMLat* 7 (1997) 178–233

GRAY, P.T.R. *The Defence of Chalcedon in the East (451–553)* (Leiden 1979)

GRAY, P.T.R. & HERREN, M.W. 'Columbanus and the Three Chapters controversy – a new approach', *The Journal of Theological Studies* n.s. 45/1 (April 1994) 160–70

GROSJEAN, P. 'Sur quelques exégètes irlandais du VIIe siècle', *Sacris Erudiri* 7 (1955) 67–98

GRUNDY, L. *Books and Grace: Aelfric's Theology* KCLMS VI (London 1991)

GUY, J-C. (ed. and tr.) *Jean Cassien: Institutions cénobitiques. Texte latin revue introduction, traduction et notes SC* 109 (Paris 1965)

GWYNN, E. 'An Irish penitential', *Ériu* 7 (1914) 121–95

GWYNN, E. (ed.) *The Rule of Tallaght* (Dublin 1927)

HADDAN, A.W. & STUBBS, W. (edd.) *Councils and Ecclesiastical Documents Relating to Great Britain and Ireland* 3 vols. (Oxford 1869–71)

HAMESSE, J. (ed.) *Roma, Magister Mundi: Itineraria Culturae Medievalis: Mélanges offerts au Père L.E. Boyle à l'occasion de son 75e anniversaire* (Louvain-la-Neuve 1998)

HAMLIN, A. 'Crosses in early Ireland: the evidence from written sources', in *Ireland and Insular Art A.D. 500–1200* ed. Ryan 138–40

HANSON, R.P.C. (ed.and tr.) *Saint Patrick: Confession et lettre à Coroticus. Introduction, texte critique, traduction et notes* (Paris 1978)

HANSON, R.P.C. *Saint Patrick: his Origins and Career* (Oxford 1968)

HARBISON, P. 'Earlier Carolingian narrative iconography: ivories, manuscripts, frescoes and Irish high crosses', *Jahrbuch des Römisch-Germanischen Zentralmuseums* 31 (1984) 455–71

HARBISON, P. 'The bronze crucifixion plaque said to be from St John's (Rinnagan), near Athlone', *The Journal of Irish Archaeology* 2 (1984) 1–17

HARBISON, P. *The High Crosses of Ireland* 3 vols. (Bonn 1992)

HARDINGE, L. *The Celtic Church in Britain* (London 1972)

HARTING-CORREA, A.L. *Walafrid Strabo's Libellus de Exordiis et Incrementis Quarundam in Observationibus Ecclesiasticis Rerum* (Leiden 1996)

HASKYNS, S. *Mary Magdalen: Myth and Metaphor* (London 1993)

HAVERFIELD, F.J. & GREENWELL, W. *A Catalogue of the Sculptured and Inscribed Stones in the Cathedral Library, Durham* (Durham 1899)

HAWKES, J. & MILLS, S. (edd.) *Northumbria's Golden Age* (Thrupp 1999)

HEFELE, C.J. *Histoire des conciles* 11 vols. (Paris 1907–52)

HENDERSON, G. *From Durrow to Kells: The Insular Gospel-Books 650–800* (London 1987)

HENDERSON, G. *Vision and Image in Early Christian England* (Cambridge 1999)

HENDERSON, I. 'The shape and decoration of the cross on Pictish cross-slabs carved in relief', in *The Age of Migrating Ideas* edd. Spearman & Higgitt 209–18

HENNECKE, E. & SCHNEEMELCHER, W. (edd.) *New Testament Apocrypha* 2 vols. tr. R. McL.Wilson (Philadelphia 1963)

HENNIG, J. 'The literary tradition of Moses in Ireland', *Traditio* 7 (1949–51) 233–61

HENRY, F. *The Book of Kells* (London 1974)

HENRY, F. *Irish Art during the Viking Invasions 800–1020 A.D.* (London 1967)

HENRY, F. *Irish Art in the Early Christian Period to 800 A.D.* (London 1965)

HERBERT, M. *Iona, Kells and Derry: the History and Hagiography of the Monastic Familia of Columba* (Oxford 1988)

HERBERT, M. & McNAMARA, M. (tr.) *Irish Biblical Apocrypha: Selected Texts in Translation* (Edinburgh 1989)

HERBERT, M. & Ó RIAIN, P. (edd. and tr.) *Betha Adamnáin: the Irish Life of Adamnán* Irish Texts Society 54 (London 1988)

HERITY, M. 'The antiquity of *an Turas* (the pilgrimage round) in Ireland', in *Lateinische Kultur im VIII. Jahrhundert* edd. Lehner & Berschin 95–143

HERREN, M.W. 'An early Irish precursor of the 'Offiziendichtung' of the Carolingian and Ottonian periods', *Euphrosyne* 22 (1994) 291–300

HERREN, M.W. 'Gildas and early British monasticism', in *Britain 400–600* edd. Bammesberger & Wollman 65–78

HERREN, M.W. (ed. and tr.) *Iohannis Scotti Eruigenae Carmina SLH* XII (Dublin 1993)

HERREN, M.W. 'Irish biblical commentaries before 800', in *Roma, Magister Mundi* ed. Hamesse 391–407

HERREN, M.W. 'Mission and monasticism in the *Confessio* of St Patrick', in *Sages, Saints and Storytellers* edd. Breatnach *et al.* 76–85

HERREN, M.W. 'On the earliest Irish acquaintance with Isidore of Seville', in *Visigothic Spain* ed. James 243–50

HERREN, M.W. 'Scholarly contacts between the Irish and the southern English in the seventh century', *Peritia* 12 (1998) 24–53

HERREN, M.W. 'The authorship, date of composition and provenance of the so-called *Lorica Gildae*', *Ériu* 24 (1973) 35–51

HERREN, M.W. (ed. and tr.) *The Hisperica Famina I: the A-Text* (Toronto 1974)

HERREN, M.W. (ed. and tr.) *The Hisperica Famina II: Related Poems* (Toronto 1987)

HERREN, M.W. 'The role of the miraculous in the earliest Irish saints' *encomia*', in *Lateinische Biographie* ed. Walz 35–40.

HERRIN, J. *The Formation of Christendom* (Princeton 1987)

HERZFELD, G. (ed.) *An Old English Martyrology* Early English Text Society 116 (London 1900)

HIGGITT, J. (ed.) *Early Medieval Sculpture in Britain and Ireland* BAR British Series 152 (Oxford 1986)

HILL, T.D. 'Invocation of the Trinity and the tradition of the *Lorica* in Old English poetry', *Speculum* 56 (1981) 259–69

HILLGARTH, J.N. (ed.) *Christianity and Paganism, 350–750: the Conversion of Western Europe* (Philadelphia PA 1986)

HILLGARTH, J.N. 'Ireland and Spain in the seventh century', *Peritia* 3 (1984) 1–16

HILLGARTH, J.N. 'Visigothic Spain and early Christian Ireland', *PRIA* 62C (1962) 167–94

HOOD, A.B. (ed. and tr.) *St Patrick, his Writings and Muirchú's Life* (London 1978)

HOWLETT, D. 'Inscriptions and design of the Ruthwell Cross', in *The Ruthwell Cross* ed. Cassidy 71–94

HUEMER, J. (ed.) *Sedulii Opera Omnia* (Vienna 1885)

HUGHES, I. (ed. and tr.) *Stair Nicoméid: the Irish Gospel of Nicodemus* The Irish Texts Society 55 (London 1991)

HUGHES, K. 'Some aspects of Irish influence on early Irish private prayer', *Studia Celtica* 5 (1970) 48–61

HUGHES, K. 'Synodus II S. Patricii', in *Latin Script and Letters* edd. O'Meara & Naumann 141–7

HUGHES, K. 'The Celtic Church: is this a valid concept?', *CMCS* 1 (1981) 1–20

HUGHES, K. *The Church in Early Irish Society* (London 1966)

HUGHES, K. & HAMLIN, A. *The Modern Traveller to the Early Irish Church* 2nd ed. (Dublin 1997)

HULL, V. '*Apgitir Chrábaid*: the alphabet of piety', *Celtica* 8 (1968) 44–89

HUNTER BLAIR, O. (ed. and tr.) *The Rule of St Benedict: Edited with an English Translation and Explanatory Notes* 5th ed. (Fort Augustus 1948)

HURST, D. (ed.) *Bedae Venerabilis Opera Exegetica, Part II. CCSL* CXIX (Turnhout 1962)

HURST, D. (ed.) *Bedae Venerabilis Opera Exegetica, Part IIA. CCSL* CXIX A (Turnhout 1969)

HURST, D. & HUDSON, J.E. (edd.) *Bedae Venerabilis Opera Exegetica, Part IIB. CCSL* CXIX B (Turnhout 1983)

IZYDORCZYK, Z. (ed.) *The Medieval* Gospel of Nicodemus: *Texts, Intertexts, and Contexts in Western Europe* Medieval & Renaissance Texts & Studies 158 (Tempe AZ 1997)

JAMES, E. (ed.) *Visigothic Spain: New Approaches* (Oxford 1980)

JAMES, J.W. (ed. and tr.) *Rhigyfarch's Life of St David* (Cardiff 1967)

JAMES, M.R. (tr.) *The Apocryphal New Testament* (Oxford 1924)

JONES, C.W. (ed.) *Bedae Opera de Temporibus* (Cambridge MA 1943)

KARKOV, C. *et al.* (edd.) *The Insular Tradition* (Albany NY 1997)

KELLY, D. 'Irish high crosses: some evidence from the plainer examples', *JRSAI* 116 (1986) 51–67

KELLY, D. 'The relationships of the crosses of Argyll: the evidence of form', in *The Age of Migrating Ideas* edd. Spearman & Higgitt 219–29

KELLY, F. *A Guide to Early Irish Law* Early Irish Law Series 3 (Dublin 1988)

KELLY, J.F. 'Augustine in Hiberno-Latin literature', *Augustinian Studies* 8 (1977) 139–49

KELLY, J.F. 'Pelagius, Pelagianism and the Early Christian Irish', *Mediaevalia* 4 (1978) 99–124

KELLY, J.F. (ed.) *Scriptores Hiberniae Minores CCSL* CVIII C (Turnhout 1974)

KELLY, J.N.D. *Early Christian Doctrines* (London 1960)

KENNEY, J.F. *The Sources for the Early History of Ireland: Ecclesiastical* (New York 1929)

KERLOUÉGAN, F. 'Grégoire le Grand et les pays celtiques', in *Grégoire le Grand* edd. Fontaine *et al.* 589–96

KERLOUÉGAN, F. *Le De Excidio Britanniae de Gildas: les destinées de la culture latine dans l'île de Bretagne au VIe siècle* (Paris 1987)

KERMODE, P.M.C. & WILSON, D. *Manx Crosses* (Balgavies 1994)

KIM, H.C. (ed.) *The Gospel of Nicodemus* Toronto Medieval Latin Texts 2 (Toronto 1973)

KIRBY, D.P. (ed.) *Saint Wilfrid at Hexham* (Newcastle upon Tyne 1974)

KLINGSHIRN, W.E. *Caesarius of Arles: the Making of a Christian Community in Late Antique Gaul* (Cambridge 1994)

KOTTJE, R. *Studien zum Einfluss des alten Testamentes auf Recht und Liturgie des frühen Mittelalters (6–8 Jahrhundert)* Bonner historische Forschungen 23 (Bonn 1970)

KRAPP, G.P. (ed.) *The Vercelli Book* (New York 1932)

KRAPP, G.P. & DOBBIE, E.V.K. (edd.) *The Exeter Book* (New York 1936)

KRUSCH, G.P. (ed.) *Ionae Vitae Sanctorum Columbani, Vedastis, Iohannis* MGH (Hanover 1905)

KUYPERS, A.B. *The Prayer Book of Aedeluald the Bishop commonly called The Book of Cerne* (Cambridge 1902)

LADNER, G.B. 'St Gregory of Nyssa and St Augustine on the symbolism of the Cross', in *Late Classical and Medieval Studies* ed. Weitzmann 88–95

LADNER, G.B. *The Idea of Reform* (New York 1967)

LAKE, K. (ed. and tr.) *Eusebius, The Ecclesiastical History* 2 vols. (Cambridge MA 1965)

LAMBKIN, B. 'Blathmac and the Céili Dé: a reappraisal', *Celtica* 23 (1999) 132–54

LAPIDGE, M. 'A seventh-century Insular Latin debate poem on divorce', *CMCS* 10 (1985) 1–23

LAPIDGE, M. 'Aediluuf and the School of York', in *Lateinische Kultur im VIII. Jahrhundert* edd. Lehner & Berschin 161–78

LAPIDGE, M. (ed.) *Archbishop Theodore* Cambridge Studies in Anglo-Saxon England 11 (Cambridge 1995)

LAPIDGE, M. (ed.) *Columbanus: Studies on the Latin Writings* Studies in Celtic History 17 (Woodbridge 1997)

LAPIDGE, M. 'Gildas' education and the Latin culture of sub-Roman Britain', in *Gildas* edd. Lapidge & Dumville 27–50

LAPIDGE, M. '*Precamur patrem*: an Easter hymn by Columbanus?', in *Columbanus* ed. Lapidge 255–63

LAPIDGE, M. 'The career of Archbishop Theodore', in *Archbishop Theodore* ed. Lapidge 1–29

LAPIDGE, M. & DUMVILLE, D. (edd.) *Gildas: New Approaches* Studies in Celtic History 5 (Woodbridge 1984)

LAPIDGE, M. & HERREN, M.W. (tr.) *Aldhelm, the Prose Works* (Cambridge 1979)

LAPIDGE, M. & ROSIER, J. (tr.) *Aldhelm, the Poetic Works* (Cambridge 1985)

LAPIDGE, M. & SHARPE, R. *A Bibliography of Celtic-Latin Literature 400–1200* (Dublin 1985)

Le GOFF, J. *The Birth of Purgatory*, tr. A. Goldhammer (Chicago IL 1984)

LEHNER, A. & BERSCHIN, W. (edd.) *Lateinische Kultur im VIII. Jahrhundert: Traube-Gedenkschrift* (St Ottilien 1989)

LEVISON, W. 'An eighth-century poem on Ninian', *Antiquity* 14 (1940) 280–91

LEWIS, S. 'Sacred calligraphy: the Chi-Rho page in the Book of Kells', *Traditio* 36 (1980) 139–59

LINDSAY, W.M. *Isidori Hispalensis Episcopi: Etymologiarum Sive Originum* 2 vols. (Oxford 1911)

LÖFSTEDT, B. Review of Cahill (ed.), *Expositio Evangelii Secundum Marcum*, *Peritia* 12 (1998) 434–6

MACALISTER, R.A.S. *The Memorial Slabs of Clonmacnois* (Dublin 1909)

MacCULLOCH, J.A. *The Harrowing of Hell: a Comparative Study of an Early Christian Doctrine* (Edinburgh 1930)

MacDONALD, A.D.S. 'Aspects of the monastery and monastic life in Adomnán's Life of Columba', *Peritia* 3 (1984) 271–302

MacGINTY, G. 'The Treatise *De Mirabilibus Sacrae Scripturae*: Critical Edition with Introduction, English Translation of the Long Recension and Some Notes', unpublished Ph.D. dissertation (Dublin, National University of Ireland 1971)

MACKIE, W.S. (ed.) *The Exeter Book Part II: Poems IX–XXXII* Early English Text Society 104 (Oxford 1934)

MacLEAN, D. 'The date of the Ruthwell Cross', in *The Ruthwell Cross* ed. Cassidy 49–70

Mac NIOCAILL, G. & WALLACE, P. (edd.) *Keimelia: Studies in Medieval Archaeology and History in Memory of Tom Delaney* (Galway 1988)

MacQUARRIE, A. *The Saints of Scotland: Essays in Scottish History A.D. 450–1093* (Edinburgh 1997)

MacQUEEN, J. *St Nynia with a Translation of the* Miracula Nynie Episcopi *and the* Vita Niniani *by Winifred MacQueen* (Edinburgh 1990)

MARKUS, R.A. 'Pelagianism: Britain and the Continent', *Journal of Ecclesiastical History* 37/2 (April 1986) 191–204

MARKUS, R.A. 'The legacy of Pelagius: orthodoxy, heresy and conciliation', in *The Making of Orthodoxy* ed. Williams 214–34

MAURER, C. 'Gospel of Peter', in *New Testament Apocrypha* edd. Hennecke & Schneemelcher, I.179–81

McCONE, K. *Pagan Past and Christian Present in Early Irish Literature* Maynooth Monographs 3 (Maynooth 1990)

McCONE, K. & SIMMS, K. (edd.) *Progress in Medieval Irish Studies* (Maynooth 1996)

McENTIRE, S. 'The devotional context of the Cross before A.D. 1000', in *Sources of Anglo-Saxon Culture* ed. Szarmach & Oggins 345–56

McGURK, P. *Latin Gospel Books from A.D. 400 to A.D. 800* (Paris 1961)

McNALLY, R.E. '*Dies dominica*: two Hiberno-Latin texts', *Medieval Studies* 22 (1960) 355–61.

McNALLY, R.E. 'The Evangelists in the Hiberno-Saxon tradition', in *Festschrift Bernhard Bischoff*, edd. Autenrieth & Brunhölzl 111–22

McNAMARA, M. *The Apocrypha in the Early Irish Church* (Dublin 1975)

McNAMARA, M. 'The inverted eucharistic formula *Conversio Corporis Christi in Panem et Sanguinis in Vinum*: the exegetical and liturgical background in Irish usage', *PRIA* 87C (1987) 573–93

McNEILL, J.J. *The Celtic Churches. A History A.D. 200 to 1200* (Chicago 1974)

MEEHAN, B. *The Book of Kells* (London 1994)

MEEHAN, B. *The Book of Durrow* (Dublin 1996)

MEEHAN, D. *Adamnan's De Locis Sanctis* (Dublin 1958)

MEEK, D.E. *The Quest for Celtic Christianity* (Edinburgh 2000)

MEYER, K. 'An Old Irish treatise *De Arreis*', *Revue celtique* 15 (1894) 485–98

MEYVAERT, P. 'An Apocalypse panel on the Ruthwell Cross', in *Medieval and Renaissance Studies* ed. Tirro 3–32

MEYVAERT, P. 'A new perspective on the Ruthwell Cross: Ecclesia and Vita Monastica', in *The Ruthwell Cross* ed. Cassidy 95–166

MILLER, M.W. (ed. and tr.) *Rufini Presbyteri Liber De Fide* (Washington DC 1964)

MOMMSEN, T. (ed.) *Chronica minora saec. IV.V.VI.VII*, MGH Auctores Anti-quissi IX (Berlin 1892)

MOREL, C. (ed. and tr.) *Gregoire le Grand: Homélies sur Ezechiel 1 (Livre I). Texte latin, introduction, traduction et notes SC* 327 (Paris 1986)

MORIN, G. 'On the opinions of the lord Caesarius against those who explain why God gives grace to some but not to others', *Revue Bénédictine* 13 (1896) 481–5

MORRIS, J.R. 'Pelagian literature', *Journal of Theological Studies* new series 16 (1965) 26–60

MULCHRONE, K. *Bethu Phátraic* (Dublin 1939)

MÜLLER, H.-G. *Hrabanus Maurus, De laudibus sanctae crucis* Beiheft zum *Mittellateinischem Jahrbuch* 11 (Dusseldorf 1973)

MUNZ, P. 'John Cassian', *Journal of Ecclesiastical History* 11 (1960) 1–22

MURPHY, D. (ed.) *The Annals of Clonmacnoise* (Dublin 1993)

MURPHY, G. (ed. and tr.) *Early Irish Lyrics: Eighth to Twelfth Century* (Oxford 1956)

NASH-WILLIAMS, V.E. *The Early Christian Monuments of Wales* (Cardiff 1950)

NERNEY, D.S. 'A study of St Patrick's sources: II – The Doctine of Divine Vocation', *Irish Ecclesiastical Record* 72 (1949) 14–26

NERNEY, D.S. 'A study of St Patrick's sources: IV – Proof of Divine Vocation', *Irish Ecclesiastical Record* 72 (1949) 265–80

NÍ CHATHÁIN, P. 'Bede's Ecclesiastical History in Irish', *Peritia* 3 (1980) 115–30

NÍ CHATHÁIN, P. & RICHTER, M. (edd.) *Irland und die Christenheit: Bibelstudien und Mission/ Ireland and Christendom: the Bible and the Mission* (Stuttgart 1987)

NÍ CHATHÁIN, P. & RICHTER, M. (edd.) *Irland und Europa: die Kirche im Frühmittelalter/ Ireland and Europe: the Early Church* (Stuttgart 1984)

NÍ DHONNCHADHA, M. '*Caillech* and other terms for veiled women in medieval Irish texts', *Éigse* 28 (1994–5) 71–96

O'BEIRNE CROWE, J. *The Amra Cholium Chilli of Dallan Forgaill* (Dublin 1871)

Ó CARRAGÁIN, É. 'Christ over the beasts and the Agnus Dei: two multivalent panels on the Ruthwell and Bewcastle Crosses', in *Sources of Anglo-Saxon Culture* edd. Szarmach & Oggins 377–403

Ó CARRAGÁIN, É. 'Liturgical innovations associated with Pope Sergius and the iconography of the Ruthwell and Bewcastle crosses', in *Bede and Anglo-Saxon England* ed. Farrell 131–47

Ó CARRAGÁIN, É. 'Meeting of Saint Paul and Saint Anthony: visual and literary uses of a eucharistic motif', in *Keimelia*, edd. MacNiocaill & Wallace 1–80

Ó CARRAGÁIN, É. 'The necessary distance: *Imitatio Romae* and the Ruthwell Cross', in *Northumbria's Golden Age* ed. Hawkes & Mills 191–203

Ó CARRAGÁIN, É. 'The Ruthwell Crucifixion poem in its iconographic and liturgical contexts', *Peritia* 6–7 (1988) 1–71

Ó CARRAGÁIN, É. '*Traditio evangeliorum* and *sustenatio*: the relevance of liturgical ceremonies to the Book of Kells', in *The Book of Kells* ed. O'Mahony 398–436

O'COLLINS, G. *Christology: a Biblical, Historical, and Systematic Study of Jesus* (Oxford 1995)

Ó CORRÁIN, D. 'Irish vernacular law and the Old Testament', in *Irland und die Christenheit* edd. Ní Chatháin & Richter 284–307

Ó CORRÁIN, D. *et al.* 'The laws of the Irish', *Peritia* 3 (1984) 382–438

Ó CRÓINÍN, D. 'Bischoff's *Wendepunkte* fifty years on', *Revue Bénédictine* 110.3–4 (2000) 204–37

Ó CRÓINÍN, D. 'New heresy for old: Pelagianism in Ireland and the papal letter of 640', *Speculum* 60/3 (July 1985) 505–16

Ó CRÓINÍN, D. 'New light on Palladius', *Peritia* 5 (1986) 276–83

Ó CRÓINÍN, D. 'The computistical works of Columbanus', in *Columbanus* ed. Lapidge 264–73

Ó CRÓINÍN, D. 'Who was Palladius "First Bishop of the Irish"?', *Peritia* 14 (2000) 206–37

Ó CUÍV, B. 'Some early devotional verse in Irish', *Ériu* 19 (1962) 1–24.

O'DWYER, P. *Céli Dé: Spiritual Reform in Ireland, 750–900* 2nd ed. (Dublin 1981)

Ó FLOINN, R. 'A fragmentary house-shaped shrine from Clonard, Co. Meath', *The Journal of Irish Archaeology* 5 (1989/90) 49–55

O'LOUGHLIN, T. 'Adomnán and Arculf: the case of an expert witness', *JMLat* 7 (1997) 127–46

O'LOUGHLIN, T. *Celtic Theology* (London 2000)

OLSON, L. *Early Monasteries in Cornwall* Studies in Celtic History 11 (Woodbridge 1989)

O'MAHONY, F. (ed.) *The Book of Kells: Proceedings of a Conference at Trinity College Dublin 6–9 September 1992* (Aldershot 1994)

Ó MAIDÍN, U. (tr.) *The Celtic Monk: Rules and Writings of Early Irish Monks* Cistercian Studies Series 162 (Kalamazoo MI 1996)

O'MEARA, J.J. & NAUMANN, B. (edd.) *Latin Script and Letters A.D. 400–900: Festschrift presented to Ludwig Bieler on the Occasion of his 70th Birthday* (Leiden 1976)

Ó NÉILL, P. '*Romani* influences on seventh-century Hiberno-Latin literature', in *Irland und Europa* edd. Ní Chatháin & Richter 280–90

Ó NÉILL, P. 'The date and authorship of the Apgitir Chrábrad', in *Irland und die Christenheit* edd. Ní Chatháin & Richter 203–15

O'RAHILLY, C. *Ireland and Wales: their Historical and Literary Relations* (London 1924)

O'RAHILLY, T.F. *The Two Patricks: a Lecture on the History of Christianity in Fifth-century Ireland* (Dublin 1942)

ORCHARD, A. '*Audite omnes amantes*: a hymn in Patrick's praise', in *St Patrick* ed. Dumville 153–73

ORCHARD, A. 'Hot lust in a cold climate: comparison and contrast in the Old Norse versions of the Life of Mary of Egypt', in *The Legend of Mary of Egypt* edd. Poppe & Ross 175–204

ORCHARD, A. *The Poetic Art of Aldhelm* Cambridge Studies in Anglo-Saxon England 4 (Cambridge 1994)

O'REILLY, J. 'Early medieval text and image: the wounded and exalted Christ', *Peritia* 6–7 (1987–8) 72–118

Ó RÍORDÁIN, S.P. 'The genesis of the Celtic cross', in *Féilscríbhinn Tórna* ed. Pender 108–14

PAINTER, K.S. *The Water Newton Early Christian Silver* (London 1977)

PELIKAN, J. *Jesus through the Centuries: his Place in the History of Culture* (New Haven CT 1985)

PELIKAN, J. *The Christian Tradition: a History of the Development of Doctrine* 4 vols. (Chicago IL 1971–)

PENDER, S. (ed.) *Féilscríbhinn Torna: Essays presented to Professor Tadhg Ua Donnchadha* (Cork 1947)

PERRIN, M. *Raban Maur: Louanges de la Sainte Croix* (Paris 1988)

PICARD, J.-M. 'The marvellous in Irish and continental saints' Lives of the Merovingian period', in *Columbanus and Merovingian Monasticism* edd. Clarke & Brennan 91–104

PICHERY, E. (ed.) *Jean Cassien Conférences SC* 42, 54, 64 3 vols. (Paris 1955–9)

PLUMMER, C. (ed.) *Baedae Opera Historica* (Oxford 1896 1975)

PLUMMER, C. (ed. and tr.) *Irish Litanies* (London 1925)

POLARA, G. (ed.) *Virgilio Marone grammatico: Epitomi ed Epistole* (Naples 1979)

PONTAL, O. *Histoire des conciles mérovingiens* (Paris 1989)

POPPE, E. & ROSS, B. (edd.) *The Legend of Mary of Egypt in Medieval Insular Hagiography* (Dublin 1996)

RYAN, M. (ed.) *Ireland and Insular Art A.D. 500–1200* (Dublin 1987)

[PROSPER], *Sancti Prosperi Aquitani S. Augustini discipuli, S. Leonis Papae Notarii, Opera Omnia ad Manuscriptos Codices, necnon ad Antiquiores et Castigatiores Emendata . . . Editio Secunda Veneta* 2 vols. (Venice 1782)

PRYCE, H. (ed.) *Literacy in Medieval Celtic Societies* Cambridge Studies in Medieval Literature 53 (Cambridge 1998)

RADNER, J.N. (ed. and tr.) *Fragmentary Annals of Ireland* (Dublin 1978)

RAMSEY, B. *John Cassian: the Conferences* Ancient Christian Writers: the Works of the Fathers in Translation 57 (New York 1997)

RCAHMS *Argyll: an Inventory of the Monuments, 4, Iona* (Edinburgh 1982)

REES, B.R. *Pelagius: a Reluctant Heretic* (Woodbridge 1988)

REES, B.R. *The Letters of Pelagius and his Followers* (Woodbridge 1991)

RICHARDSON, H. 'Number and symbol in early Christian Irish art', *JRSAI* 114 (1984) 28–47

ROE, H. 'A stone cross at Clogher, Co.Tyrone', *JRSAI* 90 (1960) 191–206

ROE, H. *Monasterboice and its Monuments* (Meath 1981)

ROE, H. *The High Crosses of Kells* (Kells 1975)

ROE, H. *The High Crosses of Western Ossory* (Kilkenny 1969)

ROE, H. 'The Irish high cross: morphology and iconography', *JRSAI* 95 (1965) 213–26

ROUSSEAU, A. & DOUTRELEAU, L. (edd. and tr.) *Irénée de Lyon: Contre les hérésies. Livre III. Édition critique. 2 Texte et traduction* SC 211 (Paris 1974)

RUSSELL, P. 'The sounds of a silence: the growth of Cormac's Glossary', *CMCS* 15 (1988) 1–30

RYAN, M. 'Decorated metalwork in the Museo del'Abbazia, Bobbio, Italy', *JRSAI* 120 (1990) 102–11

SCHALLER, D. '*De mundi transitu*: a rhythmical poem by Columbanus', in *Columbanus* ed. Lapidge 240–54

SCHAPIRO, M. 'The religious meaning of the Ruthwell Cross', *The Art Bulletin* 26 (1944) 232–45

SHANZER, D. '*Iuvenes vestri visiones videbunt*: Visions and the literary sources of Patrick's *Confessio*', *JMLat* 3 (1993) 169–201

SHARPE, R. (tr.) *Adomnán of Iona: Life of St Columba* (London 1995)

SHARPE, R. 'An Irish textual critic and the *Carmen paschale* of Sedulius: Colmán's letter to Feradach', *JMLat* 2 (1992) 44–54

SHARPE, R. 'Gildas as a Father of the Church', in *Gildas* edd. Lapidge & Dumville 193–205

SHARPE, R. *Medieval Irish Saints' Lives: an Introduction to* Vitae Sanctorum Hiberniae (Oxford 1991)

SHARPE, R. 'Saint Mauchteus, *discipulus Patricii*', in *Britain 400–600* edd. Bammesberger & Wollman 85–93

SHARPE, R. 'Some problems concerning the organization of the Church in early medieval Ireland', *Peritia* 3 (1984) 230–60

SIEGMUND, P.A. *Die Überlieferung der griechischen christlichen Literatur in der lateinischen Kirche bis zum zwölften Jahrhundert* (Munich 1949)

SIMS-WILLIAMS, P. *Religion and Literature in Western England, 600–800* Cambridge Studies in Anglo-Saxon England 3 (Cambridge 1990)

SIMS-WILLIAMS, P. 'The uses of writing in early medieval Wales', in *Literacy in Medieval Celtic Societies* ed. Pryce 15–38

SMITH, T.A. *De Gratia: Faustus of Riez's Treatise on Grace and its Place in the History of Theology* Christianity and Judaism in Antiquity 4 (Notre Dame IN 1990)

SMYTH, A.P. 'The earliest Irish annals: their first contemporary entries and the earliest centres of recording', *PRIA* 72C (1972) 1–48

SOUTER, A. (ed.) *Pelagius's Expositions of Thirteen Epistles of St Paul* (Cambridge 1922)

SPEARMAN, R.M. & HIGGITT, J. (edd.) *The Age of Migrating Ideas: Early Medieval Art in Northern Britain and Ireland* (Edinburgh 1993)

STALLEY, R. 'European art and the Irish high cross', *PRIA* 90 C/6 (1990) 135–58

STANCLIFFE, C. 'Cuthbert and the polarity between pastor and solitary', in *St Cuthbert, his cult, and his community*, edd. Bonner *et al.* 21–44

STANCLIFFE, C. 'Red, white and blue martyrdom', in *Ireland in Medieval Europe* edd. Whitelock *et al.* 21–46

STANCLIFFE, C. 'The miracle stories in seventh-century Irish saints' Lives', in *La Septième siècle: changements et continuités/The Seventh Century: Change and Continuity* edd. Fontaine & Hillgarth 87–115

STANCLIFFE, C. 'The thirteen sermons attributed to Columbanus and the question of their authorship', in *Columbanus* ed. Lapidge 93–202

STEVENS, W.O. *The Cross in the Life and Literature of the Anglo-Saxons* Yale Studies in English 22 (New York 1904)

STEVENSON, J.B. 'Altus Prosator', *Celtica* 23 (1999) 326–68

STEVENSON, J.B. 'The holy sinner: the life of Mary of Egypt', in *The Legend of Mary of Egypt* edd. Poppe & Ross 19–50

STEVENSON, J.B. *The Liturgy and Ritual of the Celtic Church* (F.E. Warren) 2nd ed. (Woodbridge 1987)

STEVENSON, J.B. 'The monastic rules of Columbanus', in *Columbanus* ed. Lapidge 203–16

STEVENSON, R.B.K. 'Brooches and pins: some seventh- to ninth-century problems', in *Ireland and Insular Art A.D. 500–1200* ed. Ryan 90–5

STEVENSON, R.B.K. 'The chronology and relationships of some Irish and Scottish crosses', *JRSAI* 86 (1956) 84–96

STEWART, C. *Cassian the Monk* (Oxford 1998)

STOKES, M. & BURTON, T.L. (edd.) *Medieval Literature and Antiquities: Studies in Honour of Basil Cottle* (Cambridge 1987)

STOKES, W. *Saltair na Rann* (Oxford 1833)

STOKES, W. 'The Bodleian *Amra Choluimb Chille*', *Revue celtique* 20 (1899) 30–55, 133–83, 248–89, 400–37

STOKES, W. *Three Irish Glossaries* (London 1862)

STOKES, W. & STRACHAN, J. (edd.) *Thesaurus Palaeo-Hibernicus: a Collection of Old-Irish Glosses, Scholia, Prose and Verse* 2 vols. (Cambridge 1901–3)

STRIJBOSCH, C. *The Seafaring Saint* (tr. T. Summerfield) (Dublin 2000)

SZARMACH, P.E. & OGGINS, Y.D. (edd.) *Sources of Anglo-Saxon Culture* (Kalamazoo MI 1986)

THACKER, A. 'Bede's ideal of reform', in *Ideal and Reality in Frankish and Anglo-Saxon Society* edd. Bullough *et al.* 130–53

THOMAS, C. *Christianity in Roman Britain to A.D. 500* (London 1981)

THOMPSON, E.A. *Who Was Saint Patrick?* 2nd edn (Woodbridge 1999)

TIBILETTI, C. 'Libero arbitrio e grazia in Fausto di Riez', *Augustinianum* 11 (1979) 259–85

TIRRO, F. (ed.) *Medieval and Renaissance Studies, IX.* Proceedings of the Southeastern Institute of Medieval and Renaissance Studies, Summer 1978 (Durham NC 1982)

URBA, C.F. & ZYCHA, J. (edd.) *Sancti Aureli Augustini CSEL* XLII (Vienna 1902)

VAN DAM, R. *Leadership and Community in Late Antique Gaul* (Berkeley 1985)

VEELENTURF, K. *Dia Brátha: Eschatological Theophanies and Irish High Crosses* (Amsterdam 1997)

VAN HAMEL, A.G. 'The foreign notes in the "Three Fragments of Irish Annals"', *Revue celtique* 36 (1915) 13–15

WALKER, G.S.M. (ed. and tr.) *Sancti Columbani Opera* (Dublin 1957)

WALPOLE, A.S. *Early Latin Hymns* (Cambridge 1922)

WALSH, M. & Ó CRÓINÍN, D. (edd. and tr.) *Cummian's Letter* De Controversia Paschali *and the* De Ratione Conputandi (Toronto 1988)

WALZ, D. (ed.) *Lateinische Biographie zwischen Antike und Neuzeit* Festschrift Walter Berschin (Heidelberg 2002)

WARD, B. *Harlots of the Desert: a Study of Repentance in Early Monastic Sources* (Kalamazoo MI 1987)

WARREN, F.E. (ed.) *Antiphonary of Bangor: an Early Irish Manuscript in the Ambrosian Library at Milan* 2 vols. Henry Bradshaw Society 4 (London 1893–5)

WASSERSCHLEBEN, H. *Die irische Kanonensammlung* (Leipzig 1885)

WEIGEL, G. *Faustus of Riez: a Historical Introduction* (Philadelphia PA 1938)

WEITZMANN, K. (ed.) *Late Classical and Medieval Studies in Honor of Albert Mathias Friend, Jr.* (Princeton 1955)

WELLDON, J. (ed.) *Sancti Aurelii Augustini Episcopi, De civitate Dei* 2 vols. (New York 1924)

WERNER, M. 'The cross-carpet page in the Book of Durrow: the cult of the True Cross, Adomnan, and Iona', *The Art Bulletin* 72/2 (1990) 174–223

WERNER, M. 'The four evangelist symbols page in the Book of Durrow', *Gesta* 8/1 (1969) 3–17

WHITELOCK, D. *et al.* (edd.) *Ireland in Early Medieval Europe: Studies in Memory of Kathleen Hughes* (Cambridge 1982)

WICKHAM, L. 'Pelagianism in the East', in *The Making of Orthodoxy* ed. Williams 200–13

WILKINSON, J. (tr.) *Egeria's Travels* (London 1971)

WILLIAMS, R. (ed.) *The Making of Orthodoxy: Essays in Honour of Henry Chadwick* (Cambridge 1989)

WILSON, D.M. *Anglo-Saxon Art from the Seventh Century to the Norman Conquest* (London 1984)

WINTERBOTTOM, M. (ed. and tr.) *Gildas: the Ruin of Britain and Other Works* (London 1979)

WOOD, I. 'The end of Roman Britain', in *Gildas* edd. Lapidge & Dumville 1–25

WORMALD, P. 'Bede and Benedict Biscop', in *Famulus Christi* ed. Bonner 141–69

WRIGHT, C. 'Bischoff's theory of exegesis and the Genesis commentary in Munich clm 6302: a critique of a critique', *JMLat* 10 (2000) 115–75

WRIGHT, C. *The Irish Tradition in Old English Literature* Cambridge Studies in Anglo-Saxon England 6 (Cambridge 1993)

WRIGHT, N. 'The *Hisperica Famina* and Caelius Sedulius', *CMCS* 4 (Winter 1982) 61–76

YOUNGS, S. *'The Work of Angels': Masterpieces of Celtic Metalwork, 6th–9th Centuries A.D.* (London 1990)

ZIMMER, H. *Pelagius in Irland: Texte und Untersuchungen zur patristischen Literatur* (Berlin 1901)

ZIMMER, H. *The Celtic Church in Britain and Ireland* (tr. A. Meyer) (London 1902)

303

INDEX

Aaron
  symbol of priesthood 254, 264–5
abbot(s)
  in orders 40
  lay abbacy in Ireland 32
  master in own house 145
  office of 32, 34, 41
  status equivalent to bishop 38
Abraham, abbot 35
Acca 207
  cross at Hexham 207–9, 237; fig. ii.a
acrostic poems 197
Acts of Peter and Paul 161–2, 165
  see also Passions of
Acts of Pilate
  Irish version of 253
Adam
  Adam and Eve 271
  burial site of 270
  created mortal 72, 92
  fall or sin of 71
  fate of 93
  imitation of sin of 71, 75, 122
  prayer of 159
  transmission of sin of 71, 75, 122
Adelphus adelpha meter, poem 94
Adomnán 223
  Life of Columba 109, 110, 120, 166, 198
  De locis sanctis 196–7
Adoptianism 51
Aelfric 197, 201
Æthelbehrt, king 38, 39
Æthelthryth, marriage dissolved 3
agapé vessels 188
Agatho, pope 55, 234
Agilulf, king of Lombardy
  and the Aquileian Schism 53, 54
Agnus Dei: see Lamb of God
Ahenny crosses 201–6, 212, 234, 237; plate 1
Aidan, monk and bishop 40, 171
  rule introduced by at Lindisfarne 41
Ailerán, *sapiens* 283
Ailred of Rievaulx 23

Alban, St 86
Alcuin 38
  Ad aram sanctae crucis 197
  Ad sanctam crucem 197
  Crux decus es mundi 197
Aldhelm 1, 38, 40, 47, 171
  Anglo-Latin rhythmical poem 146 n.146
  appointment as abbot of Malmesbury 41
  De virginitate (*On Virginity*) 43, 169
  Ecclesiastical Poems 190
  education 116, 170
  knew the *Letter to Demetrius* 97–8
  Letter to King Geraint 58–9, 60, 106, 133
  partisan of Roman orthodoxy 170
  use of martyrologies 169
allegory: see exegesis
Alpha and *Omega* 257
  see Christ
Alphabet of Piety: see *Apgitir Chrábaid*
Altus prosator, hymn 96
Ambrose, St 209, 230
  Hexaemeron 263
Amra Choluimb Chille 110, 118, 119, 120, 152, 153, 167
Anastasius 216
anchorite, anchoritic life 150, 242, 247–8
Annales Cambriae, 105
Anonymus ad Cuimnanum 115
Anglo-Saxon England
  religious art 18
ankh hieroglyph 199
Antiphonary of Bangor 156, 279, 284
Anthony and Paul of Thebes: see Paul and Anthony, hermits
Apgitir Chrábaid 99–100, 106, 117, 118
apocalyptic literature 153
Apocalypse of Paul 153, 170
Apocalypse of Peter 153
Apocalypse, scenes from 174
apocrypha: see scriptures
Apostle's Creed 156, 174, 281
Aquileian Schism 53

archiepiscopal seat
  posited for Ireland 168
Arculf
  description of cross on Golgotha 196
  voyage of 197
Ardagh chalice 192, 193, 203, 205, 206
Anglian crosses 206–7
arbor vitae: see tree of life
Arianism, heresy 51–2, 54, 64, 76
Arius 51–2
Armagh 122, 275, 279
Artbrannan 95
askesis/asceticism 5, 14, 36, 37, 71, 120,
    148, 172–4, 238, 278, 280
  see also discipline
  and *theoria* 145–6
  ascetic movements 76
  Celtic asceticism 167
  meaning of term 77
  private asceticism 279
  privileged by Christ 140
athleta Dei 14
Athlone plaque 20, 217, 219, 237, 241,
    253–6, 260; plate 12
Audite omnes amantes (hymn on St
    Patrick) 118, 119, 120, 139
Augustine of Canterbury 18, 40, 116,
    171, 205
  mission to England 22, 38
  correspondence with Pope Gregory I
    39
Augustine of Hippo 7, 11, 14, 21, 69, 70,
    73, 74, 80, 108, 122, 151, 175
  Augustinian theology,
    Augustinianism 7, 8, 13, 16, 69, 96,
    100, 155, 156, 282
  Confessions 71
  De civitate Dei (*City of God*) 162, 163,
    282
  De trinitate 71
  doctrine of grace 71, 76, 77, 78, 80
  doctrine of predestination 79
Auxilius 31
azyma (feast of unleavened bread) 59

Bangor 285
  Viking attack on 275
baptism
  forgiveness after 95, 96
  grace of 11, 71, 76, 90, 134, 151, 257–8,
    271
  not necessary for perfect life 95

of infants 5, 73, 84, 122, 134, 279
  pre-Augustinian views of 123
  removes all sins 84
  sin committed after 73, 82
Barberini Gospels 214, 227, 228, fig. iii.c,
    plate 6
Bede 1, 22, 39, 47, 56, 60, 63, 120–1, 142,
    145, 150, 153, 171, 197, 201, 205
  Commentary on Canticles 97–8, 145
  Commentary on Job 263
  Commentary on Luke 241
  Ecclesiastical History 2, 38, 61, 62,
    106, 148, 171, 173
  History of the Abbots 171, 235
  knowledge of Pelagian writings 97–8
  Life of Cuthbert 40, 149, 171, 172, 239
  lives of Felix and Anastasius 171
  On the day of Judgement, poem 154,
    177
Benedict Biscop 18, 234, 235
  abbot of SS Peter and Paul 40
  and church of St Peter 174
  as arch-abbot 41
  dissolution of marriage 43
  monasteries in Northumbria 41, 239
Benedict of Nursia 169
Benedictinism 33, 41
  Benedictine monk 148
  Benedictine Reform 38
  Benedictine Rule 33 n.65, 41, 45
Betha Adamnáin 110 n.22
Bewcastle cross 209–11, 218, 227, 232,
    235, 237, 239, fig. ii.b-d
Bigotian Penitential 127
bird
  as symbol of soul 273
  resuscitating dead Christ 282
bishops
  authority of 31, 34, 36
  presence of 32
  restricted to diocese 32
Blathmac
  Poem to Mary and her Son 157–8, 159,
    176, 177, 213, 249, 252, 262, 265,
    268, 271, 273, 274, 281, 282
bonum naturale 10, 11, 95
Book of the Angel 33, 121
Book of Armagh 228; plate 7
  prologues to Pauline Epistles 98
Book of Cerne
  poem on harrowing of hell 159
'book of the devil' 266

Book of Durrow 203, 213, 215–17, 220, 221, 224, 226, 228, 230; plates 2, 5
Book of Kells 20, 213, 214, 215-17, 221, 222, 228, 229, 230, 231, 243–50, 262, 272, 282; fig.iv, plates 3, 8, 10, 11, 15
breastplate 255–6
'breastplate of judgement' 254
Brigit, St 2
  compared to Christ 168
  miracles of 168–9
  not ascetic 169
British Church 4, 7, 25, 104, 106, 109, 117–18, 156, 189, 278
  British Christianity 25–8, 116, 278
  British Christians resident in Ireland 81
  British clergy in Ireland 104, 105
  British virgins resident in Ireland 26
  continental contacts 105
Bugga, church of 190
burial 33
  marked by crosses 192
Byzantium 53

Caedwalla, king 198
Caesarius of Arles 7, 8, 80
  treatise on grace 80
Caí Cáinbrethach 114
Cáin Domnaig (Law of Sunday) 110
Calf of Man, slab 255, fig. v
Cambrai Homily 142, 147
Candida Casa 22–3, 27
  see also Whithorn
Canterbury
  Church of the Holy Saviour 39
  Monastery of SS Peter and Paul 39–40
Cardonagh slab cross 251, 258
Carmen de ave phoenice 263
Carolingian painting/art 243, 275
'Caspari Corpus' 70, 126
Cassian of Marseilles (John Cassian) 7, 14, 24, 35, 42, 69, 106, 117, 124, 145, 147, 148, 241, 275
  Conferences 24, 77, 120, 121, 128, 143
  grace and free will 77
  influence on Faustus and Columbanus 24
  Institutes 24, 77

  on contemplative life 141–2, 143, 148, 240
  on healing 121
  on poverty 146
  scriptural preferences 117
  Second Conference 247
  Tenth Conference (on Prayer) 190
  Thirteenth Conference 77–8, 79
  writings known in Insular world 191
catechumen, catechumenate 123
Celestine, pope 81, 278
Célí Dé (culdees) 17, 35, 36–8, 43, 110, 125, 128, 192, 244, 275, 279, 280, 281
celibacy 27
  applied to clergy 29, 30, 37, 42
  partial celibacy for laity 30
Celtic, term 4
Celtic Christianity 1, 2, 4, 5, 7, 9, 13, 14, 15, 18, 19, 20, 109, 200, 264, 279
Celtic decorative motifs 19
Ceolfrid, abbot 198
  letter to Nechtan 58–9, 62
Chaeremon 78
Chi Rho 192, 193, 244, 263, 282
  see also under Christ, sacred monogram
Christ
  alpha and *omega* 187, 200, 257
  and fulfilment of the Law 63, 117
  and the two beasts 237–9, 240, 254
  as Breastplate 159, 219, 254–5, 258, 283
  as Good Shepherd 187
  as harrower of hell 138, 151–60, 177, 268–70
  as hero, heroic 16, 20, 120, 137, 138, 151–60, 177, 281
  as king 187
  as Logos 225, 226, 229, 230
  as judge 16, 20, 137, 138, 174–8, 236, 238, 242, 257, 260–7, 280
  as lawgiver 65, 75, 249, 280, 282
  as Messiah, anointed one 160, 186, 238, 254, 257
  as miracle-worker/wonder worker 120, 137, 160–74, 270–6
  as perfect monk 17, 20, 137, 138, 140–50, 177, 236–50, 260, 280
  as teacher/model/philospher 65, 75, 187, 278, 280
  at Gethsemani 245, 254

Christ (*cont.*):
  Christ/Hercules 187
  Christ/Moses 20, 245–6, 248
  Christ/Orpheus 187
  Christ/Priest 20, 254, 264
  Christ of the cross 15, 17, 280
  Christ of the desert 15, 147, 237, 239,
    266, 280
  cross as 19, 186, 189, 206, 221, 222,
    223, 224, 235, 238, 260
  crucified Christ 20, 137, 239, 250–60,
    282
  dead Christ 273
  divinity on the cross 256–60
  enthroned Christ 262, 264
  entombed Christ 273
  fish as 19, 186, 205, 225, 228, 229
  inhabited plant/vine scroll as 207, 209,
    211–12, 217, 239
  Lamb of God 230, 238, 260
  nature of (theology) 47–52, 53, 54, 55,
    64, 65, 177, 186, 253, 281, 282
  obedience of 75, 146–7
  on Mount of Olives 243–5, 254
  iudex aequitatis 16, 175, 237, 238, 260,
    280, 291
  red-backed, vengeful 16–17, 176, 262,
    265, 281, 282
  representational images of 18, 19, 20,
    189, 190, 213, 243, 251, 259, 275
  sacred monogram (*Chi Rho*) 19, 186–
    9, 205, 213, 217, 221, 224–32, 244
  Saviour, Redeemer 15, 65, 257, 266
  Second Person of the Trinity 186, 282
  Sol and *Luna* 258–9
  Sol Invictus 187
  Son of God 160, 186
  Son of Man 176, 260
  sonship of 75
  symbolic images of 18, 215, 232, 251,
    275, 281
  tree of life as 19, 207, 213, 217, 219,
    223–4, 227, 228, 232
  vine as 19, 186, 205, 207, 209, 213, 219,
    227, 228, 231, 232, 236, 244, 246,
    263
Christi autem page 226–7, 229
Christus militans 268–70, 283
Church of the Holy Saviour: see
  Canterbury
Church of the Saviour (Constantiniana):
  see Rome

Church of the Holy Sepulchre: see
  Jerusalem
clergy
  celibacy required of 30
  married 30, 32
  monastic 21, 22
  monks distinct from 29, 32, 34
  right of assigning penances 42
Clonard, monastery of 248
Clonmacnois, scripture crosses 213, 165,
  269, 273, 274
  incised cross forms fig. i
Clovesho 50
Codex Amiatinus 207
Coelestius 23, 69, 71, 72, 76, 92, 100, 156
coenobitism/coenobitic 21
Cogitosus
  Life of St Brigit 120, 167, 168–9
Collectio Canonum Hibernesium 98
Colmán, Irish bishop
  at Synod of Whitby 60, 63
colobium
  Christ depicted in 251, 258, 259
Columba/Colum-cille 2, 109–10, 120,
  198
  allegedly a Quattuordeciman 62
  Altus prosator, attrib. 50
  celebrated sabbath as well as Lord's
    Day 62
  community on Iona 34
  conversations with angels 145
  gift of prophecy 166
  journey to heaven 153
  mission to the Picts, to Alba 22, 145
  profession of faith, attrib. 50
  scriptural preferences 117
  taught by Uinniau 29, 124
Columban Church 286
Columbanus 2, 11, 24, 31, 35, 50, 99,
  105, 120, 144
  and ideal of literacy 116
  and the Three Chapters 53–4
  De mundi transitu (*On the World's
    Impermanence*) 118, 143
  Instructiones 34, 88–9, 118, 144, 145,
    175
  Letter to Pope Boniface IV 49, 53–4
  Letter to Pope Gregory I 63, 111
  lost commentary on Psalms 117 n.53,
    118
  mission to Gaul and Rhaetia 22
  Monk's Rule 34, 143, 146

omits discussion of resurrection
on obedience 147
on paschal lunar limits 60
on poverty 146
penitential of 32, 105
Precamur patrem, attrib. 285
profession of faith 47, 49
scriptural preferences 117
Sermo XI 88–9
commandements
  infractions of 107–8
  of Christ 108, 117, 126, 146
  Ten Commandments 108
Commentaries of Nicodemus (Greek) 252
common Celtic Church 3–9, 17, 18, 69,
  100, 104–34, 137–8, 146, 169,
  188–91, 206, 249, 272, 278, 279,
  282
  dissolution of 17, 106, 140, 278–9
communion
  see also eucharist
  frequent communion recommended
    127, 129
  worthiness of recipient 129
commutations (*arrae*) 125
  see also Old Irish Table of
    Commutations
Conlaeth, bishop 234
Constans II, emperor 55
Constantine, emperor 187, 191–2, 195,
  198, 203, 215, 219
Constantinople 198, 213
contemplation 141, 149, 191, 240, 275
  see also *theoria*
  equals leading a good life 144
continentes 30, 33, 37
Coptic cross: see *crux ansata*
'Cormac's Glossary' (*Sanas Cormaic*)
  114
Coroticus, British chieftain 25
Council
  see also Synods
  First Lateran (a.649) 51, 55, 56
  Lateran (a.680) 55
  of Arles 109
  of Carthage 76
  of Chalcedon 51,52
  of Constantinople I 51
  of Constantinople II (Fifth Council)
    51–3
  of Constantinople III 55
  of Ephesus 23, 51, 57, 76

  of Hatfield 50, 55–6
  of Hertford 41, 50, 58
  of Milevis 76
  of Mâcon 109
  of Nicaea 50, 57
  of Orléans 109
  of Toledo 156, 195
  of Vannes 27, 30, 32
  Quinisext 18, 250–1
cross 191–213
  see also Christ as cross
  Anglian 242
  cosmological 200, 216, 219, 268
  cult of 195–8
  cross-in-circle 193, 255
  discovery of 195–6
  double-armed 215
  equal-armed 206, 216, 220, 242
  garlanded cross 193
  incised cross slabs 193
  Irish devotion to 192
  Latin cross 195, 202, 217, 219, 221,
    256
  of the crucifixion 223, 270
  patriarchal 216
  ringed 199–201, 206, 217, 262
  'saltire cross' 221
  'scripture crosses' 213, 240, 251, 272,
    274
  'sign of the cross' 191–2
  standing high crosses 193, 195, 201,
    212
  true cross of Christ 215
  wooden 198, 199
cross carpet pages 215–20, 232, 255, 256,
  263
cross poems: see acrostic poems
cross vigil(s) 36, 192, 221, 244, 246, 258
  as 'Breastplate of Devotion' 246
crucified Christ, depictions of 250–60
crucifixion poem: see Dream of the
  Rood
crux gemmata 196, 197, 200, 202, 205,
  220
crux ansata 199, 215
crux decussata 225
Cumméne Ailbe (Cummeneus Albus)
  Liber de virtutibus sancti Columbae
  167
Cummian 2, 47, 63, 88, 106, 121, 204,
  234
  Commentary on Mark, attrib. 89

Cummian (*cont.*):
  Letter on the paschal controversy 60,
    62
  Penitential of 42, 105, 123
cura animarum: see pastoral care
curses, cursing 165–6
Cuthbert, monk and priest 40, 171
  see also St Cuthbert's coffin; and
    Bede, *Life of St Cuthbert*
  compared to Irish saints 172
  projection of Christ 150, 172
  spiritual retirement 149–50
Cuthburg, nun of Barking 43
Cynewulf
  Elene 197
Cyril, patriarch of Alexandria 55

David and his harp 267–8, 269, 270
David, St 4, 29, 87, 100
Day of Atonement 111–12
De divitiis (*On Riches*), Pelagian work
    24, 74, 85–6, 131, 189
De doctoribus malis (*On Bad Teachers*),
    Pelagian work 107
De mirabilibus sacrae scripturae (*On the
    miracles of holy scripture*), 91–4,
    96, 100, 119, 122, 162–3, 164, 279,
    280
*De sollemnitatibus et sabbatis et
    neomeniis* (*On Festivities*) 106, 111,
    114, 280
  attrib. to Jerome and Columbanus 111
De virginitate (*On Virginity*), Pelagian
    work 81
'Debate Poem' 43–4
Derrynaflan chalice and paten 192, 205
descent into hell 156, 269, 270, 272, 273
  see also harrowing of hell
  descensus 157, 267
  Irish version of 159, 167
Desert Fathers
  lives of 150
  as models of virginity 169
devil 246–7, 248–9, 258, 266, 269, 273
  see also Satan
Díchu 95
Dies dominica 100, 284–8
dietary restrictions 112–13
discipline, *disciplina* 34, 35
  see also *askesis*
Dismas 253
Dome of the Rock 207

Dream of the Rood 197, 211, 236, 242
druids
  and St Patrick 165–6
Drythelm, monk
  dissolution of marriage 43
  vision of 148, 154
Dublitir, abbot 36
Durham Gospels 213, 251, 256, 260
Durrow
  scripture cross 213, 265, 267, 269, 273,
    274
  Book of: see Book of Durrow
Dyophisite(s) 5, 54, 55–6, 65, 174, 178

Eanflaed
  marriage dissolved 41
Easter 5, 133, 177, 285
  as Christ's sacrifice 62, 138
  as Christ's triumph 88, 138
  controversy 56–64
  duty 125, 127
  'orthodox' reckoning of 111, 234, 279
Echternach Gospels 213, 226, 228
effort (*studium*)
  as a means to salvation 24, 99, 120,
    140
Egeria
  and the Holy Land 196
Egitanus 253 n.61
elect (*electi*) 134, 175
energeia ('actualisation') 55
Emchath 95
English Church 152
Epistle of James 99
eremiticism 33
eucharist 5, 230, 238, 242, 254, 263, 271,
    272
  approached by stages 128, 134, 239
  as Christ 229, 236
  inverted formula 126, 164
  institution of 243, 244, 246
  mark of perfection/reward 125, 229,
    257–8
  minimalist attitude towards 126, 211
  represented by vine 209, 211–12, 228,
    231, 263
  sacramental character 125
  spiritual refreshment 128–9
Eusebius 56, 118, 191
  Life of Constantine 196
Eutyches, heresy of 52, 55
  see Monophysitism

evangelist symbols 221–2, 224, 232
  as cross page 224
Euangelium Nicodemi: see *Gospel of Nicodemus*
'Evans Letters' 70, 126
excommunication 29, 36, 125, 130–4
  see also ostracism
exegesis, scriptural
  Alexandrian 280
  allegorical 93, 112, 164, 205
  and images of Christ 173, 243
  Antiochene 56, 280
  false 73, 119
  literal interpretation of narratives 93, 163
  principles of 163
Exeter Book
  harrowing of hell 158
exousia 161–2, 177
  see also *virtus Christi*

Fahan Mura slab cross
  and Greek doxology 195
faith 134
Farne 149, 171
Fastidius
  On the Christian Life, attrib. 80–1
Faustus of Riez 7, 24, 25, 80, 106
  On grace 79
  works known in Britain 118
Feast of the Discovery of the Cross 197
Feast of the Exaltation of the Cross 197, 198
Feast of Tabernacles 112
filioque-clause 51
Finnian: see Uinniau
First Commentary on Mark 89, 96, 115, 126, 129, 141
  Christ's miracles and resurrection 139
First Synod of St Patrick 27, 31, 32, 34
Fís Adamnáin (Vision of Adomnán) 154–5
fish (ἰχθύς): see Christ
flowering sceptre/rod 265, 270, 273
four archangels 246
four rivers of Paradise 224
four evangelical symbols: see evangelist symbols
Fragmentary Annals of Ireland 61
Frankish Church 4
Fursa 148, 153, 171
  vision of 153

Galla Placidia,
  mausoleum of: see Ravenna
Gennadius 7, 80
Germanus (speaker in the *Conferences*) 77–8, 143
Germanus of Auxerre 7, 8, 100, 189
  mission to Britain 9, 81, 278
  second mission to Britain 86, 278
Gildas 4, 6, 13, 22, 24, 47, 52, 76, 81, 87, 100, 120, 133, 278
  and Pelagian teachings 85–6
  and the monastic movement 24, 30
  and the resurrection 138
  De excidio Britanniae (*Ruin of Britain*) 28, 118, 138
  epistolary fragments 28, 120, 130–1
  floruit 27
  Lorica, attrib. 28
  on excommunication 130–1
  Preface on Penance, attrib. 28, 29
  reading of 118
  visit to Ireland, alleged 105
Golgotha *stauroteca* 218
Gospel of Nicodemus 157, 158, 159, 267–8, 285
  Irish version 252
  Latin version 253
Gospel of Peter 273
Gospel of Thomas: see *Infancy Gospel of Thomas*
grace 11, 17, 82, 89–90, 92, 100, 119, 120, 122, 151, 231, 239, 272, 278, 279
  and the eucharist 130
  as created nature 71, 95
  'enemies of grace' 69, 105
  expressed by tears 241
  fate of souls before 155
  'forgives only once' 90
  'Grace of the Law' 114
  'grace of the Redemption' 140
  irresistible 100
  Pelagian doctrine of 71, 75, 76
  'second grace' 91
graven images
  forbidden by scripture 133, 186
Gregory I, pope 38, 39, 145, 205, 241, 246
  correspondence with Augustine 40
  homily on Book of Exechiel 222
  known in Ireland 223
  on contemplation and good works 142
  policy *re* the Fifth Council 53

Gregory I, pope (*cont.*):
  support for bishops in monastic
    communities 41
Gregory of Nyssa 200
Gaulish Church 285

Hadrian
  abbot of SS Peter and Paul 40
  superintended Theodore 55
Haemgisl 148
hagiography: see saints' lives
harrowing of hell 20, 267, 268–70, 272,
  273, 281, 285
  conflation with resurrection 139, 282
  influence in Insular world 157–60
Helena, St 195
hell
  avoidance of 144–5, 151–3
  destiny of most people 76, 151
  hell-oriented Churches 152
  theology of 151
  visions of 154–5
'Help of God', depictions of 272
Heraclius, emperor 197, 198
Heron, hermit 247
Hexham 171
  crosses at 207, 209, 237; fig. ii.a
Hibernenses 3, 37, 106, 110, 123, 206,
  242, 279
  reflects common Celtic Church 109
Hilda, St
  monastery at Whitby 41, 171
Hildelith
  monastery at Barking 41
Hinton St Mary (Dorset)
  Roman villa at 188
Hisperica Famina 152
homoousion 52
Honorius, pope 55
  letter to Irish 204
house shrines
  at Bobbio 188
  at Clonmore 188
  Irish 192
Hunterston Brooch 188
Hwaetberht 198
Hymnus Sancti Hilarii de Christo 138
hypostatic union (of Christ's natures)
  253

Iasmus 253
Ibas of Odessa 53

iconoclasm 211, 235, 259
  see also images, graven images
Illtud 4, 29
'image of God' (*imago Dei*) 89
images 279, 280
  see also graven images
  as objects of contemplation 191, 281
imitation of Christ (*imitatio Christi*)
  131–2, 143, 147, 165, 172, 189, 244,
  248, 249, 250, 274, 275
inequality
  criticised by Pelagians 85–6
Infancy narratives 162, 165
Infancy Gospel of Thomas 165
inhabited vine scroll: see Christ
instruction
  as a form of grace 71
  'instructed by grace' 72
Insular art 17, 18
Iona
  and Easter 204
  and Hibernenses 106
  Church in Columba's time 109–10
  crosses on 192, 198
  monastic rule 41
  Viking raids on 267, 275
Irenaeus of Lyon 200, 222, 223
Irish Canons (*Canones Hibernenses*) 96,
  112, 113
Irish Church 4, 12, 13, 21, 31, 33, 104,
  109, 118, 128, 152, 153, 156, 169,
  189, 242, 261, 278
Irish commentary on Luke 141, 248
Irish Gospel of Thomas 162
Iserninus 31
Isidore of Seville 216, 229
  Irish knowledge of 225

Jarrow 235
  see Monkwearmouth-Jarrow
Jerome 23, 70, 114, 120, 223
  De exodo in vigilia Paschae (*On
    Exodus on the Vigil of Easter*) 64
  known in Ireland 223
  Preface to the Psalms, glosses to 96
  scriptural commentaries of 120, 222
Jerusalem 198, 199, 223, 272
  Church of the Holy Sepulchre 195–6
  heavenly Jerusalem 249, 263
  Jerusalem shrine 203
  new Jerusalem 249
  Shrine of the True Cross 195, 205

Jews, Jewish
  Christian Jews 56
  Jewish aspects of Christianity 109, 111
  Jewish Christianity 106
  restrictions applied to Christians 63
John the Baptist 238, 239, 241
John, pope-elect
  letter to northern Irish bishops and
    abbots 59–60, 62, 87–8, 89, 94, 99,
    100, 122, 278, 279
John, precentor 234
John Scottus Eriugena
  and harrowing of hell 158–9
  description of cross 197, 201
Josephus Scottus 197
Judaisers 56–65
Judaising tendencies 109–15
judgement (condemnation) 176
Julian of Acclanum, bishop 69
  commentary on Canticles 97
  De amore (*On love*) 97
  De bono constantiae (*On the good of
    constancy*) 97
  Letter to Demetrius, wrongly attrib.
    97
Justinian, emperor
  and the Fifth Ecumenical Council 53

Kells
  south scripture cross ('cross of SS
    Patrick and Columba') 213, 264,
    268
  market cross 269
Kilclispen, Cill Criospín, St Crispin's
  church 203
Kildare
  church of St Brigit 190
Killamery high cross 206, 255
kingdom of heaven, kingdom of God
  145
  in Western Christianity 151
Knappaghmanagh slab 255

Lactantius: see *Carmen de ave phoenice*
Laidcenn
  invocation of the Trinity 50
  Lorica 50, 152, 175, 255–6
laity: see also *manaig*
  'faithful laity' 14, 15, 128, 232
  included in monastic community 152
  married laity 42–3
  paramonastic laity 105

Lamb of God 236, 238, 239, 249
Last Judgement 16, 174, 177, 249, 265,
    257, 260, 262, 264–7, 268, 282, 284,
    285
  see also judgement, second coming

Laurence, archbishop
  letter to the bishops and abbots of
    Ireland 57–8, 60, 105
law
  lex naturae (law of nature) 11, 72, 85,
    91, 96, 113, 114, 231, 269, 274
  God's law promulgated in scripture 72
  knowledge of necessary 84
  Law of Moses: see Mosaic Law
  Law of Sunday: see *Cáin Domnaig*
  law versus example 131
  New Law 15, 72, 85, 108, 114, 249, 261
  obedience to 131, 139, 222, 265
  of Christ 71, 72, 91, 108, 113, 147
  Old Law 62, 63, 108, 110, 113, 114,
    116, 206, 232, 249, 261, 265, 283
  primacy of 88
  sources of divine law 106, 108
  succession of laws 94, 108, 113, 114
  theology of 151
  unity of Old and New Laws 266
Leo, pope
  Tome of 53
'Letter of Jesus concerning Sunday'
  110
Leuthere, bishop 41
Liber de virtutibus sancti Columbae
  (*Book on the virtues of St Columba*)
  280
Lichfield Gospels 213, 220, 221, 227, 228,
  265
Lindisfarne 40, 41, 171
  Viking raids on 267, 275
Lindisfarne Gospels 103, 213, 217–20,
    221, 226, 228, 255–6; plate 4
Lismore, monastery 204
litanies
  as form of private prayer 153
  Litany of Jesus 152
literacy 116
literary culture 115–22
liturgical objects 250
Longinus 217, 251–2, 253, 255, 257, 258,
    259, 271, 282
lorica: see also breastplate
  basic form of private prayer 152–3

Lullingstone (Kent)
  villa at 188
Lupus of Troyes
  mission to Britain 81
luxury, luxurious
  items used in worship 189
  strictures against 189–90

MacDurnan Gospels 221
MacRegol Gospels 213
Mael Ruain 35, 36, 247–8
magisterium 64
maiestas domini/Christi 220, 221–2, 223, 264
Maihingen Gospels 226
manaig 14, 33, 232, 270
Marcion 107–8
Marius Mercator 70
marigold pattern 193, 207–216
marriage
  dissolubility 43
Martin I, pope 51, 55–6
Martin of Tours 22, 23
martyrdom
  red, white, and green 147–8, 169
Martyrology of Tallaght 96
Mary Magdalene and Martha 236, 237, 239, 240–1
Mary of Egypt 241
Mauchteus, 'disciple of Patrick' 31
Maxentius 191
Maximus the Confessor 55, 56
Melchisadek, priest/king 254
Mellitus, bishop 40, 57
Melrose, abbey 171
  rule in use 41
mercy
  distinguished from grace 90
merit 17, 134
  see also miracles
  weighing of merits 175
metalwork, secular 189
Michael, archangel 155, 157, 160, 266, 285
Mildenhall treasure 187
miles Christi, soldier(s) of Christ 13, 38, 178, 270
millenialism 267
Milvian Bridge
  and the cross 191
miracles, the miraculous 9, 15, 16, 17, 81,
    91, 121, 133, 138, 139, 140, 169, 170, 173, 280
  'concealed in divine law'/equated with law 72, 93
  eucharistic 272
  evangelical 16, 160, 161, 169
  factual treatment of 139
  in saints' lives 119, 120, 169
  interference with created nature 72, 92, 126, 163, 279
  merited 16
  monastic 15, 150, 271, 282
  of Christ 163, 164, 169, 280, 284–8
  tokens of faith in resurrection 162
Monasterboice
  south cross (Muiredach's cross) 213, 159, 260, 264–5, 266, 267, 269, 274; fig. iii.b, plate 16
  west cross 268, 269, 270
monasteries 13, 14, 15, 21
  as hospitals 42
  double 41
  enclosures 34
monasticism
  Celtic 15, 239–40, 249
  in Anglo-Saxon England 38–44
  in Britain 22–30, 56
  in Ireland 30–8, 199
  monastic audience 231, 170
  monastic clergy 21, 22
  monastic community 20, 152, 267
  monastic *conversatio* 8, 13, 21, 22, 23, 27, 30, 134, 141, 160, 238, 239, 240, 241, 242, 255, 274
  monastic exegesis 264
  monastic images 167
  monastic instructions 118
  monastic movement 104, 106, 151
  monastic *paruchia* 168
  monastic precepts 146
  monastic rules 8, 41, 118
  monastic theology 14, 17
  monastic vows for clergy 42
  monasticised church, society 26, 37
Monastery of SS Peter and Paul: see Canterbury
'Monastery of Tallaght', rule 110
Monesan, British virgin 96
monks 8, 15, 21, 23, 27, 31, 32, 33
  distinguished from clergy 29
  not to baptise or receive alms 29
  part of the 'hundred fold' 38

separate communities/seclusion 34, 35
Monkwearmouth-Jarrow 198, 207, 234–5, 242
monogram: see Christ
Monophysitism, -ites 52, 55, 65
  see also Eutyches
monotheism, Christian 187
Monothelitism, Monothelite controversy 54–6
Moone, cross of 251, 258, 259, 272
Mosaic Law 37, 60–1, 63, 64, 71, 72, 85, 91, 107, 108, 113, 114, 190, 206, 254, 269
  translated to Ireland 114
Moses, as type of Christ: see Christ
Moslems 197, 198
moths, as resurrection symbol 230
Moylough belt shrine 192
Muirchú
  Life of Patrick 95, 120, 165, 167, 192, 198
Muiredach's cross: see Monasterboice

nature
  'blessing of' (*beneficium naturae*) 89
  'by nature' immortal 93
  created nature 92, 96, 126, 163
  grace as created nature 71, 95
  human nature 73
  Pelagian doctrine of 11, 72
Nestorianism 51, 53, 65
Nicene Creed
  knowledge required of English priests 50
nomen sacrum 225, 228, 231
Northumbria 207, 209, 212, 220, 234, 235, 236, 237, 242
  and Easter 204, 206
Novatians
  Quattuordeciman element 57
Nynia 22–3, 27
  conversion of Picts 23

Offa, king
  dissolution of marriage 43
Old Irish Penitential 128
Old Irish Table of Commutations 36, 125
opus geminatum 171
Orosius 70
Ossory, kingdom of 201, 205
  kings of 204

crosses 206, 217
ostracism 130–4
  see also excommunication
Oswald, king 198

paganism, pagan practices 31
  and law of nature 95
  pillars 195
Palladius, bishop 81, 104, 278
paradise, vision of 154
paruchia, monastic 168
paschal/pasch/pesach 57, 133, 138
Passions of Peter and Paul 161–2, 165
  see also Acts of Peter and Paul
Passio Albani 86
Passover, feast of
  abolished by Christ 111
  and Easter 56–7, 60, 62
pastoral care (*cura animarum*) 33, 172–73
patriarchal cross: see cross
Patrician Church 31
Patrick, St 2, 6, 12, 13, 30, 116, 120, 192
  and grace 82–4
  and liturgical items 190
  and monasticism 31, 33, 34
  anti-Pelagian stance 82–4, 278
  Confession 25, 26, 49, 82, 84
  inheritance 24
  Letter to Coroticus 25, 31, 82, 84
  mission to Ireland 22, 25–6, 31
  profession of faith 47, 48–9
  reading 118
  rusticity 84–5
  sin of 82
  sojourn in Gaul 27
  time of baptism 84
Paul and Anthony, hermits 236, 239–40, 270–1, 274, 282
peacock: see phoenix
Pelagianism, Pelagians 5–9, 11–12, 15, 18, 23, 52, 65, 92, 93, 104, 106, 107, 113, 115, 116, 119, 121, 131, 132, 146, 169, 189, 190, 205, 231, 232, 235, 259, 271, 272, 279
  and miracle cures 120
  'Caspari Corpus' 70, 126
  disapproval of riches 117
  'Evans Letters' 70, 126
  on the resurrection 138
  Pelagian Christ 280–1

Pelagianism, Pelagians (*cont.*):
Pelagian Church 6, 9, 104, 123, 278
Pelagian doctrines 71–80, 190, 278
Pelagian movement 69–70
Pelagian party 10, 124, 134
Pelagian theology 122, 123, 126, 282
Pelagian writings 70–1, 108, 126
Pelagianism in Ireland 69, 87–97
Pelagianism in Northumbria 97–100
theological spectrum 7, 138
Pelagius 6, 10, 11, 12, 14, 16, 17, 23, 24,
52, 57, 69, 81, 94, 96, 100, 101, 109,
139, 151, 175, 278
birthplace 23
Commentary on Epistles of Paul 9, 70,
89, 98, 99, 106–8
Letter to Demetrius 71, 77, 113, 116,
117
profession of faith 47, 48–9, 70, 76,
122, 123
saying attributed to 71
penance, penitential system(s) 36, 71,
134, 144
after baptism 96, 279
and mortification 141, 248, 258, 272
and compassion 142
as form of grace 71
as repentance 91, 120
not a sacrament 123, 125
penitential life 176, 238, 241
penitentials 6, 30, 118, 120, 124
penitents
sections of a church provided for
125
special class 27, 129
Pentateuch 115, 248
see also Mosaic Law, Torah
perfection, the *perfecti* 13, 15, 24, 37,
117, 148, 174, 222, 224, 231
and the scriptures 106
without baptism 95
three perfections 144
vita perfecta, perfect life 33, 141, 145,
239, 243, 244, 249
Peter, abbot of SS Peter and Paul 40
phoenix, resurrection symbol 263
Pictish art 19
pilgrimage, *peregrinatio* 37, 147
peregrinatio pro Christo 147
pillars
cross-incised 198
pagan 195

Potitus, grandfather of Patrick 24
poverty
absolute 36
of Christ 189
Pelagian emphasis on 74
'the first perfection' 24, 28, 146
prayer, imageless 191, 281
Precamur patrem, hymn 175, 274, 284–8
and the harrowing of hell 157–8, 274
omits resurrection 139–40, 274, 280–1,
284
predestination 17, 76, 79, 175, 278, 280
'heresy' of 80, 278
princeps/airchinnech 32
professions of faith 47–51, 70, 76, 91
prophecies 165–6
Prosper of Aquitaine 7, 100, 105
Contra Collatorem ('Against Cassian')
69, 81
Pseudo-Alcuin 201
Pseudo-Augustine
and original sin 93
'apostolic power in Christ' 161
De mirabilibus sacrae scripturae (*On
the miracles of holy scripture*) 91–4,
96, 100, 119, 122, 162–3, 164, 279,
280
distinction between *opus* and labour
92
God does nothing against nature 164
literal interpretation of biblical
narratives 93
proof of possibility of miracles 162–3
Pseudo-Bede
Collectanea 98
psychostasis 266, 267, 269
see also weighing of souls
purgatory, vision of 154

Quinisext Council 18, 250–1
Quattuordecimans 56–65, 109–10
and Pelagianism 88

Rabanus Maurus 197
Rabbula Gospels 251
Ravenna 199, 200, 270
mausoleum of Galla Placidia 200,
220
Sant'Apollinare in Classe, church of
200
redemption: see salvation
relics 17, 18, 81, 205, 280

introduced to Ireland 121–2, 279
of the martyrs 121
of the true cross 197–8
representational art
strictures against 186–90, 191
resurrection
and ascension 272
discussion avoided by Pelagians 88,
138
of Christ 15, 17, 56–65, 75, 140, 162,
178, 225, 230, 231, 264, 274, 280,
281, 284–5
overlooked in British and Irish works
138–9, 261, 282, 284
symbolised by phoenix 263
two resurrections 176–7
resuscitation
of Abraham's body (sexual) 88
from the dead 164, 173
retirement, spiritual 148–50
Rheged, British kingdom 242
Rhygyfarch
Life of St David 86–7, 100, 104
riches
Pelagian disapproval of 117
Ripon, church at 173
Rock of Calvary 203
Roman Church/Catholic Church/
Church of Rome 64, 100, 104, 106,
133, 205, 207, 211–12, 231
liturgy of 242
unity with 279
Rome 204, 209
authority of 234
Church of the Saviour
(Constantiniana) 198
Irish visits to 121, 201, 234, 237, 279
Santa Croce in Hierusalem, church of
242
Santa Pudenziana, church of 196, 220
St John Lateran, church of 242
Romani, Romanisers
Roman party in England and Britain
62, 104, 239
Irish 3, 16, 17, 36, 37, 62, 63, 106, 110,
116, 119, 120, 121, 123, 125, 127,
156, 167, 169, 176, 201, 205, 212,
232, 234, 235, 242, 274, 279, 280,
281, 282, 286
Romano-British art 17, 187, 188, 206
Rufinus the Syrian 69, 93
Rule of the *Celi Dé* 37

Rule of Tallaght 36, 128, 153, 246–7
Ruthwell cross 18, 209–13, 217, 218, 227,
232, 235, 236–43, 251, 258, 259, 270,
271; fig. iii.a, plate 9

sabbath
ended by Christ 111
observance 6, 106, 110, 133
sabbatarianism 106
Sabbath of the Trumpets 111–12
sacraments 17, 32, 73, 76, 122–30, 134,
212, 280
sacramental, -ism 231
saints' lives 119, 120, 279
earliest Irish 165
reflect images of Christ 173
resistance to 169
Saltair na Rann 176
salvation
difficulty of attainment 74, 150
God's plan for 93
impossible before Christ 155
monasticism surest road to 141, 239,
242
'salvation ethic' 151
through Christ 193
through Christ's sacrifice 207, 212,
217, 252, 258, 260, 262
through imitation of Christ's
perfection 238, 249
through obedience to the law and
good works 134, 190, 265, 272, 275,
278
Samson of Dol
Life of 119
Sant'Apollinare in Classe: see Ravenna
Santa Croce in Hierusalem: see Rome
Santa Pudenziana: see Rome
Satan: see also devil
Christ's battle with 157–60, 177, 267,
268–70, 281,
temptation of Christ by 246–7, 248
scripturalism 64, 106–9, 133, 265
scriptural commentaries 116, 118–19
scriptures
apocryphal 16, 138, 160, 162, 274, 279
as a weapon 249
canonical 16, 138
canon of Christian Bible 107
New Testament 73, 107, 141, 169, 271,
273

scriptures (*cont.*):
  Old Testament 63, 73, 92, 106, 107, 169, 205, 271, 272
  source of God's law 72, 115, 120, 278, 279
  spiritual food 116
scripture crosses: see crosses
second coming 16, 238, 242, 256, 260, 261–67, 274
  see also Last Judgement
  and the ascension of Christ 261
Sedulius, Caelius
  Carmen paschale 196, 200, 260
Sedulius Scottus
  use of Pelagius 98–9
Ségéne, abbot 204
semi-Pelagians/ -ism 6, 8, 9, 15, 16, 17, 24, 69, 79, 80, 100–01, 104, 106, 116, 19, 121, 128, 279, 281, 282
  theological spectrum 7, 138
Sergius, pope 198, 209, 238
sexual abstinence
  see also 'Three Lents'
  for laity 30, 33, 42–3, 74
sexual offences
  punishments for 42, 124
Shrine of the True Cross 195, 205
Signs before Doomsday 176, 262
Simon Magus
  contest with Peter 161–2, 165
sin
  see also Adam
  allotment of sins 73
  original sin, transmitted sin 73, 75, 76, 96
  possibility of sinless life 71, 74, 94
  sinless men before Christ 156
Sophronius 55, 56
Soiscél Molaise book shrine 222
Sol and *Luna*: see Christ
St. Cuthbert's coffin 220, 264
St Gall Gospels 213, 227, 252, 256, 257, 258, 268 272; plate 13, 14
St John Lateran, church of: see Rome
stauroteca 201
Stephanus, 'Eddius'
  Life of Wilfrid 171, 245
'Stephaton' 217, 251–2, 258–9
  represents unbelief 253
Stoicism
  in Pelagian theology 97
Stowe Missal

'Tract on the Mass' 129
sumptuary laws: see luxury
Sunday ('Lord's Day) 109, 284–6
  prohibitions (sabbatising of Sunday) 109–10, 179, 284
supernatural (praeternatural) condition 72
Sutton Hoo hoard 217
synods
  Second Synod of the Grove of Vistory 87
  Second Synod of St Patrick 34, 38, 123, 127
  Synod of Brefi 86
  Synod of Diospolis 71, 72, 73–4, 76, 92, 94
  Synod of Mag Léne 204
  Synod of North Britain 124
  Synod of Victory 86
  Synod of Whitby 12, 204

Tara brooch 203
Temptation of Christ 246, 248, 249; plate 11
temple
  as symbol of the Church 249
Tertullian 191
thaumaturgy 164, 167, 169, 170
Theodore of Mopsuestia 53
Theodore of Tarsus, archbishop 4, 40, 50
  and the Lateran Council 55
  and the Synod of Hatfield 56
  biblical glosses attrib. to 11
  penitential attrib. to 38, 41–3, 127
Theodore of Cyrrhus 53
Theodosius I, emperor
  Edicts of 388 and 392 187
Theodosius II, emperor 196
'Three Chapters' controversy 5, 52–4
theoria 145–6, 147
  see also contemplation
  vita theorica 148
Three Lents 30, 33, 37
  pre-easter and pre-christmas 'Lent' 248
Tírechán
  Life of Patrick 50, 91, 96, 120, 166, 167, 190, 198, 205
tithes 112–13, 133
tonsure, Roman 31

Transitus Mariae (*Ascension of Mary*)
155
Torah 282
see also Pentateuch
Traditio legis 274
transubstantiation 126
tree of life (*arbor vitae*) 207, 209, 211
see also Christ
Trier Gospels 221
Trinity
Christ as second person in 65
'Remaining in the Trinity' (*manens in
Trinitate*) 54
theology of 47–51
Turin Gospels 261
Tynan cross 268

Uinniau (Finnian) 4, 37, 43, 133
penitential of 30, 32, 105, 124, 125
questions regarding monastic practice
29
urbs, civitas 32
Utrecht Psalter 270

Venantius Fortunatis
Crux benedicta nitet 209
Pange lingua 196
Vexilla regis 196–7
viaticum 128
Victor, pope 56–7
Victricius of Rouen 22
Vigilius, pope
and the Fifth Ecumenical Council
53
Viking
attacks 236, 245, 248, 267, 275
Virgilius Maro Grammaticus 114–15
Vincent of Lérins 7
virginity 22, 24, 30, 74, 146

fallen virgins 27
instruction of virgins 71
part of the 'hundred fold' 38
virgins of Christ 22, 26, 31, 32, 33
virtus Christi 161
see also *exousia*
vision literature 153
Vitalian, pope 55
voluntarism 85, 86

Walafrid Strabo 127
Water Newton hoard 187
Wearmouth-Jarrow: see
Monkwearmouth-Jarrow
weighing of souls 264
see also *psychostasis*
Western Church 17, 54, 60, 152, 191
Whithorn: see *Candida Casa*
new bishopric at 242
widows, widowhood 33, 74
instruction of 71
Wilfrid 18, 40, 171
as anti-ideal to Cuthbert 173
church at Ripon 173
reforms of 207
represents Roman cause at Whitby
60–1, 62, 63
will
as part of created nature 72
freedom of 71, 77, 79, 89–90
perverted 76
Würzburg commentary on Epistles of
Paul 91, 96, 98

Zacharius, priest of Old Dispensation
266
Zosimus, pope
excommunicated Pelagius and
Coelestius 176

STUDIES IN CELTIC HISTORY

Already published

I · THE SAINTS OF GWYNEDD
Molly Miller

II · CELTIC BRITAIN IN THE EARLY MIDDLE AGES
Kathleen Hughes

III · THE INSULAR LATIN GRAMMARIANS
Vivien Law

IV · CHRONICLES AND ANNALS OF MEDIAEVAL IRELAND
AND WALES
Kathryn Grabowski and David Dumville

V · GILDAS: NEW APPROACHES
M. Lapidge and D. Dumville (edd.)

VI · SAINT GERMANUS OF AUXERRE AND THE END OF
ROMAN BRITAIN
E. A. Thompson

VII · FROM KINGS TO WARLORDS
Katherine Simms

VIII · THE CHURCH AND THE WELSH BORDER IN
THE CENTRAL MIDDLE AGES
C. N. L. Brooke

IX · THE LITURGY AND RITUAL OF THE CELTIC CHURCH
F. E. Warren (2nd edn by Jane Stevenson)

X · THE MONKS OF REDON
Caroline Brett (ed. and trans.)
XI · EARLY MONASTERIES IN CORNWALL
Lynette Olson

XII · IRELAND, WALES AND ENGLAND IN THE
ELEVENTH CENTURY
K. L. Maund

XIII · SAINT PATRICK, A.D 493–1993
D. N. Dumville and others

XIV · MILITARY INSTITUTIONS ON THE WELSH MARCHES:
SHROPSHIRE, AD 1066–1300
Frederick C. Suppe

XV · UNDERSTANDING THE UNIVERSE IN
SEVENTH-CENTURY IRELAND
Marina Smythe

XVI · GRUFFUDD AP CYNAN: A COLLABORATIVE BIOGRAPHY
K. L. Maund (ed.)

XVII · COLUMBANUS: STUDIES ON THE LATIN WRITINGS
Michael Lapidge (ed.)

XVIII . THE IRISH IDENTITY OF THE KINGDOM OF THE SCOTS IN
THE TWELFTH AND THIRTEENTH CENTURIES
Dauvit Broun

XIX · THE MEDIEVAL CULT OF ST PETROC
KarenJankulak